NOTABLE
AFRICAN AMERICAN
WRITERS

NOTABLE
AFRICAN AMERICAN
WRITERS

Second Edition

Volume 1
Ai — Nikki Giovanni

Edited by
ROBERT C. EVANS
I.B. Young Professor of English
Auburn University at Montgomery

SALEM PRESS
A Division of EBSCO Information Services, Inc.
Ipswich, Massachusetts

GREY HOUSE PUBLISHING

Cover Photos (from left to right): Toni Morrison (The U.S. Military Academy, West Point); Richard Wright (Library of Congress); Zora Neale Hurston (Library of Congress); Ralph Ellison (National Archives and Records Administration).

Publisher's Cataloging-In-Publication Data
(Prepared by The Donohue Group, Inc.)

Names: Evans, Robert C., 1955- editor.
Title: Notable African American writers / edited by Robert C. Evans, I.B. Young Professor of English, Auburn
    University at Montgomery.
Description: [Second edition]. | Ipswich, Massachusetts : Salem Press, a division of EBSCO Information Services,
    Inc.; Amenia, NY : Grey House Publishing, [2020] | "First Edition Edited by The Editors of Salem Press." |
    Includes bibliographical references and index. | Contents: Volume 1. Ai - Nikki Giovanni -- Volume 2. Alex
    Haley - Ishmael Reed -- Volume 3. Sonia Sanchez - Genre Essays, Bibliography, Indices.
Identifiers: ISBN 9781642654073 (set) | ISBN 9781642654899 (v. 1) | ISBN 9781642654905 (v. 2) | ISBN
    9781642654912 (v. 3)
Subjects: LCSH: American literature--African American authors--Dictionaries. | African American authors--
    Biography--Dictionaries. | African Americans in literature--Dictionaries. | African Americans--Intellectual
    life--Dictionaries.
Classification: LCC PS153.N5 N68 2020 | DDC 810.9/89607303--dc23

FIRST PRINTING
PRINTED IN THE UNITED STATES OF AMERICA

Contents

Publisher's Note

The three-volume set *Notable African American Writers* is a new, updated version of a reference work originally published in 2006 under the title *Magill's Choice: Notable African American Writers*. This edition not only provides 19 new articles but also includes hundreds of updates to older articles including current bibliographical resources. The essays are arranged alphabetically by the author's last name, from "Ai" to "Al Young".

Essay Length and Format

Each essay in *Notable African American Writers* profiles a different writer, and includes an overview of the writer's life and work, a detailed reading of the author's principal writings, as well as a comprehensive bibliography. The essays range in length from 3,000 to 11,000 words and contain the following sections:
- A comprehensive list of the writer's *Works*, organized by genre;
- A list of the writer's *Achievements,* comprising both specific awards and the author's larger impact on the culture;
- A detailed *Biography* of each writer;
- An in-depth *Analysis* of the writer's major works, with close readings of the author's principal texts; and
- An annotated *Bibliography* offering a generous selection of resources for further study.

Special Features

The back matter in Volume 3 contains a number of reference tools to help readers further explore the lives and works of African American writers. These include:
- Four lengthy *Essays* that provide a critical overview of African American literature by genre. Essays cover Drama, Long Fiction, Poetry, and Short Fiction.
- An updated *Bibliography* that directs readers to accessible sources for further study;
- A *Genre Index* which allows readers to search for individual authors by the type of work they've produced;
- A *Title Index* which allows readers to search for the titles of individual works; and
- A *Subject Index* which provides access to the individual essays and their content through multiple access points.

The Contributors

Salem Press extends its appreciation to all who have been involved in the development and production of this work, especially the original editorial board and Robert C. Evans, editor of the revised edition. Essays were written by academic specialists and independent scholars, whose expert contributions made this interdisciplinary project possible. Their names and affiliations appear in the front matter of this volume.

Editor's Introduction

This new, second edition of *Notable African American Writers* builds on but also substantially expands the first edition, published in 2006. Nineteen new authors have been added, including Ai, Ta-Nehisi Coates, Teju Cole, Edwidge Danticat, Michael Eric Dyson, Percival Everett, Roxane Gay, Terrance Hayes, bell hooks, Dawn Lundy Martin, James McBride, Dinaw Mengestu, Lynn Nottage, Claudine Rankine, Anna Deveare Smith, Tracy K. Smith, Natasha Trethewey, Colson Whitehead, and Jacqueline Woodson. In addition, entries included in the first edition have all been thoroughly updated. Primary and secondary bibliographies have been brought up to date, and the same is true of biographies and lists of awards and honors. Moreover, the size of the entries themselves has often been expanded. Finally, supplementary essays dealing with distinct genres have not only been expanded (in several cases doubled in size), but the comprehensive secondary bibliographies have also been brought up to date.

In the decade and a half since the publication of the first edition, African American literature became an even more vibrant part of the American literary tradition than it had already been. Some writers who had previously established themselves as major figures, such as Toni Morrison, continued to be impressively productive, while new writers who were very little known at the time of the first edition's publication have now established themselves as important authors in their own right. The range of topics, styles, and genres explored by these newer authors has been broad, and the same is true of the perspectives from which they have written. A significant number of these recent writers have been immigrants to the U.S. Many have been women. LGBT voices are increasingly part of the African American literary conversation and will almost certainly receive more attention in the years and decades to come. Many of the newer writers have strong academic affiliations, and some of them write in ways that defy expectations or easy classification. An impressive number of these writers not only explore one genre especially thoroughly but also contribute to other genres as well. Thus it is not surprising to find a fine novelist also writing important short fiction, or an impressive short fiction writer also venturing into poetry and/or drama. African American authors are now often trend-setters in the broader field of American letters, and this new, much-expanded edition of *Notable African American Writers* highlights that fact in a multitude of ways.

For assistance in updating the primary bibliographies that appear throughout this second edition, I am especially grateful to Jordan Bailey and Robert Lee. For encouragement and guidance throughout the lengthy process of preparing this second version, I am very grateful to my editor, Andrew Schenker. For the kind of encouragement and patience I have received during more than forty years of work on various academic projects, I am grateful to my wife, Ruth.

– Robert C. Evans

Complete Table of Contents

List of Contributors

Timothy Dow Adams
University of West Virginia

Heather Russell Andrade
Barry University

Karen Antell
University of Oklahoma

Philip Auslander
Georgia Tech

Philip Bader
Independent Scholar

Jane L. Ball
Independent Scholar

Janet M. Ball
The Mogollon Gazette

Beverly Ballaro
Northeastern University

Paula C. Barnes
Hampton University

Joseph F. Battaglia
Rutgers University

Cynthia S. Becerra
Humphreys College

Kate Begnal
Utah State University

Robert Bensen
Hartwick College

Alvin K. Benson
Brigham Young University

Jacquelyn Benton
Metropolitan State College of Denver

Margaret Boe Birns
The New School

Mary A. Blackmon
Hardin-Simmons University

Franz G. Blaha
University of Nebraska, Lincoln

Jo-Ellen Lipman Boon
Independent Scholar

Harold Branam
Savannah State University

Carl Brucker
Arkansas Tech University

Roland E. Bush
California State University, Long Beach

Rebecca R. Butler
Dalton College

Susan Butterworth
Oregon Health and Society University

Amee Carmines
Hampton University

Warren J. Carson
University of South Carolina, Spartanburg

Linda M. Carter
Morgan State University

Mary LeDonne Cassidy
South Carolina State University

Thomas Cassidy
South Carolina State University

Delores L. Christie
Independent Scholar

Anita Price Davis
Independent Scholar

Jodi Dean
Hobart and William Smith

Joseph Dewey
University of Pittsburgh

M. Casey Diana
University of Illinois, Urbana-Champaign

Sally S. Driscoll
Independent Scholar

Richard A. Eichwald
Independent Scholar

Thomas L. Erskine
Salisbury University

Robert C. Evans
Auburn University at Montgomery

Jack Ewing
Independent Scholar

Howard Faulkner
Washburn University

James Feast
Baruch College, City University of New York

John W. Fiero
University of Louisiana, Lafayette

T Fleischmann
DIAGRAM

Ben Forkner
Indpendent Scholar

Ann Davison Garbett
Averett College

Leslie E. Gerber
Independent Scholar

Scott Giantvalley
Independent Scholar

Dennis Goldsberry
College of Charleston

Marc Goldstein
Independent Scholar

Vincent F.A. Golphin
The Writing Company

Charles A. Gramlich
Xavier University of Louisiana

James Green
Independent Scholar

Molly Hagan
Independent Scholar

Elsie Galbreath Haley
Metropolitan State College of Denver

Nelson Hathcock
Saint Xavier University

Terry Heller
Coe College

Rebecca Bliss Herman
Independent Scholar

Cheryl Herr
Independent Scholar

Sarah Hilbert
Independent Scholar

Cynthia Packard Hill
University of Massachusetts, Amherst

James L. Hodge
Bowdoin College

Nika Hoffman
Crossroads School for Arts & Sciences

Edward Huffstetler
Bridgewater College

Theodore C. Humphrey
California Polytechnic University, Pomona

Ashleigh Imus
Independent Scholar

John Jacob
Independent Scholar

Philip K. Jason
United States Naval Academy

Shakuntala Jayaswal
University of New Haven

Alphine W. Jefferson
Randolph-Macon College

Jeffrey Jensen
Independent Scholar

Judy A. Johnson
Independent Scholar

Sheila Golburgh Johnson
Independent Scholar

Judith L. Johnston
Independent Scholar

Leslie Ellen Jones
Independent Scholar

Rhona Justice-Malloy
Central Michigan University

Deborah Kaplan
Independent Scholar

Steven G. Kellman
University of Texas at San Antonio

W.P. Kenney
Independent Scholar

Anne Mills King
Prince George's Community College

Tom Koontz
University of Washington, Tacoma

Kathryn Kulpa
Independent Scholar

Mildred C. Kuner
Huner College, City University of New York

Vera M. Kutzinski
Yale University

Eugene Larson
Los Angeles Pierce College

Donald F. Larsson
Mankato State University

Katherine Lederer
Southwest Missouri State University

Christine Levecq
University of Liege

Leon Lewis
Appalachian State University

Michael Loudon
Eastern Illinois University

R.C. Lutz
University of California, Berkeley

S. Thomas Mack
Independent Scholar

Kekla Magoon
Vermont College of Fine Arts

Daryl F. Mallett
Independent Scholar

Cheryl Lawton Malone
Lesley University

Anne B. Magnum
Independent Scholar

Charles E. May
California State University, Long Beach

Janet McCann
Texas A&M University

Paul McCann
Independent Scholar

Joanne McCarthy
Tacoma Community College

Barbara A. McCaskill
University of Georgia

Robert McClenaghan
Independent Scholar

Margaret McFadden
Colby College

Sheila McKenna
University of Pittsburgh

Joseph McLaren
Hofstra University

Julia M. Meyers
Duquesne University

Kathleen Mills
Independent Scholar

Michelle Mock-Murton
Independent Scholar

Christian H. Moe
Southern Illinois University, Carbondale

Anna A. Moore
Independent Scholar

Sherry Morton-Mollo
Independent Scholar

C. Lynn Munro
Independent Scholar

Earl Paulus Murphy
Harris-Stowe State College

John Nizalowski
Mesa State College

Emma Coburn Norris
Troy State University

Holly N. Norton
University of Delaware

Sally Osborne Norton
University of Redlands

George O'Brien
Independent Scholar

David Peck
California State University, Long Beach

Eleanor Perry
Independent Scholar

Allene Phy-Olsen
Austin Peay State University

Marjorie Podolsky
*Pennsylvania State University,
Behrend College*

Norman Prinsky
Augusta State University

Thomas Rankin
Duke University

Honora Rankine-Galloway
University of Southern Denmark

Rosemary M. Canfield Reisman
Charleston Southern University

Kenneth Robbins
Independent Scholar

Danny Robinson
Bloomsburg University

Mary Rohrberger
University of Northern Iowa

Marybeth Rua-Larsen
Independent Scholar

Irene Struthers Rush
Independent Scholar

Alexa L. Sandmann
University of Toledo

Andrew Schenker
Independent Scholar

Reinhold Schlieper
Independent Scholar

Barbara Kitt Seidman
Linfield College

D. Dean Shackelford
Concord College

Frank W. Shelton
Limestone College

Nancy Sherrod
*Armstrong Atlantic State
University*

John C. Shields
Illinois State University

Hugh Short
Independent Scholar

R. Baird Shuman
*University of Illinois,
Urbana-Champaign*

Rebecca G. Smith
Barton College

Traci S. Smrcka
Independent Scholar

Katherine Snipes
Eastern Washington University

Stephen F. Soitos
Independent Scholar

Sherry G. Southard
Oklahoma State University

P. Jane Splawn
Purdue University

Eric Sterling
Auburn University

Philip A. Tapley
Louisiana College

Judith K. Taylor
Northern Kentucky University

Thomas J. Taylor
University of Akron

Betty Taylor-Thompson
Texas Southern University

Terry Theodore
*University of North Carolina,
Wilmington*

Lorenzo Thomas
Independent Scholar

Emily Turner
Independent Scholar

Sara Vidar
Independent Scholar

Edward E. Waldron
Yankton College

Nagueyalti Warren
Emory University

Gladys J. Washington
Texas Southern University

Shawncey Webb
Taylor University

Craig Werner
University of Wisconsin

John T. West III
Grambling State University

Patricia A.R. Williams
Texas Southern University

Cynthia Wong
Western Illinois University

Lorna Raven Wheeler
Ashford University

Tyrone Williams
Xavier University

Bill Yousman
Sacred Heart University

Barbara Wiedemann
Auburn University, Montgomery

Judith Barton Williamson
Sauk Valley Community College

Gay Annette Zieger
Santa Fe Community College

Ai

(Florence Anthony)

Poet

Pseudonym: Florence Haynes; Pelorhanke Ai Ogawa

Born: Albany, Texas; October 21, 1947

Died: Stillwater, Oklahoma; March 20, 2010

POETRY: *Cruelty*, 1973; *Killing Floor*, 1979; *Sin*, 1986; *Cruelty/Killing Floor*, 1987; *Fate: New Poems*, 1991; *Greed*, 1993; *Vice: New and Selected Poems*, 1999; *Dread*, 2003; *No Surrender*, 2010

NONFICTION: *"On Being 1/2 Japanese, 1/8 Choctaw, 1/4 Black, and 1/16 Irish,"* 1974 (Ms. 6, June)

Achievements

In 1975, Ai was awarded Guggenheim and Radcliffe fellowships, followed in 1976 by fellowships from the Massachusetts Arts and Humanities Foundation. *Killing Floor* was the 1978 Lamont Selection of the Academy of American Poets, and Ai subsequently received two fellowships from the National Endowment for the Arts (NEA) in 1980 and 1985. She won an Ingram Merrill Foundation grant and an Emergency Fund for Writers award from the International Association of Poets, Playwrights, Editors, Essayists, and Novelists. *Sin* was awarded the American Book Award from the Before Columbus Foundation, and *Vice: New and Selected Poems* (1999) won the 1999 National Book Award for Poetry.

Biography

Ai (ah-EE) had a rich multicultural heritage. Her ancestry was a mixture of Choctaw, Caucasian, Japanese, African American, and Filipino. Although Anthony and her mother clearly looked black, she found it difficult to identify with any particular ethnic group. She was born at her grandparents' house after her mother's husband discovered his wife's affair and beat her. Ai lived in Tucson, Arizona, then moved to Las Vegas, Nevada, then spent two years in San Francisco, California, before returning to Tucson. Her family moved again when Ai was twelve, this time to Los Angeles, California, returning again to Tucson three years later, when Ai was fifteen.

Anthony attended an "integrated" Catholic school that was, in fact, largely black; there, some schoolmates taunted her for her mixed ethnicity. Her first poem, written when she was twelve, was about a Christian martyr fated to die the next day. At fourteen, intending to enter a contest for poems about a historical figure, Ai began writing poetry regularly.

History was Ai's best subject in her Tucson high school. At the University of Arizona in Tucson, she found her identity in the "aesthetic atmosphere" of intellectual life. She graduated in 1969 with a degree in Oriental studies and then earned an M.F.A. in creative writing from the University of California at Irvine in 1971.

At that time, she adopted the name "Ai," Japanese for "love." She held various jobs, including modeling and teaching. Her unconventional

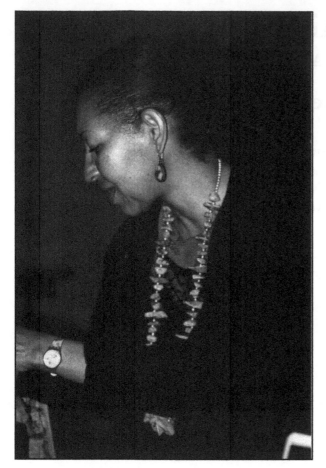

Photo courtesy of OTRS

beginnings and rage at her ethnic homelessness are clearly reflected in her poetry—work that has been both praised and attacked.

Ai once said her family's ethnic history resembles the history of America. Rather than defining her identity through ethnicity, however, she insisted on the uniqueness of personal identity. Accordingly, one aim of her work is to destroy stereotypes. When she published her poetry collection, *Cruelty*, in 1973, she became nationally known, so striking were her grimly realistic and violent poems. Although she married Lawrence Kearney in 1976, they divorced in 1984.

Following a stint as visiting associate professor at the University of Colorado, Boulder (1996-1997), Ai held the Mitte Chair in Creative

Writing during 2002-2003 at Southwest Texas State University. She then moved to Oklahoma State University in Stillwater, where serving as a professor of English and as vice president of the Native American Faculty and Staff Association.

During her final decade she continued to write poetry and comment on her life and work in interviews and articles. Far from being a voice of black or feminist literature, Ai remained her own person, not tied to any ethnic or racial group but, rather, identifying with the most intense aspects of humanity in general. She died in 2010 from breast cancer.

Analysis: Poetry

Ai's poetry is far from gentle. It emphasizes graphic violence, rape, child molestation, and murder, and has sometimes been condemned as pornographic. When *Killing Floor* (1979) received a major award, Ai had to be taken seriously, but some still rejected her graphic depictions of sex and violence. Ai was also loudly attacked by some feminists for graphically describing rape and violence against women. Although applauded for speaking to and for minorities, she was also criticized for refusing to identify with any particular group. In response, she declared, "I was forced to be loyal to myself as a multiracial person or be immersed in the black struggle for identity with which I had little in common. Except a desire to be accepted as I was." Although she chose Japanese culture as her own, her works showed she could identify with humans in general and especially with the darker aspects of human life.

Ai's poetry uses a straightforward narrative style to describe especially horrible people and events. She often assumes various voices from many times and places. Generally, though, her speakers experience the darkest parts of the human experience. Ai has changed American poetry by her forthright, often horrific renderings of some of reality's grimmer aspects. She dealt with pain and anger so well because she felt hurt and angry. Her forthright poetry pulls no punches. Her characters are murderers, child molesters, rapists, and prostitutes. Life is not necessarily pretty, and Ai shows its ugliest parts. While readers might not like to admit that the people Ai talks about exist, her work makes them impossible to ignore.

Cruelty

Ai is more concerned with social class than with racial identity or gender in her first book, *Cruelty* (1973). The book offers dramatic monologues spoken by members of the American underclass. It powerfully indicts societies that permit poverty.

Life itself is cruel for the speakers in *Cruelty*. The speaker in "Tenant Farmer" lacks crops. The couple in "Starvation" lack food. In "Abortion," a man finds his girlfriend's aborted fetus, wrapped in wax paper and thinks: "the poor have no children, just small people/ and there is room for only one man in this house." Men and women become alienated from each other in these conditions. The speaker in "Young Farm Woman Alone" no longer wants a man. In "Recapture," a man finds and beats a fleeing woman. In "Prostitute," a woman kills her husband, then seeks revenge on exploitative men. Some characters do achieve transcendence through love. The couple in "Anniversary" has managed to stay together, providing a home for their son for many years, despite never having "anything but hard times." In "The Country Midwife: A Day," the midwife delivers a woman's child for "the third time between abortions." Crying out to the Lord, the midwife lets the woman bleed. Ending the woman's cycles of pregnancy in an act of mercy, the midwife takes up the cross of guilt and suffering.

Late in *Cruelty*, Ai explores the causes and consequences of poverty in other times and places. In "Cuba, 1962," a farmer cuts off his dead wife's feet, allowing her blood to mix with sugarcane he intends to sell, so everyone can taste his grief. Medieval peasants are evoked by "The Corpse Hauler's Elegy," although the plague victims there could also be contemporary.

Violence increases in the book's final poems. In "The Deserter," a soldier kills the woman who gave him shelter: he wants to leave everything of himself behind. In "The Hitchhiker," a woman is raped and killed by a psychopath. In "The Child Beater," a mother assaults her seven-year-old daughter with a belt, then gets out her "dog's chain leash." Ai feels, and elicits, compassion for all of these people—including the killers.

Killing Floor

Killing Floor (1979) resembles *Cruelty*, but its poems are generally much longer and are more stylistically varied. Dialogues and even a few prose poems appear. Moreover, *Killing Floor*'s characters do not exist in isolation; they exist in specific environments and historical settings. Narrators include actress Marilyn Monroe and also Ira Hayes, an American Indian World War II hero who eventually died broke and drunk. Other characters are especially horrid archetypes.

The narrator of "Jericho" is a fifteen-year-old girl in bed with an older man who feeds her candy and gets her pregnant. In "The Mortician's Twelve-Year-Old Son," a boy makes love to a corpse. "Almost Grown" concerns a boy's first visit to a prostitute. Sixteen of the twenty-four narrators are men. The poet is clearly identifying with all humanity, or at least with the darker side of all human souls. An especially disturbing poem entitled "The Kid" is spoken by a highly unusual fourteen-year-old boy who splits open his father's skull, bludgeons his mother, slaughters horses, and kills his little sister. But his attitude gives this poem its power: "Yeah. I'm Jack, Hogarth's son. / I'm nimble, I'm quick. // I'm fourteen. I'm a wind from nowhere. / I can break your heart." The poem does not justify Jack, but something is obviously wrong. After killing his family, he dresses well and heads for the highway. In a terrifying twist, readers feel compelled to identify with the boy and, in some strange way, feel sorry for him. But the poem shows that even a child can be a monster. Readers can hardly excuse his acts, but they wish they could, somehow.

In these first two collections, death, violence, and sex are prominent. Children appear often but are never happy. Both books emphasize misery, but readers identify with these characters. Ai's poetry draws readers inside especially dark minds. Readers do not sympathize with these grim characters but do learn how these people feel. This is Ai's greatest strength.

Sin

In *Sin* (1986), Ai's focus becomes more overtly political and religious. "Two Brothers" features John and Robert Kennedy and emphasizes death and immortality as the Kennedys posthumously discuss their deaths. The poem ends by suggesting that death is not final and that God may be responsible for everything: humans seem only secondary. "The Prisoner," spoken by an anonymous, regularly tortured inmate, describes a jailer who calls himself "Our Father." "The Good Shepherd: Atlanta, 1981," a dramatic monologue by a mass murderer, was inspired by the case of Wayne Williams, a black man accused of murdering black children. The killer graphically describes disposing of a child's body and then goes home, makes hot cocoa, washes blood stains from his bathroom, then finishes his drink. Once again, readers are given access to this man's thoughts. Pleased by his actions, he considers himself "a good shepherd"— a god feels no guilt. *Sin* is full of such ideas, but

this poem is unusually powerful. Readers don't sympathize with the murderer, but they understand his perspective.

In "The Testimony of J. Robert Oppenheimer: A Fiction," the liberal Oppenheimer describes helping develop the atomic bomb. He recounts his early passion for science as well as his later work supervising construction of the bombs that destroyed Hiroshima and Nagasaki. He announces that when "we accept the worst in ourselves," we are "set free," as if trying to absolve himself of guilt. But he concludes that we destroy ourselves "atom by atom," leading to our ironic "transcendent annihilation."

In "The Priest's Confession," an admittedly sinful priest battles his own temptations, fearing God's wrath. Sexually attracted to a young girl, he contemplates suicide. Images of the girl and her developing body haunt him. He eventually gives in to temptation, but he still wants God's love. Confessing to a sadistic encounter with the girl, he is haunted both by her laughter and by her screams. But he still implores the Lord's help.

Fate

In this collection (1991), Ai's dark emphasis continues, as in "Eve's Story," a poem told from the viewpoint of a sixteen-year-old girl who leaves home after her father strangles a deformed kitten. She winds up in an evangelist's tent. He quickly seduces her. She becomes his servant and procuress. After being edged out of his inner circle by more photogenic women, she films him engaging in a lurid sex act and exposes his hypocrisy. Although his followers desert him, the speaker stays with him. Ai here satirizes both the preacher and the system that produced him. Unlike most of Ai's narrators, this victimized girl inspires real compassion and pity. Who is to blame? The preacher? His religion? God?

Greed

Greed (1993) explores late twentieth-century American identities. In dramatic monologues spoken by famous or obscure Americans, Ai exposes amorality in the institutions of society, business, and private life. For most of the speakers, America has not kept its promises. Truth and justice are illusions in a society made more vicious, because of greed, than the Darwinian struggle for survival among animals. Money, power, drugs, sex—these are the gods Americans worship.

To the African American speakers throughout the collection, slavery is still alive in the "big house" of white America and violence is the inevitable result. In "Riot Act, April 29, 1992," a black man threatens to "set your world on fire." In "Self Defense," Marion Barry, mayor of Washington, D.C., trapped using drugs by the FBI, warns: "The good ole days of slaves out pickin' cotton / ain't coming back no more." In "Endangered Species," a black university professor is stopped by police while driving through his own neighborhood. In "Hoover, Edgar J.," Ai indicts the long-time FBI director for abusing power. Government deceptions are implicated in poems concerning the assassination of President John F. Kennedy. In "Oswald Incognito and Astral Travels," Lee Harvey Oswald finds himself "trapped / in the palace of lies, / where I'm clothed in illusion / and fed confusion with a spoon." Other poems explore domestic violence and the sexual abuse of children. In "Finished," a woman kills her husband after repeated episodes of physical abuse. In "Respect, 1967," a man expresses rage "against the paycheck that must be saved for diapers / and milk." The priest in "Life Story" sexually abuses young boys. He was once abused by his uncle, also a priest. In "The Ice Cream Man," the speaker molests a little girl inside his truck. He tells of his own abuse by his stepfather and his mother. Ai offers little hope for the promise of America in *Greed*. She closes the book with the title poem, about the savings and loan scandal of the 1980s. The responsible working man in "Family Portrait, 1960" has little chance to succeed. Even so, he takes care of his sick wife, cooks dinner, oversees his young daughters' baths, then dozes—"chaos kept at bay" for one more day.

Vice

Subtitled "New and Selected Poems," *Vice* (1999) won the National Book Award for poetry. In the collection's 18 new poems, Ai's obsession with the dark side of human nature continues. For instance, "Sleeping Beauty: A Fiction" is dedicated to a real comatose patient raped by a medical aide. The speaker calls her abuser "furtive," violent, and eager to hide external evidence of his abuse. She worries that any baby that might result from the rape will have no real parents. But she says, "My eyes were open, / while you violated me" and "I could see / beyond the veil of your deceit." Later she ironically recalls Sleeping Beauty. She realizes that own her story will have no happy ending.

Other Literary Forms

Although best known for her poetry, Ai did write occasional nonfiction prose and participated in a number of interviews.

Bibliography

Ackerson, Duane. "Ai: Overview." In *Contemporary Poets*, edited by Thomas Riggs. 6th ed. New York: St. James Press, 1996. A brief but useful introduction.

Ai. "On Being One-Half Japanese, One-Eighth Choctaw, One-Fourth Black, and One-Sixteenth Irish." *Ms.* 6, no. 11 (May 1978): 58.

Albers, Randall. "Ai's *Killing Floor. Chicago Review* 30, no. 4 (Spring 1979): 119-22. An in-depth critical reaction to Ai's early poetry.

Bellamy, Joe David, ed. *American Poetry Observed: Poets on Their Work*. Urbana: U of Illinois P, 1984. Contains an interview of Ai by Lawrence Kearney and Michael Cuddihy.

Carruth, Hayden. "Impetus and Invention: Poetic Tradition and the Individual Talent." *Harper's* 258, no. 1548 (May 1979): 88-90. Carruth places Ai in the poetic tradition from which she springs and attempts to explain her idiosyncratic style.

Cramer, Steven. Review of *Fate*, by Ai. *Poetry* 159 (Nov. 1991): 108-11.

Field, C. Renee. "Ai." In *American Poets Since World War II, Third Series*, edited by R. S. Gwynn. Vol. 20 in *Dictionary of Literary Biography*. Detroit: Gale Group, 1992. A good overview.

Flamm, Matthew. "Ai Came, Ai Saw, Ai Conquered." *The Village Voice* 31 (22 July 1986). An interesting profile.

Forché, Carolyn. "Sentenced to Despair." *The Washington Post Book World*, 11 Mar. 1979: F2. The author comes face to face with the subjects of Ai's work: rape, sodomy, death, drowning, all in relation to the contemporary world.

Morris, John N. "Making More Sense Than Omaha." *The Hudson Review* 27, no. 1 (Spring 1974): 107-8. Examines Ai's biographical roots and compares them to the subjects of her poems.

Murray, G. E. "Book Notes: *Killing Floor*." *The Nation* 228, no. 19 (19 May 1979): 578. Another early view of the idiosyncrasies of Ai's poetry by a well-known Chicago columnist and book reviewer.

Ostriker, Alicia. Review of *Sin*, by Ai. *Poetry* 144 (Jan. 1987): 231-37.

Varnum, Janet. "An Interview with Ai." *Cimarron Review* 173 (Fall 2010): 88-122. A substantial interview published in the year of Ai's death.

Walker, Alice. " 'Like the Eye of a Horse.' " *Ms.* 2 (June 1974): 41. Walker uses a line from the poet to show the distance that Ai utilizes in describing potentially subjective events from an objective viewpoint.

Wilson, Rob. "The Will to Transcendence in Contemporary American Poet, Ai." *Canadian Review of American Studies* 17, no. 4 (Winter 1986): 437-48. A thorough critical study.

Yenser, Stephen. "New Books in Review: *Killing Floor*." *The Yale Review* 68, no. 4 (Summer 1979): 566-69. Still another attempt to explain Ai's excesses so that they might fit in the contemporary canon.

—Marc Goldstein; James Green; John Jacob;
Holly L. Norton; Robert C. Evans

Maya Angelou

(Marguerite Johnson)

Memoirist and Poet

Born: St. Louis, Missouri; April 4, 1928

Died: Winston-Salem, NC: May 28, 2014

SHORT FICTION: "Steady Going Up," 1972; "The Reunion," 1983. drama: *Cabaret for Freedom*, pr. 1960 (with Godfrey Cambridge; musical); *The Least of These*, pr. 1966; *Encounters*, pr. 1973; *Ajax*, pr. 1974 (adaptation of Sophocles' play); *And Still I Rise*, pr. 1976; *King*, pr. 1990 (musical; lyrics with Alistair Beaton, book by Lonne Elder III, music by Richard Blackford).

SCREENPLAY: *Georgia, Georgia*, 1972; *All Day Long*, 1974.

TELEPLAYS: *Black, Blues, Black*, 1968 (ten episodes); *The Inheritors*, 1976; *The Legacy*, 1976; *I Know Why the Caged Bird Sings*, 1979 (with Leonora Thuna and Ralph B. Woolsey); *Sister, Sister*, 1982; *Brewster Place*, 1990.

POETRY: *Just Give Me a Cool Drink of Water 'fore I Diiie*, 1971; *Oh Pray My Wings Are Gonna Fit Me Well*, 1975; *And Still I Rise*, 1978; *Shaker, Why Don't You Sing?*, 1983; *Poems: Maya Angelou*, 1986; *Now Sheba Sings the Song*, 1987 (Tom Feelings, illustrator); *I Shall Not Be Moved: Poems*, 1990; *On the Pulse of Morning*, 1993; *The Complete Collected Poems of Maya Angelou*, 1994; *Phenomenal Woman: Four Poems Celebrating Women*, 1994; *A Brave and Startling Truth*, 1995; *Mother: A Cradle to Hold Me*, 2006; *Celebrations of Peace and Prayer*, 2006; *His Day is Done: A Nelson Mandela Tribute*, 2014; *Complete Poetry*, 2015.

NONFICTION: *I Know Why the Caged Bird Sings*, 1970 (autobiography); *Gather Together in My Name*, 1974 (autobiography); *Singin' and Swingin' and Gettin' Merry Like Christmas*, 1976 (autobiography); *The Heart of a Woman*, 1981 (autobiography); *All God's Children Need Traveling Shoes*, 1986 (autobiography); *Wouldn't Take Nothing for My Journey Now*, 1993 (autobiographical essays); *Even the Stars Look Lonesome*, 1997; *A Song Flung Up to Heaven*, 2002 (autobiographical essays); *The Collected Autobiographies of Maya Angelou*, 2004 (autobiography); *Hallelujah! The Welcome Table: A Lifetime of Memories with Recipes*, 2004 (memoir and cookbook); *Great Food, All Day Long: Cook Splendidly, Eat Smart*, 2010 (cookbook); *Mom & Me & Mom*, 2013 (autobiography).

CHILDREN'S/YOUNG ADULT LITERATURE: *Mrs. Flowers: A Moment of Friendship*, 1986 (illustrated by Etienne Delessert); *Life Doesn't Frighten Me*, 1993 (poetry; illustrated by Jean-Michel Basquiat); *Soul Looks Back in Wonder*, 1993; *My Painted House, My Friendly Chicken, and Me*, 1994; *Kofi and His Magic*, 1996; *Izak of Lapland*, 2004; *Mikale of Hawaii*, 2004; *Renie Marie of France*, 2004; *Angelina of Italy*, 2004.

MISCELLANEOUS: *Letter to My Daughter*, 2008 (memoir, poetry, prose); *Rainbow in the Cloud: The Wisdom and Spirit of Maya Angelou*, 2014 (poetry and prose).

Achievements

Maya Angelou's work has garnered many prestigious awards. For her writing of the revue *Cabaret for Freedom*, which she and Godfrey Cambridge produced, directed, and performed in 1960 for the purpose of raising money for Martin Luther King, Jr.'s Southern Christian Leadership Conference (SCLC), she was named northern coordinator for the SCLC in 1959. She later worked with civil rights leader Malcolm X. Other honors include a nomination for a National Book Award (1970) for *I Know Why the Caged Bird Sings*; a Yale University fellowship (1970); a Pulitzer Prize nomination (1972, for *Just Give Me a Cool Drink of Water 'fore I Diiie*); Antoinette Perry ("Tony") Award nominations (1973 and 1977); a Rockefeller Foundation scholarship in Italy (1975); honorary degrees from Smith College (1975), Mills College (1975), Lawrence University (1976), and Wake Forest University (1977); the Woman of the Year in Communications award, and a listing as one of the one hundred most influential women, both bestowed by *Ladies' Home Journal* (1976); a Golden Eagle Award for documentary (1977); a Matrix Award from Women in Communications (1983); the North Carolina Award in Literature (1987); Distinguished Woman of North Carolina (1992); the Woman of the Year award from *Essence* magazine (1992); the Horatio Alger Award (1992); the Spingarn Medal (1993); a Grammy Award for Best Spoken Word or Non-Traditional Album (1994); the National Medal of Arts (2000); the prestigious Order of Kilimanjaro Award from the National Association for the Advancement of Colored People (2001); the Presidential Medal of Freedom (2011).

Angelou was appointed Reynolds Professor of American Studies at Wake Forest University in Winston-Salem, North Carolina, in 1981. She

Photo courtesy of Kingkongphoto

composed and read a poem in honor of the inauguration of President Bill Clinton at the inaugural ceremonies in January, 1993; only one poet before her, Robert Frost, had been invited to read at an inauguration ceremony. In all, she has received more than thirty honorary degrees.

While many honorary titles have been assigned to Angelou, one is especially significant to her: the modern female African American Proust. Angelou is known for addressing the world through the medium of her own life. The first volume of her autobiography made her the first African American woman to appear on nonfiction best-seller lists; six volumes followed the first.

Biography

Born Marguerite Johnson, rechristened Maya, and taking the professional name Angelou (an adaptation of the name of her first husband, Tosh Angelos), Maya Angelou studied music and dance with Martha Graham, Pearl Primus, and Ann Halprin. Her early career was as an actress and singer, to which she quickly added the roles of civil rights worker (as the northern coordinator for the SCLC, 1959-1960), editor (as associate editor for the *Arab Observer*, 1961-1962), educator (beginning with the School of Music and Drama at the University of Ghana's Institute of African Studies, 1963-1966), and finally writer—first as a reporter for the *Ghanaian Times* (1963-1965). During the late 1960s and 1970s she taught at many colleges and universities in California and Kansas. After joining the faculty at Wake Forest University in 1981, she became a sought-after speaker and was for many years regarded as America's unofficial poet laureate, although she never received that honor.

She has told much of her own life's story in her seven-volume autobiography. Undoubtedly, Angelou's legacy will be her writings: Although the best-selling *I Know Why the Caged Bird Sings* was censored, her excellent work as an author in all genres has kept her story before the world. Angelou's early years have been burned into the minds of numerous readers. A particularly striking image from *Caged Bird* centers on three-year-old Marguerite and four-year-old Bailey Johnson aboard a train, alone, traveling from California to their grandmother's home in Stamps, Arkansas, after the breakup of their parents' marriage. The two children wore their names and their destination attached to their clothes. This locomotive quest for family is both a factual part of and an apt metaphor for the life of the world-famous poet. Her first feeling of being truly at home, she has said, came in Africa, after she accompanied her second husband to Egypt and then traveled to Ghana.

A second image from Angelou's childhood involves the seven-year-old's rape by her mother's boyfriend. When no legal punishment followed, the rapist was murdered, possibly by the victim's uncles. Guilt following this incident drove Angelou inward, and she began reading the great works of literature. Reading her way through the Stamps library, she fell in love with William Shakespeare and Paul Laurence Dunbar, among others. The child of a fractured nuclear family came to see herself as a child of the fractured human family.

By age thirteen Angelou had grown closer to her mother; at sixteen she became a mother herself. To earn a living for herself and her son Guy, she became a waitress, a singer, and a dancer. These and other occupations were followed by acting, directing, producing, and the hosting of television specials. She loved to dance, but when her knees began to suffer in her early twenties, she devoted her attention to her other love: writing. She began supporting herself through her writing in 1968. Her family came to include "sister friends" and "brother friends," as her troubled brother Bailey became lost in the worlds of substance abuse and prison. She married, but she has refused to attach a number to her marriages, as that might, she says, suggest frivolity, and she insists that she was never frivolous about marriage. To "brother friend" James Baldwin she gives much credit for her becoming an autobiographer. She assisted "brother friends" Martin Luther King, Jr. and Malcolm X in their work and pursued her own work to better the entire human family.

The hope that she found so significant in the 1960s is reflected in the poem she composed for Bill Clinton's presidential inauguration. The dream of King is evident in the words written and delivered by Angelou "on the pulse of [that] morning."

Analysis: Short Fiction

Maya Angelou has produced only a few short stories, but those stories, like her multiple volumes of autobiography, deal directly and poignantly with issues of African American life in America. Since her early years, Angelou has been a political activist and educator, and she is knowledgeable and articulate about civil rights and related issues. Her fiction, like her poetry and her nonfiction, reflects social issues and conditions in the second half of the twentieth century, when racial barriers were falling but the problems behind them continued. In this sense, Angelou must be considered a social realist, for her stories demonstrate the difficulties of growing up an African American woman in an America still riven by racism and sexism. Dozens of anthologies and other collections of contemporary literature have excerpted pieces from one or another of Angelou's autobiographies because they raise so many important issues about modern America—about identity, education, gender, and race. Her short stories are only marginally more fictional and raise many of the same issues.

"Steady Going Up"

"Steady Going Up" was first published in the collection *Ten Times Black* in 1972 and has since been reprinted several times, including in Gloria Naylor's *Children of the Night: The Best Short Stories by Black Writers, 1967 to the Present* (1995). The story is a little bit dated but raises several important questions nonetheless. As the story opens, a young black man, Robert, is traveling by bus from his home in Memphis to Cincinnati. He has never before been out of Tennessee, but this is hardly a pleasure trip, for he is rushing to pick up his younger sister at the nursing school where she has suddenly become ill (possibly from kidney trouble). Robert has raised Baby Sister since their parents died within six months of each other: "He was three years older than she when, at fifteen, he took over as head of the family." Getting a job as a mechanic at a local garage, he has been able to support Baby Sister, see her through high school, and send her to nursing school. He has had to put his own life on hold (he plans to marry Barbara Kendrick when Baby Sister is

finished with school), and now her illness may further complicate his life. The bus ride is full of understandable anxiety for Robert.

When the bus makes its last stop before Cincinnati, Robert gets off to relieve himself but is cornered in the "colored" bathroom by two white men, who have also been traveling on the bus. An older black woman, who was sitting across the aisle from Robert during the trip, has already warned him about the two men, who have been drinking and staring at him. Now they confront him, accusing him of going north to find white women. Robert cannot "stand the intention of meanness" in the two men, and he decides to act so that he will not miss the bus: "He wasn't going to get left with these two crazy men." When one tries to force him to drink the bourbon that has made them both drunk, Robert kicks him in the groin and then hits the other man over the head with the bottle. Robert manages to get back on the bus, hiding the blood on his hands and shirt, and the bus pulls away with the two men still sprawled in the bathroom. There is no resolution to the story except this escape. Robert has left "those crazy men"— at least for now—but the reader wonders what will happen to him. He may be free of them for the moment, but the hatred and violence they represent will continue to follow him. The story ends with a neutral description of the continuing bus trip: "Then he felt the big motor turn and the lights darkened and that old big baby pulled away from the sidewalk and on its way to Cincinnati." Robert's problems—as for so many African Americans at this time—still lie before him.

"The Reunion"

"The Reunion" has been anthologized several times, the first time in the Amina and Amiri Baraka collection *Confirmation: An Anthology of African American Women.* The story is short (only five pages) but is a much more positive short fiction than the earlier "Steady Going Up," which lacks resolution. The story is set in 1958 and is narrated by a jazz pianist named Philomena Jenkins, who is playing the Sunday matinee at the Blue Palm Cafe on the South Side of Chicago with the Cal Callen band. It is a club filled with other African Americans, but suddenly on this day Philomena spots Miss Beth Ann Baker, a white woman sitting with Willard, a large black man. The sight sends Philomena back in memory to her painful childhood growing up in Baker, Georgia, where her parents worked for the Bakers, and she lived in the servants' quarters behind the Baker main house.

The memories are painful because these were "years of loneliness," when Philomena was called "the Baker Nigger" by other children, and she has moved a long way from "the hurt Georgia put on me" to her present success in jazz music. She fantasizes about what she will say to Beth Ann when she meets her, but when they finally face each other at the bar a little later in the story, it is Beth Ann who does all the talking. She is going to marry Willard, who is a South Side school teacher, she tells Philomena, and she claims she is very happy. However, her parents have disowned her and even forbidden her to return to Baker. It is clear that she is with Willard to spite her parents, for she sounds to Philomena like "a ten-year-old just before a tantrum," "white and rich and spoiled." When Beth Ann invites "Mena" to their wedding, the narrator replies simply, "'Goodbye Beth. Tell your parents I said go to hell and take you with them, just for company.'" When she returns to her piano after this break, she realizes that Beth Ann:

> had the money, but I had the music. She and her parents had had the power to hurt me when I was young, but look, the stuff in me lifted me up above them. No

matter how bad times became, I would always be the song struggling to be heard.

Through her tears, Philomena has had an epiphany and experienced a form of reconciliation with her true self, in the recognition that art can transcend social inequity. In the story's last lines, "The piano keys were slippery with tears. I know, I sure as hell wasn't crying for myself." Like a number of other artists (James Baldwin and Amiri Baraka, among them), Maya Angelou posits art—and thus literature—as one way of getting above and beyond the social injustices that her society has created. Philomena cannot erase the painful childhood memories, but her music can lift her and others above them to another, healthier human plane. The hurt may remain, but the "song struggling to be heard" is stronger.

Analysis: Poetry

Asked in 1983 what she hoped to achieve as a writer, Maya Angelou answered, "to remind us that we are more alike [than un-alike], especially since I've grown up in racial turbulence and unfairness." Two 1990s poems reflect the dichotomy of her declaration: "Human Family" celebrates family likeness, and "Son to Mother" denounces wrongs inflicted by various branches of the human family. Angelou in her poetry dissects and resurrects humankind: She condemns its shamefulness and rejoices in its possibilities and its glories.

Still Rising

"Some poets sing/ their melodies," writes Angelou in "Artful Pose," published in 1975, "tendering my nights/ sweetly." Angelou, in contrast, chooses to write "of lovers false" "and hateful wrath/ quickly." She adds the word "quickly" to balance and countermand "sweetly." Her style as she speaks to live audiences and to readers, whether her tone is optimistic or pessimistic, reveals a sense of "gusto." In 1982 she offered this bit of self-analysis: "If you enter a room of hostile strangers with gusto, there are few who can contain, preserve their hostility. . . . [I]t speaks immediately to the gusto in other people." European American audiences applauded her and purchased her work even as she berated them: "You may write me down in history/ With your bitter, twisted lies," she says in the opening lines of one of her most famous poems, "Still I Rise." "I'll play possum and close my eyes/ To your greater sins and my lesser lies," she writes in a jump-rope rhythm in "Bump d'Bump." "That way I share my nation's prize," she continues. "Call me a name from an ugly south/ Like liver lips and satchel mouth"; gusto, anger, and a challenge to humankind are integral ingredients in Angelou's poetry.

In "Man Bigot" Angelou writes:

> The man who is a bigot is the worst thing
> God has got except his match, his
> woman, who really is Ms. Begot.

Angelou is not unwilling to amuse as she challenges her audience. She did not leave the entertainment field behind when she turned to verse. Other entertaining and uplifting elements of her poetry are sass and the celebration of womanhood. "Men themselves have wondered/ What they see in me," says the speaker of "A Phenomenal Woman." A part of her mystery, she says, is in "the fire in my eyes," "the joy in my feet," and:

> The grace of my style.
> I'm a woman Phenomenally.
> Phenomenal woman,
> That's me.

Sass and Anger

Sass is an element in 1978's "Still I Rise," but anger consistently tempers its speaker's joy. "Does my sassiness upset you?" and "Does my haughtiness offend you?" she asks her European American readers. "Out of the huts of history's shame/ I rise," says her African American speaker. In "Miss Scarlett, Mr. Rhett, and Other Latter-Day Saints," Angelou writes:

> Animated by the human sacrifice (Golgotha in black-face)
> Priests glow purely white on the bas-relief of a plantation shrine.

In "Slave Coffle" (1983) she speaks as a slave to whom "all the earth is horror," as the speaker realizes "Before the dawning,/ bright as grinning demons" that "life was gone."

While, in her later years, Angelou claimed to interviewers to have mellowed since writing her first volume of poetry, her verse remains harsh to the reader's mind and ear. Shame and ignorance recur as significant themes. Pride, however, is at least as significant.

Pride in Ancestors

In 1975 Angelou declared "Song for the Old Ones" her favorite poem. Her celebration of those who kept her race alive remained a favorite theme. Her 1990 volume of poetry, *I Shall Not Be Moved*, has as its title the chorus to the poem "Our Grandmothers." Her sense of pride in these old ones and her sense of kinship with them is evident in the words she gives one of these grandmothers. To those who hurled ribbons of invective into the wind of history:

> She said, But my description cannot
> fit your tongue, for
> I have a certain way of being in this
> world, and I shall not, I shall not be
> moved.

In "Old Folks Laugh" (1990) she writes that old folks' laughter frees the world. The freedom that the grandmothers offer their children in "Our Grandmothers" is the freedom to be fully human: They tell them, "When you learn, teach. When you get, give." "I laugh until I start to crying, / When I think about my folks," says the speaker of "When I Think About Myself." Angelou's poetry shows that the stories of her people continued to fill and to break her heart. The title of the volume containing "Song for the Old Ones," *Oh Pray My Wings Are Gonna Fit Me Well* (1975), seems, as does the title *I Shall Not Be Moved*, to derive from her wish to be worthy of and to emulate the old ones.

That Angelou gives the final position in the 1990 volume to the poem dedicated to other, less great, old ones is significant, as is the idea of that poem: "When great souls die," she says in the final stanza:

> Our senses, restored, never to be the
> same, whisper to us.
> They existed. They existed.
> We can be. Be and be better. For they
> existed.

Unbelievable cruelty has given rise to unbelievable valor. Angelou cannot and will not forget the history of human cruelty as she feels that human beings must learn from their shared history. She continues to show human beings what they must learn, that they can be better.

Guilt and Responsibility

Crucial to Angelou's overall idea is the shared guilt and responsibility of all history's survivors. In "I Almost Remember" (1975), the speaker recalls smiling and even laughing, but now:

> Open night news-eyed I watch channels
> of hunger
> written on children's faces bursting bel-
> lies balloon
> in the air of my day room.

The speaker's garden, television, and day room suggest the luxuries and the guilt of one of the "haves" as she/he witnesses the suffering of the "have-nots" on the "channels of hunger." Similarly, "Harlem Hopscotch," with a seemingly different tone and a hopscotch rhythm, shows children singing of "good things for the ones that's got." "Everybody for hisself," they continue. The pain of both the television viewer and the children reflects the suffering as well as the scarring of the human psyche.

"Take Time Out" challenges the acceptance of the status quo, challenging the attitude of all human players of life's game:

> Use a minute
> feel some sorrow
> for the folks
> who think tomorrow is a place that they
> can call up
> on the phone.

The speaker of this poem asks that kindness be shown for the folk who thought that blindness was an illness that affected eyes alone. "We'd better see," says the speaker:

> what all our
> fearing and our
> jeering and our
> crying and
> our lying brought
> about.

Society is responsible for its children and for its own and its children's attitudes. As she shows in "Faces":

> the brown caramel days of youth Reject
> the sun-sucked tit of childhood mornings.
> Poke a muzzle of war in the trust frozen
> eyes of a favored doll.

This is what humanity has wrought and what it must not accept. Humankind must be rendered both human and kind, the poet seems to say.

New Dreams

Angelou calls repeatedly on the human race to spare itself from suffering. "There's one thing that I cry for I believe enough to die for/ That is every man's responsibility to man," says the speaker of "On Working White Liberals." "Dare us new dreams, Columbus," says the speaker of "A Georgia Song" (1983). In "America" (1975) Angelou speaks of America's promise that "has never been mined": "Her proud declarations/ are leaves in the wind." The United States, says the speaker, "entraps her children/ with legends untrue." This country of such high promise—the promise that all are equally entitled to life, liberty, and the pursuit of happiness—has not yet been discovered. Its citizens are led by their poet laureate to see that it is high time that the discovery be made.

Complete Poetry

The 2015 publication of Angelou's *Complete Poetry* offered readers the opportunity to examine the whole range of her poetic achievement and, in particular, to pay close attention to the artistic skill of her poems, which have often been examined more for their meanings than for their artistry.

One notices, for instance, the simple diction, direct address, emphatic verbs, and final symmetry of "A Conceit," which ends with the very same words with which it began. This poem, tender in tone and idea, contrasts strongly with the fiery anger of "Request," the poem that immediately follows it in this volume. The juxtaposition of these two works illustrates the sheer variety of Angelou's topics and style. Likewise, "Request" is followed by two poems whose subject matters are both related and distinct: "Africa" and "America." The side-by-side placement of these two texts demonstrates how Angelou crafts her books as well as her individual lyrics, while the understated variations in

the refrain of "Africa" again demonstrate a subtlety for which Angelou is given insufficient credit. The poem opens with the line "Thus she had lain," then moves to two uses of the phrase "Thus she has lain," and then concludes with the words "although she had lain."

Almost any poem by Angelou reveals such artistry, if artistry is what a reader looks for. Consider, for instance, the opening stanza of "For Us, Who Dare Not Dare":

> Be me a Pharaoh
> Build me high pyramids of stone and question
> See me the Nile
> at twilight
> and jaguars moving to
> the slow cool draught.

The first intriguing aspect of this poem, as in so many of Angelou's poems, is the title itself. Who, exactly, are those "Who Dare Not Dare?" In what senses do they "Dare Not Dare?" How is their absence of daring relevant to the poem's focus on Africa? Here, as in many of her poems, the title raises more questions than it ever even pretends to answer, and that fact often contributes to the intrigue of Angelou's poetry. Once again, she gives us issues to think about rather than issuing simple answers to questions.

However, once the poem itself begins, we notice further subtleties. "Be me a Pharaoh," for instance, is not correct standard American English phrasing. Presumably the speaker means something like: "Let me be a Pharaoh" or "Imagine that I am a Pharaoh." Angelou could have made such meanings clearer if she had wanted to, but she chose phrasing which, by the very fact that it is unusual, attracts attention and raises questions. There is a hint of the exotic, the foreign, the unusual and unexpected in her phrasing, as if perhaps she is imitating the kind of English a native African might speak. Whatever the explanation, the phrasing here is intriguing.

Also intriguing is the sheer length of the second line. Only three lines in the entire nineteen-line poem are notably long; they literally stick out when we look at the poem on the page. Why did Angelou choose this kind of structure? Once more, the answer is not clear, although there is no denying that the long lines attract special attention, and they illustrate Angelou's frequent tendency to innovate in form as well as phrasing. She is not the sort of poet who typically (if ever) uses traditional stanzas or traditional meter.

Nearly every poem has its own distinctive shape and rhythms. Aside from the sheer length of the second line, its meaning is fairly predictable—until, that is, we reach the very last word. It is easy to understand the command to "Build me high pyramids of stone." But then we reach the final two words, especially the final word itself: "and question." We might assume that "and question" will lead smoothly into the next line (as in "and question / the right of others to build," or some such continuation). Instead, however, the next line begins a totally new thought, so that we are left hanging with the words "and question." What, exactly, does this mean? What part of speech, exactly, is "question" playing here? Is it a verb? Is it a noun? At first, we assume it is a verb, but the more one thinks about it, the more inclined one is to read it as a noun, in which case, its meaning is especially intriguing. If "question" is a noun, it resembles the line's earlier noun ("stone"). Perhaps the speaker is implying that the ancient Egyptian pyramids were built from stone but were built as part of a kind of quest, to answer or quite literally raise questions.

The questions raised by this very word itself contribute to the real interest of Angelou's poem. Once again we find ourselves pausing to think rather than merely digesting some simple statement. The questions raised by the word "question" are then followed by relatively simple but quite vivid imagery of the Nile, twilight, and jaguars, but then the stanza concludes with a splendid bit of rhythmic inventiveness. The stanza's penultimate line "and jaguars moving to" (line 5) employs strict iambic rhythm: each even syllable is accented, and each odd syllable is unstressed. Iambic rhythm is perfectly appropriate here to the steady movement the line describes. But then no sooner is this smooth iambic rhythm established than it is violated by the heavily accented syllables of the following line "the slow cool draught" (line 6), in which every word besides "the" receives strong stress. The line itself is almost impossible to pronounce quickly, partly because of the strongly emphasized vowel sounds in "slow" and "cool" and "draught." It is as if Angelou is making the very sound of the line imitate the slowness the line describes—just another example of the ways her poetry is often at least as interesting for its sounds as for its meanings.

Other Literary Forms

In addition to being a noted autobiographer, poet, and short-story writer, Maya Angelou is an essayist, playwright, screenwriter, and the author of children's books. Along with the seven volumes of her autobiography, her collection of essays *Even the Stars Look Lonesome* was on *The New York Times* best-seller list for ten consecutive weeks. Her two-act drama *The Least of These* was produced in Los Angeles in 1966. With her screenplay *Georgia, Georgia* she became, in 1972, the first African American woman to have an original screenplay produced. In 1974 she adapted Sophocles' *Aias* (early 440s b.c.e.; *Ajax*, 1729) for the modern stage. Her children's book *My Painted House, My Friendly Chicken, and Me* was published in 1994. Her works have been translated into at least ten languages.

Bibliography

Angelou, Maya. *Conversations with Maya Angelou.* Edited by Jeffrey M. Elliot. Jackson: University Press of Mississippi, 1989. This collection of informal interviews paints an appealing personal and intellectual portrait of the poet.

Bloom, Harold, ed. *Maya Angelou's I Know Why the Caged Bird Sings.* New York: Bloom's Literary Criticism, 2009.

This is one of numerous collections of criticism, of diverse lengths, formatting, and contents, edited by Bloom and dealing with Angelou. This volume contains thirteen pieces on various topics, including several interviews with Angelou.

_____, ed. *Maya Angelou.* Philadelphia: Chelsea House, 1999. This selection of essays dealing with Angelou's poetry and prose broaches, among other subjects, the singular relationship of Angelou to her audience and her distinctively African American mode of literary expression.

Braxton, Joanne M., ed. *Maya Angelou's I Know Why the Caged Bird Sings: A Casebook.* New York: Oxford University Press, 1999.

Contains nine critical essays on Angelou's most famous work. These essays deal with such topics as geography, initiation, self-discovery, rape, racial protest, death, and other issues.

Carger, Chris Liska, and Henrietta M. Smith. "To Make a Poet Black, and Bid Him Sing." *Book Links* 12, no. 2 (December/ January, 2003): 45-46. An analysis of African American poetry for children.

Eller, Edward E. "Critical Essay on *I Know Why the Caged Bird Sings.*" In *Nonfiction Classics for Students,* edited by Elizabeth Thomason. Vol. 2. Detroit: Gale, 2001. This accessible essay examines the first of Angelou's autobiographies, paying special attention to the ways in which it has attracted its wide audience.

Hagen, Lynn B. *Heart of a Woman, Mind of a Writer, and Soul of a Poet: A Critical Analysis of the Writings of Maya Angelou.* Lanham, Md.: University Press of America, 1996. While there have been a number of scholarly works addressing the different literary forms Angelou has undertaken (most devoted to autobiography), few critical volumes have appeared that survey her entire opus; Hagen's is one of the best. Chapters include "Wit and Wisdom/Mirth and Mischief," "Abstracts in Ethics," and "Overview."

King, Sarah E. *Maya Angelou: Greeting the Morning.* Brookfield, Conn.: Millbrook Press, 1994. Includes biographical references and an index. Examines Angelou's life, from her childhood in the segregated South to her rise to prominence as a writer.

Lisandrelli, Elaine Slivinski. *Maya Angelou: More than a Poet.* Springfield, N.J.: Enslow, 1996. Lisandrelli discusses the flamboyance of Angelou, comparing her to the earlier African American author Zora Neale Hurston. Their hard work, optimism, perseverance, and belief in themselves are extolled.

Lupton, Mary Jane. *Maya Angelou: A Critical Companion.* Westport, Conn.: Greenwood Press, 1998. While focusing mainly on the autobiographies, Lupton's study is still useful as a balanced assessment of Angelou's writings. The volume also contains an excellent bibliography, particularly of Angelou's autobiographical works.

Lupton, Mary Jane. *Maya Angelou: The Iconic Self.* 2nd ed. Santa Barbara, CA: Greenwood, 2016.

This book offers general introductions to Angelou's life and works and to the genre of autobiography and then discusses six different works. It ends with an essay in memory of Angelou and also supplies a bibliography and index.

Mickel, Mildred, ed. *Maya Angelou: Critical Insights.* Ipswich, MA: Salem Press, 2016.

A wide-ranging collection of essays on numerous works and aspects of Angelou's achievements. Includes a general overview; essays on history, critical commentary, comparison and contrast, and a specific theoretical approach; and ten additional essays on deliberately diverse topics.

Pettit, Jayne. *Maya Angelou: Journey of the Heart.* New York: Lodestar Books, 1996. Includes bibliographical references and an index. Traces Angelou's journey from childhood through her life as entertainer, activist, writer, and university professor.

Shapiro, Miles. *Maya Angelou*. New York: Chelsea House, 1994. A biography describing the life and work of the celebrated writer.

Smiley, Tavis, and David Ritz. *My Journey with Maya*. New York, Little, Brown, 2015.

An autobiographical memoir by the noted journalist and television commentator.

Williams, Mary E., ed. *Maya Angelou*. San Diego, Calif.: Greenhaven Press, 1997. This collection of essays by literary scholars and noted faculty offers diverse voices and approaches to Angelou's literary canon.

— *Judith K. Taylor; David Peck; Robert C. Evans*

James Baldwin

Novelist, Essayist, and Playwright

Born: New York, New York; August 2, 1924

Died: St. Paul de Vence, France; December 1, 1987

LONG FICTION: *Go Tell It on the Mountain*, 1953; *Giovanni's Room*, 1956; *Another Country*, 1962; *Tell Me How Long the Train's Been Gone*, 1968; *If Beale Street Could Talk*, 1974; *Just Above My Head*, 1979; *Early Novels and Stories, Vol.* I, 1998; *Later Novels*, 2015.

SHORT FICTION: *Going to Meet the Man*, 1965.

DRAMA: *The Amen Corner*, pr. 1954, pb. 1968; *Blues for Mister Charlie*, pr., pb. 1964; *A Deed from the King of Spain*, pr. 1974.

SCREENPLAY: *One Day, When I Was Lost: A Scenario Based on "The Autobiography of Malcolm X,"* 1972.

POETRY: *Jimmy's Blues: Selected Poems*, 1983; *Jimmy's Blues and Other Poems*, 2014.

NONFICTION: *Notes of a Native Son*, 1955; *Nobody Knows My Name: More Notes of a Native Son*, 1961; *The Fire Next Time*, 1963; *Nothing Personal*, 1964 (with Richard Avedon); *No Name in the Street*, 1971; *A Rap on Race*, 1971 (with Margaret Mead); *A Dialogue*, 1975 (with Nikki Giovanni); *The Devil Finds Work*, 1976; *The Evidence of Things Not Seen*, 1985; *The Price of the Ticket*, 1985; *Conversations with James Baldwin*, 1989; *Collected Essays*, 1998; *James Baldwin: The Last Interview and Other Conversations*, 2014.

CHILDREN'S/YOUNG ADULT LITERATURE: *Little Man, Little Man*, 1975.

Achievements

James Baldwin's public role as a major African American spokesman of the 1950s and 1960s guarantees his place in American cultural history. Though not undeserved, this reputation more frequently obscures than clarifies the nature of his literary achievement, which involves his relationship to African American culture, existential philosophy, and the moral tradition of the world novel. To be sure, Baldwin's progression from an individualistic, universalist stance through active involvement with the integrationist Civil Rights movement to an increasing sympathy with militant Pan-Africanist thought parallels the general development of African American thought between the early 1950s and the mid-1970s. Indeed, his novels frequently mirror both Baldwin's personal philosophy and its social context. Some, most notably *Another Country*, attained a high degree of public visibility when published, leading to a widely accepted vision of Baldwin as a topical writer. To consider Baldwin primarily as a racial spokesman, however, imposes a stereotype which distorts many of his most penetrating insights and underestimates his status as a literary craftsman.

More accurate, though ultimately as limited, is the view of Baldwin primarily as an exemplar of the African American presence in the "mainstream" of the American tradition. Grouped

James Baldwin with Marlon Brando (photo courtesy of the National Archives)

with Ralph Ellison as a major "post-Wright" black novelist, Baldwin represents, in this view, the generation that rejected "protest literature" in favor of "universal" themes. Strangely at odds with the view of Baldwin as racial spokesman, this view emphasizes the craftsmanship of Baldwin's early novels and his treatment of "mainstream" themes such as religious hypocrisy, father-son tensions, and sexual identity. Ironically, many younger African American novelists accept this general view of Baldwin's accomplishment, viewing his mastery of Jamesian techniques and his involvement with continental literary culture as an indication of alienation from his racial identity. Recasting activist Eldridge Cleaver's political attack on Baldwin in aesthetic terms, the African American writer Ishmael Reed dismisses Baldwin as a great "white" novelist. A grain of truth lies in Reed's assertion; Baldwin rarely created new forms. Rather, he infused a variety of Euro-American forms, derived from Richard Wright and William Faulkner as well as from Henry James, with the rhythms and imagery of the African American oral tradition.

Baldwin's high-profile career, in both the literary and the political spheres, earned for him widespread recognition and a number of awards. Early in his career, he was granted the Eugene F. Saxton Memorial Trust Fellowship in 1945, followed by the Rosenwald Fellowship in 1948. In 1956 he was awarded a Partisan Review Fellowship, a National Institute of Arts and Letter grant for literature, and a National Institute of Arts and Letters Award, followed three years later by a Ford Foundation grant. His magazine articles earned him a George Polk Memorial Award in 1963 and in 1964 *Blues for Mister Charlie* earned a Foreign Drama Critics Award and *The Fire Next Time* was given a National Association of Independent Schools Award. *Just Above My Head* was nominated in 1980 for the American Book Award. France honored him in 1986 by naming him Commander of the Legion of Honor. He served as a member of several organizations throughout his lifetime, including the American Academy and Institute of Arts and Letters, the Authors' League, International PEN, Dramatists Guild, Actors Studio, and the Congress of Racial Equality.

Biography

James Baldwin once dismissed his childhood as "the usual bleak fantasy." Nevertheless, the major concerns of his fiction consistently reflect the social context of his family life in Harlem during the Depression. The dominant figure of Baldwin's childhood was certainly his stepfather, David Baldwin, who worked as a manual laborer and preached in a storefront church. Clearly the model for Gabriel Grimes in *Go Tell It on the Mountain*, David Baldwin had moved from New Orleans to New York City, where he married Baldwin's mother, Emma Berdis. The oldest of what was to be a group of nine children in the household, James assumed a great deal of the responsibility for the care of his half-brothers and sisters. Insulated somewhat from the brutality of Harlem street life by his domestic duties, Baldwin, as he describes in *The Fire Next Time*, sought refuge in the church. Undergoing a conversion experience—similar to that of John in *Go Tell It on the Mountain*—at age fourteen in 1938, Baldwin preached as a youth minister for the next several years. At the same time, he began to read, immersing himself in works such as *Uncle Tom's Cabin* (1852) and the novels of Charles Dickens. Both at his Harlem junior high school, where the African American poet Countee Cullen was one of his teachers, and at his predominantly white Bronx high school, Baldwin contributed to student literary publications. The combination of family tension, economic hardship, and religious vocation provides the focus of much of Baldwin's greatest writing, most notably *Go Tell It on the Mountain*, *The Fire Next Time*, and *Just Above My Head*.

If Baldwin's experience during the 1930s provided his material, his life from 1942 to 1948 shaped his characteristic approach to that material. After he graduated from high school in 1942, Baldwin worked for a year as a manual laborer in New Jersey, an experience which increased both his understanding of his stepfather and his insight into America's economic and racial systems. Moving to Greenwich Village in 1943, Baldwin worked during the day and wrote at night for the next five years; his first national reviews and essays appeared in 1946. The major event of the Village years, however, was Baldwin's meeting with Richard Wright in the winter of 1944-1945. Wright's interest helped Baldwin secure first a Eugene F. Saxton Memorial Award and then a Rosenwald Fellowship, enabling him to move to Paris in 1948.

After his arrival in France, Baldwin experienced more of the poverty which had shaped his childhood. Simultaneously, he developed a larger perspective on the psychocultural context conditioning his experience, feeling at once a greater sense of freedom and a larger

sense of the global structure of racism, particularly as reflected in the French treatment of North Africans. In addition, he formed many of the personal and literary friendships which contributed to his later public prominence. Baldwin's well-publicized literary feud with Wright, who viewed the younger writer's criticism of *Native Son* (1940) as a form of personal betrayal, helped establish Baldwin as a major presence in African American letters. Although Baldwin's first novel, *Go Tell It on the Mountain*, was well-received critically, it was not so financially successful that he could devote his full time to creative writing. As a result, Baldwin continued to travel widely, frequently on journalistic assignments, while writing *Giovanni's Room*, which is set in France and involves no black characters.

Returning to the United States as a journalist covering the Civil Rights movement, Baldwin made his first trip to the American South in 1957. The essays and reports describing that physical and psychological journey propelled Baldwin to the position of public prominence which he maintained for more than a decade. During the height of the movement, Baldwin lectured widely and was present at major events such as the March on Washington and the voter registration drive in Selma, Alabama. In addition, he met with most of the major African American activists of the period, including Martin Luther King, Jr., Elijah Muhammad, James Meredith, and Medgar Evers. Attorney General Robert Kennedy requested that Baldwin bring together the most influential voices in the black community, and, even though the resulting meeting accomplished little, the request testifies to Baldwin's image as a focal point of African American opinion. In addition to this political activity, Baldwin formed personal and literary relationships—frequently tempestuous ones—with numerous white writers, including William Styron and Norman Mailer. A surge in literary popularity, reflected in the presence of *Another Country* and *The Fire Next Time* on the best-seller lists throughout most of 1962 and 1963, accompanied Baldwin's political success and freed him from financial insecurity for the first time. He traveled extensively throughout the decade, and his visits to Puerto Rico and Africa were to have a major influence on his subsequent political thought.

Partly because of Baldwin's involvement with prominent whites and partly because of the sympathy for gay people evinced in his writing, several black militants, most notably Eldridge Cleaver, attacked Baldwin's position as "black spokesman" beginning in the late 1960s. As a result, nationalist spokesmen such as Amiri Baraka and Bobby Seale gradually eclipsed Baldwin in the public literary and political spotlights. Nevertheless, Baldwin, himself sympathetic to many of the militant positions, continued his involvement with public issues, such as the fate of the so-called Wilmington Ten, a group of Civil Rights activists who were falsely convicted, which he addressed in an open letter to Jimmy Carter shortly after Carter's election to the presidency. In his later years, though he returned periodically to the South, Baldwin lived for much of the time in France and Turkey. It was in St. Paul de Vence, France, that he died, in 1987.

Analysis: Long Fiction

Uncompromising in his demand for personal and social integrity, Baldwin charged the individual with full responsibility for his or her moral identity from the beginning of his career. Both in his early individualistic novels and in his later political fiction, he insisted on the inadequacy of received definitions as the basis for self-knowledge or social action. Echoing the existentialist principle "existence precedes essence," he intimated the underlying consistency of his vision in the introductory essay in *Notes of a Native Son*: "I think all theories are suspect, that the finest principles may have to be modified, or may even be pulverized by the demands of life, and that one must find, therefore, one's own moral center and move through the world hoping that this center will guide one aright." This insistence on the moral center and movement in the world cautions against associating Baldwin with the atheistic or solipsistic currents of existential thought. Never denying the possibility of transcendent moral power—which he frequently imaged as the power of love—he simply insisted that human conceptions must remain flexible enough to allow for the honest perception of experience. Fully recognizing the reality of existential pain and despair, Baldwin invoked honesty and self-acceptance as the necessary supports for the love capable of generating individual communication and at least the groundwork for political action.

Go Tell It on the Mountain

Go Tell It on the Mountain centers on the religious conversion and family relationships of John Grimes, whose experience parallels that of Baldwin during his youth. Although he believes himself to be the natural son of Gabriel Grimes, a preacher who, like Baldwin's stepfather, moved to New York after growing up in the South, John is actually the son of Gabriel's wife, Elizabeth, and her lover, Richard, who committed suicide prior to John's birth. Growing up under the influence of his hypocritical and tyrannical stepfather, John alternately attempts to please and transcend him. Gabriel expends most of his emotional energy on his openly rebellious son Roy, whose immersion in the violent life of the Harlem streets contrasts sharply with John's involvement with the Temple of the Fire Baptized, the storefront church where his conversion takes place. To the extent that

Baldwin organizes *Go Tell It on the Mountain* around John's attempt to come to terms with these pressures, the novel appears to have a highly individualistic focus.

The overall structure of the novel, however, dictates that John's experience be viewed in a larger context. Of the three major sections of *Go Tell It on the Mountain,* the first, "The Seventh Day," and the third, "The Threshing Floor," focus directly on John. The long middle section, "The Prayers of the Saints," a Faulknerian exploration of history, traces the origins of John's struggle to the experience of his elders, devoting individual chapters to Elizabeth, Gabriel, and Gabriel's sister Florence. Together the chapters portray the Great Migration of African Americans from South to North, from rural to urban settings. Far from bringing true freedom, the movement results in a new indirect type of oppression. As Elizabeth recognizes: "There was not, after all, a great difference between the world of the North and that of the South which she had fled; there was only this difference: the North promised more. And this similarity: what it promised it did not give, and what it gave, at length and grudgingly with one hand, it took back with the other." Even in his most individualistic phase, Baldwin is aware of the power of institutional pressures. The origins of John's particular struggle against limiting definitions go back to their impact on both Elizabeth and Gabriel.

Another Country

Another Country, Baldwin's greatest popular success, analyzes the effects of deforming pressure and experience on a wide range of characters, black and white, male and female, homosexual and heterosexual. To accommodate these diverse consciousnesses, Baldwin employs the sprawling form usually associated with political rather than psychological fiction, emphasizing the diverse forms of innocence and experience in American society. The three major sections of *Another Country,* "Easy Rider," "Any Day Now," and "Toward Bethlehem," progress generally from despair to renewed hope, but no single consciousness or plotline provides a frame similar to that of *Go Tell It on the Mountain.* Rather, the novel's structural coherence derives from the moral concerns present in each of the various plots.

Casting a Melvillean shadow over the novel is the black jazz musician Rufus Scott, who is destroyed by an agonizing affair with Leona, a white southerner recently arrived in New York at the time she meets him. Unable to forge the innocence necessary for love in a context which repudiates the relationship at every turn, Rufus destroys Leona psychologically. After a period of physical and psychological destitution, he kills himself by jumping off a bridge. His sister Ida, an aspiring singer, and his friend Vivaldo Moore, an aspiring white writer, meet during the last days of Rufus' life and fall in love as they console each other over his death. Struggling to overcome the racial and sexual definitions which destroyed Rufus, they seek a higher innocence capable of countering Ida's sense of the world as a "whorehouse." In contrast to Ida and Vivaldo's struggle, the relationship of white actor Eric Jones and his French lover Yves seems Edenic. Although Baldwin portrays Eric's internal struggle for a firm sense of his sexual identity, their shared innocence at times seems to exist almost entirely outside the context of the pressures that destroyed Rufus. The final major characters, Richard and Cass Silenski, represent the cost of the American Dream. After Richard "makes it" as a popular novelist, their personal relationship decays, precipitating Cass' affair with Eric. Their tentative reunion after Richard discovers the affair makes it clear that material success provides no shortcut to moral responsibility.

The majority of the narrative lines imply the impossibility of simple dissociation from institutional pressure. Ultimately, the intensity of Rufus's pain and the intricacy of Ida and Vivaldo's struggle overshadow Eric and Yves's questionable innocence. As Ida tells Vivaldo, "Our being together doesn't change the world." The attempt to overcome the cynicism of this perception leads to a recognition that meaningful love demands total acceptance. Ida's later question, "How can you say you loved Rufus when there was so much about him you didn't want to know?" could easily provide the epitaph for the entire society in *Another Country*.

Analysis: Short Fiction

Like the folk preacher whose voice he frequently assumed in secular contexts, Baldwin combined moral insight with an uncompromising sense of the concrete realities of his community, whether defined in terms of family, lovers, race, or nation. This indicates the deepest level of Baldwin's literary achievement; whatever his immediate political focus or fictional form, he possessed an insight into moral psychology shared by only a handful of novelists. Inasmuch as the specific circumstances of this psychology involve American racial relations, this insight aligns Baldwin with Wright, Faulkner, Mark Twain, and Harriet Beecher Stowe. Inasmuch as his insight involves the symbolic alienation of the individual, it places him with American romantics such as Nathaniel Hawthorne and European existentialists such as Albert Camus. Since his insight recognizes the complex pressure exerted by social mechanisms on individual consciousness, it reveals affinities with James Joyce, George Eliot, and Ellison. As a writer who combined elements of all of these traditions with the voice of the anonymous African American preacher, Baldwin cannot be reduced to accommodate the terms of any one of them. Refusing to lie about the reality of pain, he provided realistic images of the moral life possible in the inhospitable world that encompasses the streets of Harlem and the submerged recesses of the mind. These images are particularly evident in his works of short fiction.

"The Man Child"

Baldwin's "The Man Child," the only story in *Going to Meet the Man* that has no black characters, scathingly describes whites, especially their violent propensities. The central character is Eric, an eight-year-old. The story opens as he, his mother, and his father are giving a birthday party for Jamie, his father's best friend. In the next scene Eric and his father walk together and then return to the party. After a brief summary of intervening events, the story moves forward in time to a day when Jamie meets Eric, entices him into a barn, and breaks his neck. The story described thus, its ending seems to be a surprise, and it certainly is a surprise to Eric. In fact, his sudden realization that he is in grave danger is an epiphany. "The Man Child" is thus a coming-of-age story, an account of a young person's realization of the dark side of adult existence. Eric, however, has little time to think about his realization or even to generalize very much on the basis of his intimation of danger before he is badly, perhaps mortally, injured.

The story, however, contains many hints that violent action will be forthcoming. A reader can see them even though Eric cannot because Eric is the center of consciousness, a device perfected, if not invented, by Henry James. That is, Eric does not narrate the story so the story does not present his viewpoint, but he is always the focus of the action, and the story is in essence an account of his responses to that action. The difference between his perception of the events he witnesses (which is sometimes described and sometimes can be inferred from his actions) and the perception that can be had by attending carefully to the story encourages a reader to make a moral analysis and finally to make a moral judgment, just as the difference between Huck Finn's perception and the perception that one can have while reading *Adventures of Huckleberry Finn* (1884) at first stimulates laughter and then moral evaluation. Eric's lack of perception is a function of his innocence, a quality that he has to an even larger extent than has Huck Finn, and thus he is less able to cope in a threatening world and his injury is even more execrable. If the measure of a society is its solicitude for the powerless, the miniature society formed by the three adults in this story, and perhaps by implication the larger society of which they are a part, is sorely wanting.

To be more specific about the flaws in this society and in these persons, they enslave themselves and others, as is suggested very early in the story: "Eric lived with his father ...and his mother, who had been captured by his father on some far off unblessed, unbelievable night, who had never since burst her chains." Her husband intimidates and frightens her, and his conversation about relations between men and women indicates that he believes she exists at his sufferance only for sex and procreation. Her role becomes questionable because in the summary of events that happen between the first and last parts of the story one learns that she has lost the child she had been carrying and cannot conceive anymore. The two men enslave themselves with their notions about women, their drunkenness (which they misinterpret as male companionship), their mutual hostility, their overbearing expansiveness, in short, with their machismo. Eric's father is convinced that he is more successful in these terms. He has fathered a son, an accomplishment the

significance of which to him is indicated by his "some day all this will be yours" talk with Eric between the two party scenes. Jamie's wife, showing more sense than Eric's mother, left him before he could sire a son. Jamie's violent act with Eric is his psychotic imitation of the relation of Eric's father to Eric, just as his whistling at the very end of the story is his imitation of the music he hears coming from a tavern. Eric is thus considered by the two men to be alive merely for their self-expression. His father's kind of self-expression is potentially debilitating, although somewhat benign; Jamie's version is nearly fatal.

"Going to Meet the Man"

"Going to Meet the Man" is a companion to "The Man Child," both stories having been published for the first time in *Going to Meet the Man*. Whereas the latter story isolates whites from blacks in order to analyze their psychology, the former story is about whites in relation to blacks, even though blacks make only brief appearances in it. The whites in these stories have many of the same characteristics, but in "Going to Meet the Man" those characteristics are more obviously dangerous. These stories were written during the height of the Civil Rights movement, and Baldwin, by means of his rhetorical power and his exclusion of more human white types, helped polarize that movement.

The main characters in "Going to Meet the Man" are a family composed of a southern deputy sheriff, his wife, and his son, Jesse. At the beginning of the story they are skittish because of racial unrest. Demonstrations by blacks have alternated with police brutality by whites, each response escalating the conflict, which began when a black man knocked down an elderly white woman. The family is awakened late at night by a crowd of whites who have learned that the black perpetrator has been caught. They all set off in a festive, although somewhat tense, mood to the place where he is being held. After they arrive the black man is burned, castrated, and mutilated—atrocities that Baldwin describes very vividly. This story, however, is not merely sensationalism or social and political rhetoric. It rises above those kinds of writing because of its psychological insights into the causes of racism and particularly of racial violence.

Baldwin's focus at first is on the deputy sheriff. As the story opens he is trying and failing to have sexual relations with his wife. He thinks that he would have an easier time with a black woman, and "the image of a black girl caused a distant excitement in him. "Thus, his conception of blacks is immediately mixed with sexuality, especially with his fear of impotence. In contrast, he thinks of his wife as a "frail sanctuary." At the approach of a car he reaches for the gun beside his bed, thereby adding a propensity for violence to his complex of psychological motives. Most of his behavior results from this amalgam of racial attitudes, sexual drives, fear of impotence, and attraction to violence. For example, he recalls torturing a black prisoner by applying a cattle prod to his testicles, and on the way to see the black captive he takes pride in his wife's attractiveness. He also frequently associates blacks with sexual vigor and fecundity. The castration scene is the most powerful rendition of this psychological syndrome.

The deputy sheriff, however, is more than a mere brute. For example, he tries to think of his relation to blacks in moral terms. Their singing of spirituals disconcerts him because he has difficulty understanding how they can be Christians like himself. He tries to reconcile this problem by believing that blacks have decided "to fight against God and go against the rules laid down in the Bible for everyone to read!" To allay the guilt that threatens to complicate his life he also believes that there are a lot of good blacks who need his protection from bad blacks. These strategies for achieving inner peace do not work, and Baldwin brilliantly describes the moral confusion of such whites:

> They had never dreamed that their privacy could contain any element of terror, could threaten, that is, to reveal itself, to the scrutiny of a judgment day, while remaining unreadable and inaccessible to themselves; nor had they dreamed that the past, while certainly refusing to be forgotten, could yet so stubbornly refuse to be remembered. They felt themselves mysteriously set at naught.

In the absence of a satisfying moral vision, violence seems the only way to achieve inner peace, and the sheriff's participation in violence allows him to have sex with his wife as the story ends. Even then, however, he has to think that he is having it as blacks would. He is their psychic prisoner, just as the black man who was murdered was the white mob's physical prisoner.

Late in this story one can see that Jesse, the sheriff's eight-year-old son, is also an important character. At first he is confused by the turmoil and thinks of blacks in human terms. For example, he wonders why he has not seen his black friend Otis for several days. The mob violence, however, changes him; he undergoes a coming of age, the perversity of which is disturbing. He is the center of consciousness in the mob scene. His first reaction is the normal one for a boy: "Jesse clung to his father's neck in terror as the cry rolled over the crowd." Then he loses his innocence and it becomes clear that he will be a victim of the same psychological syndrome that afflicts his father: "He watched his mother's face . . . she was more beautiful than he had ever seen her   He began to feel a joy he had never felt before." He wishes that he were the man with the knife who is about to castrate the black captive, whom Jesse considers "the most beautiful and terrible object he had ever seen." Then he identifies totally with his father: "At that moment Jesse loved his father more than he had ever loved him. He felt that his father had carried him through a mighty test, had revealed to him a great secret which would be the key to his life forever." For Jesse this brutality is thus a kind of initiation into adulthood, and its effect is to ensure that there will be at least one more generation capable of the kind of violence that he has just seen.

"Sonny's Blues"

Whereas "The Man Child" has only white characters and "Going to Meet the Man" is about a conflict between whites and blacks, "Sonny's Blues" has only black characters. Although the chronology of "Sonny's Blues" is scrambled, its plot is simple. It tells the story of two brothers, one, the narrator, a respectable teacher and the other, Sonny, a former user of heroin who is jailed for that reason and then becomes a jazz musician. The story ends in a jazz nightclub, where the older brother hears Sonny play and finally understands the meaning of jazz for him. The real heart of this story is the contrast between the values of the two brothers, a contrast that becomes much less dramatic at the end.

The two brothers have similar social backgrounds, especially their status as blacks and, more specifically, as Harlem blacks. Of Harlem as a place in which to mature the narrator says, "boys exactly like the boys we once had been found themselves encircled by disaster. Some escaped the trap, most didn't. Those who got out always left something of themselves behind, as some animals amputate a leg and leave it in a trap." Even when he was very young the narrator had a sense of the danger and despair surrounding him:

> When lights fill the room, the child is filled with darkness. He knows that every time this happens he's moved just a little closer to that darkness outside. The darkness outside is what the old folks have been talking about. It's what they've come from. It's what they endure.

For example, he learns after his father's death that his father, though seemingly a hardened and stoical man, had hidden the grief caused by the killing of his brother.

At first the narrator believes that Sonny's two means for coping with the darkness, heroin and music, are inextricably connected to that darkness and thus are not survival mechanisms at all. He believes that heroin "filled everything, the people, the houses, the music, the dark, quicksilver barmaid, with menace; and this menace was their reality." Later, however, he realizes that jazz is a way to escape: He senses that "Sonny was at that time piano playing for his life." The narrator also has a few premonitions of the epiphany he experiences in the jazz nightclub. One occurs when he observes a group of street singers and understands that their "music seemed to soothe a poison out of them." Even with these premonitions, he does not realize that he uses the same strategy. After an argument with Sonny, during which their differences seem to be irreconcilable, his first reaction is to begin "whistling to keep from crying," and the tune is a blues. Finally the epiphany occurs, tying together all the major strands of this story. As he listens to Sonny playing jazz, the narrator thinks that

> freedom lurked around us and I understood, at last, that he could help us be free if we would listen, that he would never be free until we did. Yet, there was no battle in his face now. I heard what he had gone through, and would continue to go through.

The idea in that passage is essentially what Baldwin is about. Like Sonny, he has forged an instrument of freedom by means of the fire of his troubles, and he has made that instrument available to all, white and black. His is the old story of suffering and art; his fiction is an account of trouble, but by producing it he has shown others the way to rise above suffering.

Analysis: Drama

Baldwin's reputation as a dramatist rests primarily on *The Amen Corner,* a relatively obscure play written in the early 1950s, produced under the direction of Owen Dodson at Howard University in 1954, and brought to Broadway for a twelve-week run only in April, 1965, as an attempt to capitalize on the interest generated by Baldwin's 1964 play *Blues for Mister Charlie.* Examining the tension between religious and secular experience, *The Amen Corner* maintains some interest as an anticipation of the thematic and structural use of music in African American plays during the Black Arts movement. Although Baldwin's drama fails to live up to the standards set by his prose, the heated public discussion surrounding *Blues for Mister Charlie* attests its historical importance as one element in the political and aesthetic transition from the nonviolent universalism of African American thought in the 1950s to the militant nationalism of the 1960s.

The Amen Corner

Like *Go Tell It on the Mountain, The Amen Corner* challenges the dichotomy between the holy Temple and the sinful Street, a tension that shapes the play's entire dramatic structure. Accepted unquestioningly by most members of Sister Margaret Alexander's congregation, the dichotomy reflects a basic survival strategy of blacks making the transition from their rural Southern roots to the urban North during the Great Migration. By dividing the world into zones of safety and danger, church members attempt to distance themselves and, perhaps more important, their loved ones from the brutalities of the city. As Baldwin comments in his introduction to the play, Sister Margaret faces the dilemma of "how to treat her husband and her son as men and at the same time to protect them from the bloody consequences of trying to be a man in this society." In act 1, Margaret attempts to resolve the dilemma by forcing her son David, a musician in his late teens, into the role of servant of the Lord while consigning her estranged husband Luke, a jazz musician, to the role of worldly tempter. Having witnessed the brutal impact of Harlem on Luke, she strives to protect her son by creating a world entirely separate from his father's. Ultimately, however, the attempt fails as David's emerging sense of self drives him to confront a wider range of experience; meanwhile, Luke's physical collapse, which takes place in the "safe zone," forces Margaret to acknowledge her own evasions. The most important of these, which reveals Margaret's claim to moral purity as self-constructed illusion, involves her claim that Luke abandoned his family; in fact, she fled from him to avoid the pain caused by the death of a newborn daughter, a pain associated with sexuality and the Street.

As he did in *Go Tell It on the Mountain,* Baldwin treats the collapse of the dichotomies as a potential source of artistic and spiritual liberation. David recognizes that his development as a musician demands immersion in both the sacred and the secular traditions of African American music. Margaret attempts to redefine herself in terms not of holiness but of an accepting love imaged in her clutching Luke's trombone mouthpiece after his death. Both resolutions intimate a synthesis of Temple and Street, suggesting the common impulse behind the gospel music and jazz that sound throughout the play. The emotional implications of the collapse of the dichotomies in *The Amen Corner* are directly articulated when, following her acknowledgment that the vision on which she bases her authority as preacher was her own creation, Margaret says: "It's a awful thing to think about, the way love never dies!" This second "vision" marks a victory much more profound than that of the church faction that casts Margaret out at the end of the play. Ironically, the new preacher, Sister Moore, seems destined to perpetuate Margaret's moral failings. Although Sister Moore's rise to power is grounded primarily in the congregation's dissatisfaction with Margaret's inability to connect her spiritual life with the realities of the Street (Margaret refuses to sympathize with a woman's marital difficulties or to allow a man to take a job driving a liquor truck), she fails to perceive the larger implications of the dissatisfaction. Sister Moore's inability to see the depth of Margaret's transformed sense of love suggests that the simplifying dichotomies will continue to shape the congregation's experience.

Thematically and psychologically, then, *The Amen Corner* possesses a great deal of potential power. Theatrically, however, it fails to exploit this potential. Despite Baldwin's awareness that "the ritual of the church, historically speaking, comes out of the theater, the communion which is the theater," the structure of *The Amen Corner* emphasizes individual alienation rather than ritual reconciliation. In part because the play's power in performance largely derives from the energy of the music played in the church, the street side of Baldwin's vision remains relatively abstract. Where the brilliant prose of *Go Tell It on the Mountain* suggests nuances of perception that remain only half-conscious to John Grimes during his transforming vision, David's conversations with Luke and Margaret focus almost exclusively on his rebellion against the Temple while leaving the terms of the dichotomy unchallenged. Similarly, in Act 3, Margaret's catharsis feels static. The fact that Margaret articulates her altered awareness in her preacher's

voice suggests a lingering commitment to the Temple at odds with Baldwin's thematic design. Although the sacred music emanating from the church is theoretically balanced by the jazz trombone associated with Luke, most of the performance's power comes from the gospel songs that provide an embodied experience of call and response; taken out of its performance context, the jazz seems a relatively powerless expression. As a result, *The Amen Corner* never escapes from the sense of separation it conceptually attacks.

Other Literary Forms

Before he published his first novel, James Baldwin had established a reputation as a talented essayist and reviewer. Many of his early pieces, later collected in *Notes of a Native Son* and *Nobody Knows My Name: More Notes of a Native Son*, have become classics; his essays on Richard Wright, especially "Everybody's Protest Novel" (1949) and "Many Thousands Gone" (1951), occupy a central position in the development of "universalist" African American thought during the 1950s. Culminating in *The Fire Next Time*, an extended meditation on the relationship of race, religion, and the individual experience in America, Baldwin's early prose demands a reexamination and redefinition of received social and cultural premises. His collections of essays *No Name in the Street* and *The Devil Finds Work* reflected a more militant stance and were received less favorably than Baldwin's universalist statements. *The Evidence of Things Not Seen* is a book-length essay on the Atlanta child-murders, while *The Price of the Ticket: Collected Nonfiction 1948-1985* includes all of Baldwin's essay collections as well as a number of previously uncollected pieces. Less formal and intricate, though in some cases more explicit, reflections of Baldwin's beliefs can be found in

A Rap on Race, an extended discussion with anthropologist Margaret Mead, and *A Dialogue*, a conversation with poet Nikki Giovanni.

Baldwin also wrote children's fiction (*Little Man, Little Man*), the text for a photographic essay (*Nothing Personal*, with Richard Avedon), an unfilmed scenario (*One Day, When I Was Lost: A Scenario Based on "The Autobiography of Malcolm X"*), drama, and short stories. Although he published little short fiction after the collection *Going to Meet the Man*, Baldwin was an acknowledged master of the novella form. "Sonny's Blues" (discussed above), the story of the relationship of a jazz musician to his "respectable" narrator-brother, anticipates many of the themes of Baldwin's later novels and is widely recognized as one of the great American novellas.

Bibliography

Balfour, Katharine Lawrence. *The Evidence of Things Not Said: James Baldwin and the Promise of American Democracy*. Ithaca, N.Y.: Cornell University Press, 2001. Explores the political dimension of Baldwin's essays, stressing the politics of race in American democracy.

Berger, Joseph. "A Literary Friendship in Black and White." *The New York Times*, September 13, 2004, p. B1. Studies the relationship between Baldwin and Sol Stein. The authors had different backgrounds and lifestyles but maintained a long friendship; Stein helped convince Baldwin to release *Notes of a Native Son*.

Boyd, Herb. *Baldwin's Harlem: A Biography of James Baldwin*. New York: Atria Books, 2008. Emphasizes the crucial importance of Harlem as Baldwin's home and as a major influence on his thinking and writing.

Brim, Matt. James *Baldwin and the Queer Imagination*. Ann Arbor, MI: The U of Michigan P, 2014. Explores Baldwin in relation to queer theory in general and black queer theory in particular.

Calloway, Catherine. "Fiction: The 1930s to the 1960s." *American Literature* 77, no. 2 (June, 2005): 349-368. This chapter examines Baldwin's work and compares it to that of four other major American authors: Ralph Ellison, Chester Himes, John Steinbeck, and Richard Wright.

Campbell, James. *Talking at the Gates: A Life of James Baldwin*. Berkeley: University of California Press, 2002. The author knew Baldwin during his final years, but is still able to provide a balanced and readable perspective. A good narrative biography, with detailed notes and bibliography. This edition has a new afterword.

Dudley, Marc K. *Understanding James Baldwin*. Columbus, SC: U of South Carolina Press, 2019. Offers a solid general introduction to Baldwin and his works.

Elam, Michele, ed. *The Cambridge Companion to James Baldwin*. New York: Cambridge UP, 2015. An important collection of wide-ranging essays with pieces on such topics as Baldwin's use of the novel as a genre, his poetics, the sermonic aspects of his writings, the impact of jazz, the nature of his works for theater, his humor, and many other topics.

Field, Douglas, ed. *A Historical Guide to James Baldwin*. New York: Oxford UP, 2009. Contains a biography as well as essays on such topics as Baldwin and evangelism; music; the past; the civil rights movement; "the Other Atlantic"; an overview of Baldwin criticism; and an illustrated chronology.

Francis, Consuela. *The Critical Reception of James Baldwin, 1963-2010: "an Honest Man and a Good Writer."* Rochester, NY: Camden House, 2014. Offers a comprehensive overview of critical commentary, with emphasis on early assessments; canonization; theorizing; "Sonny's Blues"; popular reviews; and recent studies.

Harris, Trudier, ed. *New Essays on "Go Tell It on the Mountain."* Cambridge, England: Cambridge University Press, 1996. These essays examine the composition, themes, publication history, public reception, and contemporary interpretations of Baldwin's first novel.

Hobson, Christopher Z. *James Baldwin and the Heavenly City: Prophecy, Apocalypse, and Doubt.* East Lansing: Michigan State UP, 2018. Emphasizes Baldwin's Biblical language and religious ideas as keys to the hope that underlies his works.

Kaplan, Cora, and Bill Schwarz, eds. *James Baldwin: America and Beyond.* Ann Arbor: The University of Michigan Press, 2011. Contains essays on such topics as what it means to be an American; the "American confusion"; *Uncle Tom's Cabin*; cold war liberalism; and prophecy and politics. Other essays examine early and late Baldwin; the "Baldwinian diaspora"; Baldwin in Paris; and Baldwin in relation to various other places and writers.

Leming, David. *James Baldwin: A Biography.* New York: Alfred A. Knopf, 1994. A biography of Baldwin written by one who knew him and worked with him for the last quarter century of his life. Provides extensive literary analysis of Baldwin's work and relates his work to his life.

McWilliams, Susan J., ed. *A Political Companion to James Baldwin.* Lexington, KY: UP of Kentucky, 2017. Contains essays on such topics as double consciousness; segregated memory; the politics of disconnection; the politics of freedom; prophecy; and political theology. Other topics include the politics of faith; race in America; women's liberation; cosmopolitan humanism; individualism and the critique of property; violence; the Black Lives Matter movement; and technology.

Miller, D. Quentin. *A Criminal Power: James Baldwin and the Law.* Columbus: Ohio State UP, 2012. Claims to offer the first comprehensive overview of Baldwin's writings by focusing on his ideas about the law.

Miller, D. Quentin, ed. *Re-Viewing James Baldwin: Things Not Seen.* Philadelphia: Temple University Press, 2000. Explores the way in which Baldwin's writing touched on issues that confront all people, including race, identity, sexuality, and religious ideology.

Robinson, Angelo R. "The Other Proclamation in James Baldwin's *Go Tell It on the Mountain.*" *CLA Journal* 48, no. 3 (March, 2005): 338-354. This article's primary focus is on John and the implications of his homoerotic desires, particularly with respect to Pentacostalism.

Romanet, Jerome de. "Revisiting Madeleine and 'The Outing': James Baldwin's Revision of Gide's Sexual Politics." *MELUS* 22 (Spring, 1997): 3-14. A discussion of Baldwin's story "The Outing" in terms of its contrast with Gide's Calvinist guilt. Discusses sexual identity in this story and other Baldwin fictions. Argues that Baldwin's exile in France was as concerned with racial identity as with sexual emancipation.

Scott, Lynn Orilla. *James Baldwin's Later Fiction: Witness to the Journey.* East Lansing: Michigan State University Press, 2002. Analyzes the temporary decline of Baldwin's reputation after the 1960s, the ways in which critics have often undervalued his work, and the interconnected themes in his body of work.

Tomlinson, Robert. "'Payin' One's Dues': Expatriation as Personal Experience and Paradigm in the Works of James Baldwin." *African American Review* 33 (Spring, 1999): 135-148. A discussion of the effect that life as an exile in Paris had on Baldwin. Argues that the experience internalized the conflicts he experienced in America. Suggests that Baldwin used his homosexuality and exile as a metaphor for the experience of the African American.

Troupe, Quincy, ed. *James Baldwin: The Legacy.* New York: Simon & Schuster, 1989. A collection of essays by and about Baldwin, with a foreword by writer Wole Soyinka. Contains eighteen essays, five of which were written for this collection, and homage and celebration from many who were profoundly influenced by Baldwin, including Pat

Mikell's account of Baldwin's last days in St. Paul de Vence. Brief bibliography.

Ushedo, Benedict. *James Baldwin and the Short Story: Ethics, Aesthetics, Psychogeography.* Eugene, OR: Pickwick Publications, 2018.
Explores such issues as scapegoat rhetoric; tragedy; "contrast experience"; and music.

Vogel, Joseph. *James Baldwin and the 1980s: Witnessing the Reagan Era.* Champagne: U of Illinois P, 2018.
Examines such topics as black popular music; ideas about androgyny; AIDS; the religious right; and terror.

Weatherby, W. J. *James Baldwin: Artist on Fire.* New York: Donald I. Fine, 1989. A portrait by a personal friend of some twenty-eight years, this study is both insightful and scholarly. The "Baldwin on Broadway" chapter covers the production of *Blues for Mister Charlie* and *The Amen Corner,* as well as Baldwin's often stormy relationship with the Actors Studio and Lincoln Center. "Down South" discusses a thwarted dramatization of *Giovanni's Room* and Baldwin's special affection for Elia Kazan. Photos and index.

Zaborowska, Magdalena J. *James Baldwin's Turkish Decade: Erotics of Exile.* Durham: Duke UP, 2009.
Studies the decade from 1961-1971, when Baldwin spent much time in Turkey and developed a new conception of himself as a black queer writer.

_____. *Me and My House: James Baldwin's Last Decade in France.* Durham: Duke UP, 2018.
Examines time in France from 1971-1987, focusing especially on how his time there helped shape his ideas about race and sexuality.

*—Terry Heller; Robert McClenaghan;
Thomas J. Taylor; Terry Theodore;
Craig Werner; Robert C. Evans*

Toni Cade Bambara

(Miltona Mirkin Cade)

Novelist and Short-story Writer

Born: New York, New York; March 25, 1939

Died: Philadelphia, Pennsylvania; December 9, 1995

LONG FICTION: *The Salt Eaters,* 1980; *Those Bones Are Not My Child,* 1999.

SHORT FICTION: *Gorilla, My Love,* 1972; *The Sea Birds Are Still Alive: Collected Stories,* 1977; *Raymond's Run: Stories for Young Adults,* 1989.

SCREENPLAYS: *The Bombing of Osage Avenue,* 1986 (documentary); *W. E. B. Du Bois—A Biography in Four Voices,* 1995 (with Amiri Baraka, Wesley Brown, and Thulani Davis).

EDITED TEXTS: *The Black Woman: An Anthology,* 1970; *Tales and Stories for Black Folks,* 1971; *Southern Exposure,* 1976 (periodical; Bambara edited volume 3).

MISCELLANEOUS: "What It Is I Think I'm Doing Anyhow," in *The Writer on Her Work,* 1981 (Janet Sternburg, editor); *Deep Sightings and Rescue Missions: Fiction, Essays, and Conversations,* 1996.

Achievements

Toni Cade Bambara is best known for her short stories, which appear frequently in anthologies. She has also received recognition as a novelist, essayist, journalist, editor, and screenwriter, as well as a social activist and community leader. Her stories depict the daily lives of ordinary people who live in the black neighborhoods of Brooklyn, Harlem, and sections of New York City and the rural South. Although she wrote in other genres, her short stories established her reputation. In *Gorilla, My Love,* a collection of fifteen stories, Bambara focuses on the love of friends and neighborhood as she portrays the positive side of black family life and stresses the strengths of the African American community. These fast-paced stories, characterized by her use of the black dialect of the street, are full of humorous exchanges and verbal banter. *The Sea Birds Are Still Alive* is a collection of short stories that reflect Bambara's concern with people from other cultures; the title story focuses on the plight of Vietnamese refugees at the end of the Vietnam War. *Deep Sightings and Rescue Missions,* a collection of Bambara's writings, most of which never appeared before in print, was published posthumously.

Bambara received the Peter Pauper Press Award in Journalism from the *Long Island Star* in 1958, the John Golden Award for Fiction from Queens College in 1959, and the Theater of Black Experience Award in 1969. She was also the recipient of the George Washington Carver Distinguished African American Lecturer Award from Simpson College, Ebony's Achievement in the Arts Award, and the American Book Award, for *The Salt Eaters,* in 1981. *The Bombing of Osage Avenue* won the Best Documentary of 1986 Award from the Pennsylvania Association of Broadcasters and the Documentary Award from the National Black Programming Consortium in

1986. As an editor of anthologies of the writings of African Americans, Bambara introduced thousands of college students to the works of these writers. She was a founder of the Southern Collective of African American Writers and played a major role in the 1984 Conference on Black Literature and the Arts at Emory University. During the last fourteen years of her life, Bambara devoted her energies to the film industry, writing screenplays.

Biography

Miltona Mirkin Cade was born in New York on March 25, 1939, to Helen Brent Henderson Cade. She grew up in Harlem, Bedford-Stuyvesant, and Queens, where she lived with her mother and brother, Walter. She credited her mother with "cultivating her creative spirit and instilling in her a sense of independence and self-sufficiency." In 1970, after finding the name Bambara written in a sketchbook in her grandmother's trunk, she legally changed her surname to Bambara. She received a B.A. in theater arts and English literature from Queens College in 1959, and that same year her first short story, "Sweet Town," was published in *Vendome* magazine. After studying in Italy and Paris, she earned a master's degree in American literature at City College of New York and completed additional studies in linguistics at New York University and the New School for Social Research. She was a social worker for the Harlem Welfare Center and director of recreation in the psychiatric division of Metro Hospital in New York City. She taught in the Search for Education, Elevation, Knowledge (SEEK) program at City College.

In 1970, under the name of Toni Cade, she published *The Black Woman: An Anthology*, a collection of essays, short fiction, poetry, and letters exploring the experiences of black women, with emphasis on their involvement with the Civil Rights movement and the women's movement. In 1971 she edited *Tales and Stories for Black Folks*, a collection of writings from students in her composition class, along with the work of well-known authors.

As an assistant professor at Livingston College at Rutgers University from 1969 to 1974, Bambara was active in black student organizations and arts groups. She was a visiting professor in Afro-American Studies at Emory University and an instructor in the School of Social Work at Atlanta University. In 1973, on a visit to Cuba, Bambara met with the Federation of Cuban Women, and in 1975 she traveled to Vietnam. These experiences served to broaden Bambara's view of the importance of community involvement and political action and provided subject matter for stories in *The Sea Birds Are Still Alive*.

Bambara and her daughter, Karma, lived in Atlanta from 1974 to 1986, during which time Bambara continued to be active in community political and artistic organizations, hosting potluck dinners in her home and organizing writers and artists in the community. In 1986 Bambara moved to Philadelphia, where she continued her active participation in the community and worked on *The Bombing of Osage Avenue*, a 1986 documentary on the bombing of a house where a group of black nationalists lived. She also worked on a film about African American writer Zora Neale Hurston. Bambara was known as a writer, civil rights activist, teacher, and supporter of the arts. Her work represents her dedication to the African American community and her desire to portray the ordinary lives of the people who live in those communities. As a lecturer and teacher she worked to raise the consciousness of other African Americans and to encourage a sense of pride in their heritage. Bambara died of cancer in a suburb of Philadelphia on December 9, 1995.

Analysis: Long Fiction

Toni Cade Bambara's work reflects her experiences with political action committees and her belief in the necessity for social responsibility. The political activism of the 1960s and 1970s provides the subject matter for her work, as she explores the consequences of the Civil Rights movement and the divisions in the African American community. In describing this community, Bambara portrays the individual characters with affection and humor.

The Salt Eaters

Set in the 1970s, Bambara's novel *The Salt Eaters* focuses on the effects of the Civil Rights movement on the inhabitants of the small town of Claybourne, Georgia. The plot centers on the attempted suicide of its main character, Velma Henry, a community activist who has tried to kill herself by slitting her wrists and sticking her head in an oven. The other major character is Minnie Ransom, a conjure woman who uses her healing powers to restore Velma to health. Minor characters include Fred Holt, the bus driver; Obie, Velma's husband; and Dr. Julius Meadows. These members of the African American community are suffering from the fragmentation and alienation that have occurred in the wake of the Civil Rights movement. Velma was so filled with rage that she sought death as an answer to her pain. The novel traces Velma's journey from despair to mental and spiritual health. Bambara's own experiences with political activism provided her with the background for the events of the novel.

Throughout the novel, Bambara stresses the importance of choice. In the opening line of the novel, Minnie Ransom asks Velma, "Are you sure, sweetheart, that you want to be well?" Freedom of choice requires acceptance of responsibility. If Velma is to heal herself, she must make a conscious choice of health over despair.

Characters in the novel are seen in relationship to the larger community. Godmother Sophie M'Dear reminds Velma that her life is not solely her own, but that she has a connection and obligation to her family and community. Other characters are reminded of their responsibility to others. When Buster gets Nadeen pregnant, her uncle Thurston arrives with a gun, ordering Buster to attend parenting classes. Doc Serge tells Buster that abortion is not a private choice but a choice that involves the whole community. The characters echo Bambara's belief that membership in a community entails responsibilities to that community.

For most of the novel Velma sits on a stool in a hospital, suffering from depression, overwhelming fatigue, and a mental collapse. She remains immobile and seemingly frozen as scenes from the past and present play in her mind in no particular order. Other characters seem to whirl past Velma and blend into one another, reflecting the problems that have brought Velma to this hospital room. Bambara shows that these problems are a result of alienation from the community. Because of his light skin, education, and profession, Dr. Julius Meadows has lost touch with his roots, but, through a chance encounter with two young black men, Julius begins his journey back to the black community. Reflecting on the encounter, Julius feels that "whatever happened, he wasn't stumbling aimlessly around the streets anymore, at loose ends, alone." Meadows's journey back into the black community parallels Velma's journey to health. Alienation from the community had brought Velma to the brink of destruction, and realignment with the community heals her. Velma's journey is similar to the spiritual journey of Tayo, the Native American protagonist in Leslie Marmon Silko's *Ceremony* (1977). The horrors Tayo experienced as a prisoner of the Japanese during World War II and the sense of alienation he experiences when he returns to his Laguna reservation have nearly destroyed his will to survive. Through immersion in the Native American culture, traditions, beliefs, and stories, Tayo finds his way back to health. As Tayo and Velma embrace their cultural heritages, they begin to heal.

The predominant image in the novel is the vision of the mud mothers painting the walls of their cave. This recurring vision haunts Velma until she sees the cave as a symbol of cultural history and identity. Other characters reflect on the responsibility of the older generation to educate and nurture the children of the community. If the children are forgetting the values of the community, it is because the elders have failed in their responsibility to instill community values in the young.

Bambara believes that to keep traditions alive, every generation has to be nurtured and educated, has to be taught the old stories. At times the novel seems to be a catalog of African American cultural history, which includes African tribal customs and rituals, slave ships, and names of famous leaders. In the early part of the novel, Ruby, one of the most politically active characters, laments the loss of leaders and causes: "Malcolm gone, King gone, Fannie Lou gone, Angela quiet, the movement splintered, enclaves unconnected." Near the end of the novel, Velma realizes how much she has learned from the leaders and influences that are part of her background, "Douglass, Tubman, the slave narratives, the songs, the fables, Delaney, Ida Wells, Blyden, Du Bois, Garvey, the singers, her parents, Malcolm, Coltrane."

Bambara enriches the novel with background from folk legends and literary works. At times she merely mentions a name, such as Shine, the famous African American trickster, or the legendary Stagolee, who killed a man for his hat. Fred's friend Porter, borrowing a term from Ralph Ellison's novel *Invisible Man* (1952), explains his feelings about being black: "They call the Black man the Invisible Man. Our natures are unknowable, unseeable to them." The following lines show how Bambara packs cultural, historical, and political history into one sentence: "Several hotheads, angry they had been asleep in the Sixties or too young to participate, had been galvanized by the arrival in their midst of the legless vet who used to careen around Claybourne fast and loose on a hot garage dolly."

In contrast to the positive images, Bambara shows the negative side of society in describing the "boymen" who hang around women in grocery stores begging for money in a ritual she calls "market theater." In another scene, Ruby complains about the way women have had to carry the burden of improving society, "taking on drugs, prisons, alcohol, the schools, rape, battered women, abused children," while the men make no contribution to the organization.

One of the most distinctive aspects of Bambara's style is her use of black dialect, with its colorful vocabulary, playful banter, and unique phrasing and speech patterns. At times the rhythm and rhyme of phrases give a musical quality to the prose: "Cause the stars said and the energy belts led and the cards read and the cowries spread." At other times Bambara describes the atmosphere in musical terms: "the raga reggae bumpidity bing zing was pouring out all over Fred Holt" and "the music drifted out over the trees maqaam now blending with the bebop of Minnie Ransom's tapes."

The major theme of the novel is that identification with one's cultural history can be liberating and empowering. In *The Salt Eaters*, loss of cultural identity has brought despair. Bambara provides flashbacks to the civil rights struggles of the 1960s and the legacy of slavery as aids to her more central point: As they struggle for political power, African Americans must remember the past and maintain their best traditions. As Velma begins to heal she thinks that she knows "how to build resistance, make the journey to the center of the circle stay centered in the best of her people's traditions."

Analysis: Short Fiction

Toni Cade Bambara's short fiction is especially notable for its creativity with language and its ability to capture the poetry of black speech. In a conversation that was printed in her posthumous collection *Deep Sightings and Rescue Missions* as "How She Came by Her Name," she claimed that in the stories about childhood from *Gorilla, My Love*, she was trying to capture the voice of childhood, and she was surprised that readers received these efforts to use black dialect as a political act. Nonetheless, her writing (like her work as a teacher, social worker, and filmmaker) was always informed by her sense of social activism and social justice in the broadest sense. Inher later work outside the field of short fiction (in films and in her last novel) she focused on the bombing of the black neighborhood in Philadelphia where the MOVE Organization was headquartered, the life of W. E. B. Du Bois, and the Atlanta child-murders of the 1980s, all topics that were rife with political meaning.

Nonetheless, what enlivens her writing is her originality with language and a playful sense of form which aims more to share than to tell directly. Another essay from *Deep Sightings and Rescue Missions*, "The Education of a Storyteller" tells of Grandma Dorothy teaching her that she could not really know anything that she could not share with her girlfriends, and her stories seem to grow out of the central wish to share things with this target audience of black women peers. Her stories are usually digressive, seldom following a linear plot. Most of them are structured in an oral form that allows for meaningful side issues with the aim of bringing clear the central point to her audience. Though this technique can be daunting when used in the novel-length *The Salt Eaters*, it allows her to make her short stories into charming, witty, and lively artistic performances whose social messages emerge organically.

Gorilla, My Love

Gorilla, My Love was Toni Cade Bambara's first collection of her original work, and it remains her most popular book. The stories in it were written between 1959 and 1970, and as she explains in her essay, "How She Came by Her Name," she was trying to capture the language system in which people she knew lived and moved. She originally conceived it as a collection of the voices of young, bright, and tough girls of the city, but she did not want it to be packaged as a children's book, so she added some of the adult material to it. "My Man Bovane," for instance, features a matronly black woman seducing a blind man at a neighborhood political rally, while her children look on in disapproval. Similarly, among the fifteen stories (most of which are written in the first person) that make up this book is "Talkin' 'Bout Sonny," in which Betty and Delauney discuss their friend Sonny's recent breakdown and assault on his wife. Delauney claims he understands exactly how such a thing could happen, and it is left unclear how this unstable relationship between Betty and Delauney (who is married) will resolve itself.

Most of the stories, however, focus on young girls determined to make their place in the world and the neighborhood. "The Hammer Man," for example, tells of a young girl who first hides from a mentally disturbed older boy she has humiliated in public but later futilely attempts to defend against two policemen who try to arrest him. The adult themes and the childhood themes come together best in "The

Johnson Girls," in which a young girl listens in as a group of women try to console Inez, whose boyfriend has left with no promise of return. As the young narrator listens in the hope that she will not have to endure "all this torture crap" when she becomes a woman, it becomes clear that the intimate conversation between women is a form of revitalization for Inez.

A delightful preface to *Gorilla, My Love* assures the reader that the material in the book is entirely fictional, not at all autobiographical, but it is hard for a reader not to feel that the voices that populate the work speak for Bambara and the neighborhood of her youth.

The title story is also Bambara's most irresistible work. The narrator is a young girl named Hazel who has just learned that her "Hunca Bubba" is about to be married. She is clearly upset about both this news and the fact that he is now going by his full name, Jefferson Winston Vale. The story proceeds in anything but a linear manner, as Hazel sees a movie house in the background of Hunca Bubba's photos, and starts to tell about going to the movies on Easter with her brothers, Big Brood and Little Jason. When the movie turns out to be a film about Jesus instead of "Gorilla, My Love," as was advertised, Hazel gets angry and demands her money back, and not getting it, starts a fire in the lobby—"Cause if you say Gorilla My Love you supposed to mean it."

What is really on her mind is that when Hunca Bubba was baby-sitting her, he promised he was going to marry her when she grew up, and she believed him. Hazel's attempt to keep her dignity but make her feeling of betrayal known by confronting Hunca Bubba is at once both a surprise and a completely natural outgrowth of her character. Her grandfather's explanation, that it was Hunca Bubba who promised to marry her but it is Jefferson Winston Vale who is marrying someone else, is at once both compassionate and an example of the type

of hypocrisy that Hazel associates with the adult world. The example she gives in her story about going to the movie makes it clear that she has always seen her family as better than most, but she sees hypocrisy as a universal adult epidemic.

"Raymond's Run"

"Raymond's Run," a short story that was also published as a children's book, is about the relationship between the narrator, Hazel (not the same girl from "Gorilla, My Love," but about the same age), her retarded brother, Raymond, and another girl on the block, Gretchen. Hazel's reputation is as the fastest thing on two feet in the neighborhood, but coming up to the annual May Dayrun, she knows that her new rival, Gretchen, will challenge her and could win. Mr. Pearson, a teacher at the school, suggests it would be a nice gesture to the new girl, Gretchen, to let her win, which Hazel dismisses out of hand. Thinking about a Hansel and Gretel pageant in which she played a strawberry, Hazel thinks, "I am not a strawberry . . . I run. That is what I'm all about." As a runner, she has no intention of letting someone else win.

In fact, when the race is run, she does win, but it is very close, and for all her bravado, she is not sure who won until her name is announced. More important, she sees her brother Raymond running along with her on the other side of the fence, keeping his hands down in an awkward running posture that she accepts as all his own. In her excitement about her brother's accomplishment, she imagines that her rival Gretchen might want to help her train Raymond as a runner, and the two girls share a moment of genuine warmth.

The central point of the story is captured by Hazel when she says of the smile she shared with Gretchen that it was the type of smile girls can share only when they are not too busy being "flowers or fairies or strawberries instead of something honest and worthy of respect . .. you know . .. like being people." The honest competition that brought out their best efforts and enticed Raymond to join them in his way brought them all together as people, not as social competitors trying to outmaneuver one another but as allies.

"The Lesson"

"The Lesson" is a story about a child's first realization of the true depth of economic inequity in society. The main characters are Miss Moore, an educated black woman who has decided to take the responsibility for the education of neighborhood children upon herself, and Sylvia, the narrator, a young girl. Though it is summer, Miss Moore has organized an educational field trip. This annoys Sylvia and her friend, Sugar, but since their parents have all agreed to the trip, the children have little choice but to cooperate. The trip is actually an excursion to a high-priced department store, F. A. O. Schwartz.

The children look with astonishment at a toy clown that costs $35, a paperweight that sells for $480, and a toy sailboat that is priced at $1,195. The children are discouraged by the clear signs of economic inequality. When Miss Moore asks what they have learned from this trip, only Sugar will reply with what she knows Miss Moore wants them to say: "This is not much of a democracy." Sylvia feels betrayed but mostly because she sees that Sugar is playing up to Miss Moore, while Sylvia has been genuinely shaken by this trip. At the end, Sugar is plotting to split the money she knows Sylvia saved from the cab fare Miss Moore gave her, but Sylvia's response as Sugar runs ahead to their favorite ice cream shop, "ain't nobody gonna beat me at nothin,'" indicates she has been shaken and is not planning to play the same old games. However, Sylvia cannot so easily slough it off.

"Medley"

The most popular story from *The Sea Birds Are Still Alive*, "Medley" is the story of Sweet Pea and Larry, a romantic couple who go through a poignant breakup in the course of the story. Though neither of them is a musician, both are music fans, and their showers together are erotic encounters in which they improvise songs together, pretending to be playing musical instruments with each other's bodies. Sweet Pea is a manicurist with her own shop, and her best customer is a gambler named Moody, who likes to keep his nails impeccable. Because he goes on a winning streak after she starts doing his nails, he offers to take her on a gambling trip as his personal manicurist, for which he pays her two thousand dollars. Sweet Pea takes the offer, though Larry objects, and when she gets back, he seems to have disappeared from her life. Nonetheless, she remembers their last night in the shower together, as they sang different tunes, keeping each other off balance, but harmonizing a medley together until the hot water ran out.

Though Sweet Pea is faced with the choice of losing two thousand dollars or her boyfriend and chooses the money, the story does not attempt to say that she made the wrong choice. Rather, it is a snapshot of the impermanence of shared lives in Sweet Pea's modern, urban environment. This transience is painful, but is also the basis for the enjoyment of life's beauty.

Other Literary Forms

Before Toni Cade Bambara published her first collection of stories, *Gorilla, My Love*, she edited two anthologies, *The Black Woman* and *Tales and Stories for Black Folks*, under the name Toni Cade. She was also an active screenwriter whose credits include Louis Massiah's *The Bombing of Osage Avenue*, about the bombing of the Movement (MOVE) Organization's headquarters in

Philadelphia, and Massiah's *W. E. B. Du Bois: A Biography in Four Voices.* Her friend and editor, Toni Morrison, edited a posthumous collection of her previously uncollected stories and essays in 1996 called *Deep Sightings and Rescue Missions: Fiction, Essays, and Conversations,* and her final novel, *Those Bones Are Not My Child,* was published in 1999.

Bibliography

Alwes, Derek. "The Burden of Liberty: Choice in Toni Morrison's *Jazz* and Toni Cade Bambara's *The Salt Eaters.*" *African American Review* 30, no. 3 (Fall, 1996): 353-365. In comparing the works of Toni Morrison and Bambara, Alwes argues that while Morrison wants readers to participate in a choice, Bambara wants them to choose to participate. Bambara's message is that happiness is possible if people refuse to forget the past and continue to participate in the struggle.

Bone, Martyn. "Capitalist Abstraction and the Body Politics of Place in Toni Cade Bambara's *Those Bones Are Not My Child.*" *Journal of American Studies* 37, no. 2 (August, 2003): 229-247. Takes a closer look at the effects of class, race, geography, and the special role of the African American child in Bambara's novel.

Butler-Evans, Elliott. *Race, Gender, and Desire: Narrative Strategies in the Fiction of Toni Cade Bambara, Toni Morrison, Alice Walker.*

Philadelphia: Temple University Press, 1989. The first book-length study to treat Bambara's fiction to any extent, this study uses narratology and feminism to explore Bambara's works.

Collins, Janelle. "Generating Power: Fission, Fusion, and PostModern Politics in Bambara's *The Salt Eaters.*" *MELUS* 21, no. 2 (Summer, 1996): 35-47. Collins argues that Bambara's nationalist and feminist positions inform the text of the novel as she advocates political and social change.

Evans, Mari, ed. *Black Women Writers(1950-1980): A Critical Evaluation.* Garden City, N.Y.: Anchor Press/Doubleday, 1984. In the essay "Salvation Is the Issue," Bambara says that the elements of her own work that she deems most important are laughter, use of language, sense of community, and celebration.

Hargrove, Nancy. "Youth in Toni Cade Bambara's *Gorilla, My Love.*" In *Women Writers of the Contemporary South,* edited by

Peggy Whitman Prenshaw. Jackson: University Press of Mississippi, 1984. A thorough examination of an important feature of Bambara's most successful collection of short fiction— namely, that most of the best stories center on young girls.

Holmes, Linda Janet. *A Joyous Revolt: Toni Cade Bambara, Writer and Activist.* Praeger, 2014. The first full-length biography of Bambara, this book situates her in her life and times and explores her relations with others, especially her friends.

Holmes, Linda Janet, and Cheryl A. Wall, ed. *Savoring the Salt: The Legacy of Toni Cade Bambara.* Temple UP, 2007. A wide-ranging essay collection that includes thirty separate pieces by scholars, friends, and other creative writers.

Hooks, Bell. "Uniquely Toni Cade Bambara." *Black Issues Book Review* 2, no. 1 (January/February, 2000): 14-17. A tribute to the author. Hooks discusses the importance of *The Salt Eaters* and Bambara's faith in the power of revolutionary politics.

Lewis, Thabiti, ed. *Conversations with Toni Cade Bambara.* UP of Mississippi, 2012. A brief collection of interviews.

Muther, Elizabeth. "Bambara's Feisty Girls: Resistance Narratives in *Gorilla, My Love.*" *African American Review* 36, no. 3 (Fall, 2002): 447-460. Gives a good summary of the book and explores the often-fractured relationships between children and parents.

Tate, Claudia, ed. *Black Women Writers at Work.* New York: Continuum, 1983. Tate interviews fourteen African American women writers about social and political issues as well as aspects of their personal lives. In Bambara's interview, she says that she works to "applaud the tradition of struggle in our community" as she focuses on the "ordinary folks on the block."

Valerio, Anthony. *Toni Cade Bambara's One Sicilia Night: A Memoir.* Bordighera Press, 2007. The author's account of his romantic relationship with Bambara.

Vertreace, Martha M. *Toni Cade Bambara.* New York: Macmillan Library Reference, 1998. The first full-length work devoted to the entirety of Bambara's career. A part of the successful Twayne series of criticism, this book will be quite helpful for students interested in Bambara's career.

Willis, Susan. "Problematizing the Individual: Toni Cade Bambara's 'Stories for the Revolution.'" In *Specifying: Black Women Writing the American Experience.* Madison: University of Wisconsin Press, 1987. Though largely centered on an analysis of *The Salt Eaters,* this essay also has clear and informative analysis of Bambara's most important short fiction.

— *Thomas Cassidy; Judith Barton Williamson; Robert C. Evans*

Amiri Baraka

(Everett LeRoi Jones)

Playwright, Poet, and Essayist

Born: Newark, New Jersey; October 7, 1934

LONG FICTION: *The System of Dante's Hell,* 1965.

SHORT FICTION: *Tales,* 1967; *The Fiction of LeRoi Jones/Amiri Baraka,* 2000.

DRAMA: *The Baptism,* pr. 1964, pb. 1966; *Dutchman,* pr., pb. 1964; *The Slave,* pr., pb. 1964; *The Toilet,* pr., pb. 1964; *Experimental Death Unit #1,* pr. 1965, pb. 1969; *Jello,* pr. 1965, pb. 1970; *A Black Mass,* pr. 1966, pb. 1969; *Arm Yourself, or Harm Yourself,* pr., pb. 1967; *Great Goodness of Life (A Coon Show),* pr. 1967, pb. 1969; *Madheart,* pr. 1967, pb. 1969; *Slave Ship: A Historical Pageant,* pr., pb. 1967; *The Death of Malcolm X,* pb. 1969; *Bloodrites,* pr. 1970, pb. 1971; *Junkies Are Full of (SHHH ...),* pr. 1970, pb. 1971; *A Recent Killing,* pr. 1973, pb. 1978; *S-1,* pr. 1976, pb. 1978; *The Motion of History,* pr. 1977, pb. 1978; *The Sidney Poet Heroical,* pb. 1979 (originally as *Sidnee Poet Heroical,* pr. 1975); *What Was the Relationship of the Lone Ranger to the Means of Production?,* pr., pb. 1979; *At the Dim'cracker Convention,* pr. 1980; *Weimar,* pr. 1981; *Money: A Jazz Opera,* pr. 1982; *Primitive World: An Anti-Nuclear Jazz Musical,* pr. 1984, pb. 1997; *The Life and Life of Bumpy Johnson,* pr. 1991; *General Hag's Skeezag,* pb. 1992; *Meeting Lillie,* pr. 1993; *The Election Machine Warehouse,* pr. 1996, pb. 1997.

POETRY: *Spring and Soforth,* 1960; *Preface to a Twenty Volume Suicide Note,* 1961; *The Dead Lecturer,* 1964; *Black Art,* 1966; *A Poem for Black Hearts,* 1967; *Black Magic: Sabotage, Target Study, Black Art—Collected Poetry, 1961-1967,* 1969; *It's Nation Time,* 1970; *In Our Terribleness: Some Elements and Meaning in Black Style,* 1970 (with Fundi [Billy Abernathy]); *Spirit Reach,* 1972; *Afrikan Revolution,* 1973; *Hard Facts,* 1975; *Selected Poetry of Amiri Baraka/LeRoi Jones,* 1979; *Reggae or Not!,* 1981; *Transbluesency: The Selected Poems of Amiri Baraka,* 1995; *Wise, Why's, Y's,* 1995; *Funk Lore: New Poems, 1984-1995,* 1996; *S O S : Poems 1961-2013* (selected by Paul Vangelisti), 2014.

NONFICTION: "*Cuba Libre,*" 1961; *The New Nationalism,* 1962; *Blues People: Negro Music in White America,* 1963; *Home: Social Essays,* 1966; *Black Music,* 1968, 2010; *A Black Value System,* 1970; *Strategy and Tactics of a Pan-African Nationalist Party,* 1971; *Kawaida Studies: The New Nationalism,* 1971; *Raise Race Rays Raze: Essays Since 1965,* 1971; *Crisis in Boston!,* 1974; *The Creation of the New Ark,* 1975; *The Autobiography of LeRoi Jones/Amiri Baraka,* 1984; *Daggers and Javelins: Essays,* 1984; *The Artist and Social Responsibility,* 1986; *The Music: Reflections on Jazz and Blues,* 1987 (with Amina Baraka); *The Great Max Roach,* 1991; *Fearful Symmetry: The Art of Thornton Dial,* 1993; *Jesse Jackson and Black People,* 1994; *Conversations with Amiri Baraka,* 1994 (Charlie Reilly, editor); *Eulogies,* 1996; *Digging: The Afro-American Soul of American Classical Music,* 2009; *The Papers of Amiri Baraka, Poet Laureate of the Black Power Movement,* 2012; *Razor: Revolutionary Art for Cultural Revolution,* 2012; *Amiri Baraka and Edward Dorn: The Collected Letters,* 2014 (Claudia Moreno Pisano, editor).

EDITED TEXTS: *The Moderns: New Fiction in America*, 1963; *Black Fire: An Anthology of Afro-American Writing*, 1968 (with Larry Neal); *African Congress: A Documentary of the First Modern PanAfrican Congress*, 1972; *Confirmation: An Anthology of African-American Women*, 1983 (with Amina Baraka).

MISCELLANEOUS: *Selected Plays and Prose*, 1979; *The LeRoi Jones/ Amiri Baraka Reader*, 1991; Madhubuti, Haki, et al, ed. *Brilliant Flame!: Amiri Baraka: Poetry, Plays, & Politics for the People*, 2018.

Achievements

One of the most politically controversial playwrights of the 1960s, Amiri Baraka is best known for his brilliant early play *Dutchman* and for his contribution to the development of a community-based black nationalist theater. Throughout his career, he has sought dramatic forms for expressing the consciousness of those alienated from the psychological, economic, and racial mainstream of American society. Even though no consensus exists concerning the success of his experiments, particularly those with ritualistic forms for political drama, his challenge to the aesthetic preconceptions of the American mainstream and the inspiration he has provided younger black playwrights such as Ed Bullins and Ron Milner guarantee his place in the history of American drama.

Baraka has won a number of awards and fellowships, particularly for his poetry and drama (such as Italy's Ferroni Award and Foreign Poet Award in 1993 and the Playwright's Award at North Carolina's Black Drama Festival in 1997). He won the Longview Best Essay of the Year award (1961) for his essay "Cuba Libre" and the John Whitney Foundation Fellowship for poetry and fiction (1962). *Dutchman* won an Obie

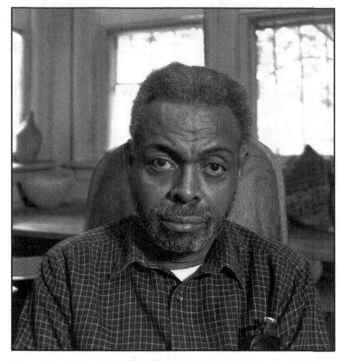
Photo by Anthony Barboza, courtesy of Getty Images

Award for Best American Off-Broadway Play and was granted a John Simon Guggenheim Memorial Foundation Fellowship. He received second prize at the International Art Festival of Dakar (1966) for his play *The Slave*; a National Endowment for the Arts grant (1966); a doctorate of humane letters from Malcolm X College in Chicago (1972); appointment as a Rockefeller Foundation Fellow in drama (1981); a National Endowment for the Arts poetry award (1981); a New Jersey Council for the Arts award (1982); and the American Book Award (Before Columbus Foundation) for *Confirmation: An Anthology of African-American Women* (1983). In 1984 he received an American Book Award, and in 1989 he won a PEN/Faulkner Award for Fiction. He has also founded or supported numerous journals (such as *Yugen* magazine), theater groups (such as the Black Arts Repertory Theatre), and other cultural organizations, especially in the African American community, and he has edited several important books on black culture, such as *Black Fire*. In 1989, Baraka was given the Langston Hughes Medal for outstanding contribution to literature. His work has been translated and published in a number of other languages and countries.

Biography

Amiri Baraka, as he has been known since 1967, was born Everett LeRoi Jones into a middle-class family in Newark, New Jersey. An excellent student whose parents encouraged his intellectual interests, Jones graduated from Howard University of Washington, D.C., in 1954 at the age of nineteen. After spending two years in the United States Air Force, primarily in Puerto Rico, he moved to Greenwich Village, where he embarked on his literary career in 1957. During the early stage of his career, Jones associated closely with numerous white avant-garde poets, including Robert Creeley, Allen Ginsberg, Robert Duncan, and Dianne DiPrima, with whom he founded the American Theatre for Poets in 1961. Marrying Hettie Cohen, a white woman with whom he edited the magazine *Yugen* from 1958 to 1963, Jones established himself as an important young poet, critic, and editor. Among the many magazines to which he contributed was *Downbeat*, the jazz journal where he first developed many of the musical interests which were to have such a large impact on his later poetry. The political interests that were to dominate Jones's later work were unmistakably present as early as 1960 when he toured Cuba with a group of black intellectuals. This event sparked his perception of the United States as a corrupt bourgeois society and seems particularly significant in relation to his later socialist emphasis. Jones's growing political interest conditioned his first produced plays, including the Obie Award winning *Dutchman* (1964), which anticipated the first major transformation of Jones's life.

Separating from Hettie Cohen and severing ties with his white associates, Jones moved from the Village to Harlem in 1965. Turning his attention to direct action within the black community, he founded the Black Arts Theatre and School in Harlem and, following his return to his native city in 1966, the Spirit House in Newark. After marrying a black woman, Sylvia Robinson (Amina Baraka), in 1966, Jones adopted his new name, which means "Prince" (Ameer) "the blessed one" (Baraka), along with the honorary title of "Imamu." Over the next half dozen years, Baraka helped found and develop the Black Community Development and Defense Organization, the Congress of African Peoples (convened in Atlanta in 1970), and the National Black Political Convention (convened in Gary, Indiana, in 1972). As a leading spokesman of the Black Arts movement, Baraka provided support for young black poets and playwrights, including Larry Neal, Ed Bullins, Marvin X, and Ron Milner. During the Newark uprising/riot of 1967, Baraka was arrested for unlawful possession of firearms. Although he was convicted and given the maximum sentence after the judge read his poem "Black People!" as an example of incitement to riot, Baraka was later cleared on appeal.

Baraka supported Kenneth A. Gibson's campaign to become the first black mayor of Newark in 1970, but he later broke with Gibson over what he perceived as the bourgeois values of the administration. This disillusionment with black politics within the American system, combined with Baraka's attendance at the Sixth Pan-African Conference at Dar es Salaam in 1974, precipitated the subsequent stage of his political evolution. While not abandoning his commitment to confronting the special problems of African Americans in the United States, Baraka came to interpret these problems within the framework of an overarching Marxist-Leninist-Maoist philosophy. In conjunction with this second transformation, Baraka dropped the title "Imamu" and changed the name of his Newark publishing firm from "Jihad" to "People's War."

Baraka has continued to teach, lecture, and conduct workshops, and he is noted not only for his writings but also for his influence on young writers and social critics. He is the editor of *Black Nation*, the organ of the League of Revolutionary Struggle, a Marxist organization. His influence extends far beyond African American culture and politics to embrace other people of color. Native American writer Maurice Kenney, for example, credited Baraka for teaching ethnic writers how to open doors to important venues for their writing, to "claim and take" their place at the cultural forefront.

Analysis: Short Fiction

Amiri Baraka's literary career has had three distinct periods. In the first period—the late 1950s and early 1960s—he was influenced by, and became a part of, the predominantly white avant-garde Beat movement in the arts. By the mid-1960s, Baraka had become a black nationalist (indicated by his rejection of the name LeRoi Jones), and many of his better-known plays, such as *Dutchman*, reflect his confrontational racial views from this period. Since the 1970s, Baraka has continued working as a political activist and writer, but his writing has increasingly encompassed a Marxist economic analysis in addition to his strong racial views. Nearly all of Baraka's short stories—although they continued to be reprinted into the 1980s and 1990s—first appeared in his earlier black nationalist period in the 1960s and reflected both the literary experiments of his Beat period and the increasingly political attitudes of his black nationalism. While many of these stories hold mainly historical interest today, the best are still compelling examples of how radical political

views and experimental prose styles could be fused in the 1960s, when a number of writers, both white and black, were trying to merge their art and their politics.

"The Screamers"

Reprinted at least a half dozen times since its appearance in *Tales*, generally in collections of African American fiction, "The Screamers" is by far Baraka's best-known short story. The narrative covers one night in a black jazz nightclub in Newark (probably in the early 1950s) from the perspective of a young man listening to "Harlem Nocturne" and other popular dance tunes. What makes this night unique is the performance by saxophonist Lynn Hope, who in an inspired moment leads the musicians through the crowd and out into the streets. "It would be the form of the sweetest revolution, to huckle-buck into the fallen capital, and let the oppressors lindy hop out." The police arrive and attack the crowd, a riot ensues, and the marchers "all broke our different ways, to save whatever it was each of us thought we loved." The story has a number of elements common to Baraka's fiction: the positive depiction of African American cultural forms (including a kind of "bop" jazz language), the conflict between this culture and white oppressors, and the metaphor of black art—here it is music, but it could as easily stand for writing—as an inspirational cultural form which, while it cannot finally overcome white oppression, at least achieves a moment of heightened consciousness for the people (here called "Biggers," in reference to the central character, Bigger Thomas, of Richard Wright's 1940 novel *Native Son*) listening to the music and moved by it.

"The Death of Horatio Alger"

The titles of Baraka's stories—such as "Uncle Tom's Cabin: Alternate Ending" or "A Chase

(Alighieri's Dream)"—often carry the larger meaning of the work, even when the story makes no further reference to it. In the case of "The Death of Horatio Alger," the tale seems a fairly simple description of a childhood fight. The narrator of the tale, Mickey, is playing dozens—a black word game of insults aimed at participants' parents—with his best friend, J.D., and in front of three white friends. J.D. misunderstands one of the insults and attacks Mickey, and then they both attack the three white boys (who do not understand the black word game to begin with). The story is thus about communication and its failure, but also about the Horatio Alger myths of equality and freedom and about the alienation Baraka's protagonists often experience. As Lloyd Brown accurately writes of the story, "In stripping himself of insensitive white friends and Horatio Alger images of American society, Mickey is putting an end to his alienation from his black identity."

Analysis: Poetry

Amiri Baraka's importance as a poet rests on both the diversity of his work and the singular intensity of his Black Nationalist period. During this period, Baraka concentrated on exposing the unstated racist premises of Euro-American art and developing an alternative "Black Aesthetic." In part because he had demonstrated mastery of Euro-American poetic modes, Baraka's Black Nationalist philosophy commanded an unusual degree of white attention. Coming from an unknown poet, his militant poetry might well have been dismissed as a naive kind of propaganda. It did, in fact, alienate many of his earlier admirers, who came to see him as an embodiment of the civil disorders of the mid-1960s. On a more profound level, however, he spurred many to ponder the complex logic of his transformation and to reassess the political implications of their own aesthetic stances.

Baraka's poetry falls into three distinctive periods, each reflecting an attempt to find a philosophy capable of responding adequately to a corrupt culture. The voice of each period is shaped in accord with a different set of assumptions concerning the nature of the cultural corruption, the proper orientation toward political action, and the poet's relationship with his audience. During his early period, Baraka built an essentially aesthetic response on premises shared primarily with white poets and intellectuals. Although Baraka always recognized the importance of his racial and economic heritage, the intricate philosophical voice of the early period sounds highly individualistic in comparison with his later work. During his middle Black Nationalist period, Baraka shifted his emphasis to the racial dimension of American culture. The associated voice—much more accessible, though not nearly so simple as it first appears—reflects Baraka's desire to relate primarily to the African American community. During his third Marxist-Leninist-Maoist period, Baraka adopted a less emotionally charged voice in accord with his stance as a scientific analyst of capitalist corruption. The diversity of Baraka's work makes it extremely difficult to find a vocabulary equally relevant to the complex postmodernism of *Preface to a Twenty Volume Suicide Note*, the militant nationalism of *Black Magic*, and the uncompromising economic analysis of *Hard Facts*.

Music

To speak with a black voice, Baraka must present a variety of shifting surfaces, both to defend against and to attack the predatory forces of his environment. These shifting surfaces are extremely elusive, deriving their meaning as much from audience as from speaker. Using musical forms and images as primary points of reference, Baraka explores this relationship between group and individual voices. His music criticism frequently refers to the primacy in African American culture of the "call and response" mode of work songs and spirituals. Playing off this dynamic, many of Baraka's nationalist poems identify his individual voice with that of a group leader calling for an affirmative response from his community. "Three Movements and a Coda," for example, concludes: "These are songs if you have the/ music." Baraka can provide lyrics, but if they are to come alive as songs, the music must be provided by the participation of a responsive community. The conclusion of "Black Art" makes it clear that this music is more than a purely aesthetic response: "Let the world be a Black Poem/ And Let All Black People Speak This Poem/ Silently/ or LOUD." If the world is to be a poem for the black community, a political response must accompany the aesthetic one.

Violence

Frequently, Baraka pictures violence in graphic images of "smashing at jelly-white faces" or "cracking steel knuckles in a jewlady's mouth." Given the unqualified intensity of these images, it hardly seems surprising that many white and less militant black readers dismiss the Baraka of this period as a reverse racist forwarding the very modes of thought he ostensibly rejects. In essence, they take the call which concludes "A Poem Some People Will Have to Understand" on a literal level. When Baraka asks "Will the machine gunners please step forward," they respond that a military race war can end only in catastrophe for both races.

As the title of the poem suggests, however, the call should not be interpreted simplistically. To be understood, it must be seen in the context of Baraka's view of the historical response of African Americans to racist oppression. Describing a society in which "the wheel, and the wheels, wont let us alone," he points out that blacks have "awaited the coming of a natural/ phenomenon" to effect a release. Only after repeating "But none has come" three times does Baraka summon the "machinegunners." The call sounds Baraka's response to what he sees as the traditional passivity of the African American community. Recognizing that practically all black experience involves direct contact with psychological racism tied to economic exploitation, Baraka treats these shared experiences hyperbolically in order to shake his community into political action. Placed in a social context where violent group rebellion has been the exception, there is much less chance than most white readers believe that his words will be acted on literally. The use of this aesthetic of calculated overstatement demonstrates Baraka's willingness to use the tradition of masking for a new set of political purposes. Where the form of most African American masks has been dictated by their relationship to white psychology, however, Baraka shapes his new masks to elicit response from blacks. Far from oversimplifying his awareness in the nationalist period, Baraka demonstrates his developing sense of the complexity of poetry designed to function in a real social and political context.

The contextual complexity, however, adds a new dimension of seriousness to attacks on Baraka's use of anti-Semitism and racism as rhetorical strategies. Baraka negotiates extremely treacherous territory when and if he expects readers to concentrate on his desire to "Clean out the world for virtue and love" in the same poem ("Black Art") that endorses "poems that kill . . . Setting fire and death to/ whitie's ass." A similar apparent paradox occurs in "Black People!" which says both "Take their lives if need be" and "let's make a world we want black children to grow and learn in." Baraka's aesthetic approach, which vests ultimate authority in the authenticating response, raises the problematic possibility that the audience's real social actions will authenticate the destructive rhetoric rather than the constructive vision.

Black Nationalism

Baraka attempts to diminish this possibility by developing his constructive vision in celebratory nationalist poems such as "It's Nation Time" and "Africa Africa Africa," which introduce a new musical/chant mode to his work. Exhortations such as "Black Art," which, like Baraka's earlier work, manipulate punctuation and syntax to express fully the urgency of an emotional experience, also anticipate the chant poems by introducing oratorical elements reflecting participation in communal ritual. "A Poem for Black Hearts," for example, varies the opening phrase "For Malcolm's eyes" to establish a focal point for audience response. "For Malcolm's words," "For Malcolm's heart," and similar phrases provide a kind of drumbeat for Baraka's meditation on the fallen leader.

In "It's Nation Time" and "Africa Africa Africa" this drumbeat, clearly the constitutive structural element, often sounds explicitly: "Boom/ Boom/ BOOOM/ Boom." Writing primarily in short lines echoing these single drumbeats, Baraka uses reiteration and rhythmical variation to stress his vision of Pan-African unity. The first thirteen lines of "Africa Africa Africa" include no words other than "Africa" and "Africans." Anticipating Baraka's developing interest in reggae music, these poems call for the transformation of the old forms of African American culture into those of a new Pan-African sensibility. "It's Nation Time" phrases this call: "get up rastus for real to be rasta fari." Baraka rejects those "rastus" figures content to wear the passive masks imposed on Africans unaware of their heritage, and celebrates the rastafarians, a Caribbean sect associated strongly with reggae.

Socialist Voice

No simple aesthetic analysis suffices to explain either Baraka's new poetic voice or his difficulty in calling forth an affirmative response from either the artistic or the working-class community. Lines such as "This is the dictatorship of the proletariat/ the total domination of society by the working class" can easily be dismissed as lacking either the intellectual complexity or the emotional power of Baraka's earlier work. Such a dismissal, however, risks avoiding the issue of cultural conditioning, which Baraka now sees as central. Arguing that capitalist control of the media deforms both the proletariat's image of itself as a revolutionary force and its response to a "pure" socialist art, Baraka attempts to shatter the psychological barriers through techniques of reiteration similar to those used in the nationalist poetry. His relationship with the proletariat audience, however, generates a new set of political and aesthetic problems. While the nationalist voice assumed authority only insofar as it was validated by the experience of the African American community, the socialist voice must take on the additional burden of convincing the proletarian audience that its interpretation of its own experience had been "incorrect." If the community does not respond to Baraka's voice as its own, the problem lies with a brainwashed response rather than with a tainted call (the source of the problem in "Leroy"). As a result, Baraka frequently adopts a "lecturer's" voice to provide the "hard facts" that will overcome resistance to political action by proving that capitalism deceives the proletariat into accepting a "dictatorship of the minority."

Analysis: Drama

Working with forms ranging from the morality play to avant-garde expressionism, Amiri Baraka throughout his career has sought to create dramatic rituals expressing the intensity of the physical and psychological violence that dominates his vision of American culture. From his early plays on "universal" alienation through his Black Nationalist celebrations to his multimedia proletarian pageants, Baraka has focused on a variety of sacrificial victims as his central dramatic presences. The dominant type in Baraka's early plays are passive scapegoats unaware of their participation in ritual actions who condemn themselves and their communities to blind repetition of destructive patterns. Their apparent mastery of the forms of European American cultural literacy simply obscures the fact of their ignorance of the underlying reality of oppression. Responding to this ironic situation, Baraka's Black Nationalist plays emphasize that the new forms of consciousness, rooted in Africa rather than in Europe, needed to free the African American community from the historical and psychological forces that enforce such blind repetition. Inverting the traditional moral symbolism of European American culture, Baraka creates rituals that substitute symbolically white scapegoats for the symbolically black victims of his earlier works. These rituals frequently reject the image of salvation through self-sacrifice (seen as a technique for the pacification of the black masses), insisting instead that only an active struggle can break the cycle of oppression.

Because the rituals of Baraka's Black Nationalist plays frequently culminate in violence directed against whites, or symbolically white members of the black bourgeois, or aspects of the individual black psyche, numerous critics have attacked him for perpetuating the violence and racism he ostensibly criticizes. These critics frequently condemn him for oversimplifying reality, citing his movement from psychologically complex ironic forms to much more explicit allegorical modes in his later drama; the most insistent simply dismiss his

post-*Dutchman* plays as strident propaganda, lacking all aesthetic and moral merit. Basing their critiques firmly on European American aesthetic assumptions, such critics in fact overlook the central importance of Baraka's changing sense of his audience. Repudiating the largely white avant-garde audience that applauded his early work, Baraka turned almost exclusively to an African American audience more aware of the storefront preacher and popular music groups such as the Temptations than of August Strindberg and Edward Albee. In adopting a style of performance in accord with this cultural perception, Baraka assumed a didactic voice intended to focus attention on immediate issues of survival and community or class defense.

The Baptism

Baraka's early plays clearly reflect both his developing concern with issues of survival and his fascination with European American avant-garde traditions. *The Baptism*, in particular, draws on the conventions of expressionist theater to comment on the absurdity of contemporary American ideas of salvation, which in fact simply mask a larger scheme of victimization. Identified only as symbolic types, Baraka's characters speak a surreal mixture of street language and theological argot. While the slang references link them to the social reality familiar to the audience, their actions are dictated by the sudden shifts and thematic ambiguities characteristic of works such as Strindberg's *Ett dromspel* (pb. 1902; *A Dream Play,* 1912) and the "Circe" chapter of James Joyce's *Ulysses* (1922).

The play's central character, named simply "the Boy," resembles a traditional Christ figure struggling to come to terms with his vocation. Baraka treats his protagonist with a mixture of irony and empathy, focusing on the ambiguous roles of the spirit and the flesh in relation to salvation. Pressured by the Minister to deny his body and by the cynical Homosexual to immerse himself in the profane as a path to the truly sacred, the Boy vacillates. At times he claims divine status; at times he insists, "I am only flesh." The chorus of Women, at once holy virgins and temple prostitutes, reinforces his confusion. Shortly after identifying him as "the Son of God," they refer to him as the "Chief Religious jelly roll of the universe." Given these irreconcilable roles, which he is expected to fulfill, the Boy's destiny as scapegoat and martyr seems inevitable; the dramatic tension revolves around the question of who will victimize him and why. Baraka uses a sequence of conflicting views of the Boy's role, each of which momentarily dominates his self-image, to heighten this tension.

Responding to the Homosexual's insistence that "the devil is a part of creation like an ash tray or senator," the Boy first confesses his past sins and demands baptism. When the Women respond by elevating him to the status of "Son of God/ Son of Man," he explicitly rejects all claim to spiritual purity. The ambiguous masquerade culminates in an attack on the Boy, who is accused of using his spiritual status to seduce women who "wanted to be virgins of the Lord." Supported only by the Homosexual, the Boy defends himself against the Women and the Minister, who clamor for his sacrifice, ostensibly as punishment for his sins. Insisting that "there will be no second crucifixion," the Boy slays his antagonists with a phallic sword, which he interprets as the embodiment of spiritual glory. For a brief moment, the figures of Christ as scapegoat and Christ as avenger seem reconciled in a baptism of fire.

Baraka undercuts this moment of equilibrium almost immediately. Having escaped martyrdom at the hands of the mob (ironically, itself victimized), the Boy confronts the Messenger, who wears a motorcycle jacket embellished with a gold crown and the words "The Man." In Baraka's dream allegory, the Man can represent the Roman/American legal system or be a symbol for God the Father, both powers that severely limit the Boy's control over events. The Boy's first reaction to the Messenger is to reclaim his superior spiritual status, insisting that he has "brought love to many people" and calling on his "Father" for compassion. Rejecting these pleas, the Messenger indicates that "the Man's destroying the whole works tonight." The Boy responds defiantly: "Neither God nor man shall force me to leave. I was sent here to save man and I'll not leave until I do." The allegory suggests several different levels of interpretation: social, psychological, and symbolic. The Boy rejects his responsibility to concrete individuals (the mob he kills, the Man) in order to save an abstract entity (the mob as an ideal man). Ultimately, he claims his right to the martyr's death, which he killed the mob in order to avoid, by repudiating the martyr's submission to a higher power. Losing patience with the Boy's rhetoric, the Messenger responds not by killing him but by knocking him out and dragging him offstage. His attitude of boredom effectively deflates the allegorical seriousness of the Boy's defiance, a deflation reinforced by the Homosexual's concluding comment that the scene resembles "some really uninteresting kind of orgy."

The Baptism's treatment of the interlocking themes of sacrifice, ritual, and victimization emphasizes their inherent ambiguity and suggests the impossibility of moral action in a culture that confuses God with the leader of a motorcycle gang. Baraka's baptism initiates the Boy into absurdity rather than responsibility. If any sins have been washed away, they are resurrected immediately in pointless ritual violence and immature rhetoric. Although he does not develop the theme explicitly in *The Baptism*, Baraka suggests that there is an underlying philosophical corruption in European American culture, in this case derived from Christianity's tendency to divorce flesh from spirit. Increasingly, this philosophical corruption takes the center of Baraka's dramatic presentation of Western civilization.

Dutchman

Widely recognized as Baraka's greatest work in any genre, *Dutchman* combines the irony of his avant-garde period with the emotional power and social insight of his later work. Clay, a young black man with a highly developed sense of self, occupies a central position in the play analogous to that of the Boy in *The Baptism*. The central dramatic action of the play involves Clay's confrontation with a young white woman, Lula, who may in fact be seen as an aspect of Clay's own self-awareness. In both thematic emphasis and dramatic structure, *Dutchman* parallels Edward Albee's *The Zoo Story* (pr., pb. 1959). Both plays focus on a clash between characters from divergent social and philosophical backgrounds, both comment on the internal divisions of individuals in American society, and both culminate in acts of violence that are at once realistic and symbolic. What sets *Dutchman* apart, however, is its intricate exploration of the psychology that leads Clay to a symbolic rebellion that ironically guarantees his real victimization. Clay *thinks* he exists as an autonomous individual struggling for existential awareness. Baraka implies, however, that this European American conception of self simply enforces Clay's preordained role as ritual scapegoat. As the Everyman figure his name suggests, Clay represents all individuals trapped by self-deception and social pressure. As a black man in a racist culture, he shares the more specific problem of those whose self-consciousness has been determined by white definitions.

The stage directions for *Dutchman* emphasize the link between Clay's situation and the decline of European American culture, describing the subway car where the action transpires as "the flying underbelly of the city . . . heaped in modern myth." Lula enters eating an apple, evoking the myth of the Fall. Together, these allusions contribute a literary dimension to the foreboding atmosphere surrounding the extended conversation that leads to Clay's sacrifice at the hands of Lula and the subway riders, mostly white but some black. Throughout, Lula maintains clear awareness of her symbolic and political intentions, while Clay remains effectively blind. Lula's role demands simply that she maintain the interest of the black man until it is convenient to kill him. Meanwhile, Clay believes he can somehow occupy a position of detachment or spiritual superiority. Changing approach frequently, Lula plays the roles of temptress, intellectual, psychologist, and racist. Clay responds variously to these gambits, sometimes with amusement, ultimately with anger and contempt. Consistently, however, he fails to recognize the genocidal reality underlying Lula's masquerade, unwittingly assuming his preordained role in the controlling ritual of black destruction. Much like the legendary ghost ship for which it was named, the *Dutchman*, Baraka implies, will continue to sail so long as blacks allow the white world to control the premises of the racial debate.

This rigged debate reflects Baraka's reassessment of his universalist beliefs and his movement toward Black Nationalism. Clay resembles the early LeRoi Jones in many ways: Both are articulate natives of New Jersey with aspirations to avant-garde artistic success. *Dutchman* implies that both are subject to fantasies about the amount of meaningful success possible for them in the realm of European American culture. Lula alternately reduces Clay to a "well-known type" and condemns him for rejecting his roots and embracing "a tradition you ought to feel oppressed by." During the first act, Clay stays "cool" until Lula sarcastically declares him the "Black Baudelaire" and follows with the repeated phrase "My Christ. My Christ." Suddenly shifting emphasis, she immediately denies his Christ-like stature and insists, "You're a murderer," compressing the two major attributes of the Boy in *The Baptism*, this time with a specifically social resonance. The sudden shift disrupts Clay's balance. Ironically restating and simplifying the thesis of Ralph Ellison's universalist novel *Invisible Man* (1922), Lula concludes the opening act with an ironic resolution to "pretend the people cannot see you...that you are free of your own history. And I am free of my history." The rapid movement from Clay as Christ and murderer—standard black roles in the fantasy life of white America—to the *pretense* of his freedom underscores the inevitability of his victimization, an inevitability clearly dictated by the historical forces controlling Lula, forces that Clay steadfastly refuses to recognize.

Admitting his hatred for whites, Clay claims a deep affinity with the explosive anger lying beneath the humorous surface of the work of the great black musicians Bessie Smith and Charlie Parker. Ridiculing Lula's interpretation of his psychological makeup, Clay warns her that whites should beware of preaching "rationalism" to blacks, since the best cure for the black neurosis would be the random murder of whites. After this demonstration of his superior, and highly rational, awareness, Clay turns to go. He dismisses Lula with contempt, saying, "we won't be acting out that little pageant you outlined before." Immediately thereafter, Lula kills him. The murder is in fact the final act of the real pageant, the ritual of black sacrifice. Seen from Lula's perspective, the entire conversation amounts to an extended assault on Clay's awareness of the basic necessities of survival. Seen from Baraka's viewpoint, the heightened racial awareness of Clay's final speech is simply an illusion, worthless if divorced from action. Clay's unwilling participation in the pageant of white mythology reveals the futility of all attempts to respond to white culture on its own terms. Regarded in this light, Baraka's subsequent movement away from the theoretical avant-garde and from European American modes of psychological analysis seems inevitable.

Other Literary Forms

Amiri Baraka is an exceptionally versatile literary figure, equally well known for his poetry, drama, and essays. In addition, he has written an experimental novel, *The System of Dante's Hell*, which includes numerous poetic and dramatic passages. Baraka's critical and political prose has been collected in *Home: Social Essays, Raise Race Rays Raze: Essays Since 1965, Selected Plays and Prose*, and *Daggers and Javelins: Essays. The Autobiography of LeRoi Jones/Amiri Baraka* was published in 1984.

Bibliography

Baker, Houston A., Jr. *The Journey Back: Issues in Black Literature and Criticism*. Chicago: University of Chicago Press, 1980. Baker sees Baraka's transformation as groundbreaking, pivotal in the development of a "Black Aesthetic" that would define itself apart from the Western white canon. The reader must use the index to find references to Baraka, as the chapters are organized historically rather than by authors considered.

Banfield, William. "Black Artistic Invisibility." *Journal of Black Studies* 35, no. 2 (November, 2004): 195-210. Discusses the work of Baraka and other authors who examine the relationship between mainstream American culture—especially musical culture—and African American musicians.

Baraka, Amiri. "Amiri Baraka." http://www.amiribaraka.com/. Accessed September 1, 2005.

Baraka's site has information about his recent activities, articles, reviews, lists of his publications, photos, video and audio clips, and a few of Baraka's own drawings.

_____. "Amiri Baraka Analyzes How He Writes." Interview by Kalamu Ya Salaam. *African American Review* 37, nos. 2/3 (Summer, 2003): 211-237. An interview with Baraka that reveals the poet's thoughts in writing and choosing the title of his poem "A System of Dante's Hell." Baraka also discusses his personal relationship to the poem.

_____. "Philistinism and the Negro Writer." In *Anger, and Beyond: The Negro Writer in the United States,* edited and with an introduction by Herbert Hill. New York: Harper & Row, 1966. This essay is useful to the student of Baraka as an articulation in prose of the commitments that were being made simultaneously in the poetry. The tone is rather quiet and reasoned, relative to Baraka's later rhetoric, but the radical central theme is clear: "The Negro writer can only survive by refusing to become a white man."

Benston, Kimberly W., ed. *Imamu Amiri Baraka (LeRoi Jones): A Collection of Critical Essays.* Englewood Cliffs, N.J.: Prentice-Hall, 1978. Benston, who has also written the full-length work *Baraka: The Renegade and the Mask* (1976), brings together essays that shed light on various aspects of his poetry and drama. Includes a bibliography.

Brown, Lloyd Wellesley. *Amiri Baraka.* Boston: Twayne, 1980. By a scholar who specializes in African, African American, and Western Indian literary studies, this is the standard critical piece on Baraka's poetic achievement. Provides a bibliography and an index.

Fox, Robert Eliot. *Conscientious Sorcerers: The Black Post-modernist Fiction of LeRoi Jones/Baraka, Ishmael Reed, and Samuel R. Delany.* New York: Greenwood Press, 1987. Chapter 2 is a discussion of Baraka's novel and the stories collected in *Tales,* in a comparative study of "three of the most important

and gifted American authors to have emerged in the tumultuous period of the 1960s."

Gwynne, James B., ed. *Amiri Baraka: The Kaleidoscopic Torch.* Harlem, N.Y.: Steppingstones Press, 1985. This collection of essays hails Baraka as torchbearer for all racial and ethnic minorities.

Harris, William J. *The Poetry and Poetics of Amiri Baraka: The Jazz Aesthetic.* Columbia: University of Missouri Press, 1985. Discusses Baraka's significance as the creator of a new artistic movement and his influence on African American artists. Includes selected bibliography and index.

Harris, William J., and Aldon Lynn Nielsen. "Somebody Blew Off Baraka." *African American Review* 37, nos. 2/3 (Summer, 2003): 183-188. Examines the controversy surrounding Baraka's selection as poet laureate of New Jersey and the criticisms of his poem "Somebody Blew Up America," whose references to the terrorist attacks of September 11, 2001, angered many.

Hudson, Theodore. *From LeRoi Jones to Amiri Baraka: The Literary Works.* Durham, N.C.: Duke University Press, 1973. This sympathetic work provides a biographical chapter based on interviews with Baraka and his parents. Other chapters examne his works, philosophy, and styles. Notes and an index are provided, along with a bibliography that lists primary and secondary works through the early 1970s.

Johnson, Charles. *Being and Race: Black Writing Since 1970.* Bloomington: Indiana University Press, 1988. Places Baraka in the tradition of Negritude and credits him as having "for the most part established the style of Cultural Nationalist poetics in the period between 1960 and 1970—for an entire generation of writers." There is no chapter devoted to Baraka, so the reader must consult the index.

Kumar, Nita N. "The Logic of Retribution: Amiri Baraka's *Dutchman.*" *African American Review* 37, nos. 2/3 (Summer, 2003): 271-280. A thorough discussion of Baraka's rejection of white sensibilities in *Dutchman*, his most highly regarded play.

Lacey, Henry C. *To Raise, Destroy, and Create: The Poetry, Drama, and Fiction of Imamu Amiri Baraka (LeRoi Jones)*. Troy, N.Y.: Whitston, 1981. Unlike other studies, which separate the works by genres, this volume divides Baraka's life into a Beat period, a transition, and a rebirth symbolized by taking on a new name. Also discusses Baraka's dramatic work in context with his writing in other genres. Supplemented by an index and a list of Baraka's works.

Oyigbenu, Amirikpa. *Racism, Citizenship and Identity Politics in African-American Drama: Celebrating Amiri Baraka and August Wilson*. Ahmadu Bello UP Limited, 2013. A detailed study by a Nigerian writer.

Reilly, Charlie, ed. *Conversations with Amiri Baraka*. Jackson: University Press of Mississippi, 1994. Offers insights into the black experience through Baraka's experiences during the turbulent later half of the twentieth century. Baraka critiques and elucidates his works and underscores his belief in the connection between art and social criticism. Includes chronology and index.

Shannon, Sandra G. "Evolution or Revolution in Black Theater: A Look at the Cultural Nationalist Agenda in Select Plays by Amiri Baraka." *African American Review* 37, nos. 2/3 (Summer, 2003): 281-300. Presents Baraka's argument against technology as it appears in his play *Home on the Range*.

Simanga, Michael. *Amiri Baraka and the Congress of African People: History and Memory*. Palgrave Macmillan, 2015. Contains thirteen chapters on such topics as Baraka's leadership, the Black Arts Movement, women, revolution, Marxism, and others.

Smethurst, James. "*Pat Your Foot and Turn the Corner:* Amiri Baraka, the Black Arts Movement, and the Poetics of Popular Avant-Garde." *African American Review* 37, nos. 2/3 (Summer, 2003): 261-270. A good analysis of the Black Arts movement and its impacts on the construction of American identity and mainstream perceptions of African Americans.

Sollors, Werner. *Amiri Baraka / LeRoi Jones: The Quest for a "Populist Modernism."* New York: Columbia University Press, 1978. In Chapter 7 of this early study, Sollors examines the themes and forms of Baraka's lone novel, his dramatic works, and his short stories. Other chapters provide detailed analyses of his plays. Good photograph section of production stills. Bibliography and index.

Watts, Jerry Gafio. *Amiri Baraka: The Politics and Art of a Black Intellectual*. New York: New York University Press, 2001. This immense volume criticizes Baraka for his political oversimplification and polemicism, at the same time outlining his influence on other writers and contrasting him with other black activists and political figures.

Woodard, K. Komozi. *A Nation Within a Nation: Amiri Baraka (LeRoi Jones) and Black Power Politics*. Chapel Hill: University of North Carolina Press, 1999. Revises the common view of Baraka as an extremist, arguing that he became a seasoned political veteran who brought together divergent black factions.

—Robert McClenaghan; David Peck; Judith K. Taylor; Thomas J. Taylor; Craig Werner; Robert C. Evans

Arna Wendell Bontemps

Novelist, Poet, and Biographer

Born: Alexandria, Louisiana; October 13, 1902

Died: Nashville, Tennessee; June 4, 1973

LONG FICTION: *God Sends Sunday*, 1931; *Black Thunder*, 1936; *Drums at Dusk*, 1939.

SHORT FICTION: *The Old South*, 1973.

DRAMA: *St. Louis Woman*, pr. 1946 (with Countee Cullen). poetry: *Personals*, 1963.

NONFICTION: *Father of the Blues*, 1941 (with W. C. Handy; biography); *They Seek a City*, 1945 (with Jack Conroy; revised as *Anyplace but Here*, 1966); *One Hundred Years of Negro Freedom*, 1961 (history); *Free at Last: The Life of Frederick Douglass*, 1971; *Arna Bontemps-Langston Hughes Letters: 1925-1967*, 1980.

CHILDREN'S/YOUNG ADULT LITERATURE: *Popo and Fifina: Children of Haiti*, 1932 (with Langston Hughes); *You Can't Pet a Possum*, 1934; *Sad-Faced Boy*, 1937; *The Fast Sooner Hound*, 1942 (with Jack Conroy); *We Have Tomorrow*, 1945; *Slappy Hooper: The Wonderful Sign Painter*, 1946 (with Conroy); *The Story of the Negro*, 1948; *Sam Patch*, 1951 (with Conroy); *Chariot in the Sky: A Story of the Jubilee Singers*, 1951; *The Story of George Washington Carver*, 1954; *Lonesome Boy*, 1955; *Frederick Douglass: Slave, Fighter, Freeman*, 1959; *Famous Negro Athletes*, 1964; *Mr. Kelso's Lion*, 1970; *Young Booker: Booker T. Washington's Early Days*, 1972; *The Pasteboard Bandit*, 1997 (with Hughes); *Bubber Goes to Heaven*, 1998.

EDITED TEXTS: *The Poetry of the Negro*, 1949, revised, 1971 (with Langston Hughes); *The Book of Negro Folklore*, 1958 (with Hughes); *American Negro Poetry*, 1963; *Great Slave Narratives*, 1969; *Hold Fast to Dreams*, 1969; *The Harlem Renaissance Remembered*, 1972.

Achievements

Arna Wendell Bontemps's finely honed poems quietly reflect his lifelong Christian beliefs. After winning several prizes for his poems and short stories in the 1920s and 1930s, Bontemps was granted the first of two Rosenwald Fellowships in Creative Writing in 1939 (the other came in 1943). In 1949 and 1954 he received Guggenheim Fellowships for creative writing. He was given the Jane Addams Children's Book Award in 1956 for *The Story of the Negro* and was also runner-up for the Newbery Award. In 1969 he was appointed writer-in-residence at Fisk University, and in 1972 he was named honorary consultant to the Library of Congress in American cultural history. Beginning in the 1960s he was a popular national speaker, and he always offered encouragement to struggling black writers. He was loved and respected by his students, wherever he served as a teacher.

Biography

Arna Wendell Bontemps's parentage was Louisiana Creole. He was born in the front bedroom of his maternal grandfather's comfortable home at the corner of Ninth and Winn Streets in Alexandria, Louisiana. The house is still

The Arna Wendell Bontemps House in Alexandria, Louisiana (photo courtesy of Farragutful)

standing, though it has been moved, and is today the Arna Bontemps African American Museum. Bontemps's father, a skilled stonemason, bricklayer, and former trombonist with a New Orleans marching band, moved with his wife, children, and in-laws to California following a racial incident in Louisiana. The elder Bontemps also served as a Seventh-day Adventist preacher after he abandoned Catholicism.

Bontemps's earliest childhood was spent happily in his grandparents' house in Alexandria. Later, in California, he recalled being greatly influenced by a great-uncle, Uncle Buddy, who came from Alexandria to stay with his relatives in California. Though Uncle Buddy was a down-at-the-heels alcoholic, he nevertheless represented, for young Bontemps, the essence of Louisiana culture, folklore, and, history with his colorful stories and speech. Self-educated, intelligent, and articulate, Uncle Buddy was a good reader and storyteller and awakened in his grand-nephew a love of hearing and telling stories and of reading and reciting poetry. Most important, Uncle Buddy reminded young Bontemps of his Louisiana and southern roots,

which were later to be a great literary storehouse for the budding author.

Bontemps's mother died when he was ten, and he and his sister went to live on his grandmother's farm near Los Angeles. Bontemps completed his secondary schooling at a private boarding school and his bachelor's degree at Pacific Union College in Northern California. In New York he joined the Harlem Renaissance, which was in full swing, and began a close, lifelong friendship with writer Langston Hughes.

Bontemps taught school in New York, married Alberta Jones when he was twenty-four, and subsequently fathered six children. In 1931 Bontemps and his family moved to Alabama, where he taught in a junior college and observed southern behavior and customs. In 1934 Bontemps and his family left Alabama because of a hostile racial climate following the trial of the Scottsboro Nine, black men who were unjustly convicted of raping two white women, and moved into his father's small house in California. There the author worked on his second novel, frequently writing outdoors with his small portable typewriter on a makeshift desk.

By 1943 he had moved to Chicago, where he earned a master's degree in library science. Accepting an appointment as full professor and head librarian at Fisk University in Nashville, he served there until the mid-1960s, when he accepted a professorship in history and literature at the University of Illinois at Chicago Circle. He also served as curator of the James Weldon Johnson Collection.

In 1969 he retired to work on his autobiography, which was unfinished at his death. In 1972 he published *The Harlem Renaissance Remembered* and returned to visit his birthplace in Louisiana. He died on June 4, 1973, and was honored at both Protestant and Catholic memorial services.

Analysis: Long Fiction

Though he lived and taught in many parts of America, Bontemps always identified with the South and set most of his fictional works there. Bontemps greatly valued his African American inheritance and tried to increase both racial pride and understanding through his many books about African American figures, life, and culture.

God Sends Sunday

In *God Sends Sunday*, set in the 1890s, Bontemps depicts a diminutive black jockey, Little Augie, who lives on a Red River plantation in Louisiana with his older sister. Because he was born with a caul over his face, he is thought to be lucky. He discovers a talent for riding horses, which serves him well when he escapes to New Orleans on a steamboat and becomes a jockey. Augie grows rich, arrogant, and ostentatious. He falls in love with a beautiful young mulatto, Florence Desseau, but learns, to his sorrow, that she is the mistress of his rich white patron. Going to St. Louis to find a woman like Florence, Augie falls in with a crowd of prostitutes, gamblers, and "sugar daddies," one of whom he murders when the man bothers Augie's woman. Returning to New Orleans, Augie at last has Florence as his lover. However, she deserts him, taking his money and possessions. Augie's luck fades, and he declines rapidly into penury and alcoholism. In California, Augie commits another "passion murder" and escapes to Mexico.

The novel exhibits a remarkable joie de vivre among its black characters, but they are primarily caricatures within a melodramatic plot. Bontemps uses black dialect and folklore effectively, making especially good use of the blues, for which Augie has a great affection.

Black Thunder

Bontemps's second novel, first published in 1936, was reissued in 1968 with a valuable introduction by Bontemps. In this essay, he describes finding a treasured store of slave narratives in the Fisk Library; he read the stories of slave insurrectionists Nat Turner, Denmark Vesey, and Gabriel Prosser. Bontemps identified Prosser as the slave-rebel-hero whose yearning for freedom most greatly resembled his own.

Black Thunder is generally acknowledged by readers and critics alike to be Bontemps's best novel; it has even been called the best African American historical novel. The French Revolution and the slave rebellion in Santo Domingo are a significant background; the story dramatizes an enslaved people's long-restrained desire for freedom. Bundy, an old black peasant, longs for the freedom that the legend of Haitian liberator Toussaint-Louverture has inspired in many slaves. When Bundy is viciously flogged to death, Gabriel Prosser, a strong young coachman, feels driven to seek freedom for himself and his people. This feeling is even held by already-freed slaves, such as Mingo, a leather worker, who plays a major role in the rebellion effort. The white Virginians, both patricians and common folk, hold Creuzot, a French painter, and Biddenhurst, a British lawyer, responsible for the slaves' disquiet. Moreover, the white population does not believe the slaves to be human; thus, they cannot understand why they would want freedom. The whites' interpretation of the Bible supports their racial beliefs.

Gabriel too is deeply religious, though not fanatical, and often echoes scripture, believing that God will free his people because Armageddon is at hand. He plans, with the assistance of free blacks, slaves, and a few sympathetic whites, to capture the arsenal at Richmond in order to seize the weapons and overpower the city. Unfortunately, a monsoon-like rainstorm on the night of the rebellion causes a delay in the insurrection. Bontemps's powers as a prose artist are especially strong as he describes, in haunting cadences, the revolt's defeat by nature's wrath. The slaves believe that it was ill luck and fateful weather that led to the revolt's collapse, though in actuality two elderly, spoiled house servants betrayed the cause. The collapse of the rebellion marks the climax of the story; what follows tells of the insurrectionists' capture and execution. Bontemps makes astute use of court records as he dramatizes Gabriel's trial.

Bontemps is in firmer control of his literary material in *Black Thunder* than in his other novels. All his characters—white planter-aristocrats, free blacks, and French zealots—are drawn with objectivity and restraint. Pro-freedom views are not praised at the expense of anti-freedom beliefs. Furthermore, Bontemps's characters, even minor ones, are richly complex. For example, Ben and Pharoah, the betrayers of the rebellion, evidence conflicting loyalties both to their aristocratic masters and to their African American brothers. In a memorable interior monologue, Ben condemns himself for the narcissism that made his own survival more important to him than that of his fellow slaves. His ironic curse is that he must live under the threat of a horrible revenge at the hands of his own people.

Bontemps's special achievement in *Black Thunder* is the skill with which he integrates Gabriel's revolt into the fabric of Virginian and American life by using a documentary style of exposition. While Virginia legislators debate further segregation of blacks as a way of dealing with race issues, quoted reports from Federalist newspapers oppose the liberal ideas of former president Thomas Jefferson and attribute Gabriel's revolt to his evil influence. These same newspapers support John Quincy Adams's presidential campaign.

Even more impressive is Bontemps's use of interior monologues and passages which present the point of view of several individual characters, Caucasian and African American. First- and third-person perspectives are blended in order to present both objective and subjective forces. Bontemps's careful synthesis of history and imagination helps him demonstrate the universal, age-old struggles of humankind to surmount barriers of race, class, and caste and gain equality, liberty, respect, and security. Because Bontemps allows Gabriel to maintain and even increase his integrity, he becomes a truly tragic figure for whom, at the end of the novel, "excellent is strength, the first for freedom of the blacks . . .[he is] perplexed but unafraid, waiting for the dignity of death."

Drums at Dusk

Drums at Dusk, like *Black Thunder*, is a historical novel in which Bontemps makes use of slave narratives and legal records to establish background for the black rebellion leading to Haiti's independence and Toussaint-Louverture's ascendancy. Bontemps centers the story on a young girl of French ancestry, Celeste Juvet, and Diron de Sautels, an aristocratic young Frenchman who claims membership in Les Amis des Noirs, embraces enthusiastically the ideas of writers of the French Revolution, and works as an abolitionist. Celeste and her grandmother reside on a large plantation where the owner's cousin, Count Armand de Sacy, abuses ailing slaves and mistreats his mistresses, abandoning them at his uncle's. De Sacy is deeply disliked, and when several slaves foment an insurrection, the aristocrats are overturned and rebel leaders successfully seize power.

Diron de Sautels's radical opinions influence young blacks, and they fight with three other groups for political control of Santo Domingo: rich aristocrats, poor whites, and free mulattos.

Drums at Dusk describes with melodramatic sensationalism the sybaritic lives of the wealthy and their sexual exploitation of light-skinned black women. Moreover, the novel describes graphically the heinous conditions on the slave ships and on many of the plantations. The patricians' cruelty and abuse lead to a rapid spread of liberal ideology and the rise of such leaders as Toussaint-Louverture.

In spite of its faults, Bontemps's last novel, like his second one, emphasizes the universal need and desire for freedom, which he intimates is as necessary for the survival of human beings as water, air, food, and shelter.

Analysis: Short Fiction

The Old South, Arna Bontemps's collection of short stories, contains fourteen selections, the firstof which is an important essay, "Why I Returned," an account of his early life in Louisiana and California and his later life in Alabama and Tennessee. All of the selections are set in the South of the 1930s (a time when this region was yet unchanged and thus "old") or concern characters from the South. Some of the stories are also autobiographical—"The Cure," "Three Pennies for Luck," "Saturday Night"—and some are sharply satirical portraits of influential white women: a wealthy patron of young black musicians in "A Woman with a Mission" and a principal of a black boarding school in "Heathens at Home." The titles of these latter stories are self-explanatory.

Bontemps was brought up in the Seventh-day Adventist Church, for which his father had abandoned the Creoles' traditional Catholicism. The boarding school and college Bontemps attended as well as the academy where he taught in Alabama were sponsored by the Adventists. Though Bontemps did not remain active in this church, he was deeply religious all his life. Several of his stories thus have religious settings and themes, including "Let the Church Roll On," a study of a black congregation's lively charismatic church service. Bontemps was early influenced by music since his father and other relatives hadbeen blues and jazz musicians in Louisiana. "Talk to the Music," "Lonesome Boy, Silver Trumpet," and "A Woman with a Mission" all concern young black musicians.

Several selections concern black folk culture and folklore: "The Cure," "Lonesome Boy, Silver Trumpet," and "The Devil Is a Conjurer." The latter story reflects the human desire to invest nature with a sense of the mysterious, which unimaginative men find foolish and unprofitable. In addition, at least seven of Bontemps's stories, including the three named above, involve a young boy or man seeking or discovering meaning and worth in family and community, which some Bontemps scholars believe was a principal desire in the author's own life. Bontemps's short stories treat sensitive political, economic, and social themes that are also employed in his two novels of slave revolts, *Black Thunder* and *Drums at Dusk.*

"Boy Blue" in *The Old South* concerns an escaped black murderer who is hunted down and killed after he commits a second homicide. The action in this story is seen from two perspectives, that of a young child and of the criminal himself. Critic Robert Bone argues that the criminal named Blue is in fact "Bontemps's apotheosis of the blues hero." In his best stories Bontemps achieves an aesthetic distance, mastery of literary form, and a belief in transcendence in spite of his characters' struggles in a world that often denies them human value. Though Bontemps's stories have been compared with those of Richard Wright, Bontemps's are less angry and acerbic.

"A Summer Tragedy"

"A Summer Tragedy," first published in *Opportunity* in 1935, is Bontemps's best-known, most frequently anthologized, and perhaps most successful short story because of its artistic interlacing of setting, symbolism, characterization, and folklore. As Bontemps's biographer, Kirkland C. Jones, has observed, this story is "to the Bontemps canon what 'Sonny's Blues' has become to Baldwin's short fiction efforts—outstanding."

An elderly black couple, Jennie and Jeff Patton, have for decades been tenant farmers on Greenbrier Plantation in an unnamed southern state. The Pattons are ill, frail, and barely ambulatory; Jennie is nearly blind. Their five adult children have all died in violent situations, none of which is specified, suggesting that life for blacks, particularly the young, was dangerous and uncertain in the South.

The opening scene reveals the old couple dressing in their clean but threadbare black "Sunday-best." Their actions are described slowly and painfully as they prepare for some great, momentous occasion. The story is set in the fullness of the green, fecund, early summer fields; all of nature—plants, animals, and birds—seems to be celebrating life, youth, warmth, and procreation, as contrasted with the aging, pinched, wintry, weary, and deathlike lives of Jennie and Jeff. Nevertheless, they affirm their love for each other and resolve to persevere in their plans, which are not clear to the reader until late in the story. At first, Bontemps's narrative seems almost naturalistic in the tradition of Theodore Dreiser as the Pattons reflect upon their lives of hard, monotonous, futile labor that has left them only more debt-ridden. Their existence seems to be a cruel trap, a vicious, meaningless struggle. They own an old, battered, hard-to-crank Model-T Ford that will later serve a vital but ominous purpose.

Yet the story is not merely documentary with dreary details. Jeff and Jennie are presented as three-dimensional characters through a psychological point of view which allows the reader to share their thoughts, feelings, and memories. Bontemps had also skillfully used folk motifs to provide both verisimilitude and foreshadowing. For example, the Pattons's sickly "frizzly" chickens, which are supposed to protect the farm from evil spirits by devouring them, seem to be as death-doomed as their owners.

Jeff reflects on the many mules he has worn out in his years of plantation toil. His stingy employer has allowed him to have only one mule at a time; thus a long succession of mules has been killed by excessive and unremitting toil. Jeff is not aware that he is symbolically a mule for whom the callous old Major Stevenson has also had no sympathy. Moreover, Jeff himself has never felt pity for a man who is too weak to work.

Passing a neighbor's house on the journey through the countryside, Jennie is silently amused to think that their neighbor, Delia, who sees the Pattons' car drive past, is consumed with curiosity to know their destination. Delia, it seems, had once made passes at Jeff when he was a young married man. By refusing to supply Delia with any information, Jennie feels she is punishing her neighbor for her long-ago indiscretion. Such details as these help humanize and individualize Bontemps's characters, making them psychologically credible. The reader gradually becomes aware that because of the couple's love for one another and their fear that one may grow too weak to help the other, they are determined to perish together.

As the Pattons near the high banks of the river levee, they can hear the rushing water. They drive over the levee and into the dark, swirling water. (Some readers contend that the stream is Louisiana's Red River, which flows near Bontemps's birthplace.) In death, Jeff and Jennie have preserved their independence and dignity. As the car sinks, one wheel sticks up out of the mud in a shallow place—fate's ironical monument to the lives and courageous deaths of Jeff and Jennie Patton. Free of histrionics and sentimentality, this well-handled story is, as Robert Bone contends, truly "compelling."

"Talk to the Music"

In the years just prior to World War I, young Norman Taylor leaves his home in Rapides Parish (where Bontemps himself was born) and travels two hundred miles to attend college in New Orleans. However, instead of enrolling in college as his parents expect, Norman informally enrolls in a real-life course in blues music, which he studies in the notorious Storyville area, where the inimitable blues singer Mayme Dupree performs in a night club. Apparently Norman has not been able to "study" the blues in Rapides Parish, where it may have been considered "the Devil's music" by good church-going folk. Norman pretends to be a waiter at the club and is finally able to hear the fabulous Mayme sing her own style of blues. Her singing moves the audience to look into their hearts and individual and collective pasts and thus both figuratively and literally "talk to" (communicate with) the music as it is performed. Later Norman confesses to Mayme that her blues touched him like Adam and Eve's wail over their innocence lost in Eden, but Mayme comments that he is "crazy." Nevertheless, "Talk to the Music" richly evokes scenes and senses in New Orleans and convincingly dramatizes the young man's struggles to hear Mayme's blues and to learn from her lips about her loves and losses—which are shared not only by African Americans but also by all humanity.

Other Literary Forms

Bontemps was a prolific author and editor. He wrote or cowrote many children's books, biographies, and histories. He edited or coedited more than a dozen works, including African American poetry anthologies, histories, slave narratives, and a folklore collection. He and Countee Cullen adapted Bontemps's novel *God Sends Sunday* for the New Yorkstage in 1946 as *St. Louis Woman*. Bontemps's forty-two-year correspondence with writer Langston Hughes was published in 1980.

Bibliography

Bone, Robert. "Arna Bontemps." *Down Home: A History of Afro-American Short Fiction from Its Beginnings to the End of the Harlem Renaissance.* New York: G. P. Putnam's Sons, 1975. Brief but incisive analyses of four of the stories from *The Old South:* "Boy Blue," "A Summer Tragedy," "The Cure," and "Three Pennies for Luck." Notes the use of nature symbolism and folklore in Bontemps's short stories.

_____. *The Negro Novel in America.* New Haven, Conn.: Yale University Press, 1965. Contains brief but perceptive comments on Bontemps's two historical novels.

Canaday, Nicholas. "Arna Bontemps: The Louisiana Heritage." *Callaloo* 4 (February-October, 1981): 163-169. Traces the significant influence of Bontemps's Louisiana great-uncle, Buddy (Joe Ward), on the author's novel *God Sends Sunday* and on "The Cure" in *The Old South.*

Davis, Mary Kemp. "Arna Bontemps' *Black Thunder:* The Creation of an Authoritative Text of 'Gabriel's Defeat.'" *Black American Literature Forum* 23, no. 1 (Spring, 1989): 17-36. Compares Bontemps's novel with three previously published versions of the Gabriel Prosser conspiracy.

Fleming, Robert E. *James Weldon Johnson and Arna Wendell Bontemps: A Reference Guide.* Boston: G. K. Hall, 1978. Contains a biography of Bontemps, as well as indexes and a bibliography.

Jones, Kirkland C. "Bontemps and the Old South." *African American Review* 27, no. 2 (1993): 179-185. Argues that the Old South is employed more greatly in Bontemps's fiction than in that of any other Harlem Renaissance writer. Brief but perceptive critiques of five of *The Old South* selections: "A Summer Tragedy," "The Cure," "Talk to the Music," "Boy Blue," and "Why I Returned."

_____. *Renaissance Man from Louisiana, A Biography of Arna Wendell Bontemps.* Westport, Conn.: Greenwood Press, 1992. The first full-scale biography of Bontemps. Treats the author's life and career in detail but only cursorily analyzes or evaluates the writings.

Reagan, Daniel. "Voices of Silence: The Representation of Orality in Arna Bontemps' *Black Thunder.*" *Studies in American Fiction* 19 (Spring, 1991): 71-83. Examines the use of African American vernacular traditions in *Black Thunder* and concludes that the novel's significant statements of black cultural identity occur in the oral discourse that Bontemps portrays through figurative language.

Stone, Albert. "The Thirties and the Sixties: Arna Bontemps's *Black Thunder.*" In *The Return of Nat Turner: History, Literature, and Cultural Politics in Sixties America.* Athens: University of Georgia Press, 1992. Examines Bontemps's successful synthesis of history and his own imagination in *Black Thunder.*

Weil, Dorothy. "Folklore Motifs in Arna Bontemps's *Black Thunder.*" *Southern Folklore Quarterly* 25, no. 1 (March, 1971): 1-14. Analyzes Bontemps's authentic use of black folklore concerning death, spirits, portents, magic, and conjuring.

Yardley, Jonathan. Review of *The Old South. The New York Times Book Review,* December, 1973, 11. Comments on the impression of informality and chattiness the reader gets on a first reading of Bontemps's stories, but a second reading reveals the author's concern about race relations while avoiding bitterness.

— *Philip A. Tapley*

Edward Kamau Brathwaite

Poet

Born: Bridgetown, Barbados, West Indies; May 11, 1930

SHORT FICTION: *Dream Stories*, 1994.

DRAMA: *Four Plays for Primary Schools*, pr. 1961; *Odale's Choice*, pr. 1962, pb. 1967.

POETRY: *Rights of Passage*, 1967; *Masks*, 1968; *Islands*, 1969; *The Arrivants: A New World Trilogy*, 1973 (includes *Rights of Passage, Masks,* and *Islands*); *Other Exiles*, 1975; *Days and Nights*, 1975; *Black + Blues*, 1977; *Mother Poem*, 1977; *Word Making Man: A Poem for Nicolas Guillen*, 1979; *Sun Poem*, 1982; *Third World Poems*, 1983; *Jah Music*, 1986; *X/Self*, 1987; *Sapph oSakyi's Meditations*, 1989; *Shar*, 1990; *Middle Passages*, 1992; *Words Need Love Too*, 2000; *Ancestors: A Reinvention of "Mother Poem," "Sun Poem," and "X/Self,"* 2001.

NONFICTION: *Folk Culture of the Slaves in Jamaica*, 1970; *The Development of Creole Society in Jamaica, 1770-1820*, 1971; *Contradictory Omens: Cultural Diversity and Integration in the Caribbean*, 1974; *Caribbean Man in Space and Time*, 1974; *Our Ancestral Heritage: A Bibliography of the Roots of Culture in the English Speaking Caribbean*, 1976; *Wars of Respect: Nanny, Sam Sharpe, and the Struggle for People's Liberation*, 1977; *Barbados Poetry, 1661-1979: A Checklist*, 1979; *Jamaica Poetry: A Checklist*, 1979; *The Colonial Encounter: Language*, 1984; *History of the Voice: The Development of Nation Language in Anglophone Caribbean Poetry*, 1984; *Roots: Essays in Caribbean Literature*, 1986; *The Zea Mexican Diary*, 1993.

EDITED TEXTS: *New Poets from Jamaica: An Anthology*, 1979.

Achievements

Edward Kamau Brathwaite is one of the most popular and critically acclaimed writers to emerge in the West Indies during the remarkable period in theregion's history and literature following World War II. He epitomizes the intensified ethnic and national awareness of his generation of writers—which includes Derek Walcott, Wilson Harris, Michael Anthony, Martin Carter, Samuel Selvon, John Hearne, and Austin Clarke, to name several of the more prominent—whose writing seeks to correct the destructive effects of colonialism on West Indian sensibility.

For his efforts, Brathwaite has earned a number of honors. He won an Arts Council of Great Britain bursary in 1967, a Camden Arts Festival prize in 1967, a Cholmondeley Award in 1970 for *Islands*, a Guggenheim Fellowship in 1972, a City of Nairobi Fellowship in 1972, the Bussa Award in 1973, a Casa de las Americas Prize for Poetry in 1976, a Fulbright Fellowship in 1982, and an Institute of Jamaica Musgrave Medal in 1983. He is also a winner of the prestigious Neustadt International Prize for Literature.

Biography

Lawson Edward Brathwaite was born in Bridgetown, Barbados, on May 11, 1930, the son of Hilton Brathwaite and Beryl Gill Brathwaite. He enrolled at Harrison College in Barbados, but won the Barbados Scholarship in

1949, enabling him the next year to read history at Pembroke College, University of Cambridge, England. He received an honors degree in 1953 and the Certificate of Education in 1955.

His earliest published poems appeared in the literary journal *Bim,* beginning in 1950. The poems of that decade, some of which are collected in *Other Exiles* and, in revised form, in *The Arrivants,* portray an estranged world fallen from grace, a world that can be redeemed through poetic vision—a creative faith that sustains the more complex fashionings of his later work. Brathwaite shared with other West Indian writers of his generation a strong sense of the impossibility of a creative life in the Caribbean, and the equal impossibility of maintaining identity in exile in England or North America. That crisis of the present he understood as a product of his island's cultural heritage fragmented among its several sources: European, African, Amerindian, and Asian.

His reading of history at Cambridge heightened both his sense of the European culture which had been the dominant official culture of the West Indies and his need to understand the African culture that had come with the slaves on the Middle Passage. His search led him to Africa, where from 1955 to 1962 he served as an education officer in Kwame Nkrumah's Ghana. His career in Ghana (and in Togoland in 1956-1957 as United Nations Plebiscite Officer) provided the historical and local images that became *Masks,* the pivotal book of *The Arrivants.* In Ghana, he established a children's theater and wrote several plays for children (*Four Plays for Primary Schools,* 1961, and *Odale's Choice,* 1962). He married Doris Welcome in 1960, and has a son, Michael Kwesi Brathwaite.

Brathwaite returned to the West Indies after an exile of twelve years to assume a post as Resident Tutor at the University of the West Indies in St. Lucia (1962-1963) and to produce programs for the Windward Islands Broadcasting Service. His return to the Caribbean supplied the focus that his poetry had lacked:

> I had, at that moment of return, completed the triangular trade of my historical origins. West Africa had given me a sense of place, of belonging; and that place . . . was the West Indies. My absence and travels, at the same time, had given me a sense of movement and restlessness—rootlessness. It was, I recognized, particularly the condition of the Negro of the West Indies and the New World.

The exploration of that sense of belonging and rootlessness in personal and historic terms is the motive for Brathwaite's subsequent work in poetry, history, and literary criticism. He began in 1963 as lecturer in history at the University of the West Indies at Kingston, Jamaica; he became a professor of social and cultural history there. He earned his Ph.D. at the University of Sussex in England (1965-1968). His dissertation became *The Development of Creole Society in Jamaica, 1770-1820,* a study of the assimilation of cultures by various groups within the colonial hierarchy.

His poetry continues to explore the cultural heritage of the West Indies in historical and personal terms. During the 1980s, Brathwaite continued to produce important literary criticism and poetry collections. The 1986 death of Brathwaite's wife, Doris, marked a critical juncture in his career. The shock came in the midst of a series of publications that year: a retrospective collection of essays (*Roots: Essays in Caribbean Literature*); a retrospective collection of poems (*Jah Music*); and Doris's own labor of love, the bibliography *EKB: His Published Prose and Poetry, 1948-1986.* Another blow came in 1988, when hurricane Gilbert virtually destroyed Brathwaite's house and buried most of his library in mud, entombing an unequaled collection of Caribbean writing as well as

Brathwaite's own papers. Even more harrowing was a 1990 break-in and physical attack against Brathwaite in his Marley Manor apartment in Kingston, Jamaica. These events helped in his decision to leave Jamaica in 1991, when he began his tenure at New York University, teaching comparative literature.

Analysis: Poetry

Brathwaite's aim, as he has described it, is to "transcend and heal" the fragmented culture of his dispossessed people through his poetry, re-examining the whole history of the black diaspora in a search for cultural wholeness in contemporary Caribbean life. Brathwaite offers his poetry as a corrective to the twin problems of the West Indian: dispossession of history and of language. The West Indian writer labors in a culture whose history has been distorted by prejudice and malice, the modern version of which is the commonplace notion, after James Anthony Froude and V. S. Naipaul, that nothing was created or achieved in the West Indies. The Afro-Caribbean's history is the record of being uprooted, displaced, enslaved, dominated, and finally abandoned. Brathwaite's reclamation of racial pride centers on rectifying the significance of the Middle Passage not as the destroyer but as the transmitter of culture.

The second problem that the writer confronts, that of language, is an aspect of cultural dispossession. The diversity of Creole languages, hybrids of many African and European tongues, reinforces the insularity of the individual and devalues the expressively rich languages that the people use in their nonofficial, personal, most intimate lives. Brathwaite's poems in Bajun dialect extend the folk traditions of Claude McKay and Louise Bennett and ground his work in the lives of the people for and about whom he writes.

The problem of language, however, is not a matter of choosing the Creole over the metropolitan language. It is a deeply political and spiritual problem, since, as Brathwaite writes, it was with language that the slave was "most successfully imprisoned by the master, and through his (mis)use of it that he most effectively rebelled." With nearly all other means of attaining personal liberty denied, the slave's last, irrevocable instrument of resistance and rebellion was language. For Brathwaite, a West Indian writer, Caliban in William Shakespeare's *The Tempest* (1611), written at the beginning of England's experiment in empire, is the archetype of the slave who turns his borrowed language against his master. To turn his instrument of rebellion into one of creation is Brathwaite's task.

"Caliban"

Accordingly, in his poem "Caliban" (*The Arrivants*), Brathwaite's persona begins by celebrating the morning of December 2, 1956, the start of the Cuban Revolution, which remains a symbol of self-determination in the region. In the second section of the poem, Brathwaite adapts Shakespeare's "'Ban Ban Caliban,'/ Has a new master" curse-chant to the hold of a slave ship, articulating a spirit of resistance which turns in the final section to an assertion of endurance. At the end of the poem, the slaves' nightly limbo on deck becomes the religious ceremony—the seed of African culture carried to the New World—of the assembled tribes, who are able to raise their ancestral gods and be for the moment a whole people.

Nation Language

What he achieves in "Caliban" Brathwaite achieves in his poetry at large: He uses his languages, both Creole and metropolitan English, to define the selfhood of the group in positive terms, contrary to the negations of the colonizers. "Within the folk tradition," Brathwaite writes, "language was (and is) a creative act in itself; the word was held to contain a secret power." His term "nation language" (defined in *History of the Voice*) for the language of the people brought to the Caribbean, as opposed to the official language of the colonial power, has profoundly influenced the theory and criticism of African American literature. Brathwaite continues in *Mother Poem* and *Sun Poem* to explore the resources of both his native Bajun dialect and contemporary standard English. In his poetry, the power of the word is to conjure, to evoke, to punish, to celebrate, to mourn, to love. He uses language boldly as one who seeks its deepest power: to reveal and heal the wounds of history.

Edward Kamau Brathwaite's early poetry in *Bim*, collected later in *Other Exiles*, with its themes of anxiety and alienation, changed under the search for racial and cultural identity while in exile. Brathwaite became surer of his European heritage while he was a student in England and recovered the remnants of his African heritage while working in Ghana. Those two great cultures, in conflict in the New World for the last four centuries, are the forces that shape Brathwaite's personal and racial history and the poetics through which he renders his quest for wholeness.

He is equally indebted to the Euro-American literary tradition through the work of T. S. Eliot and to the Afro-West Indian tradition through the work of Aime Cesaire. Brathwaite draws upon Eliot's musical form in *Four Quartets* (1943) for his own use of musical forms developed in stages of the black diaspora— work song, shanto, shango hymn, spiritual, blues, jazz, calypso, ska, and reggae—for his poetic rendering of historic and lyric moments. He also draws his aesthetic for rendering modern industrial and mercantile society in the United States and the Caribbean from Eliot's *The Waste Land* (1922). From Cesaire's *Cahier d'un retour au pays natal* (1968; *Notebook of the Return to My Native Land*, 1995), Brathwaite derives the epic and dialectical structure of his trilogy as well as the surrealistic heightening of language that propels the movement from the reality of the Caribbean as wasteland to the vision of the Caribbean as promised land.

The Arrivants

That movement can be discerned in the three books of *The Arrivants* through the poet's reconstruction of racial history and his tracing of his personal history. *Rights of Passage*, the first book of the trilogy, contains the restless isolation of his early life in Barbados that sends him into exile in England and Africa, as well as a recollection of the first phase of the black diaspora, the advent of the slave trade and the Middle Passage. The original dispersal of tribes from Ethiopia to West Africa, as well as his own search for his African origins, is the subject of *Masks*, In *Islands*, racial and personal history merge in the exile's return to the West Indies. The fruits of that return will become manifest in his planned second trilogy.

Readers of *The Arrivants* who focus on its historical dimension figure Brathwaite as the epic poet of the black diaspora, while those who focus on the autobiography make him the hero of the poem. Taking both approaches as valid, with the binocular vision that the poem requires, one can see that the central figure of the rootless, alienated West Indian in exile and in search of home is the only possible kind of hero for a West Indian epic. That questing poet's voice is, however, often transformed into the voice of a precolonial African being fired upon by a white slaver; the Rastafarian Brother Man; Uncle Tom; a *houngan* invoking Legba; or some other historic or mythic figure. Brathwaite's use of personas, or masks, derives equally from the traditions of Greek drama (dramatic monologue) and African religious practice (chant or invocation). One communal soul speaks in a multiplicity of guises, and the poet thereby recreates not only his own quest as victim and hero but also the larger racial consciousness in which he participates. The poet's many masks enable him to reconstruct his own life and the brutal history that created "new soil, new souls, new ancestors" out of the ashes of the past.

Combining racial history and personal quest in *The Arrivants*, Brathwaite has fashioned a contemporary West Indian myth. It is not the myth of history petrified into "progress" but that of a people's endurance through cycles of brutal oppression. Across centuries, across the ocean, and across the three books of this poem, images, characters, and events overlie one another to defy the myth of progress, leading in the poem only to heaven swaying in the reinforced girders of New York, and to the God of capitalism floating in a soundless, airtight glass bubble of an office, a prisoner of his own creation. For the "gods" who tread the earth below, myth is cyclical, and it attaches them to the earth through the "souls" of their feet in repetitions of exodus and arrival.

The trilogy begins with one tribe's ancient crossing of the Sahara desert, their wagons and camels left where they had fallen, and their arrival at a place where "cool/ dew falls/ in the evening." They build villages, but the cattle towns breed flies and flies breed plague, and another journey begins, for across the "dried out gut" of the riverbed, a mirage shimmers where:

> trees are cool, there
> leaves are green,
> there burns the dream
> of a fountain, garden
> of odours, soft
> alleyways.

This is the repeated pattern of their history: exodus across desert, savanna, ocean; in caravan, ship, or jet plane; visitations of plague, pestilence, famine, slavery, poverty, ignorance, volcanoes, flood. The promised land is always elsewhere, across the parched riverbed ("Prelude") or in the bountiful fields of England, not in Barbados ("The Cracked Mother").

The connections between history and biography and the difficult process of destroying the colonial heritage in favor of a more creative mode of life are evident in the six poems that constitute the "Limbo" section of *Islands*. In "The Cracked Mother," the first poem of "Limbo," the dissociation of the West Indian's sensibility—regarding attitudes toward self, race, and country— threatens to paralyze the poet's dialectical movement toward a sustaining vision. The poet's rejection of his native land in favor of England is an acceptance of the colonial's position of inferiority. That attitude is instilled in young West Indians, such historians as Walter Rodney, Frantz Fanon, and Brathwaite have argued, by the system of colonial education that taught an alien and alienating value system. The debilitating effects of such an education are the subject of "The Cracked Mother." The three nuns who take the child from his mother to school appear as "black specks . . . / Santa Marias with black silk sails." The metaphor equates the nuns' coming with that of Columbus and anticipates the violence that followed, especially in the image of the nuns' habits as the sails of death ships. With her child gone, the mother speaks in the second part of the poem as a broken ("cracked") woman reduced to muttering children's word-games that serve as the vehicle for her pain:

> See?
> She saw the sea . . .
> I saw you take my children . . .
> You gave your beads, you took

my children . . . Christ on the Cross your crucl laws teach only to divide us and we are lost.

History provides the useful equation of nuns' habits with sails and the nuns' rosary with the beads that Columbus gave to the inhabitants of his "discovered" lands, but it is Brathwaite's own biography that turns metaphor into revelation in the last two parts of the poem, showing how ruinous the colonial mentality is, even to the point of rejecting the earth under one's feet (another "cracked mother") because it is not England.

Brathwaite's corrective begins in "Shepherd," the second poem of the "Limbo" section. Having recalled the damage of his early education and having felt again some of the old abhorrence of the colonial for himself, the poet returns to the African drumbeats of *Masks* to chant a service of possession or reconnection with the gods of his ancestors. The poet then addresses his peers in proverbs, as would an elder to his tribe:

> But you do not understand.
> For there is an absence of truth like a
> good tooth drawn from the tight skull
> like the wave's tune gone from the ship's
> hull there is sand
> but no desert where water can learn of its
> loveliness.

The people have gifts for the gods but do not give them, yet the gods are everywhere and waiting. Moving in *Islands* toward the regeneration promised in *Masks*, Brathwaite continues with "Caliban" to explore the potential for liberty inherent in the Cuban Revolution, then moves at the moment of triumph back into the slave ship and the limbo that contained the seeds of African religion and identity.

The "Limbo" section ends with the beautiful poem "Islands," which proposes the alternatives that are always present in every moment of Caribbean history: "So looking through a map/ of the islands, you see/ . . . the sun's/ slums: if you hate/ us. Jewels,/ if there is delight/ in your eyes." The same dichotomy of vision has surrounded every event and personage in the poem, all infolded upon the crucial event of the Middle Passage: Did it destroy a people or create one? Brathwaite's account of the voyage in "New World A-Comin" promises "new worlds, new waters, new/ harbours" on one hand, and on the other, "the flesh and the flies, the whips and the fixed/ fear of pain in this chained and welcoming port."

The gods have crossed with the slaves to new soil, and the poet has returned to the origin of his race to discover his communal selfhood in African rite, which requires participation by all to welcome the god who will visit one of them. *The Arrivants* is a long historical and autobiographical poem, and it is also a rite of passage for the poet-priest who invites the god to ride him. Brathwaite's incantatory poems in *Masks* are his learning of the priest's ways, which restores his spirit in *Islands*. The refrain "*Attibon Legba/ Ouvri bayi pou'moi*" ("Negus") is the Voodoo *houngon*'s prayer to the gatekeeper god Legba to open the door to the other gods. The prayer is answered in the final poem "*Jou'vert*" ("I Open"), where Legba promises:

> hearts
> no longer bound to
> black and bitter ashes
> in the ground now
> waking making
> making with their
> rhythms something torn
> and new.

Mother Poem

In *Mother Poem*, the first book of Brathwaite's planned second trilogy, the central figure is not the restless poet but the mother he has left and returned to, the source of his life. The types of motherhood established in "The Cracked Mother" (*The Arrivants*) are reiterated here as the poet's human mother and his motherland, Barbados. Both "mothers" are established in the first poem, "Alpha," the origin. Barbados is the mother-island of porous limestone (thus absorbing all influence of weather and history), cut by ancient watercourses that have dried up in sterility. Her dead streams can be revived only by the transfigured human mother who "rains upon the island with her loud voices/ with her grey hairs/ with her green love." The transfiguration that occurs in the last lines of the book must wait, however, for the woman to endure the dream-killing, soul-killing life of the island that is dominated by "the man who possesses us all," the merchant, the modern agent of bondage ("nametracks").

The mother is his victim, no matter whether she "sits and calls on jesus name" waiting for her husband to come home from work with lungs covered with jute from the sugar sacks, or whether she goes out after his death to sell calico cloth, half-soled shoes, and biscuits, or persuades her daughter to sell herself to the man who is waiting: "It int hard, leh me tell you/ jess sad/ so come darlin chile/ leh me tell he you ready you steady you go" ("Woo/ Dove").

She gets no help from her men, who are crippled, destroyed, frightened, or sick from their lives of bondage to the merchant. One man goes to Montreal to work for nine years and sends back nothing ("Woo/ Dove") and another goes to work for life in the local plantation, brings nothing home, and loses three fingers in the cane-grinder ("Milkweed"). Nor does she receive comfort from her children, "wearing dark glasses/ hearing aids/ leaning on wine" ("Tear or pear shape"), who were educated by Chalkstick the teacher, a satirical composite of the colonial educator whose job is to see that his pupils "don't clap their hands, shake their heads, tap their feet" or "push bones through each others' congolese nostrils" ("Lix"). Nor does her help come from her sisters ("Dais" and "Nights"), or from her Christianity ("Sam Lord").

Rather, the restoration of her powers as life-giver begins in the guttural, elemental, incantatory uttering of "Nametracks," where, as a slave-mother beaten by her owner, she reminds herself and her huddled children in dark monosyllables like the word-game of "The Cracked Mother" that they will endure while "e di go/ e go di/ e go dead," that despite all his power, he "nevver maim what me." Her eyes rise from the plot of land she has bought with her meager earnings, the land that has sustained her and her children, to the whole island and a vision of revolutionary solidarity with her people: "de merchants got de money/ but de people got de men" ("Peace Fire"). With full realization that her child will be born to the life of "broken islands/ broken homes" ("Mid/Life"), in "Driftwood," the human mother still chooses to suffer the "pour of her flesh into their mould of bone." The poem ends with the mother recreated in clay by the potter who can work again, in stone by the sculptor whose skill has returned, and in her words gathered by the poet as rain gathering in the dry pools flows once more past the ruins of the slave and colonial world, refreshing and renewing the ancient life of the island.

Sun Poem

Brathwaite's second volume on Bajun life moves from *Mother Poem*'s focus on the female characters (and character) of the island to the male principle of the tropical sun and of the various sons of Barbados. The pun of sun/son is derived from a number of historical and mythological associations, including that of Christianity (Brathwaite renames himself Adam as the boy-hero of the poem, and spells the pronoun "his" as "ihs" or Iesu Hominum Salvator) and various African traditions. The sun, for instance, contains "megalleons of light," the invented word associating it with the Egyptian god Ra's sun-ship, the galleons of European explorers, and the enormous nuclear energy that eclipses or perhaps anticipates the holocaust that Western man has in his power. The complexity of the sun/son as controlling metaphor, as it evokes various ethnic and historical images, extends through time and geographic space the significance of the narrative, even as it complements and completes the female principle of *Mother Poem.*

The mythologies evoked in the poem contribute to the meaning of the life of the son Adam, as he begins to understand the West Indian male's sunlike course of ascent, dominance, and descent, played out through the rituals of boyhood games and identity-seeking, adolescence, adult sexual experience, marriage and paternity, and finally death. In an early encounter, Adam wrestles the bully Batto underwater in a life-or-death rite of passage that initiates him into the comradeship of his peers, but which, Brathwaite suggests, fails (as the other games that "had little meaning" fail) to prepare him for the struggles of adult manhood ("Son"). The types of fathers portrayed ("Clips") fall into roles available from Christian, bourgeois, and Rastafarian cultures that are equally dead-ended. These fathers are unable to pass on to their sons any mode of fulfilling identity or action, even as in his soliloquy the father laments his own diminishment, his being displaced as the head of his family by his own son.

The central incidents of Adam's life introduce him to the cares and costs of adulthood. On his Sunday school trip to the Atlantic coast, he enters the adult world, in part by hearing the story of Bussa's slave rebellion, a story of the painful price one pays for asserting his personhood ("Noom"). He conducts his courtship of

Esse ("Return of the Sun") with a blithe but growing awareness of the consequences of one's sexual life in determining social and political roles ("Fleches"). The death of Adam's grandfather ("Indigone"), the final event in the poem, reveals to him the cyclical nature of manhood in which he begins to locate himself: "and i looked up to see my father's eye: wheeling/ towards his father/ now as i his sun moved upward to his eye." The cultural determinants of dispossession and lack of identity that so condition the natural progress and decline of masculine life are transcended in the poem's ultimate vision of a world capable of beginning anew. The final section ("Son") returns to the cosmic, creative domain of the poem's invocation ("Red Rising"), but with a clarified focus on creation and growth as the first principles of the natural and hence human world. The image of emerging coral returns the reader to the genesis of the island at the beginning of *Mother Poem* ("Rock Seed"), completing the cycle of the poems with the "coming up coming up coming up" of his "thrilldren" to people a world renewed.

Middle Passages

A collection of fourteen poems, *Middle Passages* has a running theme regarding the effects of slavery on Caribbean culture and on the world. The title also seems to evoke the grief caused by his wife's death in 1986, an event he personally referred to as "middle passages" in his book with excerpts from his personal diary, *The Zea Mexican Diary.* Thus the title also suggests a spiritual passage that death entails for both the dead and the living. Journeys, especially those to African roots, is a recurring theme in this volume.

"Columbe" suggests the beauty that Christopher Columbus and his entourage must have discovered upon their arrival in the Caribbean: "Yello pouis/ blazed like pollen and thin waterfalls suspended in the green." Told from the perspective of an island inhabitant watching the arrival, it also asks whether Columbus understood the violence to which his discovery would lead: "But did his vision/ fashion as he watched the shore/ the slaughter that his soldiers/ furthered here?"

Music and musicians are a strong presence in the collection as well. "Duke Playing the Piano at 70" pictures Duke Ellington's wrinkled hands as alligator skins gliding along a keyboard. Brathwaite uses a number of devices to evoke a sense of music to the printed page. Several poems call on the rhythm and cadence of different instruments to heighten the theme at hand: "Flutes" lyrically describes the sounds of bamboo flutes, while "Soweto," written about the Soweto massacre, draws on the rhythm of drums.

The history of violence against Africa plays a dominant role here, as it does in so many of Brathwaite's literary works. "The Visibility Trigger" surveys European history of using guns to kill and subdue Third World peoples. Another, "Stone," is dedicated to Mickey Smith, a poet and political activist who was "stoned to death on Stony Hill, Kingston" in 1983.

Other Literary Forms

Edward Kamau Brathwaite has published scores of books, articles, and reviews as a historian and literary critic. Among his historical studies are *The Development of Creole Society in Jamaica, 1770-1820*, which was his dissertation in college in the 1960's, one chapter of which was expanded and published as *Folk Culture of the Slaves in Jamaica*; *Contradictory Omens*; *Caribbean Man in Space and Time*; and *History of the Voice*. His historical studies have delineated the historical pressures that have shaped present-day Caribbean life. He is particularly interested in the transmission of African culture to the New

World, the "'little' tradition of the ex-slave," and its promise to serve as a "basis for creative reconstruction" in postemancipation, postcolonial Creole society. His literary criticism has sought out the presence of African traditions in Caribbean literature and has helped to develop a vigorous, indigenous school of West Indian criticism. Brathwaite's work as poet, critic, and historian has made available to a wide audience the rich cultural heritage of Caribbean people.

Bibliography

Brown, Stuart. *The Art of Kamau Brathwaite.* Bridgend, Mid Glamorgan, Wales: Seren, 1995. A book of critical essays that includes some of the most informed and cogent ways to approach Brathwaite's varied body of work. It also has the distinction of looking at most of that corpus, allowing the reader to discover Brathwaite the critic, the historian, the poet, and the essayist.

Gowda, H. H. Anniah. "Creation in the Poetic Development of Kamau Brathwaite." *WorldLiterature Today* 68, no. 4 (Autumn, 1 994): 69 1. The poetry of Kamau Brathwaite is examined. He insists on the sense and value of the inheritance of the West Indies and is keen on discovering the West Indian Voice in creative arts.

McWatt, Mark A. "Edward Kamau Brathwaite." In *Fifty Caribbean Writers*, edited by Daryl Cumber Dance. New York: Greenwood Press, 1 986. While this study traces the shift of the West Indies from "wasteland" to "promised land" in Brathwaite's poetry, it more importantly recounts the critical debate over the relative merits of the poetry of Brathwaite and Derek A. Walcott in relation to West Indian society.

Otto, Melanie. "The Other Side of the Mirror: Utopian and Heterotopian Space in Kamau Brathwaite's *DreamStories*." *Utopian Studies* 16, no. 1 (2005): 27-45. Explains the concepts of utopian and heterotopian space and discusses their application in Brathwaite's work. Gives a good overview of the book, placing it in an autobiographical context and analyzing some of Brathwaite's most important literary influences.

Povey, John. "The Search for Identity in Edward Brathwaite's *The Arrivants*." *World Literature Written in English* 27 (1987): 275-289. Povey details both the historical causes of the lack of a coherent regional identity and Brathwaite's exploration of European and African elements that have shaped the region. Povey studies autobiographical aspects of *The Arrivants,*in particular the reversal of the route of the slave trade that Brathwaite's own career has made.

Rohlehr, Gordon. "'Megalleons of Light': Edward Brathwaite's *Sun Poem*." *Jamaica Journal* 16 (1983): 81-87. Rohlehr draws together *Mother Poem* and *Sun Poem* in reading their parallel movements, passages, and themes. Those poems revive the redemptive view of history taken in *The Arrivants*. Rohlehr expertly delineates the patterns of imagery and their thematic relations, particularly in the poem's depiction of the West Indian's distorted self-image and cultural dispossession.

Pathfinder: Black Awakening in "The Arrivants" of Edward Kamau Brathwaite. Tunapuna, Trinidad: Gordon Rohlehr, 1981. This lengthy work is an indispensable companion to *The Arrivants*. Rohlehr's commentary is compendious and meticulous. It clarifies what the poem's language and syntax leave obscure to a non-West-Indian reader and identifies the poem's references unfailingly, including the many musical references that are essential to Brathwaite's technique. Lack of an index, however, hampers efforts to locate specific topics.

Ten Kortenaar, Neil. "Where the Atlantic Meets the Caribbean: Kamau Brathwaite's *The Arrivants* and T. S. Eliot's *The Waste Land*." *Research in African Literatures* 27, no. 4 (Winter, 1996): 15-27. Brathwaite

has acknowledged Eliot as a poetic precursor. Parallels between Brathwaite's trilogy *The Arrivants* and Eliot's *The Waste Land* are examined.

Thomas, Sue. "Sexual Politics in Edward Brathwaite's *Mother Poem* and *Sun Poem*."*Kunapipi* 9 (1987):33-43.Inherseminal feminist reading, Thomas analyzes the sexual politics inherent in the poet's portrayal of, and commentary on, racial and sexual stereotypes. She finds Brathwaite's ideology to be patriarchal, with the liberated husband supplanting the colonizer in a continuing subordination of the West Indian woman.

Torres-Saillant, Silvio. *Caribbean Poetic: Towards an Aesthetic of West Indian Literature.* New York: Cambridge University Press, 1997.Theauthormakestheassertionsthatthereshouldbea new system of canon formation and that Caribbean discourse in European languages is a discrete entity. Offers scholarly, in-depth studies of Edward Kamau Brathwaite, Rene Depestre, and Pedro Mir.

Williams, Emily Allen."Whose Words Are These? Lost Heritage and Search for Self in Edward Brathwaite's Poetry." *CLA Journal* 40 (September, 1996): 104-108. Williams examines the search for identity in Braithwaite's work. She asserts that Brathwaite's poetry moves readers through a world of dichotomized existence brought on by the ravages of European colonization and acts as a song for the disenfranchised.

World Literature Today 68, no.4(Autumn, 1994).An entire issue is devoted to an examination of Brathwaite's contribution to the literary world and to West Indies studies.

— *Robert Bensen; Sarah Hilbert*

Gwendolyn Brooks

Poet

Born: Topeka, Kansas; June 7, 1917
Died: Chicago, Illinois; December 3, 2000

LONG FICTION: *Maud Martha*, 1953.

POETRY: *A Street in Bronzeville*, 1945; *Annie Allen*, 1949; *The Bean Eaters*, 1960; *Selected Poems*, 1963; *We Real Cool*, 1966; *The Wall*, 1967; *In the Mecca*, 1968; *Riot*, 1969; *Family Pictures*, 1970; *Aloneness*, 1971; *Black Steel: Joe Frazier and Muhammad Ali*, 1971; *Aurora*, 1972; *Beckonings*, 1975; *Primer for Blacks*, 1980; *To Disembark*, 1981; *Black Love*, 1982; *The Near-Johannesburg Boy*, 1986; *Blacks*, 1987; *Gottschalk and the Grand Tarantelle*, 1988; *Winnie*, 1988; *Children Coming Home*, 1991; *In Montgomery*, 2003; *The Essential Gwendolyn Brooks*, 2005 (edited by Elizabeth Alexander).

NONFICTION: *The World of Gwendolyn Brooks*, 1971; *Report from Part One*, 1972; *Young Poet's Primer*, 1980.

CHILDREN'S/YOUNG ADULT LITERA-TURE: *Bronzeville Boys and Girls*, 1956; *The Tiger Who Wore White Gloves*, 1974; *Very Young Poets*, 1983.

EDITED TEXTS: *Jump Bad: A New Chicago Anthology*, 1971.

Achievements

Working comfortably in relation to diverse poetic traditions, Gwendolyn Brooks was widely honored. Early in her career, she received numerous mainstream literary awards, including the Pulitzer Prize in poetry in 1950 for *Annie Allen*. She became poet laureate of Illinois in 1969 and received more than fifty honorary doctorates. Equally significant, numerous writers associated with the Black Arts movement recognized her as an inspirational figure linking the older and younger generations of black poets. Brooks's ability to appeal both to poetic establishments and to a sizable popular audience, especially among young blacks, stemmed from her pluralistic voice, which echoes a wide range of precursors while remaining unmistakably black. Her exploration of America in general and Chicago in particular links her with Walt Whitman and Carl Sandburg. Her exploration of the interior landscape of humanity in general and women in particular places her in the tradition of Emily Dickinson and Edna St. Vincent Millay. At once the technical heir of Langston Hughes in her use of the rhythms of black street life and of Robert Frost in her exploration of traditional forms such as the sonnet, Brooks nevertheless maintained her integrity of vision and voice.

This integrity assumes special significance in the context of African American writing of the 1950s and 1960s. A period of "universalism" in black literature, the 1950s brought prominence to such poets as Brooks, LeRoi Jones (Amiri Baraka), and Robert Hayden. During this period of intellectual and aesthetic integration, Brooks never abandoned her social and racial heritage to strive for the transcendent (and deracinated) universalism associated by some

A bust of Gwendolyn Brooks in a park in Chicago, Illinois (photo by Raymond Boyd, courtesy of Getty Images)

African American critics with T. S. Eliot. Responding to William Carlos Williams's call in *Paterson* (19461951) to "make a start out of particulars and make them general," Brooks demonstrated unambiguously that an African American writer need not be limited in relevance by concentrating on the black experience.

The 1960s, conversely, encouraged separatism and militancy in African American writing. Even while accepting the Black Arts movement's call for a poetry designed to speak directly to the political condition of the black community, Brooks continued to insist on precision of form and language. While Jones changed his name to Amiri Baraka and radically altered his poetic voice, Brooks accommodated her new insights to her previously established style. An exemplar of integrity and flexibility, she both challenged and learned from younger black poets such as Haki R. Madhubuti (Don L. Lee), Sonia Sanchez, Carolyn Rodgers, and Etheridge Knight. Like Hughes, she addressed the black community without condescension or pretense. Like Frost, she wrote technically stunning "universal" poetry combining clear surfaces and elusive depths.

Brooks was appointed to the Presidential Commission on the National Agenda for the Eighties and was the first black woman elected to the National Institute of Arts and Letters. She was named Consultant in Poetry to the Library of Congress for 1985-1986, received the Shelley Memorial Award in 1975 and the Frost Medal in 1989 (both awarded by the Poetry Society of America), and was awarded the Academy of American Poets Fellowship in 1999.

Biography

Gwendolyn Brooks' poetry bears the strong impress of Chicago, particularly of the predominantly black South Side where she lived most of her life. Although she was born in Topeka, Kansas, Brooks was taken to Chicago before she was a year old. In many ways she devoted her career to the physical, spiritual, and, more recently, political exploration of her native city.

Brooks' life and writings are frequently separated into two phases, with her experience at the 1967 Black Writers' Conference at Fisk University in Nashville serving as a symbolic transition. Prior to the conference, Brooks was known primarily as the first black Pulitzer Prize winner in poetry. Although not politically unaware, she held to a somewhat cautious attitude. The vitality she encountered at the conference crystallized her sense of the insufficiency of universalist attitudes and generated close personal and artistic friendships with younger black poets such as Madhubuti, Walter Bradford, and Knight. Severing her ties with the mainstream publishing firm Harper and Row, which had published her first five books, Brooks transferred her work and prestige to the black-owned and operated Broadside Press of Detroit, Third World Press of Chicago, and Black Position Press, also of Chicago. Her commitment to black publishing houses remained unwavering despite distribution problems that rendered her later work largely invisible to the American reading public.

Educated in the Chicago school system and at Wilson Junior College, Brooks learned her craft under Inez Cunningham Stark (Boulton), a white woman who taught poetry at the South Side Community Art Center in the late 1930s and 1940s. Brooks' mother, who had been a teacher in Topeka, had encouraged her literary interests from an early age. Her father, a janitor, provided her with ineffaceable images of the spiritual strength and dignity of "common" people. Brooks married Henry Blakely in 1939 and her family concerns continued to play a central role in shaping her career. The eleven-year hiatus between the publication of *Annie Allen* and *The Bean Eaters* resulted at least in part from her concentration on rearing her two children, born in 1940 and 1951. Her numerous poems on family relationships reflect both the rewards and the tensions of her own experiences. Her children grown, Brooks concentrated on teaching, supervising poetry workshops, and speaking publicly. These activities brought her into contact with a wide range of younger black poets, preparing her for her experience at Fisk. As poet laureate of Illinois, she encouraged the development of younger poets through personal contact and formal competitions.

The division between the two phases of Brooks' life should not be overstated. She evinced a strong interest in the Civil Rights movement during the 1950s and early 1960s; her concern with family continued in the 1980s. Above all, Brooks lived with and wrote of and for the Chicagoans whose failures and triumphs she saw as deeply personal, universally resonant, and specifically black. She died in Chicago on December 3, 2000, at the age of eighty-three.

Analysis: Poetry

The image of Gwendolyn Brooks as a readily accessible poet is at once accurate and deceptive. Capable of capturing the experiences and rhythms of black street life, she frequently presents translucent surfaces which give way suddenly to reveal ambiguous depths. Equally capable of manipulating traditional poetic forms such as the sonnet, rhyme royal, and heroic couplet, she employs them to mirror the uncertainties of characters or personas who embrace conventional attitudes to defend themselves against internal and external chaos. Whatever form she chooses, Brooks consistently focuses on the struggle of people to find and express love, usually associated with the family, in the midst of a hostile environment. In constructing their defenses and seeking love, these persons typically experience a disfiguring pain. Brooks devotes much of her energy to defining and responding to the elusive forces, variously psychological and social, which inflict this pain. Increasingly in her later poetry, Brooks traces the pain to political sources and expands her concept of the family to encompass all black people. Even while speaking of the social situation of blacks in a voice crafted primarily for blacks, however, Brooks maintains the complex awareness of the multiple perspectives relevant to any given experience. Her ultimate concern is to encourage every individual, black or white, to "Conduct your blooming in the noise and whip of the whirlwind" ("The Second Sermon on the Warpland").

A deep concern with the everyday circumstances of black people living within the whirlwind characterizes many of Brooks' most popular poems. From the early "Of De Witt Williams on His Way to Lincoln Cemetery" and "A Song in the Front Yard" through the later "The Life of Lincoln West" and "Sammy Chester Leaves 'Godspell' and Visits UPWARD BOUND on a Lake Forest Lawn, Bringing West Afrika," she focuses on characters whose experiences merge the idiosyncratic and the typical. She frequently draws on black musical forms to underscore the communal resonance of a character's outwardly undistinguished life. By tying the refrain of "Swing Low Sweet Chariot" to the repeated phrase "Plain black boy," Brooks transforms De Witt Williams into an Everyman figure. Brooks describes his personal search for love in the pool rooms and dance halls, but stresses the representative quality of his experience by starting and ending the poem with the musical allusion.

"We Real Cool"

"We Real Cool," perhaps Brooks' single best-known poem, subjects a similarly representative experience to an intricate technical and thematic scrutiny, at once loving and critical. The poem is only twenty-four words long, including eight repetitions of the word "we." It is suggestive that the subtitle of "We Real Cool" specifies the presence of only seven pool players at the "Golden Shovel." The eighth "we" suggests that poet and reader share, on some level, the desperation of the group-voice that Brooks transmits. The final sentence, "We/ die soon," restates the carpe diem motif in the vernacular of Chicago's South Side.

On one level, "We Real Cool" appears simply to catalog the experiences of a group of dropouts content to "sing sin" in all available forms.

A surprising ambiguity enters into the poem, however, revolving around the question of how to accent the word "we" which ends every line except the last one, providing the beat for the poem's jazz rhythm. Brooks said that she intended that the "we" *not* be accented. Read in this way, the poem takes on a slightly distant and ironic tone, emphasizing the artificiality of the group identity which involves the characters in activities offering early death as the only release from pain. Conversely, the poem can be read with a strong accent on each "we," affirming the group identity. Although the experience still ends with early death, the pool players metamorphose into defiant heroes determined to resist the alienating environment. Their confrontation with experience is felt, if not articulated, as existentially pure. Pool players, poet, and reader cannot be sure which stress is valid.

Brooks crafts the poem, however, to hint at an underlying coherence in the defiance. The intricate internal rhyme scheme echoes the sound of nearly every word. Not only do the first seven lines end with "we," but the penultimate words of each line in each stanza also rhyme (cool/school, late/straight, sin/ gin, June/ soon). In addition, the alliterated consonant of the last line of each stanza is repeated in the first line of the next stanza (Left/lurk, Strike/ sin, gin/June) and the first words of each line in the middle two stanzas are connected through consonance (Lurk/strike, Sing/thin). The one exception to this suggestive texture of sound is the word "Die" which introduces both a new vowel and a new consonant into the final line, breaking the rhythm and subjecting the performance to ironic revaluation. Ultimately, the power of the poem derives from the tension between the celebratory and the ironic perspectives on the lives of the plain black boys struggling for a sense of connection.

"The Mother"

A similar struggle informs many of Brooks's poems in more traditional forms, including "The Mother," a powerful exploration of the impact of an abortion on the woman who has chosen to have it. Brooks states that the mother "decides that *she*, rather than her world, will kill her children." Within the poem itself, however, the motivations remain unclear. Although the poem's position in Brooks' first book, *A Street in Bronzeville,* suggests that the persona is black, the poem neither supports nor denies a racial identification. Along with the standard English syntax and diction, this suggests that "The Mother," like poems such as "The Egg Boiler," "Callie Ford," and "A Light and Diplomatic Bird," was designed to speak directly of an emotional, rather than a social, experience, and to be as accessible to whites as to blacks. Re-creating the anguished perspective of a persona unsure whether she is victim or victimizer, Brooks directs her readers' attention to the complex emotions of her potential Every-woman.

"The Mother" centers on the persona's alternating desire to take and to evade responsibility for the abortion. Resorting to ambiguous grammatical structures, the persona repeatedly qualifies her acceptance with "if" clauses ("If I sinned," "If I stole your births"). She refers to the lives of the children as matters of fate ("Your luck") and backs away from admitting that a death has taken place by claiming that the children "were never made." Her use of the second person pronoun to refer to herself in the first stanza reveals her desire to distance herself from her present pain. This attempt, however, fails. The opening line undercuts the evasion with the reality of memory: "Abortions will not let you forget." At the start of the second stanza, the pressure of memory forces the persona to shift to the more honest first person pronoun.

A sequence of spondees referring to the children ("damp small pulps," "dim killed children," "dim dears") interrupts the lightly stressed anapestic-iambic meter which dominates the first stanza. The concrete images of "scurrying off ghosts" and "devouring" children with loving gazes gain power when contrasted with the dimness of the mother's life and perceptions. Similarly, the first stanza's end-stopped couplets, reflecting the persona's simplistic attempt to recapture an irrevocably lost mother-child relationship through an act of imagination, give way to the intricate enjambment and complex rhyme scheme of the second stanza, which highlight the mother's inability to find rest.

The rhyme scheme—and Brooks can rival both Robert Frost and William Butler Yeats in her ability to employ various types of rhyme for thematic impact—underscores her struggle to come to terms with her action. The rhymes in the first stanza insist on her self-doubt, contrasting images of tenderness and physical substance with those of brutality and insubstantiality (forget/ get, hair/air, beat/sweet). The internal rhyme of "never," repeated four times, and "remember," "workers," and "singers," further stresses the element of loss. In the second stanza, Brooks provides no rhymes for the end words "children" in line 11 and "deliberate" in line 21. This device draws attention to the persona's failure to answer the crucial questions of whether her children did in fact exist and of whether her own actions were in fact deliberate (and perhaps criminal). The last seven lines of the stanza end with hard "d" sounds as the persona struggles to forge her conflicting thoughts into a unified perspective. If Brooks offers coherence, though, it is emotional rather than intellectual. Fittingly, the "d" rhymes and off-rhymes focus on physical and emotional pain (dead/instead/made/afraid/said/died/cried). Brooks provides no easy answer to the anguished question: "How is the truth to be told?" The persona's concluding cry of "I loved you/ All" rings with desperation. It is futile but it is not a lie. To call "The Mother" an antiabortion poem distorts its impact. Clearly portraying the devastating effects of the persona's action, it by no means condemns her or lacks sympathy. Like many of Brooks' characters, the mother is a person whose desire to love far outstrips her ability to cope with her circumstances and serves primarily to heighten her sensitivity to pain.

Perhaps the most significant change in Brooks' poetry involves her analysis of the origins of this pervasive pain. Rather than attributing the suffering to some unavoidable psychological condition, Brooks' later poetry indicts social institutions for their role in its perpetuation. The poems in her first two volumes frequently portray characters incapable of articulating the origins of their pain. Although the absence of any father in "The Mother" suggests sociological forces leading to the abortion, such analysis amounts to little more than speculation. The only certainty is that the mother, the persona of the sonnet sequence "The Children of the Poor," and the speaker in the brilliant sonnet "My Dreams, My Works Must Wait Till After Hell" share the fear that their pain will render them insensitive to love. The final poem of *Annie Allen*, "Men of Careful Turns," intimates that the defenders of a society which refuses to admit its full humanity bear responsibility for reducing the powerless to "grotesque toys." Despite this implicit accusation, however, Brooks perceives no "magic" capable of remedying the situation. She concludes the volume on a note of irresolution typical of her early period: "We are lost, must/ Wizard a track through our own screaming weed." The track, at this stage, remains spiritual rather than political.

Politics

Although the early volumes include occasional poems concerning articulate political participants such as "Negro Hero," her later work frequently centers on specific black political spokespersons such as Malcolm X, Paul Robeson, John Killens, and Don L. Lee. As of the early 1960s, a growing anger informs poems as diverse as the ironic "The Chicago *Defender* Sends a Man to Little Rock," the near-baroque "The Lovers of the Poor," the imagistically intricate "Riders to the Blood-Red Wrath," and the satiric "Riot." This anger originates in Brooks' perception that the social structures of white society value material possessions and abstract ideas of prestige more highly than individual human beings. The anger culminates in Brooks' brilliant narrative poem "In the Mecca," concerning the death of a young girl in a Chicago housing project, and in her three "Sermons on the Warpland."

The Warpland Poems

The Warpland poems mark Brooks' departure from the traditions of Euro-American poetry and thought represented by T. S. Eliot's *The Waste Land* (1922). The sequence typifies her post-1967 poetry, in which she abandons traditional stanzaic forms, applying her technical expertise to a relatively colloquial free verse. This technical shift parallels her rejection of the philosophical premises of Euro-American culture. Brooks refuses to accept the inevitability of cultural decay, arguing that the "waste" of Eliot's vision exists primarily because of our "warped" perceptions. Seeing white society as the embodiment of these distortions, Brooks embraces her blackness as a potential counterbalancing force. The first "Sermon on the Warpland" opens with Ron Karenga's black nationalist credo: "The fact that we are black is our ultimate reality." Clearly, in Brooks' view, blackness is not simply a physical fact; it is primarily a metaphor for the possibility of love. As her poem "Two Dedications" indicates, Brooks sees the Euro-American tradition represented by the Chicago Picasso as inhumanly cold, mingling guilt and innocence, meaningfulness and meaninglessness, almost randomly. This contrasts sharply with her inspirational image of the Wall of Heroes on the South Side. To Brooks, true art assumes meaning from the people who interact with it. The Wall helps to redefine black reality, rendering the "dispossessions beakless." Rather than contemplating the site of destruction, the politically aware black art which Brooks embraces should inspire the black community to face its pain with renewed determination to remove its sources. The final "Sermon on the Warpland" concludes with the image of a black phoenix rising from the ashes of the Chicago riot. No longer content to accept the unresolved suffering of "The Mother," Brooks forges a black nationalist politics and poetics of love.

"The Blackstone Rangers"

Although her political vision influences every aspect of her work, Brooks maintains a strong sense of enduring individual pain and is aware that nationalism offers no simple panacea. "The Blackstone Rangers," a poem concerning one of the most powerful Chicago street gangs, rejects as simplistic the argument, occasionally advanced by writers associated with the Black Arts movement, that no important distinction exists between the personal and the political experience. Specifically, Brooks doubts the corollary that politically desirable activity will inevitably increase the person's ability to love. Dividing "The Blackstone Rangers" into three segments—"As Seen by Disciplines," "The Leaders," and "Gang Girls: A Rangerette"— Brooks stresses the tension between

perspectives. After rejecting the sociological-penal perspective of part one, she remains suspended between the uncomprehending affirmation of the Rangers as a kind of government-in-exile in part two, and the recognition of the individual person's continuing pain in part three.

Brooks undercuts the description of the Rangers as "sores in the city/ that do not want to heal" ("As Seen by Disciplines") through the use of off-rhyme and a jazz rhythm reminiscent of "We Real Cool." The disciplines, both academic and corrective, fail to perceive any coherence in the Rangers' experience. Correct in their assumption that the Rangers do not want to "heal" themselves, the disciplines fail to perceive the gang's strong desire to "heal" the sick society. Brooks suggests an essential coherence in the Rangers' experience through the sound texture of part one. Several of the sound patterns echoing through the brief stanza point to a shared response to pain (there/thirty/ ready, raw/sore/corner). Similarly, the accent cluster on "Black, raw, ready" draws attention to the pain and potential power of the Rangers. The descriptive voice of the disciplines, however, provides only relatively weak end rhymes (are/ corner, ready/ city), testifying to the inability of the distanced, presumably white, observers to comprehend the experiences they describe. The shifting, distinctively black, jazz rhythm further emphasizes the distance between the voices of observers and participants. Significantly, the voice of the disciplines finds no rhyme at all for its denial of the Rangers' desire to "heal."

This denial contrasts sharply with the tempered affirmation of the voice in part two which emphasizes the leaders' desire to "cancel, cure and curry." Again, internal rhymes and sound echoes suffuse the section. In the first stanza, the voice generates thematically significant rhymes, connecting Ranger leader "*Bop*" (whose name draws attention to the jazz rhythm which is even more intricate, though less obvious, in this section than in part one) and the militant black leader "*Rap*" Brown, both nationalists whose "country is a Nation on no *map*." "Bop" and "Rap," of course, do not rhyme perfectly, attesting to Brooks' awareness of the gang leader's limitations. Her image of the leaders as "Bungled trophies" further reinforces her ambivalence. The only full rhyme in the final two stanzas of the section is the repeated "night." The leaders, canceling the racist association of darkness with evil, "translate" the image of blackness into a "monstrous pearl or grace." The section affirms the Blackstone Rangers' struggle; it does not pretend to comprehend fully the emotional texture of their lives.

Certain that the leaders possess the power to cancel the disfiguring images of the disciplines, Brooks remains unsure of their ability to create an alternate environment where love can blossom. Mary Ann, the "Gang Girl" of part three, shares much of the individual pain of the characters in Brooks' early poetry despite her involvement with the Rangers. "A rose in a whiskey glass," she continues to live with the knowledge that her "laboring lover" risks the same sudden death as the pool players of "We Real Cool." Forced to suppress a part of her awareness—she knows not to ask where her lover got the diamond he gives her—she remains emotionally removed even while making love. In place of a fully realized love, she accepts "the props and niceties of non-loneliness." The final line of the poem emphasizes the ambiguity of both Mary Ann's situation and Brooks' perspective. Recommending acceptance of "the rhymes of Leaning," the line responds to the previous stanza's question concerning whether love will have a "gleaning." The full rhyme paradoxically suggests acceptance of off-rhyme, of love consummated leaning against an alley wall, without expectation of safety or resolution. Given the political tension created by the juxtaposition of the disciplines and the leaders, the "Gang Girl" can hope to find no sanctuary beyond the reach of the whirlwind. Her desperate love, the more moving for its precariousness, provides the only near-adequate response to the pain that Brooks saw as the primary fact of life.

Other Literary Forms

In addition to the poetry on which her literary reputation rests, Gwendolyn Brooks published a novel, *Maud Martha*, a book of autobiographical prose, *Report from Part One*, and volumes of children's verse. An episodic novel, *Maud Martha* makes some use of autobiographical materials and shares many of the major concerns of Brooks' poetry, particularly concerning the attempts of the person to maintain integrity in the face of crushing environmental pressures. *Report from Part One* recounts the personal, political, and aesthetic influences that culminated in Brooks' movement to a black nationalist stance in the late 1960s. She also wrote introductions to, and edited anthologies of, the works of younger black writers. These introductions frequently provide insight into her own work. Several recordings of Brooks reading her own work are available.

Bibliography

Baker, Houston A., Jr. *The Journey Back: Issues in Black Literature and Criticism.* Chicago: University of Chicago Press, 1980. The value of Baker's treatment of Brooks (accessible through the index) is his examination of the shift in her thinking and her art generated by her experience at the Fisk University Writers' Conference in 1967. Baker sets her in the context of the larger movement toward a "Black Aesthetic."

Banks, Margot Harper. *Religious Allusion in the Poetry of Gwendolyn Brooks.* Jefferson, NC: McFarland, 2012. Discusses Brooks' life, her religious ideas, and various longer works, with three chapters on short poems and a conversation with Brooks.

Blakely, Nora Brooks, and Cynthia A. Walls, ed. *Seasons: A Gwendolyn Brooks Experience.* Chicago: Third World Press Foundation, 2017. A commemorative volume full of works by Brooks on various themes, reminiscences of her, photographs and drawings, and other materials.

Bloom, Harold, ed. *Gwendolyn Brooks.* New York: Chelsea House, 2004. This slim volume contains a short biography and critical essays written by a number of top-notch critics, including Langston Hughes, D. H. Melhem, and Maria K. Mootry.

Bolden, B. J. *Urban Rage in Bronzeville: Social Commentary in the Poetry of Gwendolyn Brooks, 1945-1960.* Chicago: Third World Press, 1999. A critical analysis focused on the impact of Brooks's early poetry. Bolden examines *A Street in Bronzeville, Annie Allen,* and *The Bean Eaters* in clear historical, racial, political, cultural, and aesthetic terms.

Bryant, Jacqueline Imani, ed. *Gwendolyn Brooks and Working Writers.* Chicago: Third World Press, 2007. A collection of anecdotes about Brooks by friends, educators, and other creative writers.

"Gwendolyn's Words: A Gift to Us." *Essence* 31, no. 11 (March, 2001): A18. Discusses the career of Brooks, the first African American to win a Pulitzer Prize. Begins with an account of her early life and documents the sequence of her compositions. Also covers her professional relationship with Haki R. Madhubuti, who helped publish her works.

Hughes, Sheila Hassell. "A Prophet Overheard: A Juxtapositional Reading of Gwendolyn Brooks's *In the Mecca.*" *African American Review* 38, no. 2 (Summer, 2004): 257-281. Hughes's interest is in the relationship between Brooks's political beliefs and the artistic merit and social relevance of her poetry.

Jackson, Angela. *A Surprised Queenhood in the New Black Sun: The Life & Legacy of Gwendolyn Brooks.* Boston: Beacon Press, 2017. A biography that sets Brooks' works in the contexts of her themes, her developing career, and the social and political conditions of her era.

Kahn, Peter, et al, ed. *The Golden Shovel Anthology: New Poems Honoring Gwendolyn Brooks.* Little Rock: University of Arkansas Press, 2017, 2019. Scores of poets honor Brooks by using her poems as inspirations for their own.

Kent, George E. *A Life of Gwendolyn Brooks.* Lexington: University Press of Kentucky, 1990. This biography, actually completed in 1982 just before Kent's death, is based on interviews with Brooks and her friends and family. Integrates discussions of the poetry with a chronicle of her life. Especially valuable is an extensive recounting of the events and speeches at the 1967 Fisk conference, which changed the direction of her poetry. D. H. Melhem's afterword provides an update.

Melhem, D. H. *Gwendolyn Brooks: Poetry and the Heroic Voice.* Lexington: University Press of Kentucky, 1987. Beginning with a biographical chapter, Melhem employs a generally laudatory tone as he subsequently looks closely at the earlier poetry collections (through *Aloneness*). He surveys the later works within a single chapter, and also examines *Maud Martha* and *Bronzeville Boys and Girls.* Melhem's treatment gives attention to both structures and themes. Includes notes and an index, as well as a bibliography of her works (organized by publisher, in order to show the commitment she made to small black-run presses after the late 1960s).

Miller, R. Baxter, ed. *Black American Poets Between Worlds, 1940-1960.* Tennessee Studies in Literature 30. Knoxville: University of Tennessee Press, 1986. To this collection Harry B. Shaw contributes "Perceptions of Men in the Early Works of Gwendolyn Brooks," which looks at *A Street in Bronzeville, Annie Allen, Maud Martha,* and *The Bean Eaters* for their largely positive depictions of urban African American men. "Define . . . the Whirlwind: Gwendolyn Brooks' Epic Sign for a Generation," by R. Baxter Miller, focuses on Brooks' epic achievement "In the Mecca." Each of these essays has notes, and the book is indexed.

Mootry, Maria K., and Gary Smith, eds. *A Life Distilled: Gwendolyn Brooks, Her Poetry and Fiction.* Urbana: University of Illinois Press, 1987. An introductory overview by Mootry is followed by a look at Brooks' sense of place ("The World of Satin-Legs, Mrs. Sallie, and the Blackstone Rangers" by Kenny J. Williams), her aesthetic (essays by George E. Kent, Norris B. Clark, and R. Baxter Miller), and the militancy that emerged in her "second period" (by William H. Hansel). The middle section comprises essays on individual collections, while the book's final two essays examine *Maud Martha.* Features notes, and a selected bibliography that not only lists Brooks' works but also surveys critical sources in great detail, including book reviews and dissertations. No index is provided.

Saber, Yomna Mohamed. *Brave to Be Involved: Shifting Positions in the Poetry of Gwendolyn Brooks.* Peter Lang, 2010. Traces the development of Brooks' various voices and pays special attention to her work in relation to works by Richard Wright, Margaret Walker, Ralph Ellison, Lorraine Hansberry, Amiri Baraka and Sonia Sanchez.

Wade Gayles, Gloria, ed. *Conversations with Gwendolyn Brooks.* Jackson: University Press of Mississippi, 2003. Essays by a number of contemporary authors—including Studs Terkel, Haki Madhubuti, and Roy Newquist—provide valuable insights into Brooks' work and philosophy.

Washington, Mary Helen. "An Appreciation: A Writer Who Defined Black Power for Herself." *Los Angeles Times*, December 8, 2000, p. E1. Discusses the young Brooks, who, when just starting her writing career, attended the 1967 Fisk University Writers' Conference, encountered the young black militants led by Amiri Baraka, and was converted. She branded her earlier writing "white writing" and resolved to change.

Wright, Stephen Caldwell, ed. *On Gwendolyn Brooks: Reliant Contemplation.* Ann Arbor: University of Michigan Press, 1996. This resource judiciously selects and assembles the most important writings to date about the works of Gwendolyn Brooks in the form of reviews and essays. Three-part organization helpfully separates the reviews from the essays and the later essays from the rest.

— *Craig Werner; Robert C. Evans*

Sterling A. Brown

Poet

Born: Washington, D.C.; May 1, 1901

Died: Takoma Park, Maryland; January 13, 1989

POETRY: *Southern Road*, 1932; *The Last Ride of Wild Bill, and Eleven Narrative Poems*; 1975; *The Collected Poems of Sterling A. Brown*, 1980.

NONFICTION: *Outline for the Study of the Poetry of American Negroes*, 1931; *The Negro in American Fiction*, 1937; *Negro Poetry and Drama*, 1937; *The Negro Caravan*, 1941 (Arthur P. Davis and Ulysses Lee, editors); *A Son's Return: Selected Essays of Sterling A. Brown*, 1996 (Mark A. Sanders, editor); *A Negro Looks at the South*, 2007 (John Edgar Tidwell and Mark A. Sanders, editors).

Achievements

Sterling Brown is considered an important transitional figure between the Harlem Renaissance era and the period immediately following the Depression. Brown's fame is based not only on his poetry but also on his achievements as a critic, folklorist, scholar, and university teacher. As an acknowledged authority on African American culture, Brown served on many committees and boards and participated in numerous scholarly and research activities. Among these were the Carnegie Myrdal Study, the American Folklore Society, the Institute of Jazz Studies, the editorial board of *The Crisis*, the Federal Writers' Project, and the Committee on Negro Studies of the American Council of Learned Societies.

Brown's poems and critical essays have been anthologized widely, and he was a memorable reader of his own poetry, especially on such recordings as *The Anthology of Negro Poets* (Folkways) and *A Hand's on the Gate*. He cowrote an article with Rayford Logan on the American Negro for *Encyclopedia Britannica*. Brown was a Guggenheim Fellow (1937-1938) and a Julius Rosenwald Fellow (1942). He was an eminent faculty member at Howard University in Washington, D.C., from 1929 to 1969. In 1987, Brown won the Frost Medal, awarded by the Poetry Society of America.

Biography

Born into an educated, middle-class African American family, Sterling Allen Brown was the last of six children and the only son of Adelaide Allen Brown and the Reverend Sterling Nelson Brown. His father had taught in the School of Religion at Howard University since 1892, and the year Brown was born, his father also became the pastor of Lincoln Temple Congregational Church. The person who encouraged Brown's literary career and admiration for the cultural heritage of African Americans, however, was his mother, who had been born and reared in Tennessee and graduated from Fisk University. Brown also grew up listening to tales of his father's childhood in Tennessee, as well as to accounts of his father's friendships with noted leaders such as Frederick Douglass, Blanche K. Bruce, and Booker T. Washington.

Brown attended public schools in Washington, D.C., and was graduated from the well-known Dunbar High School, noted for its distinguished teachers and alumni; among the latter were many of the nation's outstanding black professionals. Brown's teachers at Dunbar included literary artists such as Angelina Weld Grimke and Jessie Redmon Fauset. Moreover, Brown grew up on the campus of Howard University, where there were many outstanding African American scholars, such as historian Kelly Miller and critic and philosopher Alain Locke.

Brown received his A.B. in 1922 from Williams College (Phi Beta Kappa) and his M.A. in 1923 from Harvard University. Although he pursued further graduate study in English at Harvard, he never worked toward a doctorate degree; however, Howard University, the University of Massachusetts, Northwestern University, Williams College, Boston University, Brown University, Lewis and Clark College, Lincoln University (Pennsylvania), and the University of Pennsylvania eventually granted him honorary doctorates. In September, 1927, he was married to Daisy Turnbull, who shared with him an enthusiasm for people, a sense of humor, and a rejection of pretentious behavior; she was also one of her husband's sharpest critics. She inspired Brown's poems "Long Track Blues" and "Against That Day." Daisy Turnbull Brown died in 1979. The Browns had one adopted child, John L. Dennis.

In 1927, "When de Saints Go Ma'ching Home" won first prize in an *Opportunity* writing contest. From 1926 to 1929, several of the poems that Brown later published in *Southern Road* were printed in *Crisis, Opportunity, Contempo,* and *Ebony and Topaz*. His early work is often identified with the outpouring of black writers during the Harlem Renaissance, for he shared with those artists (Claude McKay, Countee Cullen, Jean Toomer, and Langston Hughes) a deep concern for a franker self-revelation and a respect for the folk traditions of his people; however, Brown's writings did not reflect the alien-and-exile theme so popular with the writers of the Renaissance.

Brown's teaching career took him to Virginia Seminary and College, Lincoln University (Missouri), and Fisk University. He began teaching at Howard University in 1929 and remained there until his retirement in 1969. He was also a visiting professor at Atlanta University, New York University, Vassar College, the University of Minnesota, the New School, and the University of Illinois (Chicago Circle). Several years after coming to Howard University, Brown became an editor with the Works Progress Administration's Federal Writers' Project. Along with a small editorial staff, he coordinated the Federal Writers' Project studies by and about blacks. Beginning in 1932, Brown supervised an extensive collection of narratives by former slaves and initiated special projects such as *The Negro in Virginia* (1940), which became the model for other studies. His most enduring contribution to the project was an essay, "The Negro in Washington," which was published in the guidebook *Washington: City and Capital* (1937).

Brown's first fifteen years at Howard were most productive. During this period (1929-1945), he contributed poetry as well as reviews and essays on the American theater, folk expressions, oral history, social customs, music, and athletics to *The New Republic, The Journal of Negro Education, Phylon, Crisis, Opportunity,* and other journals. His most outstanding essay, "Negro Characters as Seen by White Authors," which appeared in *The Journal of Negro Education* in 1933, brought attention to the widespread misrepresentation of black characters and life in American literature. Only after Brown's retirement from Howard in 1969 did he begin reading his poems regularly there. This long neglect has been attributed to certain conservative faculty members' reluctance to appreciate a fellow professor whose interests were in blues and jazz. Brown was widely known as a raconteur. Throughout his career as a writer, he challenged fellow African American writers to choose their subject matter without regard to external pressures and to avoid the error of "timidity." He was a mentor who influenced the black poetry movement of the 1960s and 1970s, and poets such as Margaret Walker, Gwendolyn Brooks, Langston Hughes, and Arna Bontemps, along with critics such as Addison Gayle and Houston Baker, learned from him.

In the five years before his retirement, Brown began to exhibit stress caused by what he perceived to be years of critical and professional neglect as well as unfulfilled goals. Inclined toward periods of deep depression, he was occasionally hospitalized in his later years. He died in Takoma Park, Maryland, on January 13, 1989.

Analysis: Poetry

The poetry of Sterling Brown is imbued with the folk spirit of African American culture. For Brown there was no wide abyss between his poetry and the spirit inherent in slave poetry; indeed, his works evidence a continuity of racial spirit from the slave experience to the African American present and reflect his deep understanding of the multitudinous aspects of the African American personality and soul.

The setting for Brown's poetry is primarily the South, through which he traveled to listen to the folktales, songs, wisdom, sorrows, and frustrations of his people, and where the blues and ballads were nurtured. Brown respected traditional folk forms and employed them in the construction of his own poems; thus he may be called "the poet of the soul of his people."

Southern Road

Brown's first published collection of poems, *Southern Road,* was critically acclaimed by his peers and colleagues James Weldon Johnson and Alain Locke, because of its rendering of the living speech of the African American, its use of the raw material of folk poetry, and its poetic portrayal of African American folk life and thought. Later critics such as Arthur P. Davis, Jean Wagner, and Houston Baker have continued to praise his poetry for its creative and vital use of folk motifs. Some of the characters in Brown's poetry, such as Ma Rainey, Big Boy Davis, and Mrs. Bibby, are based on real people. Other characters, such as Maumee Ruth, Sporting Beasley, and Sam Smiley seem real because of Brown's dramatic and narrative talent. He is also highly skilled in the use of poetic techniques such as the refrain, alliteration, and onomatopoeia, and he employs several stanzaic forms with facility. Brown's extraordinary gift for re-creating the nuances of folk speech and idiom adds vitality and authenticity to his verse.

Brown is successful in drawing upon rich folk expressions to vitalize the speech of his characters through the cadences of southern speech. Though his poems cannot simply be called "dialect poetry," Brown does imitate southern African American speech, using variant spellings and apostrophes to mark dropped consonants. He uses grunts and onomatopoeic sounds to give a natural rhythm to the speech of his characters. These techniques are readily seen in a poem that dramatizes the poignant story of a "po los boy" on a chain gang. This poem follows the traditional folk form of the work song to convey the convict's personal tragedy.

Brown's work may be classed as protest poetry. Influenced by poets such as Carl Sandburg and Robert Frost, he is able to draw upon the entire canon of English and American poetry as well as African American folk material. Thus he is fluent in the use of the sonnet form, stanzaic forms, free-verse forms, and ballad and blues forms.

In *Southern Road*, several themes express the essence of the southern African American's folk spirit and culture. Recurring themes and subjects in Brown's poetry include endurance, tragedy, and survival. The theme of endurance is best illustrated in one of his most anthologized poems, "Strong Men," which tells the story of the unjust treatment of black men and women from the slave ship, to the tenant farm, and finally to the black ghetto. The refrain of "Strong Men" uses rhythmic beats, relentlessly repeating an affirmation of the black people's ability and determination to keep pressing onward, toward freedom and justice. The central image comes from a line of a Carl Sandburg poem, "The strong men keep comin on." In "Strong Men," Brown praises the indomitable spirit of African Americans in the face of racist exploitation. With its assertive tone, the rhythm of this poem suggests a martial song.

Some of the endurance poems express a stoic, fatalistic acceptance of the tragic fate of the African American, as can be seen in "Old Man Buzzard," "Memphis Blues," and "Riverbank Blues." Another important aspect of the endurance theme as portrayed by Brown is the poetic characters' courage when they are confronted with tragedy and injustice. In the poem "Strange Legacies," the speaker gives thanks to the legendary Jack Johnson and John Henry for their demonstration of courage.

"The Last Ride of Wild Bill"

Brown's poems reflect his understanding of the often tragic destinies of African Americans in the United States. No poet before Brown had created such a comprehensive poetic dramatization of the lives of black men and women in America. Brown depicts black men and women as alone and powerless, struggling nevertheless to confront an environment that is hostile and unjust. In this tragic environment, African American struggles against the schemes of racist whites are seen in "The Last Ride of Wild Bill," published in 1975 as the title poem of a collection. A black man falls victim to the hysteria of a lynch mob in "Frankie and Johnnie," a poem that takes up a familiar folktale and twists it to reflect a personal tragedy that occurs as a result of an interracial relationship. Brown emphasizes that in this story the only tragic victim is the black man. The retarded white girl, Frankie, reports her sexual experience with the black man, Johnnie, to her father and succeeds in getting her black lover killed; she laughs uproariously during the lynching. "Southern Cop" narrates the mindless killing of a black man who is the victim of the panic of a rookie police officer.

Yet Brown's poems show black people not only as victims of whites but also as victims of the whole environment that surrounds them, including natural forces of flood and fire as well as social evils such as poverty and ignorance. Rural blacks' vulnerability to natural disasters is revealed in "Old King Cotton," "New St. Louis Blues," and "Foreclosure." In these poems, if a tornado does not come, the Mississippi River rises and takes the peasant's arable land and his few animals, and even traitorously kills his children by night. These poems portray despairing people who are capable only of futile questions in the face of an implacable and pitiless nature. The central character of "Low Down" is sunk in poverty and loneliness. His wife has left and his son is in prison; he is convinced that bad luck is his fate and that in the workings of life someone has loaded the dice against him. In "Johnny Thomas," the title character is the victim of poverty, abuse by his parents and society, and ignorance. (He attempts to enroll in a one-room school, but the teacher throws him out.) Johnny ends up on a chain gang, where he is killed. The poem that most strongly expresses African American despair of the entire race is "Southern Road," a convict song marked by a rhythmic, staccato beat and by a blues line punctuated by the convict's groaning over his accursed fate:

> My ole man died—hunh—
> Cussin' me;
> Old lady rocks, bebby, huh misery.

Slim Greer Poems

The African American's ability to survive in a hostile world by mustering humor, religious faith, and the expectation of a utopian afterlife is portrayed in poems depicting the comical adventures of Slim Greer and in one of Brown's popular poems, "Sister Lou." The series of Slim Greer poems, "Slim Greer," "Slim Lands a Job," "Slim in Atlanta," and "Slim in Hell," reveal Brown's knowledge of the life of the ordinary black person and his ability to laugh at the weaknesses and foolishness of blacks and whites alike. With their rich exaggerations, these poems fall into the tall tale tradition of folk stories. They show Slim in Arkansas passing for white although he is quite dark, or Slim in Atlanta laughing in a "telefoam booth" because of a law that keeps blacks from laughing in the open. In "Slim Lands a Job," the poet mocks the ridiculous demands that southern employers make on their black employees. Slim applies for a job in a restaurant. The owner is complaining about the laziness of his black employees when a black waiter enters the room carrying a tray on his head, trays in each hand, silver in his mouth, and soup plates in his vest, while simultaneously pulling a red wagon filled with other

paraphernalia. When the owner points to this waiter as one who is lazy, Slim makes a quick exit. In "Slim in Hell," Slim discovers that Hell and the South are very much alike; when he reports this discovery to Saint Peter, the saint reprimands him, asking where he thought Hell was if not the South.

"Sister Lou"

In "Sister Lou," one of his well-known poems, Brown depicts the simple religious faith that keeps some blacks going. After recounting all the sorrows in Sister Lou's life, the poem pictures Heaven as a place where Sister Lou will have a chance to allow others to carry her packages, to speak personally to God without fear, to rest, and most of all to take her time. In "Cabaret," however, Brown shows the everyday reality that belies the promises God made to his people: The black folk huddle, mute and forlorn, in Mississippi, unable to understand why the Good Lord treats them this way. Moreover, in poems such as "Maumee Ruth," religion is seen as an opium that feeds people's illusions. Maumee Ruth lies on her deathbed, ignorant of the depraved life led by her son and daughter in the city, and needing the religious lies preached to her in order to attain a peaceful death.

"Remembering Nat Turner"

Sterling Brown's poems embrace themes of suffering, oppression, and tragedy yet always celebrate the vision and beauty of African American people and culture. One such deeply moving piece is "Remembering Nat Turner," a poem in which the speaker visits the scene of Turner's slave rebellion, only to hear an elderly white woman's garbled recollections of the event; moreover, the marker intended to call attention to Turner's heroic exploits, a rotting signpost, has been used by black tenants for kindling. A stoic fatalism can be seen in the poem "Memphis Blues," which nevertheless praises the ability of African Americans to survive in a hostile environment because of their courage and willingness to start over when all seems lost: "Guess we'll give it one more try." In the words of Sterling Brown, "The strong men keep a-comin' on/ Gittin' stronger . . . ."

Other Literary Forms

Sterling Brown produced several studies of African American literature: *Outline for the Study of the Poetry of American Negroes*, *The Negro in American Fiction*, and *Negro Poetry and Drama*. With Arthur P. Davis and Ulysses Lee, he edited *The Negro Caravan*. Brown also published numerous scholarly pieces in leading journals on subjects relating to African American culture and literature.

Bibliography

African American Review 31, no. 3 (Fall, 1997). An entire issue devoted to discussion of Brown's poetry and its impacts on African American and mainstream American culture.

Baker, Houston A., Jr. "Sterling's Magic: The Scholar and Poet Sterling Brown Stamped American Poetry with the Music of the Black Vernacular." *Black Issues Book Review* 3, no. 3 (May/ June, 2001): 32-34. Emphasizes Brown's many contributions to African American and southern literature and language.

Callaloo 21, no. 4 (Fall, 1998). An entire issue devoted to analysis of Brown's life and work. An excellent place to begin serious research.

Davis, Arthur P. "Sterling Brown." In *From the Dark Tower: Afro-American Writers, 1900-1960*. Washington, D.C.: Howard University Press, 1982. A comprehensive study by the dean of African American critics, who knew Brown personally and taught with him at Howard on African American writers during the 1950's. The essays on individual writers are supplemented by ample introductory material, and there is also an extensive bibliography, listed by author.

Ekate, Genevieve. "Sterling Brown: A Living Legend." *New Directions: The Howard University Magazine* 1 (Winter, 1974): 5-11. A tribute to the life and works of Sterling Brown in a magazine published by the university where he taught for forty years. This article analyzes Brown's literary influence on younger poets and assesses his importance in the African American literary canon.

Manson, Michael Tomasek. "Sterling Brown and the 'Vestiges' of the Blues: The Role of Race in English Verse Structure." *MELUS* 21, no. 1 (Spring, 1996): 21-41. Of special interest to students familiar with poetry, this essay examines the ways in which literary and linguistic theory converge in Brown's sonnet "Challenge" from the 1932 book *Southern Road*.

Redding, Saunders. *To Make a Poet Black*. Chapel Hill: University of North Carolina Press, 1939. This pioneering study gives an effective overview of the intellectual and literary influences and processes involved in the development of African American poets. Although it includes only a few pages on Brown himself, it is essential background reading in African American poetics.

Sanders, Mark A. *Afro-Modernist Aesthetics and the Poetry of Sterling A. Brown*. Athens: University of Georgia Press, 1999. Criticism and interpretation of Brown and his poetry in the context of twentieth century African American literature and intellectual life.

Thelwell, Ekwueme Michael. "The Professor and the Activists: A Memoir of Sterling Brown." *The Massachusetts Review* 40, no. 4 (Winter, 1999/2000): 617-638. A fond memoir of Brown written by one of his students at Howard University. Offers a glimpse into Brown's personality, political bent, and place as a black intellectual during the tumultuous 1960's.

Tidwell, John Edgar, and Steven C. Tracy, ed. *After Winter: The Art and Life of Sterling A. Brown*. Oxford

UP, 2009. Contains over thirty essays and other contributions by some of the most prominent scholars of African American literary study.

Wagner, Jean. "Sterling Brown." In *Black Poets of the United States, from Paul Laurence Dunbar to Langston Hughes.* Urbana: University of Illinois Press, 1973. A comprehensive and insightful study of the poetry of Brown, covering the subjects, themes, and nuances of his poetry. Wagner's writing on Brown is warm and appreciative.

— *Betty Taylor-Thompson; Robert C. Evans*

Ed Bullins

Playwright

Born: Philadelphia, Pennsylvania; July 2, 1935

Pseudonym: Kingsley B. Bass, Jr.

LONG FICTION: *The Reluctant Rapist*, 1973.

DRAMA: *Clara's Ole Man*, pr. 1965, pb. 1969 (one act); *Dialect Determinism: Or, The Rally*, pr. 1965, pb. 1973 (one act); *How Do You Do?*, pr. 1965, pb. 1968 (one act); *The Theme Is Blackness*, pr. 1966, pb. 1973 (one act); *A Son, Come Home*, pr. 1968, pb. 1969 (one act); *The Electronic Nigger*, pr. 1968, pb. 1969 (one act); *Goin' a Buffalo*, pr. 1968, pb. 1969; *In the Wine Time*, pr. 1968, pb. 1969; *Five Plays*, pb. 1969 (includes *Clara's Ole Man*, *A Son, Come Home*, *The Electronic Nigger*, *Goin' a Buffalo*, and *In the Wine Time*); *The Gentleman Caller*, pr. 1969, pb. 1970; *In New England Winter*, pb. 1969, pr. 1971; *We Righteous Bombers*, pr. 1969 (as Kingsley B. Bass, Jr.; adaptation of Albert Camus' play *Les Justes*); *A Ritual to Raise the Dead and Foretell the Future*, pr. 1970, pb. 1973; *The Pig Pen*, pr. 1970, pb. 1971; *The Duplex*, pr. 1970, pb. 1971; *Street Sounds*, pr. 1970, pb. 1973; *The Devil Catchers*, pr. 1971; *The Fabulous Miss Marie*, pr. 1971, pb. 1974; *House Party*, pr. 1973 (lyrics; music by Pat Patrick); *The Theme Is Blackness*, pb. 1973 (collection); *The Taking of Miss Janie*, pr. 1975, pb. 1981; *Home Boy*, pr. 1976 (lyrics; music by Aaron Bell); *Jo Anne!*, pr. 1976, pb. 1993; *Daddy*, pr. 1977; *Storyville*, pr. 1977, revised pr. 1979 (music by Mildred Kayden); *Sepia Star: Or, Chocolate Comes to the Cotton Club*, pr. 1977 (lyrics; music by Kayden); *Michael*, pr. 1978; *Leavings*, pr. 1980; *Steve and Velma*, pr. 1980; *A Teacup Full of Roses*, pr. 1989; *A Sunday Afternoon*, pr. 1989 (with Marshall Borden); *I Think It's Going to Turn Out Fine*, pr. 1990; *American Griot*, pr. 1991 (with Idris Ackamoor); *Salaam, Huey Newton, Salaam*, pr. 1991 (one act); *Boy X Man*, pr. 1995; *Mtumi X*, pr. 2000; *Blacklist*, pb. 2010; *The Doorway*, pb. 2010; *Snickers*, pb. 2010; *Spaces*, pb. 2010; *That Day*, pb. 2010.

SCREENPLAYS: *Night of the Beast*, 1971; *The Ritual Masters*, 1972.

POETRY: *To Raise the Dead and Foretell the Future*, 1971. edited texts: *New Plays from the Black Theatre*, 1969 (with introduction); *The New Lafayette Theater Presents: Plays with Aesthetic Comments by Six Black Playwrights*, 1974 (with introduction).

MISCELLANEOUS: *The Hungered Ones: Early Writings*, 1971 (stories and essays); *Twelve Plays & Selected Writings*, 2006 (edited by Mike Sell); *Funky Chicken: A Fragment*, 2006.

Achievements

Ed Bullins won the 1968 Vernon Rice Award for *The Electronic Nigger*, the 1971 Obie Award for *In New England Winter* and *The Fabulous Miss Marie*, and in 1975 both the Obie and the New York Drama Critics Circle Award for *The Taking of Miss Janie*. In 1997 he received the Living Legend Award from the Black Theatre Conference, and in 1999 he won the August Wilson Playwriting Award and the Garland Anderson

Playwright Award. In 2012 he received the Theatre Communications Group Visionary Leadership Award. He has also received grants from the Guggenheim Foundation (1971, 1976), the Rockefeller Foundation (1968, 1970, 1973), the Creative Artists Program Service (1973), the Black Arts Alliance (1971), and the National Endowment for the Arts (1974).

As much as any contemporary American playwright, Bullins has forged a powerful synthesis of avant-garde technique and revolutionary commitment challenging easy preconceptions concerning the relationship between politics and aesthetics. Like Latin American writers Carlos Fuentes and Gabriel Garcia Marquez and African writers Ngugi wa Thiong'o and Wole Soyinka, Bullins sees no inherent contradiction between the use of experimental techniques and the drive to reach a mass audience alienated from the dominant social/economic/racial hierarchy. Separating himself from the cultural elite that has claimed possession of the modernist and postmodernist tradition, Bullins adapts the tradition to the frames of reference and to the immediate concerns of his audience, primarily but not exclusively within the African American community. Although he frequently comments on and revises the philosophical and aesthetic concerns of European American modernism, he does so to clarify his audience's vision of an American culture riddled by psychological and political contradictions that intimate the need for a basic change.

Paralleling the political modernism advocated by Bertolt Brecht in his aesthetic and political debate with Gyorgy Lukacs, Bullins's synthesis takes on particular significance in the context of the Black Arts movement of the late 1960s. As a leading figure in the movement for specifically black cultural institutions and modes of expression, Bullins refuted through example the casual stereotypes of black

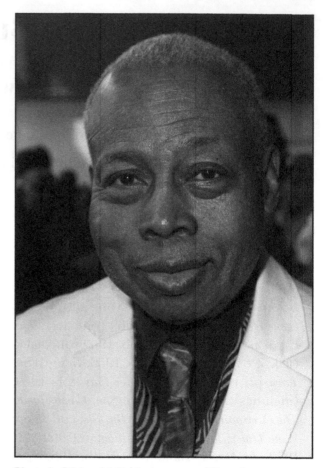

Photo by Walter McBride, courtesy of Getty Images

revolutionary artists as ideologically inflexible and aesthetically naive. Although he supports the confrontational strategies of radical playwrights committed to what he calls the "dialectic of change," he works primarily within what he calls the "dialectic of experience," which entails a sophisticated confrontation with a "reality" he understands to be in large part shaped by individual perceptions. Drawing on Brecht, Jean Genet, Albert Camus, Amiri Baraka, Eugene O'Neill, John Cage, Anton Chekhov, and Langston Hughes with equal facility, Bullins is not primarily a literary dramatist or a political agitator. Rather, he is a playwright in the classic sense, concerned above all else with bringing the experience of black Americans alive on stage in a manner that forces the audience to confront its metaphorically ambiguous but politically explosive implications. His most successful plays, such as *In New England Winter* and *The Taking of Miss Janie*, demonstrate conclusively that a revolutionary artist does not need to circumscribe his vision in order to defend a preestablished ideological position. Demonstrating his affinities with Brechtian theory as opposed to Brechtian practice, Bullins creates tensions between presentation style and content to alienate his audience, white or black, from its assumptions concerning race, class, sex, and ultimately the nature of perception.

Not surprisingly, this challenge frequently disturbs mainstream audiences and critics; typical is the response of Walter Kerr, who complained in a review of *The Taking of Miss Janie* that "no one likes having to finish—or trying to finish—an author's play for him; but that's the effort asked here." Ironically, Kerr's criticism accurately identifies the reason for Bullins's success in contexts ranging from the black community theaters of San

Francisco and New York to the La Mama theater in New York's SoHo district. Challenging the audience to confront the experience presented rather than to accept a mediated statement about that experience, Bullins rarely presents didactic statements without substantial ironic qualification. By refusing to advance simple solutions or to repress his awareness of oppression, Bullins attempts to force the audience to internalize and act on its responses. Effective as literature as well as theater, Bullins's plays have won numerous awards and grants from both African American and European American organizations. The best of them, especially the early sections of the Twentieth Century Cycle, a projected twenty-play series, have led some critics to compare Bullins with Eugene O'Neill. Although his ultimate stature depends in large part on the development of the cycle

and his continuing ability to generate new forms in response to changing audiences and political contexts, Bullins's place in the history of American and African American theater seems assured.

Biography

Intensely protective concerning the details of his private life, Ed Bullins has nevertheless been a highly visible force in the development of African American theater since the mid-1960s. Reared primarily by his civil servant mother in North Philadelphia, Bullins attended a predominantly white grade school before transferring to an inner-city junior high, where he became involved with the street gang called the Jet Cobras. Like his semiautobiographical character Steve Benson (*The Reluctant Rapist, In New England Winter, The Duplex*), Bullins suffered a near-fatal knife wound, in the area of his heart, in a street fight. After dropping out of high school, he served in the United States Navy from 1952 to 1955. In 1958, he moved to California, where he passed his high school graduation equivalency examination and attended Los Angeles City College from 1961 to 1963.

Bullins's 1963 move to San Francisco signaled the start of his emergence as an influential figure in African American literary culture. The first national publication of his essays in 1963 initiated a period of tremendous creativity extending into the mid-1970s. Actively committed to black nationalist politics by 1965, he began working with community theater organizations such as Black Arts/West, the Black Student Union at San Francisco State College, and Black House of San Francisco, which he founded along with playwright Marvin X. The first major production of Bullins's drama, a program including *How Do You Do?*, *Dialect Determinism*, and *Clara's Ole Man*, premiered at the Firehouse Repertory Theater in San Francisco on August

5, 1965. At about the same time, Bullins assumed the position of minister of culture with the Black Panther Party, then emerging as a major force in national politics. Breaking with the Panthers in 1967, reportedly in disagreement with Eldridge Cleaver's decision to accept alliances with white radical groups, Bullins moved to Harlem at the urging of Robert MacBeth, director of the New Lafayette Theater.

Bullins's first New York production, *The Electronic Nigger*, ran for ninety-six performances following its February 21, 1968, debut at the American Place Theatre, where it was moved after the original New Lafayette burned down. Combined with his editorship of the controversial "Black Theatre" issue of *The Drama Review* (Summer, 1968), the success of *The Electronic Nigger* consolidated Bullins's position alongside Baraka as a major presence within and outside the African American theatrical community. Between 1968 and 1976, Bullins's plays received an average of three major New York productions per year at theaters, including the New Lafayette (where Bullins was playwright-inresidence up to its 1973 closing), the American Place Theatre, the Brooklyn Academy of Music, Woodie King's New Federal Theatre at the Henry Street Settlement House, Lincoln Center, and the La Mama Experimental Theater.

Bullins wrote *A Sunday Afternoon* with Marshall Borden and "a pseudo-satiric monster horror play, a take-off on B-movies," called *Dr. Geechie and the Blood Junkies*, which he read at the Henry Street Settlement House in New York in the summer of 1989. The La Mama theater staged *I Think It's Going to Turn Out Fine*, based on the Tina Turner story, in 1990, and *American Griot* (coauthored with Idris Ackamoor, who also acted in the play) in 1991. *Salaam, Huey Newton, Salaam*, a one-act play on the aftermath of the black revolution, premiered at the Ensemble Studio Theater in 1991.

Bullins has also taught American humanities, black theater, and play making at Contra Costa College, in San Pablo, California. He settled in Emeryville, near Oakland, and started a theater there called the BMT Theatre (Bullins Memorial Theatre, named after his son, who died in an automobile accident).

He continued his formal education at Antioch University in San Francisco, where he received his bachelor's degree in liberal studies (English and playwriting) in 1989. After he completed his master's degree in playwriting at San Francisco State University in 1994, he was appointed professor of theater at Northeastern University in 1995, where he continues to write and direct plays. In 1996 he was made acting director of North-eastern University's Center for the Arts, and his *Boy X Man*, which premiered a year earlier in Greensboro, North Carolina, was staged at the Arts Black Box Theater in Boston. Three years later many of his plays were presented at a retrospective at the Schomberg Center for Research in Black Culture in New York.

An avid supporter of local drama, he has written two ten-minute plays for the Boston Theater Marathon, and works with the ACT Theater Group in Roxbury, where he mentors young playwrights and conducts workshops. In 2000 his play *Mtumi X* was produced, and his play *Goin' a Buffalo* was adapted to film and screened at the New York International Film and Video Festival in New York's Madison Square Garden.

Analysis: Drama

A radical playwright in both the simple and the complex senses of the term, Bullins consistently challenges the members of his audience to test their political and aesthetic beliefs against the multifaceted reality of daily life in the United States. Committed to a revolutionary black nationalist consciousness, he attacks both liberal and conservative politics as aspects of an oppressive context dominated by a white elite. Equally committed to the development of a radical alternative to European American modernist aesthetics, he incorporates a wide range of cultural materials into specifically black performances. The clearest evidence of Bullins's radical sensibility, however, is his unwavering refusal to accept any dogma, white or black, traditional or revolutionary, without testing it against a multitude of perspectives and experiences. Throughout a career that has earned for him serious consideration alongside O'Neill and Tennessee Williams as the United States' greatest dramatist, Bullins has subjected the hypocrisies and corruptions of European and African American culture to rigorous examination and reevaluation. Refusing to accept any distinctions between aesthetics and politics or between the concerns of the artist and those of the mass community, Bullins demands that his audience synthesize abstract perception and concrete experience. Providing a set of terms useful to understanding the development of these concerns in his own work, Bullins defines a constituting dialectic in the black theatrical movement that emerged in the mid-1960s:

> This new thrust has two main branches—the *dialectic of change* and the *dialectic of experience*. The writers are attempting to answer questions concerning Black survival and future, one group through confronting the Black/white reality of America, the other, by heightening the dreadful white reality of being a modern Black captive and victim.

Essentially, the dialectic of change focuses attention on political problems demanding a specific form of action. The dialectic of experience focuses on a more "realistic" (though Bullins redefines the term to encompass aspects of reality frequently dismissed by programmatic realists) picture of black life in the context in which the problems continue to condition all experience. Reflecting his awareness that by definition each dialectic is in constant tension with the other, Bullins directs his work in the dialectic of change to altering the audience's actual experience. Similarly, his work in the dialectic of experience, while rarely explicitly didactic, leads inexorably to recognition of the need for change.

Bullins's work in both dialectics repudiates the tradition of the Western theater, which, he says, "shies away from social, political, psychological or any disturbing (revolutionary) reforms." Asserting the central importance of non-Western references, Bullins catalogs the "elements that make up the alphabet of the secret language used in Black theater," among them the blues, dance, African religion and mysticism, "familial nationalism," myth, science, ritual-ceremony, and "nigger street styles." Despite the commitment to an African American continuum evident in the construction and content of his plays, Bullins by no means repudiates all elements of the European American tradition. Even as he criticizes Brechtian epic theater, Bullins employs aspects of Brecht's dramatic rhetoric, designed to alienate the audience from received modes of perceiving theatrical, and by extension political, events. It is less important to catalog Bullins's allusions to William Shakespeare, O'Neill, Camus, or Genet than to recognize his use of their devices alongside those of Baraka, Soyinka, and Derek A. Walcott in the service of "Black artistic, political, and cultural consciousness."

Most of Bullins's work in the dialectic of change, which he calls "protest writing" when addressed to a European American audience and "Black revolutionary writing" when addressed to an African American audience, takes the form of short satiric or agitpropic plays. Frequently intended for street performance, these plays aim to attract a crowd and communicate an incisive message as rapidly as possible. Influential in the ritual theater of Baraka and in Bullins's own "Black Revolutionary Commercials," this strategy developed out of association with the black nationalist movement in cities such as New York, Detroit, Chicago, San Francisco, and Newark. Reflecting the need to avoid unplanned confrontations with police, the performances described in Bullins's influential "Short Statement on Street Theater" concentrate on establishing contact with groups unlikely to enter a theater, especially black working people and individuals living on the margins of society—gang members, junkies, prostitutes, and street people. Recognizing the impact of the media on American consciousness, Bullins frequently parodies media techniques, satirizing political advertising in "The American Flag Ritual" and "selling" positive black revolutionary images in "A Street Play." Somewhat longer though equally direct, "Death List," which can be performed by a troupe moving through the neighborhood streets, alerts the community to "enemies of the Black People," from Vernon Jordan to Whitney Young. Considered out of their performance context, many of these pieces seem simplistic or didactic, but their real intent is to realize Bullins's desire that "each individual in the crowd should have his sense of reality confronted, his consciousness assaulted." Because the "accidental" street audience comes into contact with the play while in its "normal" frame of mind, Bullins creates deliberately hyperbolic images to dislocate that mind-set in a very short period of time.

When writing revolutionary plays for performance in traditional theaters, Bullins tempers his rhetoric considerably. To be sure, *Dialect Determinism,* a warning against trivializing the revolutionary impulse of Malcolm X, and *The Gentleman Caller,* a satiric attack on master-slave mentality of black-white economic interaction,

both resemble the street plays in their insistence on revolutionary change. *Dialect Determinism* climaxes with the killing of a black "enemy," and *The Gentleman Caller* ends with a formulaic call for the rise of the foretold "Black nation that will survive, conquer and rule." The difference between these plays and the street theater lies not in message but in Bullins's way of involving the audience. Recognizing the different needs of an audience willing to seek out his work in the theater but frequently educated by the dominant culture, Bullins involves it in the analytic process leading to what seem, from a black nationalist perspective, relatively unambiguous political perceptions. Rather than asserting the messages at the start of the plays, therefore, he developed a satiric setting before stripping away the masks and distortions imposed by the audience's normal frame of reference on its recognition of his revolutionary message.

Along with Baraka, Marvin X, Adrienne Kennedy, and others, Bullins helped make the dialectic of change an important cultural force at the height of the Black Nationalist movement, but his most substantial achievements involve the dialectic of experience. Ranging from his impressionistic gallery plays and politically resonant problem plays to the intricately interconnected Twentieth Century Cycle, Bullins's work in this dialectic reveals a profound skepticism regarding revolutionary ideals that have not been tested against the actual contradictions of African American experience.

Street Sounds

Street Sounds, parts of which were later incorporated into *House Party,* represents Bullins's adaptation of the gallery approach pioneered by poets such as Robert Browning, Edgar Lee Masters (*Spoon River Anthology,* 1915), Melvin B. Tolson (*Harlem Gallery,* 1969), Gwendolyn

Brooks (*A Street in Bronzeville*, 1945), and Langston Hughes (*Montage of a Dream Deferred*, 1951). By montaging a series of thirty- to ninety-second monologues, Bullins suggests the tensions common to the experience of seemingly disparate elements of the African American community. Superficially, the characters can be divided into categories such as politicians (Harlem Politician, Black Student), hustlers (Dope Seller, The Thief), artists (Black Revolutionary Artist, Black Writer), street people (Fried Brains, Corner Brother), working people (Errand Boy, Workin' Man), and women (The Loved One, The Virgin, Harlem Mother).None of the categories, however, survives careful examination; individual women could be placed in every other category; the Black Revolutionary Artist combines politics and art; the Harlem Politician, politics and crime. To a large extent, all types ultimately amount to variations on several social and psychological themes that render the surface distinctions far less important than they initially appear.

Although their particular responses vary considerably, each character in *Street Sounds* confronts the decaying community described by The Old-timer: "They changin' things, you know? Freeways comin' through tearin' up the old neighborhood. Buildings goin' down, and not bein' put up again. Abandoned houses that are boarded up, the homes of winos, junkies and rats, catchin' fire and never bein' fixed up." As a result, many share the Workin' Man's feeling of being "trapped inside of ourselves, inside our experience." Throughout the play, Bullins portrays a deep-seated feeling of racial inferiority that results in black men's obsession with white women (Slightly Confused Negro, The Explainer) and a casual willingness to exploit or attack other blacks (The Thief, The Doubter, Young West Indian Revolutionary Poet). Attempting to salvage some sense of freedom or self-worth, or simply to find momentary release

from the struggle, individuals turn to art, sex, politics, or drugs, but the weight of their context pressures each toward the psychological collapse of Fried Brains, the hypocritical delusions of the NonIdeological Nigger, or the unfounded self-glorification of The Genius. Even when individuals embrace political causes, Bullins remains skeptical. The Theorist, The Rapper, and The Liar, who ironically echoes Bullins's aesthetic when he declares, "Even when I lie, I lie truthfully I'm no stranger to experience," express ideological positions similar to those Bullins advocates in the dialectic of change. None, however, seems even marginally aware that his grand pronouncements have no impact on the experience of the black community. The Rapper's revolutionary call—"We are slaves now, this moment in time, brothers, but let this moment end with this breath and let us unite as fearless revolutionaries in the pursuit of world liberation!"—comes between the entirely apolitical monologues of Waiting and Bewildered. Similarly, the Black Revolutionary Artist's endorsement of" a cosmic revolution that will liberate the highest potential of nationhood in the universe" is followed by the Black Dee Jay's claim that "BLACK MEANS BUY!" The sales pitch seems to have a great deal more power than the nationalist vision in the lives of the Soul Sister and the Corner Brother, whose monologues frame the Black Revolutionary Artist-Black Dee Jay sequence.

One of Bullins's characteristic "signatures" is the attribution of his own ideas to characters unwilling or unable to act or inspire others to act on them. Reflecting his belief that without action ideals have little value, Bullins structures *Street Sounds* to insist on the need for connection. The opening monologue, delivered by a white "Pig," establishes a political context similar to the one that Bullins uses in the dialectic of change, within which the dialectic of experience proceeds. Reducing all blacks to a single type, the nigger, Pig wishes only to "be a this nig-gerass good." Although Bullins clearly perceives the police as a basic oppressive force in the ghetto, he does not concentrate on highlighting the audience's awareness of that point. Rather, by the end of the play he has made it clear that the African American community in actuality beats its own ass. The absence of any other white character in the play reflects Bullins's focus on the nature of victimization as experienced within and perpetuated by the black commu-nity. The Harlem Mother monologue that closes the play concentrates almost entirely on details of experience. Although she presents no hyperbolic portraits of white oppressors, her memories of the impact on her family of eco-nomic exploitation, hunger, and government indifference carry more politically dramatic power than does any abstraction. This by no means indicates Bullins's distaste for political analysis or a repudiation of the opening mono-logues; rather, it reflects his awareness that ab-stract principles signify little unless they are em-bedded in the experience first of the audience and, ultimately, of the community as a whole.

The Taking of Miss Janie

Although Bullins consistently directs his work toward the African American community, his work in the dialectic of experience inevitably in-volves the interaction of blacks and whites. *The Taking of Miss Janie*, perhaps his single most powerful play, focuses on a group of California college students, several of whom first appeared in *The Pig Pen*. In part a meditation on the heri-tage of the 1960s Civil Rights movement, *The Taking of Miss Janie* revolves around the sexual and political tensions between and within racial groups. Although most of the characters are readily identifiable types—the stage directions identify Rick as a cultural nationalist, Janie as a California beach girl, Flossy as a "soul sister"—Bullins explores individual characters in depth, concentrating on their tendency to re-vert to behavior patterns, especially when they assume rigid ideological or social roles. The central incident of the play—the "rape" of the white Janie by Monty, a black friend of long standing—provides a severely alienating image of this tendency to both black and white audi-ences. After committing a murder, which may or may not be real, when the half-mythic Jewish beatnik Mort Silberstein taunts Monty for his inability to separate his consciousness from Eu-ropean American influences, Monty undresses Janie, who does not resist or cooperate, in a rape scene devoid of violence, love, anger, or physical desire. Unable to resist the pressures that make their traditional Western claim to in-dividuality seem naive, both Janie and Monty seem resigned to living out a "fate" that in fact depends on their acquiescence. Monty accepts the role of the "black beast" who rapes and mur-ders white people, while Janie plays the role of plantation mistress. Although these intellectu-ally articulate characters do not genuinely be-lieve in the reality of their roles, their ironic at-titude ultimately makes no difference, for the roles govern their actions.

Although the rape incident provides the frame for *The Taking of Miss Janie*, Monty and Janie exist in a gallery of characters whose col-lective inability to maintain individual integrity testifies to the larger dimensions of the problem. Rick and Len enact the classic argument be-tween nationalism and eclecticism in the black political/intellectual world; Peggy tires of con-fronting the neuroses of black men and turns to lesbianism; "hip" white boy Lonnie moves from fad to fad, turning his contact with black cul-ture to financial advantage in the music busi-ness; several couples drift aimlessly into interra-cial marriages. Alternating scenes in which characters interact with monologues in which an   individual   reflects   on   his   future development, Bullins reveals his characters' inability to create alternatives to the "fate" within which they feel themselves trapped. Although none demonstrates a fully developed ability to integrate ideals and experiences, several seem substantially less alienated than others. In many ways the least deluded, Peggy accepts both her lesbianism and her responsibility for her past actions. Her comment on the 1960s articulates a basic aspect of Bullins's vision: "We all failed. Failed ourselves in that serious time known as the sixties. And by failing ourselves we also failed in the test of the times." Her honesty and insight also have a positive impact on the black nationalist Rick, who during a conversation with Peggy abandons his grandiose rhetoric on the "devil's tricknology" (a phrase adopted from the Nation of Islam)—rhetoric that masks a deep hostility toward other blacks. Although he has previously attacked her as a lesbian "freak," Rick's final lines to Peggy suggest another aspect of Bullins's perspective: "Ya know, it be about what you make it anyway." Any adequate response to *The Taking of Miss Janie* must take into account not only Peggy's survival strategy and Rick's nationalistic idealism but also Janie's willed naivete and the accuracy of Mort's claim that, despite his invocation of Mao Zedong, Malcolm X, and Frantz Fanon, Monty is still on some levels "FREAKY FOR JESUS!" Bullins presents no simple answers nor does he simply contemplate the wasteland. Rather, as in almost all of his work in both the dialectic of change and the dialectic of experience, he challenges his audience to make something out of the fragments and failures he portrays.

The Twentieth Century Cycle

The Twentieth Century Cycle, Bullins's most far-reaching confrontation with the American experience, brings together most of his theatrical and thematic concerns and seems destined to stand as his major work. Several of the projected twenty plays of the cycle have been performed, including *In the Wine Time, In New England Winter, The Duplex, The Fabulous Miss Marie, Home Boy, Daddy,* and *Salaam, Huey Newton, Salaam.* Although the underlying structure of the cycle remains a matter of speculation, it clearly focuses on the experience of a group of black people traversing various areas of America's cultural and physical geography during the 1950s, 1960s, and 1970s. Recurring characters, including Cliff Dawson, his nephew Ray Crawford, Michael Brown (who first appeared in a play not part of the cycle, *A Son, Come Home*), and Steve Benson, a black intellectual whose life story resembles Bullins's own, serve to unify the cycle's imaginative landscape. In addition, a core of thematic concerns, viewed from various perspectives, unites the plays.

In the Wine Time, the initial play of the cycle, establishes a basic set of thematic concerns, including the incompatibility of Ray's romantic idealism with the brutality and potential violence of his northern urban environment. Stylistically, the play typifies the cycle in its juxtaposition of introverted lyricism, naturalistic dialogue, technological staging, and African American music and dance. Individual plays combine these elements in different ways. *In New England Winter*, set in California, draws much of its power from a poetic image of the snow that takes on racial, geographical, and metaphysical meanings in Steve Benson's consciousness. Each act of *The Duplex* opens with a jazz, blues, or rhythm-and-blues song that sets a framework for the ensuing action. *The Fabulous Miss Marie* uses televised images of the Civil Rights movement both to highlight its characters' personal desperation and to emphasize the role of technology in creating and aggravating their problems of perception. Drawing directly on the reflexive rhetoric of European American modernism, *In New England Winter* revolves around Steve Benson's construction of a "play," involving a planned robbery, which he plans to enact in reality but which he also uses as a means of working out his psychological desires.

Ultimately, Bullins's *Salaam, Huey Newton, Salaam* extends Bullins's vision into an imaginary future to depict the former Black Panther leader down and out in the wake of a black revolution. Bullins suggests that each of these approaches reflects a perspective on experience actually present in contemporary American society and that any vision failing to take all of them into account will inevitably fall victim to the dissociation of ideals and experience that plunges many of Bullins's characters into despair or violence. While some of his characters, most notably Steve Benson, seem intermittently aware of the source of their alienation and are potentially capable of imaginative responses with political impact, Bullins leaves the resolution of the cycle plays to the members of the audience. Portraying the futility of socially prescribed roles and of any consciousness not directly engaged with its total context, Bullins continues to challenge his audience to attain a perspective from which the dialectic of experience and the dialectic of change can be realized as one and the same.

Boy X Man

In *Boy X Man* (the "X" means "times," as in an equation), Bullins constructs a memory play in which a young man's return to attend his mother's funeral prompts him to remember his boyhood with his mother and her "friend," who raised him as a son. The song "Blues in the Night," his first crib memory, provides the transition to scenes from the 1930s and 1940s. Ernie's mother, Brenda, is a single mom and dancer whose life improves dramatically when she meets Will, who lacks ambition but who

nevertheless provides his "family" with much-needed stability. The play includes a series of highly emotional vignettes, including the following: Brenda's reliving of her discovery of her dead mother; Will's reliving of his Nazi concentration camp experiences; and, to provide balance, Will's attending and listening to Negro League baseball games. Bullins provides his audience with a glimpse of the problems, prejudice, and tensions that black American families encounter; but because many of the problems are not confined to the black experience, the play reflects on American life in general.

Other Literary Forms

Although known primarily as a playwright, Ed Bullins has also worked in forms ranging from fiction and the essay to the "revolutionary television commercial." His novel *The Reluctant Rapist* focuses on the early experience of Steve Benson, the semi-autobiographical character who appears in several plays, including *In New England Winter, The Duplex*, and *The Fabulous Miss Marie*. *The Hungered Ones: Early Writings*, a collection of Bullins's early stories and essays, some of which are loosely autobiographical, provides an overview of his early perspective. Active as an editor and a theorist throughout his career, Bullins has written introductions to anthologies such as *The New Lafayette Theater Presents* and *New Plays from the Black Theatre*. Along with the introduction to his own collection *The Theme Is Blackness*, these introductions provide a powerful and influential theoretical statement on the aesthetics and politics of the African American theater during the late 1960s and early 1970s. *The Theme Is Blackness* also contains scripts for "rituals" and mixed-media productions, including "Black Revolutionary Commercials," which reflect the concern with electronic media visible in many of his later plays.

Bibliography

Armstrong, Linda. "Bullins Explains the Theme Behind His Theatrical Writings." *Amsterdam News*, April 26, 1997, p. 21-23. A brief description of Bullins's play *BoyXMan* and discussion of the play by the playwright.

Bigsby, C. W. E. *The Second Black Renaissance: Essays in Black Literature*. Westport, Conn.: Greenwood Press, 1980. A strong chapter, "Black Drama: The Public Voice," includes a protracted discussion of Bullins's work as "a moving spirit behind the founding of another black theatre institution, the New Lafayette Theatre." Index.

Bullins, Ed. "Ed Bullins: Now." http://www.edbullins.com/. Accessed September 1, 2005. Bullins's Web site has a brief biography, a list of his plays, and, most important, information on upcoming performances of his work.

DeGaetani, John L. *A Search for a Postmodern Theater: Interviews with Contemporary Playwrights*. New York: Greenwood Press, 1991. After writing more than fifty plays, Bullins still admires Samuel Beckett and still deals with the theme of "the breakdown of communications among loved ones, and misunderstanding among good intentions." Contains an excellent update of his activities and a strong discussion of the theme of rape in his work.

Hay, Samuel A. *Ed Bullins: A Literary Biography*. Detroit: Wayne State University Press, 1997. Despite the title, Hay's "biography" contains few biographical details and really focuses on Bullins's more than one hundred dramas, which he examines in some detail. The book, which was written with Bullins's approval, provides readers with the social, political, and intellectual context in which the plays were written. Hay includes an exhaustive bibliography, which helps to resolve some issues about the dates the plays were written, produced, and published. It is the only full-length treatment of Bullins's work.

_____. "Structural Elements in Ed Bullins's Plays." In *The Theater of Black Americans*, edited by Errol Hill. Vol. 1. Englewood Cliffs, N.J.: Prentice-Hall, 1980. Examines structural consistencies in *The Duplex* but adds valuable comments on earlier works. Begins with Walter Kerr's review, comparing his remarks with Bullins's structural elements, such as "desultory conversation," "unplanned and casual action," and "frequently disconnected dialogue." Compares Bullins's work with Anton Chekhov's *Tri sestry* (pr., pb. 1901; *Three Sisters*, 1920).

Herman, William. *Understanding Contemporary American Drama*. Columbia: University of South Carolina Press, 1987. A long chapter on Bullins, "The People in This Play Are Black," details his major plays to 1984. Good biographical sketch of Bullins's New Lafayette connections, including his editorship of *Black Theatre*, the theater company's journal.

Sanders, Leslie Catherine. *The Development of Black Theater in America: From Shadows to Selves*. Baton Rouge: Louisiana State University Press, 1988. Sanders devotes a lengthy chapter of the book to Bullins. The focus is on Bullins's work for the New Lafayette productions in New York and on some of his major plays: *The Taking of Miss Janie*, *A Son, Come Home*, *The Electronic Nigger*, *In the Wine Time*, *Goin' a Buffalo*, and *Clara's Ole Man*.

Sell, Mike. "Bullins as Editorial Performer: Textual Power and the Limits of Performance in the Black Arts Movement." *Theatre Journal* 53, no. 3 (October, 2001): 411-429. Analyzes Bullins's contributions to the Black Arts Movement and his efforts to promote an open dialogue on racial issues.

Williams, Mance. *Black Theatre in the 1960s and 1970s: A Historical-Critical Analysis of the Movement*. Westport, Conn.: Greenwood Press, 1985. By concentrating on theater movements rather than on the playwright, this study underlines Bullins's strong administrative and inspirational contributions to the African American theater experience. Includes discussion of his literary style, use of music, views on street theater, and his relationship with the New Lafayette Theater. Index and bibliography.

— *Thomas L. Erskine; Thomas J. Taylor;*
Craig Werner; Robert C. Evans

Octavia E. Butler

Novelist

Born: Pasadena, California; June 22, 1947

Died: Seattle, Washington; February 24, 2006

LONG FICTION: *Patternmaster,* 1976; *Mind of My Mind,* 1977; *Survivor,* 1978; *Kindred,* 1979; *Wild Seed,* 1980; *Clay's Ark,* 1984; *Dawn,* 1987; *Adulthood Rites,* 1988; *Imago,* 1989; *Parable of the Sower,* 1993; *Parable of the Talents,* 1998; *Fledgling,* 2005.

SHORT FICTION: "Crossover," 1971; "Near of Kin," 1979; "Speech Sounds," 1983; "Blood-child," 1984; "The Evening and the Morning and the Night," 1987.

NONFICTION: "Birth of a Writer," 1989 (later renamed "Positive Obsession"); "Furor Scribendi," 1993.

MISCELLANEOUS: *Bloodchild, and Other Stories,* 1995 (collected short stories and essays).

Achievements

Broad and growing popularity among readers of science fiction greeted first Octavia E. Butler's Patternist series of novels and then her Xenogenesis series. She won multiple prizes for her short fiction as well as critical acceptance for her longer work. Her portrayal of the "loner" of science and adventure fiction is given depth and complexity by the implied treatment of sexual and racial prejudices and the direct treatment of social power structures. Entertaining stories with alien settings, sometimes narrated by alien characters, provided a platform for her contemplative approach to human dynamics. Love and miscegenation, male-female roles, the responsibilities of power, and the urge to survive are among the recurring themes that insistently invite the reader to reexamine long-standing attitudes.

Biography

Octavia E. Butler grew up in a family that reflected some of the hard realities for African Americans. Her father, who died when she was very young, shined shoes; her mother, who had been taken from school at the age of ten, supported herself by working as a maid.

Reared by her mother, grandmother, and other relatives, Butler felt most comfortable in the company of her adult relatives, even while she was uncomfortable with a social system that routinely denied their humanity. She was tall for her age, shy, bookish, and further set off from her peer group by strict Baptist prohibitions against dancing and the use of makeup. Her escape from a less-than-satisfactory everyday life was provided by her ability to write. She began writing when she was about ten years old and began to experiment with science fiction one day at age twelve, when she decided that she could write a better story than the one of the poor science-fiction film she was watching on television.

Her family did not support her decision to write, and her teachers did not support her choice of science fiction as a medium. She attended Pasadena City College and then

Photo by Malcolm Ali, courtesy of Getty Images

California State College at Los Angeles, where she was unable to major in creative writing but took a potpourri of other subjects. After attending evening writing classes at the University of California at Los Angeles (UCLA), she met science-fiction writer Harlan Ellison through the Writers Guild of America, and he brought her to the Clarion Science Fiction Writers Workshop in 1970. Butler continued her study of science-fiction writing in classes taught by Ellison at UCLA. Although she had sold some of her science fiction as early as 1970, her breakthrough publication came in 1976 with *Patternmaster,* with which she began the Patternist series. She went on to fashion a successful career that was cut short by a fatal stroke in 2006.

Analysis: Long Fiction

Octavia E. Butler presented a version of humanity as a congenitally flawed species, possibly doomed to destroy itself because it is both intelligent and hierarchical. In this sense, her work does not follow the lead of Isaac Asimov's *Foundation* series (1951-1993), Arthur C. Clarke's *2001: A Space Odyssey* (1968), and similar science fiction in offering an optimistic, rational, and agreeable view of humanity. As Butler herself said, she did not believe that imperfect human beings can create a perfect world.

Butler's diverse societies are controlled by Darwinian realities: competition to survive, struggle for power, domination of the weak by the strong, parasitism, and the like. Within this framework, there is room for both pain and hope, for idealism, love, bravery and compassion, for an outsider to challenge the system, defeat the tyrant, and win power. There is, however, no happy ending but a conclusion in which the lead characters have done their best and the world (wherever it is) remains ethically and morally unchanged.

In contemplative but vividly descriptive prose, Butler tells her story from the first- or third-person perspective of someone who is passive or disfranchised and is forced by events or other characters to take significant action. In order to fulfill her destiny, often the protagonist—most often a black woman—must do or experience something not only unprecedented but also alien and even grotesque. What begins as an act of courage usually ends as an act of love, or at least understanding. Through an alien, alienated, or excluded person, a crucial compromise is struck, civilization is preserved in some form, and life goes on.

Butler's fiction reflects and refracts the attempts—and failures—of the twentieth century to deal with ethnic and sexual prejudice. She frequently used standard images of horror, such as snakelike or insectlike beings, to provoke an aversion that the reader is unable to sustain as the humanity of the alien becomes clear. Being human does not mean being faultless—merely familiar. Therefore, each of her human, non-human, and quasihuman societies displays its own form of selfishness and, usually, a very clear power structure. The maturity and independence achieved by the protagonists imply not the advent of universal equality and harmony but merely a pragmatic personal obligation to wield power responsibly. Characters unable to alter or escape the order of things are expected to show a sort of noblesse oblige.

Kindred

Butler's most atypical work in terms of genre is *Kindred*, published in 1979. While the protagonist is shuttled helplessly back and forth between 1824 and 1976 in a kind of time travel, this device is of no intrinsic importance to the message of the story. At one point, the heroine, Edana, asks herself how it can be that she—the as yet unborn black descendant of a nineteenth century slaveholder—can be the instrument of keeping that slaveholder alive until he fulfills his destiny and fathers her ancestor. By asking, she preempts the reader's own curiosity, and when there is no answer, the story simply moves forward.

Kindred uses a black woman of the 1970s and her white husband to probe beneath the surface stereotypes of "happy slave" on the one hand and "Uncle Tom" on the other. When Edana and Kevin are separated by the South of 1824 into slave and master, they each begin unwillingly to imbibe the feelings and attitudes of the time from that perspective. The impact of the novel results from Butler's ability to evoke the antebellum South from two points of view: the stubborn, desperate attempts of blacks to lead meaningful lives in a society that disregards

family ties and disposes of individuals as marketable animals; and the uncomprehending, sometimes oppressively benevolent ruthlessness of a ruling class that defines slaves in terms of what trouble or pleasure they can give.

The Patternist Series

Butler began her science-fiction novels with the Patternist series, and in this series the reader can observe the beginning of her development from a writer of well-crafted science/adventure fiction to a writer who recalls in her own way the reflectiveness of Ray Bradbury.

First written but third published was *Survivor*, the tale of an orphaned Afro-Asian girl who becomes a "wild human" in order to survive in a harsh environment. She is found and adopted, in an atypical act of reaching out, by two members of the Missionaries—a nouveau-Fundamentalist Christian sect. The Missionaries's escape from a hostile Earth takes them to a planet inhabited by furred bipeds, whom they regard as less than human. These beings are, in fact, a science-fiction version of the noble savage, but the protagonist is alone in recognizing their nobility. Internally untouched by Missionary dogma, she is truly socialized as a captive of the Tehkohn and, in the end, chooses them as her own people. Her survival and success require an understanding of the color classes of fur among the Tehkohn, where blue is the highest color, suggesting a tongue-in-cheek reference to "blue blood." She makes her own way by dint of qualities often found in protagonists of adventure novels: physical agility, courage, and adaptability.

Patternmaster features an appealing duo, with the younger son of the Patternmaster—the psychic control-central of a society of advanced human beings—confronting and defeating his brutal older brother in an unwanted competition to succeed their father. His helper, mentor, and lover is a bisexual Healer; he trusts her enough to "link" with her in order to pool their psionic power. She teaches him that Healing is, paradoxically, also a deadly knowledge of the body with which he can defeat his brother. Thus, trust and cooperation overcome ambition and brutality. The "mutes" of this novel are nontelepathic human beings whose vulnerability to cruelty or kindness and inability to control their own destinies reflect the earlier status of slaves in America.

Mary, in *Mind of My Mind*, is a "latent" who must undergo a painful transition in order to become a full-fledged telepath. The pain and danger of this passage from adolescence to adulthood are emblematic of the turmoil of coming of age everywhere and of the physical or psychological pain that is required as the price of initiation in many, if not all, societies. The deadened, sometimes crazed, helplessness of latents who cannot become telepaths but must continue to live with the intrusive offal of other people's thoughts is a powerful metaphor for people trapped in poverty, and some of the horrors Butler paints are familiar.

Mary has no choice at first. The founder of her "people," a nontelepathic immortal named Doro, prescribes her actions until she acquires her power. He senses danger only when she reaches out reflexively to control other, powerful telepaths, thus forming the first Pattern. Mary's destruction of the pitiless Doro, like the death of the older brother in *Patternmaster* and of the rival alien chief in *Survivor*, is foreordained and accomplished with a ruthlessness appropriate to the society and to the character of the victim. The incipient change in Butler's style is evident here in the comparative lack of adventure-action sequences and in the greater concentration on psychological adaptation to and responsible use of social power.

The technique of historical reconstruction is seen again in *Wild Seed*, whose evocation of Ibo

West Africa owes something to the work of writers such as Chinua Achebe. *Wild Seed* traces Doro and Anyanwu from their seventeenth century meeting in West Africa to the establishment of Doro's settlements in America. Doro is a centuries-old being who lives by "taking" another man's or woman's body and leaving his previous body behind. Anyanwu is a descendant of Doro. She is a "wild seed" because she has unexpectedly developed the power to shape-shift, becoming young or old, an animal, fish, or bird, at will. Their relationship is completely one-sided, since Doro could "take" her any time he chose, although he would not acquire her special abilities. His long life and unremitting efforts to create a special people of his own have left him completely insensitive to the needs and desires of others. Anyanwu finally achieves some balance of power simply by being willing to die and leave Doro without the only companion who could last beyond a mortal lifetime.

The last Patternist novel, *Clay's Ark*, introduces the reader to those brutish enemies of both Patternist and "mute" humanity, the Clayarks, so named because the disease that created them was brought back to Earth on a spaceship called "Clay's Ark." The disease culls its victims, killing some and imbuing others with a will to live that overcomes the horror of their new existence. They become faster and stronger, and their children evolve even further, taking on animal shapes and attributes of speed, power, and heightened senses, but retaining human thought and use of their hands. In the guise of a horror story, *Clay's Ark* follows the first Clayarks' attempt to come to terms with their condition and live responsibly, shut off from civilization. Their failed attempt demonstrates that it is not possible to contain cataclysmic natural change, but the story enlists the reader's sympathy for human beings who suffer even as they afflict others.

The Xenogenesis Series

With the exception of *Clay's Ark*, where there is much action, the pace of Butler's novels slows progressively; action is increasingly internalized and psychological. Moral judgments and the contest of right versus wrong dwindle to insignificance. The next, and quite logical, development is the Xenogenesis series: *Dawn, Adulthood Rites,* and *Imago*. This series confirmed Butler as a science-fiction writer of sufficient depth to be of significance beyond the genre.

The change from her originally projected title for the series is informative. "Exogenesis" would have implied merely genesis effected from outside humanity. "Xenogenesis" has both text and subtext. Its meaning is the production of an organism altogether and permanently unlike the parent. The subtext is a function of the best-known English word built on the same root: xenophobia, fear and dislike of that which is foreign or alien. Butler makes the series title a statement of the thesis she will address.

Many of the techniques and themes of her earlier, developing style come to fruition here: the alternating use of first- and third-person narrative, the slow pace of a plot laden with psychological development and sensory perceptions, the meticulous foreclosure of value judgments, the concern with hierarchy and responsibility, the objective observation of feelings of revulsion for that which is alien, and those feelings' gradual dissipation as the alien becomes familiar and therefore less threatening. Action in the series is sparse, normally kept to the minimum necessary to maintain the pace of psychological and social observation. In some ways, it is a chilling series of seductions of human beings by an alien, benevolent oppressor. In some ways, it is a demonstration of the infinite capacity of humanity to seek satisfaction in the destruction of itself and others.

Words used to describe two of Butler's shorter works in the 1984 and 1987 issues of *The Year's Best Science Fiction* may serve here as a characterization of the Xenogenesis series: "strange, grotesque, disturbing . . . and ultimately moving," a "tale of despair, resignation, and, most painfully, hope." It is apparently to examine the capacity of human beings to adapt, to survive, and perhaps stubbornly to pursue a self-destructive course of action that Butler has created the nightmarish situation that the reader encounters in *Dawn*.

Dawn

In a world devastated by nuclear exchange between East and West, the dying remnants of humanity survive largely in the Southern Hemisphere. The heroine of *Dawn* is an African, Lilith, whose name suggests the demonic goddess of Hebrew tradition, the famous medieval witch who appears in Johann Wolfgang von Goethe's *Faust* (1808, 1833), and the medieval, alternate "first mother" who was put aside in favor of Eve.

Enter the Oankali, a nonviolent race of benevolent parasites and genetic engineers, who exist for the opportunity of combining with other species to acquire new cellular "knowledge" and capabilities. They live for miscegenation. They are trisexual: male, female, and ooloi. The ooloi is the indispensable link between male and female, channeling, altering, or amplifying all genetic material and sexual contact, including transfer of sperm and pleasurable sensations. The ooloi is capable of internal healing; for example, one cures Lilith of a cancer and finds the cancer to be an exciting new biological material with which to work.

The Oankali blend with another species by linking a male and female of that species and a male and female Oankali through an ooloi.

Thereafter, independent conception is not possible for those members of that species. The progeny are "constructs," who, at least at first, resemble their direct parents but carry genetic change within them. Lilith's first husband is killed in *Dawn*, but she bears his child posthumously because Nikanj, the ooloi that has chosen her, has preserved his seed. The resultant humanoid male child is the protagonist of *Adulthood Rites*, while a much later child of Lilith with another husband and the same Oankali parents is the protagonist of *Imago*.

Lilith is at first appalled by even the more humanoid Oankali, with their Medusan tentacles and sensory arms. She is gradually acclimated to them, cooperates with them to save humanity, bears children with them, is overwhelmed by the sensory pleasure they can give, and becomes sympathetic to their need to unite with other species, but she is never fully resigned. In *Imago*, Lilith compares the Oankali's description of the "flavors" of human beings to physical cannibalism and implies that the spiritual equivalent is no less predatory.

Lilith's conversion from complete repugnance in *Dawn*, a stylistic tour de force, shapes the following novels, as human beings are ultimately allowed a choice of living with the Oankali, staying behind on a doomed and barren Earth, or living in an experimental, all-human world on Mars. The Oankali, who seem to make decisions as a kind of committee-of-the-whole, foresee that the same old combination of intelligence and hierarchical tendencies (in a rather Darwinian sense) will lead this last outpost of humanity to destroy itself. No one convincingly denies it.

Adulthood Rites and Imago

Butler's stylistic virtuosity also extended to narrative person. *Dawn* is a third-person account of Lilith's absorption into the Oankali social structure; *Adulthood Rites* is the third-person narrative of Akin, a male-human construct, who convinces the more rational human beings left on Earth to trust the Oankali, and convinces the Oankali to offer the humans the choice of planetary residences; *Imago* is a first-person account of Jodahs, a child whose transformation to adulthood reveals it to be an ooloi. Use of the first-person narrative to tell the story of an apparent human who becomes wholly alien in both psychology and physiology is risky but rewarding. Through the eyes of a being routinely referred to as "it" in its own society, the reader observes its benevolent stalking and drug-induced brainwashing of human mates and the final planting of a seed that will grow into an organic town and then an organic spaceship, which will carry Jodahs and his people to new worlds for new genetic blendings.

Imago's conclusion serves as a reminder that Butler's imaginary worlds are primarily arenas for hard, necessary decisions in the business of survival. There is compassion as well as bitterness, and love as well as prejudice, but there is no triumph or glory. There is only doing what must be done as responsibly as possible.

Parable of the Sower

Parable of the Sower was published in 1993. It is set in California in 2024. The narrator is a fifteen-year-old African American girl who lives with her family in the fictitious town of Robledo, some twenty miles from Los Angeles. At the time of the story, the social order has nearly disintegrated. Society consists of "haves" and "have-nots." The haves live in walled and fortified neighborhoods; the have-nots roam outside the walls along with packs of wild dogs and drug addicts called "Paints," whose addiction imbues them with an orgasmic desire to burn things. Apparently due to the follies of humankind, the climate has been altered, and the entire world is in a state of near-collapse. Disease is rampant, natural disasters are frequent, and though there are stores, some jobs, and even television programming, the social order, at least in California, is almost gone.

Against this backdrop, the heroine, Lauren Olamina, founds anew religion named Earthseed. The novel takes the form of a journal Lauren keeps. Entries are dated and each chapter is prefaced with a passage from the new religion, the essence of which is that everything changes, even God. In fact, God is change.

Butler said that humankind is not likely to change itself, but that humans will go elsewhere and be forced to change. When the Paints destroy Lauren's neighborhood and most of her family, she treks north toward Canada, and new members join her group, one by one. Most survive and reach their destination, a burned farm in Oregon. The ending is a classic Butler resolution: There is no promised land; people who have not changed generally perish. Lauren has changed nothing in society; she has merely adapted and learned to survive. The structure, style, and plot of *Parable of the Sower* are all deceptively simple. Beneath the surface of the story, the novel deals directly with social power, its use and abuse, and its possible consequences.

Other Literary Forms

In addition to her long fiction, Octavia E. Butler contributed short stories to various science-fiction collections and periodicals, including *Isaac Asimov's Science Fiction Magazine*, *Future Life*, and *Clarion*. Her story "Speech Sounds" won the Hugo Award in 1984; a short work of fiction, "Bloodchild," was honored with the Hugo and various other prizes in 1985.

Bibliography

Butler, Octavia E. "Interview with Octavia E. Butler." Interview by Larry McCaffery. In *Across the Wounded Galaxies*. Urbana: University of Illinois Press, 1990. Among the best of numerous Butler interviews.

Call, Lewis. "Structures of Desire: Erotic Power in the Speculative Fiction of Octavia Butler and Samuel Delany." *Rethinking History* 9, nos. 2/3 (June, 2005): 275-297. Discusses the power of Butler and Delany's works to both criticize traditional forms of slavery and also present alternative, positive forms of slavery.

Canavan, Gerry. *Octavia E. Butler*. Champagne: University of Illinois Press, 2016. Traces the development of Butler's career in chronological order, focusing of such matters as themes, politics, and Butler's refusal of easy answers to the questions she explored.

Crossley, Robert. Introduction to *Kindred*, by Octavia Butler. Boston: Beacon Press, 1988. One of the more scholarly critical appreciations of *Kindred*. Crossley deals with the political and social content of Butler's writing, noting how few science-fiction writers have been able to treat questions of race and sex without a patronizing attitude.

Curtis, Claire P. "Rehabilitating Utopia: Feminist Science Fiction and Finding the Ideal." *Contemporary Justice Review* 8, no. 2 (June, 2005): 147-163. The author studies the concept of utopia as it is presented in Butler's work, noting that Butler's tolerance and tendency toward pluralism make her utopian vision more sustainable.

Foster, Frances Smith. "Octavia Butler's Black Female Future Fiction." *Extrapolation* 23 (Spring, 1982): 37-49. A very early article, published before Butler had completed the *Patternmaster* series. The article outlines the way "Butler consciously explores the impact of race and sex on future society." Unfettered by the pretentious writing common to much later Butler criticism, Foster illuminates the early texts and, with Sandy Govan's articles, remains among the best Butler criticism.

Francis, Conseula, ed. *Conversations with Octavia Butler*. Jackson: UP of Mississippi, 2010. A collection of interviews ranging from 1980 to 2006 in which Butler discusses such matters as race, sex, and her rare position among science fiction writers of her era.

Govan, Sandra Y. "Connections, Links, and Extended Networks: Patterns in Octavia Butler's Science Fiction." *Black American Literature Forum* 18 (1984): 82-87. Demonstrates how Butler used elements of slave narratives and historical novels to produce a new kind of science fiction, one which "features black characters in major significant roles" and also "features black women as heroic characters, protagonists who either share power with men or who maintain their right to wield power on an equal basis." Govan's clear and convincing demonstration is enlightening and thought provoking.

Hampton, Gregory Jerome. *Changing Bodies in the Fiction of Octavia Butler: Slaves, Aliens, and Vampires.* Lanham, MD: Lexington Books, 2010. Explores various works by Butler; discusses her responses to Wole Soyinka and W. E. B. DuBois; and examines her thinking about such matters as migration, religion, vampires, utopia, race, and gender.

Hampton, Gregory Jerome, and Wanda M. Brooks. "Octavia Butler and Virginia Hamilton: Black Women Writers and Science." *English Journal* 92, no. 6 (July, 2003): 70-75. Brief discussion of works by Butler and Hamilton.

Jesser, Nancy. "Blood, Genes, and Gender in Octavia Butler's *Kindred* and *Dawn.*" *Extrapolation* 43, no. 1 (Spring, 2002): 3662. Using the characters of Lilith and Edana, Jesser looks at the ways in which Butler integrated feminism and theories of genetic development.

Long, Lisa A. "A Relative Pain: The Rape of History in Octavia Butler's *Kindred* and Phyllis Alesia Perry's *Stigmata.*" *College English* 64, no. 4 (March, 2002): 459-484. Discusses the many representations of pain and slavery in Butler's works.

Peppers, Cathy. "Dialogue Origins and Alien Identities in Butler's *Xenogenesis.*" *Science Fiction Studies* 22 (1995): 47-62. Peppers's article carefully lays out the way Butler used origin stories and the African American story of diaspora and slavery. An illuminating article with too much postmodern and poststructural verbiage.

Phillips, Jerry. "Title: The Intuition of the Future: Utopia and Catastrophe in Octavia Butler's *Parable of the Sower.*" *Novel: A Forum on Fiction* 35, nos. 2/3 (Spring/Summer, 2002): 299312. An interesting discussion of Butler's views on futurism, fascism, and California.

Reed, Brian K. "Behold the Woman: The Imaginary Wife in Octavia Butler's *Kindred.*" *CLA Journal* 47, no. 1 (September, 2003): 66-75. Provides a brief analysis of *Kindred*'s plot and delves into the conflict between the maternal instinct to protect a child and concern for a plantation's slaves.

Sands, Peter. "Octavia Butler's Chiastic Cannibalistics." *Utopian Studies* 14, no.1 (2003): 1-14. The author contends that Butler's use of cannibalism is in some ways a metaphor that facilitates discussion of mind-body dualism.

Shinn, Thelma. "The Wise Witches: Black Woman Mentors in the Fiction of Octavia E. Butler." In *Conjuring: Black Women, Fiction, and Literary Tradition*, edited by Marjorie Pryse and Hortense Spillers. Bloomington: Indiana University Press, 1985. An interesting discussion of some of Butler's early heroines. Shinn draws on Annis Pratt's work, which defines archetypal patterns in women's fiction. She then demonstrates convincingly how Butler employed wise witches in her fiction.

Steinberg, Marc. "Inverting History in Octavia Butler's Postmodern Slave Narrative." *African American Review* 38, no. 3 (Fall, 2004): 467-477. The author views *Kindred* as a starting point for discussion of literacy issues. Asserts that literacy and study of history are essential survival tools for those battling repression and violence.

Stillman, Peter G. "Dystopian Critiques, Utopian Possibilities and Human Purposes in Octavia Butler's *Parables.*" *Utopian Studies* 14, no. 1 (2003): 15-36. An analysis of the utopian vision presented in *Parable of the Sower* and *Parable of the Talents.*

Yaszek, Lisa. "'A Grim Fantasy': Remaking American History in Octavia Butler's *Kindred.*" *Signs: Journal of Women in Culture & Society* 28, no. 4 (Summer, 2003): 1053-1067. Presents *Kindred* as a mechanism for presenting African American women's stories and doing so in a way that frees them from many of the constraints of race and gender.

— James L. Hodge; John T. West III;
Robert C. Evans

Bebe Moore Campbell

Novelist and Memoirist

Born: Philadelphia, Pennsylvania; February 18, 1950

Died: Los Angeles, California; November 27, 2006

LONG FICTION: *Your Blues Ain't Like Mine*, 1992; *Brothers and Sisters*, 1994; *Singing in the Comeback Choir*, 1998; *What You Owe Me*, 2001; *72 Hour Hold*, 2005.

NONFICTION: *Successful Women, Angry Men: Backlash in the Two-Career Marriage*, 1986, revised 2000; *Sweet Summer: Growing Up with and Without My Dad*, 1989.

CHILDREN'S/YOUNG ADULT LITERA-TURE: *Sometimes My Mommy Gets Angry*, 2003 (Earl B. Lewis, illustrator); *Stompin' at the Savoy*, 2006 (Richard Yarde, illustrator); *I Get So Hungry*, 2008 (Amy Bates, illustrator).

SELECTED ARTICLES AND ESSAYS: "Staying in the Community," 1989; "Daddy's Girl," 1992; "Remember the 60s?," 1992; "Brothers and Sisters," 1993; "I Felt Rage-Then Fear," 1993; "Only Men can Prevent Spousal Abuse," 1994; "Coming Together: Can We See Beyond the Color of Our Skin?," 1995; "The Boy in the River," 1999; "Poor Health of African Americans," 2000.

Achievements

Bebe Moore Campbell has been called one of the most important African American authors of the twentieth century, and she has received numerous awards and grants and earned national attention and praise. She won the Body of Work Award from the National Association of Negro Business and Professional Women in 1978, received a National Endowment for the Arts Literature grant in 1980, was awarded the Mayor's Certificate of Appreciation from Los Angeles Mayor Tom Bradley, and won the National Association for the Advancement of Colored People (NAACP) Award for fiction in 1994. She had two radio dramas produced by the Midwestern Radio Theater, earning first place in one of its Workshop Competitions.

Biography

Though she did not grow up in a traditional two-parent family, Bebe Moore Campbell never felt an absence of love and understanding from either her mother or father. Her school months in Philadelphia were slightly constrained because of the close supervision of her mother, grandmother, and aunt, who oversaw her every move. They instructed her in proper speech, manners, and behavior. Summers with her father and his mother in North Carolina were much more carefree. There she felt total love and acceptance.

When she was in third grade, a teacher recognized her potential, placing her in a special creative-writing class. She began sending letters to her father that were intended to intrigue him—installments of stories—all of them calling for a response. She wanted to keep his interest alive all year long. Her idealization of her father ended abruptly when, at fourteen, she learned that his speeding had caused the crash that

Photo by Tom Herde, courtesy of the Boston Globe and Getty Images

resulted in his paralysis and lifelong need for a wheelchair and that he was responsible for another accident in which a young boy had been killed. Her initial anger abated, but the relationship suffered.

Campbell earned a B.S. degree in elementary education at the University of Pittsburgh, later teaching elementary school for ten years in Pittsburgh, Atlanta, and Washington, D.C. An early marriage ended in divorce. Campbell, as her mother had, assumed the responsibilities of a single parent. Her writing career began when the editor of *Essence* gave a lecture at Howard University. Campbell hurriedly handed her young daughter, Maia, to a friend for care so that she could chase the woman to the ladies room and tell her of her writing aspirations. The woman, impressed, helped Campbell enter the publishing world. Campbell moved to Los Angeles in the early 1980s. There she married a banker, Ellis Gordon, Jr., who also had a child, a son named Ellis Gordon III.

Analysis: Long Fiction

Bebe Moore Campbell's fiction is based largely on her own experiences as a female member of a racial minority in a white, male-dominated culture. Her works are sociopolitical, generally dealing with matters of race, class, and gender. They cover such issues as sexism and sexual harassment in the workplace, racism—black to black, white to black, and black to white—and issues of racial solidarity versus gender solidarity. Her works have received widespread approval, with only minor criticisms for a tendency to create somewhat one-dimensional characters and, at times, to present slightly unflattering pictures of women. She is considered a serious writer, who, while popular, never popularizes by resorting to superhuman characters in glamorous sexual situations. Her white characters, as well as her black ones, ring true. Some have questioned how she could enter the minds of people of a different race. In response, she has explained that she socializes with people of all races and classes and has close white friends who help her gain the perspective she needs.

Your Blues Ain't Like Mine

Your Blues Ain't Like Mine appeared on bestseller lists and was chosen by *The New York Times* as one of the most notable books of 1992. It is based on the actual 1955 Mississippi murder of Emmett Till, a black teenager who dared to speak to a white woman. Campbell's fictionalized account has a black northern boy, Armstrong Todd, staying with his southern grandmother while his divorced mother attempts to pull her life together in Chicago. Unfamiliar with the deep-seated racism in this part of the country, he teasingly recites some harmless French phrases to a bored, obviously bemused, white woman as she stands in a barroom door waiting for her husband. The woman, despite being ordered to stay in the truck by her abusive husband, had ventured toward the sounds of laughter and gaiety, so sadly lacking in her own life.

Her husband, Floyd Cox, himself a victim of constant verbal abuse from his father and brother (the favored son), sees obtaining retribution for this slight as a way of gaining his family's respect. He hunts down Armstrong because he wants to please his father. For a short while in the truck, drinking and laughing after they had just terrorized, beaten, and shot to death the frightened black fifteen-year-old, Floyd seems to have gained his father's acceptance. The sense of closeness is fleeting, however, since, upon his arrest, his father and brother all but abandon him.

Southern justice being what it was in the 1950s, Floyd Cox's punishment is minimal, and he is soon released from jail. The subsequent ruination of his family strongly interests Campbell. She wants to show their suffering as well as the suffering of the victim and his family. Campbell's point is that racism hurts the racist as well as the victim. She said that she chose to present both sides of the story because she firmly believes that until people understand the ramifications of racism, they cannot begin to deal with it. Through seeing and feeling the pain of others, even of unsympathetic characters, people will recognize that bias is hateful and ultimately harmful to all.

Campbell also explores the efforts of the murdered boy's family to make some sense out of what is left of their lives. The mother determines to have another son, one who will have a chance to experience a full life. However, this boy yields to the lure of the streets and soon has gang affiliations; his chances of survival are slim. Hopelessness and despair have turned black men against one another and each man against himself. The future seems bleak, with only a hint of promise when the son responds slightly to his father's initiative of friendship.

Brothers and Sisters

Brothers and Sisters takes place in Los Angeles, in the aftermath of the Rodney King verdict riots. It is a novel of relationships, most notably that between a black bank manager, Esther Jackson, and Mallory Post, a white loan officer. Mallory holds a position coveted by Esther but denied her because of racism. These two women are cautious friends, neither completely comfortable with the other race—one filled with underlying anger, the other always fearful of appearing racially insensitive. Esther is the sort of woman who will not date "down": She is insistent on running a kind of financial background check on her suitors. Mallory urges Esther to relax her demand for upward mobility and to date the mail-truck driver because he is nice and will treat her well. Campbell notes that Mallory, as a middle-class white woman, has "the freedom to exercise these choices because she's not so clutched about trying to get to the next rung on the ladder and thinking she's got to be with the proper partner to get there."

Campbell hoped that the novel would "serve as a kind of blueprint, to help people foster racial understanding." She says that "our strengths lie in saluting our differences and getting along." While she is aware that many of the problems in the black community have to do with institutionalized racism, she also feels that "African-Americans need to begin to look really closely and make some movement toward changing the problems" and to recognize that some of them are the result of choices they have made. The response to *Brothers and Sisters* was uncommon, in that hundreds of discussion groups formed to come to terms with its issues. In Prince George's County, Maryland, an area with a large black population as well as a relatively stable white one, the book became the basis of a community project: People studied the impact of bias and sought ways to deal effectively with communication breakdowns between races.

Campbell laments the abandonment of the old neighborhoods, feeling that integration should not entail embracing white communities at the expense of black ones. She urges middle-class blacks to stay in touch with those less fortunate, to mentor the young. She feels that men, in particular, must take steps toward regaining control of their children and of the streets. In an interview with Martha Satz published in the *Southwest Review* (Spring, 1996), she observed that the Million Man March, with its resultant reawakening of moral, ethical, familial, and racial responsibilities, may have been responsible for the dramatically lower number of arson incidents in Detroit on Halloween of that year.

Singing in the Comeback Choir

Singing in the Comeback Choir is the story of Malindy Walker, a once-famous entertainer who has fallen ungracefully into old age, with its sometimes attendant sense of the pointlessness of the battle. Her life consists mainly of stealthily smoking and drinking, despite admonitions from her doctor. Based loosely on Alberta Hunter, jazz legend of the 1940s and 1950s, Malindy is a fiercely independent soul who has no intention of bowing to her granddaughter's wish to have her cared for (and closely supervised) in a senior citizen compound. The old neighborhood in which she lives has fallen into ruin, but Malindy's friends are there; memories of her great triumphs, of her sequined gowns and the applause, seem to sustain her. Her underlying sadness is over her diminished singing ability. She sees herself as finished, so she partakes of the fleeting pleasures of alcohol and nicotine.

Her granddaughter, Maxine Lott McCoy, a highly successful television producer with a relatively good marriage and a child on the way, is a professional who bears some resemblance to Campbell herself. She comes to the rescue of her grandmother, only to find that she herself is the one who needs to be rescued—from the high-powered yet insular and protected world in which she has lost touch with her origins. Therein lies the point of the novel. The old neighborhoods are dying because they have been abandoned by those who could give them life, the ones who are capable of regeneration. Maxine is saddened by what is left of her grandmother's street and by the dead eyes of the neighborhood boy she once knew; now grown and playing at being a man, he curses her and makes sexually threatening gestures. She confronts him but sees that he is the wave of the future unless others can intervene and help.

Part of Campbell's intent in the novel was "to talk about the work that needs to be done" in order to salvage and rebuild the decaying neighborhoods and despairing lives. She has noted that she wants "black folks to do the hard work that we've done in the past that we haven't been doing as much in the years following the Civil Rights movement."

Other Literary Forms

Bebe Campbell's early works were primarily nonfiction. Her first book, *Successful Women, Angry Men: Backlash in the Two-Career Marriage,* delves into the effect of the feminist movement on family structure, most notably the shifting gender roles that result when women, either of necessity or in quest of self-actualization, seek work outside the home, sometimes upsetting the balance within. Her second work, *Sweet Summer: Growing Up with and Without My Dad,* is her memoir as a child of divorce having to spend the school year with her mother in Philadelphia and summer with her father in North Carolina. The book was hailed for showing loving relationships in the black community and for stressing the importance of men or male figures in young girls' lives. Poet Nikki Giovanni praised it for providing "a corrective to some of the destructive images of black men that are prevalent in our society" and doing so with great vitality and clarity. Campbell has produced nonfiction articles for a wide range of publications, including *Essence, The New York Times, The Washington Post,* the *Los Angeles Times, Black Enterprise, Working Mother, Adweek, Ms.,* and *Glamour;* she was a contributing editor for *Essence, Black Enterprise,* and *Savvy.* In the 1990s, she became a regular commentator on National Public Radio's *Morning Edition.*

Bibliography

Brown, Rosellen. "Race-Blind Angst." *New Leader* 88, no. 3 (May/June, 2005): 41-42. A thoughtful analysis of *72 Hour Hold.*

Campbell, Bebe Moore. "Bebe Moore Campbell." http://www .bebemoorecampbell.com/. Accessed September 1, 2005. Campbell's sophisticated Website offers answers to typical interview questions, articles about mental health and bipolar disorder, as well as a biography and links to sites that sell her books.

_____. "I Hope I Can Teach a Little Bit: An Interview with Bebe Moore Campbell." Interview by Martha Satz. *Southwest Review* 81 (Spring, 1996): 195-213. An in-depth discussion (which occurred in November, 1995) of Campbell's views on the need for African Americans to stay in touch with the old neighborhoods, particularly with the children who are still there and need mentoring.

_____. "An Interview with Bebe Moore Campbell." Interview by Jane Campbell. *Callaloo* 22, no. 4 (Fall, 1999): 954-973. A revealing portrait of the author's career and upbringing that provides valuable insights into the importance of geography (particularly the East Coast) in her novels and her most dominant influences.

Chambers, Veronica. "Which Counts More, Gender or Race?" *The New York Times Magazine,* December 25, 1994, 16-19. Chambers moderates a conversation between Bebe Moore Campbell and Joyce Carol Oates dealing with Black English, interracial dating, liberal white guilt, and the historic importance of the black church.

Edgerton, Clyde. "Medicine for Broken Souls." *The New York Times Book Review,* September 20, 1992, p. 13. Edgerton offers an interesting review of Campbell's *Your Blues Ain't Like Mine.*

Harwell, Osizwe Raena Jamila. *This Woman's Work: The Writing and Activism of Bebe Moore Campbell.* UP of Mississippi, 2016. Discusses Campbell's interests in various kinds of activism (such as campus, community, student, and mental health) and pays special attention to her first and last novels.

Head, John. "New Novel Centers on Issue Blacks Fail to Discuss: Mental Health." *The New Crisis* 112, no. 4 (July/August, 2005): 50-52. A brief but worthwhile look at Campbell's book *72 Hour Hold.*

Ladson-Billings, Gloria. "*Your Blues Ain't Like Mine:* Keeping Issues of Race and Racism on the Multicultural Agenda." *Theory Into Practice* 35, no. 5 (Fall, 1996): 248-256. Takes a closer look at Campbell's novel and at William Wilson's 1978 analysis of the roles of race and class to argue that discussion of racism must assume a higher priority on any multiculturalist agenda.

Olendorf, Donna, ed. *Contemporary Authors.* Vol. 139. Detroit: Gale, 1993. A brief biographical entry on Campbell appears on pages 76-77.

Powers, Retha. "A Tale of Two Women." *Ms.,* September/October, 1994, 78. An article discussing the merits of *Brothers and Sisters.*

See, Lisa. "Bebe Moore Campbell." *Publishers Weekly,* June 30, 1989, 82-83. Includes a discussion of *Sweet Summer: Growing Up with and Without My Dad* and an interview with Campbell.

White, Evelyn C. "Bebe Moore Campbell on Mental Illness." *Essence* 36, no. 3 (July, 2005): 149-151. The writer explains why she chose to deal with mental health in her latest book and gives advice to African Americans who struggle with mental health issues.

Winter, Kari J. "*Brothers and Sisters,* by B. M. Campbell." *African American Review* 31, no. 2 (Summer, 1997): 369-372. A comparative review of Bebe Moore Campbell's *Brothers and Sisters* and Gita Brown's *Be I Whole* (1995) in which Brown fares better. Campbell is charged with "replicating many of the objectifying, spiritually bankrupt attitudes of American capitalism" and using "cliche-ridden prose."

—*Gay Annette Zieger; Robert C. Evans*

Barbara Chase-Riboud

Novelist, Poet, and Artist

Born: Philadelphia, Pennsylvania; June 26, 1939

LONG FICTION: *Sally Hemings,* 1979; *Valide: A Novel of the Harem,* 1986, revised 1988; *Echo of Lions,* 1989; *The President's Daughter,* 1994; *Hottentot Venus,* 2003.

POETRY: *From Memphis and Peking,* 1974; *Portrait of a Nude Woman as Cleopatra,* 1987; *Every Time a Knot is Undone, a God is Released: Collected and New Poems, 1974-2011,* 2014.

Achievements

Barbara Chase-Riboud became a popular writer almost overnight, with the publication of *Sally Hemings,* which sold more than one million copies and won the Janet Heidinger Kafka Prize for best novel by an American woman in 1979. Ten years later, *Echo of Lions* sold 500,000 copies and confirmed Chase-Riboud's reputation as a solid historical novelist who likes to bring historical figures out of an undeserved obscurity.

Her original literary vocation, though, was in poetry. *From Memphis and Peking* combines a strong sensual appeal with the expression of a desire to travel through time, in the form of a quest for her ancestry, and space, in an exploration of the cultures of Africa, America, and China. In 1988, she won the Carl Sandburg Poetry Prize for *Portrait of a Nude Woman as Cleopatra,* a tortured unveiling of the Egyptian queen's public and private lives. Even before becoming a poet, Chase-Riboud was a sculptor with an international reputation. She received many fellowships and awards for her work, including a John Hay Whitney Foundation Fellowship in 1957-1958 for study at the American Academy in Rome, a National Endowment for the Arts Fellowship in 1973, and a Van der Zee Award in 1995. Her several honorary doctorates include one from Temple University in 1981. In 1996 she received a Knighthood for Contributions to Arts and Letters from the French government. In 2004 she was nominated for the Hurston-Wright Legacy Award (Fiction) for *Hottentot Venus,* a novel which won the 2005 "Best Fiction Book of 2004" award from the Black Caucus of the American Library Association. In 2007, she was given a lifetime achievement award by the College Art Association Women's Caucus for Art as well as the Alain Locke Award from Detroit Institute of Arts.

Biography

Barbara DeWayne Chase-Riboud was born and raised in Philadelphia, the only child of a building contractor and a medical assistant. She won her first art prize at age eight. She received a bachelor's of fine arts from Temple University in 1957 and a master's of fine arts from Yale University in 1960. In 1961 she married the French photojournalist Marc Eugene Riboud, with whom she had two sons, David and Alexis. She made her home in Europe, mostly in Paris and Rome. After her divorce in 1981, she married Sergio Tosi, an Italian art historian and expert. She traveled widely in Africa and the Near and Far East and was the first American woman to be admitted to the People's Republic of China after the revolution in 1949. Asked if she felt like an expatriate, she answered: "It takes me three hours to get from Paris to New York, so I don't really believe in expatriatism anymore."

Analysis: Long Fiction

Chase-Riboud's historical novels offer a strongly diversified exploration of power relationships as they are shaped by race, gender, and social and political needs. Slavery figures prominently in each novel, not only in its aberrations and its violence but also in the complex configurations of relationships it produces. The hairsplitting legal separation of the races is rendered incongruous by the intertwined blood ties exemplified in the extended interracial Jefferson family. More controversially, the notions of slave and master lose their sharp distinction in front of multiple forms of attraction and manipulation. It is the theme of profoundly mixed heritage and history, embodied in miscegenation, that ultimately dominates. The "outing" of hidden or mysterious women, such as Sally Hemings or Valide, bespeaks a desire to shake taboos and renew our understanding of world history.

Chase-Riboud's intellectual inquisitiveness, her multilingual and multicultural experience, and her artistic sensibility successfully collaborate in these recreations of large portions of world history, whose visual power is attained through precise and often poetic descriptions of places, events, clothes, and physiognomies. Especially engaging are the nuanced renderings of the characters' psychological and emotional turmoil, whether Catherine the Great or the African Joseph Cinque. These are historical novels in the pure Scottian tradition, which depict a welter of official historical events while bringing them to life with invented but eminently plausible depictions of the private lives that lie in the gaps. The sense of wide-ranging tableau is enhanced by a narrative technique that often jumps between numerous characters'

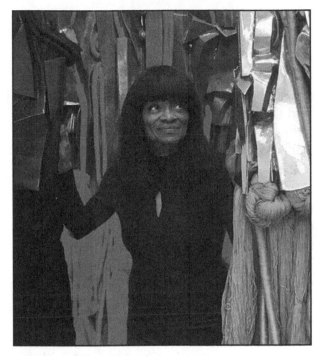

Photo courtesy of Nikitag94

perspectives in successions of relatively short chapters. One can even hear echoes from one novel to another, as Sally Hemings is discussed by John Quincy Adams in *Echo of Lions* or Thomas Jefferson figures in *Valide*'s Tripoli episode, and *The President's Daughter* even reproduces scenes from *Sally Hemings*.

In October, 1997, Chase-Riboud filed a plagiarism suit against film director Steven Spielberg, accusing him of stealing "themes, dialogue, characters, relationships, plots, scenes, and fictional inventions" from *Echo of Lions* for his 1997 film *Amistad*. The suit ended with an out-of-court settlement, but during the controversy plagiarism charges were turned against Chase-Riboud, for both *Echo of Lions* and *Valide*. Although she admitted that not mentioning her sources was an inexperienced writer's oversight, she pointed out that she often weaves "real documents and real reference materials" into her novels; *The President's Daughter* contains nine pages of author's notes on historical sources.

Sally Hemings

This novel is a fictional biography of Sally Hemings, President Thomas Jefferson's slave mistress (in November, 1998, a *Nature* magazine article revealed, thanks to deoxyribonucleic acid [DNA] evidence, that Jefferson had at least fathered Hemings's last child). Primarily inspired by Fawn M. Brodie's 1974 biography *Thomas Jefferson: An Intimate History* and by the Hemings family's oral testimony, Chase-Riboud recreates known historical events and characters, filling them out with nuanced and convincing psychological and emotional texture. The official facts are: Sally Hemings accompanied Jefferson's daughter Maria to Paris in June of 1787 to join him there and they all came back to America in October of 1789. A scandal broke out during Jefferson's first term as president, when he was accused of having a son with his slave Sally, an allegation Jefferson never publicly denied; all seven of Sally's children were conceived when Jefferson was present at Monticello, his estate in Virginia, and all her children were either allowed to run away or freed by Jefferson's will. According to Sally's son Madison Hemings, whose memoirs appeared in the Pike County (Ohio) *Republican* in 1873, his mother was pregnant with Jefferson's child when they came back from Paris, and Jefferson had promised her that he would free their children when they turned twenty-one.

The novel, which is told mostly from Sally's point of view, explores with great subtlety the emotional torture involved in a love story between a slave mistress and her master. Her alternate references to him as "my master" or "my lover" reflect her changing evaluation of herself as someone who gave up her freedom for love. A reminder of her surrender is provided by her brother James, who exhorts her to stay in France, where they are legally free, who keeps reproaching her for choosing a golden prison,

and who ultimately dies in mysterious circumstances. The relationship with Jefferson is presented realistically, as Sally occupies the underside of his public life, which echoes back into her life though remains frustratingly out of reach. Her rare excursions into public spaces lead to unpleasant confrontations with future vice president Aaron Burr and future First Lady Dolley Madison, reminding her of the limits imposed on her identity by the outside world. The recurring silences between her and her lover, which become a motif in the book, symbolize the extent of her invisibility and powerlessness. As a consequence she starts wielding power indirectly and subversively, as she takes over the keys of the house from her mother and decides to methodically attain freedom for each of her children. Ultimately, though, it is the love that defines her more than her slavehood.

Sally's story is told as a flashback, after the census taker Nathan Langdon visits her in her cabin in 1830 and decides to mark her and her two sons down as white, thereby replaying the white world's many attempts to erase her identity. The novel thus explicitly defines itself as a response to the silences and taboos of American history, as signified by the burning of letters and the ripping up of portraits. Langdon's interviews with sixth president John Quincy Adams, Burr, and painter John Trumbull, inserted in the middle of the novel, ensure a definite link between Sally Hemings's private life and the representatives of public history and lend her story long-overdue weight and legitimacy.

Although Jefferson remains an elusive figure throughout the book, some personality traits come out forcefully, such as the strength of his desires and passions under a facade of equanimity and his streak of despotism despite his egalitarian principles. The Jefferson family, and Virginia society more generally, are shown to be shot through with violence and decay, as evidenced by Jefferson's granddaughter's death at the hands of an abusive husband and George Wythe's and his mulatto son's murders by his nephew. The theme of lying to oneself and to others in order to preserve a semblance of social order would remain a dominant one in Chase-Riboud's oeuvre.

Valide

In *Valide*, Chase-Riboud transports her exploration of power relationships under slavery to the Ottoman Empire at the turn of the nineteenth century. The novel starts with the death of the sultana Valide in 1817, then retraces her rise from American slave of sultan Abdulhamid I after her capture by Barbary pirates to Ikbal (favorite) to Kadine (official wife) to Valide, queen mother. The subtle political and psychological analysis uncovers the complex usages of power and powerlessness in a profoundly hierarchical and ritualistic social structure. Under her new name, Naksh-i-dil ("embroidered tongue"), she becomes slowly acquainted with the intrigues, alliances, and corruption that condition survival in the harem, and which constitute the only possible form of resistance against engulfment by boredom and lassitude. She learns to use her body to wield power over the sultan and her female companions, and love is shown to be merely "a mixture of need and power, lust and loneliness."

The microcosmos of the harem reflects the wider geopolitical struggles of the empire with France, England, and Russia. As a young woman, Naksh-i-dil realizes that the sultan himself is a slave, whose power oscillates between treasons, alliances, and demonstrations of military prowess. Later, as Valide, she displays more political insight than her son and becomes his mastermind; for example, she forces a peace treaty with the Russians as an alliance against French emperor Napoleon I. The parallels and contrasts with Russian empress Catherine the Great, whose triumphant trip through the newly acquired Crimea turns out to be an illusion of grandeur, intensify the theme that "there was no absolute tyranny, just as there was no absolute slavery." By zeroing in on numerous historical figures, such as Russian statesman Grigory Aleksandrovich Potemkin, the sultan Selim III, and American admirals, the novel skillfully captures the intermingling of public and private lives. Detailed descriptions of settings (including a map of the harem), as well as information on social mores, help place this book in the best tradition of the historical novel.

Echo of Lions

Echo of Lions recounts the true ordeal of fifty-three kidnapped Mende Africans taken to Havana and sold to two Cuban planters, Jose Ruiz and Pedro Montez. On their way to the plantation aboard the *Amistad*, the Africans rebelled and killed the captain and the cook, while two sailors escaped. The Spaniards, kept alive to help steer the ship back to Africa, tricked the mutineers by navigating east by day and northwest by night. After their capture off Long Island, the Africans underwent three trials for murder and piracy, the last one in the Supreme Court in March, 1841, which declared them free. The *Amistad* story, which fascinated the American public at the time, put forth the view of slaves as mere property to be returned to their owners, according to a treaty with Spain, against their constitutional rights as persons illegally captured from their home country. The novel presents a skillful mixture of public and private history, providing minute descriptions of the slaves' tribulations, their court trials, their incarceration conditions, the New England abolitionist scene, and political debates, all the while infusing them with the historical characters' intimate thoughts and perspectives. Joseph Cinque, the Africans' charismatic leader, who, even though the case did little for the abolition of slavery in America, became a symbol of black pride and the right to freedom, as well as John Quincy Adams, who defended the case before the Supreme Court, receive a splendidly nuanced psychological treatment. In occasionally poetic passages Cinque tries to make sense of his new surroundings, recalls the beauty of his native land, and dreams of his wife; excerpts from Adams's diary bring to light his anxious but intense commitment. Several fictional characters, such as a wealthy black abolitionist and his beautiful daughter, help provide social and emotional texture to the wide-ranging historical material.

The President's Daughter

A follow-up to *Sally Hemings, The President's Daughter* chronicles the life of Harriet Hemings, Thomas Jefferson's white-skinned, red-haired slave daughter, as she leaves Monticello, travels through Europe, and marries a pharmacist in Philadelphia. After his death and burial in Africa, she marries his twin brother and raises seven children, passing as a white woman until her death. This novel of epic proportions gives Harriet's life a wide public resonance by associating it closely with a stream of historical events, such as Jefferson's death, the legal twists and turns of the institution of slavery, the Civil War (the Gettysburg battle, in particular), even the European presence in South Africa. Its descriptions of various social circles, such as Philadelphian high society and abolitionist groups, its renderings of long conversations on issues of the day, and its lengthy time span, give it a nineteenth century novel's consistency. Its themes, though, are painfully contemporary. Besides the continued exploration of filial love and power relationships, the novel concentrates on the psychological tortures of Harriet as an impostor and betrayer of her two families, the white and the black. The motif of fingerprints as an unmistakable bearer of identity is complicated when Harriet loses hers after burning her hand and sees the signs of her identity thus irrecoverably lost. The local theme of slavery as an institution based on fake premises and dependent on duplicity and lies reaches a philosophical dimension when Jefferson's Paris lover, Maria Cosway, whom Harriet visits in her Italian convent, teaches her that "nothing is real" and "everything is illusion." The theme of race relations receives a more bitter treatment in this sequel, as even love cannot seem to rise above gulfs of incomprehension.

Bibliography

Loke, Margarett. "Writer Who Cried Plagiarism Used Passages She Didn't Write." *The New York Times,* December 19, 1997, p. A1. Reports on Chase-Riboud's admission that parts of *Valide* contain sections taken from a nonfiction book called *The Harem* (written by another author). Includes Chase-Riboud's comments on the issue.

Peterson, V. R. "Word Star Barbara Chase-Riboud Rewriting History." *Essence* 25, no. 8 (December, 1994): 56-59. Examines the revisionist view of history presented in the novel *Sally Hemings.* Includes responses from scholars of American history.

Rushdy, Ashraf H. A. "'I Write in Tongues': The Supplement of Voice in Barbara Chase-Riboud's *Sally Hemings.*" *Contemporary Literature* 35, no. 1 (1994): 100-135. Examines the complex interplay of orality and literacy in the novel.

___ . "Representing the Constitution: Embodiments of America in Barbara Chase-Riboud's *Echo of Lions.*" *Critique: Studies in Contemporary Fiction* 36, no. 4 (Summer, 1995): 258-280. Sophisticated investigation of the critique of the American Constitution embedded in the novel.

Wells, Monique Y. "Barbara Chase-Riboud, Visionary Woman: In Words and Art the Renowned Author and Sculptor Breathes Life into the History of the Forgotten Female." *Black Issues Book Review* 7, no. 2 (March/April, 2005): 64-66. This article will be especially interesting to those looking for information about Chase-Riboud's artistic career. Discusses her work for the Museum of Contemporary Art in Shanghai.

Zeitchik, Steven M. "Chase-Riboud Drops *Amistad* Copyright Suit." *Publishers Weekly,* February 16, 1998, 105-110. A good summary of the legal battle between Chase-Riboud and *Amistad* director Steven Spielberg. Also touches on the plagiarism accusations leveled against Chase-Riboud.

— *Christine Levec; Robert C. Evans*

Charles Waddell Chesnutt

Short-story Writer and Novelist

Born: Cleveland, Ohio; June 20, 1858

Died: Cleveland, Ohio; November 15, 1932

LONG FICTION: *Mandy Oxendine*, wr. 1897, pb. 1997; *The House Behind the Cedars*, 1900; *The Marrow of Tradition*, 1901; *The Colonel's Dream*, 1905; *Paul Marchand, F.M.C.*, wr. 1921, pb. 1998; *The Quarry*, wr. 1928, pb. 1999; *A Business Career* (2005); *Evelyn's Husband* (2005).

SHORT FICTION: *The Conjure Woman*, 1899; *The Wife of His Youth, and Other Stories of the Color Line*, 1899; *The Northern Stories*, 2004.

NONFICTION: *The Life of Frederick Douglass*, 1899; *The Journals of Charles W. Chesnutt*, 1993; *To Be an Author: The Letters of Charles W. Chesnutt, 1889-1905*, 1997; *Charles W. Chesnutt: Essays and Speeches*, 1999; *Selected Writings*, 2001 (Sally Ann H. Ferguson, editor).

Achievements

In 1872, when he was fourteen years old, Charles Waddell Chesnutt's first story was published serially in a local black weekly. The publication of "The Goophered Grapevine" (August, 1887) in *The Atlantic Monthly* marked Chesnutt's first appearance in a major American literary magazine. Three more short stories followed: "Po' Sandy," "The Conjurer's Revenge," and "Dave's Neckliss." The publication of these four Uncle Julius stories were his entering wedge into the literary world—a world of which Chesnutt had long dreamed of being a part as a novelist. In 1900, Chesnutt published his first novel, *The*

House Behind the Cedars, which sold about two thousand copies in its first two months. His next two published novels (*The Marrow of Tradition* and *The Colonel's Dream*) were not as well received. Although he was honored as a writer by being asked to be a guest at Mark Twain's seventieth birthday party, he retired from writing as a profession in 1905. After that time, none of his creative work was published.

Chesnutt achieved a great deal in nonliterary areas. He was active politically and socially and wrote many controversial essays and speeches on race. In 1913, he received an honorary degree from Wilberforce University. In 1928, he was awarded the National Association for the Advancement of Colored People (NAACP) Spingarn Medal, an award given to African Americans who distinguish themselves in their fields. The gold medal commemorated Chesnutt for his "pioneer work as a literary artist depicting the life and struggles of Americans of Negro descent and for his long and useful career as a scholar, worker, and freeman of one of America's greatest cities [Cleveland]."

Biography

When Charles Waddell Chesnutt was nine years old, his family moved to Fayetteville, North Carolina, where he spent his youth. Although he was of African American descent, his features barely distinguished him from Caucasians. He

Photo courtesy of the Cleveland Public Library Image Collection

learned, however, that family blood was very important in determining a person's social and economic prospects.

Chesnutt's mother died in 1871, when he was thirteen years old. Two years later, he left school to teach in order to supplement the family income. In 1878, he married Susan Perry, a fellow teacher and daughter of a well-to-do black barber in Fayetteville. He had begun teaching in 1877 at the new State Colored Normal School in Fayetteville, and in 1880 he became principal of the school.

On a job-hunting trip to Washington, D.C., in 1879, Chesnutt was unable to find work. He had been studying stenography and hoped to obtain a job on a newspaper. In 1883, he was able to begin a new career as a stenographer and reporter in New York City, and shortly afterward he moved to Cleveland, where he was first a clerk and then a legal stenographer. Two years later, he began studying law, and in 1887, he passed the Ohio bar examination with the highest grade in his group. He opened his own office as a court reporter in 1888.

Between 1887 and 1899, beginning with the publication of "The Goophered Grapevine" by *The Atlantic Monthly,* he achieved some success as a short-story writer. In 1899, when Houghton Mifflin published two collections of his short stories, he gave up his profitable business and began writing novels full time— something he had dreamed of doing for many years.

His first published novel, *The House Behind the Cedars,* had some commercial success, but the next, *The Marrow of Tradition,* did not. In 1901, two years after he had closed his stenographic firm, he reopened it. Deciding to write short stories once more in 1903 and 1904, he sent them to *The Atlantic Monthly,* where he had found success earlier, but only one, "Baxter's Procrustes," was accepted. His novel *The Colonel's Dream,* published in 1905, failed to attract the attention of the public. The public of the early 1900s was not ready for the controversial subject matter of his novels and later short stories or for the sympathetic treatment of the black characters in them. It did not want to read literature that had African Americans as the main characters, that presented their problems in a predominantly white world, and that were written with a sympathy for blacks rather than whites. Chesnutt retired from creative writing as a profession in 1905, and thereafter he published only nonfiction.

During the rest of his life, Chesnutt concentrated on managing his business affairs, on participating in civic affairs, and on working on behalf of black people. He was an active member of the Rowland Club, an exclusive male literary group in Cleveland, although at first he was denied membership in this club because of his race. During the last twenty-seven years of his life, he managed to find time to travel in Europe and to help educate his three children. He was a member of the Cleveland Chamber of Commerce and the National Arts Club; he also helped establish Playhouse Settlement (now Karamu House).

Before 1905, he had been politically and socially active in helping to advance the cause of black people, and he continued to be active throughout his life. In 1901, he contributed greatly to having W. H. Thomas's *The American Negro* withdrawn from circulation. That same year, he chaired the Committee on Colored Troops for the 35th National Encampment of the Grand Army of the Republic in Cleveland. In 1904, he became a member of the Committee of Twelve, organized by Booker T. Washington, and in 1905 he was a member of the Cleveland Council of Sociology. He addressed the National Negro Committee, which later became the NAACP, and served as a member of its General Committee. He protested the showing of the film *The Birth of a Nation* (1915), which glorified the Ku Klux Klan, and, more important, he protested the treatment of black soldiers. He participated in the First Amenia Conference, called by Joel Spingarn in 1916. He was awarded the Spingarn Medal by the NAACP in 1928.

Analysis: Long Fiction

Charles Waddell Chesnutt wrote three novels that were published and several that were not. He was a much more skillful short-story writer than a novelist, and although he developed most of his novels from short stories, one of the novels is exceptional as a literary work. Those reading his novels should remember, however, that some of the matters for which he is criticized today—thin, idealized characters and the use of plot manipulations such as foreshadowing and coincidence—were standard in the fiction of the late 1800s and were accepted by the readers of the day.

Chesnutt dreamed of being a novelist, and he believed that racial issues such as the problems of passing, miscegenation, and racial assimilation had to be the subject of serious fiction. He found, though, that if he tried to write novels that would be commercially successful, publishers would not accept them, and if he tried to write works that examined racial issues honestly and with sympathy for blacks, the public would not accept these topical but controversial novels.

Chesnutt is notable for being the first African American fiction writer to gain a reputation for examining honestly and in detail the racial problems of black people in America after the Civil War. Many Americans in the last part of the nineteenth century preferred to ignore the problems of the African American and especially did not want a presentation as sympathetic toward blacks as that given by Chesnutt.

Chesnutt may have been a victim, just as his characters sometimes are. The themes that he could present most effectively and that he felt compelled to present were ones that the public would not accept; thus, he did not continue to write novels and may have been prevented from developing as a literary artist. In addition, he may have had to compromise to get his views before readers in America. Chesnutt believed that Americans had an unnatural fear of miscegenation. Because of this fear, the person of mixed blood was an outcast in society and was almost forced by society to pass for white to try to obtain the American Dream. Ironically, those forced into passing and marrying whites began again the miscegenation cycle that was so feared by whites. Anglo-Saxon racial purity was something that should not be preserved, Chesnutt believed. Intermingling and integration would improve humanity biologically, but more important, blacks would then be able to have the rights they should have as human beings. Only by eliminating laws against intermarriage and social interaction between the races would blacks gain true social, economic, and political equality.

The House Behind the Cedars

Between 1890 and 1899, Chesnutt greatly expanded and revised "Rena Walden," a short story, until it became *The House Behind the Cedars*. At first, he focused on how color consciousness can destroy an interracial marriage and then on the predominant issue of whether a mulatto should cross the "color line." In March, 1899, he wrote journalist and diplomat Walter Hines Page that the Rena Walden story was the strong expression of a writer whose themes dealt primarily with the American color line. When he wrote to his daughters in the fall of 1900, he indicated that he hoped for "a howling success" from *The House Behind the Cedars*, "a strong race problem novel." The story of Rena Walden and her brother was the first in which the problems of Americans concealing their African heritage were studied with a detached and compassionate presentation of individuals on the various sides of the issue.

The novel can be divided into two parts: Rena in white society, in which her brother is the major focus, and Rena in black society, in which she becomes the focus. The novel is set in Patesville, North Carolina, a few years after the Civil War. John Warwick, who has changed his name from Walden, has left Patesville and gone to South Carolina, where he has become a lawyer and plantation owner, acquiring wealth and position. He and his sister Rena are the children of a quadroon mother Molly and a white man who has died. John has returned to Patesville to help his beautiful sister escape the restrictions of color by teaching her how to pass for white. She is a success at the boarding school in South Carolina to which he takes her. As proof of her success in passing, George Tryon, a good friend of John and a white, wants to marry Rena, but she is not sure she should marry him without telling him of her mixed blood. John and Rena indirectly discuss the pros and cons of passing and intermarriage. A series of coincidences leads to an unexpected meeting between George and Rena; he learns of her heritage, and the engagement is broken. Rena returns home to her mother and the house behind the cedars.

A chapter interlude that gives the Walden family history separates the first part of the novel from the second. John tries to persuade his sister to return to South Carolina with him or to take money and go North or West, where she can pass for white and marry someone even better than George, but she refuses to leave Patesville. She has decided to accept her destiny and be of service to her people, whom she has rediscovered. After this point, the reader is told little more about John.

Rena meets Jeff Wain, an influential and prosperous mulatto from a rural county, who is seeking a schoolteacher. Rena accepts the position, not realizing Jeff has a personal as well as a professional interest in her. Jeff is not as admirable a character as he first appears. As he pays her more and more attention, she is upset and repulsed. Once again, coincidence plays a part in the plot. George Tryon happens to learn of her presence near a place he is visiting. When he sees her, he realizes that he loves her and that his love is stronger than his racial prejudice. The same day that George decides to declare his love, Jeff decides to do so too. Rena fears both of the men and leaves hastily for her mother's house behind the cedars. After exposure and fatigue have overcome her, Frank Fowler, a childhood friend and a conscientious black workman, finds her and carries her to her home, where she dies. Rena realizes before she dies that Frank loved her the best.

Chesnutt seeks to lead his readers to share his perspective rather than lecturing them. He delays revealing that John and Rena are mulattoes. To create sympathy for them first, he presents them simply as persons of humble origins who are attempting to achieve prosperity and happiness. Chesnutt passes John and Rena for white with the reader before he lets the reader know that they are mulattoes who have chosen or will deliberately choose to pass for white.

John Walden is the first black character in American fiction to decide to pass for white and, at the same time, to feel that his decision is legally and morally justified. Believing that the color of his skin tells him that he is white, he has no psychological problems concerning his choice to pass. He is not a stereotype. Intelligent and industrious, he patiently trains himself so that he can achieve the American Dream. At the beginning of the novel, the reader learns that he has become a prosperous lawyer and plantation owner after leaving Patesville; in the second part of the novel, after he has not been successful in helping Rena pass for white, he returns to South Carolina to regain his position.

The characters are not fully developed and remain stick figures, although Chesnutt is partially successful in creating human interest for them. While Chesnutt attempts to create pity for her, Rena is simply a victim who accepts her fate, like other antiassimilationist mulattoes of the time. Another character, Dr. Green, is no more than a vehicle to present the traditional southern viewpoint. Two figures, Molly Walden and George Tyron, retain some individuality. Molly, as an unprotected free black woman in the slave South, is a product of her environment. With the circumstances that she faces, she can do little other than be the kept mistress for the white plantation owner, who has died but left her the house behind the cedars. Chesnutt does not want the reader to feel contempt for her or to be repulsed by her actions; her

position is rendered dispassionately. George Tyron, on the other hand, undergoes great emotional upheaval and has a change of view that is probably meant to be instructive. He is tied to the traditional code of the southern gentleman but is not deluded about his prerogatives as a southern aristocrat. Rather, he is meant to be the best of the new South. His realization that he loves Rena and that her racial heritage is not important comes too late; she dies before he is able to do anything about it. He does not blame her for passing, and Chesnutt expects the reader not to blame her.

The Marrow of Tradition

The Marrow of Tradition is the story of two families: The Carterets stand for the New South aristocracy with its pride and prejudice, and the Millers, who are of mixed blood, represent the qualities of the new black. The lives of the families are intertwined because the wives are half sisters. Janet Miller, however, has been cheated of her inheritance by Olivia Carteret, and Olivia constantly struggles with the problem of accepting Janet as her rightful sister.

The novel's message—a study of white supremacist politics in a small southern town after the Civil War—is more relevant to the problems encountered by the husbands than those facing the wives. Dr. Adam Miller is a brilliant young surgeon denied opportunity in his hometown of Wellington (Wilmington, North Carolina). Major Philip Carteret, editor of the town's newspaper, seeks to seat a white supremacist regime in the local government. If he is successful, Adam Miller's position will be even more intolerable than it has been.

At the end of the novel, Major Carteret stirs up a riot during which Dr. Miller's son is killed. Immediately after the death of the Millers' child, the son of the Carterets becomes ill, and Adam Miller is the only person who can perform the surgery necessary to save the child's life. At first, Miller refuses, but after Olivia Carteret humbles herself before her half sister and pleads with her to help save the Carterets' son, Janet Miller convinces her husband to change his mind and operate. The child is saved.

The Marrow of Tradition was too controversial a novel for the public. Americans were not ready for the subject of white supremacist politics and the political injustice existing in the South. Chesnutt himself was concerned that the novel approached fanaticism. He believed that he should not speak so plainly concerning these matters if he hoped to succeed as a fiction writer.

Analysis: Short Fiction

Chesnutt's short fiction embraces traditions characteristic of both formal and folk art. Indeed, the elements of Chesnutt's narrative technique evolved in a fashion that conspicuously parallels the historical shaping of the formal short story itself. The typical Chesnutt narrative, like the classic short story, assumes its heritage from a rich oral tradition immersed in folkways, mannerisms, and beliefs. Holding true to the historical development of the short story as an artistic form, his early imaginative narratives were episodic in nature. The next stage of development in Chesnutt's short fiction was a parody of the fable form with a folkloric variation. Having become proficient at telling a story with a unified effect, Chesnutt achieved the symbolic resonance characteristic of the Romantic tale, yet his awareness of the plight of his people urged him toward an increasingly realistic depiction of social conditions. As a mature writer, Chesnutt achieved depth of characterization, distinguishable thematic features, and a rare skillfulness in creation of mood, while a shrewdly moralizing tone allowed him to achieve his dual goal as artist and social activist.

"The Goophered Grapevine"

Chesnutt's journal stories constituted the first phase of his writing career, but when *The Atlantic Monthly* published "The Goophered Grapevine" in 1888, the serious aspects of his artistic skill became apparent. "The Goophered Grapevine" belongs to a tradition in Chesnutt's writings which captures the fable form with a folkloric variation. These stories also unfold with a didactic strain which matures significantly in Chesnutt's later writings. To understand clearly the series of stories in *The Conjure Woman* of which "The Goophered Grapevine" is one, the reader must comprehend the allegorical features in the principal narrative situation and the thematic intent of the mythic incidents from African American lore.

The Conjure Woman contains narratives revealed through the accounts of a Northern white person's rendition of the tales of Uncle Julius, a former slave. This storytelling device lays the foundation for Chesnutt's sociological commentary. The real and perceived voices represent the perspectives he wishes to expose, those of the white capitalist and the impoverished, disadvantaged African American. The primary persona is the capitalist, while the perceived voice is that of the struggling poor. Chesnutt skillfully melds the two perspectives.

Chesnutt's two volumes of short stories contain pieces which are unified in theme, tone, and mood. Each volume also contains a piece which might be considered the lead story. In *The Conjure Woman*, the preeminent story is "The Goophered Grapevine." This story embodies the overriding thematic intent of the narratives in this collection. Chesnutt points out the foibles of the capitalistic quest in the post-Civil War South, a venture pursued at the expense of the newly freed African American slave. He illustrates this point in "The Goophered Grapevine" by skillfully intertwining

Aunt Peggy's gains as a result of her conjurations and Henry's destruction as a result of man's inhumanity to man. Chesnutt discloses his ultimate point when the plantation owner, McAdoo, is deceived by a Yankee horticulturist and his grape vineyard becomes totally unproductive.

Running episodes, such as Aunt Peggy's conjurations to keep the field hands from consuming the grape crop and the seasonal benefit McAdoo gains from selling Henry, serve to illustrate the interplay between a monied white capitalist and his less privileged black human resources. McAdoo used Aunt Peggy to deny his field laborers any benefit from the land they worked, and he sold Henry every spring to increase his cash flow and prepare for the next gardening season.

The central metaphor in "The Goophered Grapevine" is the bewitched vineyard. To illustrate and condemn man's inhumanity to man, Chesnutt contrasts the black conjure woman's protection of the grape vineyard with the white Yankee's destruction of it. McAdoo's exploitation of Henry serves to justify McAdoo's ultimate ruin. Through allegory, Chesnutt is able to draw attention to the immorality of capitalistic gain through a sacrifice of basic humanity to other people.

"Po' Sandy"

Following the theme of inhumanity established in "The Goophered Grapevine," "Po' Sandy" highlights the abuse of a former slave laborer. Accordingly, a situation with a folkloric variation is used to convey this message. Sandy, Master Marabo's field hand, is shifted from relative to relative at various points during the year to perform various duties. During the course of these transactions, he is separated from his second common-law wife, Tenie. (His first wife has been sent to work at a distant plantation.) Tenie is a conjurer. She transforms Sandy into a

tree, and she changes him back to his original state periodically so that they can be together. With Sandy's apparent disappearance, Master Marabo decides to send Tenie away to nurse his ailing daughter-in-law. There is therefore no one left to watch Sandy, the tree. The dehumanizing effects of industrialization creep into the story line at this point. The "tree" is to be used as lumber for a kitchen at the Marabo home. Tenie returns just in time to try to stop this transformation at the lumber mill, but she is deemed "mad."

Sandy's spirit thereafter haunts the Marabo kitchen, and no one wants to work there. The complaints are so extensive that the kitchen is dismantled and the lumber donated toward the building of a school. This structure is then haunted, too. The point is that industrialization and economic gain diminish essential human concerns and can lead to destruction. The destruction of Sandy's marital relationships in order to increase his usefulness as a field worker justifies this defiant spirit. In his depiction of Sandy as a tree, Chesnutt illustrates an enslaved spirit desperately seeking freedom.

"The Conjurer's Revenge"

"The Conjurer's Revenge," also contained in *The Conjure Woman,* illustrates Chesnutt's mastery of the exemplum. The allegory in this work conveys a strong message, and Chesnutt's evolving skill in characterization becomes apparent. The characters' actions, rather than the situation, contain the didactic message of the story. Some qualities of the fable unfold as the various dimensions of characters are portrayed. Consequently, "The Conjurer's Revenge" is a good example of Chesnutt's short imaginative sketch. These qualities are also most characteristic of Chesnutt's early short fiction.

"The Conjurer's Revenge" begins when Primus, a field hand, discovers the conjure man's hog alone in a bush one evening.

Concerned for the hog and not knowing to whom the animal belongs, Primus carries it to the plantation where he works. Unfortunately, the conjurer identifies Primus as a thief and transforms Primus into a mule. Chesnutt uses this transformation to reveal Primus's personality. As a mule, Primus displays jealousy when other men show an attraction to his woman, Sally. The mule's reaction is one of shocking violence in instances when Sally is approached by other men. The mule has a tremendous appetite for food and drink, an apparent compensation for his unhappiness. Laying the foundation for his exemplum, Chesnutt brings these human foibles to the forefront and illustrates the consequences of even the mildest appearance of dishonesty.

The conjurer's character is also developed more fully as the story progresses. After attending a religious revival, he becomes ill, confesses his act of vengeance, and repents. During the conjurer's metamorphosis, Chesnutt captures the remorse, grief, and forgiveness in this character. He also reveals the benefits of human compassion and concern for other human beings. A hardened heart undergoes reform and develops an ability to demonstrate sensitivity. Nevertheless, the conjurer suffers the consequences of his evil deed: He is mistakenly given poison by a companion and he dies before he completely restores Primus's human features, a deed he undertakes after repenting. The conjurer dies prematurely, and Primus lives with a club-foot for the rest of his life.

Features of Chesnutt's more mature writing emerge in the series of narratives which make up *The Wife of His Youth, and Other Stories of the Color Line.* The stories in this collection center on the identity crisis experienced by African Americans, portraying their true human qualities in the face of the grotesque distortions wrought by racism. In order to achieve his goal, Chesnutt abandons his earlier imaginative posture and embraces realism as a means to unfold his message. The dimensions of his characters are therefore appropriately self-revealing. The characters respond to the stresses and pressures in their external environment with genuine emotion; Mr. Ryder in "The Wife of His Youth" is no exception.

"The Wife of His Youth"

"The Wife of His Youth" follows the structural pattern which appears to typify the narratives in the collection. This pattern evolves in three phases: crisis, character response, and resolution. The crisis in "The Wife of His Youth" is Mr. Ryder's attempt to reconcile his new and old ways of life. He has moved North from a southern plantation and entered black middle-class society. Adapting to the customs, traditions, and mores of this stratum of society is a stressful challenge for Mr. Ryder. Tensions exist between his old life and his new life. He fears being unable to appear as if he belongs to this "blue vein" society and exposing his lowly background. This probable eventuality is his constant preoccupation.

The "blue veins" were primarily lighter-skinned blacks who were better educated and more advantaged than their darker counterparts. Relishing their perceived superiority, they segregated themselves from their brothers and sisters. It is within this web of social clamoring and essential self-denial that Mr. Ryder finds himself. The inherent contradictions of this lifestyle present a crisis for him, although a resolution is attained during the course of the narrative.

Mr. Ryder's efforts to fit into this society are thwarted when his slave wife appears at his doorstep on the day before a major social event that he has planned. He is about to introduce the Blue Vein Society to a widow, Mrs. Dixon, upon whom he has set his affections. The appearance of Liza Jane, his slave wife, forces Mr.

Ryder to confront his new life. This situation also allows Chesnutt to assume his typically moralizing tone. Mr. Ryder moves from self-denial to self-pride as he decides to present Liza Jane to his society friends instead of Mrs. Dixon. The narrative ends on a note of personal triumph for Mr. Ryder as he proudly introduces the wife of his youth to society.

"The Passing of Grandison"

Chesnutt does not totally relinquish his allegiance to the use of myth in *The Wife of His Youth, and Other Stories of the Color Line*. The myth of the ascent journey, or the quest for freedom, is evident in several stories in the collection, among them "The Passing of Grandison" and "Wellington's Wives." Following the structured pattern of crisis, character response, and resolution, "The Passing of Grandison" is a commentary on the newly emerging moral values of the postbellum South. Colonel Owens, a plantation owner, has a son, Dick, who is in love with a belle named Charity Lomax. Charity's human values reflect the principles of human equality and freedom, and the challenge that she presents to Dick Owens becomes the crisis of the narrative.

Dick is scheduled to take a trip North, and his father insists on his being escorted by one of the servants. Grandison is selected to accompany his young master. Charity Lomax challenges Dick to find a way to entice Grandison to remain in the North and receive his well-deserved liberation. Charity's request conflicts with the values held by Dick and Grandison. Dick believes that slave/master relationships are essential to the survival of the South. Grandison holds that servants should be unequivocally loyal to their masters.

In spite of Dick's attempts to connect Grandison unobtrusively with the abolitionist movement in the North, the former slave remains loyal to Dick. Grandison's steadfastness perplexes Dick because his proposed marriage to

Charity is at risk if he does not succeed in freeing Grandison. After a series of faulty attempts, Dick succeeds in losing Grandison. Dick then returns home alone and triumphant. Grandison ultimately returns to the plantation. He had previously proven himself so trustworthy that goodwill toward him is restored. To make the characterization of Grandison realistic, however, Chesnutt must have him pursue his freedom.

In a surprise ending typical of Chesnutt, Grandison plans the escape of all of his relatives who remain on the plantation. They succeed, and in the last scene of the narrative, Colonel Owens spots them from a distance on a boat journeying to a new destination. "The Passing of Grandison" successfully achieves the social and artistic goals of *The Wife of His Youth, and Other Stories of the Color Line*. Chesnutt creates characters with convincing human qualities and captures their responses to the stresses and pressures of their environment. While so doing, he advocates the quest for human freedom.

"Uncle Wellington's Wives"

"Uncle Wellington's Wives" contains several of the thematic dimensions mentioned above. The story concerns the self-identity of the African American and the freedom quest. Wellington Braboy, a light-skinned mulatto, is determined to move North and seek his freedom. His crisis is the result of a lack of resources, primarily financial, to achieve his goal.

Braboy is portrayed as having a distorted view of loyalty and commitment. He justifies stealing money from his slave wife's life savings by saying that, as her husband, he is entitled to the money. On the other hand, he denies his responsibility to his slave wife once he reaches the North. In order to marry a white woman he denies the legality of a slave marriage.

Chesnutt takes Braboy on a journey of purgation and catharsis as he moves toward resolution. After being subjected to much ridicule and humiliation as a result of his mixed marriage, Braboy must honestly confront himself and come to terms with his true identity. Abandoned by his wife for her former white husband, Braboy returns to the South. This journey is also a symbolic return to himself; his temporary escape from himself has failed.

Milly, Braboy's first wife, does not deny her love for him, in spite of his previous actions. Milly receives and accepts him with a forgiving spirit. Chesnutt capitalizes on the contrast between Braboy's African and Anglo wives. The African wife loves him unconditionally because she has the capacity to know and understand him, regardless of his foibles. Braboy's Anglo wife was frustrated by what she considered to be irreparable inadequacies in his character and abandoned him.

"Cicely's Dream"

In his character development, Chesnutt repeatedly sought to dispel some of the stereotypical thinking about African Americans. An example of his success in this effort is found in "Cicely's Dream," set in the period of Reconstruction. Cicely Green is depicted as a young woman of considerable ambition. Like most African Americans, she has had very little education and is apparently limited in her capacity to achieve. She does have, however, many dreams.

Cicely's crisis begins when she discovers a wounded man on her way home one day. The man is delirious and has no recollection of who he is. Cicely and her grandmother care for the man until his physical health is restored, but he is still mentally distraught. The tenderness and sensitivity displayed by Cicely keep the stranger reasonably content. Over a period of time, they become close and eventually pledge their love to each other. Chesnutt portrays a caring, giving relationship between the two lovers, one which

is not complicated by any caste system which would destroy love through separation of the lovers. This relationship, therefore, provides a poignant contrast to the relationships among blacks during the days of slavery, and Chesnutt thereby exposes an unexplored dimension of the African American.

Typically, however, there is a surprise ending: Martha Chandler, an African American teacher, enters the picture. She teaches Cicely and other black youths for one school term. During the final program of the term, the teacher reveals her story of lost love. Her lover had been killed in the Civil War. Cicely's lover's memory is jolted by the teacher's story, and he proves to be the teacher's long-lost love. The happy reunion is a celebration of purely committed love. Again, Chesnutt examines qualities in African Americans which had largely been ignored. He emphasizes the innate humanity of the African American in a natural and realistic way, combining great artistic skill with a forceful moral vision.

Other Literary Forms

Chesnutt also wrote a biography (*The Life of Frederick Douglass*), a play (*Mrs. Darcy's Daughter*), and a few poems. He wrote essays and speeches that were published in national magazines. These writings were primarily political and didactic: "What Is a White Man?," "A Plea for the American Negro," and "The White and the Black." His essay on "The Disfranchisement of the Negro" appeared as a part of a book entitled *The Negro Problem*, whose subtitle announced that it was *A Series of Articles by Representative American Negroes of Today* and whose list of contributors included such men as Booker T. Washington, W. E. B. Du Bois, T. Thomas Fortune, and Paul Laurence Dunbar.

Chesnutt's correspondence and many of his writings have not been published. Most of these unpublished works, as well as many of the published ones, are in the Charles Waddell Chesnutt Collection of the Erastus Milo Cravath Memorial Library, Fisk University, Nashville, Tennessee.

Bibliography

Ashton, Susanna, and Bill Hardwig, ed. *Approaches to Teaching the Works of Charles W. Chesnutt*. New York: The Modern Language Association of America, 2017. Deals with such matters as critical reception, available editions, and the challenges of teaching Chesnutt. Includes more than twenty essays on a wide variety of topics.

Chesnutt, Charles Waddell. *"To Be an Author": Letters of Charles W. Chesnutt, 1889-1905*, edited by Joseph R. McElrath, Jr., and Robert C. Leitz III. Princeton, N.J.: Princeton University Press, 1997. The six-part organization is particularly useful to a student of Chesnutt's fiction and of his career development: "Cable's Protege in 1889-1891," "A Dream Deferred, 1891-1896," "Page's Protege in 1897-1899," "The Professional Novelist," "Discontent in 1903-1904," and "The Quest Renewed, 1904-1905." Includes a comprehensive introduction and detailed index.

Duncan, Charles. *The Absent Man: The Narrative Craft of Charles W. Chesnutt*. Athens: Ohio University Press, 1998. This informative volume includes bibliographical references and an index.

Filetti, Jean. "The Goophered Grapevine." *Explicator* 48 (Spring, 1990): 201-203. Discusses the use of master-slave relationships within the context of storytelling and explains how Chesnutt's "The Goophered Grapevine" relates to this tradition. Indicates that one of Chesnutt's concerns was inhumanity among people, but the story is told from a humorous perspective with the newly freed slave outwitting the white capitalist.

Gleason, William. "Chesnutt's Piazza Tales: Architecture, Race, and Memory in the Conjure Stories." *American Quarterly* 51 (March, 1999): 33-77. Argues that Chesnutt counters historical amnesia with concrete memories from the piazza that represents a simpler past.

Izzo, David Garrett, and Maria Orban, ed. *Charles Chesnutt Reappraised: Essays on the First Major African American Fiction Writer*. Jefferson, NC: McFarland & Co., 2009. Contains more than fifteen essays on such topics as race riots, realism, genre, racial passing, folklore, classical literature, phenomenology, black readers, historical memory, epics. tricksters, Africa, mobility, uplift, martyrdom, and motherhood.

Keller, Frances Richardson. *An American Crusade: The Life of Charles Waddell Chesnutt*. Provo, Utah: Brigham Young University Press, 1978. The most helpful and important biographical resource on Chesnutt available.

Kulii, Elon A. "Poetic License and Chesnutt's Use of Folklore." *CLA Journal* 38 (December, 1994): 247-253. Discusses Chesnutt's use of the hoodoo tradition in "Goophered Grapevine." Claims that Chesnutt communicates the inner tale as a story from the hoodoo tradition, but that the episodic core of the tale is not of the oral tradition.

Lehman, Cynthia L. "The Social and Political Views of Charles Chesnutt: Reflections on his Major Writings." *Journal of Black Studies* 26, no. 3 (January, 1996): 274-287. Argues that Chesnutt's writing helped propel African Americans toward a more Africa-centered conciousness.

McFatter, Susan. "From Revenge to Resolution: The (R)evolution of Female Characters in Chesnutt's Fiction." *CLA Journal* 42 (December, 1998): 194-211. Discusses the theme of female revenge in Chesnutt's fiction, showing how female characters respond to racism and patriarchal paradigms in various ways. Argues that Chesnutt's women use intelligence and instinct for survival to manipulate their repressive environments.

Moddelmog, William E. "Lawful Entitlements: Chesnutt's Fictions of Ownership." *Texas Studies in Literature & Language* 41, no. 1 (Spring, 1999):

47-80. Analysis of Chesnutt's fiction from a perspective concerned largely with ownership— particularly self-ownership—and entitlements.

Petrie, Paul R. *Conscience and Purpose: Fiction and Social Consciousness in Howells, Jewett, Chesnutt, and Cather.* Tuscaloosa: University of Alabama Press, 2005. Explores the influence of W. D. Howells on Chesnutt and two other major American writers of the era.

Render, Sylvia. *Charles W. Chesnutt.* Boston: Twayne, 1980. A good general introduction to the life and writing of Charles Chesnutt. Render discusses Chesnutt's major concerns with narrative technique, social justice, and the place of the African American in American society.

Simmons, Ryan. *Chesnutt and Realism: A Study of the Novels.* Tuscaloosa: University of Alabama Press, 2006. Explores such topics as Chesnutt's northern novels, his interest in "tragic mullatas," his use of both simple and complex discourse, and his authorship of a "radical" text.

Sollers, Werner. "Thematics Today." In *Thematics Reconsidered: Essays in Honor of Horst S. Daemmrich,* edited by Frank Trommler. Amsterdam: Rodopi, 1995. A detailed discussion of the themes in "The Wife of His Youth." Argues that contemporary thematic readings that stress race and gender are less likely to identify other themes such as marriage, fidelity, and age difference. Suggests that Chesnutt's special way of treating the race and age themes needs more attention.

Sollors, Werner, ed. *The Marrow of Tradition: Authoritative Text, Contexts, Criticism.* New York: W. W. Norton & Co., 2012. An edition containing much contextual material as well as many reactions to the novel from both early and recent writers.

Stepto, Robert B., and Jennifer Rae Greeson, ed. *The Conjure Stories: Authoritative Texts, Contexts, Criticism.* New York: W. W. Norton & Co., 2012. Part of the highly respected Norton Critical Editions series, widely known for presenting superb versions of literary classics.

Watson, Reginald. "The Tragic Mulatto Image in Charles Chesnutt's *The House Behind the Cedars* and Nella Larsen's *Passing.*" *CLA Journal* 46, no. 1 (September, 2002): 48-71. Provides important insights into the portrayal of mixed-blood subjects in literature.

White, Jeannette S. "Baring Slavery's Darkest Secrets: Charles Chesnutt's *Conjure Tales* as Masks of Truth." *Southern Literary Journal* 27, no. 1 (Fall, 1994): 85-140. Analyzes the use of masks in African American fiction as tools for conveying controversial messages. Uses *The Conjure Woman* as a case study of Chesnutt's methods for understanding slave psychology.

Wilson, Matthew. *Whiteness in the Novels of Charles W. Chesnutt.* Jackson: University Press of Mississippi, 2004. Comments on such topics as Chesnutt's racial non-fiction, theorizing race, melodrama and popular fiction, and mulatta fiction. Offers readings of five major works.

Wonham, Henry B. "Plenty of Room for Us All? Participation and Prejudice in Charles Chesnutt's 'Dialect Tales.'" *Studies in American Fiction* 26 (Autumn, 1998): 131-146. Argues that the dialect tales deal in a subtle way with the restriction of African American rights in the post-Reconstruction South; asserts Chesnutt focuses on a historical moment between Reconstruction and the return of white racism.

Wright, Susan Prothro, and Ernestine Pickens Glass, ed. *Passing in the Works of Charles W. Chesnutt.* University Press of Mississippi, 2010. Contains nine essays on such topics as history, teaching, narrative and technical strategies, D. W. Griffith, performing race, mixed-race characters, conscience, and historicizing whiteness.

—Earl Paulus Murphy; Sherry G. Southard; Patricia A. R. Williams; Robert C. Evans

Alice Childress

Playwright

Born: Charleston, South Carolina; October 12, 1916

Died: New York, New York; August 14, 1994

LONG FICTION: *A Short Walk*, 1979.

SHORT FICTION: *Like One of the Family: Conversations from a Domestic's Life*, 1956.

DRAMA: *Florence*, pr. 1949, pb. 1950; *Just a Little Simple*, pr. 1950; *Gold Through the Trees*, pr. 1952; *Trouble in Mind*, pr. 1955, pb. 1971; *Wedding Band: A Love/Hate Story in Black and White*, pr. 1966 (staged), pr. 1973 (televised), pb. 1973; *The World on a Hill*, pb. 1968; *Wine in the Wilderness*, pr. 1969 (televised), pb. 1969, pr. 1976; (televised); *String*, pr. 1969 (staged), pb. 1971, pr. 1979 (televised; adaptation ofa Guy de Maupassant story); *The Freedom Drum*, pr. 1969 (music by Nathan Woodard; retitled *Young Martin Luther King*); *Mojo: A Black Love Story*, pr. 1970, pb. 1971; *The African Garden*, pb. 1971 (with Woodard); *When the Rattlesnake Sounds*, pb. 1975 (for children); *Let's Hear It for the Queen*, pb. 1976 (for children); *Sea Island Song*, pr. 1979 (with Woodard; pr. 1984 as *Gullah*); *Moms: A Praise Play for a Black Comedienne*, pr. 1987 (with Woodard); *After the Last Supper*, 2008; *Gullah*, 2008; *A King Remembered*, 2008; *Man Bearing a Pitche*, 2008; *A Portrait of Fannie Lou Hamer*, 2008; *Selected Plays*, 2011 (Kathy A Perkins, editor).

SCREENPLAY: *A Hero Ain't Nothin' but a Sandwich*, 1978.

CHILDREN'S/YOUNG ADULT LITERATURE: *A Hero Ain't Nothin' but a Sandwich*, 1973; *Rainbow Jordan*, 1981; *Those Other People*, 1989.

EDITED TEXTS: *Black Scenes: Collection of Scenes from Plays Written by Black People About Black Experience*, 1971.

Achievements

Alice Childress's *Gold Through the Trees* was the first play by an African American woman to be produced professionally with union actors. In 1956 Childress became the first woman to receive an Obie Award, for *Trouble in Mind*. She was appointed to the Radcliffe Institute (now the Mary Ingraham Bunting Institute) for Independent Study (1966-1968) and was awarded a graduate medal for writing produced there. Her novel *A Hero Ain't Nothin' but a Sandwich* was named the ALA Best Young Adult Book of 1975, and it received the Jane Addams Award for a young adult novel in 1974.

Biography

Alice Childress was five years old when her parents separated and she was sent to live with her maternal grandmother, who had seven children of her own. Although Grandmother Eliza was a poverty-stricken former slave with only a fifth-grade education, she was intellectually curious and self-educated. Childress credited her grandmother with teaching her how to observe and encouraging her to write. Her grandmother also took her to Salem Church in Harlem, where Alice learned storytelling from the Wednesday night testimonials. Childress was educated in New York public schools, leaving before she graduated from high school. She encountered racial prejudice at school but recalled several teachers who made a difference, encouraging her to read and introducing her to the library.

Childress revealed little about her private life, but it is known that she married and divorced Alvin Childress, who played Amos on television's *Amos 'n' Andy Show*. The couple had a daughter, Jean, born on November 1, 1935, who was raised by her mother. To support herself and her child while she tried to establish her writing and acting career, Childress held a variety of jobs, including domestic servant, salesperson, and insurance agent. Through these jobs, she became acquainted with numerous working-class people, whose lives became the basis of characters in her later plays and novels.

In 1941 Childress joined the American Negro Theatre (ANT), which met in the Schomburg Library in Harlem. Like all ANT members, Childress participated in all aspects of theater, though her main interest was acting. She stayed with ANT for eleven years but was frustrated by the emphasis on issues important to black men and the consequent neglect of black women's issues and roles. When she tried to act in the theater at large, she ran into problems because she was considered too light-skinned to play black roles but not fair enough to play whites. Although she starred in the Broadway production of *Anna Lucasta* (1944-1946) and did some work in radio and television, Childress finally

Alice Childress, front, with James Broderick and Ruby Dee, stars of her play, *Wedding Band* (photo by Jack Mitchell, courtesy of Getty Images)

concluded that she would be better able to express herself as a writer.

Interested in creating complex and realistic black female characters, Childress wrote *Florence*, a one-act play that she hoped would show that African American drama did not have to be sensational to be significant. This drama, about a working-class black woman on her way to New York to rescue her daughter from a failed career in the theater, opened new areas to African American theater, eventually influencing Amiri Baraka's Black Revolutionary Theater and woman-centered African American dramatists such as Ntozake Shange. Childress's next plays did not focus on women, however. One was a reworking of Langston Hughes's serialized articles, *Simple Speaks His Mind*, published in the *Chicago Defender*, as a musical review titled *Just a Little Simple*.

In 1955, Childress returned to her controversial subjects and assertive black women characters with *Trouble in Mind*, a play about a black actress trying to maintain her dignity while playing menial roles. The play was well received Off-Broadway, but Broadway options were abandoned because producers considered it too risky for the commercial theater. It was presented twice by the British Broadcasting Corporation (BBC), however. Childress received the Obie Award for *Trouble in Mind* in 1956, becoming the first woman to receive the award.

Also in 1956, Childress published *Like One of the Family: Conversations from a Domestic's Life*, a series of vignettes or monologues that incorporated sketches from her *Baltimore Afro-American* column "Here's Mildred," which she would write through 1958. The column and book centered on Mildred, a domestic servant modeled on Childress's aunt. On July 17, 1957, she married a musician named Nathan Woodward. She and Woodward collaborated on a number of projects; he wrote music for her play *Sea Island Song*, later produced as *Gullah*.

During the 1960s, Childress focused on writing plays. She chose to ignore white audiences and focused on controversial topics, which made production difficult. During this period, she wrote *Wedding Band: A Love/Hate Story in Black and White*, which focused on interracial lovers; *The Freedom Drum* (later retitled *Young Martin Luther King*); *String*, an adaptation of Guy de Maupassant's story "A Piece of String"; and *Wine in the Wilderness*, on revolution and black males' problematic attitudes toward black women.

Also during this period, Childress participated in a variety of communities of writers and scholars. In 1965 she was part of a BBC panel discussion, "The Negro in American Theater," which also included James Baldwin, LeRoi Jones (Amiri Baraka), and Langston Hughes. The writer Tillie Olsen recommended Childress for an appointment at the Radcliffe Institute for Independent Study, where she worked on her writing from 1966 to 1968.

During the 1970s Childress traveled extensively to study drama and other arts: to the Soviet Union in 1971; to Beijing and Shanghai, China, in 1973; and to Ghana, West Africa, in 1974. She also shifted the focus of her own writing at this time, producing a young adult novel, *A Hero Ain't Nothin' but a Sandwich* and its screenplay; two plays for children, *When the Rattlesnake Sounds*, about a summer in the life of escaped slave Harriet Tubman, and *Let's Hear It for the Queen*; and *A Short Walk*, a novel. Also in 1979, Childress's play *Sea Island Song*, which had been commissioned by the South Carolina Arts Commission, was presented in Columbia and Charleston, South Carolina, during the observance of Alice Childress Week.

In the 1980s, Childress continued to write and speak out. She wrote her second young adult novel, *Rainbow Jordan*, in 1981. She was artist-in-residence at the University of Massachusetts, Amherst, in 1984. Her final works were *Moms: A Praise Play for a Black Comedienne*, based on the life of comedienne "Moms" Mabley, and a novel, *Those Other People*. Her daughter Jean died of cancer in May, 1990. Four years later, Childress died of cancer, in Queens.

Analysis: Drama

Alice Childress's playwriting career spanned four decades, an achievement in itself. Even more important, she broke with tradition followed by both male and female playwrights, which held that significant African American drama dealt with sensational topics such as lynching and focused on male concerns such as the disenfranchisement of the black man. Childress chose instead to write about the concerns of black women. A major theme is the female psychological journey; it applies equally to her domestics such as Mildred in *Like One of the Family* and disappointed artists such as Wiletta Mayer in *Trouble in Mind*.

Childress addressed issues of gender and race through her black female characters. She worked against stereotypes prevalent in both black and white American literature to present ordinary women—strong, searching for their identities, and standing up to prejudices based on class, gender, and race. Even when she wrote about controversial topics such as miscegenation, her characters and the situations were realistic and believable. Her explorations laid the groundwork for later African American women playwrights such as Ntozake Shange and Sonia Sanchez.

Childress's unwillingness to compromise her principles or play to white audiences cost her in terms of production and visibility. However, she attracted the attention of feminist scholars in the 1980s and 1990s, and she has always had the attention of African American theater people. Elizabeth Brown-Guillory calls her the mother of African American professional theater, and the debt that those who followed her owe to her pioneering work in presenting realistic and complex black women characters supports that title.

Trouble in Mind

Childress uses two tried and true theatrical devices in *Trouble in Mind*—a play-within-a-play and metadrama, focusing on an examination of theater itself. Placed in the larger context of the Civil Rights movement, with allusions to Rosa Parks and Martin Luther King, Jr., the play features Wiletta Mayer, a veteran actress who has been cast in an antilynching drama written by a white playwright. Although Wiletta and the

other veteran black actors have been conditioned to accept the denigrating conditions of working in white-controlled theater, she cannot justify her character's advising her son to give himself up to a lynch mob. When she argues against the play and its portrayal of blacks, the cast is dismissed with the clear implication that Wiletta will not be called for the next rehearsal. The play-within-the-play, however, has made clear the problems of stereotypes of African Americans.

Wedding Band

This play about the ten-year romantic relationship of a black seamstress, Julia, and a white baker, Herman, was not well received either by blacks, who saw it as integrationist, or whites, who were offended by the topic of miscegenation. In the world of the play, Julia receives little support from her black neighbors, who do not see her relationship with Herman as positive in any way, or from Herman's mother and sister, who make racist comments and try to sabotage the relationship. When Herman develops influenza, collapsing in Julia's home, the situation is serious because the same laws that have prevented Julia and Herman's marriage will result in their prosecution if the relationship is discovered. Julia calls in Herman's mother, but instead of help, she gets abuse. She does stand up to her, though, claiming her place as her daughter-in-law. The play examines problematic relationships between black and white women and between black women themselves, as well as the interracial love relationship.

Wine in the Wilderness

Wine in the Wilderness is set in the apartment of a middle-class black artist during a 1960s Harlem riot. Childress depicts the arrogance and ignorance of the black middle class in the artist's treatment of a young lower-class black woman,

Tommy (Tomorrow Marie). The artist, Bill, has been working on a triptych dedicated to black womanhood—as Bill understands it. He has completed two of the panels, one depicting "innocent" black girlhood, the second a beautiful, regal woman representing an idealized Mother Africa. He has been looking for a model for the third panel—the "lost" black woman of his imagination, rude and vulgar, the antithesis of the African queen. His neighbors find Tommy during the riot, and she, believing that she is to be the model for an ideal woman in the artist's work, goes with them to his apartment. When she realizes the truth, she confronts the group. Finally Bill understands his shortsightedness and persuades "his" Tomorrow to pose for the new center panel as woman of the future. The middle-class assimilationists learn to value an assertive black woman.

Other Literary Forms

Although she wrote many plays, Alice Childress is perhaps better known for her young adult novels, especially *A Hero Ain't Nothin' but a Sandwich.* Childress wrote the screenplay for the film based on this book, which premiered in 1978. Her other novels include *Rainbow Jordan* and *Those Other People,* both for young adults, and *A Short Walk.*

Bibliography

Austin, Gayle. "Alice Childress: Black Woman Playwright as Feminist Critic." *Southern Quarterly* 25 (Spring, 1987): 53-62. Focuses on Childress as social critic and transformer of images of black women. Discusses *Trouble in Mind* and *Wine in the Wilderness* in the context of Elizabeth Abel's three stages of feminist criticism.

_____. "Black Women Playwrights Exorcizing Myths." *Phylon* 48 (Fall, 1997): 229-239. Examines the work of Childress, Lorraine Hansberry, and Ntozake Shange in dispelling stereotypical myths of African American characters, such as the tragic mulatto and the comic Negro, and in presenting new constructions, such as the black militant and the evolving black woman.

Brown-Guillory, Elizabeth. *Their Place on the Stage: Black Women Playwrights in America.* Westport, Conn.: Greenwood Press, 1988. Contains summaries and comparisons of the work of Alice Childress, Lorraine Hansberry, and Ntozake Shange.

Dugan, Olga. "Telling the Truth: Alice Childress as Theorist and Playwright." *The Journal of Negro History* 81 (1996): 123-137. Examines Alice Childress's essays as a reflection of her theory of a black self-determinist theater, in which individual black playwrights should use black culture and history in plays that demonstrate black self-determination. Childress believed such plays should focus on realistic situations and conditions under which African Americans live.

Hawkins, Alfonso W. "The Nurture of African American Youth in the Fiction of Ann Petry, Alice Childress, and Gloria Naylor." *CLA Journal* 46, no. 4 (June, 2003): 457-478. Provides interesting insights into the influence that nurture—and many other societal forces—have over African American youths, both in fiction and in life.

Jennings, LaVinia Delois. *Alice Childress.* New York: Twayne, 1995. A comprehensive and accessible critical introduction to Childress's life and work. Contains a discussion of Childress's life and career in the theater as well as summaries and critiques of individual works. Especially helpful are a succinct chronology of Childress's life and work and a bibliography, which is divided into primary sources—Childress's novels, plays, productions in other media, and her articles, essays, and interviews—and secondary sources.

"The Refusal of Motherhood in African American Women's Theater." *MELUS* 25, nos. 3/4 (Fall/Winter, 2000): 117-136. An interesting review of several plays, including Childress's *Mojo.*

— Elsie Galbreath Haley; Robert C. Evans

Lucille Clifton

Poet and Novelist

Born: Depew, New York; June 27, 1936

POETRY: *Good Times,* 1969; *Good News About the Earth,* 1972; *An Ordinary Woman,* 1974; *Two-Headed Woman,* 1980; *Good Woman: Poems and a Memoir, 1969-1980,* 1987; *Next: New Poems,* 1987; *Quilting: Poems, 1987-1990,* 1991; *The Book of Light,* 1993; *The Terrible Stories,* 1996; *Blessing the Boats: New and Selected Poems, 1988-2000,* 2000; *Mercy,* 2004; *Collected Poems,* 2012.

NONFICTION: *Generations: A Memoir,* 1976.

CHILDREN'S/YOUNG ADULT LITERA-TURE: *The Black BC's,* 1970; *Some of the Days of Everett Anderson,* 1970; *Everett Anderson's Christmas Coming,* 1971; *All Us Come Cross the Water,* 1973; *The Boy Who Didn't Believe in Spring,* 1973; *Everett Anderson's Year,* 1974; *The Times They Used toBe,* 1974; *My Brother Fine with Me,* 1975; *Everett Anderson's Friend,* 1976; *Three Wishes,* 1976; *Amifika,* 1977; *Everett Anderson's 1-2-3,* 1977; *Everett Anderson's Nine Month Long,* 1978; *The Lucky Stone,* 1979; *Sonora Beautiful,* 1981; *Everett Anderson's Goodbye,* 1983; *One of the Problems of Everett Anderson,* 2001.

Achievements

In 1988, Lucille Clifton became the only poet ever to have two books chosen as finalists for the Pulitzer Prize in the same year: *Next: New Poems* and *Good Woman: Poems and a Memoir, 1969-1980.* Lucille Clifton won the National Book Award for *Blessing the Boats: New and Selected Poems, 1988-2000;* previously, she was a National Book Award finalist for *The Terrible Stories.* She also won the Coretta Scott King Award for *Everett Anderson's Goodbye* in 1984. Other honors include an Emmy Award from the American Academy of Television Arts and Sciences, the Shelley Memorial Award, the Charity Randall Citation, the Shestack Prize from the American Poetry Review, the Lannan Literary Award, and two creative writing fellowships from the National Endowment for the Arts. She holds honorary degrees from the University of Maryland and Towson State University. Clifton was elected to the American Academy of Arts and Sciences and appointed chancellor of the Academy of American Poets in 1999. In 1991, Clifton became a distinguished professor of humanities at St. Mary's College in Columbia, Maryland.

Biography

Thelma Lucille Sayles Clifton, daughter of Samuel L. and Thelma Moore Sayles, was born in New York, near Buffalo, and grew up with two half sisters and a brother. Her father worked for the New York steel mills. Her mother was a launderer, homemaker, and aspiring poet but once had to burn all her poems because her husband told her, "Ain't no wife of mine going to be no poetry writer."

Ironically, by both parents, Clifton was encouraged to be anything she wanted to be. She was named for her great-grandmother, who, according to her father, was the first black woman to be legally hanged in the state of Virginia. The first in her family to finish high school or consider attending college, at sixteen, Clifton entered college at Howard University, having earned a full scholarship. After majoring in drama and attending for two years, Clifton lost her scholarship. She told her father," I don't need that stuff. I'm going to write poems. I can do what I want to do! I'm from Dahomey women!"

After transferring to Fredonia State Teachers College in 1955, Clifton worked as an actor and began her writing career. While at Fredonia, she met novelist Ishmael Reed at a writers' group, and he showed some of her poems to Langston Hughes, who was the first to publish Clifton's writing.

In 1958 she married Fred James Clifton. They had six children, four daughters, Sidney, Fredrica, Gillian, and Alexia, and two sons, Channing and Graham. In 1969, poet Robert Hayden entered her poems into competition for the Young Men's-Young Women's Hebrew Association Poetry Center Discovery Award. Clifton won the award and with it the publication of her first volume of poems, *Good Times*, which was chosen as one of the ten best books of the year by *The New York Times*. Prior to 1971, when she became poet in residence at the historically black Coppin State College in Baltimore, Maryland, Clifton worked in state and federal government positions. She remained at Coppin until 1974. From 1979 through 1982, she was poet laureate of the state of Maryland. From 1982 to 1983, she was a visiting writer at Columbia University School of the Arts and at George Washington University. Subsequently, she taught literature and creative writing at the University of California at Santa Cruz, and later at St. Mary's College. Besides appearing in more than one hundred anthologies of poetry, her poems have come to popular attention through her numerous television appearances.

Photo courtesy of *Afro Newspaper* and Getty Images

Analysis: Poetry

Distinguished by her minimalist style, Clifton is sometimes compared with poets Gwendolyn Brooks and Emily Dickinson. Clifton is usually considered one of the prominent Black Aesthetic poets, along with Sonia Sanchez and Amiri Baraka, who were consciously breaking with Eurocentric conventions in their work. The characteristics of Clifton's craft—her concise, often untitled free verse, use of vernacular speech, repetition, puns and allusions, lowercase letters, sparse punctuation, and focused use of common words—have become her trademark style, which is clearly unfettered by others' expectations. Without worrying about convention, about boundaries—created either physically or emotionally—Clifton shares her perceptions of life by writing about the feelings humans share. Her rationale for writing poetry is to assert the importance of being human. In an interview with Michael Glaser, Clifton stated that:

> writing is a way of continuing to hope. When things sometimes feel as if they're not going to get any better, writing offers a way of trying to connect with something beyond that obvious feeling . . . a way of remembering I am not alone.

She states further that she sees writing as a way to bear witness, to hold back the darkness by acknowledging the pain of the past and then choosing a more joyful future.

Good Times

Clifton's early work was frequently inspired by her family, especially her children, and was often a celebration of African American ancestry, heritage, and culture. In the title poem of this collection, Clifton reminds all children, "oh children think about the/ good times." She juxtaposes society's perceptions and her own in the opening poem of the collection—"in the inner city/ or/ like we call it/ home"—in order to honor the place she lives. Believing in the humanity of all people, she calls on each person, regardless of ancestry, to take control of his or her life. Of Robert, in the poem by the same name, she states he "married a master/ who whipped his mind/ until he died," suggesting through the image that the union was one of mutual consent. Her impatience with humans of all kinds who do not strive to improve their lot is a theme begun with this collection and continued throughout her more than three

decades of publishing. Another theme that arises here is optimism, as in "Flowers": "Oh/ here we are/ flourishing for the field/ and the name of the place/ is Love."

Good Woman: Poems and a Memoir

One theme of the poems in this collection involves Clifton's ethnic pride, as is reflected in "After Kent State": "white ways are/ the way of death/ come into the/ black/ and live." This volume also contains a section called "Heroes," which directly extends this first theme, and ends the book with a section called "Some Jesus:"

> I have learned
> some few things
> like when a man
> walk manly
> he don't stumble
> even in the lion's den.

While the gender is male, Clifton would not limit the message to men. Overall, her early work heralds African Americans for their resistance to oppression and their survival of racism.

An Ordinary Woman

An Ordinary Woman includes poems divided into two sections, beginning with "Sisters," a celebration of family and relationships. "The Lesson of the Falling Leaves" includes the following line:

> the leaves believe such letting go is love
> such love is faith such faith is grace such
> grace is god i agree with the leaves.

It is a testimony to hope, a theme that runs throughout her work. Consistently juxtaposing past with present, Clifton provides wisdom to guide the future, as in the example of "Jackie Robinson":

ran against walls
without breaking.
in night games
was not foul
but, brave as a hit
over whitestone fences,
entered the conquering dark.

Two-Headed Woman

Two-Headed Woman, which invokes the African American folk belief in a "Two-Headed Woman," with its overtones of a voodoo conjurer, begins with a section titled "Homage to Mine," moves onto "Two-Headed Woman," and concludes with "The Light That Came to Lucille Clifton." While Clifton's works often have allusions to Christianity, as in the "Some Jesus" series in *Good News About the Earth*, she refers to other faiths as well, including the Hindu goddess Kali, from "An Ordinary Woman," providing evidence of her openness to multiple ways of knowing. As a "Two-Headed Woman," in the opening poem of that section, Clifton says she has "one face turned outward/ one face/ swiveling slowly in." Spirituality and mysticism pervade this collection, as the final poem attests, with its reference to the "shimmering voices" of her ancestors, whom the poet has heard singing in the "populated air."

Quilting

In five parts, each of the first four named for traditional quilt patterns, "Log Cabin," "Catalpa Flower," "Eight-Pointed Star," and "Tree of Life," *Quilting* seems pieced together, as a quilt. It ends with a single poem, "Blessing the Boats," in "prayer," as if the spiritual life serves as the connecting threads. Clifton honors those whose roles in history have brought about change, like "February 11, 1990" dedicated to "Nelson Mandela and Winnie," and "Memo" which is dedicated "to Fannie Lou Hamer." The poem's

"questions and answers" ends with "the surest failure/ is the unattempted walk."

The Terrible Stories

In *The Terrible Stories*, Clifton chronicles the terrible stories of her own life, which include her struggle with breast cancer, and the terrible stories of her people, which include slavery and the prejudice that has survived time. The book ends with a section called "From the Book of David," which ends with a question from the poem "What Manner of Man." Referring to the biblical David, the poet asks how this David will be remembered "if he stands in the tents of history/ bloody skull in one hand, harp in the other?" Clifton's ability to look at history—ancient, contemporary, or personal—and find redemption in it gives humanity a way to face and survive its failures; this perspective shows her consistent faith in grace.

Blessing the Boats

This anthology includes new poems as well as selected poems from *Next*, sometimes called a collection of sorrow songs, as loss is the overriding theme. Once more, "New Poems," the opening section of the anthology, records and comments on contemporary events of the twentieth century, such as school shootings, referred to in "The Times," and the bombing of black churches, referred to in "Alabama 9/15/63." It also addresses private occurrences, such as the traumas that gave rise to such poems as "Dialysis" and "Donor."

Other Literary Forms

In addition to her poetry, Lucille Clifton has written prose, often for children but also for adults. *Generations: A Memoir*, is included as apart of *Good Woman: Poems and a Memoir, 1969-1980*. She began publishing for children in 1970 with *Some of the Days of Everett Anderson*, short poems in a picture-book format that spawned a series about the life of a young black boy. *The Times They Used to Be* is written as a narrative poem. She has written other picture books in prose: *The Boy Who Didn't Believe in Spring, All Us Come Cross the Water, My Brother Fine with Me, Three Wishes*, and *Amifika*, as well as a short novel, *The Lucky Stone*. In response to questions her own six children had, Clifton wrote *The Black BC's*, an alphabet book which blends poetry with prose. A departure from her usual perspective, *Sonora Beautiful* features a white girl as the protagonist.

Bibliography

Anaporte-Easton,Jean." Healing Our Wounds: The Direction of Difference in the Poetry of Lucille Clifton and Judith Johnson." *Mid-American Review* 14, no. 2 (1994). This essay suggests that Clifton's voice is distinctive because of her use of physical imagery, particularly of the body, in order to write a work that seeks to unite it with both mind and spirit.

Bennett, Bruce. "Preservation Poets." *The New York Times Book Review*, March 1, 1992, p. 22-23. Poet and critic Bennett discusses Clifton's *Quilting*, noting that the first four sections are named after traditional quilting designs, yet the final section, "prayer," consists of a single poem. He believes readers familiar with Clifton's work will witness recurrent themes section by section: importance of history on the present and future, celebration of women, and life as a personal journey of spiritual growth and discovery.

Cahill, Susan, ed. *Writing Women's Lives: An Anthology of Autobiographical Narratives by Twentieth Century American Women Writers*. New York: HarperPerennial, 1994. This collection of narratives, more than five hundred pages in length, provides extensive points of comparison as the careers of nearly fifty female writers are featured. The women included cut across cultures and span the century, but all are contemporaries of Clifton.

Carger, Chris Liska, and Henrietta M. Smith. "To Make a Poet Black, and Bid Him Sing." *Book Links* 12, no. 2 (December/ January, 2003): 45-46. An analysis of African American poetry for children.

Clifton, Lucille. "I'd Like Not to Be a Stranger in the World: A Conversation/Interview with Lucille Clifton." Interview by Michael Glaser. *The Antioch Review* 58, no. 3 (2000): 310-328. In an extensive interview, Clifton discusses why she writes and explores the genesis of the topics about which she writes. She emphasizes the importance of family in her writing, particularly her heritage and the storytelling tradition, epitomized in her husband's last words to her: "Tell my story."

Davis, Eisa. "Lucille Clifton and Sonia Sanchez: A Conversation." *Callaloo* 25, no. 4 (Fall, 2002): 1038-1075. An interesting interview with two ofthe most important figures in contemporary literature.

Holladay, Hillary. "Black Names in White Space: Lucille Clifton's South." *Southern Literary Journal* 34, no. 2 (Spring, 2002): 120-134. This article focuses on the South as it is portrayed in Clifton's work. Beyond its discussion of slavery, the article also explores the relevance of names and the information they convey.

Holladay, Hilary. *Wild Blessings: The Poetry of Lucille Clifton*. Louisiana State UP, 2004. Deals with such topics as Sylvia Plath, menstruation, biblical poems, dialogism, and selfhood and contains an interview with Clifton.

Jordan, Shirley, ed. *Broken Silences: Interviews with Black and White Women Writers*. New Brunswick, N.J.: Rutgers University Press, 1993. In an interview format, Jordan and Clifton explore the differences in perception between black and white women and how that impacts how each approaches their writing. Focuses on *Sonora Beautiful*, one of the few works by a female African American writer told from the perspective of a white protagonist.

Kriner, Tiffany Eberle. "Conjuring Hope in a Body: Lucille Clifton's Eschatology." *Christianity & Literature* 54, no. 2 (Winter, 2005): 185-204. A thought-provoking look at the role of hope in Clifton's poetry. Explains the concept of eschatology and its application in Clifton's work.

Lupton, Mary Jane. *Lucille Clifton: Her Life and Letters.* Praeger, 2006. Deals with such issues as children, teaching, politics, and Clifton's legacy.

Whitley, Edward. "'A Long Missing Part of Itself': Bringing Lucille Clifton's *Generations* into American Literature." *MELUS* 26, no. 2 (Summer, 2001): 47-65. An interesting article that explores Clifton's autobiography and compares her work with that of Walt Whitman.

— *Alexa L. Sandmann; Robert C. Evans*

Ta-Nehisi Coates

Essayist, Cultural Critic, and Comic Book Author

Born: Baltimore, Maryland; September 30, 1975

LONG FICTION: *The Water Dancer: A Novel,* 2019

POETRY: *Asphalt Sketches,* 1990

ESSAYS: "This Is How We Lost to the White Man," 2008; "Fear of a Black President," 2012; "The Case for Reparations," 2014; "The Black Family in the Age of Mass Incarceration," 2015

NONFICTION: *The Beautiful Struggle,* 2008; *Between the World and Me,* 2015; *We Were Eight Years in Power: An American Tragedy,* 2017

COMIC BOOKS: *Black Panther,* vol. 6 nos. 1-18, and nos.166-171, 2016-2018; *A Nation Under Our Feet* nos. 1-12; *A Nation Under Our Feet,* Book 1, 2016; *A Nation Under Our Feet,* Book 2, 2017; *A Nation Under Our Feet,* Book 3, 2017; *Avengers of the New World,* nos. 13-18 and nos. 166-171; *Avengers of the New World,* Book 1, 2017; *Avengers of the New World,* Book 2, 2018; *Black Panther: World of Wakanda,* nos. 16, 2016 (with Roxane Gay and Yona Harvey); *Vol. 1: Dawn of the Midnight Angels,* 2017; *Black Panther and the Crew,* nos. 1-6, 2017 (with Yona Harvey); *Vol. 1: We Are the Streets,* 2017; *Black Panther,* vol. 7, no.1, 2018–; *Captain America,* vol. 9, no. 1, 2018–

Achievements

Ta-Nehisi Coates has had an enormous impact on American culture in the twenty-first century, not only as an essayist and cultural critic but also as the writer for various influential comic books. One comic book series, *Black Panther,* was turned into a highly acclaimed and very popular 2018 Hollywood film. Probably more people are familiar with Coates's work in comics and film than with his essays and nonfiction books, but his work in all genres has been widely praised. His essays and other nonfiction, in particular, often become topics of important national conversations and debates.

Coates has won a nonstop string of significant awards and prizes. These include a 2012 Hillman Prize for Opinion and Analysis Journalism; a 2013 National Magazine Award for Essays and Criticism; a 2014 George Polk Award for Commentary; a 2015 Harriet Beecher Stowe Center Prize for Writing to Advance Social Justice; and a 2015 Visiting Fellowship at the American Library in Paris. Other honors have included a 2015 National Book Award for Nonfiction; a prestigious 2015 "genius" grant from the John D. and Catherine T. MacArthur Foundation; a 2015 Kirkus Prize for Nonfiction; a 2018 Dayton Literary Peace Prize in Nonfiction; and a 2018 Eisner Award for Best Limited Series (shared with Roxane Gay and Alitha E. Martinez). He has taught at the Massachusetts Institute of Technology, the City University of New York, and New York University.

Biography

Ta-Nehisi Coates was born on September 30, 1975. He spent his childhood in Baltimore, Maryland, a city marked by urban poverty, drug abuse, and one of the highest murder rates in

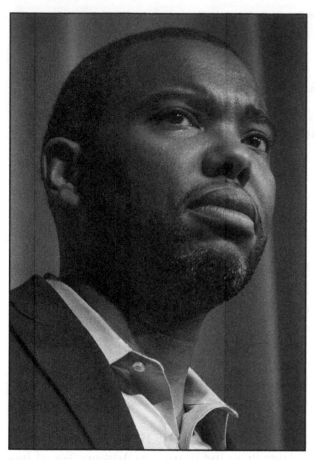

Photo courtesy of Eduardo Montes-Bradley

among other national newspapers and magazines.

Coates's father, William Paul Coates, was a Vietnam veteran and a former member of the Black Panther Party. His mother, Cheryl Waters, was a teacher. The influence of both his parents on Coates's education and politics is apparent. William Paul Coates founded a small Afrocentric publishing endeavor and ran the operation from the basement of their home in Baltimore. Later, he would become a librarian at Howard University, where the younger Coates enrolled in accordance with his parents' wishes. As a young man, Coates was an indifferent student who was more interested in popular culture—such as video games, television, comic books, fantasy novels, gaming, and professional sports—than in academic study per se. Much of Coates's education came from outside formal settings. His mother insisted that he write self-reflective essays as a form of discipline for behavior she disliked, such as his lack of attention to schoolwork, disrespect of teachers, and fighting.

Although Coates clearly loves and respects both his parents, his childhood was difficult at times. He was one of seven children that his father had with four women. The children were close despite going back and forth between the homes of their father and mothers. Coates always lived with his father, a strict disciplinarian who was willing to utilize corporal punishment, but also a person who emphasized the importance of education and black pride.

After a spotty high school career, Coates was admitted to Howard but left before completing his degree to accept a position with the *Washington City Reporter*, where he began to make a name for himself as a promising young journalist. Eventually he became highly regarded in journalistic and literary circles. Nevertheless, Coates is not without his critics, especially many conservative writers but also the progressive

the United States. Emerging from a middle-class background, Coates became a highly regarded journalist and author. In addition to numerous blog posts and magazine features, he has also published a book of poetry, *Asphalt Sketches* (1990), several well-received nonfiction books, and written contributions to many popular comic books, including the *Black Panther* series.

Coates has been a senior editor and national correspondent for the *Atlantic*, a publication he initially joined as a blogger after previous stints with *The Washington City Reporter*, the *Philadelphia Weekly*, and high-profile publications such as the *Village Voice* and *Time*. He has also published pieces in the *New York Times Magazine*, the *Washington Post*, and *O: The Oprah Magazine*, scholar Cornel West, who called his writing immature and superficial and accused him of proffering "linguistic glitz."

Coates lives in New York with his wife, Kenyatta Matthews, whom he met at Howard University, and their son, Samori Maceo-Paul Coates.

Analysis

If there is one consistent theme that cuts through Coates's writings, it is the paradoxical and contradictory relationship between white supremacy and democracy. Coates turns an unflinching and often pessimistic eye on the racial issues of his time. Much of his writing focuses on issues such as police violence and the repression of black people. Beyond this, his interests as a writer also reflect a type of postmodern blurring of high culture and popular culture, as alongside his online posts on history, democracy and inequality, police brutality in black communities, the legacies of white supremacy and slavery, and the connections between poverty and racism, readers also find commentary on sports, movies, and comic books. Coates has also authored numerous comic books himself.

The Atlantic Essays

Beginning in 2008, Coates began publishing a series of long essays in the *Atlantic* that were focused on controversial issues involving racism and structural inequality in the United States. The first of these essays, "This Is How We Lost to the White Man," takes a critical look at Bill Cosby's "personal responsibility" speaking tour, in which he exhorted black men to stop blaming whites for their problems and "pull themselves up by their own bootstraps." Four years later, in 2012, Coates similarly took on the conservative rhetoric of Barack Obama, contending that throughout most of his first term in office, Obama had refused to talk about racism at all.

Building on this 2012 essay, in 2014, Coates dove even deeper into the history of white supremacy and the consequences of centuries of separate and unequal treatment for black individuals and communities. He did so in a long cover story for the *Atlantic*, "The Case for Reparations," which argues fiercely for the economic, political, and social need for compensating blacks for past racism.

In 2015, Coates published another long cover story in the *Atlantic* titled "The Black Family in the Age of Mass Incarceration." Coates calls America's prisons the Gray Wastes, and he documents the havoc that mass incarceration of black men has on African American communities.

The Beautiful Struggle

The Beautiful Struggle was Ta-Nehisi Coates's first nonfiction book. Published in 2008, it is a poignant memoir of his youth in Baltimore. The book covers his childhood and teenage years, ending just as Coates is about to leave for Howard University, a place he calls the Mecca as a homage to his mother's faith that Howard was the ultimate and rightful destination for her beloved son.

Much of the book is set in the 1980s, the decade during which crack cocaine invaded America's cities and added a heightened dimension of danger to the urban experience. Although Coates reminisces about life at school and in his neighborhood, his memoir primarily focuses on family. His father, William Paul Coates, looms like an angry but loving giant throughout the book's pages. An essential force in shaping the kind of intellectual Coates would become, the elder Coates was both feared and adored by his children. A veteran of the Vietnam War and a former member of the Black Panther Party, he would brook no nonsense or dissent from his children and was staunch in his mission to educate them about black history and the proud legacy of their ancestors.

Coates's mother, Cheryl Waters, also nurtured the writer and man Coates would become. Waters made her peace with a paternalistic and controlling husband who continued to be involved with other women even after their marriage. But she was also a strong and independent person in her own right. As Coates conveys in his memoir, his mother played a significant role in both his formal and informal education, utilizing corporal punishment just like his father, checking his homework and assigning him extra, holding him accountable, teaching him about the world he would inhabit, and insisting that he attend Howard University.

Aside from his parents, the other key figure in his memoir is Coates's older brother, Bill. Coates looked up to Big Bill, but he was a completely different sort of person from young Ta-Nehisi. Where Bill found a sense of identity in parties, drugs, alcohol, clothes, jewelry, basketball, and girls, Coates eventually found his in literature, history, and African drumming. As a young man, Bill carried a gun, while Ta-Nehisi carried a book or a drum. The main thing they shared besides a father was a love for rap music. Surviving his troubled teenage years through a combination of wits and luck, Bill managed to get accepted to Howard University and, unlike Coates, he ended up staying and he was able to achieve a modicum of success. Despite this hopeful outcome, Bill is portrayed primarily as a tragic figure in *The Beautiful Struggle*, a young man trapped by false idols of masculinity, driven by hedonistic urges, too smart to fall victim to the streets but unable to escape their allure: "Bill was moved by laws of survival. He was a soldier, insistent that he would not be caught out there. But the 'out there' was bigger than he ever dreamed."

Between the World and Me

The ominous "out there" that Coates alluded to in *The Beautiful Struggle* is precisely what he turned his attention to in his next book, *Between the World and Me*, first published in 2015. Garnering much critical praise and honors, including the National Book Award for Nonfiction, *Between the World and Me* was also a finalist for the Pulitzer Prize for General Nonfiction. Upon publication it became an instant best seller while making Coates a nationally recognized media figure.

Coates's second book reflects his pessimism about race relations in the United States. It was partially motivated by a meeting Coates had with Barack Obama in 2013, when the president pulled him aside, pushed back against a critique Coates had published in the *Atlantic* in 2012, and urged him to be more optimistic about racial progress—advice Coates resisted.

As he had in his 2008 memoir, Coates recalls that he always needed to be wary of bodily harm from multiple sources: his father, the police, and other young black men. This precarious nature of the black body is one of Coates's central themes in *Between the World and Me* as he repeatedly refers to bodies under siege, bodies exploited by white supremacy, bodies that hurt and are hurt by other bodies.

Although ostensibly writing to his teenage son in an attempt to educate him, Coates treats the boy as an adult and spares him no truth about the damage that has been inflicted on black bodies by white supremacy. He also tells his son that he found no solace in the myths of religion that simply offer false promises of a better world somewhere beyond our bodily senses. Religion's focus on the spirit cannot address the victimization of bodies that Coates laments.

In his view whiteness, too, is a sort of myth. Coates refers to the privileges of whiteness as The Dream. In contrast to racial reformers like Obama, Coates believes that racism is not a bug in the American system; it is a persistent feature. It is not a dysfunctional aberration but a functional aspect of a society built on a foundation of racist ideologies and practices.

Myths such as The Dream offer Coates no comfort but knowledge does. In college, he developed a ravenous appetite for black authors, an appetite that had first been whetted by his father. His voracious reading opened up as many questions as it provided answers, and he became obsessed with expanding his knowledge base, and on exploring more and more perspectives on black history and philosophy.

But the second section of *Between the World and Me* turns bleak again as Coates shares his painful memories of a friend from Howard, Prince Jones, who was killed by a police officer. Coates's hard lesson to his son is that police murders of black people are endemic to a society built on white supremacy.

In some of its most controversial pages, Coates also offers his son naked honesty when reflecting on his own rejection of the general response to the 9/11 terrorist attacks: "I kept thinking about how southern Manhattan had always been Ground Zero for us. They auctioned our bodies down there, in that same devastated, and rightly named, financial district. . . . Bin Laden was not the first man to bring terror to that section of the city. I never forgot that. Neither should you."

Late in the book, Coates takes a surprising turn, moving his gaze outward and alluding to the dangers that await the planet in the postindustrial age. Coates warns his son and, by extension, all future generations that while white supremacy is based on the plunder of black bodies, it is also devoted to the plunder of the earth's natural resources. Coates's message to his young son is not optimistic. He is a realist, and the reality he sees is a bleak one for people of color and whites alike.

We Were Eight Years in Power

The essays included in *We Were Eight Years in Power*, which were originally published in the *Atlantic*, explore a diverse range of subjects. Separate profiles of Michelle and Barack Obama act as bookends to the forty-fourth president's time at the White House: the second piece in the collection, titled "American Girl," captures the feeling of hope the First Lady and her husband provided African Americans in the first year of Obama's presidency; the final essay, "My President Was Black," examines the actual impact of the Obama administration as it was winding down. Coates is painstakingly honest and critical in the way that he writes about the Obamas, and this sharp, unfiltered perspective infuses the narrative with a bittersweet tone. He admits that the Obamas allowed him to feel proud about being American for the first time in his life, but he is also quick to point out the president's shortcomings. Coates criticizes Obama for his "color-blind" policies, which he feels allowed the president to cater too much to white fears. In addition to exploring the significance of African American cultural and political figures, *We Were Eight Years in Power* also features a number of essays that directly address major issues in race politics, including "Why Do So Few Blacks Study the Civil War?"

Before each essay, Coates includes a short autobiographical sketch, each designed to introduce and contextualize the essay that follows. This introduction of the memoiristic element proves to be a powerful literary device, one that definitively ties the disparate essays together. Each autobiographical sketch leaps a year into the future, thereby chronicling Coates's journey from a struggling writer on unemployment to one of the country's most famous journalists.

The story of his ascent reinforces one of the book's central arguments: that while Obama's presidency did not eradicate racism, it did facilitate the wave of African American journalists and artists who broke through to the mainstream during this time. As Coates states in the book's introduction, he was a fortunate member of this wave.

Other Literary Forms

Coates's writing for various comic books and comic book series has probably been among his most widely influential contributions to American culture. This is especially true since the *Black Panther* series has resulted in a major film and seems likely to become an ongoing Hollywood franchise. More people have experienced Coates's ideas in theaters than have ever read his nonfiction books, and his involvement in films and television programs seems only to have just begun. Such involvement seems likely to take up increasing amounts of his time and energies. His first novel, *The Water Dancer*, was published on September 24, 2019.

Bibliography

Daniels, Anthony. "Coates Contra Mundum." *The New Criterion* 34, no. 2 (Oct. 2015): 4-9. Daniels compares and contrasts Coates's *Between the World and Me* with a 1963 essay by James Baldwin. Daniels accuses Coates of ignoring all the real progress African Americans have made in recent decades.

De Loera-Brust, Antonio. "Can We Overcome Racism?" *America* 217 (13 Nov. 2017): 52-53. De Loera-Brust asserts that in his book *We Were Eight Years in Power*, "Coates is at his best when exploring the multitude of ways in which black people have navigated, survived and resisted racism over the centuries. He lets us intimately witness his struggles with his own pessimism about African-Americans' place in the United States when faced with Obama's optimistic vision of inclusion."

Lewis, Thabiti. "How Fresh and New Is the Case Coates Makes?" *African American Review* 49, no. 3 (Fall 2016): 192-96. Lewis contends that "issues broached in [*Between the World and Me*] comprise the regular diet of black studies courses and scholarship. The problem is that while Coates's style fresh, his opinion is seen as the only opinion because black folk do not control the message, or the mechanisms by which it is delivered."

O'Donnell, Patrick A. "Still Dreaming." *America* 214, no. 9 (14 Mar. 2016): 32-34. O'Donnell suggests that there "is still a tendency in the national media to speak of racism as a specter of the past, as something that has a few kinks to be worked out, but is largely solved." He thinks this tendency "is deeply misleading; even when it is not obvious, racism (and more particularly, anti-blackness) lives in the very cracks and fissures of our social structure, and it always has. Books like *Between the World and Me* pry at these fissures and confront us with a troubling but important truth: All of us keep dreaming at our peril."

—Bill Yousman; Emily Turner; Robert C. Evans

Teju Cole

(Obayemi Onafuwa)

Novelist

Born: Kalamazoo, Michigan; June 27, 1975

LONG FICTION: *Every Day Is for the Thief*, 2007, 2014; *Open City*, 2012

NONFICTION: *Known and Strange Things: Essays*, 2016

PHOTOGRAPHY: *Punto d'Ombra*, 2016 (published in English as *Blind Spot*, 2017)

Achievements

Cole's literary talents have won him many distinctions. *Open City* was named one of 2011's "Best Books of the Year" by *Time Magazine*, was a finalist in 2012 for the National Book Critics Circle Award; received a 2012 Hemingway Foundation/PEN Award; was short-listed for the 2012 Ondaatje Prize; and was also a *Morning News* Tournament of Books finalist. In 2015 Coles won $150,000 as part of the Windham–Campbell Literature Prize in Fiction. *Every Day Is for the Thief* was named one of the best books of the year in *The New York Times*, the *San Francisco Chronicle*, National Public Radio, the London *Telegraph*, and the Toronto *Globe and Mail*. It was also a finalist for the Phillis Wheatley Book Award. *Known and Strange Things* was a finalist for the PEN/Diamonstein-Spielvogel Award for the Art of the Essay and PEN/Jean Stein Book Award.

Biography

Teju Cole was born Obayemi Onafuwa in 1975 at the Borgess Medical Center in Kalamazoo,

Michigan. His parents were originally from Nigeria and had married during their time in Michigan. His father earned an M.B.A. at Kalamazoo's Western Michigan University (WMU) while his mother taught French. Cole and his mother returned to Nigeria by the end of 1975, and his father joined them several months later. His parents later had three additional children.

Cole recalls "invent[ing] memories" of what his first year of life must have been like back in Kalamazoo. He convinced himself the he "could remember our one-bedroom apartment, on Howard Street." He says that while growing up in Lagos, his nation's capital, he was "a regular middle-class Nigerian kid." His "first language was Yoruba," and he "had Nigerian citizenship from birth." Yet he was also the only member of his family who was, by law, officially an American as well, a fact in which his parents took pride. He remembers defending the United States during boyhood political debates and championing American teams during the Olympics. His father, in particular, assumed that someday his son would return to the United States and succeed there, probably in some way connected to science.

"In the nineteen-eighties," Cole notes, "Nigeria went from being the hope of Africa to being a poor and perpetually tense place. Inflation dragged most Nigerians into poverty." A dictatorship soon flourished and then fell and a brutal civil war broke out. Coles' parents began assuming that their son might *have* to return to

Photo courtesy of the U.S. State Department

the United States. Eventually, however, it was not war but socioeconomic paralysis and decay that led Cole to leave Nigeria: "We faced … a corrupt ruling class, crumbling institutions, armed robberies, bad universities, despair." After finishing high school, Cole was sent by his parents back to Kalamazoo in 1992, where he immediately felt isolated and in some ways homesick. He began to recall Nigeria, sometimes with longing but sometimes with relief that he was no longer there.

Encouraged and inspired by both the words and the example of an art professor at Kalamazoo College (where Cole had transferred after a year at WMU), he planned to become an art historian, not the scientist his father had envisioned. He soon became interested in all kinds of arts, including music and film but especially photography. He enjoyed the college's small, peaceful campus and spent much time in the library, reading widely. A trip to Boston helped him develop of love of walking through cities—a topic featured in *Open City*. He has said that "Very early on, you are told you have to choose a

major, become an expert in something. But my own natural inclination was to take all the world as mine." His officially declared interests were in "studio art, art history and pre-med," but his deepest interests were far more wide-ranging. Remembering his time at the college, he has remarked that his professors "were very encouraging people, and it was a very positive place to be." He later abandoned medical studies at the University of Michigan in order to write fiction, study art, and pursue his interests in photography. He earned a master's degree in art history at the University of London and later began working on a doctorate in the same field at Columbia University.

Coles' skills as a writer helped him become a regular contributor to the *New Yorker* magazine, a successful novelist, and a professor of creative writing at Harvard University. He has said that he is especially interested "in the ability of individuals choosing which way they want to go. I admire Emerson, Thoreau, Kierkegaard, Camus, the idea of marching to the beat of a different drum. I want to explore something of what it's like to be an individual."

Analysis: Long Fiction

Coles' fiction often deals with such topics as multiculturalism, immigration, life in large cities, and the experience of protagonists who enjoy exploring unfamiliar places while also feeling somewhat threatened in such locations. Racism, social corruption, psychological complexities, cultural complexities, relations within families, and relations between the past and present are also typical concerns.

Every Day Is for the Thief

Cole's first book, a novella, follows a young American medical student who returns to his home city of Lagos, Nigeria. The text, which consists of vignettes and photographs taken by Cole himself, reads like an autobiography and captures Lagos in all of its vibrancy and lawlessness. The work opens at the Nigerian consulate in New York City, where Cole's unnamed narrator attempts to renew his Nigerian passport and encounters the first of many corrupt situations in which bribes are required. He bemoans his fellow Nigerians' "casual complicity" in their country's "informal economy." Corruption is rampant and pervasive in Nigeria, a nation that has suffered under colonial and military rulers for years. While quick to defend the creativity, ingenuity, and ultimately the humanity of its people, the narrator is frustrated by the country's lack of progress. The stagnation is self-perpetuating. The narrator recalls a family friend who worked as an immigration officer. The man refused to take bribes at his new rural post, but his honorable stance cost his colleagues money, so they requested that he be transferred to a different location to hurt people there financially. The same culture of necessary lawlessness in Nigeria is referenced in the book's title, taken from a Yoruba proverb that says, "Every day is for the thief, but one day is for the owner."

The unwieldy nature of public life in Lagos, Nigeria's most populous city, contributes to the narrator's heightened sense of being. In one vignette, he tries to hold two essential truths about the city at once: Lagosians are family oriented, often fervently religious, and, on the surface, happy; yet many Lagosians have known tremendous grief as a result of arbitrary acts of violence. Armed home invasions were common in the 1990s, and the narrator recalls hiding in the bathroom with his family while robbers tried to break into their home. But people who have suffered such pain often show little obvious sign of it even though they feel deep-rooted fear. "The barely concealed panic that taints so many interactions here is due precisely to the fact that nobody is in control, no one is ultimately responsible," Cole writes.

This panic is assuaged by the embrace of superstitious and spiritual beliefs, particularly evangelical Christianity in the south and extreme Islam in the north. The narrator reports that shortly before he visited Nigeria, the country was named the world's most religious country, its people the happiest, and its government the third most corrupt, an unusual combination of superlatives. Nigerians feel tremendous pressure to say they are happy, to express optimism or expect miracles. Various episodes illustrate the random cruelty of existence in Nigeria and how quickly the tide of violence can rise up and overtake one's life.

Like the author, Cole's narrator loves taking pictures. Cole's own photos appear throughout the book. Most are voyeuristic street scenes. Some are blurry or off-center, as if Cole only had time to shoot a picture quickly before hastily pulling his camera back down. The images, compelling in their own right, are particularly striking in juxtaposition with Cole's semifictional narrative; they are the souvenirs of a place where truthfulness means many things, the ephemera of a city in constant transformation.

Open City

Open City is the story of Julius, a thirty-two-year-old Nigerian German psychiatrist in residency at Columbia Presbyterian Hospital in New York City. The story begins in 2006 and continues into the following year, as he studies the relationship between depression and apoplexy in the elderly. Stressed by a full schedule and professional responsibilities, Julius begins to take therapeutic walks in the evenings, exploring various neighborhoods in Manhattan, where he reflects on their architecture and history, as well as the sociopolitical issues that engulf their residents' lives. He visits art museums and stores, attends movies and concerts, and explores the waterfront, Ground Zero, and other significant sites, usually offering commentary with the demeanor of a tour guide but with a much deeper sensitivity and breadth of knowledge.

The novel is a collection of vignettes, a blending of the narrator's peripatetic ramblings, dreams, conversations with friends and colleagues, flashbacks to his youth in Nigeria, and philosophical observations on numerous political and social issues. It is fiction and nonfiction, essay and poetry, reading more like an elaborate, stream-of-consciousness journal than a plot-infused novel. Most reviewers noted similarities to the work of J. M. Coetzee, V. S. Naipaul, and W. G. Sebald.

The novel reads so much like a diary that it should be remembered that this *is* a work of fiction. While Julius is a psychiatrist, Cole is an art historian and photographer. But otherwise Julius could be Cole's alter ego. They are each in their early thirties, intelligent, and professional men of Nigerian descent who came to the United States for their education and spent time in New York City, Cole at Columbia University and Julius at the fictitious Maxwell College. Like Cole, Julius deeply appreciates art history and has a keen eye for light and detail. Both are world travelers and introverts given to observation and reflection. Only Cole knows where his work of imagination truly begins and ends.

The book's title alludes in part to Brussels being an "open city" during World War II. By surrendering and negotiating with Germany, the city avoided bombardment and thus preserved its ancient historic structures. The connotations of an "open city," however, are both negative and positive. When Julius visits Brussels, searching for his estranged German grandmother, he witnesses the problems of a modern open city, especially the influx of African and Middle Eastern Muslim immigrants, whose cultural and religious values challenge the status quo. Hate crimes against nonwhites are rampant, and Julius, himself black, also feels insecure. However, he is not targeted while in Brussels; instead, he is robbed and beaten back in New York City, ironically by African American boys whom he had casually acknowledged just moments earlier.

The parallels between Brussels and New York City are central to the book. Cole confronts the benefits and difficulties of living in a multicultural world, as well as problems related to immigration and assimilation in the post–September 11 climate. While many New Yorkers have focused on preventing additional terrorist acts by Islamic fundamentalists, Cole alludes to many other threats to the open city, including ignorance, mental illness, indifference, poverty, economic recessions, and even bed bugs. Clearly, some of these threats result from openness and the ongoing influx of new people, ideas, and beliefs.

The marginalization of immigrants is another prominent theme. Julius frequently notes the plight of the foreigner – alienated, impoverished, and forgotten by much of society. As a psychiatrist, he is naturally interested in other people's mental health, but his sympathy for social outcasts also reflects his own sense of alienation and "otherness." Another key theme is the exploration of place as a palimpsest, or how easily and routinely history is erased or forgotten. While visiting Ground Zero, as plans are being drawn up for new buildings and a memorial, Julius mentions the diverse history of the property. Related to the idea of palimpsests is the propensity of the expunged past to haunt successive generations. But Julius, although proud of his Nigerian past, has all but severed ties with his family there and knows little about his German background. He also, however, refuses to identify with African Americans, as he is not American or descended from slaves, and he resents being called "brother" by other black people. When a cab driver states, "I'm African, just like you," Julius is in "no mood for people who try to lay claims on me." Similarly, when an African American postal worker calls him "brother" and recites his own amateur, black-angst-infused poetry, Julius plans "to avoid that particular post office in the future."

Julius's trip to Brussels is central to his search for identity. He has not seen his grandmother in decades and does not know if she is even alive; his father is deceased, and Julius and his mother are estranged. The search for his "oma" is short-lived, though, as he gets distracted by the old-world culture and meets new characters, who share their insights into the urban milieu. In particular, he encounters Farouq, a Moroccan graduate student who works at an Internet café, and Khalil, his employer, who together engage Julius in politically charged discussions on Islam, Palestinian American activist Edward Said, issues concerning Palestine, communitarianism, and dictators, among other subjects. The grandmother becomes little more than a pretext for the novel to expose other issues, and the novel ends with no obvious resolution.

In much of the book, Julius tries to make sense of his Nigerian past. Through the protagonist's dreams, interior monologues, and dialogues with Nigerian friends, readers learn about his schooling, family dynamics, and certain important events in his life. At times, these memories seem extraneous or disparate, complicating a book already bursting with ideas, even as the memories round out the larger collection of vignettes.

However, a major revelation near the end of the book has struck certain reviewers as a flaw,

an element perhaps resulting from editorial interference or from insufficient editing. Some readers may feel manipulated or deceived. But the scene demonstrates another theme: an individual's personal history is always evolving and can easily be compromised by new experiences.

Fortunately for Cole, Julius remains an especially memorable character. His astute, often poetic observations concerning migrating birds, paintings, and architecture will satisfy readers who appreciate fine turns of phrase. His attention to serious philosophy is intriguing, and he also gives one of the best walking tours of New York City ever to appear in fiction

Other Literary Forms

In addition to writing fiction, Cole has also published numerous essays, especially in the *New Yorker*. Many of his essays from that magazine and elsewhere have been collected in *Known and Strange Things*. Their topics deal with such issues as race, photography, literature, music, travel, and politics. They also respond to various other artists of different sorts, including writers and photographers. "This book," Cole has written, "contains what I have loved and witnessed, what has seemed right and what has brought joy, what I have been troubled and encouraged by, and what has fostered my sense of possibility."

Bibliography

Cole, Teju. "Home, Strange Home." *The New Yorker* 18 Apr. 2011: n.p., https://www.newyorker.com/magazine/2011/04/18/home-strange-home. In this autobiographical essay, Cole provides important information about his early life in Nigeria and his college years in the United States.

DeRitter, Margaret. "From New Yorker Envy to Literary Acclaim." BeLight, the eZine of Kalamazoo College, 2012, https://web.archive.org/

web/20150225172638/http://www.kzoo.edu/beLightArchive/articles/?issueid=33&id=126. Both this article and the other by DeRitter cited below contain interviews with Cole, information about his life, and commentary on his works.

_____. "Teju Cole, a K-College Grad, Writes What He Observes through Narrator in 'Open City.'" Be-Light, the eZine of Kalamazoo College, 2011, https://web.archive.org/web/20150225175753/http://www.mlive.com/entertainment/kalamazoo/index.ssf/2011/05/teju_cole_a_k-college_grad_wri.html.

Kirsch, Adam. "Restless Amid the Ruins." *The New Statesman* 140, no. 5065 (8 Aug. 2011): 44-45. In this review of *Open City*, Kirsch concludes by focusing on "the book's constant question: is the hero's refusal to be claimed—by ideology, community, family—a moral victory, or a surrender? Even more than his perfectly sustained tone and his ruminative intelligence," Kirsch argues, "it is Cole's ability to keep that question open which makes *Open City* such a compelling book."

Thomson, Ian. "First Class Traveller." *The New Statesman* 145, no. 5328 (19 Aug. 2016): 45. Reviewing *Known and Strange Things*, Thomson observes that the "55 short pieces here, written over a period of eight years, display a cosmopolitan range of interest as Cole explores evidence of racism in Rio de Janeiro, Boko Haram's feared encroachment on Lagos, and the Australian Outback-influenced music of the late Peter Sculthorpe," among many other topics, with often a special interest in the visual.

—*Molly Hagan; Sally S. Driscoll; Robert C. Evans*

Countee Cullen

Poet

Born: New York, New York; May 30, 1903

Died: New York, New York; January 9, 1946

LONG FICTION: *One Way to Heaven*, 1932.

DRAMA: *Medea*, pr., pb. 1935 (translation of Euripides); *One Way to Heaven*, pb. 1936 (adaptation of his novel); *St. Louis Woman*, pr. 1946 (adaptation of Arna Bontemps's novel *God Sends Sunday*); *The Third Fourth of July*, pr., pb. 1946 (with Owen Dodson).

POETRY: *Color*, 1925; *The Ballad of the Brown Girl: An Old Ballad Retold*, 1927; *Copper Sun*, 1927; *The Black Christ, and Other Poems*, 1929; *The Medea, and Some Poems*, 1935; *On These I Stand: An Anthology of the Best Poems of Countee Cullen*, 1947; *Collected Poems*, 2013.

CHILDREN'S/YOUNG ADULT LITERATURE: *The Lost Zoo (A Rhyme for theYoung, butNot Too Young)*, 1940; *My Lives and How I Lost Them*, 1942.

EDITED TEXTS: *Caroling Dusk*, 1927.

Achievements

Countee Cullen's literary accomplishments were many. While he was a student at DeWitt Clinton High School in New York City, he published his first poems and made numerous and regular contributions to the high school literary magazine. From DeWitt, whose other distinguished graduates include Lionel Trilling and James Baldwin, Cullen went to New York University. There he distinguished himself by becoming a member of Phi Beta Kappa and in the same year, 1925, by publishing *Color*, his first collection of poems. In June, 1926, the poet took his second degree, an M.A. in English literature from Harvard University. In December, 1926, *Color* was awarded the first Harmon Gold Award for literature, which carried with it a cash award of five hundred dollars. Just before publication in 1927 of his second book, *Copper Sun*, Cullen received a Guggenheim Fellowship for a year's study and writing in France. While in France, he worked on improving his French conversation by engaging a private tutor and his knowledge of French literature by enrolling in courses at the Sorbonne. Out of this experience came *The Black Christ, and Other Poems*. In 1944, the poet was offered the chair of creative literature at Nashville's Fisk University, but he refused in order to continue his teaching at the Frederick Douglass Junior High in New York City.

Biography

Despite his several trips abroad, Countee Cullen lived most of his life in New York City, spending his childhood years with his grandmother. When he reached adolescence, he was adopted by the Reverend and Mrs. Frederick A. Cullen; Reverend Cullen was minister of the Salem Methodist Episcopal Church of Harlem. The years spent with the Cullens in the Methodist parsonage made a lasting impression on the young poet; although he experienced periods of intense self-questioning, Cullen appears never to have discarded his belief in Christianity.

During his undergraduate years at New York University, the young poet became heavily involved with figures of the Harlem Renaissance; among these Harlem literati were Zora Neale Hurston, Langston Hughes, Carl Van Vechten (a white writer who treated black themes), and Wallace Thurman. After the appearance of *Color* in 1925 and the receipt of his Harvard M.A. in June, 1926, Cullen assumed the position of literary editor of *Opportunity*. At the end of October, 1926, he wrote one of the most important of his "Dark Tower" essays about the appearance of that great treasure of the Harlem Renaissance, the short-lived but first black literary and art quarterly *Fire* (issued only once). He contributed one of his best poems, "From the Dark Tower," to *Fire*. About the solitary issue, Cullen wrote that it held great significance for black American culture, because it represented "a brave and beautiful attempt to meet our need for an all literary and artistic medium of expression.

On April 10, 1928, Cullen married Nina Yolande Du Bois, daughter of one of the most powerful figures of twentieth century black American culture, W. E. B. Du Bois; the two were married at Salem Methodist Episcopal Church. This star-crossed union proved to be of short duration, however; while Cullen was in Paris on his Guggenheim Fellowship, Yolande was granted a decree of divorce. The marriage had not lasted two years. Much of Cullen's poetry deals with disappointment in love, and one senses that the poet was himself often disappointed in such matters.

In 1940, however, after Cullen had taught for several years at the Frederick Douglass Junior High School of New York, he married a second time; on this occasion he chose Ida Mae

Photo courtesy of the Bettmann Archive and Getty Images

Roberson, whom he had known for ten years. Ida Mae represented to the poet the ideal woman; she was intelligent, loyal, and empathetic, if not as beautiful and well-connected as his former wife.

When Cullen died of uremic poisoning on January 9, 1946, only forty-two years old, the New York newspapers devoted several columns to detailing his career and praising him for his distinguished literary accomplishments. Yet in later years, Houston A. Baker deplored (in *A Many-Colored Coat of Dreams: The Poetry of Countee Cullen*, 1974) the fact that to date no collection of Cullen's poetry had been published since the posthumous *On These I Stand*, nor had any of his previously published volumes been reprinted. Indeed, many volumes of this important Harlem Renaissance poet can be read today only in rare-book rooms of university libraries.

Analysis: Poetry

In his scholarly book of 1937, *Negro Poetry and Drama*, Sterling Brown, whose poems and essays continue to exert formidable influence on black American culture, remarked that Countee Cullen's poetry is "the most polished lyricism of modern Negro poetry." About his own poetry and poetry in general, Cullen himself observed: "good poetry is a lofty thought beautifully expressed. Poetry should not be too intellectual. It should deal more, I think, with the emotions." In this definition of "good poetry," Cullen reflects his declared and constant aspiration to transcend his color and to strike a universal chord. Yet the perceptive poet, novelist, essayist, and critic James Weldon Johnson asserted that the best of Cullen's poetry "is motivated by race. He is always seeking to free himself and his art from these bonds."

The tension prevalent in Cullen's poems, then, is between the objective of transcendence—to reach the universal, to enter the "mainstream"—and his ineluctable return to the predicament his race faces in a white world. This tension causes him, on one hand, to demonstrate a paramount example of T. S. Eliot's "tradition and the individual talent" and, on the other, to embody the black aesthetic (as articulated during the Harlem Renaissance); in his best poems, he achieves both. Transcending the bonds of race and country, he produces poetry that looks to the literature and ideas of the past while it identifies its creator as an original artist; yet, at the same time, he celebrates his African heritage, dramatizes black heroism, and reveals the reality of being black in a hostile world.

"Yet Do I Marvel"

"Yet Do I Marvel," perhaps Cullen's most famous single poem, displays the poet during one of his most intensely lyrical, personal moments; yet this poem also illustrates his reverence for tradition. The sonnet, essentially Shakespearean in rhyme scheme, is actually Petrarchan in its internal form. The Petrarchan form is even suggested in the rhyme scheme; the first two quatrains rhyme *abab, cdcd* in perfect accord with the Shakespearean scheme. The next six lines, however, break the expected pattern of yet another quatrain in the same scheme; instead of *efef* followed by a couplet *gg*, the poem adopts the scheme *eeffgg*. While retaining the concluding couplet (*gg*), the other two (*eeff*) combine with the final couplet, suggesting the Petrarchan structure of the sestet. The poem is essentially divided, then, into the octave, wherein the problem is stated, and the sestet, in which some sort of resolution is attempted.

Analysis of the poem's content shows that Cullen chooses the internal form of the Petrarchan sonnet but retains a measure of the Shakespearean form for dramatic effect. The first eight lines of the poem express by means of antiphrastic statements or ironic declaratives that the poem's speaker doubts God's goodness and benevolent intent, especially in his creation of certain limited beings. The poem begins with the assertion that "I doubt not God is good, well-meaning, kind" and then proceeds to reveal that the speaker actually believes just the opposite to be true; that is, he actually says, "I do doubt God is good." For God has created the "little buried mole" to continue blind and "flesh that mirrors Him" to "some day die." Then the persona cites two illustrations of cruel, irremediable predicaments from classical mythology, those of Tantalus and Sisyphus. These mythological figures are traditional examples: Tantalus, the man who suffers eternal denial of that which he seeks, and Sisyphus, the man who suffers the eternal drudgery of being forced to toil endlessly again and again only to lose his objective each time he thinks he has won it.

The illustration of the mole and the man who must die rehearses the existential pathos of modern human beings estranged from God and thrust into a hostile universe. What appeared to be naive affirmations of God's goodness become penetrating questions that reveal Cullen himself in a moment of intense doubt. This attitude of contention with God closely resembles that expressed by Gerard Manley Hopkins in his sonnet "Thou Art Indeed Just, Lord." The probing questions, combined with the apparent resolve to believe, are indeed close; one might suggest that Cullen has adapted Hopkins's struggle for certainty to the black predicament, the real subject of Cullen's poem. The predicaments of Tantalus and Sisyphus (anticipating Albert Camus's later essay) comment on a personal problem, one close to home for Cullen himself. The notion of men struggling eternally toward a goal, thinking they have achieved it but having it torn from them, articulates the plight of black artists in America. In keeping with the form of the Petrarchan sonnet, the ninth line constitutes the *volta* or turn toward some sort of resolution. From ironic questioning, the persona moves to direct statement, even to a degree of affirmation. "Inscrutable His ways are," the speaker declares, to a mere human being who is too preoccupied with the vicissitudes of his mundane existence to grasp "What awful brain compels His awful hand," this last line echoing William Blake's "The Tyger." The apparent resolution becomes clouded by the poem's striking final couplet: "Yet do I marvel at this curious thing:/ To make a poet black, and bid him sing!"

The doubt remains; nothing is finally resolved. The plight of the black poet becomes identical with that of Tantalus and Sisyphus. Like these figures from classical mythology, the black poet is, in the contemporary, nonmythological world, forced to struggle endlessly toward a goal he will never, as the poem suggests,

be allowed to reach. Cullen has effectively combined the Petrarchan and the Shakespearean sonnet forms; the sestet's first four lines function as an apparent resolution of the problem advanced by the octave. The concluding couplet, however, recalling the Shakespearean device of concentrating the entire poem's comment within the final two lines, restates the problem of the octave by maintaining that, in the case of a black poet, God has created the supreme irony. In "Yet Do I Marvel," Cullen has succeeded in making an intensely personal statement; as James Johnson suggested, this poem "is motivated by race." Nevertheless, not only race is at work here. Rather than selecting a more modern form, perhaps free verse, the poet employs the sonnet tradition in a surprising and effective way, and he also shows his regard for tradition by citing mythological figures and by summoning up Blake.

Regard for Tradition

Cullen displays his regard for tradition in many other poems. "The Medusa," for example, by its very title celebrates once again the classical tradition; in this piece, another sonnet, the poet suggests that the face of a woman who rejected him has the malign power of the Medusa. In an epitaph, a favorite form of Cullen, he celebrates the poetry of John Keats, whose "singing lips that cold death kissed/ Have seared his own with flame." Keats was Cullen's avowed favorite poet, and Cullen celebrates him in yet a second poem, "To John Keats, Poet at Spring Time." As suggested by Cullen's definition of poetry, it was Keats's concern for beauty which attracted him: "in spite of all men say/ Of Beauty, you have felt her most."

"Heritage"

Beauty and classical mythology were not the only elements of tradition which Cullen revered. Indeed, he forcefully celebrated his own African heritage, exemplifying the first of the tenets of the Black Aesthetic. "Heritage" represents his most concentrated effort to reclaim his African roots. This 128-line lyric opens as the persona longs for the song of "wild barbaric birds/ Goading massive jungle herds" from which through no fault of his own he has been removed for three centuries. He then articulates Johnson's observation that this poet is ever "seeking to free himself and his art" from the bonds of this heritage. The poem's speaker remarks that, although he crams his thumbs against his ears and keeps them there, "great drums" always throb "through the air." This duplicity of mind and action force upon him a sense of "distress, and joy allied." Despite this distress, he continues to conjure up in his mind's eye "cats/ Crouching in the river reeds," "silver snakes," and "the savage measures of/ Jungle boys and girls in love." The rain has a particularly dramatic effect on him; "While its primal measures drip," a distant, resonant voice beckons him to "'strip!/ Off this new exuberance./ Come and dance the Lover's Dance!'" Out of this experience of recollection and reclaiming his past comes the urge to "fashion dark gods" and, finally, even to dare "to give You [one God, the]/ Dark despairing features."

The Black Christ

The intense need expressed here, to see God as literally black, predicts the long narrative poem of 1929, *The Black Christ*. This poem, perhaps more than any other of Cullen's poems, represents his attempt to portray black heroism, the second tenet of the Black Aesthetic. Briefly the poem tells the tale of Jim, a young black man who comes to believe it is inevitable that he will suffer death at the hands of an angry lynch mob. Miraculously, after the inevitable lynching

has indeed occurred, the young man appears to his younger brother and mother, much as Jesus of Nazareth, according to the Gospels, appeared before his disciples. Christ has essentially transformed himself into black Jim. Although the poem contains such faults as a main character who speaks in dialect at one point and waxes eloquent at another and one speech by Jim who, pursued by the mob, speaks so long that he cannot possibly escape (one may argue that he was doomed from the start), it has moments of artistic brilliance.

Jim "was handsome in a way/ Night is after a long, hot day." He could never bend his spirit to the white man's demands: "my blood's too hot to knuckle." Like Richard Wright's Bigger Thomas, Jim was a man of action whose deeds "let loose/ The pent-up torrent of abuse," which clamored in his younger brother "for release." Toward the middle of the poem, Jim's brother, the narrator, describes Jim, after the older brother has become tipsy with drink, as "Spring's gayest cavalier"; this occurs "in the dim/ Half-light" of the evening. At the end, "Spring's gayest cavalier" has become the black Christ, Spring's radiant sacrifice, suggesting that "Half-light" reveals only selective truths, those one may be inclined to believe are true because of one's human limitations, whereas God's total light reveals absolute truth unfettered. Following this suggestion, the image "Spring's gayest cavalier" becomes even more fecund. The word cavalier calls up another poem by Hopkins, "The Windhover," which is dedicated to Christ. In this poem, the speaker addresses Christ with the exclamation, "O my chevalier!" Both cavalier and chevalier have their origins in the same Latin word, *caballarius*. Since Cullen knew both French and Latin and since Hopkins's poems had been published in 1918, it is reasonable to suggest a more than coincidental connection. At any rate, "Spring's gayest cavalier" embodies an example of effective foreshadowing.

Just before the mob seizes Jim, the narrator maintains that "The air about him shaped a crown/ Of light, or so it seemed to me," similar to the nimbus so often appearing in medieval paintings of Christ, the holy family, the disciples, and the saints. The narrator describes the seizure itself in an epic simile of nine lines. When Jim has been lynched, the younger brother exclaims, "My Lycidas was dead. There swung/ In all his glory, lusty, young,/ My Jonathan, my Patrocles." Here Cullen brings together the works of John Milton, the Bible, and Homer into one image which appears to syncretize them all. Clearly, the poet is attempting to construct in Jim a hero of cosmic proportions while at the same time managing to unify, if only for a moment, four grand traditions: the English, the biblical, the classical, and the African American.

Interpreting "The Black Experience"

While *The Black Christ* dramatizes black heroism, it also suggests what it means to be black in a hostile, white world. Not all the black experience, however, is tainted with such unspeakable horror. In "Harlem Wine," Cullen reveals how blacks overcome their pain and rebellious inclinations through the medium of music. The blues, a totally black cultural phenomenon, "hurtle flesh and bone past fear/ Down alleyways of dreams." Indeed the wine of Harlem can its "joy compute/ with blithe, ecstatic hips." The ballad stanza of this poem's three quatrains rocks with rhythm, repeating Cullen's immensely successful performance in another long narrative poem, *The Ballad of the Brown Girl*.

Although not as notable a rhythmic performance as "Harlem Wine" or *The Ballad of the Brown Girl*, "From the Dark Tower" is, nevertheless, a remarkable poem. It contains a profound

expression of the black experience. Important to a reading of the poem is the fact that the Dark Tower was an actual place located on New York's 136th Street in the heart of Harlem; poets and artists of the Harlem Renaissance often gathered there to discuss their writings and their art. Perhaps this poem grew out of one of those gatherings. The poem is more identifiably a Petrarchan or Italian sonnet than "Yet DoI Marvel"; as prescribed by the form, the octave is arranged into two quatrains, each rhyming *abbaabba*, while the sestet rhymes *ccddee*. The rhyme scheme of the sestet closely resembles that in "Yet Do I Marvel."

"From the Dark Tower"

The octave of "From the Dark Tower" states the poem's problem in an unconventional, perhaps surprising manner by means of a series of threats. The first threat introduces the conceit of planting, to which the poem returns in its last pair of couplets. The poet begins, "We shall not always plant while others reap/ The golden increment of bursting fruit." The planting conceit suggests almost immediately the image of slaves working the fields of a Southern plantation. Conjuring up this memory of the antebellum South but then asserting by use of the future tense ("We *shall* not") that nothing has changed—that is, that the white world has relegated today's African Americans to their former status as slaves, not even as good as second class citizens—Cullen strikes a minor chord of deep, poignant bitterness felt by many contemporary blacks. Yet, what these blacks produce with their planting is richly fertile, a "bursting fruit"; the problem is that "others reap" this "golden increment." The poet's threat promises that this tide of gross, unjust rapine will soon turn against its perpetrators.

The next few lines compound this initial threat with others. These same oppressed people will not forever bow "abject and mute" to such treatment by a people who have shown by their oppression that they are the inferiors of their victims. "Not everlastingly" will these victims "beguile" this evil race" with mellow flute"; the reader can readily picture scenes of supposedly contented, dancing "darkies" and ostensibly happy minstrel men. "We were not made eternally to weep" declares the poet in the last line of the octave. This line constitutes the *volta* or turning point in the poem. All the bitterness and resentment implied in the preceding lines is exposed here. An oppressed people simply will not shed tears forever; sorrow and self-pity inevitably turn to anger and rebellion.

The first four lines of the sestet state cases in defense of the octave's propositions that these oppressed people, now identified by the comparisons made in these lines as the black race, are "no less lovely being dark." The poet returns subtly to his planting conceit by citing the case of flowers which "cannot bloom at all/ In light, but crumple, piteous, and fall." Cullen takes his reader from the infinite heavens to finite flowers of earth, grasping universal and particular significance for his people and thereby restoring and bolstering their pride and sense of worth.

Then follow the piercing, deep-felt last lines: "So, in the dark we hide the heart that bleeds,/ And wait, and tend our agonizing seeds." As with "Yet Do I Marvel," Cullen has effectively combined the structures of the Petrarchan and Shakespearean sonnets by concluding his poem with this trenchant, succinct couplet. The planting conceit, however, has altered dramatically. What has been "golden increment" for white oppressors will yet surely prove the "bursting fruit" of "agonizing seeds." The poem represents, then, a sort of revolutionary pre-declaration of independence. This "document" first states the offenses sustained by the downtrodden, next asserts their worth and significance as human beings, and finally argues that

the black people will "wait" until an appropriate time to reveal their agony through rebellion. Cullen has here predicted the anger of James Baldwin's *The Fire Next Time* (1963) and the rhetoric of the Black Armageddon, a later literary movement led by such poets as Amiri Baraka, Sonia Sanchez, and Nikki Giovanni.

Whereas these figures of the Black Armageddon movement almost invariably selected unconventional forms in which to express their rebellion, Cullen demonstrated his respect for tradition in voicing his parallel feelings. Although Cullen workably displays his knowledge of the traditions of the Western world, from Homer to Keats (and even Edna St. Vincent Millay), it equally enunciates his empathy with black Americans in its celebration of the Black Aesthetic. At the same time that his poetry incorporates classicism and English Romanticism, it affirms his black heritage and the black American experience.

Other Literary Forms

Countee Cullen wrote nearly as much prose as he did poetry. While serving from 1926 through most of 1928 as literary editor of *Opportunity*, a magazine vehicle for the National Urban League, Cullen wrote several articles, including book reviews, and a series of topical essays for a column called "The Dark Tower" about figures and events involved in the Harlem Renaissance. He also wrote many stories for children, most of which are collected in *My Lives and How I Lost Them,* the "autobiography" of Cullen's own pet, Christopher Cat, who had allegedly reached his ninth life. Earlier, in 1932, the poet had tried his hand at a novel, publishing it as *One Way to Heaven.* In addition to articles, reviews, stories, and a novel, the poet translated or collaborated in the writing of three plays, one of them a musical. In 1935, Cullen translated Euripides' *Medea* for the volume by the same name; in

1942, Virgil Thomson set to music the seven verse choruses from Cullen's translation. With Owen Dodson, Cullen wrote the one-act play *The Third Fourth of July*, which appeared posthumously in 1946. The musical was produced at the Martin Beck Theater on Broadway, where it ran for 113 performances; this production also introduced Pearl Bailey as the character Butterfly.

Bibliography

Braddock, Jeremy. "The Poetics of Conjecture: Countee Cullen's Subversive Exemplarity." *Callaloo* 25, no. 4 (Fall, 2002): 1250-1272. Traces the use of subversion through Cullen's works, paying special attention to its use in depicting notions of sex and death.

Carger, Chris Liska, and Henrietta M. Smith. "To Make a Poet Black, and Bid Him Sing." *Book Links* 12, no. 2 (December/ January, 2003): 45-46. An analysis of African American poetry for children.

Corti, Lillian. "Countee Cullen's *Medea*." *African American Review* 32, no. 4 (Winter, 1998): 621-634. Places Cullen's play *Medea* in context of the Harlem Rennaissance.

Evans, Robert C. *Crisis of Faith: Critical Insights.* Ipswich, MA: Salem Press, 2013. Contains an essay dealing with Cullen and other Harlem Renaissance writers in relation to the crisis of faith theme.

Ferguson, Blanche E. *Countee Cullen and the Negro Renaissance.* New York: Dodd, Mead, 1966. The only book-length study of Countee Cullen for many years, this volume is a highly fictionalized biography. In a pleasant and simple style, Ferguson walks readers through major events in Cullen's life. Includes eight photographs, a brief bibliography, and an index.

Goldweber, David E. "Cullen, Keats, and the Privileged Liar." *Papers on Language & Literature* 38, no. 1 (Winter, 2002): 29-49. Examines Cullen's technique and Keats's influence on Cullen's work.

Molesworth, Charles. *And Bid Him Sing: A Biography of Countee Cullen.* The University of Chicago Press, 2012. The first major scholarly biography of Cullen; by a major scholar of modern poetry.

Onyeberechi, Sydney. *Critical Essays: Achebe, Baldwin, Cullen, Ngugi, and Tutuola.* Hyattsville, Md.: Rising Star, 1999. A collection of Onyeberechi's criticism and interpretation of the work of several African American authors. Includes bibliographic references.

Perry, Margaret. *A Bio-bibliography of Countee Cullen.* Westport, Conn.: Greenwood Press, 1971. After a brief biographical sketch, Perry offers a valuable bibliography of Cullen's works and a sensitive reading of the poetry.

Powers, Peter. "'The Singing Man Who Must Be Reckoned With': Private Desire and Public Responsibility in the Poetry of Countee Cullen." *African American Review* 34, no. 4 (Winter, 2000): 661-679. A very interesting article that examines Cullen's interest in using primitive themes in his poetry, which the author contrasts with Cullen's privileged background and class-consciousness.

Schwarz, A. B. Christa. *Gay Voices of the Harlem Renaissance.* Bloomington: Indiana University Press, 2003. Schwarz examines the work offour leading writers from the Harlem Renaissance—Countee Cullen, Langston Hughes, Claude McKay, and Richard Bruce Nugent—and their sexually non-conformist or gay literary voices.

Sheasby, Ronald E. "Dual Reality: Echoes of Blake's Tiger in Cullen's Heritage." *CLA Journal* 39, no. 2 (December, 1995): 219-228. Takes an in-depth look at William Blake's influence on Cullen as shown in the poem "The Tyger."

Tuttleton, James W. "Countee Cullen at 'The Heights.'" In *The Harlem Renaissance: Revaluations,* edited by Amritjit Singh, William S. Shiver, and Stanley Brodwin. New York: Garland, 1989. Examines Cullen's years at New York University and analyzes his senior honors thesis on Edna St. Vincent Millay. Tuttleton argues that this period was very important to Cullen's emergence as a poet.

Whitted, Qiana. "In My Flesh Shall I See God: Ritual Violence and Racial Redemption in 'The Black Christ.'" *African American Review* 38, no. 3 (Fall, 2004): 379-394. Focuses on Cullen's work as a catalyst for discussion of theology, particularly through use of Christ-related imagery.

                    —John C. Shields; Robert C. Evans

Edwidge Danticat

Novelist and Poet

Born: Port-au-Prince, Haiti; January 19, 1969

LONG FICTION: *Breath, Eyes, Memory,* 1994; *The Farming of Bones,* 1998; *The Dew Breaker,* 2004; *Claire of the Sea Light,* 2013

SHORT FICTION: *Krik? Krak!,* 1995; *Everything Inside,* 2019

DRAMA: *The Creation of Adam,* pr. 1992; *Dreams Like Me,* pr. 1993; *Children of the Sea,* pr. 1997.

POEMS: *Standing Tall: Portraits of the Haitian Community in Miami, 2003-2010,* 2010 (with photographs by Bruce Weber)

NONFICTION: *After the Dance: A Walk Through Carnival in Jacmel Haiti,* 2002 *Brother, I'm Dying,* 2007; *Create Dangerously: The Immigrant Artist at Work,* 2010; *Tent Life: Haiti,* 2010 (with photographs and journal by Wyatt Gallery); The *Art of Death: Writing the Final Story,* 2017; *Conversations with Edwidge Danticat,* 2017

EDITED TEXTS: *The Butterfly's Way: Voices from the Haitian Dyaspora in the United States,* 2001; *Haiti Noir,* 2011; *Best American Essays, 2011,* 2011; *Haiti Noir 2: The Classics,* 2013

CHILDREN'S LITERATURE: *Anacaona: Golden Flower, Haiti, 1490,* 2005; *Mama's Nightingale,* 2015; *Untwine,* 2015.

TRANSLATION(S): *In the Flicker of an Eyelid,* 2002 (with Carrol F. Coates; by Jackes Stephen Alexis)

Achievements

Through her award-winning writings, Edwidge Danticat has brought an awareness of Haitian culture and Haitian immigrant experience to readers in the United States. Her short fiction won a Pushcart Prize, and her first novel, *Breath, Eyes, Memory,* led to her selection as one of *Granta*'s Twenty Best Young American Novelists in 1996. The novel also was selected for Oprah Winfrey's Book Club in 1998. Danticat's short-story collection *Krik? Krak!* was nominated for a National Book Award in 1995. *The Farming of Bones* was written with the help of a Lila Wallace-Reader's Digest Foundation grant and won an American Book Award from the Before Columbus Foundation. *The Dew Breaker* was nominated for a National Book Critics Circle Award in 2004 and a PEN/Faulkner Award in 2005. *Brother, I'm Dying* won the National Book Critics Circle Award for autobiography in 2007. In 2009, she was awarded a prestigious MacArthur "genius grant"; in 2011 she won the Langston Hughes medal given by the City College of New York; in 2013 she was granted an honorary doctorate by Yale University; and in 2014 she won the PEN Oakland Josephine Miles Literary Award. In 2017 she was awarded the Neustadt International Prize for Literature.

Danticat also has written professionally and worked as an educator. She has taught creative writing at New York University and the University of Miami, edited anthologies, and worked with filmmakers on documentaries about Haiti and Haitian art.

Danticat's writings, which have been translated into several languages, form a whole and complement one another to create a larger picture of Haitian and Haitian American

Photo courtesy of Library of Congress Life

experience. She is considered a leading voice for Haitian American women and has been embraced by feminists, the Haitian American community, the literary establishment, and the general reading public.

Biography

Edwidge Danticat was born in Port-au-Prince, Haiti, in 1969. Like many Haitian children of her generation, she was born into a poor family and was left in the care of relatives when her parents emigrated to the United States in search of better opportunities. Danticat's father left first, when she was two years old; her mother followed two years later. Danticat's parents settled in Brooklyn, New York, and found work—her father as a cab driver, her mother as a textile worker. They had two more children, both boys, before sending for their older children in Haiti. In 1981, when Danticat was twelve years old, she and her younger brother were reunited with their parents in Brooklyn.

As a child in Haiti, Danticat spoke Haitian Creole, or Kreyol, a language that is based mainly on French but includes influences from West African languages as well. Creole is still the language that Danticat speaks at home with her parents in Brooklyn. Danticat recalls that storytelling was one of the favorite pastimes in Haiti when she was young. Older relatives would ask "Krik?" to inquire whether the children were ready to hear stories and the children would reply "Krak!" to indicate that they were ready to listen. Danticat believes that her love of writing stems from her immersion in the culture of storytelling as a child.

When Danticat arrived in Brooklyn, she spoke no English. In school in Haiti, she had learned to read and write in French. English was her third language, which she learned in bilingual classes at Brooklyn's Intermediate School 320. Her teen years were difficult. Danticat felt like an outsider at school, because she was very shy, and her Haitian background made her feel different from most of her classmates. In addition to adjusting to living in a new country, Danticat had to adjust to living with her parents again after eight years of separation. Although she was glad to be reunited with them, she did not remember them well, and it took some time to get to know them again.

During her first few years in Brooklyn, Danticat spoke very little, partly out of shyness, partly because she was ashamed of her accent. She quickly learned to read and write English, however, and she found consolation in the world of books at her local public library. Some of her favorite authors were Alice Walker, Richard Wright, and James Baldwin. Danticat began writing during her adolescence, at first keeping journals, later writing for a high school publication, and even starting on the book that would become her first novel, *Breath, Eyes, Memory* (1994).

Danticat's parents hoped that she would become a nurse, and she enrolled in a special high school for students planning to enter the health professions. To her parents' disappointment, though, Danticat was much more interested in writing than nursing. Her parents worried that writing would not help Danticat earn a living. However, Danticat attended Barnard College and excelled in writing. Some of the stories in her first collection of short stories, *Krik? Krak!* (1995), were written while she was at Barnard. After graduating from college in 1990, Danticat enrolled at Brown University and earned an M.F.A. degree in creative writing in 1993.

Returning to Brooklyn, she published her first two books in 1994 and 1995 and quickly achieved both popular and critical success. She was named by *Granta* magazine as one of the twenty "Best of American Novelists" in 1996, a remarkable accomplishment for a writer in her twenties. Several of her books have won literary awards. In 1998 Danticat's first novel, *Breath, Eyes, Memory* was selected for the Oprah Winfrey Book Club and became a best-seller. Later, Danticat published the novels *The Farming of Bones* (1998) and *The Dew Breaker* (2004).

Danticat is easily the best-known Haitian American writer. However, she is not comfortable with the idea that her writing "represents" the experience of Haitian Americans. In an interview with Garry Pierre-Pierre for the *New York Times*, Danticat said, "I don't really see myself as the voice for the Haitian American experience. . . . There are many. I'm just one."

Analysis: Short Fiction

The constraining power of social class is a theme repeated in many of Danticat's short stories. In "A Wall of Fire Rising," a story in *Krik? Krak!*, a young couple living in poverty in Haiti dream of a better life for their young son, a gifted student. However, they disagree strenuously about what "a better life" means. The boy's father, who works intermittently at best and has always dreamed of a permanent job at the local mill, wants to place his son on the waiting list for millwork so that "maybe by the time he becomes a man he can be up for a job." The boy's mother, on the other hand, is opposed to this; to her, a better life means education and a life beyond millwork and poverty. Placing the boy on the waiting list, she feels, will condemn him to a life of millwork. This conflict in their marriage ultimately turns tragic: The boy's father kills himself by leaping from a hot-air balloon, symbolically demonstrating to his wife what he thinks will happen to the boy if she aims too high for him.

Danticat frequently places her characters in real historical settings that depict the often violent political situation in Haiti and the Dominican Republic. A particular strength of her writing is the skill with which she portrays the effect of political violence on individual lives. The importance of the mother-daughter relationship is another common theme in Danticat's work. Often in her fiction, daughters lose their mothers to death, emigration, or prison. Inevitably daughters are damaged by being motherless. In "Nineteen Thirty-Seven," a story in *Krik? Krak!*, Josephine becomes mute when her mother is imprisoned for having witch-like powers. Marie, the main character in *Krik? Krak!*'s "Between the Pool and the Gardenias," is unable to have children of her own after her mother dies. Instead, she finds a dead baby girl lying in a gutter and carries its body home, taking care of it like a living baby until it starts to decompose.

The damage of being motherless can be overcome, however. In "The Missing Peace," from *Krik? Krak!*, Lamort is a teenager whose name means "death" because her mother died giving birth to her. After she meets and helps a woman who is searching for her own missing mother, Lamort gains confidence and decides to change her name to Marie Magdalene after her mother, symbolically claiming her own life. In Danticat's writing, no other relationship can quite compare to the tenderness of the mother-daughter bond, but healing can be found in friendships with surrogate-mother figures.

Krik? Krak!

Krik? Krak! opens with the story "Children of the Sea," which consists of an "exchange" of letters between two young lovers. Hauntingly, the letters are written, but never actually exchanged, because the young man is on a small boat with a group of people who are trying to escape Haiti, where they are wanted by the police for speaking out against the government. The reader learns at the end of the story that the young man is being forced to throw his letters overboard to make the boat lighter, because it has sprung a leak.

The reader also suspects that the boat and its inhabitants will not survive this journey. For all its tragedy, this story has a tender side. In their writing, the young lovers reveal the depth of their feelings for each other—the unconditional love that the young woman's parents have for her, and the young man's commitment to justice despite its cost.

Many of the other stories in *Krik? Krak!* are similarly bittersweet. The prostitute in "Night Women" dreads the night, when her "suitors" come to visit. Yet, to protect her young son from the truth about her work, she invents magical stories about visiting angels to explain why she dresses up and puts on make-up at night when she is not planning to go out. "Nineteen Thirty-Seven" also transforms tragedy into tenderness. Josephine's mother's "crime" is purportedly being a witch and having the ability to fly. Josephine is devastated by her mother's imprisonment and she finds that she cannot talk when she visits her mother. When her mother dies, Josephine, nurtured by a friend, realizes that the mother-daughter bond is not broken even by death, and that she might one day be reunited with her mother.

The most complicated story in *Krik? Krak!* is "A Wall of Fire Rising," in which Lili and Guy's young son, a good student, is chosen for the lead role in a school play. In their pride over their son's accomplishments the parents dream of a better life for him than the poverty, hunger, and unemployment that mark their lives.

Ironically, the son's school play is about Boukman, a leader of the slave rebellion that won Haiti its independence from France in 1804. In the play, Boukman's passionate speeches about freedom are written not in the Creole dialect of native Haitians but by a European who has the slave speak in "European phrasing." As the symbol of the boy's aptitude for learning, the play hints that Lili's dreams of an education for her son will make him less Haitian and more European. Most tragically, the reader learns in a later story that Lili "killed herself in old age because her husband had jumped out of a flying balloon and her grown son left her to go to Miami."

Analysis: Long Fiction

Danticat's fiction is informed by her own experiences as a Haitian American and as an immigrant. But she infuses her experience with a compelling voice and well-drawn characters that illustrate the complex themes that are woven into her work. Her writing explores how people can "live between two worlds," how social class and color exert powerful forces on people's lives, how the major upheavals of history affect individuals, and how the mother-daughter relationship resonates throughout the lives of women. Most of all, Danticat's work centers on relationships and the ways that relationships are affected by difficult times. To be certain, many of her characters undergo great hardships and tragedies. Most of the time, the bitterness is tempered with a share of sweetness or tenderness.

The Farming of Bones

In *The Farming of Bones,* Amabelle loses her lover, Sebastien, and almost loses her own life in the great massacre of 1937, a historical event in which almost twenty thousand Haitians were murdered in the Dominican Republic and thousands of others were driven out of the country.

Orphaned as a child, she was adopted by a Dominican family and raised almost as a sister to Senora Valencia, who is the same age as Amabelle. However, even though Amabelle feels at home with Valencia and her father, even calling the father "Papi," she is not quite "family." Her position in the household is that of a servant, and Valencia remarks frequently that Amabelle's skin color is darker than that of her Dominican family. As an immigrant, she lives between two physically separate countries, but she also lives between two different roles in her household—sister and servant—and between two different social classes, as identified by skin color.

The main character in *The Farming of Bones* Amabelle, is a young Haitian woman living with her adoptive family in the Dominican Republic in the 1930s. Orphaned at the age of eight when her parents drowned, Amabelle is haunted by dreams and nightmares about her childhood. In the happy dreams, she recalls the tender memories of family life with loving parents, but in the nightmares, she relives the moment when her mother reached out to her as she was drowning. Amabelle is never sure whether her mother was motioning for her to enter the river to die with her parents or warning her to stay back.

As a child, Amabelle was taken in by a Dominican widower and his small daughter, Valencia. Although Amabelle calls her adoptive father "Papi" and feels almost like part of the family, she also realizes that her role is that of a servant. Now in her twenties, she has found a lover, Sebastien, who is also a Haitian living in the Dominican Republic. Sebastien's patience and soothing presence help Amabelle heal the scars of her childhood.

However, soon after the couple has become engaged to be married, violence erupts in the Dominican Republic. The Dominican dictator, General Trujillo, has incited his people to force the Haitians out of the country. In the ensuing chaos, Amabelle and Sebastien become separated from each other, and Amabelle makes her way to the border without him. There, she is brutally beaten and barely makes it across the Massacre River alive.

However, she is nursed back to health by Man Rapadou, a friend's mother, and she settles into Man Rapadou's household much like she once settled into Papi and Valencia's household. This time though, she is in a Haitian household, with a surrogate-mother figure, and she is an equal, not a servant.

Amabelle spends the next years searching for some scrap of information about Sebastien, but to no avail. When she finds the priest with whom Sebastien was last seen, she is hopeful that she will find out for sure whether Sebastien died or survived the massacre. The priest, however, has gone insane as a result of being tortured, and all he can do is babble the racist words of the dictator: "Our motherland is Spain; theirs is darkest Africa. . . . We, as Dominicans, must have our separate traditions and our own ways of living." Because these words are uttered in a priest's voice, it is as if even God has abandoned the Haitians.

In late middle age, Amabelle journeys back to the Dominican Republic, both to revisit the place where she knew Sebastien and to try to find additional information about him. She visits Valencia during this trip, but now they are "neither strangers nor friends." Although she learns nothing about Sebastien's fate, she visits the waterfall where she used to meet him, and this brings her a sense of closure. On the way back to Haiti, Amabelle enters the Massacre River once again, symbolically reliving the massacre but also undergoing a rebirth of sorts. "The water was warm for October, warm and shallow, so shallow that I could lie on my back in it with my shoulders only half submerged. . . . cradled by the current, paddling like a newborn in a washbasin."

The Dew Breaker

The Dew Breaker looks at Haitian political violence from another perspective. It tells the story of a Haitian man who was a "dew breaker"—a torturer—but then emigrated to Brooklyn and established a new, peaceful life as a barber and family man. In a series of interrelated stories, the novel explores the lives of several people affected by the dew breaker's violence. Although it provides no straightforward answers, the novel raises the question of whether a person can be forgiven for a brutal past.

It is not entirely accurate to call *The Dew Breaker* a novel. It is really a collection of interrelated stories. Each story has its own plot, setting, and group of characters. Each story also sheds light on the main character of the novel, a mild-mannered Haitian American barber and family man who had been a "dew breaker," or torturer, during the dictatorship of Francois Duvalier during the 1960's. (These torturers were known as "dew breakers" because they made their arrests very early in the morning breaking the dew on the grass with their footsteps.)

The book opens with an encounter between Ka Bienaime, a sculptor and teacher, and her father the dew breaker. Ka has grown up believing that her father was once a prisoner in Haiti, and that his scarred face is a result of torture. She has created a sculpture of her father

in which she has tried to capture his experience as a prisoner, and a famous Haitian American actress has expressed interest in purchasing the sculpture. However, just before Ka is to deliver the sculpture her father suddenly disappears with it. He returns some hours later, saying that he has dumped the sculpture into a lake because he does not "deserve a statue" and confessing the truth to his daughter: He was never in prison. He was a torturer who killed and maimed people and rounded them up for prison. His scar is the result of a fight with a prisoner whom he murdered.

The chapters that follow let the reader glimpse the perspectives of several people whose lives were changed by the dew breaker. Dany, a Haitian immigrant to Brooklyn, returns to Haiti after ten years to tell his aunt that he has met the man who blinded her and killed his parents. At first, Dany wants to kill the dew breaker, but this desire fades with time, and Dany realizes that what he really wants is to know "why one single person had been given the power to destroy his entire life." Dany gains some insight into the dew breaker's character when he gets to know Claude, a young Haitian American who, at the age of fourteen, killed his parents for drug money and spent time in prison. Upon hearing Claude's story, Dany says, "I'm sorry," but Claude responds, "Sorry? . . . I'm the luckiest f——er alive. I've done something really bad that makes me want to live the rest of my life like a f——ing angel now."

In another chapter, "The Bridal Seamstress," the reader meets Beatrice, another character whose life is uprooted by the dew breaker. Now an old woman living in Brooklyn, Beatrice was once arrested and beaten in Haiti by the dew breaker simply because she refused to date him. Since moving to Brooklyn Beatrice still lives in fear because she sees the dew breaker everywhere she goes and thinks he is looking for her. She does not know that he has reformed and she plans to move away so that he will not be able to find her.

In the end, after hearing the truth about her father Ka asks her mother, "How do you love him?" but she also asks, "Is there more?" expressing her willingness to hear another side of her father's story. After all, her father's brutal past scarred not only his victims but his own face as well. The book does not leave the reader with any answers about whether such brutality can be forgiven. At the very least, it leaves open the possibility that a person can make the transformation from a monster to a human being.

Other Literary Forms

Danticat has published in a wide variety of literary forms. Her early plays were produced while she was still a graduate student at Brown University, and her short-story collection *Krik? Krak!* was published in 1995. Her short stories also have been published in major periodicals and in anthologies. She has edited, written forewords to, and translated the works of other Haitian writers. She has also published novels for children and young adults, including *Anacaona, Golden Flower* (2005).

Danticat's nonfiction works include *After the Dance: A Walk Through Carnival in Jacmel, Haiti* (2002), which examines her first visit to carnival in Haiti, and *Brother, I'm Dying* (2007), an autobiographical account of her elderly uncle's emigration to Miami and his encounter with the U.S. Department of Homeland Security.

Brother, I'm Dying

In *Brother, I'm Dying,* Danticat recounts an acutely personal story of her family's struggles both with the politically challenging and poverty-ridden context of modern Haiti and with the land of immigrant promise in the United States. This is a story of pain and passion, of family devotion and government oppression. Ultimately, it is a story of hope.

The book opens with the dual disclosure that Edwidge is pregnant with her first child and that her father, Mira, is suffering from a well-advanced pulmonary fibrosis. His cough and weight loss signal a bleak prognosis. Two years before, her father had urged her not to leave New York for Miami. His rationale was that Edwidge should not move away from her family, an important support system. Mira knows the absence of family support only too well. As a young man, he had traveled alone to the United States to start a new life, leaving his wife and two small children in Haiti to be cared for by family members. It is only later that the young writer realizes that Mira's concern is less about her need for family than about his as yet unshared knowledge that he is dying.

When she is four and still living in Haiti, Edwidge is placed in the care of her Uncle Joseph and Aunt Denise. Her mother had finally been allowed to join her father in New York. Sadly, because of restrictive immigration rules, the young couple is unable to take their two small children with them. In the manner of many cultures, Edwidge and her baby brother, Bob, are welcomed into the household of relatives. Joseph is the pastor of a small Baptist church, built in part with his own hands. Denise is his lifelong love. The extended family lives in a modest salmon-colored house—the color ubiquitous inside and out—built on the site of an ancient battle for independence between the indigenous people and the occupying French. It is a home of family syncretism and political ferment. Bedrooms, family tribulations, and modest celebrations are shared by anyone sheltered there at any one time. Food prepared by Aunt Denise and homemade liquor are offered to political activists who are forced to bring their own chairs to crowded meetings in this welcoming home.

Only in his mid-fifties, Joseph is diagnosed with throat cancer. He finds it difficult to preach to his congregation. With a tumor-impaired voice, he announces to Mira, "Brother, I'm dying."After a difficult journey to consult doctors in Haiti who can do little for him, Joseph travels to the United States to have the tumor removed. A radical laryngectomy is necessary, leaving him dependent on an artificial voice box in order to speak. Rather than take the easier and perhaps more sensible road and remain in the United States close to family and good medical care, he returns to Haiti to continue his ministry. Young Edwidge, at this time still part of Joseph's household, becomes his interpreter. On one of her trips with him to a local bank, the teller asks Joseph if the young girl with him is his daughter: "Ta fille?" ("Your daughter?") Uncle Joseph realizes that she is indeed his daughter. He responds to the teller with "the same blissful nod he used to indicate agreement when something was suddenly clear to him. He smiled broadly, while patting [Edwidge's] tightly plaited hair."

Eventually, Edwidge and Bob are able to join their parents in America. It is an awkward transition, since neither know their biological parents nearly as well as they know their custodial parents. To make matters more complicated, two siblings whom Edwidge and Bob did not even know existed have joined the family. Food and humor smooth the transition as the older children from Haiti take up residence in New York.

While the story of Mira's illness and anticipated death is the first to be introduced in the queue of tragic tales, it is Joseph's story that most grips the reader. Still, even the account of the suffering connected with the pastor's journey while seeking treatment for his throat tumor pales in contrast to what happens to him on his final trip to the United States. His beloved city of Bel Air is overrun with uncontrolled thugs, in a long line of political oppressors who disrupt the lives of the ordinary Haitian populace. People are slaughtered, Joseph's church is destroyed, and even his clothing and family possessions are looted. It is made clear that his life is in jeopardy. Friends smuggle him away from the danger.

With only his Bible, his papers, and some money, he takes the advice of friends and travels to the United States. When he arrives in Florida, still shaken from all that he has just experienced in Haiti, he meets immigration authorities. A fund-raising trip to America had already been planned, but given the conditions in Haiti he concludes reluctantly that it is time to leave the country permanently. He is eighty-one, his wife is dead, and many of his relatives live in New York. There is little left for him in his native land. The reader is reduced to a sense of horror and impotent anger as the author describes what happens to this vulnerable old man as he enters the United States. He has lost nearly everything but his dignity. As he moves through the immigration process, his hands grasp only hope and his passport and visa. It is too late for fund-raising for a destroyed church; he asks for asylum.

Unbelievably, the authorities do not immediately allow him to pass. Joseph is detained, awaiting determination of his status and the efficacy of his request for sanctuary. His medicines are taken from him; his son, Maxo, who has traveled with him and who at one time had lived in the United States, is likewise detained and separated from the elderly man. Joseph, who has worked a lifetime for peace, who has brought dignity to anyone who needed him, is treated with less care than a stray dog. At the hearing to determine whether he should be granted asylum, deprived of his medicines and of adequate food, he turns violently ill, vomits in the court, and becomes unconscious. The medic who comes to examine him accuses him of faking the condition. Joseph is placed in the prison ward of a hospital, likely shackled, and soon dies. Using official documents, Danticat, who has been prevented from being at his side during the ordeal, describes in horrible detail the lacunae in his medical care and the perfidy in the records of the immigration interviews. The reader is spellbound, if profoundly offended and grieved, by the account of treatment Joseph receives in the United States.

Mira's final days are much more humane. He is cared for at home. As death knocks gently at the sickroom door, the dying man asks for some food. His deteriorating body is well beyond hunger, but unexpectedly he says he would like some rice. He eats a small amount and then passes the plate to his daughter. "You have some," he insists. The concerned daughter urges that he eat more. Then it becomes clear that nourishment of the body is not the issue. What the dying Mira craves is the companionship: someone to *share* food with him. While he is well cared for, during his illness family members have brought meals to him in his sickroom. Inadvertently, he has been denied the pleasure of eating with others, and Mira soon dies. The author describes the paramedics' attempts to resuscitate the frail body. Danticat tells of the police officer standing by, whose job it was to determine that this death was natural and not caused by foul play. Such is the ironic contrast to the final hours of Uncle Joseph.

Edwidge Danticat is both the author and the anchor of the book. The story of the two brothers, their fraternal bond, and the parallels of their medical decline are held together by the common thread of the observing but never detached daughter of them both. Young Edwidge accompanies Uncle Joseph as he learns to deal with the loss of his voice. At the end, the adult Edwidge is the vocal witness to the ignominious story of his tragic death. With her father, she is caregiver and family support. Eventually, both slip from her life.

The theme of dying permeates the text. The atrocities of power that infest the changing governments in Haiti become real not only in the suffering of her uncle but also in the violent death of Edwidge's cousin Madeline, a clinic nurse. Madeline has been a consistent member of the family in the salmon-colored house, the "adopted" daughter of Joseph and Denise. Her extended story is one of the many poignant narratives that the author sprinkles throughout the text.

The book's ending leaves the faint odor of hope. The baby announced in the first chapter, a girl named Mira, is brought to the bedside of her dying grandfather. He is so weak that he can barely hold her, yet he rallies briefly to get out of bed to have a photograph taken of the two Miras. The frail man clutches this tiny promise of hope. It is unfortunate that this photograph, which embodies the pain and the possibility that the book narrates, is not included in the family pictures that decorate the book's cover.

Create Dangerously

Even before the catastrophic 7.0-magnitude earthquake that struck on January 12, 2010, leaving more than 230,000 dead and obliterating its infrastructure, Haiti, the poorest country in the Western Hemisphere, had long been beset by oppression, corruption, storms, and diseases. Since attaining its independence in 1804 after a successful slave rebellion against France, Haiti has been what, in Creole, Danticat calls "*tè glise*, slippery ground." Pointing to the political and meteorological upheavals that have rendered life in her hurricane-prone native land so precarious, she explains that "[e]ven under the best of circumstances, the country can be stable one moment and crumbling the next."

Create Dangerously, which is based in part on the Toni Morrison Lectures that Danticat delivered at Princeton University in 2008, reflects on life and death in Haiti and on the ambiguous position of a writer who attempts to serve as a bridge between her native and adopted lands. A translingual person who comes to English as her third language, Danticat, "writing in this language that is not mine," nevertheless shapes her thoughts in a graceful, engaging style. Her book is less a coherent argument than a series of loosely connected, but vivid, incidents and reflections.

Danticat announces her artistic credo in her title: *Create Dangerously*. It is an injunction she acknowledges borrowing from Albert Camus, whose play *Caligula* (wr. 1938-1939, pb. 1944, pr. 1945; English translation, 1948) she notes, was performed in Haiti clandestinely, as an act of defiance against the brutal dictatorship of François "Papa Doc" Duvalier. "Create dangerously," Danticat urges herself and others, "for people who read dangerously. This is what I've always thought it meant to be a writer. Writing, knowing in part that no matter how trivial your words may seem, someday, somewhere, someone may risk his or her life to read them." For Danticat, as for Camus, who defied the Nazi occupation of France by editing an underground newspaper, creating dangerously "is creating as a revolt against silence, creating when both the creation and the reception, the writing and the reading, are dangerous undertakings, disobedience to a directive."

In the United States, which enjoys constitutional safeguards for freedom of expression, writing does not usually entail a mortal risk, but Danticat pays tribute to Haitian writers and artists who put their lives in jeopardy in order to bear witness to injustice. She salutes Daniel Morel, a courageous photojournalist who became the target of assassination attempts because he showed the world images of Haiti's harsh realities. Conversations with Morel persuade Danticat that "to create dangerously is also to create fearlessly, boldly embracing the public and private terrors that would silence us, then bravely moving forward even when it feels as though we are chasing or being chased by ghosts."

Morel dared to photograph the bodies of Marcel Numa and Louis Drouin, two gifted young men who gave up comfortable lives in the United States to try to liberate Haiti. They were put to death by firing squad because of their opposition to the Duvalier regime. *Create Dangerously* begins with an account of their public execution on November 12, 1964, and it uses that gruesome scene as a touchstone for much of Danticat's insistence on the urgency of art and on the obligations of Haitian expatriates.

Despite its subtitle, *The Immigrant Artist at Work*, the book is not a generic study of creativity in exile nor does it provide an historic overview of the phenomenon. Instead, Danticat's focus is personal, her method anecdotal. While she does discuss the experiences of other displaced Haitians such as the writers Jacques Stephen Alexis, Louis-Philippe Dalembert, Dany Laferrière, and Marie Vieux-Chauvet; the radio commentator Jean Dominique; and Morel, Danticat mentions only in passing immigrant artists from other times and other places such as Frantz Fanon, Wole Soyinka, and Isabel Allende. The book is an expression of its author's privileged, unstable, and awkward position within what, using the Creole term, she calls the Haitian *dyaspora*.

One of Danticat's cousins, who she calls Marius in this book, was living in exile in Miami when he died of AIDS. She recounts how Marius's mother, whom she calls Tante Zi, implores her to arrange for the return of his body for burial in Port-au-Prince. Because Marius entered the United States surreptitiously by boat and never obtained legal papers, Danticat struggles against bureaucratic obstacles to his posthumous repatriation to Haiti. However, she eventually succeeds in fulfilling her grieving aunt's request to have her dead son sent back home. However, when Danticat arrives in Haiti, Tante Zi is suspicious of her literary niece. "People talk," says the aunt. "They say that everything they say to you ends up written down somewhere." Danticat is troubled by the accusation she faces repeatedly: "You are a parasite and you exploit your culture for money and what passes for fame." However, as she admits to her aunt: "the immigrant artist, like all other artists, is a leech, and I needed to latch on. . . . I wanted to ask her forgiveness for the essay that in my mind I was already writing." Without abandoning her essay or even apologizing for planning it, she does promise Tante Zi that she will disguise her name and Marius's name when she writes about them. However, Danticat also recounts an arduous trek into the mountains in 1999 to see her seventy-five-year-old Tante Ilyana, who, though illiterate, beams with pride in the knowledge that her visitor is a writer.

There is an element of the vampire in all writers, who obtain sustenance for their art from the human lives they encounter, but Danticat suggests that artists who relocate abroad are particularly vulnerable to the charge of being foreign expropriators of native lives. They are gifted with a valuable double consciousness; Danticat can bring to her writing the perspective of a Haitian who spent her first dozen years under the ruthless tyranny of the Duvaliers, but she also sees through the eyes of the American she has been for most of her life. When Hurricane Katrina wreaks havoc on the American Gulf coast, she is able to observe that, like Haiti, even the United States is not immune to humanitarian and ecological disaster.

However, immigrant artists also suffer the alienation of dislocation. Divided loyalties can make them question any loyalty. Danticat seems to express some of her own anxieties of identity when she quotes an immigrant photographer: "I have no country now," states Jean Daniel, trying to eke out a living after moving to the United States. "I can't live in Haiti and I can't live in the U.S. In Haiti they called me *jounalis la, atis la*, the journalist, the artist. . . . Here, I feel like I have little value."

Create Dangerously provides valuable witness to the rich culture and dreadful tribulations of its author's native land. Long before its misery in the aftermath of the devastating 2010 earthquake, Haiti was burdened with onerous debts as the immediate price for independence from France. It has endured vicious dictatorships, violent coups, exploitation by foreign corporations, and a nineteen-year military occupation by the United States. Danticat describes her return to Haiti for the burial of her beloved, vibrant cousin Maxo, a victim of the 2010 earthquake. She also recalls the funeral in 2000 of Dominique, who was assassinated in the parking lot of the radio station from which he broadcast his provocative views.

However, the most heartrending section of the book, chapter 5, is devoted to an account of her encounter with Alèrte Bélance, a Haitian refugee in her late twenties living in New Jersey with her husband and three young children. In 1991, paramilitary men working for the latest junta abducted, slashed, and dismembered Bélance, a supporter of the ousted President Jean-Bertrand Aristide. Left for dead, she survived to describe her ordeal, how they sliced her up with machete strokes, cutting out her tongue, slashing through an eye and ear and severing her right arm. "She looked like chopped meat," her young son explains. Nonetheless, Bélance is undaunted. Pregnant again, she declares: "They tried to take my life away, but not only couldn't they do that, I'm producing more life."

While pained and appalled by her condition, Danticat clearly admires Bélance's tenacity and defiance, finding in it a model for the immigrant artist who, spanning two worlds but at home in neither, is particularly well positioned to speak truth to both her nation of origin and her nation of residence. Danticat recalls a childhood in which she became enamored of literature despite and because of the fact that, in a repressive society, just to open a book was to read dangerously. She also notes that, for all the myriad misfortunes that Haiti has undergone in more than two centuries, the 2010 earthquake created a dividing point from which there is no turning back. Going forward, she states: "Perhaps we will write with the same sense of fearlessness or hope. Perhaps we will continue to create as dangerously as possible, but our muse has been irreparably altered. Our people, both inside and outside of Haiti, have changed. In ways that I am not yet fully capable of describing, we artists too have changed."

Create Dangerously comes as the partial, provisional testimony of a forty-one-year-old immigrant artist who presumably still has many more productive years ahead. In forthcoming fictions, it will be fascinating to observe the ways in which her artistry changes. In the final paragraphs of this book, Danticat describes her return to Miami after visiting Haiti immediately after the earthquake. After producing her American passport, she boards a plane at the Port-au-Prince airport named for Toussaint-L'Ouverture, the leader of the Haitian rebellion against France. When the flight attendant proclaims: "God bless America," Danticat cries out: "God bless, Haiti, too." As the plane gains altitude, she bids farewell to Haiti, but qualifies her valediction with the final words of the book: "At least for now." She is still a work in progress.

Bibliography

Bell, Madison Smartt. "A Hidden Haitian World." *The New York Review of Books* 17 June 2008. A leading writer about Haiti discusses Danticat's work, especially *The Farming of Bones*, in the context of other Haitian writers who are lesser known outside Haiti. In discussing the role of translation in bringing Haitian authors to a wider audience, Bell positions Danticat as an exception, a Haitian writer who writes in English.

Bennett, Ian A. B., ed. *Four Writers: Women Writing the Caribbean*. San Juan, PR: Sargasso, 2005. Includes an interview with Danticat titled "Haiti: History, Voice, Empowerment" and a review of *The Dew Breaker* among essays on the works of Merle Hodge, Jamaica Kincaid, and Paule Marshall.

Campbell, Elaine. *The Whistling Bird: Women Writers of the Caribbean*. Boulder, CO: Lynne Rienner, 1998. Includes a useful discussion of Danticat.

Charters, Mallay. "Edwidge Danticat: A Bitter Legacy Revisited." *Publishers Weekly* 245, no. 33 (17 Aug. 1998): 42-43. A profile of the novelist. Discusses the experiences that led to the writing of *Breath, Eyes, Memory* and her other novels.

Clitandre, Nadege T. *Edwidge Danticat: The Haitian Diasporic Imaginary*. Charlottesville: U of Virginia P, 2018. Clitandre "argues that Danticat … articulates a diasporic consciousness that acts as a form of social, political, and cultural transformation at the local and global level." She uses "the echo trope to approach Danticat's narratives and subjects."

Corelli, Marie. "*Breath, Eyes, Memory*." *Belles Lettres: A Review of Books by Women* 10, no. 1 (Fall 1994): 36ff. Argues that the novel serves two important purposes: It is a celebration of a Haitian culture likely to disappear in the not-too-distant future, and it is a plea for mothers to welcome their daughters into the world the same way they welcome their sons, to stop the cycle of abuse that they perpetuate because of their own suffering at the hands of their own mothers.

Danticat, Edwidge. "The Dangerous Job of Edwidge Danticat: An Interview." Interview by Renee H. Shea. *Callaloo* 19, no. 2 (17 Jan. 1996): 382-89. Interview focuses on the centrality of mother-daughter relationships in Danticat's work.

_____. "An Interview with Edwidge Danticat." Interview by Bonnie Lyons. *Contemporary Literature* 44, no. 2 (Summer 2003): 181-98. An extensive interview of Danticat in a respected academic journal.

Francis, Donette A. "'Silences Too Horrific to Disturb': Writing Sexual Histories in Edwidge Danticat's *Breath, Eyes, Memory*." *Research in African Literatures* 35, no. 2 (Summer 2004): 75ff. Provides the history of the women's movement in Haiti, which is seen as closely tied to the U.S. occupation and Duvalier regimes. To make her case for the relationship between scenes of sexual violence and the postcolonial state, Francis closely examines five key moments of abuse, beginning with the rape of Martine in a cane field.

Hoey, Jr., Danny M., et al., eds. *Approaches to Teaching the Works of Edwidge Danticat*. New York: Routledge, 2019. Essay topics include evil John Glover; Haitian youth; genre; local oral history; gender; the black female body; generational trauma and healing; history; transnational communities; global classrooms; cross-cultural communication; community; experiences from a class in Ghana; criticism; thematic analysis; teaching as activism; postnationalism; cultural sensitivity; and public sphere pedagogy.

Laforest, Marie-Hélène. *Diasporic Encounters: Remapping the Caribbean*. Naples, Italy: Liguori Editore, 2000. Criticism and interpretation of the works of Danticat, as well as Jamaica Kincaid and Michelle Cliff, by an authority on twentieth-century Caribbean literature.

Loichot, Valerie. "Edwidge Danticat's Kitchen History." *Meridians* 5, no. 1 (2004): 92-116. Sees food as the central link between the individual and community, claiming that Martine's loss of Haitian recipes, like Sophie's bulimia, results from her cultural isolation. Places Danticat in the company of other feminist writers who use food as a metaphor for the female body and who equate literacy and writing with female power.

Munro, Martin. *Exile and Post-1946 Haitian Literature: Alexis, Depestre, Ollivier, Laferrière, Danticat*. Liverpool, UK: Liverpool UP, 2007. Discusses the role of writers in exile and their relationship to a Creole identity.

Munro, Martin, ed. *Edwidge Danticat: A Reader's Guide*. Charlottesville: U of Virginia P, 2010. Essay topics include Danticat's Haitian precursors; Danticat and Caribbean women writers; Danticat and the African American women's literary tradition; diasporic politics; Danticat's young adult fiction; travel; specific works by Danticat; violence, nation, and memory; concealment, displacement, and disconnection; Danticat and her peers. Includes a brief biography; an interview; and bibliographies.

N'Zengou-Tayo, and Marie-José. "Rewriting Folklore: Traditional Beliefs and Popular Culture in Edwidge Danticat's *Breath, Eyes, Memory* and *Krik? Krak!*" *Macomère* 3 (2000): 123-40. Explains many of the novel's allusions to Haitian myths and the meaning of names used for characters and places. Translates key Creole words, identifies important Haitian proverbs, and offers an analysis of dreams and omens.

Shea, Renee H. "Traveling Worlds with Edwidge Danticat." *Poets and Writers Magazine* 25, no. 1 (Jan.-Feb. 1997): 42-51. An overview of Danticat's life and writings.

Shemak, April. "Remembering Hispaniola: Edwidge Danticat's *The Farming of Bones*." *Modern Fiction Studies* 48, no. 1 (Spring 2002): 83-113. Analysis of the novel and detailed discussion of its historical context.

"Three Young Voices." Interview with Edwidge Danticat, Veronica Chambers, and Sheneska Jackson. *Essence*, May, 1996. Danticat discusses her childhood and her life as a writer.

Wucker, Michele. "Edwidge Danticat: A Voice for the Voiceless." *Americas* 52, no. 3 (May/June 2000): 40. Discussion of Danticat's activism.

Karen Antell, Susan Butterworth;
Delores L. Christie; Steven G. Kellman;
Robert C. Evans

Samuel R. Delany

Novelist and Critic

Born: New York, New York; April 1, 1942

LONG FICTION: *The Jewels of Aptor*, 1962; *Captives of the Flame*, 1963, revised 1968 (as *Out of the Dead City*); *The Towers of Toron*, 1964; *City of a Thousand Suns*, 1965; *The Ballad of Beta-2*, 1965; *Empire Star*, 1966; *Babel-17*, 1966; *The Einstein Intersection*, 1967; *Nova*, 1968; *The Fall of the Towers*, 1970 (includes revised versions of *Out of the Dead City*, *The Towers of Toron*, and *City of a Thousand Suns*); *The Tides of Lust*, 1973 (also known as *Equinox*); *Dhalgren*, 1975; *Triton*, 1976 (also known as *Trouble on Triton*); *Empire*, 1978; *Tales of Neveryon*, 1979; *Neveryona: Or, The Tale of Signs and Cities*, 1983; *Stars in My Pocket Like Grains of Sand*, 1984; *Flight from Neveryon*, 1985; *The Bridge of Lost Desire*, 1987 (also known as *Return to Neveryon*); *Hogg*, 1993; *They Fly at Çiron*, 1993; *The Mad Man*, 1994; *Dark Reflections*, 2007; *Through the Valley of the Nest of Spiders*, 2012; *Phallos: Enhanced and Revised Edition*, 2013; *Bread & Wine: An Erotic Tale of New York*, 2013 (graphic novel); *A, B, C: Three Short Novels*, 2015; *The Atheist in the Attic: plus "Racism and Science Fiction" and "Discourse in an Older Sense": Outspoken Interview*, 2018 (novella and nonfiction).

SHORT FICTION: *Driftglass: Ten Tales of Speculative Fiction*, 1971, revised and expanded 2003 (as *Aye and Gomorrah*); *Distant Stars*, 1981; *Atlantis: Three Tales*, 1995.

NONFICTION: *The Jewel-Hinged Jaw: Notes on the Language of Science Fiction*, 1977; *The American Shore: Meditations on a Tale of Science Fiction by Thomas M. Disch*, 1978; *Heavenly Breakfast: An Essay on the Winter of Love*, 1979; *Starboard Wine: More Notes on the Language of Science Fiction*, 1984; *The Straits of Messina*, 1987; *The Motion of Light in Water: Sex and Science-Fiction Writing in the East Village, 1957-1965*, 1988 (memoir); *Silent Interviews*, 1994; *Longer Views*, 1996; *Bread and Wine: An Erotic Tale of New York City, an Autobiographical Account*, 1998; *Shorter Views: Queer Thoughts and the Politics of the Paraliterary*, 1999; *Times Square Red, Times Square Blue*, 1999; *Nineteen Eighty-Four: Selected Letters*, 2000; *About Writing: Seven Essays, Four Letters, and Five Interviews*, 2005; *Starboard Wine: More Notes on the Language of Science Fiction*, 2012; *The Journals of Samuel R. Delany: In Search of Silence. Volume 1, 1957-1969*, 2017; *Letters from Amherst: Five Narrative Letters*, 2019.

EDITED TEXTS: *Quark: A Quarterly of Speculative Fiction*, 1970-1971 (with Marilyn Hacker).

Achievements

Samuel R. Delany is one of a handful of science-fiction writers to have been recognized by the academic community as well as by authors and fans of the genre (he won both the Hugo and Nebula Awards). Delany studied and taught at the State University of New York—Buffalo and the University of Wisconsin—Milwaukee and served as a contributing editor to the scholarly journal *Science-Fiction Studies*. Unlike mainstream (or "mundane," as Delany prefers)

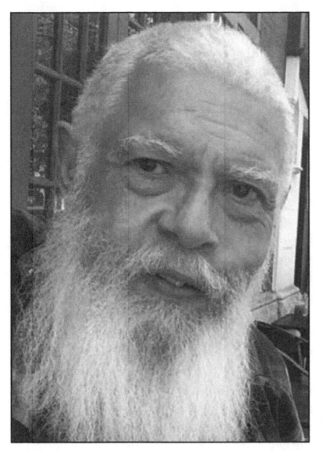

Photo courtesy of Samuel Delany

Throughout Samuel R. Delany's career, his work has been recognized as far above the level of "pulp" science fiction. Many of his novels and short stories have been nominated for Nebula or Hugo Awards, including *The Ballad of Beta-2*, "The Star Pit," "Driftglass," *Nova, Dhalgren, Triton,* and "Prismatica." *The Einstein Intersection,* "Aye and Gomorrah," and "Time Considered as a Helix of Semiprecious Stones" won the Nebula Award. "Time Considered as a Helix of Semiprecious Stones" also won a Hugo Award. In 1980, Delany was honored with an American Book Award nomination for his *Tales of Neveryon,* and he was given the Science Fiction Research Association's Pilgrim Award in 1985. *The Motion of Light in Water* was awarded a Hugo Award for Nonfiction in 1989, and in 1996 he received the Lambda Literary Award in Science Fiction and Fantasy for *Atlantis.* In 1993, Delany received the William Whitehead Award for his lifetime contribution to gay and lesbian literature. In 2010 he won the third J. Lloyd Eaton Lifetime Achievement Award in Science Fiction from the academic Eaton Science Fiction Conference at UCR Libraries. The Science Fiction Writers of America named him its 30th SFWA Grand Master in 2013.

authors such as Walker Percy and John Barth, who have dabbled in science fiction, or science-fiction writers such as Kurt Vonnegut, Jr., who would reject that label, Delany is known as a vigorous defender and promoter of the equality of science fiction with other genres. In his criticism as well as in his practice, he has continually stressed the importance of care, thought, and craft in writing. His own work, like that of those writers he most consistently praises (including especially Joanna Russ, Thomas Disch, and Roger Zelazny), is marked by its attention to language and its concern with issues beyond "hard science" and technology, particularly with the roles of language and myth in society and the potential of and constraints on human behavior within different social constructs.

Biography

Samuel Ray Delany, Jr., was born April 1, 1942, into a middle-class, professional family (two uncles were well-known judges in New York City) in Harlem, New York. His father, Samuel Ray Delany, Sr., was a funeral director, and his mother, Margaret Carey Delany (nee Boyd), was a clerk in a local library. At summer camp one year, he chose the nickname "Chip" for himself and has been called that ever since.

Delany's early education took place at Dalton, an exclusive, primarily white school on the East Side. He then attended the Bronx High School of Science, where the average intelligence quotient of the students was 140. Although his scores in most subjects were excellent (particularly in math), Delany's school career was often made more difficult by what would much later be diagnosed as dyslexia. His parents had forced him to become right-handed, and, partially as a result, Delany had immense difficulty with spelling, with a particular propensity for writing words backward. A broken and jumbled mishmash of misspellings, his writing was opaque even to him once he had forgotten the intended meaning of the words. His parents always encouraged him to write, however, because they had been told by a tutor that if Delany wrote as much as possible his spelling would have to improve. His mother read to him constantly, and his father even read aloud Mark Twain's *Adventures of Huckleberry Finn* (1884), chapter by chapter.

Toward the end of his Dalton years, Delany began to write short stories. He also began reading science fiction, including the works of such writers as Theodore Sturgeon, Alfred Bester, and Robert Heinlein. After being graduated from Dalton in 1956, Delany attended the Bronx High School of Science, where he was encouraged in his writing by some of his teachers and by a fellow student and aspiring poet, Marilyn Hacker. After high school graduation in 1960, Delany received a fellowship to the Breadloaf Writers' Conference in Vermont, where he met Robert Frost and other professional writers.

He continued to write, supporting himself as a folksinger in Greenwich Village clubs and cafes. On August 24, 1961, he and Marilyn Hacker were married. Although their marriage of more than thirteen years was open and loosely structured (the couple often lived apart), Hacker and Delany were highly influential on each other as he developed his fiction and she her poetry (Hacker's influence is especially strong in *Babel-17*). Delany submitted his first published book, *The Jewels of Aptor*, to Ace

Books, where Hacker worked, at her suggestion. Hacker herself is the model for Rydra Wong, the heroine of *Babel-17*. Delany attended City College in New York City (now City University of New York) in 1960 and again from 1962 to 1963, but dropped out to finish *Babel-17* (1966).

Delany's life in New York over the next several years, including his personal relationships and a near nervous breakdown in 1964, figures in a number of his works from *Empire Star* to *Dhalgren*. After *The Jewels of Aptor*, he completed a trilogy, *The Fall of the Towers*, and in 1964 reenrolled at City College of New York, where he edited the campus poetry magazine, *The Promethean*. He soon dropped out again and in 1965, after completing *The Ballad of Beta-2*, went with a friend to work on shrimp boats in the Gulf of Mexico.

At this point, Delany's writing was beginning to return enough to help support him, and, after completing *Babel-17* and *Empire Star*, he used the advance money to tour Europe and Turkey during 1965 and 1966, an experience which influenced both *The Einstein Intersection* and *Nova*.

When he returned to the United States, Delany became more involved in the science-fiction community, which was beginning to take notice of his work. He attended conferences and workshops and met both established science-fiction writers and younger authors, including Joanna Russ and Thomas Disch, who would both become good friends. In 1967, The Science Fiction Writers of America awarded *Babel-17* the Nebula Award for best novel (shared with *Flowers for Algernon* by Daniel Keyes), and in 1968 the award again went to Delany, this time for both *The Einstein Intersection* and the short story "Aye and Gomorrah."

During the winter of 1967, while Hacker was living in San Francisco, Delany moved in with a New York rock group called The Heavenly

Breakfast, who lived communally. This experiment in living, recorded in *Heavenly Breakfast*, is reflected in *Dhalgren*. By 1968, Delany was becoming firmly established as an important science-fiction writer. He had won three Nebulas; had a new book, *Nova*, published; had begun to receive critical acclaim from outside science-fiction circles; and had spoken at the Modern Language Association's annual meeting in New York. During the next few years, while working on *Dhalgren*, he devoted himself to a number of other projects, including reviewing and film-making. He received the Hugo Award in 1970 for his short story "Time Considered as a Helix of SemiPrecious Stones," and in the same year began coediting, with Marilyn Hacker, *Quark: A Quarterly of Speculative Fiction*. The journal—which published writers such as Russ, Disch, R. A. Lafferty, and others who experimented with both form and content in the genre—ceased publication in 1971 after four issues.

In 1972, Delany worked for D. C. Comics, writing the stories for two issues of *Wonder Woman* and the introduction of an anthology of *Green Lantern/ Green Arrow* comics. In 1973, he joined Hacker in London, where he continued to work on *Dhalgren* and sat in at the University of London on classes in language and philosophy which profoundly influenced his later writing. Completing *Dhalgren*, Delany began work on his next novel, *Triton*, which was published in 1976.

On January 14, 1974, Hacker gave birth to a daughter, Iva Hacker-Delany, in London. Delany, with his family, returned to the United States late in 1974 to take the position of Visiting Butler Chair Professor of English, SUNY—Buffalo, a post offered him by Leslie Fiedler. At this time, Hacker and Delany agreed to a separation and Hacker returned to London (they were divorced in 1980). Delany completed *Triton* and in September, 1976, accepted a fellowship at the University of Wisconsin—Milwaukee's Center for Twentieth Century Studies. In 1977, he collected some of his critical essays in *The Jewel-Hinged Jaw* and in 1978 published *The American Shore*, a book-length study of a Disch short story.

During the 1980's, Delany spent much of his time in New York, writing, looking after Iva, and attending conferences and conventions. His major project in that decade was the creation of a "sword-and-sorcery" fantasy series, comprising *Tales of Neveryon, Neveryona, Flight from Neveryon*, and *The Bridge of Lost Desire*. The impact of the acquired immunodeficiency syndrome (AIDS) crisis is seen in the latter two books, especially *Flight from Neveryon*. In 1984, Delany collected more of his criticism in *Starboard Wine* and also received the Pilgrim Award for achievement in science-fiction criticism from the Science Fiction Research Association. Delany's only science-fiction work in that decade was *Stars in My Pocket Like Grains of Sand*, the first part of a planned "dyptich." In 1988, he published his autobiographical recollections about his earlier years in *The Motion of Light in Water*, and he became a professor of comparative literature at the University of Massachusetts at Amherst.

During the 1990s Delany produced a great deal of writing and gained the recognition of being, in the words of critic and author James Sallis," among our finest and most important writers." The most controversial of Delany's 1990s publications are his erotic novels—*Equinox, Hogg*, and *The Mad Man*—and his 1998 comic-book-format erotic autobiography, *Bread and Wine*. *Equinox* appeared briefly in 1973, and *Hogg*'s scheduled publication that same year was canceled. Both went back into print in themid-1990s, along with the release of *The Mad Man*, the only one of the three erotic novels composed in the 1990s. While these books have disturbed and challenged many readers and scholars of Delany's work, a number of critics, most notably Norman Mailer, have defended them as examples of Delany's belief in pushing the boundaries of literature and of dealing with sexual subjects with absolute openness.

Delany also published two important nonfiction works in the 1990s: *Silent Interviews*, a collection of Delany's written interviews with subjects ranging from racism to aesthetic theory; and *Longer Views*, a collection of Delany's major essays on art, literature, and culture. Finally, there were two new works of fiction: *Atlantis*, a collection of three mainstream stories set in the 1920s, and *They Fly at Çiron*, a fantasy novel which appeared in 1993 but became widely available two years later. Delany also won the William Whitehead Award for Lifetime Achievement in Gay Literature in 1993 and was the guest of honor at the World Science-Fiction Convention at London, England, in 1995. That year he was also a visiting writer at the universities of Minnesota and Idaho, and in 1997 he was a visiting professor at Michigan State University. In January of 2000, he joined the faculty in the English department at the State University of New York at Buffalo.

Analysis: Long Fiction

Rather than seeking the meaning and value of science fiction by detecting the presence of "literary" elements and properties, Delany insists that the reader and critic must employ a set of "reading protocols" as a methodology for tapping the richness and complexity of science fiction. The protocols one applies to reading science fiction of necessity must be different from the protocols one applies to "mundane" literature, if only in how the reader must constitute whole worlds and universes as background for any narrative.

As an example, first noted by Harlan Ellison, Delany frequently cites a sentence from a

Robert Heinlein novel: "The door dilated." Given only these three words, one can make a wealth of suppositions about a culture which needs doors that dilate rather than swing or slide open and shut and which has the technology to manufacture and operate them. The more profound implications of the "protocol of reading" which science fiction necessitates can be seen in another example often mentioned by Delany. In another Heinlein novel, *Starship Troopers* (1959), it is casually revealed two-thirds of the way through the book that the first-person narrator is Hispanic, not white. Placed so casually in the narrative and read in the context of American society in the 1950s—when Delany himself read it—such a revelation must have been disruptive, all the more so for a reader such as Delany. The fact that a society can be imagined in which race is no longer a major factor in determining social position opens to question the social fabric of the society in which the book is read and thereby generates potential for change. Indeed, it may come as a surprise that requires such a shift in understanding for some of Delany's readers to realize that virtually none of his major protagonists is white.

To read through Delany's novels is to trace the growth and coming to maturity of a literary artist as well as to see the development and mutation of prevalent themes and images. Up through *Dhalgren*, his works usually center on a quest for identity undertaken or observed by a young man (*Babel-17*, with its female hero, is a notable exception). More often than not, the novel's center of consciousness is an artist, usually a writer or musician. These characters themselves are in varying stages of development and their quest usually culminates in their reaching a new level of awareness. In *The Ballad of Beta-2*, the young scholar-protagonist not only discovers behind an apparently trivial piece of space folklore a meaning which will alter humanity's future and knowledge of the universe but also discovers the dangers of glib preconceptions and the value of dedicated work. In *Empire Star*, the young Comet Jo advances from "simplex" to "multiplex" levels of thought in a tale which is also a neat twist on the paradoxes of time travel.

A major concern throughout Delany's career up through *Tales of Neveryon* has been the function of language and myth. The power of language in shaping awareness is the major thematic concern of *Babel-17*. Its heroine, the poet and space captain Rydra Wong (fluent in many languages, including those of body movements) is sent to interpret and discover the source of an enemy alien language, Babel-1 7. In so doing, she discovers a way of thinking which is highly analytical and marvelously efficient and compact but which is also dangerous—having no concept of "I" or "you," the language can induce psychotic and sociopathic behavior in those who use it.

Myth is employed to varying degrees in Delany's novels, most heavily in *The Einstein Intersection, Nova,* and *Dhalgren*—so much so that the three almost form a trilogy of meditations on the subject. In *The Einstein Intersection*, aliens have populated a ruined earth deserted by human beings. Before these new inhabitants can create their own culture, though, they must first act through the myths—from those of Orpheus and Jesus to those of Billy the Kid and Jean Harlow—which they have inherited from humanity. In *Nova*, space captain Lorq von Ray self-consciously sets out on a Grail-like quest for Illyrion, an element found at the heart of exploding stars, in order to change the social and economic structure of the entire universe. In *Dhalgren*, media and rumor elevate characters to legendary status almost overnight. The book effectively examines the disjuncture between myth and experience without denying the reality or validity of either.

Myth reappears in a different form in the Neveryon cycle. Although three of the books— *Tales of Neveryon, Flight from Neveryon,* and *The Bridge of Lost Desire* (in addition to *Neveryona)*— are collections of "tales," they have to be read as complete fictions whose individual parts create a greater whole. In fact, the tetralogy can be considered one complete text in itself; however, in keeping with Delany's insistence on the importance of the provisional, the random, and the contradictory as features to be accepted in life and in literature, the parts do not always cohere and may be read indifferent orders. Myth is the very subject of these writings, inspired in part by Robert Howard's Conan the Barbarian books but also playing with numerous utopian concepts. (The name Neveryon itself—"never/ there"—is a play on the word utopia—"no place.") The books themselves are further framed within the context of an ongoing mock-scholarly analysis, "Some Informal Remarks Toward the Modular Calculus" (which actually began as part of *Triton*), suggesting that *Neveryon* is an extrapolation of an ancient text, possibly the beginning and source of all writing.

Dhalgren

Dhalgren begins with an archetypal scenario: A young man, wear-ing only one sandal and unable to remember his name, wanders into Bellona, a midwestern city which has suffered some nameless catastrophe. In the course of the novel's 880 pages, he encounters the city's remaining residents; goes through mental, physical, and sexual adventures; becomes a local legend; and leaves. In its complexity and its ambitious scope, *Dhalgren* invites comparison with a handful of contemporary novels, including Vladimir Nabokov's *Adaor Ardor* (1969) and Thomas Pynchon's *Gravity's Rainbow* (1973), which make Joycean demands of the reader. Unlike many other science-fiction novels set in a post-holocaust society, *Dhalgren* is not concerned with the causes of the breakdown, nor does it tell of an attempt to create a new society out of the ashes of the old. There is no need for such a reconstruction. Bellona's catastrophe was unique; the rest of the country and the world are unaffected. Separated from outside electronic communication and simply abandoned by the larger society, Bellona has become a center of attraction for outcasts and drifters of all descriptions as well as remaining a home to its own disenfranchised, notably the city's black population. The city has become a place of absolute freedom, where all can do and be whatever they choose, yet it is not in a state of anarchy. There are rules and laws that govern the city, but they are not recorded or codified.

To the newcomer (and to a first reader of the book), these "rules" seem random and unpredictable. Clouds obscure the sky, so that time of day has little meaning, and the days themselves are named arbitrarily. Direction in this city seems constantly to shift, in part because people change the street signs at whim. Fires burn throughout the city, but listlessly and without pattern. When the clouds do part, they might reveal two moons in the night sky or a sun which covers half the sky. The protagonist (who comes to be known simply as The Kid) must define his identity in terms of these shifting relationships, coping with the ever-fluid patterns Bellona offers.

The price of failing to work within the web and to accommodate reality—even an unreal reality—is exemplified by the Richards family, white middle-class citizens who try to maintain a semblance of the life they had known and are going mad as a result. The Kid begins his stay in Bellona by working for the Richardses, helping them to move upstairs in their apartment complex, away from a "nest" of "Scorpions," the mostly black street gangs who wander through the city. (The Scorpions themselves are almost

as annoyed and bothered by the Richardses.) The move is futile—the Richardses are no happier or saner in their new apartment, and their son accidentally dies during the move; The Kid is not paid his promised wages (in any case, money is useless in Bellona). Still, the job has helped The Kid to adjust to Bellona's society, and he has begun to write poetry in a notebook he has found. As he nears the end of his job, he finds himself becoming, almost by accident, a Scorpion and eventually the leader of a "nest." His poetry is published, and he becomes, within the city, famous.

The characters and events of *Dhalgren* are rich and detailed enough in themselves to make the book notable. It is Delany's attention to form, though, that makes the book so complex and the act of reading it so disruptive. Not only are the city and its events seemingly random, but the plot and characterization are likewise unpredictable. Questions remain unanswered, few elements are fully resolved, and the answers and resolutions which are given are tentative and possibly misleading. Near the end of the novel, The Kid believes that he has discovered his name, but this is never confirmed. He leaves Bellona at the end of the book, but his fate is left obscure. The Kid is, moreover, an unreliable center of consciousness. He was once in a mental institution, so the reader must doubt his perceptions (he unaccountably loses stretches of time; after his first sexual encounter early in the book, he sees the woman he was with turn into a tree).He is also ambidextrous and possibly dyslexic, so that the random ways in which Bellona seems to rearrange itself may be the result of The Kid's own confusion. At the same time, though, Delany gives the reader reason to believe The Kid's perception; others, for example, also witness the impossible double moons and giant sun.

Dhalgren is not a book that will explain itself. A palimpsest, it offers new explanations on each reading. The Kid's notebook contains observations by an unknown author which tempt the reader to think that they are notes for the novel *Dhalgren*; there are minor but significant differences, however, between notes and text. The last phrase of the novel, "...I have come to," runs into the first, "to wound the autumnal city," recalling the circular construction of *Finnegans Wake* (1939). Unlike the river of James Joyce's dream book, though, *Dhalgren* does not offer the solace of such a unitary construction. The two phrases do not, after all, cohere, but overlap on the word "to." If anything, the construction of the book echoes the "optical chain" made of mirrors, prisms, and lenses which The Kid and other characters wear. Events and phrases within the book do not exactly repeat, but imprecisely mirror, one another. Certain events and phenomena, such as the giant sun, are magnified as if by a lens; others are fragmented and dispersed, as a prism fragments light into the visible spectrum.

Ultimately, Delany's Bellona is a paradigm of contemporary society. Within this seeming wasteland, though, the author finds not solace and refuge in art and love, as so many modern authors have, but the very source and taproot of art and love. Delany's epigraph reads, "You have confused the true and the real." Whatever the "reality" of the city, the book's events, or The Kid's ultimate fate, "truth" has been discovered. The Kid no longer needs the city, and his place is taken by a young woman entering Bellona in a scene that mirrors The Kid's own entrance. Even the "reality" of this scene is not assured, as The Kid's speech fragments into the unfinished sentences of the notebook. "Truth," finally, is provisional, whatever is sufficient for one's needs, and requires to be actively sought and separated from the "real."

Triton

Delany's next novel, *Triton*, has some similarities to *Dhalgren* but turns the premises of the earlier novel inside out. Once again, a protagonist is introduced into a society of near-total freedom. This time, however, the setting is an established, deliberately and elaborately planned society on Neptune's moon Triton in the year 2112, and the protagonist, Bron Helstrom, is a worker in "metalogics" for a company (termed a "hegemony") on that moon. Triton is at least as free a society as Bellona—indeed, more so, since people are not only free to behave and live in almost any social, sexual, or religious pattern but also may change their residences, their physical sex, and their psychological sexual orientation almost at will.

In the novel's course, Triton joins with the other Outer Satellites of the worlds beyond Jupiter in a war against Mars and Earth, but Delany subverts one's expectations in his treatment of this conflict. The war involves no soldiers, causes the deaths of millions, and is over quickly; it is also peripheral to the book's main focus, a psychological study of Bron Helstrom. Helstrom, a seemingly normal individual and a recent emigrant from Mars, is out of place on this moon, which has a place for everybody. He meets a roaming actress and theatrical producer called The Spike and becomes romantically obsessed with her, but she ultimately rejects him. This rejection, caused by and coupled with Helstrom's narcissism and obsession with correct responses to codes, conventions, and patterns of behavior, drives him deeper into himself. Unable, as he thinks, to find a woman who will suit his ideal, he has a sex-change operation to become that ideal himself, one who will then be available for a man like himself. His (or now her) rules of conduct, though, require complete passivity. Helstrom must wait for the right man and can make no sign to him, so she must wait forever, all the more so because she has falsely idealized a code of "correct" male and female behavior. The end reveals a total solipsism: The one man who could meet Bron Helstrom's standards is himself, just as she is the one woman who could meet his.

Triton is, in its way, an illustration of Godel's theorem: No logical system is sufficient to explain itself, and thus every system is incomplete and open to paradox. Triton's social system, designed to accommodate everyone (one of its rules even requires a place where no rules apply) still cannot accommodate someone such as Helstrom who, coming from Mars, does not share the presuppositions on which that system is founded. Helstrom's logic of male-female relationships, on the other hand, stems from his failure to operate on Triton's terms and is paradoxical and incomplete within itself too.

The contradictions of modern American society—tending toward libertarianism on one hand and repression on the other—are extrapolated into the future interplanetary society of *Triton*. Triton itself is an idealized extension of aspects of Delany's experiences in New York's East Village, San Francisco, and elsewhere in the 1960s and early 1970s. Earth, however, remains mired in its dominant hierarchical, patriarchal culture. Helstrom, from Mars, is sufficiently distant from Earth's culture to be shocked at its brutality and bemused by its adherence to money. Helstrom, though, patterns his own models of sex-role behavior on sexist and patriarchal assumptions about the supposedly innate natures of men and women, behavior which is rendered ridiculous by a society in which "male" and "female" are simply categories of choice. It should be noted that, in its depictions of Helstrom's behavior, *Triton* is often richly comic.

Delany's probing goes even further. He reminds the reader that *he* is presenting models too. The novel includes two appendixes, one a collection of notes and omitted segments from the novel and the other a segment of lectures bya Martian scholar, Ashima Slade, entitled "Some Informal Remarks Toward the Modular Calculus, Part Two." These additions are integral to the novel. They serve to remind the reader that the book is a made object, subject to work and revision, and they also comment on the method of the models provided in the "novel" itself. They also give hints of possible answers to some of the questions raised by the text while raising new ones in turn.

Analysis: Short Fiction

In *The Motion of Light in Water,* Delany spoke of himself as: "A black man. A gay man. A writer." Though these three truths do not "explain" Delany's life, they are the primary roots from which his writings have sprung. Delany's work often features marginalized characters, people outside society's mainstream, such as slaves or those who have been modified (through tattooing or piercing, for example).

Delany himself—in his lifestyle, chosen profession, and chosen genre—is outside the American mainstream. Yet, he has found away, through writing, to express and empower himself. This has not been easy, and many of the characters in his early short stories, whose tales were often narrated in first person, were as full of longing—or more so—at the end of the story as at the beginning. In Delany's later stories, particularly in *Tales of Neveryon,* the characters often do find a place and a purpose for themselves.

"Aye and Gomorrah"

Though Delany is primarily known for his novels, his short stories form a critical body of-work that must be considered. One of his best-known stories is "Aye and Gomorrah," which was written in September, 1966, while Delany was at the Milford Science Fiction Writers Conference in Connecticut. It was immediately bought by Harlan Ellison for an influential anthology called *Dangerous Visions*, published in 1967. It was the story that, as Delany himself noted, helped him to make the transition from "an unknown to a known entity."

This very brief story takes place mainly in Istanbul, Turkey, but its setting is clearly secondary to its subject: the neutering of people who work in space and those who, because of a syndrome called free-fall-sexual-displacement complex, worship them sexually. The former, known as spacers, are attracted to the latter, called frelks, only for the money that the frelks will give them to perform acts that are not specified in the story but that have clearly sexual undertones. Yet, the androgynous nature of the frelks prevents any real sexual relationship.

While on the spacer equivalent of "shore leave," the young protagonist of "Aye and Gomorrah" meets a Turkish girl, who wants to seduce the spacer but does not have the money necessary to bribe him. She is open about her obsession with spacers, although she does not like being a frelk—she believes that she is a "pervert" in the sense that a "pervert substitutes something unattainable for "normal' love: the homosexual, a mirror, the fetishist, a shoe or a watch or a girdle."

The idea of being a sexual outcast is a frequent theme in Delany's work, perhaps stemming from his coming to terms with his homosexuality. In *Triton*, for example, the main character, Bron, undergoes a sex change, ostensibly to be able to understand women better, but instead becomes even more confused about his (or her) own sexuality. "Aye and Gomorrah" focuses on the retarded sexuality of the spacers and the futile sexual longings of the frelks. In "The Tale of the Small Sarg" the character of Gorgik, a former slave who has become "civilized," reveals that he cannot function sexually unless either he or his partner is wearing some physical sign of ownership, such as a slave collar.

Yet, Delany often applies a light touch to these issues in his stories. In "Aye and Gomorrah," the young spacer is constantly being corrected because of his tendency to assign the wrong gender of the word "frelk" in different languages." *Une*frelk," he is told by a Frenchman, and he learns from a Latina that it is *frelko* in Spanish.

"Time Considered as a Helix of Semiprecious Stones"

"Time Considered as a Helix of Semiprecious Stones," which was written in Milford in July of 1968 and published in 1969, also presents a mocking approach to modern society. The main character, who changes his identity almost with each page, comments, often bitingly (in parentheses within the text) on the world as it passes by: "A very tanned, very blond man . . . came down the rocks (artificial) between the ferns (real) growing along the stream (real water; phony current)." Later, he notes that "automation has become the upper crust's way of flaunting the labor surplus."

The subject of the story is the behavior of a criminal once it has been predicted that he will commit a specific crime. Interwoven with this theme is that of the Singers, who are "people who look at things, then go and tell people what they've seen. What makes them Singers is their ability to make people listen." One Singer, a youth named Hawk, is a familiar Delany character all the way down to his deeply bitten fingernails. Unable to love in a "normal" way, he prefers pain to pleasure, much to the protagonist's dismay. The protagonist, meanwhile, characterizes his own aberration, the "will" to steal, as "an impulse toward the absurd and the tasteless." But this is a *want*, a *need*—like the need for love—and it cannot be forever denied.

Tales of Neveryon

Not all Delany's stories are science-fiction tales set in the future. For example, the loosely related stories found in the *Tales of Neveryon* collection are set in a mythical past. These stories owe much to the genre of swashbuckling fantasy fiction called sword-and-sorcery, though they depart as radically from the conventions of that genre as *Dhalgren* does from science fiction.

Sword-and-sorcery is, itself, a marginalized literature. It has received little respect from mainstream critics, even those willing to admit, grudgingly, that science fiction has something to offer. However, in the hands of some writers (Robert E. Howard, Fritz Leiber, Karl Edward Wagner) sword-and-sorcery has achieved notable commercial success and generated enough small press scholarship to deserve broader critical consideration.

Delany is, according to James Sallis in *Ash of Stars: On the Writing of Samuel R. Delany* (1996), "the man who would intellectualize" sword-and-sorcery. Certainly, Delany's *Neveryon* stories have contributed two things to the genre. First, while sword-and-sorcery must develop a historical "feel," most writers achieve this with descriptions of walled cities, ruins, and sword fights. The focus is on large-scale, dramatic events—war being a favorite. A common criticism here is that readers seldom see how armies are fed or how cities survive in the absence of an economy other than trade.

Delany's *Neveryon* stories, in contrast, develop a sense of history by focusing on exactly those details that other writers neglect. In "The Tale of Gorgik," the first *Neveryon* story, the reader learns of docks and warehouses, of sailors and slaves. The main trade item described is not jewels or exotic furs but little rubber balls.

"The Tale of Old Venn" shows readers the ship builders and fishing boats. The astrolabe's invention is part of the story's background, and the development of an early writing system leads one character, Norema, to thoughts on origins and philosophy.

Although sword-and-sorcery is generally set at a time when cultures are moving from barter to monetary economies and from rural to urban societies, most writers use these facts only to force characters into motion. Delany makes the change to a monetary economy a major focus of such stories as "The Tale of Potters and Dragons," where attempts to control the rubber-ball trade and the change from three-legged to four-legged pots are important plot developments. Is it coincidence that one character is named Madam Keyne (reminiscent of John Maynard Keynes, the economist)?

Delany's second contribution to sword-and-sorcery is his far greater emphasis on character than on the plot and action that drives most work in the genre. In fact, there is little plot at all in the *Neveryon* stories. There are certainly no larger-than-life characters. Gorgik, who appears in most of the tales and is the closest Delany comes to a barbarian warrior, is, in fact, a "civilized" man and has the psychological scars to prove it. Only "The Tale of Dragons and Dreamers" has much fighting, and it is not an imprisoned Gorgik who does it. It is Small Sarg, a youth, who handles the killing.

Many characters in the *Neveryon* stories are women, but not in the usual roles of princess, harlot, or woman warrior (the only woman warrior is named Raven). Instead, women are merchants, inventors, and fishers. There is a part-time prostitute whose story is told in "The Tale of Rumor and Desire"; this is Clodon, a man.

Other Literary Forms

Samuel R. Delany is known for his work in a number of other literary forms, including autobiography, and, more notably, literary criticism and theory. *Heavenly Breakfast: An Essay on the Winter of Love* is a memoir describing Delany's experiences as a member of a commune in New York. *The Motion of Light in Water: Sex and Science-Fiction Writing in the East Village, 1957-1965* is an autobiography covering Delany's youth and the early part of his writing career. Delany also published a number of important essays on science fiction, some of which have been collected in *The Jewel-Hinged Jaw, Starboard Wine, The Straits of Messina*, and *Longer Views*. In addition to other, uncollected essays, introductions, and speeches, Delany wrote *The American Shore: Meditations on a Tale of Science Fiction by Thomas M. Disch*, a structuralist-semiotic study of Disch's short story "Angouleme," and *Silent Interviews*, a collection of what Delany calls "written interviews." Delany worked in other forms as well: With his then-wife, Marilyn Hacker, he coedited the speculative-fiction journal *Quark* from 1970 to 1971; he wrote for comic books, including a large-format "visual novel," *Empire*, and he made two experimental films, *Tiresias* and *The Orchid*.

Bibliography

Barbour, Douglas. *Worlds Out of Words: The SF Novels of Samuel R. Delany*. London: Bran's Head Books, 1979. This fairly early critique of Delany's works gives a brief biography of Delany and a general discussion of his works, before concentrating on different aspects such as cultural, literary, and mythological allusions and some individual works. Includes notes and primary bibliography.

Call, Lewis. "Structures of Desire: Erotic Power in the Speculative Fiction of Octavia Butler and Samuel Delany." *Rethinking History* 9, nos. 2/3 (June, 2005): 275-297. Discusses the power of Butler and Delany's works to both criticize traditional forms of slavery and also present alternative, positive forms of slavery.

Cyclopedia of Literary Characters, 4th ed. Ipswich, MA: Salem Press, 2015. Contains numerous brief essays on characters in Delany's fiction.

DeGraw, Sharon. *The Subject of Race in American Science Fiction*. Routledge, 2007.

Dery, Mark. "Black to the Future: Interviews with Samuel R. Delany, Greg Tate, and Tricia Rose." *The South Atlantic Quarterly* 92 (Fall, 1993): 735-778. Examines why so few African Americans write science fiction, since it is a genre in which encounters with the Other are central; discusses these matters with Delany and others.

Di Filippo, Paul, editor. *Critical Survey of Science Fiction and Fantasy Literature*. 3rd edition. Amenia, NY: Salem / Grey House, 2018. Three hefty volumes that contain essays on numerous works by Delany.

Fox, Robert Elliot. *Conscientious Sorcerers: The Black Postmodernist Fiction of LeRoi Jones/Amiri Baraka, Ishmael Reed, and Samuel R. Delany*. New York: Greenwood Press, 1987. Fox's text is useful for comparing and contrasting Delany's writing with that of his contemporaries in black fiction. Despite the gulf between their genres, Fox manages to find some similarity in the styles and subjects of these writers. Contains bibliographical information and an index.

Freedman, Carl, ed. *Conversations with Samuel R. Delany*. University Press of Mississippi, 2009. Contains twelve different discussions with Delany, dealing with such topics as race, homosexuality, science fiction, and particular works by Delany.

Gawron, Jean Mark. Introduction to *Dhalgren*, by Samuel R. Delany. Reprint. Boston: Gregg Press,

1977. Gawron's forty-three-page introduction to this edition is an excellent starting point for readers wishing to deal with the complexities of Delany's longest single work. The Gregg Press reprint series includes textually accurate hardbound editions of Delany's major works through *Triton*. The introductions by various critics and scholars are especially helpful.

Kelso, Sylvia. "'Across Never': Postmodern Theory and Narrative Praxis in Samuel R. Delany's Neveryon Cycle." *Science-Fiction Studies* 24 (July, 1997): 289-301. Argues that Derridean theory supplies the "Symbolic Order" of the blurred margins and centerless structure of Delany's *Neveryon* cycle and that Michel Foucault's use of sadomasochistic experience is imaged in the cycle's "homoerotic Imaginary."

McEvoy, Seth. *Samuel R. Delany.* New York: Frederick Ungar, 1984. An accessible overview which concentrates on Delany's work through *Dhalgren*, though some later works are discussed briefly. Emphasizes the impact of Delany's dyslexia on his development as a writer and corrects some biographical inaccuracies in earlier critical studies. Includes sketchy notes; the bibliography merely consists of a listing of Delany's books in print as of 1983, though it does refer the reader to Peplow and Bravard's bibliography (see below).

Malmgren, Carl. "The Languages of Science Fiction: Samuel Delany's *Babel-17.*" *Extrapolation* 34, no. 1 (Spring, 1993): 528. Studies the relationship between language and science fiction and the possibilities that science fiction creates for new uses of language and new views of reality.

Peplow, Michael W., and Robert S. Bravard. *Samuel R. Delany: A Primary Bibliography, 1962-1979.* Boston: G. K. Hall, 1980. This exhaustive bibliography is the best starting reference book about Delany's early life and career. The introduction includes a lengthy biographical sketch, and the primary and secondary bibliographies list virtually all writings by and about Delany up to 1979.

Reid-Pharr, Robert F. "Disseminating Heterotopia" *African American Review* 28 (Fall, 1994): 347-357. Discusses how Delany confronts traditional ideas of proper identity and community politics, deconstructing lines between black and white communities and homosexual and heterosexual communities.

Review of Contemporary Fiction 16 (Fall, 1996). Special issue on Delany with essays on his novels and his science-fiction theory and criticism. Features an essay on his tales and an interview with Delany in which he discusses his theory of science fiction and his ideas about science fiction as a genre and a way of reading.

Sallis, James. "Samuel R. Delany." *Review of Contemporary Fiction* 16, no. 3 (1996): 90-171. The same year that *Ash of Stars* appeared, the *Review of Contemporary Fiction* released this collection of articles on Delany. While a few essays appear in both publications and the critical ground covered is similar, more of the *Contemporary Fiction* pieces focus on biographical critique and Delany's early work. This collection also features a Delany interview and an excerpt from *The Splendor and Misery of Bodies, of Cities*, the purported sequel to *Stars in My Pocket Like Grains of Sand*.

_____, ed. *Ash of Stars: On the Writing of Samuel R. Delany.* Jackson: University Press of Mississippi, 1996. This first major collection of critical work on Delany includes everything from straightforward appreciations to dense, deconstructionist analysis. *Ash of Stars* features essays on *Babel-17, Stars in My Pocket Like Grains of Sand, Triton, Dhalgren, Neveryon,* Delany's erotic novels, and his critical work. Sallis's introduction is an insightful critical overview of Delany's career.

Slusser, George Edgar. *The Delany Intersection: Samuel R. Delany Considered as a Writer of Semi-precious Words.* San Bernardino, Calif.: Borgo Press, 1977. This text sets out the structuralist interpretation of Delany's works, using Delany's literary criticism pieces to judge his own writing. Also traces the evolution of Delany's work from heroic epics to psychological fiction and beyond. Brief biographical and bibliographical notes.

Tucker, Jeffrey Allen. *A Sense of Wonder: Samuel R. Delany, Race, Identity, and Difference.* Wesleyan UP, 2004. Deals with such matters as homosexuality, race, identity, and psychological approaches to difference.

Weedman, Jane. *Samuel R. Delany.* Mercer Island, Wash.: Starmont House, 1982. Weedman discusses a wide range of subjects, including influences on Delany's writing, biographical events, stylistic and critical concepts, and Delany's development as a writer. A detailed chronology can be found at the beginning of the book, and annotated primary and secondary bibliographies have been included at its end. Also includes an index.

—Donald F. Larsson; Jo-Ellen Lipman Boon; John Nizalowski; Robert C. Evans

Toi Derricotte

Poet

Born: Hamtramck, Michigan; April 12, 1941

POETRY: *The Empress of the Death House*, 1978; *Natural Birth*,1983; *Captivity*, 1989; *Tender*, 1997; *The Undertaker's Daughter*, 2011; *I: New and Selected Poems*, 2019.

NONFICTION: *Creative Writing: A Manual for Teachers*, 1985 (with Madeline Bass); *The Black Notebooks: An Interior Journey*, 1997.

Achievements

Toi Derricotte has forced the American poetry establishment to rethink its assumptions about African Americans and women. Her work evolved through the 1970s, during the rise in black feminist awareness and what some scholars call the second Renaissance in black writing, or the Black Arts movement. She first won recognition from the New School for Social Research with its 1973 Pen and Brush Award for an untitled poetry manuscript. She went to on to win recognition and fellowships from the Academy of American Poets in both 1974 and 1978. The National Endowment for the Arts bestowed awards in 1985 and 1990. She won the nomination for the 1998 Pushcart Prize, a Folger Shakespeare Library Poetry Book Award, a Lucille Medwick Memorial Award from the Poetry Society of America, and a United Black Artists' Distinguished Pioneering of the Arts Award. In 2012 she won a PEN/Voelcker Award for Poetry and was also elected a Chancellor of the Academy of American Poets. In 2016, she was a corecipient of an award from the National Book Foundation. Other honors have included the Paterson Award for Sustained Literary Achievement for Previous Winners of the Paterson Poetry Prize and fellowships from the Guggenheim Foundation and the Rockefeller Foundation. In 2019 her book, *I: New and Selected Poems,* was named a finalist for the National Book Award.

Biography

Born April 12, 1941, into a Detroit-area family separated from most of the city's African American community by class and lighter skin, Toinette Derricotte wrote as a way to find solace in an existence filled with alienation. "Tender," the title poem of her fourth major collection, opens, "The tenderest meat comes from the houses where you hear the least squealing." This insight says much about what it was like to be the daughter of Benjamin Sweeney Webster, a mortician, and Antonia Banquet Webster Cyrus, a systems analyst. The young girl quickly learned to hide her thoughts on the page.

Writing is a first passion, but after high school, the shy teen studied psychology at Wayne State University with visions of a doctorate. Plans changed in December, 1961, when she gave birth to son Anthony, and in July, 1962, Derricotte married artist Clarence Reese. The union lasted two years. In 1967, she married banker Bruce Derricotte. They separated in 1991.

Parenthood's realities led Derricotte to major in special education. She started teaching in

1964 with the Manpower Program. She finished a bachelor's degree in 1965. In 1966, Derricotte became a teacher for mentally and emotionally retarded students at Detroit's Farand School. In 1969, Derricotte left her hometown to teach remedial reading at Jefferson School in Teaneck, New Jersey. The job lasted a year.

She taught for money, but always wrote. In 1973, Derricotte began a four-year stint on the *New York Quarterly* staff. The following year she started a fifteen-year residency with the New Jersey State Council on the Arts Poet-in-the-Schools program. Those years set the direction of her life as author, mentor, and teacher.

The Empress of the Death House, her first collection, was published in 1978. The next year she founded a retreat to foster the development of African American poets in a culturally sensitive atmosphere. That involvement ended in 1982 but was reborn in 1996, when she collaborated with Cornelius Eady to create Cave Canem, a summer workshop in upstate New York.

In 1983, *Natural Birth* was published. Derricotte was graduated from New York University with a master's degree in creative writing the next year. The 1985 publication of *Creative Writing: A Manual for Teachers,* coauthored with Madeline Bass, followed.

In 1988, twenty-one years after she left home for New Jersey, Derricotte moved to Norfolk, Virginia, to teach at Old Dominion. The next year, *Captivity* was published. In 1990, she spent a year as Commonwealth Professor in the English department of George Mason University in Fairfax, Virginia. In 1991, she moved to the University of Pittsburgh.

Throughout her writing career, Derricotte immersed herself in classes, readings, and contributions to various magazines and journals, such as *Pequod, Iowa Review, Ironwood, Northwest Review, Poetry Northwest, American Poetry Review, Bread Loaf Quarterly, Massachusetts Review, Ploughshares,* and *Feminist Studies.* Many of her poems

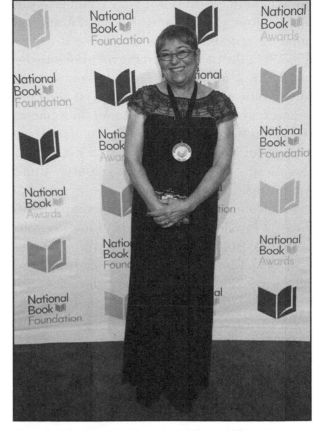

Photo by Dimitrios Kambouris, courtesy of Getty Images

and essays appear in anthologies as well.

During 1992 and 1993, she served on faculties of summer workshops at Squaw Valley, the University of South Florida, and the College of Charleston. The decade ended with the publication of *Tender,* the 1997 memoir *The Black,* in 2000, a reissue of *Natural Birth.*

In 1996 she, with Cornelius Eady, cofounded the Cave Canem Foundation to promote achievement in African American poetry; it has had a major impact in the decades since it was founded. She taught creative writing at the University of Pittsburgh, from which she is now retired.

Analysis: Poetry

Toi Derricotte's candor has been compared with the simple clarity of Emily Dickinson and honest communication of Walt Whitman—but only by those unfamiliar with African American poetry. Derricotte's blunt eloquence is typical of poets in the period from the mid-1960s to the mid-1970s, known as the Black Arts movement, which some scholars have considered to be the counterpart of the Black Power movement. Derricotte's style and themes are more similar to those of Nikki Giovanni or Mari Evans than to those of nineteenth century white Americans.

Derricotte is unique in her confessional treatment of racial identity. "My skin causes certain problems continuously, problems that open the issue of racism over and over like a wound," she once wrote. That statement hangs over her photograph on the African American Literature Book Club website as tribute to the talent she displays in the ability to turn poignant racial episodes into instruments that sometimes strike readers' consciences with jackhammer force and, at other times, soothe their souls.

"I'm not an Emily Dickinson scholar, but I have loved her for many, many years, for many reasons," she wrote in *Titanic Operas: A Poet's Corner of Responses to Dickinson's Legacy* (edited by Martha Nell Smith and Laura Elyn Lauth): "One of the reasons is because of her great courage to look at things—the most terrifying, the most beautiful—without flinching."

"Her poems begin in ordinary experiences," Jon Woodson writes of Derricotte in *Contemporary Women Poets*, "but she dissects the routine definitions supplied by society as a way towards making discoveries about what unsuspected resources the self actually contains." That aptly describes what a reader will find in any of the author's poems.

The prizewinning writer treats womanhood and race as media through which she bares her torments and forces readers to look more closely than ever before at often evaded aspects of the human experience. She writes about being an African American woman in the late twentieth century, but the work is likely to resonate with readers in any culture and time who understand that life holds more questions than answers.

The Empress of the Death House

Derricotte's early works focused on death and birth. The theme is heavy in her first book, *The Empress of the Death House*, where "The Grandmother Poems" discuss her childhood experiences in her grandparents' Detroit funeral home. Her mother's stepfather owned the business. Although she was sickly, the woman used two thousand dollars of her own money to send Derricotte's father to mortuary school, so that he might join a more stable line of work.

The Empress of the Death House grapples with the plight of women who survive abuse in an effort to sort out her feelings about her grandmother and mother. The understanding was a step on the path to self-awareness and helped her to understand her personal reactions to motherhood. In the *American Book Review*, reviewer Joe Weixlmann, who wrote about *Natural Birth*, said *The Empress of the Death House* opens readers' eyes to the "indifference or contempt" with which the world treats African American women.

Natural Birth

Natural Birth, in both its 1983 and 2000 editions, is an extension of Derricotte's investigation into African American women. The collection candidly probes the birth process as an experience that hurts too much and humiliates. This poem is a "tour de force, at once a book-length experimental poem, an exploration of the extremes of human experience, and an examination of the social construction of identity," Woodson wrote of the 1983 Crossing Press version. Of the 2000 edition, Eileen Robinson wrote in *Black Issues Book Review*.

Natural Birth is a triumph of one woman's spirit that will appeal to readers who are looking for depth, emotion, originality and truth. . . . Derricotte has completed a moving testament to teenage mothers, and mothers everywhere, who survive the miracle of birth. It is also a special gift to their children who grow stronger for understanding the very human fears and pains of the women who brought them here.

Natural Birth takes writings about death, birth, and transcendence to another level. Derricotte reaches for the truth that most unwed mothers might like to tell. She reaches inside the experience of childbirth for the thoughts that most mothers might want to share.

In *Contemporary Authors*, Derricotte is quoted as saying that her Catholic school education taught that confession made a person "whole" or "back into a state of grace." She concludes:

> As a black woman, I have been consistently confused about my "sins," unsure of which faults were in me and which faults were the results of others' projections. ...truthtelling in my art is also a way to separate my "self" from what I have been taught to believe about my "self," the degrading stereotypes about black women.

Captivity

Captivity shifted the focus from gender to race, sliding from portraits of general poverty to intricate sketches of urban students. The book places the U.S. slave experience at the root of many issues in today's black experience. The dehumanization and commercialization of African Americans' slave ancestors has been cited as a root cause of black poverty, fractured family structures, violence, and continued oppression. *Village Voice* reviewer Robyn Selman called the

book "a personal exploration yielding truths that apply to all of us."

Captivity is divided into four sections: "Blackbottom," "Red Angel," "The Testimony of Sister Maureen," and "The Terrible Bright Air." The first section's opening poem, "The Minks," describes the animals the poet's uncle raised for sale in five hundred cages in the backyard of the house she lived in on Norwood Steet as a child. Derricotte describes in painstaking detail the effects of such captivity on essentially wild animals:

> Sometimes, they paced compulsively; sometimes, the mothers snapped the necks of their kits; often, they hid in their wooden houses. In the fall, the minks were slaughtered for their skins, which returned to the yard pinned by their mouths to metal hangers.

In front of company, Derricotte's uncle would take out the skins and blow on them, parting the hairs to show their bright "underlife." The poet uses this image to end the poem in a lovely simile comparing the "underlife" to people's souls, shining and manifesting their inner life. Written in forty lines of uneven length with no stanza separations and no rhymes, the poem reads like a story, yet, because of its brevity, personification of the animals, and striking similes, it retains the condensation and impact of fine poetry.

The second poem, "Blackbottom," is the poem for which the section is named. Black Bottom is an old African American neighborhood close to Detroit that developed during the 1920s through the 1940s. Although Black Bottom is usually described as a crime-and-poverty-ridden area, it was also a vibrant center of racial and cultural identity, well known to Derricotte, who grew up in Detroit and graduated from Wayne State University.

The poem describes a middle-class African American family who left the area for a nice suburb, Conant Gardens, in northeast Detroit. They return to Black Bottom's streets to immerse themselves in the sights, sounds, and smells of their old neighborhood, knowing that on Monday they will be safe at their jobs and schools back in their new, middle-class home. The old neighborhood excites them and makes them proud. They realize they have lost something, for hearing the music of the streets makes them realize:

> We had lost our voice in the suburbs, in Conant Gardens,
> where each brick house delineated a fence of silence;
> we had lost the right to sing in the street and damn creation.

The remainder of the first section's poems deal with Derricotte's youth. They include poems for her mother and father, a poem about the house on Norwood Street, fires in childhood, her high school, and the concluding poem of "Blackbottom," "The Struggle," a meditation on her confusion about the racial aspirations of her family.

The poems in the second section, "Red Angel," deal with a later period of Derricotte's life. They cover adult topics such as sex, marriage, friendship, and the problems that occur in adult life. The last three poems in the section include one about Derricotte's mother and two about her father. The poems are still composed of varied-length lines with no apparent form, except for "Squeaky Bed," which is divided into three stanzas, and "Touching / Not Touching: My Mother," which is divided into two sections rather than stanzas.

"The Testimony of Sister Maureen," the third section of the book, is based on the story of a teaching nun with the Sisters of St. Joseph who was tried in court for manslaughter in the death of her newborn son in 1976. She was found not guilty. The poem, narrated in the first person, is surreal, beginning in the clerestory of the nun's convent, where she is advised by another woman to confess the identity of her lover. In the second part of the poem, the nun describes the changes she undergoes, her skin growing black and the miracle of God burning in her bones. More formal elements shape this poem: The stanzas are divided into seven sections, the narrator uses italics to comment on key scenes, and the spacing of words on the page becomes more varied and innovative as the poem reaches its final epiphany.

The fourth and final section of *Captivity* contains poems about children, school, Allan Ginsberg, Walt Whitman, black female corpses, and, finally, a stunning poem titled "A Note on My Son's Face," which turns into a meditation on skin color. The poems make more explicit use of formal elements in this last section, as in "For the Dishwasher at Boothman's," which is divided into three-and four-line stanzas and concluded with two couplets for emphasis. The poems about Ginsberg and Whitman use long lines in the style of the poets themselves, and "On the Turning Up of Unidentified Black Female Corpses" is divided into nine four-line stanzas.

Tender

Derricotte's fourth book of poetry, *Tender*, does a similar favor. The uncharacteristically short title poem appears to talk about meat and begins:

> The tenderest meat comes from the houses where you hear the least squealing.

It does not take much reflection to see the metaphor about pain-filled lives. In the collection's preface, Derricotte urges readers to use the poem as a hub in exploring, as she describes the book's structure, "a seven-spoked wheel." The poet continues to wrestle with the meanings of death, birth, and transcendence. She writes, "Violence is central to our lives, a constant and unavoidable reality."

Derricotte's enduring legacy might be that, as she herself observed of Emily Dickinson, she does not flinch, whether the subject is political or sexual, and that courage is especially well demonstrated in *Tender*. For example, in "Clitoris,"she discusse soral sex and her emotional response to it graphically and with lush imagery.

Like many in her generation, Derricotte never let go of the optimism of the 1960s about a positive evolution in U.S. attitudes toward and treatment of women and blacks. At the same time, she does not hesitate to display bitter disappointment at where we are along the road. For example, in "After a Reading at a Black College," also from *Tender*, she looks forward with both hope and skepticism:

> Maybe one day we will have written about this color thing until we've solved it. To-night when I read my poems about looking white, the audience strains forward with their whole colored bodies . . . .
> . . . though frightened,
> I don't stop the spirit.
> *Hold steady*, Harriet Tubman whispers,
> *Don't flop around.*

Once again, the best part of Derricotte's work is that, no matter how scathing, it is unapologetic. "People would like inspiring books that tell them what to do, something like *Five Steps Not to Be a Racist*," she told Don Lee in a 1996 interview in *Ploughshares*, the Emerson College literary journal." That's just not the truth. The easy solutions don't really prepare one for the hard work that needs to be done." She goes on:

> I feel the need to represent what's not spoken. ...I discover a pocket in myself that hasn't been articulated, then I have to find a form to carry that. Speaking the

unspeakable is not that hard. The difficulty is in finding a way to make it perfect, to make it have light and beauty and truth inside it.

Other Literary Forms

A 1997 memoir, *The Black Notebooks: An Interior Journey*, is Toi Derricotte's most popular nonfiction work. The book, expanded from twenty years of diaries, reveals how it feels to look white and be black in the United States. The work met appropriate controversy during a time when the nation, at the behest of then-president Bill Clinton, was trying to generate a dialogue on racial abuses past and present. Derricotte also cowrote with Madeline Tiger Bass *Creative Writing: A Manual for Teachers*, published by the New Jersey State Council on the Arts. The Library of Congress's *The Poet and the Poem from the Library of Congress: Toi Derricotte* is an archival recording produced in October, 1998, by the Library of Congress's Magnetic Recording Laboratory in Washington, D.C. It is one of four video or audio presentations that profile Derricotte's life and work.

Bibliography

Andrews, William, et al., eds. *The Oxford Companion to African American Literature*. New York: Oxford UP, 1996. Contains a thorough, concise resume of the author's life.

Okoampa-Ahoofe, Kwame, Jr. "The Inner Logic of Blackness." *Amsterdam News* 21 Oct. 1999: 26. Discusses notions of blackness, self-acceptance, U.S. popular culture, and the African diaspora as they are presented in *The Black Notebooks: An Interior Journey*.

Pettis, Joyce Owens. *African American Poets: Lives, Works, and Sources*. Westport, CT: Greenwood Press, 2002. Contains a helpful section on Derricotte.

Powers, William F. "The Furious Muse: Black Poets Assess the State of Their Art." *The Washington Post* 1 Oct. 1994: H1. "For lots of reasons we have felt shut out of poetry that sits up there in the traditional canon," iconoclastic Derricotte says. The article reports on a Harrisburg, Virginia, gathering of 30 African American poets and about 250 writers, critics, and scholars to define qualities that set black poetry apart from the American mainstream. The feature story offers insight into the author's personality.

Robinson, Caudell M. "Where Poets Explore Their Pain While Others Beware the Dog." *American Visions* 14, no. 5 (Oct. 1999): 30. Profiles Derricotte's thoughts on writing and efforts to promote the art among African Americans through a summer workshop in upstate New York.

—Vincent F. A. Golphin;
Sheila Golburgh Johnson; Robert C. Evans

Owen Dodson

Playwright, Poet, and Novelist

Born: Brooklyn, New York; November 28, 1914

Died: New York, New York; June 21, 1983

LONG FICTION: *Boy at the Window*, 1951 (also known as *When Trees Were Green*, 1967); *Come Home Early, Child*, 1977

SHORT FICTION: "The Summer Fire," 1956

DRAMA: *Deep in Your Heart*, pr. 1935; *Including Laughter*, pr. 1936; *The Shining Town*, wr. 1937, pb. 1991; *Divine Comedy*, pr. 1938, pb. 1974 (music by Morris Mamorsky); *The Garden of Time*, pr. 1939 (music by Shirley Graham); *Everybody Join Hands*, pb. 1943; *New World A-Coming*, pr. 1943, pb. 1944; *The Third Fourth of July*, pb. 1946 (with Countee Cullen); *Bayou Legend*, pr. 1948, pb. 1971; *Medea in Africa*, pr. 1959; *Till Victory Is Won*, pr. 1965 (with Mark Fax; opera); *Freedom, the Banner*, pb. 1984

SCREENPLAYS: *They Seek a City*, 1945

RADIOPLAYS: *Old Ironsides*, 1942; *Robert Smalls*, 1942; *The Midwest Mobilizes*, 1943; *Dorrie Miller*, 1944; *New World A-Coming*, 1945; *St. Louis Woman*, c. 1945 (adaptation of Countee Cullen and Arna Bontemps's play); *The Dream Awake*, 1969

POETRY: *Powerful Long Ladder*, 1946; *Cages*, 1953; *The Confession Stone*, 1968 (revised and enlarged as *The Confession Stone: Song Cycles*, 1970); *The Harlem Book of the Dead*, 1978 (with James Van Der Zee and Camille Billops)

NONFICTION: "Twice a Year," 1946-1947; "College Troopers Abroad," 1950; "Playwrights in Dark Glasses," 1968; "Who Has Seen the Wind? Playwrights and the Black Experience," 1977; "Who Has Seen the Wind? Part II," 1980

Achievements

Owen Dodson's writing talents garnered diverse honors. He was the recipient of various writing grants including the General Education Board (1937), Rosenwald Fellowship (1943), Guggenheim Fellowship (1953), and the Rockefeller Fellowship (1968). In 1942 *The Garden of Time* earned for Dodson Stanford University's Maxwell Anderson Verse Drama Award (second prize). In 1956 "The Summer Fire," the first chapter from *Come Home Early, Child*, placed second in the *Paris Review*'s 1956 short-story contest and was included in *Best Short Stories from the Paris Review* (1959). Bates College bestowed additional honors on its distinguished alumnus; he was elected to Phi Beta Kappa in 1951 and was awarded an honorary doctorate of letters in 1967. Dodson also received an honorary doctorate from Missouri's Lincoln University in 1978.

Paying tribute to Dodson's literary legacy, Glenda Dickerson and Mike Malone created *Owen's Song*, a collage of his plays and poems. *Owen's Song* was performed in 1974 at the Last Colony Theater, Washington, D.C.; the Harlem Cultural Center, New York; and the Eisenhower Theater in the John F. Kennedy Center for the

Performing Arts, Washington, D.C. One year later, Dodson received the New York Black Theater Alliance's AUDELCO (Audience Development Company) Outstanding Pioneer Award in recognition of his contributions to the growth and development of African American theater.

Biography

Owen Vincent Dodson, the grandson of former slaves and the ninth child of Nathaniel and Sarah Dodson, was born on November 28, 1914, in Brooklyn, New York. His father was a syndicated columnist and director of the National Negro Press. Before Owen's thirteenth birthday, death claimed four siblings and both parents; as a result, Owen and the other Dodson children lived with their older sister Lillian, an elementary school teacher. Dodson graduated from Thomas Jefferson High School in 1932, earned a B.A. from Bates College in 1936 and an M.F.A. degree from the Yale School of Fine Arts's School of Drama in 1939.

At Bates, Dodson's passion for poetry and drama was evident. In response to his criticism of a sonnet by John Keats, his professor directed him to write sonnets himself, which Dodson did at the rate of four sonnets a week during his undergraduate years. This output enabled him to become a published poet while still an undergraduate. Also at Bates, he wrote and directed plays, and during his senior year, he staged *The Trojan Women.*

At Yale, two of Dodson's best-known plays, *Divine Comedy* and *The Garden of Time,* were first produced. Dodson, recognized as a promising poet, soon gained attention as an up-and-coming dramatist. Talladega College commissioned him to write a play, *Amistad,* commemorating the hundredth anniversary of the slave-ship mutiny led by Joseph Cinque.

After Dodson received his graduate degree from Yale, he began his career as an educator.

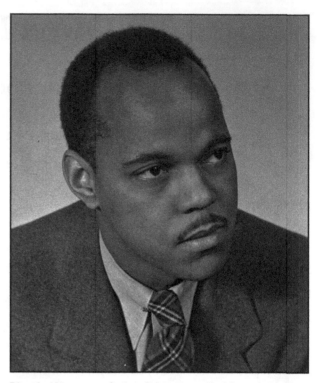

Photo courtesy of the Bettmann Archive and Getty Images

He was employed by Spelman College and later at Hampton University. Dodson was one of the founders of the Negro Playwright Company in 1940. In 1942, during World War II, he enlisted in the Navy. While stationed at the Great Lakes Naval Training Center in Illinois, Dodson wrote and directed *Heroes on Parade,* a series of plays, including *Robert Smalls, John P. Jones, Booker T. Washington, Lord Nelson, Dorrie Miller, Everybody Join Hands, Old Ironsides, Don't Give Up the Ship, Freedom, the Banner,* and *Tropical Fable.* Some of these plays were performed by other military drama groups in the United States and abroad. Dodson received a medical discharge in 1943.

On June 26, 1944, twenty-five thousand people saw *New World A-Coming* at Madison Square Garden. Based on the production's success, Dodson was appointed executive secretary of the American Film Center's Committee for Mass Education in Race Relations. Other prominent committee members were Arna

Bontemps, Langston Hughes, and Richard Wright. Dodson was a prolific dramatist. He collaborated with the well-known Harlem Renaissance poet Countee Cullen and wrote *The Third Fourth of July* and *Medea in Africa,* an adaptation of Euripides' *Medea* (431 BCE; *Medea,* 1781) that was based on Cullen's play *Medea* (pr., pb. 1935) and Dodson's *The Garden of Time.* Dodson also collaborated with composer Mark Fax and wrote two operas: *A Christmas Miracle* and *Till Victory Is Won.*

In 1947 Dodson joined the faculty of Howard University, and a decade later he was appointed chair of the drama department. He taught during the day and directed during the night. Indeed, during his long career he directed more than one hundred plays. In the fall of 1949, Dodson, Anne Cooke, and James Butcher led the Howard Players on a three-month tour of northwestern Europe. After the group's return to Washington, D.C., the United States government presented Howard University with the American Public Relations Award. During the 1954-1955 season, Dodson directed the premier performance of James Baldwin's *The Amen Corner* nine years before its Broadway debut. He also staged productions of plays by former Howard students, including Amiri Baraka (then known as LeRoi Jones).

In 1970, Dodson retired from Howard. However, his passion for the theater and poetry remained steadfast. He continued to direct plays and write poetry, including *The Confession Stone* and *The Harlem Book of the Dead.* Dodson taught at City College of New York and at York College in Queens. He died on June 21, 1983, in New York. Memorial services were held in Washington, D.C. and New York.

Analysis: Drama

Although Owen Dodson—teacher, director, and critic—made many valuable contributions

to African American drama as he encouraged and trained actors and playwrights, his plays remain his most significant theatrical accomplishment. Dodson, the author of at least thirty-seven plays and a dominant director in African American university theater for more than thirty years, was not the first black dramatist; however, he was one of the first black playwrights to consistently write and direct serious African American plays. Therefore, he is a literary forefather of younger generations of black playwrights such as Lorraine Hansberry and August Wilson as well as black directors, including Lloyd Richards. He has been hailed as the dean of African American drama.

In Dodson's plays, themes, plot, and characters are upstaged by language. His most widely known theatrical works are verse plays. He was one of the first playwrights, white or black, to effectively use verse drama. Even when Dodson wrote other types of plays, language remains, more often than not, the most potent element.

The epigraph ("It takes a powerful long ladder to climb to the sky / An catch the bird of freedom for the dark") for Dodson's first volume of verse, *Powerful Long Ladder,* has relevance for his plays. The ladder is a metaphor for whatever individuals need, and the bird of freedom represents goals and desires. In *The Shining Town,* black women need to endure in order to reach financial stability. In *Divine Comedy,* the churchgoers need to turn away from a con man and empower themselves to obtain life's basic necessities. In *The Garden of Time,* the characters must realize that racism affects love. In *Bayou Legend,* Dodson's second full-length play, which critics have described as a fantasy and an allegorical poetic legend, Reve Grant fails to learn until it is too late that to compromise one's life is to compromise one's soul. He "chose the kingdom of compromise, of nothing, of mediocrity" as he longed for wealth and power.

The Shining Town

The setting of this one-act play is a subway station in the Bronx during the Depression. New York is no "shining town" for the women who participate in a twentieth century version of a slave auction. African American domestic workers compete with each other for daily jobs offered by white women who pay extremely low wages. As the black women wait for their potential employers to arrive at the station, the atmosphere of gloom increases. The dark station corresponds with the women's despair. Dodson suggests that Abby, a little girl who accompanies her mother on her quest for employment, is doomed to the same fate. Dodson completed this play at Yale, but it was not produced there. One scholar, James V. Hatch, speculates that Dodson's less than flattering images of white women may be the reason *The Shining Town* was not produced at Yale.

Divine Comedy

Divine Comedy is another drama that Dodson completed at Yale. It premiered at Yale, was reviewed favorably in *Variety*, and remains one of his best-known plays. This verse play in two acts portrays a character based on Father Divine, the self-proclaimed religious leader. Dodson boldly focuses on an infamous black character at a time when a number of African American writers and scholars advocated positive images only. *The Shining Town*'s Depression era time period is repeated here, and despair is also prevalent in this play. For example, a mother realizes she is rocking a dead baby. However, unlike *The Shining Town*, *Divine Comedy* does not have a pessimistic ending. The characters eventually realize they have to make their own lives better instead of depending on a religious charlatan. At the end, the characters proclaim: "We need no prophets. / This Winter is Autumn. / We need no miracles. / We *are* the miracle." Love is

also an important factor in this play, as Cyril Jackson demonstrates the extremes to which a son will go to protect his mother.

The Garden of Time

This three-act verse play, completed and produced at Yale, is Dodson's interpretation of Euripides' *Medea*. *The Garden of Time*, a drama of interracial relationships, begins in ancient Greece, and midway through the play, the characters are in Georgia and Haiti. Concurrent with the shift in settings is the transformation of characters. Medea becomes Miranda, a Haitian, and Jason becomes John, a plantation owner's son. When *The Garden of Time* was staged at Yale, Shirley Graham was the play's only black actor. Graham, who was also enrolled in Yale's School of Drama, wrote the music for the play. *The Garden of Time* is one of Dodson's best-known plays and the winner of the Maxwell Anderson Verse Drama Award (second place) at Stanford University in 1942, yet ironically, it remains unpublished.

Dodson's plays provide insight into African American life, yet they are not limited to the black experience. Achieving universality in his writing was of primary importance to Dodson. His plays transcend cultures and time. *The Garden of Time*'s choral refrain, which was later titled "Circle One" and published in Dodson's *Powerful Long Ladder*, applies to the universality of life found in his plays: "Nothing happens only once, / Nothing happens only here, / . . . All the lands repeat themselves, / Shore for shore and men for men."

Analysis: Poetry

Although Dodson is primarily known for his dramas, he also wrote a number of collections of poetry. Of these, his 1946 collection *Powerful Long Ladder* is the best known.

Powerful Long Ladder

Powerful Long Ladder is concerned with human struggle, particularly with the struggle of black people in a society that first enslaved and then simultaneously exploited and ignored them. At the time the book was published, segregation was widespread. Dodson had recently been discharged from the Navy, where he belonged to a segregated company at the Great Lakes Naval Training Station outside Chicago.

The book, divided into five sections, takes its title from the Dodson poem "Someday We're Gonna Tear Them Pillars Down," a seven-page verse drama that uses dramatic technique to the utmost. The pillars are symbolically akin to the wall in Robert Frost's famous poem "Mending Wall"; they are barriers that serve as points of demarcation between people—in the Dodson poem, between African Americans and the dominant society.

Dodson has often been compared to Frost. In a sense, however, this comparison may be misleading because of Dodson's deep personal involvement on a daily basis with the inequities of segregation and discrimination, which continually devoured his spirit. Robert Frost could afford a philosophical detachment that no African American person of Owen Dodson's period could reasonably enjoy.

The first section of *Powerful Long Ladder* contains a dozen poems of from two to six pages each. The range of these poems is remarkable. Some focus on individuals; others deal broadly with topics ranging from racial tension to death to the accomplishments of African Americans. Many of them are dialect poems. The first poem, "Lament," which is not in dialect, is particularly interesting, beginning with an imperative to a dead boy to wake and tell how he died. What the poem essentially conveys is the hopelessness of trying fully to understand life's common abstractions—love, freedom, terror, death.

A more complicated view of human existence emanates from "Guitar," a ballad about a black man jailed for hitting a white person. Society decrees that, without solid evidence, the black man should be adjudged guilty. This poem has strong metrical overtones from "The Weary Blues" by Langston Hughes. The tone of the poem is one of despair tempered by resignation. The black man has no recourse as society is constituted.

Among the best-known Dodson poems is "Black Mother Praying," a war poem about a mother whose sons have left to defend their country. She compares her sacrifice to Christ's crucifixion, her sons to the son of Mary. The rub is that when her sons come home—if they come home—the freedom they fought to ensure will, because of their color, extend neither to her nor to them. This poem is a precursor of Dodson's *The Confession Stone*, in which Dodson makes the Virgin Mary and her son quite ordinary people dealing with the details of daily life. Mary admonishes the young Jesus not to play with Judas when he goes out.

The second section of *Powerful Long Ladder* contains a substantial excerpt from Dodson's verse play, *Divine Comedy*, which is an ironic presentation of the kind of hope that the evangelist Father Divine offered his hapless followers, most of them black, for several decades. Dodson as a boy went to one of Father Divine's meetings with his brother Kenneth and never forgot the experience. Like Jesus feeding the five thousand, Father Divine fed his followers. He drew milk from a seemingly bottomless well. When the crowd had dispersed, however, Kenneth lifted the tablecloth to find that a black boy was underneath pumping milk into the vat from which Father Divine magically extracted it.

Surely this experience provided an initial stimulus for *Divine Comedy*, which also has many structural elements borrowed from Dante's masterpiece. Dodson's verse drama provides, in essence, a startling insight into how black people, stripped of much of their hope, can be exploited and duped, as Father Divine's followers usually were, even by their fellow black people.

The other sections of *Powerful Long Ladder*, "Poems for My Brother Kenneth," "All This Review," and "Counterpoint," develop the racial themes that Dodson examines in the earlier sections. The latter sections, though, show a growing artistic maturity on the author's part, particularly in the lyricism with which he approaches his material.

The twenty-four-year hiatus between *Powerful Long Ladder* and *The Confession Stone* occurred because Dodson was serving as professor of drama at Howard University. During this period—1947 until 1969—Dodson concentrated primarily on writing plays, although he did write two novels, *Boy at the Window*, published in 1951, and *A Bent House*, completed when a Guggenheim Fellowship in 1953 enabled Dodson to spend an extended period in Italy. This novel did not appear until 1977, retitled *Come Home Early, Child.*

Owen Dodson was caught between two compelling movements, a part of neither. The Harlem Renaissance had run its course by the time Dodson began to emerge as a literary figure. Ahead lay the black militancy of the 1960s and early 1970s.

When *Powerful Long Ladder* appeared in 1946, some critics considered it too much concerned with issues of race, although these critics, including John Holmes, who reviewed the book for the *New York Times*, found considerable promise in Dodson's writing. Alfred Kreymborg commented on the notable dramatic qualities in Dodson's poetry, observing that the poet could infuse old topics such as estranged love with "fire, wisdom, and dignity." Richard Eberhart, on the basis of this first volume, called Dodson the best black poet in the United States.

The poems in *Powerful Long Ladder* are largely concerned with the effects of continuing poverty and prejudice upon a race transplanted from its own continent, enslaved, and freed only to endure humiliation and repression from mainstream society. Obviously, in a poem such as "Autumn Chorus: After the Prophet Has Been Killed," the poet uses such dramatic devices as dialogue and a chorus to sustain a plaint that seems eerily prescient: Malcolm X and Martin Luther King, Jr. were alive but were scarcely known to the public at the time that this chilling poem was written.

To those nonblack critics who suggest that Dodson was too much concerned with race, one can only say that a cauldron of racial tension was simmering and was soon to boil over in America. Dodson was daily exposed to the tensions that within twenty years would result in the violence that darkened the 1960s. He could not ignore the strife he saw around him.

On the other hand, Dodson did not consciously fan the fires that were smoldering. He was being objective, but his objectivity was from the black rather than the white point of view. Therefore, his stance seemed to many whites to be more extreme than it was.

The most personal and, in some ways, the most deeply felt poems in *Powerful Long Ladder* are those contained in the section entitled "Poems for My Brother Kenneth," in which Dodson reflects on personal memories and relives portions of his youth. The racial tone in these poems is more subdued than in the other sections of this collection, although it necessarily intrudes even upon these poems.

Other Literary Forms

During Owen Dodson's undergraduate years at Bates College, his poetry appeared in such publications as *Opportunity*, *New Masses*, and the *New York Herald Tribune*. Over the decades, numerous periodicals and anthologies have published his verse. His three volumes of verse are *Powerful Long Ladder*, which includes excerpts from his *Divine Comedy* verse play; *The Confession Stone*, which was revised and enlarged as *The Confession Stone: Song Cycles*; and *The Harlem Book of the Dead*, which features Dodson's poetry and James Van Der Zee's photographs.

Dodson also wrote two novels. *Boy at the Window* is an autobiographical novel about Coin Foreman, a nine-year-old Brooklyn boy. When the novel was published in paperback in 1967, the title was changed to *When Trees Were Green*. In his second novel, *Come Home Early, Child*, Foreman is now an adult. Although his novels received favorable commentary from critics, his poetry and drama earned him greater acclaim.

Bibliography

Als, Hilton. *The Women*. New York: Farrar, Straus & Giroux, 1996. Als, a well-known writer, reflects on his own close relationship with Dodson, who had a major impact on Als' life.

Dodson, Owen. "An Interview with Owen Dodson." Interview by Charles H. Rowell. *Callaloo* 20, no 3. (Summer 1997): 627-40. Contains biographical information and gives an overview of Dodson's work and experiences.

Grant, Nathan L. "Extending the Ladder: A Remembrance of Owen Dodson." *Callaloo* 20, no 3 (Summer 1997): 640-46. A tribute to the poet that also includes interesting information on Dodson's beliefs and writing style.

_____. "The Unpublished Poetry of Owen Dodson." *Callaloo* 20, no. 3 (Summer 1997): 619-28. Takes a look at some of Dodson's unpublished poetry, noting his ability to write in different places and under different circumstances and his consistent return to death as a theme in his work.

Hatch, James V. *Sorrow Is the Only Faithful One: The Life of Owen Dodson*. Urbana: U of Illinois P, 1993. Authorized biography by the preeminent Dodson scholar. Contains a chronology of Dodson's involvement in the theater as writer, director, set designer, and actor.

Hatch, James V., and Omanii Abdullah, eds. *Black Playwrights, 1823-1977: An Annotated Bibliography of Plays*. New York: R. R. Bowker, 1977. Categorizes and provides production information for Dodson's plays. Contains entries for more than thirty of Dodson's plays.

Peterson, Bernard L., Jr. *Contemporary Black American Playwrights and Their Plays: A Biographical Directory and Dramatic Index.* New York: Greenwood Press, 1988. Contains production information for Dodson's plays written, produced, or published after 1950.

_____. "The Legendary Owen Dodson of Howard University: His Contributions to the American Theatre." *The Crisis* 86 (1979): 373-78. Contains biographical and critical commentary. Speculates that Dodson's greatest literary legacy will be his drama rather than his poems.

_____. "Owen Dodson." *Early Black American Playwrights and Dramatic Writers: A Biographical Directory and Catalog of Plays, Films, and Broadcasting Scripts*. Westport, CT: Greenwood Press, 1990. Contains a brief biographical entry. Categorizes and provides production information for Dodson's plays written, produced, or published before 1950.

— *Linda M. Carter; R. Baird Shuman; Robert C. Evans*

Frederick Douglass

Orator, Autobiographer, Journalist, and Editor

Born: Tuckahoe, Talbot County, Maryland; February, 1817?

Died: Washington, D.C.; February 20, 1895

NONFICTION: *Narrative of the Life of Frederick Douglass, an American Slave, Written by Himself,* 1845; *What to a Slave Is the Fourth of July?,* 1852; *The Claims of the Negro Ethnologically Considered,* 1854; *The Anti-Slavery Movement: A Lecture,* 1855; *My Bondage and My Freedom,* 1855; *Two Speeches by Frederick Douglass,* 1857; *The Constitution of the United States: Is It Pro-Slavery or Anti-Slavery? A Speech,* 1860; *Life and Times of Frederick Douglass, Written by Himself,* 1881, revised 1892; *The Lessons of the Hour,* 1894; *Frederick Douglass: Selected Speeches and Writings,* 1999 (Philip S. Foner, editor); *Narrative of the Life of Frederick Douglass,* 2010 (Angela Y. Davis, editor); *Narrative of the Life of Frederick Douglass,* 2011 (David W. Blight, editor); *Narrative of the Life of Frederick Douglass,* 2016 (John R. McKivigan, et al., editors); *Narrative of the Life of Frederick Douglass,* 2017 (William L. Andrews, editor); *Narrative of the Life of Frederick Douglass,* 2017 (David W. Blight, editor).

LONG FICTION: *The Heroic Slave,* 1853; *The Heroic Slave: A Cultural and Critical Edition,* 2015 (Robert S. Levine, et al., editors).

EDITED TEXTS: *North Star,* 1847-1851; *Frederick Douglass' Paper,* 1851-1860; *Douglass' Monthly,* 1859-1863; *New National Era,* 1870-1874.

MISCELLANEOUS: *The Frederick Douglass Papers,* 1979-1992 (5 volumes); *The Oxford Frederick Douglass Reader,* 1996 (William L. Andrews, editor); *The Frederick Douglass Papers.*

Series Three, Correspondence, 2009 (John R. McKivigan, editor); *The Essential Douglass: Selected Writings & Speeches,* 2016 (Nicholas Buccola, editor); *The Portable Frederick Douglass,* 2016 (John Stauffer and Henry Louis Gates, Jr., editors).

Achievements

Cedar Hill, Frederick Douglass's home in Washington, D.C., and a national historic site, has been open to the public since 1972. As visitors tour the fifteen-acre estate, they honor the memory of the abolitionist and statesman who, as orator and writer, was the nineteenth century's most influential African American, a progenitor of African American prose, and a founding father of African American autobiography.

Biography

Frederick Douglass, the son of a slave mother and an unknown white man, was born a slave in Talbot County, Maryland. Douglass spent the first twenty years of his life in bondage. In 1838, while working as a caulker in Baltimore, he became engaged to Anna Murray, a free African American. That same year, Douglass escaped to New York. Murray then traveled to New York; the couple married and moved to New Bedford, Massachusetts, where Douglass worked as a laborer. The Douglasses had five children.

Photo courtesy of the National Archives and Records Administration

Douglass's work as an abolitionist began soon after his arrival in New Bedford. He was a full-time lecturer for the Massachusetts Anti-Slavery Society for four years. After the publication of his first autobiography, *Narrative of the Life of Frederick Douglass, an American Slave, Written by Himself* (1845), Douglass feared that slave catchers would seize him and take him back to Maryland; thus he lectured in England and Ireland for two years. After Douglass's British friends purchased his freedom in 1846, he returned to the United States in 1847.

Douglass and his family moved to Rochester, New York, where he founded and edited *The North Star*, a weekly newspaper that was renamed *Frederick Douglass' Paper* and was published until 1860. In 1859, he created *Douglass' Monthly*, which was produced until 1863. Douglass's printing shop in Rochester was a stop on the Underground Railroad, and he helped more than four hundred fugitive slaves escape to Canada.

Fire destroyed Douglass's home on June 2, 1852, and the family eventually moved to Washington, D.C., where Douglass received four presidential appointments from Ulysses Grant, Rutherford Hayes, James Garfield, and Benjamin Garfield, respectively: Assistant Secretary of the Commission on the Annexation of Santo Domingo in 1871, District of Columbia Marshall in 1877, Recorder of Deeds of the District of Columbia, and Consul General to Haiti in 1889.

After Anna died in 1882, Douglass married Helen Pitts, a white woman and a former clerk at the Office of Deeds and Records. They traveled to Europe and Africa in 1884. On February 20, 1895, Douglass died at his Washington home after suffering a heart attack. Church services were held in Washington as well as in Rochester, and prior to the second funeral service, Douglass's body lay in state in Rochester's City Hall.

Analysis: Nonfiction

After the publication of *Narrative of the Life of Frederick Douglass, an American Slave*, Douglass wrote two additional autobiographies: *My Bondage and My Freedom* and *Life and Times of Frederick Douglass, Written by Himself*. Douglass's subsequent autobiographies are expanded versions of *Narrative of the Life of Frederick Douglass* as he elaborates upon his mental and physical journey from slavery to freedom. Douglass's trilogy reveals his evolving persona: slave, fugitive slave, abolitionist, free man, and statesman. Collectively, the three works form an autobiographical *Bildungsroman* that is more than Douglass's coming-of-age narrative because the autobiographies offer eloquent accounts of an individual who chooses to live his life as a free man instead of living his life as a slave.

Narrative of the Life of Frederick Douglass

Slave narratives, which are defined as first-person, written or oral accounts of African American bondage, are the earliest form of African American prose and more specifically, African American autobiography. According to Frances Smith Foster, author of *Witnessing Slavery: The Development of Antebellum Slave Narratives* (1979), the total number of slave narratives ranging from single-page interviews to books is at least six thousand. Of these thousands of slave testimonies, *Narrative of the Life of Frederick Douglass* is the preeminent slave narrative. Regarded as a classic in African American autobiography, it was one of the most influential books of the nineteenth century. Its initial edition of five thousand copies was sold in four months, and more than thirty thousand copies were purchased during the first five years that the book was in print. Two centuries later, *Narrative of the Life of Frederick Douglass* remains the most well known and widely read slave narrative.

The book's subtitle, *An American Slave,* is an indictment against the United States; Douglass audaciously accuses the nation of his birth of hypocrisy since the United States, "the land of the free," allows slavery to exist within its borders. The subtitle reflects Douglass's tendency to criticize boldly, vehemently, and harshly the nation's tolerance of slavery. Douglass's speech *What to a Slave Is the Fourth of July?* is another well-known example of his verbal attack on American hypocrisy. *Written by Himself,* also included in the title, is of interest for two reasons. Douglass was motivated to write his autobiography because a number of audience members who heard him speak at antislavery events could not fathom that such an accomplished orator was a slave. By including *Written by Himself* in his title, Douglass attempted to silence his second set of detractors: those who doubted that a fugitive slave could write such an eloquent autobiography.

Chapters 1 through 9 of the book reveal slavery's horrors. At birth, Douglass becomes a slave because the law dictated that if the mother were a slave, her child would be a slave regardless of the father's status. As a child of slavery, Douglass is denied knowledge of his birthday and is separated from his mother. Douglass's mother, Harriet Bailey, walks twelve miles from the neighboring plantation to spend too brief a time with her young son before she has to walk twelve miles home before sunrise. Although these efforts on Bailey's behalf are testament of a mother's love, Douglass writes that upon learning of his mother's death when he is seven or eight years old, he is unable to grieve because he saw her only four or five times.

Douglass describes the inhumane treatment of slaves such as their being fed like animals, clothed inadequately, and ranked together with animals at valuations. Douglass, acknowledging that his treatment by masters and overseers was not as draconian as the abuse suffered by his fellow slaves, documents the tribulations of other slaves. Among these are the beating of his Aunt Hester, which Douglass witnesses as a child and considers his initiation into slavery; the fatal shooting of Demby because, after he receives yet another whipping from his master, he runs into a creek and refuses to come out; and a slave mistress's beating her fifteen- or sixteen-year-old slave girl to death because she sleeps while the mistress's baby cries. Douglass writes that people who committed such crimes were not punished because little value was placed on African American life.

The book's most memorable events are found in chapters 6, 7, and 10. In chapter 6, Douglass, no more than eight years old, arrives in Baltimore, where he resides with Hugh and Sophia Auld and is ordered to take care of their two-year-old son. When Auld discovers that his wife is teaching Douglass to read, he demands that she cease instructing him because literacy would make Douglass unfit to be a slave. Hugh Auld's termination of Douglass's reading lessons leads to Douglass's realization that literacy is a slave's pathway to freedom. Indeed, in chapter 7, Douglass reveals how he continues to learn to read with the help of neighborhood white boys. Although Douglass is a slave, he is better fed than many of the poor white children whom he encounters. He gives them bread in exchange for their help in learning to read. Also in chapter 7, when Douglass is approximately twelve years old, he realizes that his young white friends, who are indentured servants, will be free when they reach the age of twenty-one, while he will be "a slave for life." Since the nineteenth century, many people have considered Douglass a hero, yet it is interesting to note that in *Narrative of the Life of Frederick Douglass*, he does not refrain from revealing his weak moments. When Douglass becomes aware that slave society expects him to live his entire life in bondage, he becomes so despondent that he wishes he were dead. During this period, Douglass obtains a copy of *The Columbia Orator* and finds its speeches on liberty inspirational. The hope of freedom prevents him from killing himself.

In chapter 10, Douglass, at the age of seventeen, is hired out to Edward Covey, a Talbot County farmer known for his ability to abuse slaves physically as well as break their spirit. In one of the best-known scenes in slave narratives, Douglass, who has described how a boy becomes a slave in the first nine chapters, now reveals how a slave becomes a man. Although Covey drives Douglass to the point that his suicidal thoughts return, he overcomes such thoughts. Douglass, who has received frequent beatings from Covey, fights Covey in August, 1834, and after what Douglass states is nearly a two-hour fight, he is never beaten again. In the same manner that Hugh Auld, years earlier,

makes Douglass cognizant that literacy is the pathway to freedom, Covey's cruel treatment of Douglass reawakens his desire for freedom. Douglass describes the battle with Covey as his turning point; he is now determined that while society still considers him a slave, he regards himself as a free man.

Chapter 11, the final chapter, ends with Douglass's successful escape to the North and his initial involvement with the antislavery movement. Although its dominant theme is the horrors of slavery, the book also reveals human resiliency and the determination to be free. These themes are repeated in Douglass's subsequent autobiographies. Although *Narrative of the Life of Frederick Douglass* is his shortest and consequently least detailed autobiography, it continues to overshadow his second and third autobiographies as well as all the slave narratives produced by his contemporaries.

My Bondage and My Freedom

Douglass's second autobiography was published eight years after his British friends purchased his freedom. Of the twenty-five chapters in *My Bondage and My Freedom*, the first twenty-two include events from *Narrative of the Life of Frederick Douglass*, such as his escape and early days as an abolitionist. *My Bondage and My Freedom* also includes chapters on Douglass's introduction to other abolitionists and his twenty-one-month stay in Great Britain, and the final chapter, "Various Incidents," includes his founding of *The North Star* and his family's move to Rochester. The appendix includes excerpts from Douglass's orations in England and the United States; his speech *What to a Slave Is the Fourth of July?* is also included. The appendix also contains Douglass's letter to his former master Thomas Auld; Douglass ends the letter by writing that he is a man and not Auld's slave.

Life and Times of Frederick Douglass

Douglass's third autobiography extends coverage of his life to 1891, four years prior to his death. Thus *Life and Times of Frederick Douglass* describes a century in which Douglass is born into slavery during the second decade and attains the status of statesman during the seventh and eighth. Part 1 ends with Douglass fleeing slavery in 1838. He provides more details about his escape in *Life and Times of Frederick Douglass* than in *Narrative of the Life of Frederick Douglass* and *My Bondage and My Freedom*. In part 2, Douglass offers more insight into his career as an abolitionist than he revealed in his previous autobiographies. His activities prior to the Civil War, during the war, and after the war are included; two instances are Douglass's recruitment of African American troops for the Fifty-fourth and Fifty-fifth Colored Regiments for the Civil War and his White House meeting with President Abraham Lincoln on behalf of the African American troops. Highlighted in parts 2 and 3 are Douglass's presidential appointments and his trip to Europe. As in *My Bondage and My Freedom*, *Life and Times of Frederick Douglass* provides glimpses into African American middle-class life as the Douglasses reside in New Bedford, Rochester, and Washington, D.C. Critics have stated that Douglass wrote *Life and Times of Frederick Douglass*, published decades after slavery's end, in order to remind people of slavery's injustices.

Other Literary Forms

As founder and editor of *The North Star*, Douglass wrote most of the newspaper's articles and editorials. Among his writings in *The North Star/ Frederick Douglass' Paper* are "Our Mind Is Made Up" (1847), a request for African American authors, editors, and orators to spearhead the quest for liberty and equality; "Colorphobia—A

Law of Nature?" (1848), an attack on America's preoccupation with skin color; "The Rights of Women" (1848), a report on the first United States women's rights convention; and "Here We Are, and Here We Stay" (1849), an assertion against the deportment of African Americans. Douglass was arguably the most eloquent nineteenth century orator, and during his lifetime, his speeches were printed in his publications as well as in other sources such as the *National Anti-Slavery Standard* and *Pennsylvania Freeman*. Douglass's best-known speech is *What to a Slave Is the Fourth of July?* delivered in 1852. The next year, Douglass created *The Heroic Slave*, a historical novella based on a slave ship mutiny that is recognized as one of the first works of long fiction in African American literature.

Bibliography

Andrews, William L., ed. *Critical Essays on Frederick Douglass*. Boston: G. K. Hall, 1991. Includes reviews of Douglass's three autobiographies, as well as articles focusing on the autobiographies, *The Heroic Slave*, and Douglass's other works, by such prominent literary critics as Andrews, Houston Baker, and Henry Louis Gates, Jr.

Barnes, L. Diane, ed. *Frederick Douglass: A Life in Documents*. Charlottesville: University of Virginia Press, 2013. Includes biographical and historical writings by Douglass and many others.

Barnes, L. Diane. *Frederick Douglass: Reformer and Statesman*. New York: Routledge, 2013. A short, accessible biography of Douglass that places his life in some of its central historical contexts.

Baxter, Terry. *Frederick Douglass's Curious Audiences: Ethos in the Age of the Consumable Subject*. New York: Routledge, 2004. Discusses how Douglass, as a speaker, managed to make himself and his speeches persuasive to both white and black people of his time.

Bernier, Celeste-Marie, and Andrew Taylor. *If I Survive: Frederick Douglass and Family in the Walter O.*

Evans Collection: A 200 Year Anniversary. Edinburgh: Edinburgh UP, 2018. Focuses on the private lives of Douglass and members of his family.

Bernier, Celeste-Marie and Bill E. Lawson, ed. *Pictures and Power: Imaging and Imagining Frederick Douglass.* Liverpool: Liverpool UP, 2017. Offers deliberately diverse perspectives on Douglass and his legacy.

Blight, David W. *Frederick Douglass: Prophet of Freedom.* New York: Simon Schuster, 2018. At nearly a thousand pages in length, this is a major scholarly biography of Douglass and has won numerous important prizes.

Buccola, Nicholas. *The Political Thought of Frederick Douglass: In Pursuit of American Liberty.* New York: New York University Press, 2012. Discusses Douglass in terms of politics, liberalism, liberal democracy, mutual responsibility, and education.

Chander, Harish. "Frederick Douglass." In *African American Autobiographers: A Sourcebook,* edited by Emmanuel S. Nelson. Westport, Conn.: Greenwood Press, 2002. Offers a biography of Douglass and an overview of Douglass's three autobiographies and their themes as well as a summary of criticism of the autobiographies.

Colaiaco, James A. *Frederick Douglass and the Fourth of July.* New York: Palgrave Macmillan, 2006. Recreates the contexts of an important speech Douglass delivered on July 5, 1852.

Coulson, Joseph, et al, ed. *Reader's Guide to Narrative of the Life of Frederick Douglass, an American Slave.* Chicago: Great Books Foundation, 2004. Presents detailed questions to help readers engage thoughtfully with Douglass's text.

Dilbeck, D. H. *Frederick Douglass: America's Prophet.* Chapel Hill: The University of North Carolina Press, 2018. A brief biography that explores Douglass's life in relation to his religious thought.

Ernest, John, ed. *Douglass in His Own Time: A Biographical Chronicle of His Life, Drawn from Recollections, Interviews, and Memoirs by Family, Friends, and Associates.* Iowa City: University of Iowa Press, 2014. Tells the story of Douglass's life by relying on the public and private writings of people who actually knew him.

Finkenbine, Roy E. "Frederick Douglass." In *African American Lives,* edited by Henry Louis Gates, Jr., and Evelyn Brooks Higginbotham. New York: Oxford University Press, 2004. Presents a concise biography of Douglass and stresses that Douglass agitated America's conscience.

Fought, Leigh. *Women in the World of Frederick Douglass.* Oxford: Oxford UP, 2017. Explores the impact of all sorts of women—black and white, rich and poor—and Douglass's development and achievements.

Gass, T. Anthony. "Frederick Douglass." In *Notable Black American Men,* edited by Jessie Carney Smith. Detroit: Gale, 1999. 326-331. Presents a concise biography of Douglass and acknowledges that his greatest legacy is his autobiographical trilogy.

Gibson, Danjuma G. *Frederick Douglass, a Psychobiography: Rethinking Subjectivity in the Western Experiment of Democracy.* New York: Palgrave Macmillan, 2018. Looks at the extreme conditions of Douglass's life and times, asks how he managed to cope with them so effectively, and explores this theme in several of his most important works.

Higbee, Mark, and James Brewer Stewart. *Frederick Douglass, Slavery, and the Constitution, 1845.* New York: W. W. Norton & Company, 2019. Offers a role-playing approach to Douglass's life and times.

Lee, Maurice S., ed. *The Cambridge Companion to Frederick Douglass.* Cambridge: Cambridge UP, 2009. An important collection of essays that deals with such issues as abolition, identity, rhetoric, faith, violence, manhood, war, human law, higher law, sentimentality, Romanticism, foreign nations, racial politics, and Douglass's legacies.

Levine, Robert S. *The Lives of Frederick Douglass.* Cambridge, MA: Harvard UP, 2016. A deliberately revisionist biographies the examines the various ways in which Douglass presented himself.

Levine, Robert S., and Samuel Otter, ed. *Frederick Douglass & Herman Melville: Essays in Relation.*

Chapel Hill: University of North Carolina Press, 2008. An essay collection that explores such topics as revolution, labor, justice, dance, music, authorship, insurrection, and civil rights.

McFeely, William S. *Frederick Douglass.* New York: W. W. Norton, 1991. McFeely's work adds to the research on Douglass's life spearheaded by Benjamin Quarles (see below). Benefits from scholarship produced since Quarles's 1968 study. Includes rare pictures and an extensive bibliography.

Myers, Peter C. *Frederick Douglass: Race and the Rebirth of American Liberalism.* Lawrence: University Press of Kansas, 2008. Explores Douglass's interest in natural rights philosophy.

Preston, Dickson J. *Young Frederick Douglass: The Maryland Years.* Baltimore: Johns Hopkins University Press, 1980. Preston's work is acknowledged as the first Douglass biography to focus on his childhood and teenage years up to his escape. Provides information about Douglass's return visits to Maryland in 1864, 1877, 1878, 1881, and 1893.

Preston, Dickson J. *Young Frederick Douglass: The Maryland Years.* Baltimore: Johns Hopkins UP, 2018. Draws on original documents to explore Douglass's life from 1818-1838.

Quarles, Benjamin. *Frederick Douglass.* Englewood Cliffs, N.J.: Prentice-Hall, 1968. The seminal biography of Douglass by the leading Douglass scholar of the twentieth century and one of the first African American historians. Remains essential reading even though it was originally published in 1948 and reprinted twenty years later. Includes an extensive bibliography.

Roberts, Neil, ed. *A Political Companion to Frederick Douglass.* Lexington: UP of Kentucky, 2018. A collection of essays on such topics as modernity, the master-slave dialectic, liberation, politics, Reconstruction, natural law, rational hopefulness, intersectionality, law, God's law, and democracy.

Sweeney, Fionnghuala. *Frederick Douglass and the Atlantic World.* Liverpool: Liverpool University Press, 2007. Focuses on Douglass's travels outside the U.S., including trips to Egypt, Haiti, and especially Ireland.

Thompson, Julius E., et al, ed. *The Frederick Douglass Encyclopedia.* Greenwood Press, 2010. This reference work offers a chronology and bibliography and articles on numerous topics.

Yothers, Brian. *Reading Abolition: The Critical Reception of Harriet Beecher Stowe and Frederick Douglass.* Camden House, 2016. An important overview of critics' reactions to two of the most influential nineteenth-century opponents of slavery.

— *Linda M. Carter; Robert C. Evans*

Rita Dove

Poet

Born: Akron, Ohio; August 28, 1952

LONG FICTION: *Through the Ivory Gate*, 1992

SHORT FICTION: *Fifth Sunday*, 1985

DRAMA: *The Darker Face of the Earth,* pb. 1994, revised pb. 2000

POETRY: *The Yellow House on the Corner,* 1980; *Museum,* 1983; *Thomas and Beulah,* 1986; *Grace Notes,* 1989; *Selected Poems,* 1993; *Mother Love,* 1995; *On the Bus with Rosa Parks,* 1999; *American Smooth,* 2004; *Sonata Mulattica: A Life in Five Movements and a Short Play: Poems,* 2009; *Collected Poems, 1974-2004,* 2016

NONFICTION: *The Poet's World,* 1995

EDITED TEXTS: *The Best American Poetry, 2000,* 2000; *Conversations with Rita Dove,* 2003 (Earl G. Ingersoll, editor)

Achievements

Rita Dove's literary honors include grants and fellowships from the National Endowment for the Arts, the Academy of American Poets, the Guggenheim Foundation, and the General Electric Foundation. She spent 1988-1989 as a Senior Mellon Fellow at the National Humanities Center in North Carolina. In 1987 her collection *Thomas and Beulah* made her the first black woman since Gwendolyn Brooks to win the Pulitzer Prize. She has also been awarded the National Medal in the Humanities, the Heinz Award in the Arts and Humanities, and the Sara Lee Frontrunner Award. Dove served as poet laureate of the United States from 1993 to 1995. She was awarded the 1998 Levinson Prize from *Poetry* magazine and the 1999 John Frederick Nims Translation Award (together with Fred Viebahn).

In 2006, she received the Common Wealth Award of Distinguished Service in Literature; in 2007, a Chubb Fellowship at Yale University; in 2008, the Library of Virginia Lifetime Achievement Award; and in 2009 both the Fulbright Lifetime Achievement Medal and the Premio Capri. She was presented with the 2011 National Medal of Arts and received the Carole Weinstein Prize in poetry in 2014. In 2015, she won a Chinese "Poetry and People Prize" and in 2016 was a finalist for the National Book Award and won the National Association for the Advacement of Colored People (NAACP) Image Award in poetry. Awards from *Callaloo* magazine (2017) and the *Kenyon Review* (2018) followed, and in 2019 she received the Wallace Stevens Award from the Academy of American Poets and the W.E.B. Du Bois Medal from Harvard University. Other distinctions are too numerous to mention.

Biography

Born in 1952 in Akron, Ohio, Rita Dove is the daughter of Ray and Elvira (Hord) Dove. She received a B.A. in 1973 from Miami University (Ohio) and then, on a Fulbright Fellowship, attended the University of Tubingen, Germany, to study modern European literature. She returned to the United States to earn an M.F.A. at the highly regarded University of Iowa Writers' Workshop in 1977. She then held a number of

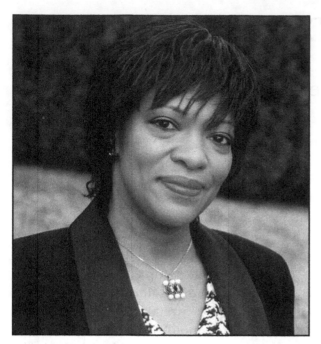

Photo courtesy of Fred Viebahn

teaching posts and traveled widely in Europe and the Middle East, later becoming a professor of English at the University of Virginia. During the summer of 1998, the Boston Symphony Orchestra performed her song cycle of a woman's life, *Seven for Luck*, with music by John Williams. Along with all of her other activities, she writes a weekly column, "Poet's Choice," for the *Washington Post*. Dove married Fred Viebahn, a writer, and with him had a daughter, Aviva Chantal Tamu Dove-Viebahn.

Analysis: Poetry

In a period when much American poetry is condemned as being merely an exercise in solipsistic navel gazing, and when African American poetry more specifically seems to have lapsed into hibernation after the vigorous activity of the Black Arts movement, Rita Dove steps forth with a body of work that answers such criticism resoundingly. Hers is a poetry characterized by discipline and technical proficiency, surprising breadth of reference, a willingness to approach emotionally charged subjects with aesthetic objectivity, and a refusal to define herself only in terms of blackness. She combines a novelist's eye for action and gesture with the lyric poet's exalted sense of language. Rita Dove's distinguishing feature is her ability to turn a cold gaze on the larger world with which she has to interact as a social being—and as an African American woman. That gaze is filtered through an aesthetic sensibility that regards poetry as a redemptive force, a transformational power.

The startling scope of Dove's learning opens for her poetry a correspondingly vast range of topics and concerns, but the most persistent, and the one that most distinguishes her work from that of poets in the 1970s and 1980s, is history. She is constantly laboring to bring into focus the individual struggle in the ebb and flow of the historical tide. A second major concern is cultural collision, the responses of an outsider to a foreign culture, and she pursues this theme in a number of travel poems. Dove also plumbs the circumstances of her life as a way of confronting the puzzle of her own identity—as an African American, as a woman, as a daughter, as a parent—but she manages self-dramatization without self-aggrandizement.

Dove has been lauded for her technical acumen. While much contemporary poetry is best characterized by a certain casualness and laxity, she has created poetry in which no verse is "free." Each poem gives the impression of having been chiseled, honed, and polished. Her poems evolve into highly individual structures, rather than traditional forms, although it is possible to find an occasional sonnet neatly revised and partially hidden. More often she stresses rhythm and sound and uses interior rhyme, slant rhyme, and feminine rhyme to furnish her stanzas with a subtle organizing principle, what she calls the "sound cage" of a poem. Her idiom is predominantly colloquial, but she can adopt the stiffened, formal diction of the eighteenth and nineteenth centuries when evoking personas from those periods. In her mastery of the craft, Dove reveals an attitude toward poetry itself—a deeply felt love and respect—that also influences the approach a reader must take to it. Her work makes demands upon the reader because of that love.

Dove's first two volumes, *The Yellow House on the Corner* and *Museum*, both provide a balance between the personal or individual and the social or cultural. Each is divided into sections that allow the author to address concerns that she wishes for now to remain separate. Yet it has also been noted that the titles of these two books signal a shift in Dove's emphasis from the homely and familiar, "the yellow house," to the more sophisticated and arcane "museum." This generalization should not, however, obscure the fact that the poet's interests in these books overlap considerably. *Museum* is the more consciously organized, with its sections pointedly titled and each dealing with a central topic—history and myth, art and artifact, autobiography and the personal past, life in the modern world.

Dove's next volume, *Thomas and Beulah*, represents her coming of age critically, a step into the position of a leading African American poet. It allows her to extend her continual dissertation on the single person striving in the midst of historical flux; at the same times she can pursue her abiding interest in her own family romance, the question of heritage. Following *Thomas and Beulah*, and still availing itself of a variety of themes, *Grace Notes* is by far the most intensely autobiographical of her works, becoming a study in limitation and poignant regret. How, she seems to ask here, does one grant to daily life that ornament or variation that magically transforms it? *On the Bus with Rosa Parks* examines the panoply of human endeavor, exploring the intersection of individual fates with the grand arc of history.

The Yellow House on the Corner

Poems in *The Yellow House on the Corner* often depict the collision of wish with reality, of heart's desire with the dictates of the world. This collision is made tolerable by the working of the imagination, and the result is, for Dove, "magic," or the existence of an unexplainable occurrence. It is imagination and the art it produces that allow the speaker in "This Life" to see that "the possibilities / are golden dresses in a nutshell." "Possibilities" have the power to transform this life into something distinct and charmed. Even the woman driven mad with grief over the loss of her son (or husband?) in "The Bird Frau" becomes a testament to possibility in her desire to "let everything go wild!" She becomes a bird-woman as a way of reuniting with her lost airman, who died in the war over France. While her condition may be perceived as pathetic, Dove refuses to indulge sentimentality, instead seeing her madness as a form of undying hope.

The refusal to indulge sentimentality is a mark of Dove's critical intelligence. It allows her to interpose an objectifying distance between herself and the subject. She knows the absolute value of perspective, so that while she can exult in the freedom that imagination makes possible, she recognizes that such liberty has its costs and dangers too. Two poems in particular reveal this desire and her wariness: "Geometry" and "Sightseeing." In the former, Dove parallels the study of points, lines, and planes in space with the work of the poet: "I prove a theorem and the house expands: / the windows jerk free to hover near the ceiling, / the ceiling floats away with a sigh." Barriers and boundaries disappear in the imagination's manipulation of them, but that manipulation has its methodology or aesthetic: "I *prove* a theorem . . . ."

In "Sightseeing" the speaker, a traveler in Europe after World War II, comes upon what would seem to be a poem waiting to happen. The inner courtyard of a village church has been left just as it was found by the villagers after an Allied bombing raid. It is filled with the shattered cherubim and seraphim that had previously decorated the inner terrace of the building: "What a consort of broken dolls!" Yet the speaker repudiates any temptation to view the sight as the villagers must—"A terrible sign. . ." Instead she coolly ponders the rubble with the detached air of a detective: "Let's look / at the facts." She "reads" the scene and the observers' attention to it as a cautionary lesson. The "children of angels" become "childish monsters." Since she distinguishes herself from the devout villagers, she can also see herself and her companion in the least flattering light: "two drunks" coming all the way across the town "to look at a bunch of smashed statues."

This ability to debunk and subvert expectations is a matter of artistic survival for Dove and a function of her calm intelligence. As an African American poet she is aware of the tradition of letters she steps into. Two other poems imply that this tradition can be problematic. In "Upon Meeting Don L. Lee, in a Dream" Dove encounters Lee (now known as Haki R. Madhubuti), a leading figure in the Black Arts movement, which attempted to generate a populist, specifically black aesthetic. The figure that emerges from Dove's poem, however, is unable to change except to self-destruct: "I can see caviar / Imbedded like buckshot between his teeth." Her dream-portrait of Lee deflates not only his masculinity but his status as cultural icon as well. In "Nigger Song: An Odyssey" Dove seems to hark back further for a literary forebear and finds one in Gwendolyn Brooks, the first black woman to win the Pulitzer Prize. Although by 1967 Brooks would have come to embrace the black nationalism that Lee embodied, Dove's poem echoes the Brooks of an earlier time, the composer of "We Real Cool." In her evocation of "the nigger night" Dove captures the same vibrant energy that Brooks both celebrates and laments with the realization that the energy of urban African American youth is allowed no purposeful outlet and will turn upon itself. She writes: "Nothing can catch us. / Laughter spills like gin from glasses."

Some of the most compelling poems in Dove's first book are in a group of vignettes and portraits from the era of American slavery. These poems not only reveal her historical awareness but also allow her to engage the issue of race from a distance. Dove wants her poetry to produce anger, perhaps, but not to be produced only by anger. One example of this aesthetic distance from emotion might be "The Abduction," a brief foray in the voice of Solomon Northrup. Northrup is a free black lured to Washington, D.C., by "new friends" with the promise of good work, and then kidnapped and sold into bondage. Dove dwells on the duplicity of these men and Northrup's susceptibility to them. Yet no pronouncements are made. The poem ends with the end of freedom, but that ending has been foreshadowed by the tightly controlled structure of the poem itself, with each stanza shortening as the scope of the victim's world constricts to this one-line conclusion: "I woke and found myself alone, in darkness and in chains." The indignation and disgust that such an episode could call forth are left entirely to the reader.

Museum

Dove's next volume, *Museum*, is itself, as the title suggests, a collection of historical and aesthetic artifacts. The shaping impulse of the book seems to be retrospective, a looking back to people and things that have been somehow suspended in time by legend, by historical circumstance, by an all-too-human emotional wish. Dove intends to delve beneath the publicly known side of these stories—to excavate, in a sense, and uncover something forgotten but vital. The book is filled with both historical and mythical figures, all sharing the single trait of muted voice. Thus, "Nestor's Bathtub" begins: "As usual, legend got it all / wrong." The private torment of a would-be martyr is made public in "Catherine of Alexandria." In "The Hill Has Something to Say" the poet speculates on the buried history of Europe, the cryptic messages that a culture sends across time. In one sense, the hill is a metaphor for this book, a repository of signs and images that speak only to that special archaeologist, the reader.

In the section titled "In the Bulrush" Dove finds worthy subjects in unlikely places and draws them from hiding. "Banneker" is another example of her flair for evoking the antebellum world of slavery, where even the freeman is wrongly regarded because of his race. In the scientist Benjamin Banneker she finds sensitivity, eloquence, and intelligence, all transformed by prejudice into mere eccentricity. Banneker was the first black man to devise an almanac and served on Thomas Jefferson's commission to lay out the city of Washington, D.C., but the same qualities that lifted him to prominence made him suspect in the eyes of white society. Dove redeems this crabbed conception of the man in an alliterative final passage that focuses attention on his vision:

> Lowering his eyes to fields
> sweet with the rot of spring, he could see
> a government's domed city
> rising from the morass and spreading in
> a spiral of lights . . .

A third section of the book is devoted entirely to poems about the poet's father, and they represent her efforts to understand him. It is a very personal grouping, made to seem all the more so by the preceding sections in which there is little or nothing directly personal at all.

In the final section, "Primer for the Nuclear Age," Dove includes what is one of her most impressive performances. Although she has not shown herself to be a poet of rage, she is certainly not inured to the social and political injustice she observes. Her work is a way of channeling and controlling such anger; as she says in "Primer for the Nuclear Age": "if you've / got a heart at all, someday / it will kill you." "Parsley," the final poem of *Museum*, summons up the rank insanity of Rafael Trujillo, dictator of the Dominican Republic, who, on October 2, 1957, ordered twenty thousand black Haitians killed because they could not pronounce the letter *r* in *perejil*, Spanish for parsley. The poem is divided into two sections; the first is a villanelle spoken by the Haitians; the second describes General Trujillo on the day of his decision. The second section echoes many of the lines from the Haitians' speech, drawing murderer and victim together, suggesting a disturbing complicity among all parties in this episode of unfettered power. Even though Dove certainly wants to draw attention to this event, the real subject here is the lyric poet's realm—that point at which language intersects with history and actually determines its course.

Thomas and Beulah

Thomas and Beulah garnered the Pulitzer Prize, but it is more important for the stage it represents in Dove's poetic development. Her first two books reveal a lyric poet generally working within the bounds of her medium. The lyric poem denies time, process, change. It becomes a frozen moment, an emotion reenacted in the reading. In *Thomas and Beulah* she pushes at the limitations of the form by stringing together, "as beads on a necklace," a whole series of these lyric moments. As the poems begin to reflect upon one another, the effect is a dramatic unfolding in which the passing of time is represented, even though the sequence never establishes a conventional plot. To accomplish this end Dove creates a two-sided book: Thomas's side ("Mandolin," twenty-one poems) followed by Beulah's ("Canary in Bloom," twenty-one poems).

The narrative moves from Thomas's riverboat life and the crucial death of his friend Lem to his arrival in Akron and marriage, through the birth of children, jobs, illness, and death. Beulah's part of the book then begins, moving through her parents' stormy relationship, her courtship with Thomas, marriage, pregnancy, work, and death. These two lives transpire against the historical backdrop of the great migration, the Depression, World War II, and the March on Washington; however, these events are practically the only common elements in the two sides of the story. Thomas and Beulah seem to live separate lives. Their communication with each other is implicit in the survival of the marriage itself. Throughout, Dove handles the story through exacting use of imagery and character.

Thomas emerges as a haunted man, dogged by the death of his friend Lem, which occurs in the opening poem, "The Event." Thomas drunkenly challenges Lem to swim from the deck of the riverboat to an island in the Mississippi. Lem drowns in the attempt to reach what is probably a mirage, and Thomas is left with "a stinking circle of rags / the half-shell mandolin." In "Courtship" he begins to woo Beulah, but the poem implies that the basis of their relationship will be the misinterpreted gesture and that Thomas's guilt has left him with a void. He casually takes a yellow silk scarf from around his neck and wraps it around her shoulders; "a gnat flies / in his eye and she thinks / he's crying." Thomas's gift, rather than a spontaneous transfer of warmth, is a sign of his security in his relative affluence. The show of vulnerability

and emotional warmth is accidental. The lyric poet in Dove allows her to compress this range of possibility in the isolated gesture or image. Beulah's life is conveyed as a more interior affair, a process of attaining the wisdom to understand her world rather than to resist it openly. In "The Great Palace of Versailles" Beulah's reading becomes her secret escape from the nastiness of the whites for whom she works in Charlotte's Dress Shoppe. As she lies dying in the final poem, "The Oriental Ballerina," the contemplation of the tiny figurine seems a similar invitation to fantasy, but her sensibilities have always been attuned to seeing the world as it is, as it has to be, and the poem ends in a brief flurry of realistic details and an air of acceptance; there is "no cross, just the paper kiss / of a kleenex above the stink of camphor, / the walls exploding with shabby tutus . . . ."

Grace Notes

Grace Notes marks Dove's return to the purely lyric mode, but an autobiographical impulse dominates the work to an unprecedented degree. More than in any of her previous collections, the poet can be seen as an actor in her own closet drama, whether as a young child learning a rather brutal lesson in the Southern black school of survival ("Crab-Boil") or as a mother groping for a way to reveal feminine mysteries to her own little girl ("After Reading *Mickey in the Night Kitchen* for the Third Time Before Bed"). The willingness to become more self-referential carries with it the danger of obscurity, the inside joke that stays inside. Dove, however, seems to open herself to a kind of scrutiny and challenge that offer no hiding place, and that assay extends to her own poetic practice. In "Dedication," a poem in the manner of Czesław Miłosz, Dove seems to question the veracity of her own technical expertise: "What are music or books if not ways / to trap us in rumors? The freedom of fine cages!"

In the wickedly ironic "Ars Poetica" she places herself on the literary chain of being with what might pass for self-deprecation. Her ambition is to make a small poem, like a ghost town, a minute speck on the "larger map of wills." "Then you can pencil me in as a hawk: / a traveling x-marks-the-spot." Yet this hawk is not a songbird to be taken lightly. The very next poem in the book unleashes the bird of prey in Dove (a pun she surely intends); in the aptly titled "Arrow," she exposes the sexism and racism of an "eminent scholar" in all of its condescending glory. This focus on the autobiographical element is not to imply that the range of subjects in *Grace Notes* is not still wide-ranging and surprising. Echoes of her earlier books sound clearly; so does the wit that makes them always engaging: "Here's a riddle for Our Age: when the sky's the limit, / how can you tell you've gone too far?"

Mother Love

In *Mother Love,* Dove survives her overused source material, the myth of Demeter and Persephone, by transforming it into something deeply personal. She allows herself to be inhabited by the myth, and Dove's Demeter consciousness reveals that every time a daughter walks out the door, the abduction by Hades begins again. Dove's persona adopts Persephone's stance in "Persephone in Hell"; here, Dove recalls, at twenty, enjoying the risks of visiting Paris. She felt her mother's worry but asserts, "I was doing what she didn't need to know," testing her ripeness against the world's (man's) treachery. Dove employs loose sonnet shapes in these poems, giving herself license in order to provide authentic contemporary voices. At once dramatic, narrative, and highly lyrical, these poems more than fulfill the expectations

of those who anointed her at the outset of her career.

On the Bus with Rosa Parks

On the Bus with Rosa Parks is a more miscellaneous collection, but with several cohesive groupings. The "Cameos" sequence provides sharply etched vignettes of working-class life, a recurrent subject in Dove's writings. The closing sequence, from which the entire collection takes its name, explores the interface of public and private lives in contemporary African American history. As ever, Dove is a superb storyteller whose movie-like poems are energized by precise imagery and tonal perfection.

Sonata Mullatica

In her preface to *Sonata Mulattica,* Rita Dove reminds her readers that all the major characters in this work are historical figures, including the principle character, George Augustus Polgreen Bridgetower. Actual historical events also form the background for the book. Even Black Billy Waters can claim a real place in history, and the relationship between Bridgetower and his mentor Ludwig van Beethoven was a real one as attested to by Beethoven's original dedication to Bridgetower of what is now known as the "Kreutzer" Sonata. The narrative that joins these historical bits makes the poetry. Dove, herself a musician, has a natural interest in music, and she was intrigued when she saw a black violinist appear briefly on the screen in *Immortal Beloved* (1994), a film biography of Beethoven. She filed away in her memory the idea of investigating Bridgetower's life. Years later, *Sonata Mulattica* was the result.

Readers familiar with Dove's work will recall that she employed a related strategy in *Thomas and Beulah* (1986), a biography-in-poems of her grandparents. In that volume, however, she was working with the materials of family history. In

Sonata Mullatica, she must invent almost everything but the bare facts. In her invention, she creates a variety of voices and scenes to represent a past world, one in which she speculates on motives that no one recorded. In doing so, she manages to make a coherent and imaginative representation of that world.

A major theme in this volume is the position of Bridgetower himself—the ultimate outsider in a world where even Joseph Haydn was little more than a servant to the powerful Esterházy family. The elder Bridgetower, the musician's father and evidently a man of great social skills, can scarcely have been more than a graceful curiosity to the family he served, as an African (he may have portrayed himself as a prince) in the white world of northern Europe. His biracial child at first may not even have risen to the level of curiosity, though he too was good looking and acquired polished manners. (As Dove portrays him, the elder Bridgetower found gambling and women more compelling than his son.) Dove's picture of young Bridgetower suggests that he remained an outsider throughout his life, even during the times of his greatest reputation. Part of that theme, of course, is related to his presence as a black man in a white world, a fact Dove explores in various ways.

That Bridgetower disappeared almost completely from public awareness in his later life gives rise to another of Dove's themes—an examination of the fleeting nature of fame and of what fame means to the celebrity. After death, even Haydn was subject to grave robbers, who stole his head out of an interest in phrenology (his skull was returned to his coffin only in 1954, 145 years after his death). Meanwhile, the beggar Black Billy Waters was celebrated in a Staffordshire figurine.

To accomplish her explorations, Dove uses the musical form of the sonata, as her title suggests, covering the events of Bridgetower's career in the five movements associated with such compositions. These include an introduction, the exposition of the themes, an elaboration and development of those themes, a recapitulation that resolves them, and a coda. Into this structure, Dove interposes a "Short Play for the Common Man," in which she dramatizes the crisis of Bridgetower's relationship with Beethoven. Two poems in the Prologue set out some of the themes Dove intends to explore. "The Bridgetower" speculates on what might have happened if Bridgetower and Beethoven had not quarreled, if their friendship had prospered and Bridgetower had "sailed his fifteen-minute fame / straight into the record books." The second poem, "Prologue of the Rambling Sort," introduces the other characters in the narrative and promises, playfully, to "leave out the boring parts." (Dove's poetic forms and tones vary widely in this volume and include playfulness.)

The first movement of the collection focuses on Bridgetower's life as a child in the Esterházy court. Haydn suggests that he has musical talent, and his father gladly turns the child over to the composer instead of returning him to his mother as he had intended. A poem in the boy's voice, "Recollection, Preempted," recalls his time there and indicates his passion for the music he learned. The poems trace Bridgetower's growing ability, dramatizing his initial concert in Paris and following him on to England, where Mrs. Papendiek's diary offers two entries about the boy's impressive musical performance. In "The Wardrobe Lesson," the voice of Bridgetower's father discusses the social value of living up to English assumptions about Africans' love of color; he recommends a cape for impressing women.

The second movement, "Bread & Butter, Turbans & Chinoiserie," begins with a poem exploring London's fondness for the exotic ("Hear Ye!") and follows that with "The Lesson: Adagio," the form of which suggests the slow bowing of a violin ("To bow / is to breathe"). "Black Pearl" examines the presence of Africans in London in 1790. Poems that suggest that black faces are cultivated as a sort of social decoration alternate with poems dealing with music. In "Pulling the Organ Stops," for instance, the voices of Bridgetower, Haydn, and Franz Clement (another prodigy) alternately describe the effects of the organ in St. Paul's Cathedral. Next is a pantoum, "Black Billy Waters, at His Pitch," in which the peg-legged black street musician proclaims "All men are beggars, black or white; / Some worship gold, some peddle brass," suggesting a sort of identity between him and Bridgetower. This section records Bridgetower's abandonment by his father and his life as a refugee at court. Dove provides useful notes to many of her poems and an even more useful chronology for tracing the events they depict.

"Sturm und Drang" (storm and stress) makes the sonata's third movement, the one in which Bridgetower meets Beethoven at a time when the famous composer is experiencing increasing deafness. In "Vienna Spring," Beethoven praises Bridgetower, who has renewed his faith in the violin, which he had previously renounced as "a tiny querulous beast" fit only for peg-legged street musicians. In "Augarten, 7 a.m." and "The Performer," Dove records first the various responses (ranging from vacuous to irrelevant to thoughtful) to a concert given by Beethoven and Bridgetower and then the voice of Bridgetower himself. Bridgetower in the latter poem declares that music is "what it is like / to be a flame."

At this point, Dove offers a bit of "Volkstheater," the play called "Georgie Porgie, or A Moor in Vienna." She heads it with a "Cast of Characters (& I mean characters!)" that includes Bridgetower and Beethoven, his copyist, a barmaid, and "a chorus of bad girls." In the first scenes, Dove suggests a rivalry between the copyist and the director of the Augarten concerts against Bridgetower, whom they see as an interloper who has displaced them in Beethoven's attention. The tone is satiric as Bridgetower responds to their stereotypes by doing some fraternity stepping. In a later scene at the Prater, an amusement park, Bridgetower flirts with a barmaid whom Beethoven has admired. When she agrees to meet Bridgetower later that night, Beethoven explodes, calling him an abomination and implying that he has insulted her. At the end, Beethoven strikes him with the score of his current violin concerto, quoting the dedication: "Mulatto Sonata, composed / for the mulatto Bridgetower, / great lunatic and mulatto composer." This is the sonata that he rededicates to violinist Rudolphe Kreutzer, whom Dove quotes as saying that Beethoven did not "understand the violin."

In the fourth movement, Dove explores the aftermath of the falling-out between Bridgetower and Beethoven. "Tail Tucked" gives voice to Bridgetower's philosophical resignation to what has happened. "Esterháza, Prodigal" records his return to the court where Haydn gave him his first lessons. "*Andante con Variazioni*" is Bridgewater's meditation on music and love in London. The fifth section, "Nomadia," chronicles the end of Bridgetower's career. The section's first poem, "Half-Life" sets the tone: "Dull / the days before me, / slack the reins, my horse run off." The section contains another poem in Black Billy Waters' voice, claiming that the "world's jig" demands that one "Fall in step / or be left behind." This section includes a poem on the sad fate of Haydn's head and one that maps Bridgetower's aimless travels through Europe's capitols. In "#8 Victory Cottages, Peckham, 1860," Bridgetower faces his own death: "I loved only / what my fingers could do...."

The last poem in the book, "The End, with MapQuest" records Dove's effort to find

Bridgetower's house in Peckham. After a frustrating search, she is cheered by the gaudy sign of a kebab shop. She confesses her inability to know such an elusive figure. She mulls whether his music was really miraculous or whether people were simply drawn to the spectacle "of all / that darkness swaying close enough to *touch,* / palm tree and Sambo and glistening tiger. . . ." Her final poignant question, "How does a shadow shine?" is answered by the poems of this book.

Collected Poems, 1974-2004

Dove is a master of conjuring situations and worlds that seem utterly convincing, even on those occasions when they also seem hauntingly enigmatic. Her poems almost always seem to contain layers of meaning even if their surface meanings are not particularly clear. Her phrasing, punctuation, and syntax are all impressively lucid, and although her writing has obviously changed in various ways over the course of her long career, it has rarely been anything less than compelling. Her earliest poems hold up very well when compared to her most recent writings, and vice versa, and seeing so many very fine poems preserved between the covers of a fairly long book is impressive indeed. Dove has written well from the very beginning, and the three decades' worth of poetry included in this volume will send many readers out looking for her newer writings to witness her more recent accomplishments.

The specific strengths of this book are unusually numerous. Dove often creates vivid personal narratives, as she does in "In the Old Neighborhood." Effective humor appears in many poems, such as "Planning the Perfect Evening," and sometimes that humor is self-deprecating, as in "Genetic Expedition." References to violence, such as those in "The Bird Frau," help complicate the overall tone of the volume.

The poems often deal with experiences to which most people can easily relate—especially experiences involving families, since relations between family members is one of the most frequent themes of the volume, as in "Taking in Wash." Relations between parents and children are especially prominent concerns, and Dove does a particularly impressive job of getting inside the heads of the many father figures who appear in her poems. She also deals more frequently with common middle-class life than is often the case in contemporary American poetry.

Sometimes the poems have a political edge, as in "Belinda's Petition," and issues of race appear, especially in some of the early poems. But no single issue or tone seems dominant or predictable in this volume; the book as a whole displays a dazzling diversity of concerns, tones, and techniques. Dove shows a real skill for evoking historical contexts and historical personalities, particularly in some of her poems written about eighteenth- and nineteenth-century African Americans. In poems such as these, Dove displays the talents of a novelist or dramatist; she inhabits the minds and souls of people she never personally knew, showing the same abilities for empathy and connection as when she draws on experiences from her own family and personal history. Many of the poems seem rooted in autobiography, but rarely do they seem self-indulgent or merely self-involved. Often Dove creates a vivid sense of presence, not only in poems rooted in recent experience but in those rooted in myths or legends, such as "Nestor's Bathtub." The poems are often informed by readings that are both wide and deep; Dove draws allusions from the classics, from Christian lore, and from historical narratives. She is also familiar with many different nations and cultures, from Chinese to Egyptian, from German to Mexican. She often creates recurring characters, among them a man named

Thomas, and many memorable women—especially mothers and daughters—appear between the covers of this book. "The Bistro Styx," for example, uses contemporary-sounding conversation between a mother and daughter to re-tell the legend of Persephone.

But it is less the themes, personalities, or topics of Dove's poems that make them so memorable than it is the sheer accomplishment of her phrasing. "In the Old Neighborhood," for instance, almost immediately displays her talent for alliteration, but rarely is that technique (or any other sound effect) intrusively overused. In that poem and in many others, italics are employed to create a variety of tones and voices, so that the poems often contain varied dialects and achieve a truly dialogical effect. Dove's poems often open emphatically, frequently by jumping immediately into the midst of things, and almost every single poem concludes with an impressively memorable ending.

Dove knows how to get into a poem, but she especially knows how to get out in ways that will often leave readers astonished by the sheer skill of her conclusions. Her imagery is consistently vivid, as in "Straw Hat," which features the lines "He used to sleep like a glass of water / held up in the hand of a very young girl," or in "A Hill of Beans," where the simple lines "he ate / straight down to the blue / bottom of the pot" create an immediate mental image of the pot in question. The visual details in these poems are often sharp and vivid, but so is practically every other aspect of these texts, especially the sounds of distinctive voices or the specifics of precise settings and particular atmospheres. Dove's line lengths tend to be short; her shifts from line to line are often masterful, as in the shift to the final stanza of "This Face"; and the diction of her poems alternates between the colloquial, the sophisticated, and sometimes even the slangy.

She has a real gift for creating memorable metaphors and striking similes—in the fourth line of "Augustus Observes the Sunset," the sun is likened to "a dragon spreading its tail"—and both the structures and the rhythms of her poems are frequently masterful. One notices, for instance, the isolated final line of "The Abduction," the skillful trochaic meter of "The Sahara Bus Trip," the effectively abrupt lines of "His Shirt," and the emphatic brevity (both of individual lines and of the overall text) of a short poem such as "Pithos."

Dove alternatively creates such effects as curiosity and suspense, as in the opening of "Great Uncle Beefheart"; a strong sense of paradox, as in the conclusion of "Nestor's Bathtub"; a vivid sense of memorable action, as in the middle of "Magic"; and images that are almost literally unforgettable, such as the line "The doctor's teeth are beavery, yellow," from the poem titled "Stitches," or the image of a newly married couple who face "rice drumming / the both of them blind" in the poem "Promises." Mostly her poems are unrhymed, but when she does rhyme she does it well, as in "Used." That poem, like many others in the second half of this book, is a kind of sonnet, and in fact Dove shows a real talent in using and experimenting not only with the sonnet form but with many other kinds of forms and structures. Her poems almost always have clear stanza divisions, but they rarely seem mechanical or contrived in structure. She varies between prose poems, long poems, very short poems, and many linked poems that essentially are poetic sequences. She includes at least one sestina, a form that can often seem artificially contrived but that Dove deftly makes work. And she also includes what might be called a "corona" of linked poems.

Especially interesting are her various experiments with form, as in such poems as "Depression Years," "Homework," and "Painting the

Town," among others. One of the most visually striking poems in the whole book is simply titled "Chronology," formatted like a timeline in a history book; this poem seems to provide a key for understanding many of Dove's other texts, although it comes late in the sequence of works to which it is most relevant.

Other Literary Forms

Rita Dove has published *Fifth Sunday*, a collection of short stories; *Through the Ivory Gate*, a novel; and *The Poet's World*, a collection of essays. *The Darker Face of the Earth*, a verse drama, appeared in 1994.

Bibliography

Dove, Rita. "Coming Home." Interview by Steven Schneider. *The Iowa Review* 19 (Fall 1989): 112-23. This interview is devoted almost entirely to a discussion of *Thomas and Beulah* and the process of its creation.

_____. Interview by Judith Kitchen et al. *Black American Literature Forum* 20 (Fall 1986): 227-40. In this fine interview the bulk of attention is paid to Dove's *Museum*, especially the poem "Parsley," and to *Thomas and Beulah*. Dove is quite forthcoming in revealing certain writerly decisions and her method of working. She also discusses her short stories in *Fifth Sunday*.

_____. "An Interview with Rita Dove." Interview by Malin Pereira. *Contemporary Literature* 40, no. 2 (Summer 1999): 182-213. This wide-ranging interview includes Dove's comments on the writings of Breyten Breytenbach, the Black Arts movement, her own literary influences, and her experience living in the South.

Harrington, Walt. "A Narrow World Made Wide." *The Washington Post Magazine* 7 May 1995: 13-19, 28-29. Harrington provides a close examination of Dove in the process of writing. Her ambitions, work habits, and revision strategies receive a clear, sympathetic, and nonacademic treatment.

Ingersoll, Earl G., ed., *Conversations with Rita Dove*. Jackson: UP of Mississippi, 2003. Contains thirteen different interviews with Dove ranging over 15 years of her career.

McDowell, Robert. "The Assembling Vision of Rita Dove." *Callaloo: A Black South Journal of Arts and Letters* 9 (Winter 1986): 61-70. This article provides an excellent overview of Dove's accomplishments in her first three books and places her in the larger context of American poetry. McDowell argues that Dove's distinction is her role as "an assembler," someone who pulls together the facts of this life and presents them in challenging ways.

Newson, Adele S. Review of *On the Bus with Rosa Parks*, by Rita Dove. *World Literature Today* 74, no. 1 (Winter 2000): 165-66. Newson examines the collection section by section, suggesting that the book forms an overall story bonded by related imagery and linked through digressions. In it, we hear "the voice of a community's history and human response."

Pereira, Malin. *Rita Dove's Cosmopolitanism*. Urbana: U of Illinois P, 2003. A critical analysis of Dove's poetry, literary criticism, drama, and fiction. Pereira states that Dove is most responsible for initiating a new era in African American poetry.

_____. "'When the pear blossoms / cast their pale faces on / the darker face of the earth': Miscegenation, the Primal Scene, and the Incest Motif in Rita Dove's Work." *African American Review* 36, no. 2 (Summer 2002): 195-212. Discusses Dove's experiences in writing the play and analyzes the primal scene.

Rampersad, Arnold. "The Poems of Rita Dove." *Callaloo: A Black South Journal of Arts and Letters* 9 (Winter 1986): 52-60. In one of the best articles yet written on Dove, Rampersad places her in the context of African American poetry on the basis of her first two books of poetry (this article precedes *Thomas and Beulah*). He emphasizes particularly the tight control of emotion that is implicit in her poetic practice.

Righelato, Pat. *Understanding Rita Dove.* Columbia: U of South Carolina P, 2006. A deliberately introductory volume that devotes roughly thirty pages each to various collections, ranging from *The Yellow House on the Corner* to *American Smooth.*

Shea, Renee H. "American Smooth: A Profile of Rita Dove." *Poets & Writers* 32, no. 5 (September/October 2004): 38-44. An interesting biographical sketch that includes history of Dove's career, writing style, and personal life.

Shoptaw, John. Review of *Thomas and Beulah,* by Rita Dove. *Black American Literature Forum* 21 (Fall 1987): 335-41. Although this is only a review of Dove's Pulitzer Prize-winning volume, it is still one of the best sources for isolating specific verbal tactics that Dove employs. It also addresses the problem of narrative and the difficult task Dove set for herself in telling the story as she did.

University of Virginia. "English Department Faculty Page: Rita Dove." http://www.engl.virginia.edu/faculty/dove.html. Contains a complete list of her works, interests, and degrees.

— Nelson Hathcock; Philip K. Jason; Ann D. Garbett; Robert C. Evans

W. E. B. Du Bois

Essayist and Novelist

Born: Great Barrington, Massachusetts; February 23, 1868

Died: Accra, Ghana; August 27, 1963

LONG FICTION: *The Quest of the Silver Fleece,* 1911; *Dark Princess,* 1928; *The Ordeal of Mansart,* 1957; *Mansart Builds a School,* 1959; *Worlds of Color,* 1961 (previous 3 novels comprise the trilogy *The Black Flame*).

NONFICTION: *The Suppression of the African Slave-Trade to the United States of America, 1638-1870,* 1896; *The Conservation of Races,* 1897; *The Philadelphia Negro,* 1899; *The Souls of Black Folk: Essays and Sketches,* 1903; *John Brown,* 1909; *Darkwater: Voices from Within the Veil,* 1920; *The Gift of Black Folk: The Negroes in the Making of America,* 1924; *Black Reconstruction: An Essay Toward a History of the Part Which Black Folk Played in the Attempt to Reconstruct Democracy in America, 1860-1880,* 1935; *Black Folk Then and Now: An Essay in the History and Sociology of the Negro Race,* 1939; *Dusk of Dawn: An Essay Toward an Autobiography of a Race Concept,* 1940; *Color and Democracy: Colonies and Peace,* 1945; *The World and Africa: An Inquiry into the Part Which Africa Has Played in World History,* 1947; *In Battle for Peace: The Story of My Eighty-Third Birthday,* 1952 (with Shirley Graham); *The Autobiography of W. E. B. Du Bois: A Soliloquy on Viewing My Life from the Last Decade of Its First Century,* 1968 (first pb. in Russian as *Vospominaniia,* 1962); *W. E. B. Du Bois Speaks: Speeches and Addresses, 1920-1963,* 1970 (Philip S. Foner, editor); *The Education of Black People: Ten Critiques, 1906-1960,* 1973 (Herbert Aptheker, editor); *Du Bois on Religion,* 2000 (Phil Zuckerman, editor); *Du Bois on Education,* 2002 (Eugene F. Provenzo, Jr., editor).

Achievements

Among the most outstanding black intellectuals of his time, W. E. B. Du Bois was editor of *The Crisis,* the official organ of the National Association for the Advancement of Colored People (NAACP). He wrote several influential books, including his celebrated *The Souls of Black Folk,* and helped initiate the Harlem Renaissance of the 1920s and early 1930s. Throughout the Depression of the 1930s, Du Bois's skepticism about capitalism grew, as did his sympathy for communism. During the excesses of Joseph McCarthy's charges against alleged communists, Du Bois came under considerable pressure and, in 1951, was indicted on charges of participating in subversive activities. In 1961, Du Bois defiantly applied for Communist Party membership. President Kwame Nkruma of Ghana invited him to relocate in his country, whose Academy of Learning offered support for his pet project, his *Encyclopedia Africana.* Du Bois and his wife moved to Ghana in 1961.

Biography

Racism was not overt in Great Barrington, Massachusetts, the Berkshire mountain town where William Edward Burghardt Du Bois was born and raised. He was close to his mother, Mary Burghardt Du Bois. His father, Alfred Du Bois, left Mary shortly after their son's birth.

Educated in integrated schools, Du Bois, a child prodigy, was not immune from an occasional racial slur, but was generally insulated from the sort of racism that pervaded much of the United States (particularly the post-Civil War South). In 1885, when he enrolled as a sophomore at Fisk University, an institution for blacks in Nashville, Tennessee, Du Bois first encountered racial segregation. At Fisk, however, he became aware of the rich fabric of black folk culture. He taught in black schools when the university was not in session and developed a considerable appreciation for the black communities where he taught.

After graduating from Fisk in 1888, Du Bois entered Harvard University, where he remained until 1892. In that year, a grant from the Slater Fund gave him the means to study at the University of Berlin for two years and to complete his doctoral dissertation, published in 1896 as *The Suppression of the African Slave-Trade to the United States of America*. In 1895, he received a Ph.D. in history from Harvard, having benefited from close contact with some of the leading intellectuals of his day: William James, George Santayana, Max Weber, and Albert Bushnell Hart.

With his Ph.D. in hand, Du Bois began teaching at Wilberforce University. In 1896, he accepted a fifteen-month appointment to do field work in Philadelphia's largely black seventh ward. Upon completing that appointment, he joined the faculty at Atlanta University, where he served from 1897 to 1910 and again as chair of the department of sociology from 1934 until 1944.

In *The Souls of Black Folk*, one of his earliest and most famous books, Du Bois called upon educated blacks to actively work for the betterment of their race. He crossed swords with

Photo courtesy of National Portrait Gallery

Booker T. Washington, who accepted segregation and urged blacks to learn trades such as bricklaying and carpentry so that they could survive economically in a predominantly white society. Du Bois denounced Washington's view of blacks as second-class citizens.

From 1897 until 1910, Du Bois was editor of the annual proceedings of the Atlanta University Conferences, a job that eventually led to his becoming editor of *The Crisis*. Under Du Bois' leadership, *The Crisis* soon became the preeminent black publication in the United States.

In 1905, Du Bois spearheaded the Niagra movement, a militant forerunner of the NAACP. He grew increasingly skeptical of capitalism, and Du Bois joined the Socialist Party in 1910. His political views continued to shift to the left as blacks suffered through the Great Depression of the 1930's. Although World War II brought about greater employment and economic opportunities for blacks, the cancer of virulent racism began to affect many northern communities to which black workers had migrated during the war.

At the end of World War II, black demographics had changed considerably, but segregation and the suppression of blacks were facts of life. When Senator Joseph McCarthy inflamed the nation with his self-serving anti-Communist crusades, Du Bois was pushed more in the direction of Communism and grew increasingly restive about the status of blacks in the United States as well as the suppression of blacks in European-dominated African nations.

DuBois had long harbored the dream of publishing the *Encyclopedia Africana* as a comprehensive chronicle of the black race. As his ideas gained acceptance among several influential African leaders, Du Bois became a celebrated figure in such nations as Ghana and Nigeria. Now under indictment for his activities with the left-leaning Peace Information Center, Du Bois, whose passport was withdrawn by the U.S. Department of State, entertained the notion of resettling in Africa.

In the late 1950s, Ghanaian president Kwame Nkruma offered Du Bois a house in the best section of Accra and government research assistance for his projected *Encyclopedia Africana*. Du Bois and his second wife, Shirley Graham Du Bois, moved to Ghana and took Ghanaian citizenship. Du Bois died in Accra on August 27, 1963, soon after the celebration of his ninety-fifth birthday, on which the University of Ghana awarded him an honorary doctorate.

Analysis: Nonfiction

Much of Du Bois' nonfiction attempts to correct misconceptions about black people and to emphasize their contributions to American society. His first book showed how the African slave trade provided cheap labor that strengthened capitalism in the South at the expense of slaves' well-being. In *The Souls of Black Folk*, he called on gifted, educated black people—"the talented tenth"—to devote their efforts to spreading education among blacks who were not well-educated. His nonfiction essentially sought to correct misconceptions white scholars and politicians had perpetuated about blacks and to rouse educated blacks to concerted action in the interests of their race.

The Philadelphia Negro

Du Bois' second book is an impressive sociological study of blacks in Philadelphia resulting from fifteen months of field work the author did in Philadelphia's seventh ward in 1896 and 1897. Although this book has received less recognition than *The Souls of Black Folk* and *The Autobiography of W. E. B. Du Bois*, it deserves consideration.

This study was proposed by Susan B. Wharton, a member of the Executive Committee of the Philadelphia Settlement, who approached the provost of the University of Pennsylvania suggesting a scholarly investigation of the status of Philadelphia's black population. Du Bois, already well-reputed as a black scholar, was an obvious choice to undertake this project. He agreed to leave his chairmanship of the classics department at Wilberforce University to undertake this investigation under the auspices of the University of Pennsylvania.

In August, 1896, Du Bois and his bride, Nina Gomer, moved into a small apartment in one of

Philadelphia's worst neighborhoods and remained there for a year conducting door-to-door interviews with area residents (Du Bois estimated that he met with over five thousand people). He distributed and collected hundreds of questionnaires while simultaneously undertaking an in-depth study of the social history of Philadelphia so that his findings would reflect the broader environment in which his subjects lived and worked.

Du Bois ran statistical analyses of situations affecting black people. He studied the proportion of black to white inmates in Philadelphia's Eastern Penitentiary and found that 62 percent of the inmates were black, a shocking disparity given the city's proportion of blacks to whites. The reasons for this disparity, he concluded, were a lack of education and of vocational opportunities for blacks in Philadelphia. By extension, it could be assumed that similar disparities existed elsewhere in the North.

This book was the first thorough, scholarly study of the problems blacks faced at the turn of the century. It made considerable social and political impact and became a model for many future sociological studies based on fieldwork.

The Souls of Black Folk

The Souls of Black Folk, a collection of revised and rearranged articles, remains Du Bois' best-known and most-frequently read book. It issues a passionate call to black and white society for social action. This collection helped Du Bois become known as a civil rights leader, one who went on to help organize the Niagara Conference in 1905 and subsequent such conferences until 1909, when the group's fifth and last conference in Sea Isle, New Jersey, resulted in the formation of the NAACP.

Du Bois deplored the lack of recognition black Americans received from the dominant white society. He blamed this invisibility on the refusal of whites to recognize blacks as worthy individuals rather than on black indifference. Blacks encountered barriers erected by whites at all social and economic levels, which limited their ability to advance; hence the inclusion of the word "advancement" in the title of the NAACP.

Du Bois' editing and rearranging of his essays resulted in his producing a coherent book, rather than just a collection of essays. His skillful, artistic construction produces a compelling analytical statement reflecting Du Bois' most deeply held beliefs, but never does he resort to diatribe or racial self-pity. He demonstrates an ability to communicate with his readers directly while simultaneously retaining an appropriate distance between them and himself. Just as a veil of color—to which he frequently refers—separates whites from blacks, so does he create a subtle veil of restraint between himself and his readers.

Du Bois examines the philosophy and ideas of both black and white society, honing in on the psychology of a people who have emerged from involuntary servitude—slavery—into a world that often appeared dismissive of them and seemed utterly dedicated to impeding their progress. Whereas immigrant groups from eastern and southern Europe had been assimilated into American society within a generation or two, racist attitudes had long prevented blacks from being similarly assimilated.

In this book, Du Bois identified the color line as the most significant problem of the emerging twentieth century. He begins his book with soft persuasion, maintaining an almost-apologetic and ever-conciliatory stance. This tone was necessary to attract white readers, to whom the book was directed just as much as it was to blacks.

Published in 1903, forty years after Abraham Lincoln freed the slaves in the Emancipation Proclamation, *The Souls of Black Folk* explores several interconnected themes. Among these are an assessment of the particular difficulties African Americans face in America, black citizens' attempts to rise above the prejudice that impedes their progress, the contributions that blacks have made to American society, and the ways in which African Americans can best achieve equality. Du Bois gleaned the irony that existed because blacks were not fully accepted in the only society they knew. Despite their ancestral origins, they were Americans, not Africans.

In essence, *The Souls of Black Folk* is autobiographical; it is the autobiography of the African American race. The theme to which Du Bois returns throughout this book is the need for blacks to improve their educations. He calls upon educated African Americans to help those whose education is limited. He counted on the generosity of educated blacks, the "talented tenth," to provide this kind of help, but he overestimated the consciences and generosity of educated African Americans and, in a speech later in his career, acknowledged his error.

Black Reconstruction in America: 1860-1880

This historical study is a product of Du Bois' later years. Published in 1935, it is sometimes referred to as the author's most important work. In it, as in his doctoral dissertation and its subsequent publication in 1896 as *Suppression of the African Slave-Trade to the United States of America*, his chief objective is to correct much that has been written by white scholars about black history.

The post-Civil War era was generally depicted as a period during which freed slaves gained power and misused it. Most previous scholars depicted this as a period marked by scandal and corruption. Du Bois, however, writing his revisionist history in the depths of the Great Depression, believed that Reconstruction epitomized what democracy is really about. He chronicles how blacks who gained power imposed necessary reforms and worked toward the redistribution of wealth, thereby reflecting Du Bois' move toward Communism in response to the economic crises African Americans faced during the Depression.

Du Bois followed this study in 1947 with *The World and Africa*, which was a further attempt to correct historical inaccuracies that portrayed his race in a less than favorable light. In both of these works, he emphasizes the exploitation of blacks by members of the dominant white society.

Other Literary Forms

Du Bois excelled in writing the deeply felt, passionate nonfiction that exposed the injustices his race suffered following the Emancipation Proclamation of 1863. He was, however, a novelist as well as an essayist. Among his published novels are *The Quest of the Silver Fleece* and the Black Flame trilogy, which consisted of *The Ordeal of Mansart, Mansart Builds a School,* and *Worlds of Color.* None of these works of fiction, however, achieves the literary quality of Du Bois's nonfiction.

Bibliography

Alridge, Derrick P. *The Educational Thought of W. E. B. Du Bois: An Intellectual History.* New York: Teachers College Press, 2008. Claims to be the first sustained examination of Du Bois's thinking about education, drawing on numerous unpublished sources.

Appiah, Kwame Anthony. *Lines of Descent: W. E. B. Du Bois and the Emergence of Identity.* Cambridge, MA: Harvard University Press, 2014. Explores the impact of Du Bois' time and experiences in Germany on the development of his social thought.

Balfour, Lawrie. *Democracy's Reconstruction: Thinking Politically with W. E. B. Du Bois.* Oxford: Oxford University Press, 2011. Argues that race, often neglected in American political thinking, deserves greater attention in the discipline of political science.

Bass, Amy. *Those About Him Remained Silent: The Battle Over W. E. B. Du Bois.* Minneapolis: University of Minnesota Press, 2009. Explores Du Bois' early life and also some controversies that arose after his death.

Blum, Edward J. *W. E. B. Du Bois: American Prophet.* Philadelphia: University of Pennsylvania Press, 2007. Emphasizes the impact of Du Bois' religious ideas on his social ideals.

Dorrien, Gary. *The New Abolition: W. E. B. Du Bois and the Black Social Gospel.* New Haven: Yale University Press, 2015. Traces the rise of a black social gospel and its relations to modern Christianity.

Douglas, Andrew J. *W. E. B. Du Bois and the Critique of the Competitive Society.* Athens: University of Georgia Press, 2019. Connects market capitalism to racist causes and racist outcomes.

Fontenot, Chester J., Jr., and Mary Alice Morgan, eds. *W. E. B. Du Bois and Race.* Macon, Ga.: Mercer University Press, 2001. The nine essays comprising this volume are varied and interesting. Especially relevant is Dolan Hubbard's "Riddle Me This: Du Bois, the Sphinx, and the Crisis of Identity."

Gillman, Susan, and Alys Eve Weinbaum, eds. *Next to the Color Line: Gender, Sexuality, and W. E. B. Du Bois.* Minneapolis: University of Minnesota Press, 2007. A collection of essays on such topics as juxtaposition, transnational politics, gendered allegory, interracial romance, internationalism, eroticism, black men, heterosexuality, criminality, and maternity.

Horne, Gerald, and Mary Young, eds. *W. E. B. Du Bois: An Encyclopedia.* Westport, Conn.: Greenwood Press, 2001. A comprehensive, one-volume encyclopedia that exhaustively covers Du Bois' life and career.

Johnson, Terrence L. *Tragic Soul-Life: W. E. B. Du Bois and the Moral Crisis Facing American Democracy.* Oxford: Oxford University Press, 2012. Explores relations between Du Bois' thought and the kind of liberalism associated with philosopher John Rawls.

Kahn, Johnathan S. *Divine Discontent: The Religious Imagination of W. E. B. Du Bois.* Oxford: Oxford University Press, 2009. Disputes the common idea that Du Bois was hostile to religion, instead claiming that it had a deep impact on his thinking and writing.

Kirschke, Amy Helene. *Art in Crisis: W. E. B. Du Bois and the Struggle for African American Identity and Memory.* Bloomington: Indiana University Press, 2007. Emphasizes the visual imagery featured in the magazine (*The Crisis*) Du Bois edited.

Kirschke, Amy Helene, and Philipp Luke Sinitiere, ed. *Protest and Propaganda: W. E. B. Du Bois, The Crisis, and American History.* Columbia: University of Missouri Press, 2014. Focuses especially on the magazine (*The Crisis*) Du Bois edited for many years.

Lewis, David Levering. *W. E. B. Du Bois: Biography of a Race, 1868-1919.* New York: Henry Holt, 1993. This, the most complete biography to date, focuses on Du Bois' first fifty-one years and was awarded the 1994 Pulitzer Prize in biography. It details Du Bois' growing appreciation of the black soul and his role in the NAACP, whose official publication, *The Crisis,* he edited.

_____. *W. E. B. Du Bois: The Fight for Equality and the American Century, 1919-1963.* New York: Henry Holt, 2001. Presents an excellent, detailed account of Du Bois' association with *The Crisis.* Also traces his move toward Communism, his eventual departure from the United States, his involvement in the *Encyclopedia Africana,* and his resettlement in Ghana.

_____. *W. E. B. Du Bois: A Biography.* Henry Holt and Co., 2009. A condensed, one-volume version of a work originally published in two large volumes.

Marable, Manning. *W. E. B. Du Bois: Black Radical Democrat*. Paradigm Publishers, 2005. An updated version of a biography first published in 1986.

McAuley, Christopher A. *The Spirit Vs. The Souls: Max Weber, W. E. B. Du Bois, and the Politics of Scholarship*. South Bend, IN: University of Notre Dame Press, 2019. Explores the connections of two major intellectuals, drawing particularly on their correspondence.

Moore, Jack B. *W. E. B. Du Bois*. Boston: Twayne, 1981. Despite its age, this compact assessment of Du Bois is pertinent and serviceable. It offers a fine, accessible overview.

Morris, Aldon D. *The Scholar Denied: W. E. B. Du Bois and the Birth of Modern Sociology*. Berkeley: University of California Press, 2015. Argues that Du Bois played a key role in the development of sociology – a role suppressed partly because of the influence of Booker T. Washington.

Moses, Wilson Jeremiah. *Creative Conflict in African American Thought: Frederick Douglass, Alexander Crummell, Booker T. Washington, W. E. B. Du Bois, and Marcus Garvey*. New York: Cambridge University Press, 2004. An excellent book; analyzes the writings of these important authors in the contexts of Jeffersonian and Jacksonian democracies as well as through the philosophy of social Darwinism.

Mullen, Bill V. *Un-American: W. E. B. Du Bois and the Century of World Revolution*. Philadelphia: Temple University Press, 2015. Explores Du Bois' career during the period of the Cold War.

Porter, Eric. *The Problem of the Future World: W. E. B. Du Bois and the Race Concept at Midcentury*. Duke University Press, 2010. Focuses on DuBois' writings from the 1940s and 1950s.

Reed, Adolph L., Jr. *W. E. B. Du Bois and American Political Thought*. New York: Oxford University Press, 1997. Reed offers excellent insights, particularly in "From Historiography to Class Ideology" and in the concluding section, "A Generativist Approach to the History of Political Thought."

Shaw, Stephanie J. *W. E. B. Du Bois and the Souls of Black Folk*. Chapel Hill: University of North Carolina Press, 2013. Relates Du Bois' most important work to the philosophy of Hegel.

Wolters, Raymond. *Du Bois and His Rivals*. Columbia: University of Missouri Press, 2002. An important chronicle of Du Bois' controversies with Booker T. Washington, Marcus Garvey, Walter White, and the NAACP.

Zamir, Shamoon, ed. *The Cambridge Companion to W. E. B. Du Bois*. Cambridge: Cambridge University Press, 2008. An important essay collection dealing with such topics as Du Bois' major works of fiction and non-fiction, black leadership, civil rights, race, diversity, economics, culture, pan-Africanism, European intellectual history, Marxism, and colonialism.

—R. Baird Shuman; Robert C. Evans

Paul Laurence Dunbar

Poet

Born: Dayton, Ohio; June 27, 1872

Died: Dayton, Ohio; February 9, 1906

LONG FICTION: *The Uncalled*, 1898; *The Love of Landry*, 1900; *The Fanatics*, 1901; *The Sport of the Gods*, 1902.

SHORT FICTION: *Folks from Dixie*, 1898; *The Strength of Gideon, and Other Stories*, 1900; *In Old Plantation Days*, 1903; *The Heart of Happy Hollow*, 1904; *The Best Stories of Paul Laurence Dunbar*, 1938.

POETRY: *Oak and Ivy*, 1893; *Majors and Minors*, 1895; *Lyrics of Lowly Life*, 1896; *Lyrics of the Hearthside*, 1899; *Lyrics of Love and Laughter*, 1903; *Lyrics of Sunshine and Shadow*, 1905; *Complete Poems*, 1913.

MISCELLANEOUS: *In His Own Voice: The Dramatic and Other Uncollected Works of Paul Laurence Dunbar*, 2002 (Herbert Woodward Martin and Ronald Primeau, editors).

Achievements

Paul Laurence Dunbar's literary career was brilliant, extending roughly across two decades. He can be credited with several first-time accomplishments: He was the first to use dialect poetry as a medium for the true interpretation of African American character and psychology, and he was the first African American writer to earn national prominence. Championed for the dialect verse and stories of the plantation folk he was unequaled in rendering but which he himself despised as limited and compliant with existing stereotypes, Dunbar was hailed by the leading literary minds of his day. In range of style and form, Dunbar remains the most versatile of African American writers.

Biography

Paul Laurence Dunbar was born to former slaves Joshua and Matilda J. Murphy Dunbar on June 27, 1872. He spent his early childhood in Dayton, Ohio, where he attended Central High School. His younger sister died when he was three and his father when Paul was twelve. In high school, he was the only African American, but perhaps both despite and because of this he became president of his class, managing editor of his school newspaper, president of the school literary club, and class poet. Dunbar began to write at age sixteen and gained early patronage for his work, and he was introduced to the Western Association of Writers in 1892.

While still in high school, he published poems in local newspapers and served as editor for the *Dayton Tattler*, published by classmate Orville Wright, coinventor of the airplane. Despite Dunbar's scholastic excellence, Dayton's discriminatory policies forced the young graduate to take a menial position as an elevator operator while he continued to write. Encouraged by other writers and a former teacher, Dunbar published privately his first collection of poetry, *Oak and Ivy*. His second collection, *Majors and*

Photo from *The Life and Works of Paul Laurence Dunbar*

Minors, won William Dean Howells's praise and sent him on the road to fame, but for Dunbar it was for all the wrong reasons.

These years found him in the presence of great black leaders. He met Frederick Douglass, Mary Church Terrell, and Ida B. Wells at the World's Columbian Exposition in Chicago in 1893. He met W. E. B. Du Bois in 1896 and Booker T. Washington in 1897. These encounters influenced Dunbar's literary tone and perspective significantly. He blended the creative perspective of Booker T. Washington with the social philosophy of Du Bois in order to present a valid scenario of African Americans after the Civil War.

Major James B. Pond, a Dunbar enthusiast, sponsored a trip to England for the writer that extended from February to August of 1897. Upon his return to the United States, Dunbar married Alice Ruth Moore, a Creole writer from New Orleans, and decided to earn his living as a writer. (The childless couple separated in 1902.) Between 1898 and 1903, Dunbar wrote essays for newspapers and periodicals, primarily addressing the issues of racial equality and social justice in America. During the latter years of his life, Dunbar wrote lyrics, including those for the school song for Tuskegee Institute. Dunbar died in 1906, at the age of thirty-three, of tuberculosis, of the effects of the alcohol prescribed to treat it, and of the melancholy brought on by his belief that his life had been a failure.

Analysis: Short Fiction

Paul Laurence Dunbar's life and writing were both impeded and tempered by the racial politics of his day. It was his greatest sorrow as an artist that his public wanted to read only his dialect verse and his stories in the plantation tradition, which were comic, sentimental, depicting black people as ignorant children. The fact that so much of his work contributed to negative stereotypes of his people has compromised his legacy and sometimes eclipsed the fact that, if he had not complied with those stereotypes, the work for which he is justly revered would not have been published at all. For African Americans of his day, his literary success was a symbol of the entire race's intellectual and creative abilities, hitherto unrecognized by white Americans, and his trials and fortunes were theirs: to suffer, to condemn, and to praise.

The roots of Dunbar's short fiction are to be found in the stories his parents told him of their Kentucky home and servitude. His mother told him gentle stories about plantation community life, but his father had been a fugitive, had fought with the Fifty-fifth Massachusetts

Infantry Regiment during the Civil War, and his stories were not sentimental. Dunbar's best short fiction is informed by the spirit and example of these stories and by the customs, traditions, and mores of the transplanted black southern community from which he came.

Dunbar's short fiction is often compared with that of his contemporary, Charles Waddell Chesnutt, who was also black and who wrote some accomplished plantation-based tales of black life. Chesnutt's stories are often peopled with characters who resist, undermine, and outsmart the white people, who think they know them. The majority of Dunbar's black characters tend instead to manipulate and subvert white opposition and gain white approval by a show of sterling character: honesty, integrity, faithfulness, loyalty, love, redemptive suffering, forgiveness. Worse, some Dunbar stories cast uneducated black people as the ignorant, minstrel buffoons his white readers preferred. Yet nestled among this packing were also great stories for which he is well remembered, stories which reveal righteous anger over ignorance and racial injustice and contempt for those who perpetuate them.

Folks from Dixie

There is plenty of "packing" in Dunbar's first story collection. Several stories, such as "Mount Pisgah's Christmas 'Possum," represent uneducated black people as ludicrous bumpkins or grateful, indebted servants. "The Colonel's Awakening" is an extremely sentimental tale, dripping with the sort of pathos Thomas Nelson Page whipped into his plantation tales. In "Anner 'Lizer," Dunbar pokes fun at religious hypocrisy, while affirming the fact that people's emotional and spiritual needs are often deeply linked. "Jimsella," "Aunt Mandy's Investment," and "Nelse Hatton's Revenge" were written primarily for his post-Reconstruction black

readers, who were still figuring out how to live now that the structure and restrictions of slavery no longer dictated their circumstances. Timely issues, which these stories address, were family responsibility, honesty, and integrity in businesses, which should serve the black community, and remembering and living the results of slavery and emancipation in ways that are not self-destructive.

"The Ordeal at Mt. Hope" and "At Shaft 11" are satisfying, well-constructed stories. The former is interesting for its autobiographical elements, its social commentary, and its "bootstrap economic" and educational philosophies as advocated by Booker T. Washington. The Reverend Howard Dokesbury steps off the train at Mt. Hope to take up his new post as Methodist preacher. The station house is run-down and filthy, like the rest of the town, and the indolent blacks, whites, and dogs view him with suspicion and malice. Dokesbury, understanding that any reconstruction of this community must happen one individual at a time, befriends 'Lias, one of the defeated young men. They collaborate on a small agricultural venture, and 'Lias gains confidence, feelings of self-reliance and self-esteem, and the financial base to go to the new industrial school to expand his skills. One by one, the townspeople are anxious to follow his example. Possibly Dunbar considered this story to be a blueprint for the betterment of the black masses, though he became increasingly critical of Washington's ideas, and by 1903 he warned of "educating the hand to the exclusion of the head." Dunbar gives Dokesbury his own physical characteristics, an occupation that Dunbar himself seriously considered, and even more important, some of his doubts and feelings of estrangement:

> He had always been such a loyal Negro, so proud of his honest brown...but...was he, after all, different from the majority

of the people with whom he was supposed to have all thoughts, feelings, and emotions in common?

Increasingly, Dunbar discovered that education and class standing were great dividers among his people, and color-consciousness made it all much worse.

"At Shaft 11" takes place in a mining community in West Virginia where a strike is being broken with a crew of black miners. Violence erupts, and two heroes emerge: the Scottish foreman, Jason Andrews, and the black foreman, Sam Bowles, who unite for common cause and mutual benefit. Less believable than the previous story, it is a blueprint for how things might have been in a more perfect world but rarely were. Still, it is revealing as a Dunbar story: The black men fight back here, meeting violence with necessary violence, and winning their share of the American pie.

The Strength of Gideon, and Other Stories

Dunbar's second collection of short stories reveals a wide spectrum of his thought and style. The title work and "Mammy Peggy's Pride" typify the plantation stories that champion the virtues of the race, such as honor, loyalty, dignity, faithfulness, selflessness, and a sense of duty and responsibility. Mammy Peggy, still the faithful, post-emancipation house servant, so identifies with her owners' former aristocratic place in southern society that she almost cannot adapt to the alliances and reconciliation necessary for a new day. Gideon's strength is his sense of duty and responsibility in keeping his word to his old master, even though he loses the woman he loves and who loves him. Dunbar's intent is to glorify race relations of an earlier day in the interest of race relations of his own day, which were marked by increasing enmity and violence. It is as if he hopes to calm

would-be lynchers and segregationists, and reassure potential friends of the race, with the admonition to "remember who these people are."

"The Ingrate" is based on Dunbar's father's experiences as a slave, a fugitive on the underground railroad to Canada, and a Union soldier. The former slaveholder sees his former slave's name on a Union roster and feels grievously abused that he taught "the ingrate" to read and cipher because he used these accomplishments against him. "The Case of 'Ca'line,'" subtitled "A Kitchen Monologue," is a sassy piece, which anticipates Langston Hughes's Simple and Alberta K. Johnson stories.

Though there is enough melodramatic action in "The Tragedy at Three Forks" for a novel, this antilynching story is not entirely unsuccessful. Reflecting the usual circumstances of lynchings, the two victims are innocent, and the reader understands that this evil bloodthirst will continue as long as white people are motivated by guilt, ignorance, immorality, cruelty, base instincts, and mob violence. Other stories point out other kinds of white injustice. In "One Man's Fortunes," a worthy black college graduate goes out to get a job and, like Dunbar himself, meets defeat and deception in the white world. Others warn of the folly of migrating to the urban North, where hardship and evil await. The last story in the collection, "Silas Jackson," could have been a prototype for the beginnings of James Weldon Johnson's *Autobiography of an Ex-Colored Man* (1912) and Ralph Ellison's *Invisible Man* (1952). Here, too, the young, country innocent has a vision of a better life, and, through a series of ever more blinding incidents involving white "benefactors" and black charlatans, he finds himself in New York City, where he thinks he has "made something of himself." Here Silas's fortunes take a characteristic Dunbarian turn, and he returns home "spent, broken, hopeless, all contentment and simplicity gone." Portending death more than reunion with "the old folks at home," it is an ambiguous, unsettling end to the collection.

In Old Plantation Days

This collection is in the plantation tradition, though there are a couple of stories worth reading. "The Finding of Martha" is really the second half of "The Strength of Gideon," which ended so unsatisfactorily in the previous collection, and "The Memory of Martha," which, despite certain weaknesses (omission of painful details of slavery, oversentimentality), is still an affecting love story.

The Heart of Happy Hollow

These stories take place during and after Reconstruction and are concerned with the strengths and weaknesses of the southern black community in the aftermath of slavery and the strained, even violent circumstances it was forced to endure as it claimed the benefits of freedom. "The Scapegoat" is Dunbar's most successful story about how African Americans were, and are, used as America's political pawns. It is also one of the first stories by a black writer to locate an alternate, undermining seat of power in the barbershop/newsstand. "The Lynching of Jube Benson" is Dunbar's other antilynching story, this one narrated by one of the lynchers, as in James Baldwin's work. Though its impact is fueled by sentiment, it is unrelenting and unforgiving in its indictment. Other stories, primarily for a black audience, warn of the dangers of boastfulness, vanity, cowardice, self-pity, class and color consciousness, and the reactionary fear of change and difference. Stories such as "The Promoter" and "The Boy and the Bayonet" reveal that Dunbar had discovered how to use humor and pathos without sacrificing his characters' humanity. At the time of his death, his strongest work was no longer in poetry but in short fiction, a genre that allowed him to be more realistic, relevant, and true to himself and his people.

Analysis: Poetry

The body of poetry produced by Paul Laurence Dunbar illustrates some of the best qualities found in lyrical verse. It is obvious that the poet concentrated on a creation of mood and that he was an innovator who experimented with form, meter, and rhyme. Equally apparent is the fact that Dunbar's creative style was influenced by the great British poetic innovators of the seventeenth and nineteenth centuries. Dunbar's commitment to speak to his people through his verse is reflected in his dialect poetry. Writing in all the major lyrical forms—idyll, hymn, sonnet, song, ballad, ode, and elegy—Dunbar established himself as one of the most versatile poets in American literature.

The more than four hundred poems written by Dunbar are varied in style and effect. It is clear, however, that his dominant aim was to create an empathetic poetic mood resulting from combinations of elements such as meter, rhyme, diction, sentence structure, characterization, repetition, imagery, and symbolism. His most memorable poems display the influence of such masters as William Wordsworth; Robert Herrick; Alfred, Lord Tennyson; John Donne; Robert Browning; and John Keats.

Such an array of influences would ordinarily render one's genius suspect. There are common threads, however, that organically characterize the poetic expressions of Paul Laurence Dunbar. The undergirding strain in his poetry is his allegiance to lyrical qualities. He carries mood through sound patterns, he creates images that carry philosophical import, he shapes dramatic events in the pattern of movement in his syntactic forms, and he develops a rhythmic pattern that is quite effective in recitation.

These lyrical qualities predominate in the best of Dunbar's poetry. Indeed, one might easily classify Dunbar's poetry in typical Romantic lyrical categories: The bulk of his poems can be classified as love lyrics, reflective lyrics, melancholic lyrics, or nature lyrics. Sometimes these moods overlap in a single poem. Consequently, an analysis of the features in Dunbar's poetry is necessarily complex, placing his lyrical qualities in the poetic traditions that shape them.

Love Lyrics: Lyrics of the Hearthside

Dunbar's lyricism is substantially displayed in his love poetry. In "A Bridal Measure," from *Lyrics of the Hearthside*, the poet's persona beckons maidens to the bridal throne. His invitation is spirited and triumphant yet controlled, reminiscent of the tradition in love poetry established by Ben Jonson. The tone, however, more closely approximates the carpe diem attitude of Robert Herrick:

> Come, essay a sprightly measure,
> Tuned to some light song of pleasure.
> Maidens, let your brows be crowned
> As we foot this merry round.

The rhyming couplets carry the mood and punctuate the invitation. The urgency of the moment is extended further in the direct address: "Phyllis, Phyllis, why be waiting?/ In the woods the birds are mating." The poem continues in this tone, while adopting a pastoral simplicity:

> When the year, itself renewing,
> All the world with flowers is strewing,
> Then through Youth's Arcadian land,
> Love and song go hand in hand.

The accentuation in the syntactic flow of these lines underlines the poet's intentions. Though the meter is irregular, with some iambs and some anapests, the force of the poet's exhortation remains apparent.

Dunbar frequently personifies abstractions. In "Love and Grief," also from *Lyrics of the Hearthside*, Dunbar espouses a morbid yet redemptive view of love. While the reflective scenario presented in this poem recalls Tennyson's meditations on death and loss, the poetic event echoes Wordsworth's faith in the indestructibility of joy. Utilizing the heroic couplet, Dunbar makes an opening pronouncement:

> Out of my heart, one treach'rous winter's day,
> I locked young Love and threw the key away.
> Grief, wandering widely, found the key,
> And hastened with it, straightway, back to me.

The drama of grief-stricken love is thus established. The poet carefully clarifies his position through an emphatic personification of Grief's behavior: "He unlocked the door/ and bade Love enter with him there and stay." Being a lyric poet of redemptive sensibility, Dunbar cannot conclude the poem on this note. The "table must turn," as it does for Wordsworth in such situations. Love then becomes bold and asks of Grief: "What right hast thou/ To part or parcel of this heart?" In order to justify the redemptive quality he presents, Dunbar attributes the human frailty of pride to Love, a failing which invites Grief. In so doing, the poet's philosophical intuitiveness emerges with a measure of moral decorum. Through the movement in the syntactic patterns, the intensity of the drama is heightened as the poem moves to resolution. Dunbar utilizes a variety of metrical patterns, the most significant of which is the spondee. This poetic foot of two accented syllables allows the poet to proclaim emphatically: "And Love, pride purged, was chastened all his life." Thus, the principal emotion in the poem is redeemed.

The brief, compact lyrical verse, as found in Browning, is among Dunbar's typical forms. "Love's Humility," in *Lyrics of the Hearthside*, is an example:

> As some rapt gazer on the lowly earth,
> Looks up to radiant planets, ranging far,
> So I, whose soul doth know thy wondrous
> worth Look longing up to thee as to a
> star.

This skillfully concentrated simile elevates love to celestial heights. The descriptive detail enhances the power of the feeling the poet captures and empowers the lyrical qualities of the poem with greater pathos.

Lyrics of Love and Laughter

Dunbar's *Lyrics of Love and Laughter* isnot the best of his collections, but it contains some remarkable dialect verse. "A Plea" provides an example of this aspect of his reputation. Speaking of the unsettling feelings experienced by one overcome with love, Dunbar exhorts a lover's love object to "treat him nice.":

> I ain't don a t'ing to shame,
> Lovahs all ac's jes de same:
> Don't you know we ain't to blame? Treat
> me nice!

Rendering a common experience in the African American idiom, Dunbar typifies the emotionally enraptured lover as one who has no control over his behavior:

> Whut a pusson gwine to do,
> W'en he come a-cou'tin' you All a-trimblin' thoo and thoo?
> Please be nice.

The diction in this poem is not pure dialect. Only those portions which describe the emotions and behavior of the lover are stated in dialect, highlighting the primary emotions and enhancing the pathetic mood, which is apparently Dunbar's principal intent. Typical of Dunbar's love lyrics, "A Plea" is rooted in the experience of a particular culture yet remains universal in its themes. Through his use of diction, meter, and stanzaic form, Dunbar captures fundamental human emotions and renders them with intensity and lyrical compassion.

Reflective Lyrics: Lyrics of Lowly Life

Reflective lyrics form a large segment of Dunbar's poetry. Some of his best poems of this type are found in *Lyrics of Lowly Life*, including the long stanzaic poem "Ere Sleep Comes Down to Soothe the Weary Eyes." This poem utilizes one sensory impression as a focal point for the lyrical evolution in the style of Keats. The sleep motif provides an avenue through which the persona's imagination enters the realm of reflection.

Through sleep's dream the persona is able to "make the waking world a world of lies—/ of lies palpable, uncouth, forlorn." In this state of subconscious reflection, past pains are revisited as they "come thronging through the chambers of the brain." As the poem progresses, it becomes apparent that the repetitive echo of "ere sleep comes down to soothe the weary eyes" has some significance. This refrain begins and ends each stanza of the poem except the last. In addition to serving as a mood-setting device, this expression provides the channel of thought for the literary journey, which is compared with the "spirit's journeying." Dunbar's audience is thus constantly reminded of the source of his revelations.

Dunbar reveals his poetic thesis in the last stanza. He uses images from the subconscious state of life, sleep, to make a point about death. Prior to making this point, Dunbar takes the reader to the realm of reflective introspection: "So, trembling with the shock of sad surprise,/ The soul doth view its awful self alone." There is an introspective confrontation of the soul with itself, and it resolves:

> When sleep comes down to seal the
> weary eyes,
> Ah, then, no more we heed
> the sad world's cries,
> Or seek to probe th' eternal mystery,
> Or fret our souls at long-withheld
> replies.

The escape from pain and misery is death; there is no intermediary state which will eradicate that fact of life. Dunbar presents this notion with sympathy and sincerity. His metaphorical extensions, particularly those relative to the soul, are filled with compassion. The soul is torn with the world's deceit; it cries with "pangs of vague inexplicable pain." The spirit, an embodiment of the soul, forges ahead to seek truth as far as fancy will lead. Questioning begins then, and the inner sense confronts the inner being until truth emerges. Dunbar's presentation of the resolution is tender and gentle.

Dunbar wrote reflective lyrics in the vernacular as well. Espousing the philosophy of divine intention, Dunbar wrote "Accountability," a poem also found in *Lyrics of Lowly Life.* In this poem, the beliefs and attitudes of the persona are revealed in familiar language:

> Folks ain't got no right to
>   censuah othah
>   folks about dey habits;
> We is all constructed diff'ent,
>   d'ain't no two of
>   us de same;
> But we all fits into places dat no
>   othah ones
>   could fill.

Each stanza in this poem presents a thesis and develops that point. The illustrations from the natural world support a creationist viewpoint. The persona obviously accepts the notion that everything has a purpose. The Creator gave the animals their members shaped as they are for a reason and so, "Him dat giv' de squr'ls de bushtails made de bobtails fu' de rabbits." The variations in nature are by design: "Him dat built de gread big mountains hollered out de little valleys"; "Him dat made de streets an' driveways wasn't shamed to make de alley." The poet establishes these notions in three quatrains, concluding in the fourth quatrain: "When you come to think about it, how it's all planned out it's splendid./ Nuthin's done er evah happens, dout hit's somefin' dat's intended." The persona's position that divine intention rules the world is thereby sealed.

Introspection is a feature of Dunbar's reflective lyrics. In "The Lesson," the persona engages in character revelation, interacts with the audience toward establishment of appropriate resolution, and participates in the action of the poem. These qualities are reminiscent of Browning's dramatic monologues. As the principal speaker sits by a window in his cottage, reflecting, he reports:

> And I thought of myself so sad and lone,
> And my life's cold winter that knew no
> spring;
> Of my mind so weary and sick and wild,
> Of my heart too sad to sing.

The inner conflict facing the persona is revealed in these lines and the perspective of self-examination is established. The persona must confront his sadness and move toward resolution. The movement toward resolution presents the dramatic occasion in the poem: "A thought stole into my saddened heart,/ And I said, 'I can cheer some other soul/ By a carol's simple art.'" Reflective introspection typically leads to improved character, a fundamental tenet in the Victorian viewpoint. Sustained by his new conviction and outlook, the persona "sang a lay for a brother's ear/ In a strain to soothe his bleeding heart."

The lyrical quality of "The Lesson" is strengthened by the movement in the poet's syntactic patterns. Feelings of initial despair and resulting joy and hope are conveyed through the poet's syntax. The sequential conjoining of ideas as if in a rushing stream of thought is particularly effective. The latter sections of the poem are noteworthy in this regard. This pattern gives the action more force, thereby intensifying the feeling. Dunbar presents an emphatic idea— "and he smiled ..."—and juxtaposes it to an exception "Though mine was a feeble art." He presents a responsive result—"But at his smile I smiled in turn"—connected to a culminating effect—"And into my soul there came a ray." With this pronouncement, the drama comes full circle from inner conflict through conversion to changed philosophical outlook. Dunbar captures each moment with appropriate vigor.

Melancholy: "Yesterday and To-morrow"

The subjects of love and death are treated in Dunbar's lyrics of melancholy, the third major mood found in the poet's lyrical verse. "Yesterday and To-morrow," in *Lyrics of Sunshine and Shadow*, is an example of Dunbar's lyric of melancholy. The mood of this poem is in the tradition of the British Romantic poets, particularly that of Wordsworth. Dunbar treats the melancholy feelings in this poem with tenderness and simplicity. The persona expresses disappointment with the untimeliness of life's events and the uncertainties of love. This scenario intimates a bleak future.

"Yesterday and To-morrow" is developed in three compact quatrains. Each quatrain envelops a primary emotion. The first stanza unfolds yesterday's contentment in love. The lover remembers the tender and blessed emotion of closeness with his lover: "And its gentle yieldingness/ From my soul I blessed it." The second stanza is reminiscent of the metaphysical questionings and imagery of Donne: "Must our gold forever know/ Flames for the refining?" The lovers' emotions are compared with precious metal undergoing the fire of refinement: Their feelings of sadness are released in this cynical question.

In the third quatrain, Dunbar feeds the sad heart with more cynicism. Returning to the feelings of disappointment and uncertainty, the persona concludes: "Life was all a lyric song/ Set to tricksy meter." The persona escapes in cynicism, but the poem still ends on a hopeless note.

"Communion"

"Communion," which is collected in *Lyrics of the Hearthside*, is another of Dunbar's melancholy lyrics and focuses on the theme of love and death. The situation in the poem again evokes a cynical attitude, again reminiscent of Donne. The poem presents a struggle between life's memories and death. Life's memories are primarily of the existence of the love relationship, and death symbolizes its demise. This circumstance unfolds in a dramatic narrative in the style of Browning.

The first two stanzas of the poem introduce the situation and the mood begins to evolve in stanza three. The poet uses images from nature to create the somber mood. The "breeze of Death," for example, sweeps his lover's soul "Out into the unsounded deeps." On one hand, the Romantic theme of dominance of nature and man's helplessness in the face of it creeps through; on the other hand, faith in love as the superior experience resounds. The conflict between conquering Death, symbolized in nature, and Love creates tension in the poem. Consequently, though the breeze of Death has swept his bride away, the persona announces that "Wind nor sea may keep me from/ Soft communing with my bride." As these quatrains of iambic pentameter unfold, the poem becomes somewhat elegiac in tone.

The persona solemnly enters into reflective reminiscence in the fifth stanza and proclaims: "I shall rest my head on thee/ As I did long days of yore." Continuing in stanza 6, he announces: "I shall take thy hand in mine,/ And live o'er the olden days." Leading up to the grief-stricken pledge of eternal love, the melancholic feeling is intensified. The mourner details his impression as follows:

> Tho' the grave-door shut between, Still
> their love lights o'er me steal.
> I can see thee thro' my tears,
> As thro' rain we see the sun.

The comfort which comes from such memories brings a ray of light; the lover concludes:

> I shall see thee still and be Thy true lover
> evermore,
> And thy face shall be to me Dear and
> helpful as before.

The drama cannot end unless the persona interacts with his audience. The audience is therefore included in the philosophical conclusion: "Death may vaunt and Death may boast,/ But we laugh his pow'r to scorn." Dunbar illustrates an ability to overcome the causes of melancholy in his lyrics of this mood. He works with contrasting feelings, cynicism, and determinism to achieve this goal. His melancholic mood is therefore less gloomy than one might expect.

Nature Lyrics: "In Summer"

Since he was greatly influenced by the British Romantic writers, it is not surprising that Dunbar also wrote nature lyrics. "In Summer," from *Lyrics of the Hearthside*, and "The Old Apple-Tree," from *Lyrics of Lowly Life*, are representative of his nature lyrics. "In Summer" captures a mood of merriment which is stimulated by nature. The common man is used as a model of one who possesses the capacity to experience this natural joy. Summer is a bright, sunny time; it is also a time for ease, as presented in the second stanza. Introducing the character of the farmer boy in stanza 3, Dunbar presents a model embodiment of the ease and merriment of summer. Amid the blades of green grass and as the breezes cool his brow, the farmer boy sings as he plows. He sings "to the dewy morn" and "to the joys of life." This behavior leads to some moralizing, to which the last three stanzas of the poem are devoted. The poet's point is made through a contrast:

> O ye who toil in the town.
> And ye who moil in the mart,
> Hear the artless song, and your faith
> made strong Shall renew your joy of
> heart.

Dunbar admonishes the reader to examine the behavior of the farm boy. Elevation of the simple, rustic life is prevalent in the writings of early British Romantic poets and postbellum African American writers alike. The admonition to reflect on the rustic life, for example, is the same advice Wordsworth gives in "The Old Cumberland Beggar." Both groups of writers agree that there are lessons to be learned through an examination of the virtues of the rustic life. In this vein, Dunbar advises: "Oh, poor were the worth of the world/ If never a song were heard." He goes further by advising all to "taunt old Care with a merry air."

"The Old Apple-Tree"

The emphasis on the rustic life is also pervasive in "The Old Apple-Tree." The primary lyrical quality of the poem is that the poetic message evolves from the poet's memory and imagination. Image creation is the medium through which Dunbar works here: His predominant image, dancing in flames of ruddy light, is an orchard "wrapped in autumn's purple haze."

Dunbar proceeds to create a nature scene which provides a setting for the immortalization of the apple tree. Memory takes the persona to the scene, but imagination re-creates events and feelings. The speaker in the poem admits that it probably appears ugly "When you look the tree all over/ Unadorned by memory's glow." The tree has become old and crooked, and it bears inferior fruit. Thus, without the nostalgic recall, the tree does not appear special at all.

Utilizing the imaginative frame, the speaker designs features of the simple rustic life, features which are typically British Romantic and peculiarly Wordsworthian. The "quiet, sweet seclusion" realized as one hides under the shelter of the tree and the idle dreaming in which one engages dangling in a swing from the tree are primary among these thoughts. Most memorable to the speaker is the solitary contentment he and his sweetheart found as they courted beneath the old apple tree:

> Now my gray old wife is Hallie, An I'm grayer still than she,
> But I'll not forget our courtin'
> 'Neath the old apple-tree.

The poet's ultimate purpose, to immortalize the apple tree, is fulfilled in the last stanza. The old apple tree will never lose its place in nature or its significance, for the speaker asks:

> But when death does come a-callin,' This my last request shall be,—
> That they'll bury me an' Hallie 'Neath the old apple-tree.

The union of man and nature at the culmination of physical life approaches a notion expressed in Wordsworth's poetry. This tree has symbolized the ultimate in goodness and universal harmony; it symbolizes the peace, contentment, and joy in the speaker's life. Here Dunbar's indebtedness to the Romantic traditions that inform his entire oeuvre is most profoundly felt.

Other Literary Forms

Though Paul Laurence Dunbar is best known for his poetry, he was a fiction writer as well. His achievements in fiction include his short stories and four novels. Criticism of Dunbar's short fiction suggests that the stories contained in *Folks from Dixie* represent his best accomplishment in this literary form. His novels *The Uncalled* and *The Sport of the Gods* acquired more critical acclaim than his other two novels, *The Love of Landry* and *The Fanatics*.

In addition to his work in these more traditional literary forms, Dunbar wrote an assortment of lyrics and libretti for a variety of theatrical productions. He also wrote essays for newspapers and attempted to establish a periodical of his own.

Bibliography

Alexander, Eleanor. *Lyrics of Sunshine and Shadow: The Tragic Courtship and Marriage of Paul Laurence Dunbar and Alice Ruth Moore.* Albany: New York University Press, 2004. Traces the tempestuous romance of America's most noted African American literary couple. Assistant professor of history Alexander draws on love letters, diaries, journals, and autobiographies to tell the story of Dunbar and Moore's tumultuous affair, elopement, Dunbar's abuse of Moore, their passionate marriage, and the violence that ended it. An examination of a celebrated couple in the context of their times, fame, and cultural ideology.

Best, Felton O. *Crossing the Color Line: A Biography of Paul Laurence Dunbar.* Dubuque, Iowa: Kendall/ Hunt, 1996. One of the Dunbar biographies. Short fiction is discussed as evidence of Dunbar's restrictions and intentions.

Bone, Robert. *Down Home: Origins of the Afro-American Short Story.* New York: Columbia University Press, 1988. Discusses the "strictures" of Dunbar's time and the "travesties" of his fictional response. Judges Dunbar to be a "purveyor of dead forms."

Brawley, Benjamin. *Paul Laurence Dunbar: Poet of His People.* Port Washington, N.Y.: Kennikat Press, 1967. A dated but still useful early biographical and critical study of Dunbar, this book is a reprint of a 1936 edition. After placing Dunbar in his historical context, Brawley gives a chronological overview of Dunbar's life and career, with some general observations about individual poems. Includes some personal correspondence of the poet, as well as an appendix and a bibliography of primary and secondary material.

Braxton, Joanne M., ed. *The Collected Poetry of Paul Laurence Dunbar.* Charlottesville: University Press of Virginia, 1993. Though collection is of poetry, biographical introduction is insightful and useful to researchers in any Dunbar genre.

Gayle, Addison, Jr. *Oak and Ivy: A Biography of Paul Laurence Dunbar.* Garden City, N.Y.: Doubleday, 1971. This study of the life and work of Dunbar focuses particularly on the "mask" of the "Negro poet" that Dunbar assumed while desiring to be a much more serious, innovative poet. Contains excellent discussions of individual poems and short stories, a chronology of Dunbar's life, and a primary and secondary bibliography.

Gentry, Tony. *Paul Laurence Dunbar: Poet.* Los Angeles: Melrose Square, 1993. Covers Dunbar's personal life and his literary accomplishments, with excerpts from his works to exemplify his ideas. Heavily illustrated, providing a sense of his times. Well geared to the needs of younger and student audiences, as well as those new to Dunbar.

Harrell, Jr., Willie J., ed. *We Wear the Mask: Paul Laurence Dunbar and the Politics of Representative Reality.* Kent State UP, 2010. A collection of essays dealing with such issues as African aesthetics, masking, national memory, the arts, war poetry, black soldiers, minstrelsy, dialect poetry, rhetoric, *The Century Magazine,* masculinity, and and realism.

Hudson, Gossie Harold. *A Biography of Paul Laurence Dunbar.* Baltimore: Gateway Press, 1999. In-depth biography with biographical references.

Keeling, John. "Paul Dunbar and the Mask of Dialect." *Southern Literary Journal* 25, no. 2 (Spring, 1993): 24-39. Takes a closer look at how plantation life is portrayed in Dunbar's poems.

Lawson, Victor. *Dunbar Critically Examined.* Washington, D.C.: Associated Publishers, 1941. Though somewhat dated, Lawson's book provides an excellent introduction to Dunbar's poetry and prose. Attempts to determine Dunbar's significance to American poetry and places him in his historical context, including the earlier and contemporary poetic traditions which influenced him, especially the works of Alfred, Lord Tennyson, and Edgar Allan Poe. Separates the literary and dialect poems for purposes of discussion. The bibliography is short and largely outdated.

Martin, Jay, ed. *A Singer in the Dawn: Reinterpretations of Paul Laurence Dunbar.* New York: Dodd, Mead, 1975. This collection of critical essays and personal reminiscences on Dunbar contains essays by Saunders Redding, Arna Bontemps, Darwin T. Turner, Dickson D. Bruce, Jr., and others. Four essays are devoted to Dunbar's poetic achievement, with especially important essays on myths about Dunbar's poetry and on Dunbar and the African American folk tradition. Also included are notes, a foreword by Jay Martin, and an afterword by Nikki Giovanni.

Okeke-Ezigbo, Emeka. "Paul Laurence Dunbar: Straightening the Record." *California Library Association Journal* 24 (1980/ 1981): 481-496. Arguing against the traditional myths concerning Dunbar the man and the poet, Okeke-Ezigbo demonstrates that Dunbar's dialect poetry reveals his condescending attitude toward African Americans. The comparisons between Dunbar and his mentor, James Whitcomb Riley, and literary predecessors such as Robert Burns, Geoffrey Chaucer, and James Russell Lowell help place Dunbar in a literary tradition. Some references lead to sections of books which include short discussions of Dunbar.

Ramsey, William M. "Dunbar's Dixie." *Southern Literary Journal* 32, no. 1 (Fall, 1999): 30-46. Analyzes the role of the South in Dunbar's work. Dunbar did not feel entirely comfortable writing about the region and its people.

Randall, Dudley. *The Black Poets.* New York: Bantam, 1971. According to Randall, "not only does this book present the full range of Black poetry, but it presents most poets in depth, and in some cases presents aspects of a poet neglected or overlooked before. Turning away from White models and returning to their roots has freed Black poets to create a new poetry. This book records their progress." Dunbar is covered along with most other major black poets.

Revell, Peter. *Paul Laurence Dunbar.* Boston: Twayne, 1979. An excellent introduction to the life and works of Dunbar, this study is organized according to the genres in which Dunbar wrote: "Poetry in Literary English," "Poetry in Dialect," "Black Theater," "The Short Stories," and "The Novels." Includes analyses of individual poems, both those in literary English and those in dialect, and an assessment of Dunbar as an important figure in African American literary history. Notes, references, and a selected annotated bibliography make this a considerable contribution to Dunbar scholarship.

Turner, Darwin T. "Paul Laurence Dunbar: The Rejected Symbol." *Journal of Negro History*, January, 1967, 1-13. Provides a balanced response to the pros and cons of Dunbar's work. Points out the restrictions under which Dunbar worked and his artistic ideals. Concludes that "readers have demanded too much of Dunbar as a symbol."

Wagner, Jean. "Paul Laurence Dunbar." In *Black Poets of the United States from Paul Laurence Dunbar to Langston Hughes,* translated by Kenneth Douglas. Urbana: University of Illinois Press, 1973. After a lengthy introduction placing Dunbar in his historical context as an African American poet, Wagner devotes an entire chapter of this important work to Dunbar's poetry. Gives an excellent over view of Dunbar's career as a poet and some quite useful analyses of individual poems. Includes a short bibliography of secondary materials on Dunbar.

— *Cynthia Packard Hill; Patricia A. R. Williams; Robert C. Evans*

Michael Eric Dyson

Writer and Cultural Critic

Born: Detroit, Michigan; October 23, 1958

NONFICTION: *Reflecting Black: African-American Cultural Criticism*, 1993; *Making Malcolm: The Myth and Meaning of Malcolm X*, 1995; *Race Rules: Navigating the Color Line*, 1996; *Between God and Gangsta Rap: Bearing Witness to Black Culture*, 1997; *I May Not Get There with You: The True Martin Luther King, Jr.*, 2000; *Holler if You Hear Me: Searching for Tupac Shakur*, 2002; *Open Mike: Reflections on Philosophy, Race, Sex, Culture and Religion*, 2002; *Why I Love Black Women*, 2002; *The Michael Eric Dyson Reader*, 2004; *Mercy, Mercy Me: The Art, Loves and Demons of Marvin Gaye*, 2005; *Is Bill Cosby Right? Or Has the Black Middle Class Lost Its Mind?*, 2005; *Pride: The Seven Deadly Sins*, 2006; *Come Hell or High Water: Hurricane Katrina and the Color of Disaster*, 2006; *Debating Race*, 2007; *Know What I Mean? Reflections on Hip Hop*, 2007; *April 4, 1968: Martin Luther King's Death and How it Changed America*, 2008; *Can You Hear Me Now? The Inspiration, Wisdom, and Insight of Michael Eric Dyson*, 2009; *The Black Presidency: Barack Obama and the Politics of Race in America*, 2016; *Tears We Cannot Stop: A Sermon to White America*, 2017; *What Truth Sounds Like*, 2018; *JAY-Z: Made in America*, 2019

EDITED TEXTS: *Born to Use Mics: Reading Nas's Illmatic* (with Sohail Daulatzai, coeditor), 1994

Achievements

Dyson's work has frequently been honored by critics and associations. In 2004, 2006, and 2007 he won NAACP Image Awards in nonfiction; in 2007 he received an American Book Award; and in 2018 he won the Southern Book Prize.

Biography

Dyson was born in Detroit, Michigan to Addie Mae Leonard, from Alabama, and was adopted by his stepfather, Everett Dyson. He has described himself as a promising student from the ghetto who was admitted to a prestigious private school on an academic scholarship on the condition that he repeat eleventh grade. However, he has said he felt unwelcome and picked upon by other students, most of whom were white, and has reported that he was expelled from that school during his second year because of his resulting poor performance. He finished his schooling at Northwestern High School in Detroit.

In 1977 he married Theresa Taylor, became a teenage father (his son, Michael Eric Dyson II, was born in 1978), worked in the auto industry, and did not begin college until 1979, when he was almost twenty-one. He has said that he divorced Taylor in that same year after moving to Knoxville, Tennessee to attend historically black Knoxville College. Already an ordained Baptist minister at this time, he has said that he served as pastor at three different churches in Tennessee while completing his studies at Carson-Newman College, near Knoxville, where he focused on studying philosophy. From there he went to Princeton University, where he earned his master's and doctoral degrees in religion. He was able to study at Princeton partly on the

Photo courtesy of Medill DC

recommendation of Cornel West, a philosopher and theologian who was one of the university's most prominent African American alumni at the time. Dyson has described his admiration of West, his long-standing friendship with him, and the impact West's ideas and example had on Dyson's own thinking and academic career.

As that career has flourished, Dyson has gone from one major academic appointment to another: he was an assistant professor at Brown University from 1993-1995; a professor at the University of North Carolina at Chapel Hill from 1995-1997; and a visiting distinguished professor at Columbia University from 1997-1999. Subsequent academic appointments included positions at DePaul University; the University of Pennsylvania; Georgetown University; and others. Dyson has become a consistently best-selling author, has hosted a radio program; has made frequent appearances on television; and has written for many different magazines. He has been married three times.

Analysis: Nonfiction

As his list of publications shows, Dyson's interests have been wide-ranging. He has said that he wants to reach a wide audience rather than writing simply for other academics. He has combined academic study with an abiding concern with popular culture and has linked his interest with history to his commitment to commenting on, and attempting to influence, contemporary social and political culture.

Between God and Gangsta Rap

Defining himself as an ordained Baptist minister, a university professor, a radical democrat, and a public intellectual, Dyson can claim to live at the intersection of varied expressions of American society and black culture and to bring to the study of that culture, in its internal structures and in its relationships to the society at large, a viewpoint constructed out of multiple perspectives. His abiding position is that, while differences must be acknowledged and affirmed, all segments of black culture can learn from the others and from the larger world. As a black writer who engages in sustained dialogue with the white community, he obviously implies further that the larger world has much to learn from black culture.

Dyson's religious commitment is most explicitly expressed in the "Invocation" and "Benediction" that constitute this book's first and last chapters and in his tribute to Gardner Taylor, a great African American preacher. The "Invocation," in substance an open letter to Dyson's brother in prison, and the "Benediction," addressed to the author's wife, both give poignant personal application to one of Dyson's compelling themes, the struggle to achieve authentic intimacy. In the tribute to Taylor, Dyson celebrates his subject's prophetic witness, his charismatic personality, and his style.

"Style" perhaps suggests a secular turn, from the concerns of the Christian to those of the critic. Sensitive readers will recognize, however, that for Dyson this is a false distinction. Thus, his criticism of secular culture—of "gangsta rap," for example—is constantly informed by an active and uncloistered faith. There is, for Dyson, no point at which the religious yields to the secular; rather, the secular can be truly seen only in the light of the spiritual. His attentiveness to style in the music reviews he includes, as in his essay on Taylor, urges us to recognize in style the epiphany of spirit.

I May Not Get There with You

Calling Martin Luther King Jr. "the greatest American who ever lived," Dyson objects to the sentimentality King's name often evokes. He maintains that "we have sanitized his *ideas*, ignoring his mistrust of white America, his commitment to black solidarity and advancement, and the radical message of his later life." Moreover, by raising King to the level of a saint, Americans have "lost the chance to connect the man's humanity, including his flaws, to the young people of today, especially our despised black youth." Thus, Dyson thinks King-as-he-was must be rediscovered. In his view, this need forces readers to see the man as conflicted and contradictory—and nonetheless (or all the more) wholly remarkable.

The volume's thirteen chapters are organized into three parts: "Ideology," "Identity," and "Image." Despite Dyson's suggestion that his analysis works from "biographical details and life episodes," he writes for those who know the King story thoroughly and who worry about such matters as the impact of Malcolm X on the later strategies of the Southern Christian Leadership Conference (SCLC), the wisdom of King's stance against the Vietnam War, the difficulties King's staff had in moving from civil to

economic rights, and the challenge of the northern ghetto to King's nonviolent ideals. Dyson also assumes that the reader knows something (and is uneasy) about King's several acts of academic plagiarism and chronic womanizing.

Dyson sees his subject as having supported "affirmative action" long before that policy was named and implemented. Indeed, he thinks King would have advocated the (now unthinkable) idea of reparation and compensation for the descendants of slaves. But in Dyson's view, King was not the naïve liberal that proponents of black power accused him of being. That he believed deeply in the possibility of "black and white together" and the ringing promises of the Declaration of Independence is clear enough. Bitter experience (especially in Chicago) convinced him that the struggle would be a very long one. In an August, 1967, speech, he said: "I am sorry to have to say that the vast majority of white Americans are racists, either consciously or unconsciously."

This being the case, why would nonviolent protest even work? Dyson appears to accept the view that King began to use Gandhian strategies more for tactical considerations than on the basis of principle, departing from the latter's emphasis on the need for means to be as pure as the ends they serve. If true, King would indeed be a radical—a radical who compromised his deepest principles.

Discussing King's early opposition to the Vietnam War (beginning in the spring of 1965) and its increasing intensity until his martyrdom in 1968, Dyson strengthens the image of King's radicalism. King had everything to lose here. His chief opponent was none other than the greatest benefactor African Americans had ever known: Lyndon B. Johnson. Both Johnson's advisers and King's associates urged him to stay out of foreign policy. The attacks on him by the established press were relentless and hurtful.

However, as Dyson shows, King saw that the war and the struggles of black folk could not be separated: War spending cut into the Great Society, and black soldiers were vastly overrepresented in combat units. Further, the war could not pass the "just war" standards articulated by generations of Christian ethicists and therefore threatened the entire nation's moral health. Dyson reminds readers that King "could not encourage black youth to avoid violence while condoning its use in Vietnam, a contradiction many youths readily cited when King came crusading in their burned up ghettos."

The titles of chapters 4 and 5—"America Must Move Toward a Democratic Socialism: A Progressive Social Blueprint" and "We Did Engage in a Black Power Move: An Integrationist Embraces Enlightened Black Nationalism"— nicely reveal Dyson's strategy. Dyson's King emerges as one who became committed to a transformed economic system requiring massive transfers of wealth to the poor—without sacrificing democratic procedures and traditions. King also clearly heard what those standing in the nationalist tradition of Marcus Garvey were saying: that integration into a white world is impossible because African Americans are a separate (if humiliated) people with a world of their own to build.

Dyson succeeds brilliantly in showing the complex terrain through which King had to march. Since his early campaigns coincided with the McCarthy era, King could always be labeled "Communist" by his opponents—the most virulent being J. Edgar Hoover and the Federal Bureau of Investigation (FBI). King, therefore, always had to be circumspect about his views of capitalism and the sources of poverty. However, as his victories mounted in the battle over voting and legal segregation, King turned increasingly to the plight of black farmers, workers, and, indeed, poor Americans as such. Tellingly, at the time of his assassination, he was supporting striking garbage workers and laying plans for the Poor People's Campaign.

For Dyson, this leftward turn means that Jesse Helms was right in labeling King an "action-oriented Marxist," but only if King is thought of as one who "appreciated Marx's insights about class and economic inequality and, more important, *put them into practice*, without being a communist."

Our media-enhanced fascination with scandal means that most readers will read chapters 7 through 10 first. Here is where Dyson confronts King's history of plagiarism, sexual misconduct, and patriarchy. Given that Dyson aims to demonstrate King's status as the greatest American, he might have been expected to be less than candid here. On the contrary: He seems determined to hunt down every last rumor and anecdote. One of his motives is to allow hip-hop culture to finally dialogue with the world of King. Thus, Dyson writes, "The bitter truth is that at a certain level, Snoop Doggy Dogg wants what Martin Luther King, Jr., enjoyed: sexual freedom. Because of King, Snoop can now choose to say so."

The "sexual personae in the revolution" King presented were complex. On one level, he was the unbridled womanizer, cheating on Coretta Scott just before their marriage; having countless liaisons, even at times when such actions jeopardized the movement; and rendezvousing with at least two women on the night before his assassination at the Lorraine Motel. In this area, he was, indeed, everything his bitterest foe said he was (since Hoover was a thoroughly promiscuous gay male, one wonders what his indictment really meant).

King knew his actions were despicable and was tormented by guilt. Dyson does not excuse King because of this. He does sort through a number of salient factors, however. With the success of the Montgomery bus boycott, King became the appointed savior of his race at the age of twenty-seven. From then on, he was in perpetual danger and constantly on the road raising money for his campaigns. Anxiety (often depression) and loneliness assailed him. His relationship with Coretta was never ideal, as she sought to have a role in the struggle, too, and exhibited an assertiveness that made King deeply uncomfortable. Very patriarchal (like most civil rights heroes), King had the additional problem of freeing himself from his own mother's influence. In the words of Andrew Young, "Martin's problem in the early days of the movement was directly related to his need to be free of that strong maternal influence."

Dyson also points out that King's sexual excesses "grew in part out of a subculture of promiscuity that is rampant among clergy and religious figures in every faith." (Temptation is probably greater in the black church because of the huge disproportion between females and males—something to which Dyson only alludes.) In addition, King, like the rappers Dyson wants to relate him to, became an overnight international superstar and "a sexual magnet for women of every race . . . who longed to bask in his limelight and in his affectionate, lustful embrace." Most persuasive, however, is the fact that more than any other black leader, King had to fashion the persona of "the good, upstanding Negro, the shining embodiment of black perfection, the exemplary exhorter of moral excellence."

In the middle of his trysts he would say, "I'm not a Negro tonight." He was, rather, the man first revealed in Ralph David Abernathy's biography—a cut-up, jokester, lewd talker, jive master—in short, a "natural man." So, "King's chronic womanizing was a complex affair that allowed him at once to reinforce his ministerial machismo, satisfy his lust, assuage his loneliness, temper his fear of death, provisionally escape his burden of racial representation, and

reduce his anxieties." Dyson provides no excuses for his hero here, deploring especially his dismissive attitude toward the possibility of female leadership and basic equality. He also condemns "the violence, misogyny and vulgarity that for many youths marks 'real' black identity." He sees in this tragic flaw a way to make King truly available to young black people—the means to a renewed conversation on the sexual devastations wrought on black people by whites and by themselves through the persistence of misogynistic messages in hip-hop culture.

By the end of *I May Not Get There with You,* few topics related to Martin Luther King Jr., remain open for exploration. The quality of his patriotism, the attempts by many to commodify him, the continuing controversies about how to mark the King holiday, the "resistant amnesia" that prevents a majority of Americans from facing up to slavery—all of these are treated. This is exactly what blemishes a book that is, in most respects, a major contribution and an intellectual tour de force. Dyson has too much to say, indulges too many ideas, preaches too hard, takes on too many issues, and coins too many phrases.

His passion and the provocative character of his ideas make the book's excessiveness more forgivable. Nevertheless, one wants more analysis trained on fewer issues. For example, the weakest chapter in the book is certainly the one on King's Christian faith. A scant thirteen pages, it is as much a lament about the misfortunes of the National Baptist Convention under the disgraced Henry Lyons as it is about King's religious development. That King had to establish his views on nonviolence against the background of Reinhold Niebuhr's pessimistic assessment of such strategies meant that King necessarily dealt with human sin in a very nuanced way. It seems especially surprising that Dyson, a minister himself, covers so little theology in a book about a man for whom theology was breath itself. Yet many will feel that Dyson has produced a book that everyone with the slightest concern about race in this country must take into account.

Tears We Cannot Stop

In *Tears We Cannot Stop: A Sermon to White America,* Dyson delivers a dose of tough love to white America. He adopts the format of a sermon—a challenging yet surprisingly effective strategy. While Dyson is not always successful in defining his audience and making his ideas fit his chosen structure, his address enables a powerful personal voice to come through and includes valuable practical examples toward the book's end.

The book is divided into nine parts that correspond to the stages of the type of Christian sermons that Dyson has long preached, beginning with the "Call to Worship" and ending with a "Closing Prayer." In the opening section, Dyson explains that he tried to write a more traditional book based on analysis and scholarship, but he kept failing. He describes being called, instead, to write a sermon, arguing that "if we stick with the sermon—through its pitiless recall of our sin, its relentless indictment of our flaws—we can make it to the uplifting expression and redeeming practices that make our faith flow from the pulpit to the public, from darkness to light." Faithful to the form, he does, indeed, deliver "pitiless recall" and "relentless indictment," as he rails against the ideology and practice of whiteness as an evil that simply will not die because white people refuse to let it go.

Many readers may be shocked at his blunt statements, such as that "there is no such thing as white people" (because, as he argues, race is an invented construct) and that "you are emotionally immature about race." Equally likely to shock is his explanation that African Americans feel so terrorized in the United States that they

perceive the police in the way that many white Americans perceive the terrorist group Islamic State of Iraq and Syria (ISIS). Expiation requires waking up and repenting, and Dyson knows how to get there.

Getting there, in part, requires a personal address, and this is one of the book's most notable features. That Dyson chooses to write to and for "white America" should not be taken for granted. One of the great developments in late twentieth-century African American literature was its focus on black readers. Writer Toni Morrison, who won the Nobel Prize for literature in 1993, declared that she has always written specifically about and for African Americans. This is not to say that white readers are discouraged from reading, but, rather, that she does not write primarily for their benefit. This shift proved to be revolutionary because, by claiming this freedom, Morrison vastly expanded the imaginative limits of fiction about African American life and culture. It became possible to tell the truth about race in America in new and perhaps more healing ways. The early twenty-first century brings an old set of challenges with new awareness, as racial injustice and tensions continue to plague the nation and technology and politics enable wider awareness of key issues such as police brutality. In this moment, Dyson uses a sermon to speak directly to white readers about their stubborn resistance to the ideology of whiteness. The direct address is thus a gift but also implies the existence of readers who will listen. Most importantly, it allows Dyson to speak hard truths directly to those who need to hear it.

This surprising rhetorical strategy, however, could prove to be tricky for some readers. To address "white America," Dyson must make assumptions about his audience, and the general assumption is of a reader who is largely ignorant about matters of race and about black life and culture. Thus, Dyson assumes that his audience does not know, for example, that Martin Luther King Jr. did not simply advocate peace and racial unity but also held radical views; for example, his opposition to the Vietnam War and his growing emphasis, toward the end of his life, on the scourge of poverty in America. Many of Dyson's white readers do know this, and they also know that whiteness is an invented ideology, which Dyson acknowledges, but he insists that knowing is not enough. "Yet you also know that whiteness for the most part remains invisible to many white folk," he argues. His point, therefore, is that white people must act on their knowledge to a greater extent than they have.

Yet Dyson's definition of his audience is sometimes uneven. While he sometimes assumes very little knowledge on the part of the audience, at other times he makes statements that would baffle such readers. For example, when discussing the O. J. Simpson trial, he compares Simpson's behavior to that of Clarence Thomas, saying, "Even Clarence Thomas is blacker than O. J.," before writing, "But Thomas was reviled by black culture for his dark skin." Here, he gets into the politics of skin color and victimhood within the black community. If white readers do not know some of the basics of racism, as Dyson assumes, statements like this will likely confuse such readers. This unevenness might be less problematic if readers consider that Dyson directs his rhetoric to white America as an ideology, which includes individual readers but does not necessarily rigidly define them. He addresses the collective behaviors of a group and their pernicious effects while urging individuals to take to heart his call for action.

The effect of the sermon structure is also more successful in some sections than in others. In the section "Hymns of Praise," the praise is directed not toward God but toward popular singers such as KRS-One, Lauryn Hill, Tupac Shakur, Jay Z, Beyoncé, and Kendrick Lamar. Dyson describes them as "our griots" who "answer the reign of terror that consumes our days." This rhetorical twist is refreshing, as Dyson praises the artists engaging in necessary protest, but some readers may object to the linking of such music, with its at times graphic and offensive language, to a traditionally religious form. The second chapter of the fifth section, titled "Sermon," outlines the "five stages of white racial grief." These include pleading ignorance about black life and culture, denial, appropriation, revising racial history, and diluting the effects of race.

Most importantly, Dyson makes many excellent, subtle points in this chapter, such as his distinction between freedom of expression and appropriation, a difficult concept for even the most well-intentioned white readers. He also explains why the claim of "not seeing color" is actually an expression of privilege and the damage done by those who would revise racial history (such as the claim that the Civil War was not about slavery but about defending states' rights). Similarly, he argues forcefully that those who balk at affirmative action must realize that white people have enjoyed de facto affirmative action for centuries. Yet, it is not at all clear why these "stages" are ordered as such, and Dyson offers no explanation of them as a larger process. Rather, these acts seem to represent some of the most prevalent and enduring racist behaviors. Nonetheless, he ends the chapter with an exhortation ringing with clarity, telling white people to "give up myths about yourself, about your history. That you are resolutely individual, and not part of a group. That you pulled yourselves up by your bootstraps." Such powerful messages make up for the structural deficit.

Ultimately, Dyson's message is that the solution is love, not hateful vengeance. He makes this clear when he eloquently writes, "The idolatry of whiteness and the cloak of innocence that shields it can only be quenched by love—a public expression of love that holds us all accountable. Justice is what love sounds like when it speaks in public." Despite—or perhaps because of—the anger that infuses Dyson's frank words, he is able to see past the rage and despair to a solution. But first, he asks readers to share the pain of the racism he has endured. His sermon format and direct address to the reader allow him to share personal stories—many truly shocking—of the profound damage that racism has inflicted on him and on black communities. He tells of the first time, as a seven-year-old, that he was referred to in racist terms and denied service in a roadside restaurant; of being pulled over by the police after disciplining his child; of being refused service and publicly humiliated at his own bank; of having police brutally threaten to kill him for no reason; and of the stream of deeply disturbing, profanity-laced hate mail he receives on a regular basis (of which he includes specific and therefore especially effective examples). The stories are heartbreaking and enraging. They also inspire deep sympathy and help readers to seriously consider the practical suggestions that Dyson presents in his final chapters.

These suggestions, in the "Benediction" section of the sermon, are perhaps the most helpful part of the book for sympathetic readers, as Dyson offers concrete ideas for how to examine beliefs and take action. While his suggestion for this seems somewhat forced, the suggestions are inspiring. Dyson believes that, even if the government fails to make reparations for the enduring damage caused by centuries of slavery, white individuals can do so in many ways, such as by paying black professionals a bit more for their services, donating scholarship money for students and to summer camps, sponsoring school trips for black children, and so forth. He also urges white people to educate themselves about black life and culture and provides a

reading list to help people get started. At the same time, he insists that white people must also educate others, participate in rallies and events, make friends with black people, speak up about injustice, and so forth.

This practical section tempers the sense of shock and outrage that some readers may experience earlier in the book and communicates that Dyson's direct address to "white America" is not something he uses as a convenient rhetorical strategy. The title *Tears We Cannot Stop* becomes a literal exhortation to white Americans to put an end to the violence that Dyson and other African Americans have endured their entire lives. By the end of the book, he has shown that his sermon does far more than lament and pray—he is in this journey of healing for the long haul.

Other Literary Forms

Although Dyson is known mostly for his nonfiction prose, he has a strong interest in popular music and popular culture, especially television, on which he has appeared many times as a commentator and interviewee.

Bibliography

Dyson, Michael Eric. "The Ghost of Cornel West." *The New Republic* 19 Apr. 2015: n.p. https://newrepublic.com/article/121550/cornel-wests-rise-fall-our-most-exciting-black-scholar-ghost. Dyson discusses his early life, his early admiration for Cornel West, and his later disagreements with West about the presidency of Barack Obama.

Griffin, Paul R. "A Question of Academic Integrity." *Diverse: Issues in Higher Education* 22, no. 19 (3 Nov. 2005): n. p. Asserts that Dyson is more a media figure than a serious intellectual and claims that his supposed shallowness as a thinker brings discredit to the field of black studies and to the real academics who possess the kind of in-depth knowledge Dyson allegedly lacks.

Jones, Meta DuEwa. "An Interview with Michael Eric Dyson." *Callaloo* 29, no. 3 (2006): 786-802. A detailed interview covering such topics as folk literature; folk poetry; folk song; rap music; and African Americans.

Kelley, Robin D. G. "'P.P.P.C.' in Blackademe." *The Nation* 257, no. 9 (27 Sep. 1993): 320-23. An early positive assessment of Dyson as a public intellectual who writes for a wide audience.

McWhorter, John. "Something 2 Die 4?" *The New Republic* 225, no. 17 (22 Oct. 2011): 30-36. While reviewing a book in which Dyson celebrates Tupac Shakur and other rap singers, McWhorter, an African American scholar, writes, "We decry the criminalization of black men, the racialization of poverty, the subtle diminishment of black boys in schools, the high rate of teen pregnancy among young black women—but most black Americans under forty, regardless of class, income, or educational attainment, see a stirring reflection of their identities in a music that celebrates poor, violent, and woman-hating young black men as heroes." McWhorter suggests that most consumers of rap music are young whites who unfortunately form their images of African Americans from such music.

— *Ashleigh Imus; Leslie E. Gerber;*
W. P. Kenney; Robert C. Evans

Cornelius Eady

Poet

Born: Rochester, New York; January 7, 1954

DRAMA: *Running Man*, pr. 1999 (libretto).

POETRY: *Kartunes*, 1980; *Victims of the Latest Dance Craze*, 1985; *BOOM BOOM BOOM*, 1988 (limited edition chapbook); *The Gathering of My Name*, 1991; *You Don't Miss Your Water*, 1995; *The Autobiography of a Jukebox*, 1996; *Brutal Imagination*, 2001; *Hardheaded Weather: New and Selected Poems*, 2008; *Book of Hooks*, 2013; *Singing While Black*, 2015.

EDITED TEXTS: *Words for Breakfast*, 1998 (with Meg Kearney, Norma Fox Mazer, and Jacqueline Woodson); *Vinyl Donuts*, 2000 (with Kearney, Mazer, and Woodson); *Gathering Ground: A Reader Celebrating Cave Canem's First Decade* (with Toi Derricotte).

Achievements

Cornelius Eady emerged within the first generation of African American poets to succeed the formidable work of the Black Arts movement of the mid-twentieth century. That literary movement, an extension of the era's Civil Rights movement, created new interest in black identity. Eady continued that exploration, using his own working-class upbringing and his position as a black poet in late twentieth century America. That compelling honesty, coupled with his experiments in the sheer music of language, has garnered Eady two nominations for the Pulitzer Prize; in addition to *Running Man*, *The Gathering of My Name* was nominated for the poetry prize. *Victims of the Latest Dance Craze* was given the Lamont Prize from the Academy of American Poets in 1985. A career academic, Eady has received fellowships from the Guggenheim Foundation (1993), the National Endowment for the Arts (1985), the Rockefeller Foundation (1993), and the Lila Wallace-Reader's Digest Foundation (1992-1993).

Biography

Born in Rochester, New York, Cornelius Eady began writing poems when he was only twelve. As chronicled in *You Don't Miss Your Water*, Eady's father posed a formidable emotional problem. High-school educated, the father, employed by the city water department, had difficulty accepting literature as a valid vocation. Consequently, Eady would struggle with feelings of estrangement until his father's death in 1993. After graduating from Empire State College and then earning his M.F.A. from Warren Wilson College, Eady held teaching appointments at Sweet Briar College, the College of William and Mary, Sarah Lawrence College, Tougaloo College, and City College of New York. While at the State University of New York at Stony Brook in the 1990s, he served as director of its famous poetry center. In 1999, Eady became distinguished writer-in-residence in the M.F.A. program at New York City's innovative New School. In 1996, along with poet Toi Derricotte, Eady founded the Cave Canem (literally, "Beware of the Dog"), a popular program of summer workshops for African American poets.

Photo courtesy of Slowking

He has taught at the University of Notre Dame and also holds the Miller Chair in Poetry at the University of Missouri.

Analysis: Poetry

Cornelius Eady's poetry concerns the construction of identity, the dynamics of memory and reflection as part of the interrogation of the self, and the importance of recording that complex process. Like the blues, Eady's poetry centers on the struggle to define the isolated self within a chaotic world that harbors little possibility for redemption. Yet, like jazz, Eady's poetry also responds to a world that, given its essential unpredictability, can sustain authentic ecstasy. That texture, the self sustained between sadness and exuberance, is central to Eady's work. His poetry explores the roles he himself has played in the construction of his own identity. Not surprisingly, over the time Eady has been writing, this interrogation of the self has become more complex. Initially, Eady explored his role as urban poet; later, he examined more complex relational roles, that of husband, lover, teacher, and, supremely, son; he later began to confront his role as an African American, specifically the struggle to construct a viable black self amid the historical and social pressures of late-twentieth century America.

The poetic line for such an investigation into the self is appropriately individual and resists conventional expectations of structure and sound. Rhythmic but not metric, Eady's lines can appear deceptively simple, direct, even conversational. However, it is freedom within a tightly manipulated form. Like improvisational jazz, which can, at first hearing, seem easy and effortless, Eady's poetry is a complex aural event. His poems consciously manipulate sounds, unexpected syncopations and cadences, enjambment, irregular spacings and emphasis, line length, and sound repetition to create an air of improvisation that is nevertheless a carefully textured sonic weave.

Kartunes

Kartunes is a portrait of the self as young poet, an exercise in testing the reach of the imagination and celebrating the role of a cocksure poet responding originally to the world. "I want to be fresh," he proclaims, "I want words/ to tumble off my lips/ rich enough/ to fertilize/ the ground." Giddy with imaginative possibilities, Eady improvises his narrative "I" into outlandish personas (the "cartoons" suggested by the title), many culled from pop culture: He is at turns an inept terrorist, a nerdy librarian, an unhappy woman forced into a witness protection program, a dying philanthropist anxious about the approaching afterlife, a man contemplating torching his own house, the legendary Headless Horseman selecting the appropriate pumpkin to hurtle, Popeye's nemesis Bluto groomed for a date, even Adolf Hitler posing before a mirror and dreaming of greatness.

Given such wild fluctuations in the narrative center, the poetry is given over to irreverent exuberance. Despite often centering on alienated characters existing within a contemporary environment of absurdity and brutality, the poems resist surrendering to emotional heaviness. The poems, themselves innovative in structure and sound (witness the wordplay of the collection's title), offer as resolutions the sheer animation of the engaged imagination, the possibility of love, and the ability of the world to stun with its unchoreographed wonder. With the confident insouciance of a young man, Eady argues that nothing is nobler than "laughing/ when nothing/ is funny anymore."

Victims of the Latest Dance Craze

The interest in defining the poet and that confident sense of play animates Eady's follow-up collection, thematically centered on the metaphor of the dance. Here the world is in constant motion—the title poem, for example, details a pulsating urban neighborhood. Like William Carlos Williams (whose influence Eady has acknowledged), the poet responds to the seductive suasion of the world that too often goes unnoticed—to a cloud passing overhead, crows battling a strong wind, a waitress's purple nail polish, the leaden feel of November, the faint stirrings of April: "an entire world," he trumpets, "on the tip of my tongue." To respond to that world is to dance, a suggestive metaphor for the body's irresistible, spontaneous response to being alive, the electric moment of the "hands . . . / Accidentally brush[ing] against the skirts of the world." Such animation, makes problematic the life of the poet so vital in *Kartunes.*

In the closing poem, "Dance at the Amherst County Public Library," the poet describes himself as a "dancing fool who couldn't stay away from words." He concedes his jealousy over those who live so effortlessly and of his own poor efforts to capture secondhand that rich experience within his poetry, his "small graffiti dance." Yet the poetic lines here boldly strive to match the urgent call to respond originally to the world, capturing the improvisational feel of jazz: irregular patterning of lines, multiple stops and starts, a delightful matching of sounds, and wildly unanticipated rhythms.

The Gathering of My Name

In Eady's ambitious third major collection, the tone considerably darkens as jazz gives way to the slower pull of the blues. In the opening poem, "Gratitude," Eady audaciously proffers love to those who have not welcomed him nor his poetry and confesses his greatest weakness is his "inability/ to sustain rage." It is a familiar brashness, and, indeed, the second poem ("Grace") offers one of those unexpected moments when the world sparkles: the sight of the neighborhood reflected in the waxed hood of a black sedan.

Yet quickly the poems concede to a more disturbing world that crushes dreams and sours love. For the first time, Eady addresses race. Poems introduce figures such as the tormented blues singer Leadbelly or jazz great John Coltrane in the aftermath of the 1963 bombing of a Baptist church in Birmingham, Alabama. In others, a waitress in Virginia refuses to serve a black man, a passing motorist hurls racial epithets at a black man's white wife, a car breaks down in the "wrong" neighborhood. Like the blues, these are poems of pain and bad luck, the curse of awareness, the dilemma of disappointment, and the need to define the self in a harsh world. What is the poet to do? "Get it all out," Eady demands in "The Sheets of Sounds," the remarkable closing piece that is a tour de force of metrical audacity. Here, Eady captures in language the technical virtuosity and improvisational sound of Coltrane himself: "What do I have to lose,/ Actually,/ By coming right out/ And saying/ What I mean/ To say?" Honesty then compels the poet/jazz artist to let loose the spirit in all its outrage, to push art if only for a moment into uncompromising expression, the "loud humility" of a man giving himself the right to claim, as a refrain insists with typographical variations: "This is who I am."

You Don't Miss Your Water

Appropriately, then, in Eady's fourth collection readers feel (for the first time in his work) the nearness of the poet himself. Dropping his elaborate personas, Eady speaks forthrightly of his own life. The twenty-one prose poems are stark narratives without poetic frills and without clean chronological sequencing. The reader is given an unblinking record of a son's estrangement from a father in the face of mortality, the honest struggle to come to terms with the difficult wisdom of the blues lines, "You don't miss your water/ 'til your well runs dry." Eady refuses to sentimentalize the father (he is at turns miserly, stubborn, distant, even unfaithful) or himself (he cremates the body to save money), or even death (he records the indignities of hospital treatment and the impersonal efficiency of agencies that manage the paperwork). Titles recall traditional blues songs, and the mood is elegiac, sobering, eloquent: "This is how life, sharpened to a fine point, plunges into what we call hope."

If Eady's first three volumes speak of how the imagination takes hold of the world and shapes individual identity, here he acknowledges the depth of the inevitable experience of loss and how that experience is as well part of any construction of identity. In the volume's rich closing poem, "Paradiso," Eady decides that language

itself, disparaged in his earlier work as second-hand graffiti, is the sole conjurer of the afterlife, that the "key to any heaven is language."

The Autobiography of a Jukebox

The Autobiography of a Jukebox is a kind of summary text. It is divided into four sections, each of which centers on themes drawn from earlier works: the heavy intrusion of loss; the ugly realities of racism; the glorious transcendence of art, specifically jazz, within this environment of oppression; and those small unexpected moments that trigger deep emotional responses and make such a world endurable. The volume begins where *You Don't Miss Your Water* ends: dealing with harsh loss—indeed, opening poems linger within recollections of Eady's father. With bluesy feel, other poems follow characters who discover the wounding of love, the certainty of bad luck, and the humiliations of poverty.

In the second section, Eady confronts the angry indignation over the 1991 beating of citizen Rodney King by Los Angeles police officers, the federal trial in which the white officers were acquitted, and the riots that followed. It is Eady's first lengthy examination of the social dimension of the self and specifically how black identity must be defined within an oppressive white culture. To maintain dignity and to touch grace within such an environment, Eady offers in the third section portraits of jazz artists (and pioneer rocker Chuck Berry), black musicians who forged from such oppression the stuff of their art: "What/Hurts is beautiful, the bruise/ Of the lyric" However, it is not sufficient simply to relish such aesthetic artifacts.

In the closing section Eady quietly affirms what his first two volumes trumpeted: the imagination's ability to be stunned by the accidental encounter with something that triggers a minor epiphany in a flawed world that still permits awe—a woman with dreadlocks crossing a street, a tray of cornbread at a posh reception, the electric flow of an urban mall, the tangy smells of a bakery. Yet, hard on the death of Eady's father and the anger over the King beating, these slender moments of grace are suddenly significant in ways the earlier volumes could not suggest.

Brutal Imagination

In *Brutal Imagination* Eady's career-long interest in defining the self takes on new maturity as he projects himself, within two unrelated poem cycles, out of the matrix of his own experience. In the first section Eady conjures the spirit, and voice, of the black kidnapper that mother Susan Smith invented as an alibi to cover the 1994 murder of her two infant sons. Eady uses that lie to investigate the white culture of anger, bigotry, and anxiety within which all black identity must be fashioned. In a biting middle section, Eady suggests the dimensions of this dilemma by giving voice to the sorry racist stereotypes fashioned by a white imagination unwilling to grant blacks the dignity and complexity of legitimate selfhood: Uncle Tom, Uncle Ben, Aunt Jemina, Buckwheat, Stepin Fetchit. The faux-kidnapper—witty, articulate, probing, caring—dominates the cycle and, specifically, the symbiotic relationship between Smith and her invention, Eady suggesting how necessary the black stereotype is for whites. In the closing poem, "Birthing," which draws excerpts from Smith's actual confession, the conjured kidnapper extends compassion to the mother, imagining the actual killing and the desperate loneliness of Smith herself driven to do the unimaginable.

The second section contains pieces from the libretto of *Running Man*. Although offered without the haunting jazz score of the original production and without the dramatic interplay of performance, the pieces nevertheless succeed in a conjuring of a sort far different from Susan Smith's. A southern black family, devastated by the death of its only son, struggles to explain why such a promising young man succumbed to the very life of crime that made credible the vicious lie of Susan Smith. Within the interplay of their elegiac recollections, the poetic line tightly clipped for maximum effect, the young man himself is conjured and speaks of his own promise lost to the anger of limited social expectations within the white system and to the easy out of drug addiction and crime. He is the "running man" never sure where he was running from or to: "Where I come from/ A smart black boy/ Is like being a cat/ With a duck's bill." Chained to history—the cycle begins in an old slave cemetery—blacks, whatever their talent or aspirations, must withstand the larger predatory white culture that can leave them helpless, like "fish, scooped from a pond." It is a powerful assessment of black identity at the twentieth century's close.

The Autobiography of a Jukebox

The Autobiography of a Jukebox consists of four parts: "Home Front," "Rodney King Blues," "The Bruise of the Lyric," and "Small Moments." While the poems could easily be read as autobiographical scenes, they may also be somewhat fictionalized. The poems are written in free verse and produce strongly focused images. They describe women coping with the tensions of economic concerns and emotionally unstable relationships; a cousin who is a "crackhead"; a woman who begs in a dangerous part of town for shopping money; and a father who loves the poet's sister so much that he must beat her with a belt. This paternal ambivalence echoes when the father also fells a large tree that, the mother says, may have invaded the foundations of their house. The poems offer no answers and no analyses; they draw readers into reflection upon such ambivalence.

The rest of the poetry in "Home Front" deals with relationships. The father threatens to leave. The mother and sister do indeed, and the narrator speculates about feelings that his father does not show when he sees the empty house. Two poems focus on men standing up for themselves. The speaker's father responds to a racially charged incident, and his grandfather calmly stands on his own land with shotgun in hand while resisting the badgering of officials. Such actions also explain the hardness of the characters.

Several poems in "Rodney King Blues" reveal the narrator's feelings of anger about the beating of Rodney King by Los Angeles police officers in 1991 and about the riots that broke out in 1992 after the officers were tried and found not guilty. The poems also deal with people who lost property to the riots, a truck driver who was assaulted by a mob during the riots, double-talk that sought to justify the officer's actions, and the helpless feeling of being a victim in the inner city. Eady isolates from these events several sharply focused scenes whose verisimilitude pulls readers into the genuine turmoil of life without engaging in tedious moralizing.

"The Bruise of the Lyric" introduces pictures of musical artists, each one drawn in words. John Coltrane and Kenny Burrell's jazz piece "Why Was I Born?" is redrawn in Eady's words. Percussionist Max Roach is pictured in words. "Miles Davis at Lennies-on-the-Turnpike" contains the memorable words "Death is one hell/ Of a pickpocket." Eady commemorates Dexter Gordon's saxophone, Milt Jackson's vibraphone, Eric Dolphy's saxophone, and Chuck Berry's "frenzy of the word go"—in the singer's "Johnny B. Goode"—as well as his jukebox point of view in "Roll Over Beethoven."

"Small Moments" builds details taken from everyday life into reflections about poetry. One poem focuses on the image of a young white woman in dreadlocks; the next follows the narrator's evolving hairstyles, from "nappy," to Afro, to "relaxed," to "vengeful" dreadlocks, to a barber alienated by the confrontation with "urban steel wool" and "industrial-strength kink." The other poems in this section reflect upon poetry. Like Eady's work, Charles Simic's poems focus on sharp images. In "Cornbread," the narrator finds cornbread at a poetry reading by Charles Simic, a connection that may be self-reflective. Particularly interesting is Eady's reference to Walt Whitman, who, Eady says, should have seen some of his posthumous success as a poet. Several poems in this section also reflect on the altered experience of self and others when poets extricate themselves from the American environment and see themselves in the context of Europe.

The first poem of "Home Front" focuses on mother and father, a focus that is generalized as the predicament of women seeking security from emotionally unstable men. The man the speaker's mother turned down "made my father look good,/ That's how bad it was." The poem's characters are forced to choose between bad alternatives. Vacant gaps of emotion are filled with the caulk of religion: "Jesus, the man my daddy once saw/ Lying next to her/ On her old army cot." Enmity characterizes the relationship between the genders. The mother wins at a lottery; the father and a cousin pick up the winnings; the mother loses the money to the two, and she acquires a pervasive and lasting feeling of having been cheated. In "The Yankee Dollar," the mother expects to receive royalties from a book she wrote. She distrusts all offers of temporary financial help to keep her afloat until the royalties arrive, even an offer from her son. She distrusts "male money," because such money represents male control over her.

"The House," a poem that represents the enmity between the sexes from the male perspective, comments:

By then he was
A pensioner,
Who would spend his days
Asleep in a Cadillac
To escape his wife
A woman who would
Glower at him . . .
Wondering when he
Was going to give
Her life back

In another strong image, the narrator's mother falls to her knees at the welfare office because something has gone wrong, a circumstance that the poem's five-or six-year-old speaker is too young to understand. Patterns repeat themselves for the sister: "Old, and toothless, he's the man who helps her to pay her bills." The sister's only alternative is to go back home to a father whose controlling behavior is equally undesirable.

"I Want to Fly Like Superman" is about a little girl who has been told that no one wants her, her mother having abandoned her for Florida. The little girl jumps off the garage. She survives the fall to tell how much she would have liked to have bled to death on the pavement. "She will learn that the main rule of this family is: there is no obligation to save a fool." Eady creates an unbearable tension between the compassion one has for the girl and the hardness of circumstances.

"Rodney King Blues" begins with a dramatic monologue by a cab driver, praising the United States. Even Timothy Leary, the cabbie insists, returned after a short while living abroad. He says that beggars are simply lazy people who should be banished from the country, so they will understand how good their life in the United States actually is. The rant of prejudice and misinformation culminates in the lines: "I don't hold nothin'/ Against no one./ Hey, I picked you up," alluding to the African American identity of the hearer.

"I'll Fly Away" is a poem included in "Small Moments." In it, a young African American man in Venice, Italy, loses a coin. A white woman picks it up to hand back to him. The scene paralyzes the young man, as he interprets it through the cognitive dissonance of his memory. He recognizes that what is innocent in Venice is fraught with dangerous meaning back home in the United States.

Eady's sharp scenes and images from ordinary life give readers a very clear view of the realities of African American experience. Many poems focus on the ambivalences of family life, as the poet's affectionate sensitivity wavers and vacillates between sundry attentions. These scenes from everyday life are also generalized and so take on more general meaning for humanity. All the poems of "Home Front" give voice to the human experience of poverty, and the pressures of economic reality on family life are experienced by many people outside the African American community. "Rodney King Blues" and "The Bruise of the Lyric" are most clearly related to African American experience. While "Rodney King Blues" addresses the blatant injustice in the distribution of wealth and resources for African Americans, "The Bruise of the Lyric" celebrates the tremendous contribution of African Americans to cultural experience throughout the world. Eady explores his poetry, his identity, and his metamorphosed sense of self in "Small Moments," concluding the section self-consciously by considering the meaning and significance of the poetic art.

Eady has created for himself a lasting place in African American literature, but his sharp imagery also reaches beyond that literature to the larger literary canon. Already noteworthy, his poetry will become increasingly important as it gains recognition and depth. The poems celebrate African American experience—in the family, in society, in culture, and in poetic practice and identity—thereby broadening the scope and understanding of that experience.

Other Literary Forms

Given his willingness to experiment with bringing to the written word the rhythms of both jazz and blues and his belief in poetry as performed (that is, heard) art, it is not surprising that Cornelius Eady has produced two experimental theater pieces, part of a projected trilogy for the New York City-based Music-Theater Group, both of which involved original scores written by jazz cellist and longtime friend Diedre L. Murray. The first production, in 1997, was a staged recitation based on *You Don't Miss Your Water,* Eady's cycle of prose poems that recounts his father's death. In 1999 Eady provided the libretto for an experimental jazz opera based on the story of Murray's brother, a gifted man lost to a life of crime and heroin addiction. That production, *Running Man,* won two Obie Awards and was shortlisted for both the New York Drama Critics Circle Award and the Pulitzer Prize. In 2001, *Brutal Imagination* was a finalist for the National Book Award in Poetry.

Bibliography

Carroll, Rebecca. *Swing Low: Black Men Writing.* New York: Carol Southern Books, 1995. This book features interviews with sixteen authors along with excerpts from their work. Included are Eady, Charles Johnson, Yusef Komunyakaa, Ishmael Reed, and August Wilson.

Eady, Cornelius. "Cornelius Eady." Interview by Patricia Spears Jones. *BOMB* 79 (Spring, 2002): 48-54. Discusses the relationship between Eady's poetry and classical Greek theater.

Eady, Cornelius. "Cornelius Eady: Lyric and Dramatic Imagination." Interview by Reamy Jansen. *The Bloomsbury Review* 22, no. 1 (January/February, 2002): 3-11. Includes a useful discussion of Eady's purpose in the "Small Moments" section of *The Autobiography of a Jukebox.*

Harper, Michael S., and Anthony Walton, eds. *Every Shut Eye Ain't Asleep: An Anthology of Poetry by African Americans Since 1945.* Boston: Little, Brown, 1994. Contains a selection of Eady's poetry with brief critical commentary within an anthology of Eady's generation of African American poets.

Hawkins, Shayla. "Cave Canem: A Haven for Black Poets." *Poets & Writers* 29, no. 2 (March/April, 2001): 48-53. Discusses the Cave Canem workshop and retreat founded by Eady and Toi Derricotte. Eady and Derricotte recognized the need for a "haven" for black writers.

Peters, Erskine. "Cornelius Eady's *You Don't Miss Your Water*: Its Womanist/Feminist Perspective." *Journal of African American Men* 2, no. 1 (Summer, 1996): 15-31. Discusses Eady through the lens of African American feminism (a branch of feminism for which Alice Walker coined the phrase "womanist").

Quashie, Kevin Everod. "Cornelius Eady." In *New Bones: Contemporary Black Writers in America,* edited by Joyce Lausch, Keith Miller, and Quashie. Saddle River, N.J.: Prentice-Hall, 2001. A helpful overview of Eady's career. The introduction assesses issues and themes of Eady's generation.

Tretheway, Natasha. "About Cornelius Eady." *Ploughshares* 28, no. 1 (Spring, 2002): 193-198. Gives a good overview of Eady's family and educational history and career highlights.

Young, Kevin, ed. *Giant Steps: The New Generation of African-American Writers.* New York: Perennial, 2000. A comprehensive introduction to Eady's generation.

—Joseph Dewey; Reinhold Schlieper;
Robert C. Evans

Lonne Elder III

Playwright and Screenwriter

Born: Americus, Georgia; December 26, 1931

Died: Woodland Hills, California; June 11, 1996

DRAMA: *Ceremonies in Dark Old Men*, pr. 1965, revised pr., pb. 1969; *Charades on East Fourth Street*, pr. 1967, pb. 1971 (one act); *Splendid Mummer*, pr. 1988.

SCREENPLAYS: *Melinda*, 1972; *Sounder*, 1972 (adaptation of William H. Armstrong's novel); *Sounder, Part Two*, 1976; *Bustin' Loose*, 1981 (with Richard Pryor and Roger L. Simon; adaptation of a story by Pryor).

TELEPLAYS: *Camera Three*, 1963 season; *The Terrible Veil*, 1963; *N.Y.P.D.*, 1967-1968 season; *McCloud*, 1970-1971; *Ceremonies in Dark Old Men*, 1975 (adaptation of his play); *A Woman Called Moses*, 1978 (miniseries based on Marcy Heidish's book); *The Negro Ensemble Company*, 1987.

NONFICTION: "Comment: Rambled Thoughts," in *Black Creation*, 1973; "Lorraine Hansberry: Social Consciousness and the Will," in *Freedomways*, 1979.

Achievements

Lonne Elder III's playwriting reputation rests solidly on the drama *Ceremonies in Dark Old Men*, not because his formidable theatrical talents faltered after he created this early work but because he turned from the stage to write for film and television. *Ceremonies in Dark Old Men* interweaves psychological and social themes in describing an African American family. Elder presents a careful dissection of the love and power relations within that family, while also, looked at more broadly, showing the adverse situation of African Americans living in a racially torn nation. Though his themes are somber, Elder injects his work with humor and affection, carefully balancing his audience's sympathy for the disparate characters. Although the play ends tragically, presenting the family's partial dissolution, it carries a positive undercurrent insofar as it charts the family's heroic resistance against difficult circumstances and portrays how a number of characters mature during the struggle.

Elder received numerous awards, including the American National Theatre Academy Award (1967), the Outer Circle Award (1970), the Vernon Rice Award (1970), and the Stella Holt Memorial Playwrights Award (1970).

Biography

Lonne Elder III was born in Americus, Georgia, on December 26, 1931, to Lonne Elder II and Quincy Elder. While he was still an infant, his family moved to New York and New Jersey. He was orphaned at the age of ten and ended up living with relatives on a New Jersey farm. Rural life, however, was not for him, and, after he ran away a few times, he was sent to live with his uncle, a numbers runner, in Jersey City.

In 1949, Elder entered New Jersey State Teachers College, where he stayed less than a year. He then moved to New York City and took courses at the Jefferson School and the New School for Social Research, while becoming involved in the movement for social equality for black people. In 1952, he was drafted into the United States Army. While stationed near Fisk University, in Nashville, Tennessee, he met the poet and playwright Robert Hayden, who encouraged Elder with his writing.

Back in New York City in 1953, Elder shared an apartment with the aspiring playwright Douglas Turner Ward and began studying acting. Supporting himself through jobs as a dock-worker, waiter, and poker dealer, among other things, he pursued his acting career, appearing on Broadway in 1959 in *A Raisin in the Sun* and with the Negro Ensemble Company (cofounded by Ward) in Ward's play *Day of Absence* (pr. 1965). During this time, he met such prominent black writers as Lorraine Hansberry and John Oliver Killens, married Betty Gross (in 1963), and wrote his first play. This work, "A Hysterical Turtle in a Rabbit Race," written in 1961 but never performed or published, broached Elder's favored topic of how a black family can be pulled apart by prejudice and false standards.

In 1965, his masterpiece, *Ceremonies in Dark Old Men*, was performed, earning for him fame and critical success. Along with his other ventures, such as writing television scripts for such shows as *N.Y.P.D.* and *McCloud*, it netted for him a number of awards and honors, including a fellowship to the Yale School of Drama in 1966-1967. His next play to be produced was the one-act *Charades on East Fourth Street*, which did not have the impact of his previous drama. It was performed in 1967.

In 1970, sick of New York City, Elder moved with his second wife, Judith Ann Johnson, whom he had married in 1969, to California. He was hoping to improve the depiction of African Americans in Hollywood productions, and he did just that in his screenplay *Sounder* in

Photo courtesy of the Bettmann Archive and Getty Images

1972. After the critical success of this film, he continued working in the industry, producing more serious work about black life and tradition, such as his follow-up television script *Sounder, Part Two* (1976) and his television presentation about Harriet Ross Tubman, *A Woman Called Moses* (1978), as well as writing an occasional comedy, such as the 1981 Richard Pryor film *Bustin' Loose*.

In 1988, Elder returned briefly to the theater with *Splendid Mummer*, a historical play about a black expatriate actor who left the United States in the 1820s to practice his art in Europe. The play was liked by critics but was not a popular success and was not published. Elder continued to be primarily devoted to his goal of working in television and film to provide a positive and realistic view of African American life until his death in 1996.

Analysis: Drama

In all of Lonne Elder III's writings, such as his screenplay *Sounder*, his depictions of family life have been outstanding for their realism, compassion, and penetration, while those works that do not describe family connections, such as his play *Charades on East Fourth Street*, have been notably lacking in inspiration.

Ceremonies in Dark Old Men

His major play, *Ceremonies in Dark Old Men*, deals with the survival of the black family under duress. For Elder, the family is not a collection of autonomous individuals but a dynamic set of relationships. In *Ceremonies in Dark Old Men*, Elder focuses on how each family member's decisions crucially hinge on the words and actions of each other member. The playwright indicates, moreover, that under stressful conditions, the equilibrium of such a black family is a fragile thing, because the family is a working unit in a larger society that is controlled by white people to the disadvantage of black persons. The drama records how, under increasing pressure, the family disintegrates in some ways while it grows in others. Thus, Elder combines social criticism with a subtle look at the inner workings of families.

In much of post-World War II American theater, including such works as Arthur Miller's *Death of a Salesman* (pr., pb. 1949) and Tennessee Williams's *The Glass Menagerie* (pr. 1944, pb. 1945), the family is portrayed as entrapping and destructive of individualism. The family may stifle a son by forcing him to support it, as in Williams's play, or it may ruin his life by giving him false views, as happens to Biff in Miller's work; in either case, however, the family is inimical to self-reliance. By contrast, in *Ceremonies in Dark Old Men*, each family member has a role that is both constricting and sustaining, while each member either grows or diminishes as a result of the family's overall adaptation to the outside world.

At first sight, the family in Elder's play is organized in stereotypical "culture of poverty" fashion, with a female, the daughter Adele, being the de facto head of the house, since she supports the other, male family members. The two sons with the father, the nominal ruler of the house, are shiftless characters; the father, Russell, presides over a defunct barbershop, while his elder son, Theo, is a hapless loser, and the younger one, Bobby, a sneak thief. As the story develops, however, the audience learns that the three are not as parasitical as they first appeared. The father, for example, had been the mainstay of the family, earning a living as a professional dancer until his legs failed and he was unceremoniously dropped from his place. When viewers see the father returning from a day of job-hunting humiliation, they also learn that, as an over-the-hill black man, he has little hope of finding work.

The thrust of the play, however, is not to exonerate any individual but to show that the current operation of the family is, given the way the odds are stacked against prosperity for minority group members, probably the best possible. This view is shown by the simple, but fundamental, device of ending the first act with the beginning of a basic change in the household arrangements (as Theo sets up a viable, if illegal, business) and then jumping ahead a few months for the second act. In this way, in the second act, the audience can see how Theo's changed status, as he takes on a more manly role in the family and supports the others by working long hours, affects the personalities and actions of each of the others, often adversely. Adele, for example, no longer having to bear tremendous responsibility, lets herself go, running around with a notorious skirt chaser. Bobby, who never felt threatened by his brother, since Theo was as ambitionless as he was, now begins sullenly competing with him, becoming a big-time hoodlum.

This is not to say that, because there is more tension in the family after Theo begins working than previously, the old organization was better. Rather, Elder indicates—especially toward the end of the second act, when the family begins to calm down and Adele gives up her playboy boyfriend—that each set of family relationships is highly interdependent and serves as an essential means to help the members orient themselves to the outside world. Elder also indicates that each transition between different familial "steady states" will involve special periods of stress.

In his plays, it is clear that Elder is critical of the position that black persons are forced to occupy in the American economy, and it also may be evident that his anger is more latent than expressed. Rather than have his characters complain about the system, he makes the audience experience the constant feeling of failure that hovers over a family whose members are not fully employed, especially when, to a large degree, their unemployment is not their fault. In relation to one character, however, Elder's social criticism is less oblique. This character, Blue Haven, is a self-styled black activist, who, curiously, is not interested in fighting injustice and oppression through protests and political action; rather, he prefers to steal the clients of white people's liquor and gambling establishments by setting up bootleg and numbers operations of his own. In this portrayal, Elder reveals a satirical side to his talent and shows that he is as critical of black persons as he is of white ones, insofar as he shows that black residents of Harlem are more interested in supporting Blue Haven's "enterprises" than the businesses run by more bona fide progressives.

Elder's treatment of this character also reveals another point about his methods. Throughout most of the play, Blue Haven obtains little sympathy from the audience, being not only a sharper but also a hypocrite. Yet in a powerful monologue that he delivers in a confrontation with Theo, who accuses Blue Haven of exploiting him, Blue Haven presents his own tortured dreams, showing that he is capable of much deeper feeling than it would have been thought possible. This emotional monologue lifts him in the audience's estimation and establishes Elder's goal of giving every character his or her due.

The generosity in Elder's treatment of his characters, seen not only in the way he allows each to develop a voice but also in his mutualistic conception of the family, does have certain drawbacks. As none of the characters is larger than the others, none, in this tale of wrecked hopes, gains the type of tragic stature obtained by the leading characters in the Williams and Miller plays mentioned above. That is to say, none has the broken splendor of a Willy Loman, because, as each family member's choices are heavily dependent on others' situations, no character ever has to face the anxiety of bearing total responsibility for his or her actions. Thus, a character can never rise to the grandeur associated with an acceptance of such responsibility. Furthermore, as a number of critics have noted, Elder's evenhandedness sometimes hints at a distance between him and his creations, since his equal treatment of each problem reveals that he was not aroused by any of his characters' tribulations. Such an attitude can lead to the pathos and power of a given dramatic situation not being fully asserted.

One compensation for these drawbacks is compassion. Elder refuses to make any of his characterizations, even of such comic figures as Blue Haven, into caricatures. He extends to each a measure of respect and understanding. Further, Elder's undistorted, accepting view of his characters and their world matches their general realism. His characters are aware of their own and others' limitations and are largely accustomed to, though hurt by, their social inferiority. The family members tend to treat each new vicissitude with relatively good humor. Thus, near the end of the first act, when everyone is momentarily glum about future prospects, the father, having leeringly accepted Theo's proposal that he work with Blue Haven but being none too happy about it, engages in a little tap dancing. Although his steps are clumsy, the boys cheer him on, caught up in their infectious attempt to celebrate a dubious alliance. The frequent joking of the father and sons works to this same end, lightening the burdens they must bear.

Charades on East Fourth Street

Elder's ability to create a multisided situation is found in his other published drama, *Charades on East Fourth Street*. This play belongs to a genre, delved into by black playwrights of the 1960s, that might be called "ritual drama." Ritual dramas were a component of the rebellious Black Arts movement that emphasized theater as a social ritual, such as the Catholic Mass, that worked to renew symbolically a society's cohesion. These works provided a way of going back to the sources of theater, as is evident in such dramas as the medieval mystery plays. Ritual dramas retold the story of Christ's passion, and, as the centerpiece of a worldview, its reenactment served to rededicate viewers to a common purpose as they re-empathized with their binding social myth. Numerous modern authors, such as T. S. Eliot, have turned back to the roots of drama, but African American writers often gave this turn a perverse twist. Undoubtedly, one of the most brilliant of the black writers' ritual dramas was *Dutchman* (pr., pb. 1964) by LeRoi Jones (who later changed his name to Amiri Baraka). In this play, a black college student flirts with an initially willing white

woman on a subway, but the game turns ugly, and she stabs him. All the other white passengers join her in disposing of the corpse. The ritual, then, is the sacrifice of a young African American male, portrayed as the glue holding together white society. Thus, *Dutchman*, pretending to reveal white America's ideological foundations, actually serves up an indictment of how, it claims, the United States can unite only by scapegoating its minorities.

It may be surmised from this plot recapitulation that such plays could easily become shrill. Although this is not the case with *Dutchman*, because of the author's use of three-dimensional characters, with the woman becoming a fury only in the last minutes, the same cannot be said for Elder's *Charades on East Fourth Street*. At points, his characters grow strident when they lecture one another about police brutality. This short play revolves around the actions of a band of black youths who have kidnapped a white policeman who they believe is guilty of raping a teenage girl. Then, in keeping with the title, *Charades on East Fourth Street*, the youths force the officer to act out a series of degrading scenes. For example, they strip him and put him in bed with a teenage girl, saying that they will send photographs to his wife. It can be seen that in this sexual charade, he is acting out the same part that he supposedly plays in his oppression of the African American community.

As the play progresses, it grows more complex. It turns out, for example, that the gang has grabbed the wrong police officer. Furthermore, the audience learns that the majority of these black teenagers are not convinced of the utility of this kidnapping and are involved in it only because they have been pressured into acting by their leader. In a short (one-act) play such as this one, however, there is no room for excessive ambiguity. The fact that Elder does not give his black revolutionaries much conviction—the kind of fanaticism that Baraka's characters often display—takes the wind out of the story's sails. Without the time to develop the gang's interplay or the anger to make the play an indictment, Elder heroically fails at a genre for which he has no aptitude.

It could be said that Elder's lack of success at agitational drama indicates that, for him, to write well he must follow his bent, which comes from depicting the complexity of characters and the networks they form. His defense of the African American family in his most important play, *Ceremonies in Dark Old Men*, does not rest on any encomiums of individual family members' virtues but on an insistence on the value of the family as a mechanism offering support and solidarity in the face of a hostile society. The worth of Elder's works lies in the evocative power of his affirmation, which itself rests on a sophisticated analysis of how a family functions as one, composed of the relationships of people rather than of people standing alone.

Other Literary Forms

Lonne Elder III also wrote screenplays and television scripts. His screenplays include *Melinda*, *Sounder, Part Two*, and *Bustin' Loose*, with Roger L. Simon and Richard Pryor. Among his teleplays are *Ceremonies in Dark Old Men*, based on his play of the same title, and *A Woman Called Moses*, based on a book by Marcy Heidish.

Bibliography

Arkatov, Janice. "Ceremonies Mark Tribute to Black History Month: Judyann Elder Directs Husband's Classic Play That Offers Sad but Hopeful Statement." *Los Angeles Times*, February 5, 1988, p. 12. A conversation with Elder's wife, Judyann Elder, on her directing of a revival of *Ceremonies in Dark Old Men* for Black History Month. She discusses the African American experience, contrasting the conditions in 1969 with those in 1988.

Eckstein, George. "Softened Voices in the Black Theater." *Dissent* 23 (Summer, 1976): 306-308. Eckstein analyzes the changes through which black drama has gone, from the heady, often outspokenly nationalist and/or revolutionary drama of the mid-1960s to the more reserved drama of the mid-1970s, which puts a greater stress on mere survival and family values. He chooses the works of Elder, as they have evolved in the transition from stage to screen, to signal these changes.

Harrison, Paul Carter. *The Drama of Nommo*. New York: Grove Press, 1972. This highly original look at black drama studies it within categories developed from African aesthetics. Harrison discusses *Ceremonies in Dark Old Men*, finding the play weak because it does not sufficiently bring to light the characters' own recognition of the moral implications of their actions.

Jeffers, Lance. "Bullins, Baraka, and Elder: The Dawn of Grandeur in Black Drama." *CLA Journal* 16 (September, 1972): 32-48. Looking at *Ceremonies in Dark Old Men*, Jeffers points to the resilience of the characters as they face oppressive circumstances. He states that one of Elder's themes is "that the genius and energy of young black America are thwarted and trampled upon, but they remain alive."

Oliver, Myrna. "Lonne Elder III: Award-Winning Writer." *Los Angeles Times*, June 14, 1996, p. 28. This obituary sums up Elder's life and touches on his works for the theater, television, and screen.

—James Feast

Ralph Ellison

Novelist

Born: Oklahoma City, Oklahoma; March 1, 1914

Died: New York, New York; April 16, 1994

LONG FICTION: *Invisible Man*, 1952; *Juneteenth*, 1999 (John F. Callahan, editor); *Three Days Before the Shooting*, 2010 (a revised version of *Juneteenth*; John F. Callahan and Adam Bradley, editors)

SHORT FICTION: *Flying Home, and Other Stories*, 1996

NONFICTION: *Shadow and Act*, 1964; *The Writer's Experience*, 1964 (with Karl Shapiro); *Going to the Territory*, 1986; *The Collected Essays of Ralph Ellison*, 1995 (John F. Callahan, editor); *Conversations with Ralph Ellison*, 1995 (Maryemma Graham and Amritjit Singh, editors); *Trading Twelves: The Selected Letters of Ralph Ellison and Albert Murray*, 2000; *Living with Music: Ralph Ellison's Jazz Writings*, 2001 (Robert O'Meally, editor); *Ralph Ellison: A Life in Letters* (John Callahan and Marc Conner, editors)

Achievements

Ralph Waldo Ellison occupied a central position in the development of African American literature and of contemporary American fiction. Equally comfortable with the influences of Fyodor Dostoevsky, Mark Twain, Louis Armstrong, Igor Stravinsky, James Joyce, and Richard Wright, Ellison was the first African American writer to attain recognition as a fullfledged artist rather than as an intriguing exotic. Whereas Caucasian critics had previously, and unjustly, condescended to African American writers such as Langston Hughes, Zora Neale Hurston, and Richard Wright, most granted Ellison the respect given European American contemporaries such as Norman Mailer and Saul Bellow. A 1965 *Book World* poll identifying *Invisible Man* as the most distinguished postwar American novel simply verified a consensus already reflected in the recurrence of the metaphor of invisibility in countless works by both European and African Americans during the 1950s and 1960s.

Within the African American tradition itself, Ellison occupies a similarly prominent position, although his mainstream acceptance generates occasional reservations among some African American critics, particularly those committed to cultural nationalism. A *Black World* poll, reflecting these reservations, identified Wright rather than Ellison as the most important black writer. The discrepancy stems in part from the critical image in the late 1960s of Ellison and James Baldwin as leading figures in an anti-Wright "universalist" movement in African American culture, a movement that some critics viewed as a sellout to European American aesthetics. In the late twentieth century, however, both European American and African American critics recognized Ellison's synthesis of the oral traditions of black culture and the literary traditions of both his black and his white predecessors. The consensus of that time viewed Ellison as clearly more sympathetic than Wright

Photo courtesy of the U.S. Bureau of Public Affairs

to the African American tradition. As a result, Ellison seems to have joined Wright as a major influence on younger black fiction writers such as James Alan McPherson, Leon Forrest, Toni Morrison, and David Bradley.

Ellison's most profound achievement—his synthesis of modernist aesthetics, American Romanticism, and African American folk culture—embodies the aspirations of democratic pluralists such as Walt Whitman, Mark Twain, and Langston Hughes. His vernacular modernism earned for Ellison an international reputation while exerting a major influence on the contemporary mainstream. With a reputation resting almost entirely on his first novel, Ellison's career is among the most intriguing in American literary history.

Ellison won a Rosenwald grant in 1945 on the strength of his short fiction, and two of his short stories, "Flying Home" and "King of the Bingo Game," are among the most commonly anthologized short stories in twentieth century American literature. *Invisible Man* won the National Book Award and the Russwurm Award, and, in 1975, Ellison was elected to the American Academy of Arts and Letters, which in 1955 awarded him a Prix de Rome Fellowship. He received the French Chevalier de l'Ordre des Arts et des Lettres in 1970 and the National Medal of Arts in 1985. In 1984 he was awarded the Langston Hughes medallion by City College in New York for his contributions to arts and letters.

Biography

Despite Ralph Ellison's steadfast denial of the autobiographical elements of *Invisible Man* and his insistence on the autonomy of the individual imagination, both the specific details and the general sensibility of his work clearly derive from his experience of growing up in a southern family in Oklahoma City, attending college in Alabama, and residing in New York City during most of his adult life. Ellison's parents, whose decision to name their son after Ralph Waldo Emerson reflects their commitment to literacy and education, moved from South Carolina to the comparatively progressive Oklahoma capital several years before their son's birth. Reflecting on his childhood, which was characterized by economic hardship following his father's death in 1917, Ellison emphasizes the unusual psychological freedom provided by a social structure that allowed him to interact relatively freely with both whites and blacks. Encouraged by his mother Ida, who was active in socialist politics, Ellison developed a frontier sense of a world of limitless possibility rather than the more typically southern vision of an environment filled with dangerous oppressive forces.

During his teenage years, Ellison developed a serious interest in music, both as a trumpet player and as a composer-conductor. Oklahoma City offered access both to formal classical training and to jazz, which was a major element of the city's nightlife. The combination of European American and African American influences appears to have played a major role in shaping Ellison's pluralistic sensibility. After he graduated from high school in 1933, Ellison accepted a scholarship to the Tuskegee Institute, founded by Booker T. Washington, where he remained for three years, studying music and literature, until financial problems forced him to drop out. Although he originally planned to finish his studies, his subsequent relocation to New York City marked a permanent departure from the South.

Arriving in the North in 1936, Ellison established contacts with African American literary figures, including Langston Hughes and Richard Wright, who encouraged him to develop his knowledge of both the African American literary world and European American modernism, especially that of T. S. Eliot and James Joyce. Never as deeply involved with leftist politics as Wright, Ellison nevertheless began developing his literary ideas in reviews and stories published in radical magazines such as the *New Masses.* In 1938, Ellison, who had previously supported himself largely as a manual laborer, worked for the Federal Writers' Project, which assigned him to collect urban folklore, providing direct contact with northern folk culture to complement his previous knowledge of southern folkways. Ellison's short fiction began appearing in print in the late 1930s and early 1940s. After a short term as managing editor of *Negro Quarterly* in 1942, he briefly left New York, serving in the merchant marine from 1943 to 1945. Awarded a Rosenwald Fellowship to write a novel, Ellison returned to New York and married Fanny McConnell in 1946.

Invisible Man, which took Ellison nearly seven years to write, was published in 1952, bringing him nearly instantaneous recognition as a major young writer. The novel won the National Book Award in 1953, and its reputation has continued to grow. Starting in 1952, Ellison taught at Bard College, Rutgers University, New York University, and other institutions. In addition, he delivered public lectures, wrote essays, and worked on a second novel. Though Ellison would publish two well-received collections of essays, *Shadow and Act* and *Going to the Territory,* he would never follow up his first novel with a second in his lifetime. He began writing his next novel around 1958, and over the years he was to publish numerous excerpts from it as a work-in-progress. A fire at his Plainsfield, Massachusetts, summer home destroyed much of the manuscript in 1967, causing him to have to painstakingly reconstruct it. Though he was to work on this project for the rest of his life, he never found a final form for the novel with which he felt comfortable, and it remained unfinished when he died of a heart attack in 1994. His literary executor, John F. Callahan, published his short fiction in one volume as *Flying Home, and Other Stories* in 1996 and a self-contained portion of his final novel as *Juneteenth* in 1999.

Less inclined to direct political involvement than contemporaries such as Amiri Baraka and James Baldwin, Ellison participated in the Civil Rights movement in a relatively quiet manner. He nevertheless attracted political controversy during the rise of the African American nationalist movements in the mid-1960s. Refusing to endorse any form of cultural or political separatism, Ellison was attacked as an aesthetic European and a political reactionary, especially after accepting appointments to the American Institute of Arts and Letters (1964) and to the National Council on the Arts and Humanities, acts which were interpreted as support for the Johnson Administration's Vietnam policy. During the mid-1970s, however, these attacks abated as nationalist critics such as Larry Neal rose to Ellison's defense and a new generation of African American writers turned to him for aesthetic inspiration. Ellison retired from full-time teaching during the 1980s and worked on *Juneteenth*, his unfinished novel, until his death on April 16, 1994, in New York.

Analysis: Long Fiction

A masterwork of American pluralism, Ralph Ellison's *Invisible Man* insists on the integrity of individual vocabulary and racial heritage while encouraging a radically democratic acceptance of diverse experiences. Ellison asserts this vision through the voice of an unnamed first-person narrator who is at once heir to the rich African American oral culture and a self-conscious artist who, like T. S. Eliot and James Joyce, exploits the full potential of his written medium. Intimating the potential cooperation between folk and artistic consciousness, Ellison confronts the pressures that discourage both individual integrity and cultural pluralism.

Invisible Man

The narrator of *Invisible Man* introduces Ellison's central metaphor for the situation of the individual in Western culture in the first paragraph: "I am invisible, understand, simply because people refuse to see me." As the novel develops, Ellison extends this metaphor: Just as people can be rendered invisible by the willful failure of others to acknowledge their presence, so by taking refuge in the seductive but ultimately specious security of socially acceptable roles they can fail to see *themselves*, fail to define their own identities. Ellison envisions the escape from this dilemma as a multifaceted quest demanding heightened social, psychological, and cultural awareness.

The style of *Invisible Man* reflects both the complexity of the problem and Ellison's pluralistic ideal. Drawing on sources such as the blindness motif from *King Lear* (1605), the underground man motif from Fyodor Dostoevsky, and the complex stereotyping of Richard Wright's *Native Son* (1940), Ellison carefully balances the realistic and the symbolic dimensions of *Invisible Man*. In many ways a classic *Kunstlerroman*, the main body of the novel traces the protagonist from his childhood in the deep South through a brief stay at college and then to the North, where he confronts the American economic, political, and racial systems. This movement parallels what Robert B. Stepto in *From Behind the Veil* (1979) calls the "narrative of ascent," a constituting pattern of African American culture. With roots in the fugitive slave narratives of the nineteenth century, the narrative of ascent follows its protagonist from physical or psychological bondage in the South through a sequence of symbolic confrontations with social structures to a limited freedom, usually in the North.

This freedom demands from the protagonist a "literacy" that enables him or her to create and understand both written and social experiences in the terms of the dominant European American culture. Merging the narrative of ascent with the *Kunstlerroman*, which also culminates with the hero's mastery of literacy (seen in creative terms), *Invisible Man* focuses on writing as an act of both personal and cultural significance. Similarly, Ellison employs what Stepto calls the "narrative of immersion" to stress the realistic sources and implications of his hero's imaginative development. The narrative of immersion returns the "literate" hero or heroine to an understanding of the culture he or she symbolically left behind during the ascent. Incorporating this pattern in *Invisible Man*, Ellison emphasizes the protagonist's links with the African American community and the rich folk traditions that provide him with much of his sensibility and establish his potential as a conscious artist.

The overall structure of *Invisible Man*, however, involves cyclical as well as directional patterns. Framing the main body with a prologue and epilogue set in an underground burrow, Ellison emphasizes the novel's symbolic dimension. Safely removed from direct participation in his social environment, the invisible man reassesses the literacy gained through his ascent, ponders his immersion in the cultural art forms of spirituals, blues, and jazz, and finally attempts to forge a pluralistic vision transforming these constitutive elements. The prologue and epilogue also evoke the heroic patterns and archetypal cycles described by Joseph Campbell in *Hero with a Thousand Faces* (1949). After undergoing tests of his spiritual and physical qualities, the hero of Campbell's "monomyth"—usually a person of mysterious birth who receives aid from a cryptic helper—gains a reward, usually of a symbolic nature involving the union of opposites. Overcoming forces that would seize the reward, the hero returns to transform the life of the community through application of the knowledge connected with the symbolic reward. To some degree, the narratives of ascent and immersion recast this heroic cycle in specifically African American terms: The protagonist first leaves, then returns to his or her community bearing a knowledge of European American society potentially capable of motivating a group ascent. While it emphasizes the cyclic nature of the protagonist's quest, the frame of *Invisible Man* simultaneously subverts the heroic pattern by removing him from his community. The protagonist promises a return, but the implications of the return for the life of the community remain ambiguous.

This ambiguity superficially connects Ellison's novel with the classic American romance that Richard Chase characterizes in *The American Novel and Its Tradition* (1975) as incapable of reconciling symbolic perceptions with social realities. The connection, however, reflects Ellison's awareness of the problem more than his acceptance of the irresolution. Although the invisible man's underground burrow recalls the isolation of the heroes of the American romance, he promises a rebirth that is at once mythic, psychological, and social:

> The hibernation is over. I must shake off my old skin and come up for breath. . . . And I suppose it's damn well time. Even hibernations can be overdone, come to think of it. Perhaps that's my greatest social crime, I've overstayed my hibernation, since there's a possibility that even an invisible man has a socially responsible role to play.

Despite the qualifications typical of Ellison's style, the invisible man clearly intends to return to the social world rather than to light out for the territories of symbolic freedom.

The invisible man's ultimate conception of the form of this return develops out of two interrelated progressions, one social and the other psychological. The social pattern, essentially that of the narrative of ascent, closely reflects the historical experience of the African American community as it shifts from rural southern to urban northern settings. Starting in the Deep South, the invisible man first experiences invisibility as a result of casual but vicious racial oppression. His unwilling participation in the "battle royal" underscores the psychological and physical humiliation visited upon southern blacks. Ostensibly present to deliver a speech to a white community group, the invisible man is instead forced to engage in a massive free-for-all with other blacks, to scramble for money on an electrified rug, and to confront a naked white dancer who, like the boys, has been rendered invisible by the white men's blindness. Escaping his hometown to attend a black college, the invisible man again experiences humiliation when he violates the unstated rules of the southern system—this time imposed by blacks rather than whites—by showing the college's liberal northern benefactor, Mr. Norton, the poverty of the black community. As a result, the black college president, Dr. Bledsoe, expels the invisible man. Having experienced invisibility in relation to both blacks and whites and still essentially illiterate in social terms, the invisible man travels north, following the countless southern blacks involved in the "Great Migration" to the northern and western sections of the United States.

Arriving in New York, the invisible man first feels a sense of exhilaration resulting from the absence of overt southern pressures. Ellison reveals the emptiness of this freedom, however, stressing the indirect and insidious nature of social power in the North. The invisible man's experience at Liberty Paints, clearly intended as a parable of African American involvement in the American economic system, emphasizes the underlying similarity of northern and southern social structures. On arrival at Liberty Paints, the invisible man is assigned to mix a white paint used for government monuments. Labeled "optic white," the grayish paint turns white only when the invisible man adds a drop of black liquid. The scene suggests the relationship between government and industry, which relies on black labor. More important, however, it points to the underlying source of racial blindness/invisibility: the white need for a black "other" to support a sense of identity. White becomes white only when compared to black.

The symbolic indirection of the scene encourages the reader, like the invisible man, to realize that social oppression in the North operates less directly than that in the South; government buildings replace rednecks at the battle royal. Unable to mix the paint properly, a desirable "failure" intimating his future as a subversive artist, the invisible man discovers that the underlying structure of the economic system differs little from that of slavery. The invisible man's second job at Liberty Paints is to assist Lucius Brockway, an old man who supervises the operations of the basement machinery on which the factory depends. Essentially a slave to the modern owner/master Mr. Sparland, Brockway, like the good darkies of the Plantation Tradition, takes pride in his master and will fight to maintain his own servitude. Brockway's hatred of the invisible man, whom he perceives as a threat to his position, leads to a physical struggle culminating in an explosion caused by neglect of the machinery. Ellison's multifaceted allegory suggests a vicious circle in which blacks uphold an economic system that supports the political system that keeps blacks fighting to protect their neoslavery. The forms alter but the battle royal continues. The image of the final explosion from the basement warns against passive acceptance of the social structure that sows the seeds of its own destruction.

Although the implications of this allegory in some ways parallel the Marxist analysis of capitalist culture, Ellison creates a much more complex political vision when the invisible man moves to Harlem following his release from the hospital after the explosion. The political alternatives available in Harlem range from the Marxism of the "Brotherhood" (loosely based on the American Communist Party of the late 1930s) to the black nationalism of Ras the Exhorter (loosely based on Marcus Garvey's Pan-Africanist movement of the 1920s). The Brotherhood promises complete equality for blacks and at first encourages the invisible man to develop the oratorical talent ridiculed at the battle royal. As his effectiveness increases, however, the invisible man finds the Brotherhood demanding that his speeches conform to its "scientific analysis" of the black community's needs. When he fails to fall in line, the leadership of the Brotherhood orders the invisible man to leave Harlem and turn his attention to the "woman question." Without the invisible man's ability to place radical politics in the emotional context of African American culture, the Brotherhood's Harlem branch flounders. Recalled to Harlem, the invisible man witnesses the death of Tod Clifton, a talented coworker driven to despair by his perception that the Brotherhood amounts to little more than a new version of the power structure underlying both Liberty Paints and the battle royal. Clearly a double for the invisible man, Clifton leaves the organization and dies in a suicidal confrontation with a white policeman. Just before Clifton's death, the invisible man sees him selling Sambo dolls, a symbolic comment on the fact that blacks involved in leftist politics in some sense remain stereotyped slaves dancing at the demand of unseen masters.

Separating himself from the Brotherhood after delivering an extremely unscientific funeral sermon, the invisible man finds few political options. Ras's black nationalism exploits the emotions the Brotherhood denies. Ultimately, however, Ras demands that his followers submit to an analogous oversimplification of their human reality. Where the Brotherhood elevates the scientific and rational, Ras focuses entirely on the emotional commitment to blackness. Neither alternative recognizes the complexity of either the political situation or the individual psyche; both reinforce the invisible man's feelings of invisibility by refusing to see basic aspects of his character. As he did in the Liberty Paints scene, Ellison emphasizes the destructive, perhaps apocalyptic, potential of this encompassing blindness. A riot breaks out in Harlem, and the invisible man watches as Du-Pree, an apolitical Harlem resident recalling a number of African American folk heroes, determines to burn down his own tenement, preferring to start again from scratch rather than even attempt to work for social change within the existing framework. Unable to accept the realistic implications of such an action apart from its symbolic justification, the invisible man, pursued by Ras, who seems intent on destroying the very blackness he praises, tumbles into the underground burrow. Separated from the social structures, which have changed their facade but not their nature, the invisible man begins the arduous process of reconstructing his vision of America while symbolically subverting the social system by stealing electricity to light the 1,369 light bulbs on the walls of the burrow and to power the record players blasting out the pluralistic jazz of Louis Armstrong.

As his frequent allusions to Armstrong indicate, Ellison by no means excludes the positive aspects from his portrayal of the African American social experience. The invisible man reacts strongly to the spirituals he hears at college, the blues story of Trueblood, the singing of Mary Rambro after she takes him in off the streets of Harlem. Similarly, he recognizes the strength wrested from resistance and suffering, a strength asserted by the broken link of chain saved by Brother Tarp.

These figures, however, have relatively little power to alter the encompassing social system. They assume their full significance in relation to the second major progression in *Invisible Man*, which focuses on the narrator's psychological development. As he gradually gains an understanding of the social forces that oppress him, the invisible man simultaneously discovers the complexity of his own personality. Throughout the central narrative, he accepts various definitions of himself, mostly from external sources. Ultimately, however, all definitions that demand he repress or deny aspects of himself simply reinforce his sense of invisibility. Only by abandoning limiting definitions altogether, Ellison implies, can the invisible man attain the psychological integrity necessary for any effective social action.

Ellison emphasizes the insufficiency of limiting definitions in the prologue when the invisible man has a dream-vision while listening to an Armstrong record. After descending through four symbolically rich levels of the dream, the invisible man hears a sermon on the "Blackness of Blackness," which recasts the "Whiteness of the Whale" chapter from Herman Melville's *Moby Dick* (1851). The sermon begins with a cascade of apparent contradictions, forcing the invisible man to question his comfortable assumptions concerning the nature of freedom, hatred, and love. No simple resolution emerges from the sermon, other than an insistence on the essentially ambiguous nature of experience. The dream-vision culminates in the protagonist's confrontation with the mulatto sons of an old black woman torn between love and hatred for their father. Although their own heritage merges the "opposites" of white and black, the sons act in accord with social definitions and repudiate their white father, an act that unconsciously but unavoidably repudiates a large part of themselves. The hostile sons, the confused old woman, and the preacher who delivers the sermon embody aspects of the narrator's own complexity. When one of the sons tells the invisible man to stop asking his mother disturbing questions, his words sound a leitmotif for the novel: "Next time you got questions like that ask yourself."

Before he can ask, or even locate, himself, however, the invisible man must directly experience the problems generated by a fragmented sense of self and a reliance on others. Frequently, he accepts external definitions, internalizing the fragmentation dominating his social context. For example, he accepts a letter of introduction from Bledsoe on the assumption that it testifies to his ability. Instead, it creates an image of him as a slightly dangerous rebel. By delivering the letter to potential employers, the invisible man participates directly in his own oppression. Similarly, he accepts a new name from the Brotherhood, again revealing his willingness to simplify himself in an attempt to gain social acceptance from the educational, economic, and political systems. As long as he accepts external definitions, the invisible man lacks the essential element of literacy: an understanding of the relationship between context and self.

His reluctance to reject the external definitions and attain literacy reflects both a tendency to see social experience as more "real" than psychological experience and a fear that the abandonment of definitions will lead to total chaos. The invisible man's meeting with Trueblood, a sharecropper and blues singer who has fathered a child by his own daughter, highlights this fear. Watching Mr. Norton's fascination with Trueblood, the invisible man perceives that even the dominant members of the European American society feel stifled by the restrictions of "respectability." Ellison refuses to abandon all social codes, portraying Trueblood in part as a hustler whose behavior reinforces white stereotypes concerning black immorality. If Trueblood's acceptance of his situation (and of his human complexity) seems in part heroic, it is a heroism grounded in victimization. Nevertheless, the invisible man eventually experiments with repudiation of all strict definitions when, after his disillusionment with the Brotherhood, he adopts the identity of Rinehart, a protean street figure who combines the roles of pimp and preacher, shifting identities with context. After a brief period of exhilaration, the invisible man discovers that "Rinehart's" very fluidity guarantees that he will remain locked within social definitions. Far from increasing his freedom at any moment, his multiplicity forces him to act in whatever role his "audience" casts him. Ellison stresses the serious consequences of this lack of center when the invisible man nearly becomes involved in a knife fight with Brother Maceo, a friend who sees only the Rinehartian exterior. The persona of "Rinehart," then, helps increase the invisible man's sense of possibility, but lacks the internal coherence necessary for psychological, and perhaps even physical, survival.

Ellison rejects both acceptance of external definitions and abandonment of all definitions as viable means of attaining literacy. Ultimately, he endorses the full recognition and measured acceptance of the experience, historical and personal, that shapes the individual. In addition, he recommends the careful use of masks as a survival strategy in the social world. The crucial problem with this approach, derived in large part from African American folk culture, involves the difficulty of maintaining the distinction between external mask and internal identity. As Bledsoe demonstrates, a protective mask threatens to implicate the wearer in the very system he or she attempts to manipulate.

Before confronting these intricacies, however, the invisible man must accept his African American heritage, the primary imperative of the narrative of immersion. Initially, he attempts to repudiate or to distance himself from the aspects of the heritage associated with stereotyped roles. He shatters and attempts to throw away the "darky bank" he finds in his room at Mary Rambro's. His failure to lose the pieces of the bank reflects Ellison's conviction that the stereotypes, major aspects of the African American social experience, cannot simply be ignored or forgotten. As an element shaping individual consciousness, they must be incorporated into, without being allowed to dominate, the integrated individual identity. Symbolically, in a scene in which the invisible man meets a yam vendor shortly after his arrival in Harlem, Ellison warns that one's racial heritage alone cannot provide a full sense of identity. After first recoiling from yams as a stereotypic southern food, the invisible man eats one, sparking a momentary epiphany of racial pride. When he indulges the feelings and buys another yam, however, he finds it frostbitten at the center.

The invisible man's heritage, placed in a proper perspective, provides the crucial hints concerning social literacy and psychological identity that allow him to come provisionally to terms with his environment. Speaking on his deathbed, the invisible man's grandfather offers cryptic advice that lies near the essence of Ellison's overall vision: "Live with your head in the lion's mouth. I want you to overcome 'em with yeses, undermine 'em with grins, agree 'em to death and destruction, let 'em swoller you till they vomit or bust wide open." Similarly, an ostensibly insane veteran echoes the grandfather's advice, adding an explicit endorsement of the Machiavellian potential of masking:

> Play the game, but don't believe in it—that much you owe yourself. Even if it lands you in a strait jacket or a padded cell. Play the game, but play it your own way—part of the time at least. Play the game, but raise the ante, my boy. Learn how it operates, learn how *you* operate. . . . that game has been analyzed, put down in books. But down here they've forgotten to take care of the books and that's your opportunity. You're hidden right out in the open—that is, you would be if you only realized it. They wouldn't see you because they don't expect you to know anything.

The veterans understands the "game" of European American culture, while the grandfather directly expresses the internally focused wisdom of the African American community.

The invisible man's quest leads him to a synthesis of these forms of literacy in his ultimate pluralistic vision. Although he at first fails to comprehend the subversive potential of his position, the invisible man gradually learns the rules of the game and accepts the necessity of the indirect action recommended by his grandfather. Following his escape into the underground burrow, he contemplates his grandfather's advice from a position of increased experience and self-knowledge. Contemplating his own individual situation in relation to the surrounding society, he concludes that his grandfather "*must* have meant the principle, that we were to affirm the principle on which the country was built but not the men." Extending this affirmation to the psychological level, the invisible man embraces the internal complexity he has previously repressed or denied: "So it is that now I denounce and defend, or feel prepared to defend. I condemn and affirm, say no and say yes, say yes and say no. I denounce because though implicated and partially responsible, I have been hurt to the point of abysmal pain, hurt to the point of invisibility. And I defend because in spite of all I find that I love. In order to get some of it down I *have* to love."

"Getting some of it down," then, emerges as the crucial link between Ellison's social and psychological visions. In order to play a socially responsible role—and to transform the words "social responsibility" from the segregationist catch phrase used by the man at the battle royal into a term responding to Louis Armstrong's artistic call for change—the invisible man forges from his complex experience a pluralistic art that subverts the social lion by taking its principles seriously. The artist becomes a revolutionary wearing a mask. Ellison's revolution seeks to realize a pluralist ideal, a true democracy recognizing the complex experience and human potential of every individual. Far from presenting his protagonist as a member of an intrinsically superior cultural elite, Ellison underscores his shared humanity in the concluding line: "Who knows but that, on the lower frequencies, I speak for you?" Manipulating the aesthetic and social rules of the European American "game," Ellison sticks his head in the lion's mouth, asserting a blackness of blackness fully as ambiguous, as individual, and as rich as the whiteness of Herman Melville's whale.

Juneteenth

Forty-seven years after the release of *Invisible Man*, Ellison's second novel was published. Ellison began working on *Juneteenth* in 1954, but his constant revisions delayed its publication. Although it was unfinished at the time of his death, only minor edits and revisions were necessary to publish the book.

Juneteenth is about a black minister, Alonzo Hickman, who takes in and raises a little boy as black, even though the child looks white. The boy soon runs away to New England and later becomes a race-baiting senator. After he is shot on the Senate floor, he sends for Hickman. Their past is revealed through their ensuing conversation.

The title of the novel, appropriately, refers to a day of liberation for African Americans. Juneteenth historically represents June 19, 1865, the day Union forces announced emancipation of slaves in Texas; that state considers Juneteenth an official holiday. The title applies to the novel's themes of evasion and discovery of identity, which Ellison explored so masterfully in *Invisible Man*.

Analysis: Short Fiction

Because most of Ralph Ellison's short fiction was written before his career as a novelist began, his short stories are often analyzed biographically, as the training ground for the novelist he was to become. This is not entirely unjustified because a biographical overview of his literary output reveals that he tried out the voices, techniques, and ideas that he was to present so boldly in *Invisible Man* and almost completely abandoned the form after his success as a novelist, devoting himself to his essays and to his never-completed second novel.

It is true that in his two most accomplished stories, "King of the Bingo Game" and "Flying Home," he develops themes of the chaos of the modern world and the affliction of racial conflict that would later be combined and expanded in his famous novel. On the other hand, his earlier stories show him working out many of the same ideas from different perspectives. While the voice that informs his most accomplished work is a mature voice that is uniquely Ellison's own, the voices in his other stories show more clearly the influences of Ernest Hemingway, Richard Wright, and James Joyce.

In relating his short fiction to his overall work, Edith Schor in *Visible Ellison: A Study of Ralph Ellison's Fiction* (1993) has aptly observed that Ellison's short stories provided experimental laboratories for testing the translation of the forms and experiences of African American life into literature. In evaluating the stories themselves, however, Robert Bone best summarized their lasting value when he observed in "Ralph Ellison and the Uses of Imagination" (1966) that Ellison's short stories are about "adventurers" testing "the fixed boundaries of southern life."

Flying Home, and Other Stories

Flying Home, and Other Stories is a posthumous collection of stories edited by Ralph Ellison's literary executor, John F. Callahan, which brings together in one volume all of the principal short fiction Ellison wrote (excepting pieces that were published as excerpts of his novels). Callahan arranged the stories according to the age of the main characters, thereby highlighting the stories' thematic unity regarding the growth of young persons' ideologies, which might not otherwise be evident.

The collection opens with "A Party Down at the Square," a story told in an intentionally flat style by a young man from Cincinnati who visits his uncle in Alabama and witnesses a lynching on a stormy night. Confused by the cyclone that moves through the town, an airplane pilot mistakes the fire of the lynching for an airport flare and flies too low through the town, knocking loose a wire and electrocuting a white woman. Undaunted, the crowd continues with the lynching and the anonymous narrator watches a nameless black man being burned, marveling at the victim's resiliency but showing no moral awareness of the horror of the act.

Four of the stories in the collection focus on two young friends, Buster and Riley, as they explore their world and their friendship. The first story, "Mister Toussan," finds them making up imaginary exploits for Haitian liberator Toussaint Louverture, a name they have heard but with which they have only vague associations and upon which they hang various fantasies. Similarly, "Afternoon" and "That I Had the Wings" find the boys involved in imaginative games to stave off boredom. "A Coupla Scalped Indians" focuses on Riley, who has just been "scalped" (circumcised) at the age of eleven, having a sexually charged encounter with old Aunt Mack, an eccentric healer Riley sees naked in her shack as he is making his way home from a carnival. "All was real," Riley tells the reader after leaving her shack, in wonderment about his discovery of the encroaching adult reality.

"Hymie's Bull" and "I Did Not Learn Their Names" are stories about riding freight trains, and together with "The Black Ball" and "A Hard Time Keeping Up," they are about young men finding their way in a world that can be violent and harsh but that can also contain friendship and tenderness in unexpected places. The importance of learning to discern the tenderness amid the harshness of the world becomes the central theme of two of the most important stories in the collection, "In a Strange Country" and "Flying Home." "King of the Bingo Game," by contrast, is a story about a young man trying to make his way in a world that offers little in the way of tenderness and much in the way of danger. Though "Flying Home" and "King of the Bingo Game" are the most significant stories in this collection, the collection offers a startling group of works, each of which is a semi-precious jewel and which, when taken together, mark the growth of the author's artistry.

"King of the Bingo Game"

One of Ellison's most durable statements about the harsh chaos of the modern world can be found in "King of the Bingo Game." The main character is an unnamed black North Carolina man living in Harlem, who has wandered into a cinema in the hope of winning the door prize that might pay for a doctor for his wife. By playing his own and several discarded Bingo cards simultaneously, he manages to win the bingo portion of the game, which gives him the opportunity to spin the bingo wheel. While on stage, he spins the bingo wheel by pressing a button but is then unable to take the chance of letting the button go. Only double zero will win the jackpot of $36.90, and he realizes that so long as he keeps the wheel spinning, he has not lost, so he refuses to let the wheel stop. The wheel takes on the symbolic importance of a mandala, a wheel of life, something the main character realizes when he exclaims, "This is God!" Because he has taken much too long to let go of the button, security guards try to take it from him and knock him out in an altercation. The wheel stops at double zero, but as he fades into unconsciousness, he realizes that he will not get the prize he sought. Though this story is among Ellison's harsher fictions, it is also one of his most poetic presentations of the unfeeling chaos of the modern world.

"In a Strange Country"

Though not as artistically satisfying as the longer "Flying Home," "In a Strange Country" tells a similar tale of self-discovery through the acceptance of a previously despised group identity. Parker is an intelligent black merchant seaman who lands in Wales during World War II only to be promptly attacked by a group of American soldiers simply for being a black man. A group of Welshmen, led by Mr. Catti, rescues him but not before his eye is injured and begins to swell. Over several drafts of ale, Catti learns that Parker is a music enthusiast and takes him to a singing club. There, Parker is swept up in the emotions of the songs about Welsh national pride but reminds himself that he is from Harlem, not Wales. He feels at first alienated and then deeply connected to the men around him, who, he believes, see his humanity much more clearly than do his fellow Americans who are white. As the evening is ending, the band begins to play "The Star-Spangled Banner" in his honor, and he finds himself singing along with deep feeling.

On one hand, the "strange country" of the title is Wales, but on a deeper level, it is the part of himself that is opened up by the bonding of common humanity he shares with these Welshmen and which, for the first time in his life, disallows any easy cynicism.

"Flying Home"

Ralph Ellison's longest short story, "Flying Home," is also his most richly satisfying accomplishment in the form. At the center of the story is Todd, a young black man whose lifelong dream of becoming a pilot crashes along with his plane when he flies into a buzzard on a training flight. Jefferson, an old black man who comes to Todd's rescue after the crash, tells him the buzzards are called "jim crows" locally, setting up an important level of symbolism about what has really caused Todd's crash. In fact, Todd has been training with the Tuskegee Airmen, a group of black World War II pilots who trained at the famed Tuskegee Institute but were only reluctantly deployed for combat missions. For Todd, this crash landing on a routine flight almost certainly means he will never get another chance to fly and, in his mind, will become the common black man he considers Jefferson to be, the worst fate he can imagine for himself.

Despite the younger man's hostility, Jefferson distracts the injured Todd by telling him a story about dying, going to heaven, and flying around so fast as to cause "a storm and a couple of lynchings down here in Macon County." In his story-within-a-story, Jefferson is stripped of his wings for flying too fast and is sent down to earth with a parachute and a map of Alabama. Todd, seeing only that this story has been twisted to mirror his own situation, snaps, "Why are you making fun of me?"—which, in fact, the old man is not doing. A feverish dream into which Todd drifts reveals not only the depth of his lifelong desire to fly but also the power of his grandmother's admonition:

> Young man, young man Yo arm's too
> short To box with God.

To Todd, becoming a pilot means taking a position higher than the majority white culture wants to allow black men of his time to occupy; it is the equivalent of boxing with God in his mind. To have failed as a pilot means not only to have made a mistake but also to have let down his entire race, something he cannot allow to happen.

So when Dabney Graves, the racist landowner on whose property Todd has crashed, arrives at the site, Todd snaps at the man and places his own life in danger. Jefferson, though, saves him

by intervening and telling Graves that the army told Todd never to abandon his ship. Graves's temper is assuaged, and Jefferson and a young boy are allowed to take Todd to safety on a stretcher. The final image is of Todd watching a buzzard flying against the sun, glowing like a bird of flaming gold. This image suggests that though Todd will never fly again, his spirit will rise up like a phoenix from the ashes of his defeat, a victory made possible by the current of goodwill he can now allow himself to feel for Jefferson. Todd will begin to learn to love himself for who he is by loving others for who they are.

Other Literary Forms

Ralph Ellison's reputation rests primarily on *Invisible Man,* but *Shadow and Act,* a collection of nonfiction prose, established him as a major force in the critical theory of pluralism and in African American aesthetics. Arranged in three thematically unified sections, the essays, most of which appeared originally in journals such as *Antioch Review, Partisan Review,* and the *New Republic,* emphasize the importance of folk and popular (especially musical) contributions to the mainstream of American culture. Several of the essays from *Shadow and Act* are recognized as classics, notably "Richard Wright's Blues," "Change the Joke and Slip the Yoke," and "The World and the Jug." A collection of essays, *Going to the Territory,* was published in 1986.

Essays

As an essayist and critic, Ellison held to an optimistic view of the possibilities of American life, celebrated African American cultural contributions, especially in jazz and blues, and criticized sociological views that emphasized the bleakness of African American life. His first essay collection, *Shadow and Act* (1964), serves as something of an intellectual autobiography in which he discusses the formative influences of his childhood in Oklahoma City, touching upon themes of racial and cultural identity, folklore, music, and literature. The book's title alludes both to a line from T. S. Eliot's "The Hollow Men" ("Between the motion / And the act / Falls the Shadow") and to the role of cinema as a cultural mythmaker. Ellison comments in his introduction that the essays are concerned "with literature and folklore, with Negro musical expression—especially jazz and the blues—and with the complex relationship between the Negro American subculture and North American culture as a whole." There are three sections in *Shadow and Act*: "The Seer and the Seen," with ten mainly literary reviews; "Sound and the Mainstream," with seven essays on jazz and the blues; and "The Shadow and the Act," with five essays on African American culture. The entire collection includes Ellison's essays and reviews from 1942 to 1964.

Throughout his essays, Ellison stresses the freedom and creative possibilities inherent in African American culture. A tough-minded individualist, Ellison is more the product of the frontier than the ghetto, more influenced by the library than the storefront church. He is more concerned with the possibilities inherent in his life as a writer than with the limitations. He views the question of identity as universal, not as limited by race, class, or culture. Ellison has always insisted upon his right to define himself, to choose his identity, in the broadest and most expansive terms, rather than to accept the limitations of a sociological description of African American culture. On this point Ellison defines himself most clearly in opposition to Richard Wright's artistic vision. He insists upon the richness of the African American experience and rejects any sense of impoverishment of spirit, insisting upon his broader literary connections with other American and European writers such as Mark Twain, Henry James,

Stephen Crane, Ernest Hemingway, T. S. Eliot, William Faulkner, André Malraux, and Fyodor Dostoevsky.

The two essential essays by Ellison on the question of the African American writer's identity are "The World and the Jug" and "Hidden Name and Complex Fate." The second is a fascinating personal and critical essay about Ellison's reasons for becoming a writer and the formative influences upon him. He defines the act of becoming a writer as a complex act of choice and will. Writers may be "forged in injustice," Ellison observes, but they transform that experience into a significant art form, rather than insisting upon the importance of the experience itself. In the end, it is the quality of the African American writer's art, rather than his political engagement, that is primary.

Ellison consciously chooses the stance of the African American writer as artist—which is to a certain degree isolating, even alienating—but he disparages what he calls the "stylized recitals" of the African American writer's past, because that suffering is not necessarily of special interest in itself. Ellison asserts that the process of claiming one's identity, what he calls making "our names . . . our own," is basically a personal experience, often an intensely private one. Here is where the writer must struggle to master his or her own craft. Better, he claims, to accept the ironies implicit in one's condition than to invent an entirely new, untainted identity. In this way, he leads up to a discussion of what it meant for him to be named by his father after Ralph Waldo Emerson. It was at first a puzzlement, a burden, an embarrassment for "such a small brown nubbin of a boy carrying around such a heavy moniker," but it later became a source of pride. Emerson's transcendentalism, he implies, provided an ideal inspiration for the young African American writer determined to transcend the barriers of racism and claim his freedom and identity as an artist.

Accepting his identity as a writer, however, also entailed certain obligations—to master a bit of technique, to develop a sense of taste, and to address the central cultural issues of his nation and his time. This is what it means to be an American writer. One of the most important of these themes is the disparity between national ideals and the actual behavior and practices of the American people. Ellison insists upon the importance of the African American writer working within the American literary tradition, not outside it. He addresses a broader question of identity beyond that of individual peculiarities—how Americans are all, despite their differences, recognizably "American," and what that means for the society and for its literature. Thus he would enrich his art as an American writer with the resources of African American speech, folklore, and music to express the complex reality of American experience. Ellison concludes "Hidden Name and Complex Fate" by alluding to Henry James, affirming that being an American is an arduous task, and that difficulty begins with one's name.

Ellison takes great pains to deny that there is a separate African American tradition or aesthetic in American literature. This distinction becomes clear in his essay "The World and the Jug," in which he answers critic Irving Howe's attack on Ellison and James Baldwin for ignoring Richard Wright's militant tradition. Ellison castigates Marxist critics who would tell the African American writer how to think and feel. He rejects the notion that the African American experience is limited to suffering and deprivation, and that to be "authentic" the African American writer must write only of these things. As Ellison insists, the real question is "How does the Negro writer participate _as a writer_ in the struggle for human freedom?" Works of literature are less ideological weapons than affirmations of life, or a particular vision of life.

Ellison also warns against any "literary apartheid" of artistic performance or evaluation. African American culture is not a steel jug; it does not isolate the African American writer from white cultural experience. Richard Wright freed himself to become a writer because he had the talent and imagination to do so, not because of any segregated view of his identity or aspirations. His novels are his most important achievement, but his characters should not be confused with the author himself. Nor should Wright's rather bleak artistic vision be held up as a standard for subsequent African American writers. Ellison insists upon the right to those dimensions of his identity as a writer that do not depend upon race. He refuses to be cast as a protest writer and argues furthermore that what the African American writer must guard against is not lack of anger or indignation but failure of craft—bad writing. Ellison's goal has been to transcend the conditions of his fate, not be bound by them.

In part 2, "Sound and the Mainstream," Ellison offers portraits of jazz, gospel, and blues performers such as Mahalia Jackson, Charlie Parker, Charlie Christian, and Jimmy Rushing. These _Saturday Review_ sketches from the late 1950s show Ellison to be a keen and appreciative critic of a variety of African American musical traditions. He praises the improvisational freedom and discipline of the jazz musician as growing out of a musical tradition as demanding as that of European classical music. "The Golden Age/Time Past" offers a nostalgic reminiscence of the Harlem jazz scene in the 1940s, especially of Minton's Playhouse on 118th Street, the home of bebop. In "On Bird, Bird-Watching, and Jazz," he criticizes the followers of Charlie Parker for promoting Parker's self-destructive side without really understanding the sources of inner pain that drove the legendary jazz performer to become a kind of sacrificial figure for a decadent and culturally disoriented public. Ellison much prefers the quiet, underappreciated talent of jazz guitarist Charlie Christian or the funky exuberance of blues and big-band singer Jimmy Rushing.

Going to the Territory

Ellison's second essay collection, *Going to the Territory* (1986), continues his interest in literature, music, and cultural identity. Lacking an introduction or subsections, the book is not as well organized as *Shadow and Act,* but it does contain sixteen additional essays, speeches, interviews, and book reviews that Ellison wrote between 1957 and 1985. The title of the collection alludes to the end of Mark Twain's *Adventures of Huckleberry Finn* (1884), when Huck announces that he is going to light out for "the Territory," as well as to a blues song by Bessie Smith with the same theme.

The book's first essay first essay, "The Little Man at Chehaw Station," is based on an autobiographical recollection of his music teacher at Tuskegee, Hazel Harrison, a highly respected concert pianist and teacher who insisted that Ellison must always play his best, regardless of the audience. The essay's title comes from the image of a hypothetical little man behind the stove at the railway station at Tuskegee who can recognize a poor performance because he knows the music, the traditions, and the standards of performance. Regardless of the supposedly egalitarian nature of American culture, there will always be someone in the audience with high aesthetic standards who can recognize a mediocre performance. Ellison uses this argument to affirm the "melting pot" metaphor of cultural integration, asserting that some knowledge of high culture works its way down through the layers of a democracy. Using the image of a young African American with an eclectic wardrobe, Ellison observes that Americans have continually ransacked and

appropriated each other's cultural forms and modes of expression.

In his West Point talk "On Initiation Rites and Power," Ellison discusses some of the formative influences from his Oklahoma boyhood in shaping his later art. He affirms the richness and diversity of his native Southwestern culture, despite the burden of segregation, and implies that in the tendency to ignore the variety of their society's cultural expression, Americans are victims of inadequate conceptions of themselves. Ellison affirms the importance of America's geographical diversity in shaping its national identity, and he reminds his audience that American society cannot define the role of the individual, because "it is our fate as Americans to achieve that sense of self-consciousness through our own efforts."

In the talk "What These Children Are Like," given at the Bank Street School of Education, Ellison talks about the rich linguistic skills of culturally deprived children and reminisces about the rich jazz traditions to which he was exposed as a child. He emphasizes that the term "culturally deprived" is relative, and that, as he discovered in his teaching at Bard College, even white, middle-class college students can be culturally deprived if their education does not adequately prepare them for the real world that they will enter.

"The Myth of the Flawed White Southerner" is a defense of Lyndon Baines Johnson against attacks from black militants, and "If the Twain Shall Meet" reflects on the discontinuities of southern history. The title essay, "Going to the Territory," was originally given at Brown University as part of the Ralph Ellison Festival and as a tribute to the African American educator Inman Page, the principal of Douglass High School in Oklahoma City, which Ellison attended.

"An Extravagance of Laughter" presents Ellison's recollection of a Broadway production based upon Erskine Caldwell's *Tobacco Road* (1932). The essay is both a brilliant discussion of the nature of humor and a passionate plea to recognize the full humanity of all Southerners. Ellison points out that he found the production hilarious and laughed to the point of embarrassing his host because he found Caldwell's poor white stereotypes, grotesques, and caricatures to be so similar to southern racist stereotypes of African Americans. He talks about the power of laughter in defeating discrimination and recalls the "laughing barrels" that boisterous Negroes were required to use in small southern towns so as not to offend white sensibilities.

"Remembering Richard Wright," given as a talk at the University of Iowa in 1971, pays tribute to Wright's early influence on Ellison, dating back to their initial meeting in New York in 1937. Ellison acknowledges Wright's impressive self-education and his influence on Ellison's intellectual development. Ellison argues that Wright had enough confidence in his talent and ability to accept the artistic challenge of making America conscious of itself, especially in regard to race.

"Homage to Duke Ellington on His Birthday" pays tribute to the great African American composer and arranger who demonstrated through his work that American jazz possessed a range of expressiveness comparable to that of European classical music. Ellison regrets that, because of the musical and racial prejudices of some of the members of the awards committee, Ellington did not receive a special Pulitzer Prize in music.

In his last three essays, Ellison shows a keen knowledge and appreciation of the American literary tradition. "Society, Morality and the Novel" offers a theoretical discussion of the nature of the novel and the social responsibility of the novelist. Ellison differs from Richard Wright and critics such as Irving Howe in insisting that the novel has a broader mandate than merely to serve as a vehicle for social change. In "The Novel as a Function of American Democracy," Ellison affirms that the health of the novel reflects the health of society. He praises Hemingway and Faulkner for their truthful depictions of American life. The United States is only a partially achieved nation, Ellison affirms, but in times of change people lose their sense of who they are and look to the novel and other art forms for reassurance. He criticizes contemporary literature for its cynicism and lack of optimism about the possibilities of American life. In "Perspectives of Literature," he celebrates the African American as the keeper of the American conscience, the symbol of American hope. The creative imagination of the writer is essential for American democracy because laws and freedom expand in response to the challenges posed by American writers.

In *Shadow and Act* and *Going to the Territory*, Ellison demonstrates his growth as an American literary and social critic, from the young Marxist-oriented Works Progress Administration (WPA) worker of the 1930s to the polished and mature novelist and essayist of the 1980s. Throughout his essays, Ellison remained a consistent cultural integrationist, insisting upon the central contributions and importance of the African American writer and resisting calls by Black Nationalists for a new black separatist literary aesthetic. Working in the mainstream of American literature helped him, he wrote, to avoid any "segregation of the mind."

Bibliography

Anderson, Paul Allen. "Ralph Ellison on Lyricism and Swing." *American Literary History* 17, no. 2 (Summer 2005): 280-306. An interesting short biography of the author.

Applebome, Peter. "From Ellison, a Posthumous Novel, with Additions Still to Come." *The New York Times* 11 Feb. 1999. This article gives information on the origins of *Juneteenth*, both historical and personal to Ellison.

Benston, Kimberly, ed. *Speaking for You: The Vision of Ralph Ellison.* Washington, DC: Howard UP, 1987. A useful resource of responses to Ellison's fiction and essays. Also includes an extensive bibliography of his writings.

Bloom, Harold, ed. *Modern Critical Views: Ralph Ellison.* New York: Chelsea House, 1986. Though this widely available collection of essays focuses mainly on *Invisible Man*, it provides insights from which any reader of Ralph Ellison may profit, and Berndt Ostendor's essay, "Anthropology, Modernism, and Jazz," offers much to the reader of "Flying Home."

_____. *Ralph Ellison.* New York: Chelsea House, 1986. A good collection of essays on Ellison's writings, with an introduction by Bloom.

Bone, Robert. "Ralph Ellison and the Uses of Imagination." *Triquarterly* 6 (1966): 39-54. An important essay on the uses of transcendentalism and jazz in Ellison's fiction and of his writing's importance to the Civil Rights movement and black culture in general.

Bradley, Adam. *Ralph Ellison in Progress: From Invisible Man to Three Days Before the Shooting.* New Haven, CT: Yale UP, 2010. Drawing on previously unstudied material, this book reexamines Ellison's whole career in light of his work on never-finished second novel.

Busby, Mark. *Ralph Ellison.* Boston: Twayne, 1991. An excellent introduction to Ellison's life and work.

Callahan, John F., ed. *Flying Home, and Other Stories.* New York: Random House, 1996. Callahan's introduction to this collection of fiction is essential reading for anyone interested in Ellison's fiction, not only for the literary insights it provides but also for the basic editorial information about how these stories were selected and edited.

Calloway, Catherine. "Fiction: The 1930s to the 1960s." *American Literature* 77, no. 2 (June 2005): 349-68. This chapter examines Ellison's work and compares it to that of four other major American authors: James Baldwin, Chester Himes, John Steinbeck, and Richard Wright.

Conner, Marc C., and Lucas E. Morel, ed. *The New Territory: Ralph Ellison and the Twenty-First Century.* Jackson: UP of Mississippi, 2016. A collection of essays dealing with such topics as the politics of love, performance and public spaces, subjectivity, blindness, visibility, fatherhood, and the blues.

Evans, Robert C., ed. *Invisible Man: Critical Insights.* Ipswich, MA: Salem, 2018. An essay collection dealing with such topics as segregation, Black Lives Matter, efforts to ban *Invisible Man*, critical responses to the novel from the 1950s to the twenty-first century, sensation, making sense, the Bible, Ellison on good writing, early interviews, anger, action, art, race and individualism, politics, Reconstruction, the dramatized version of *Invisible Man*, reviews of a documentary on Ellison, and Ellison's legacy.

Foley, Barbara. *Wrestling with the Left: The Making of Ralph Ellison's Invisible Man.* Durham, NC: Duke UP, 2010. Traces the impact of left-wing politics (and Ellison's movement away from radicalism) on the composition and reception of *Invisible Man*.

Germana, Michael. *Ralph Ellison: Temporal Technologist.* Oxford: Oxford UP, 2018. Deals with the philosophical, sociological, and political dimensions of Ellison's ideas about time.

Harriss, M. Cooper. *Ralph Ellison's Invisible Theology.* New York: New York UP, 2017.

Jackson, Lawrence. *Ralph Ellison: Emergence of Genius.* New York: Wiley, 2002. The first book-length study of Ellison's life. A good background source for the novelist's early life and career. Jackson, however, ends his study in 1953, shortly after the publication of *Invisible Man*.

Morel, Lucas E., ed. *Ralph Ellison and the Raft of Hope: A Political Companion to Invisible Man.* Lexington: UP of Kentucky, 2004. This volume provides an in-depth discussion of Ellison's own political views, the views he expresses in *Invisible Man*, and the political debate that the book has engendered.

Nadel, Alan. *Invisible Criticism: Ralph Ellison and the American Canon*. Iowa City: U of Iowa P, 1988. A look at Ellison's place in the study of American literature.

O'Meally, Robert G. *The Craft of Ralph Ellison*. Cambridge, MA: Harvard UP, 1980. Traces Ellison's development as a writer and includes considerations of his fiction published after *Invisible Man*.

_____, ed. *New Essays on "Invisible Man."* New York: Cambridge UP, 1988. A collection of essays which includes many responses to questions raised by earlier critics.

Parr, Susan Resneck, and Pancho Savery, eds. *Approaches to Teaching Ellison's "Invisible Man."* New York: Modern Language Association, 1989. Part 1 surveys reference books, critical studies, and background studies. Part 2 provides several different interpretations of the novel by noted critics. Other sections explore the novel in the context of African American, American, and European traditions, ways to teach the novel thematically, and sample study guides.

Parrish, Timothy. *Ralph Ellison and the Genius of America*. Amherst: U of Massachusetts P, 2012. Emphasizes the importance on Ellison's thinking of the 1954 Supreme Court decision that desegregated public schools. Argues that this decision helped shape Ellison's ideas about civil rights and his influence on the struggle for such rights.

Posnock, Ross, ed. *The Cambridge Companion to Ralph Ellison*. Cambridge: Cambridge UP, 2005. An important collection of essays on such topics as Ellison's ancestry, the black church, the gospel, photography, invisibility, music, the Constitution, politics, melancholy, leadership, experimentation, women, and Ellison's unfinished second novel.

Purcell, Richard. *Race, Ralph Ellison and American Cold War Intellectual Culture*. New York: Palgrave Macmillan, 2013. Discusses issues of race in the 1950s and 1960s—both their influence on Ellison and his influence on the issues.

Rampersad, Arnold. *Ralph Ellison: A Biography*. New York: Alfred A. Knopf, 2007. A lengthy, magisterial discussion of Ellison's life and career. A finalist for the National Book Award.

Rankine, Patrice D. *Ulysses in Black: Ralph Ellison, Classicism, and African American Literature*. Madison: U of Wisconsin P, 2006. Argues that many important African American writers, including Ellison, have been influenced by classical literature and that such influence need not be considered Eurocentric.

Schor, Edith. *Visible Ellison: A Study of Ralph Ellison's Fiction*. Westport, CT: Greenwood Press, 1993. Published a year before Ellison's death, this is an excellent full-length study of the fiction that was generally available at the time, including his short fiction, which had not yet been collected in book form. This is probably the best place for the serious scholar of Ralph Ellison to begin.

Skerret, Joseph. "Ralph Ellison and the Example of Richard Wright." *Studies in Short Fiction* 15 (Spring 1978): 145-53. An examination of the influence of Richard Wright on Ralph Ellison's short fiction.

Tracy, Steven C. *A Historical Guide to Ralph Ellison*. New York: Oxford UP, 2004. This collection of previously unpublished essays examines Ellison's political, musical, and literary influences and impacts. Includes a biography and chronology.

Trimmer, Joseph F., ed. *A Casebook on Ralph Ellison's "Invisible Man."* New York: Thomas Y. Crowell, 1972. An invaluable aid to students and teachers, this volume is a collection of social and literary background material useful for understanding the traditions that inform *Invisible Man*. Also contains critical essays.

Valiunas, Algis. "The Great Black Hope." *Commentary* 119, no. 3 (Mar. 2005): 61-66. An interesting article that discusses several books about African American boxers, including *Invisible Man*.

Watts, Jerry Gafio. *Heroism and the Black Intellectual: Ralph Ellison, Politics, and Afro-American Intellectual*

Life. Chapel Hill: U of NC P, 1994. Chapters exploring critic Harold Cruse's influential interpretation of black intellectuals, the biographical background to *Invisible Man*, the relationship between the novel and black music, the responsibilities of the black writer, and a discussion of heroism conceived as an artistic antidote to racism. Includes notes and bibliography.

Wright, John S. *Shadowing Ralph Ellison.* Jackson: UP of Mississippi, 2006. Examines the development of Ellison's life and career, particularly emphasizing his interest in jazz and the blues.

Yaszek, Lisa. "An Afrofuturist Reading of Ralph Ellison's *Invisible Man.*" *Rethinking History* 9, nos. 2/3 (June 2005): 297-314. A reinterpretation of Ellison's novel in the light of Afrofuturism, which looks at the future through a perspective that avoids viewing technological advancement as an inherently European American phenomenon.

—Thomas Cassidy; Craig Werner;
Andrew J. Angyal; Robert C. Evans

Percival Everett

Novelist

Born: Augusta, Georgia; December 22, 1956

LONG FICTION: *Suder*, 1983; *Walk Me to the Distance*, 1985; *Cutting Lisa*, 1986; *For Her Dark Skin*, 1990; *Zulus*, 1990; *God's Country*, 1994; *Watershed*, 1996; *Frenzy*, 1997; *The Body of Martin Aquilera*, 1997; *Glyph*, 1999; *Erasure*, 2001; *Grand Canyon, Inc.*, 2001 (novella); *A History of the African-American People (Proposed) by Strom Thurmond*, 2004 (with James Kincaid); *American Desert*, 2004; *Wounded*, 2005; *The Water Cure*, 2007; *I Am Not Sidney Poitier*, 2009; *Assumption: A Novel*, 2011; *Percival Everett by Virgil Russell*, 2013; *So Much Blue*, 2017; *Telephone: A Novel*, 2020

CHILDREN'S LITERATURE: *The One That Got Away*, 1992

POETRY: *Re: f (gesture)*, 2006; *Abstraktion und Einfühlung*, 2008; *Swimming Swimmers Swimming*, 2010; *The Book of Training by Colonel Hap Thompson of Roanoke, VA, 1843: Annotated from the Library of John C. Calhoun*, 2019.

SHORT FICTION: *The Weather and Women Treat Me Fair*, 1987; *Big Picture*, 1996: *Damned If I Do*, 2004; *Half an Inch of Water*, 2015

Achievements

Percival Everett's novel *Zulus* won the New American Writing Award, and *Erasure*, his biting parody of race in the world of publishing, received the Hurston/Wright Legacy Award. Everett has also been the recipient of a PEN USA Literary Award and of a Literature Award from the American Academy of Arts and Letters. He has held fellowships from the Lila Wallace-Reader's Digest Foundation and from the University of New Mexico. He won a second Hurston/Wright Legacy Award for Fiction for *I Am Not Sidney Poitier: A Novel* as well as such other honors as a Guggenheim Fellowship in Fiction (in 2015).

Biography

Percival Leonard Everett was born in 1956 in Fort Gordon, Georgia, and was raised in Columbia, South Carolina, where he graduated from A. C. Flora High School. His father was a sergeant in the U.S. Army when Everett was born on the military base just outside Augusta, but he went on to become a dentist. Everett received a B.A. in philosophy with a minor in biochemistry in 1977 from the University of Miami, Florida, and continued the study of philosophy at the University of Oregon from 1978 to 1980. He left the study of philosophy for creative writing, moving to Brown University, where he earned an M.A. in fiction in 1982.

For brief periods, Everett worked as a jazz musician, as a hand on a sheep ranch, and as a high school teacher. He served as an associate professor on the faculty of the University of Kentucky from January, 1985, to January, 1988, and then joined the faculty of the University of Notre Dame as a full professor. He left Notre Dame in 1991 for the University of California, Riverside, and finally moved to the University of Southern California in 1998, where he was named a distinguished professor of English in March, 2007. He has also taught at Bennington College and the University of Wyoming.

Analysis: Long Fiction

Percival Everett has developed a reputation for surprising readers and critics with each new work he brings to the public. The experimental chances he takes in his writing make his novels difficult to classify and therefore difficult to publish through mainstream presses. Although he has made the shift to major publishers, he has repeatedly been published by the small, nonprofit Graywolf Press.

Everett's first novel, *Suder*, met with success in part because it was readily identifiable as "African American" literature. The main character plays third base for the Seattle Mariners baseball team and embarks on a series of unlikely encounters during a dry spell in his career; Suder works in the tradition of the picaresque, and he is not unlike Charles Johnson's protagonist in *Middle Passage* (1990). Everett readily acknowledges his debt to Laurence Sterne, and in particular to that author's *The Life and Opinions of Tristram Shandy, Gent.* (1759-1767), an eighteenth-century classic considered by many critics as the first postmodern novel.

Critiques of Everett's work often question his reconstruction of the dialogue around race. Novels such as *Cutting Lisa* and *Frenzy* contain no racial markers, and others, such as *Glyph*, *Wounded*, and *Erasure*, implicitly or explicitly challenge many common assumptions about race. The writing of *Erasure*, in fact, was partly motivated by Everett's wish to respond more fully to what he regards as the narrow categorization of his fiction.

Everett also thematizes violence in his novels, sometimes in the form of dark humor and sometimes in more troubling ways. In *Erasure*, the narrator's sister is the victim of random violence in the poor Washington, D.C., neighborhood she serves as a doctor. In *Frenzy*, the bloody rites of the worshipers of Bacchus are vividly detailed, and *For Her Dark Sin* incorporates the murders associated with the stories of Medea, including the murders of her children. This theme surfaces in *Watershed* and *Wounded* in the more traditional setting of the murder mystery, but even so Everett brings out the moral dilemma raised by the need for self-defense and revenge.

With each successive novel, Everett has changed paradigms; *Walk Me to the Distance* and *Cutting Lisa* in some ways fit the genre of the problem novel, featuring troubled characters struggling with their own violent natures. *Zulus* operates within the expectations of science fiction but bends those expectations. Everett revises the story of Medea in *For Her Dark Skin* and takes up the stories surrounding the god Dionysus in *Frenzy*. With *Watershed* and *Wounded*, Everett continues the revisionist reading of the American West that he began in *God's Country*.

Despite Everett's reputation as an iconoclast, each of the novels contains a recognizable narrative thread around human relationships; even *Frenzy*, which features a god as its central character, narrates through a character who is struggling to become human and to connect with the all-too-human worshipers and enemies of his master, Dionysus.

Suder

This short novel follows two narrative threads: baseball player Craig Suder's quixotic adult adventures and his childhood memories. Each contemporary moment is informed by some action in the past; chapters shift from one narrative line to the other.

The first story line begins with a strikeout, but Craig Suder's problems in batting are only the beginning of his worries. His poor performance on the field is letting down his team and embarrassing his son; his poor performance in bed is driving his wife Thelma to her exercycle and perhaps to another man. After he is conveniently put on the disabled list, not for any physical injury but for his supposed jinx on the team, Craig uses his long leave of absence to examine his life. He does not like what he sees. Only with his discovery of what he assumes is Thelma's infidelity does he decide to abandon his responsibilities. He leaves, taking only his baseball bat, saxophone, record player, and a recording of Charlie Parker's "Ornithology." Herein begins a series of episodic, seriocomic experiences.

The second narrative line, tracing Suder's childhood memories, offers commentary on the main plot and illuminates the character of the protagonist.

Much of the frantic propulsion of the story derives from its first-person narration, which is marked by short sentences and the active voice. In some ways, Suder's clipped narrative voice emulates the pacing of bebop jazz. Having worked as a jazz musician, Everett has intimate knowledge of the art form that pervades this novel, especially the staccato phrasing of Charlie Parker's "Ornithology." "I could feel the push of the song, a tension," Suder admits as a young boy hearing Powell play the tune. Much the same can be said of the plot of his own life. It is full of twists and turns, abrupt changes of direction, and unpredictable complexities.

In the final analysis, it is Craig Suder's character that dominates the book. The narrative centers on his mad dash to define himself, to be himself. Beyond the labels of "black man" or "ballplayer," Suder insists on being true to his own unique identity.

Suder is Everett's first novel. Subsequent works were not greeted with as much popular enthusiasm and critical praise. The book has

been contrasted to the fiction of other modern African American novelists such as Richard Wright and James Baldwin, whose vision of the African American experience can be labeled nothing less than somber. Suder, on the other hand, has been hailed by such critics as Carolyn See as a happy work of "sustained and glittering incandescence."

In the opposite camp, however, are critics who believe that the novel is nothing more than escapist fare that fails to tackle the important issues confronting the main character. In this regard, some reviewers assert that flight, real or imagined, is not a valid option for real people in the real world.

Walk Me to the Distance

Returning from the Vietnam War to his native Savannah, Georgia, David Larson feels as "unremarkable" as when he left. This general sense of detachment is evidenced by his unemotional response to the loss of his parents in a traffic accident during his absence and the subsequent ease with which he distances himself from his sister because of her antiwar sympathies. Purchasing a used car, David motors west. Chance lands him in Slut's Hole, Wyoming, after he damages the car's radiator while shooting at a jackrabbit. Forced to spend two weeks in town until his car is repaired, David acquires, in quick succession, a job and a place to stay. His time is largely divided among his undemanding caretaker chores at a highway rest area, his forays into Laramie, and his experiences on the nearby Sixbury ranch.

The reader must look to sources in Western literature for some clue as to authorial intention in regard to the creation and development of this character. At one point in the narrative, David spends time at his desk reading a copy of *The Virginian* (1902) by American author Owen Wister. In Wister's novel, the first serious fictional treatment of the American cowboy, the title character makes a place for himself in the town of Sunk Hole, Wyoming. Like David, the Virginian becomes one with the people and the landscape of his adopted state, and he must face a difficult moral decision when he participates in the hanging of a cattle rustler who had been his friend. As in *The Virginian*, the setting of *Walk Me to the Distance* underscores the main character's development and defines the community that he encounters.

The landscape of Wyoming is depicted as a living presence. Having himself worked on a sheep ranch, Everett knows the country he describes. A sense of collective identity, which one character summarizes by saying "it's like we're a tribe here," is the central quality that draws David to consider the place as home and the people as his family. The land itself demands of the people who dwell there a kind of strength, a determination to make their own way, to dispense their own brand of justice. Some of that inner strength and assuredness can be seen in the laconic speech of the region, a verbal reticence that Everett himself tries to emulate in his narrative style. These are a people who live by deed and not by word.

In the wake of his first novel, the much-praised, humorously picaresque *Suder* (1983), Percival Everett made a dramatic shift when he published the more traditional, more serious *Walk Me to the Distance*. In some ways, the second novel may be regarded as an answer to his first: *Suder* offers flight as an option in dealing with life's problems; *Walk Me to the Distance* offers the antidote of home and family.

Walk Me to the Distance has not benefited from the positive critical reception of Everett's first, most popular novel. Many reviewers, for example, have missed in this book the comic creativity they found in *Suder*. Even those who felt at times moved by Everett's second novel nevertheless reacted negatively to what they saw as a narrative style that was too terse, a brevity of expression that perhaps masked a shallowness of content. At least one reviewer, moreover, lamented that the main character was not African American and that Percival Everett, though an African American writer, had chosen not to confront the issue of racial identity.

God's Country

In *God's Country*, a parody of the traditional Western, Everett pairs black scout Bubba with broadly drawn white rancher Curt Marder to set off on an eventful exploration of the myth of the West. Everett characterizes this novel as following in the tradition of Thomas Berger's *Little Big Man* (1964) and E. L. Doctorow's *Welcome to Hard Times* (1960) in terms of its manipulation of the conventions of the Western. The novel opens with the narrator, Marder, looking at the ruins of his ranch, which has been destroyed by "fake Indians." This evocation of John Wayne's role in the 1956 film *The Searchers* is quickly undercut by the encounters between Marder and his peers, which show his lack of heroic qualities and the contempt in which they hold him. The scout, Bubba, emerges as the hero, and the surprise ending of the novel suggests that he is larger than life: Marder shoots him repeatedly but is unable to kill him. Bubba may well represent the inescapable presence of racism in white society while at the same time embodying the resilience of African Americans within that racist world.

Glyph

With *Glyph*, Everett takes up the parody of the academy, joining that tradition as represented in *Lucky Jim* (1954) by Kingsley Amis and more recently revised in David Lodge's *Small World* (1984) and Ishmael Reed's *Japanese by Spring* (1993). The protagonist, baby Ralph, embodies the novel's critique of poststructuralist theory because Ralph is, himself, a sign, a glyph. He comes into the world fully formed in terms of written language and is able to read anything. This prodigy chooses writing as his only form of communication. Ralph, like the figures in many of Everett's novels, rushes through a series of unexpected and hilarious adventures. He is kidnapped and caged by a psychology researcher who wants to study him, then taken by federal agents, and is finally rescued by a childless couple who want him to become their own son. Here, as in all the novels, violence plays a role, however humorous it may seem. The reader may laugh while Ralph manages to elude exploitation by scientists and government officials, but the fact that he is imprisoned as a baby still evokes a darker response.

Douglas, Ralph's father, is a university professor angling for tenure who considers himself a sophisticated poststructuralist theorist, only to have his pretensions undercut by his infant son. His self-image is further eroded by a wickedly funny encounter with Roland Barthes, one of the major figures of poststructuralist thought. The marriage between Ralph's parents falls apart in tandem with the disintegration of Douglas's career. As Douglas becomes more uncertain of his intellectual ground, Ralph's mother begins to explore her gift for visual art. She makes herself independent of her husband and can then offer Ralph a home. Reunited with his mother in a chaotic final clash of all the forces that pursue him, Ralph makes the decision to step away from his identity in writing and become an ordinary human baby. This choice is mediated by Everett's interruption of Ralph's story with quotations, poetry, and imaginary dialogues between famous figures. These apparent digressions provide a running interpretive commentary on the main narrative. *Glyph* closes with the single observation "The line is all," returning to Everett's commitment to that narrative thread of human experience through time.

Erasure

Having long grown accustomed to the fact that his experimental, intellectually challenging novels will probably never find a popular readership, Thelonious Ellison is nevertheless dismayed by the relative success of those African American fiction writers who, in his eyes, exploit cultural stereotypes and reinforce a monolithic vision of the African American experience. When his sister is murdered by a fanatical antiabortion activist, Thelonious is forced to take a leave of absence from his college professorship: With his sister gone, he must move back into his family home in Washington, D.C., to take primary responsibility for his increasingly disabled mother's health. Ellison thus finds himself with no money and plenty of time. Dismayed by the twentieth rejection of his latest fictional work, in which two ancient Greek dramatists murder a rival and "then contemplate the death of metaphysics," Ellison writes a parody novel, initially entitled *My Pafology*, that embraces all the "demeaning and soul-destroying drivel" that he finds in most supposedly realistic depictions of contemporary inner-city life.

Most of *Erasure* takes the form of Ellison's journal—interrupted by the text of a paper on experimental fiction that the main character delivers at an academic conference under his own name and by the ten-chapter manuscript of *My Pafology*, penned under the pseudonym Stagg R. Leigh. Patterned in part after Bigger Thomas in Richard Wright's *Native Son* (1940), the juvenile protagonist of *My Pafology*, Van Go Jenkins, is an illiterate, self-loathing, oversexed, and hyperviolent African American man trapped in an urban jungle, victimized by socioeconomic conditions and bedazzled by pop culture.

The text that Ellison generates in anger and personally characterizes as "offensive, poorly written, racist and mindless" soon earns a publishing contract, garners a host of glowing critical reviews, and attracts a multimillion-dollar movie deal. At the public ceremony to celebrate the novel's having won the prestigious Book Award, Ellison, who, as a member of the judging panel, tried to sabotage the text's prizewinning prospects, confronts his own imminent exposure.

The often farcical plotline focuses on the fate of Ellison's parody novel and the consequent erasure of the identity that he has cultivated since his youth. This persona—encouraged by his late father, who compelled his son's future as an artist—is counterbalanced by the protagonist's evolving discovery of his past. In returning to his native city, he confronts long-held family secrets and is forced to redefine his place not only in the family unit but also in the larger world. He had always been treated by his father differently from his two siblings, but he eventually discovers the root of his father's preference. Ellison is, in effect, the accidental byproduct of an affair that his father conducted during the Korean War; when the woman he loved refused to be with him, Benjamin Ellison returned to his wife, and the child conceived during the course of their reunion was Thelonious.

Thelonious offers an object lesson in the difficulty of establishing an individual identity. Accused time and time again of being "not black enough" because he does not conform to popular cultural expectations, Ellison is the product of generations of education and economic privilege. Even as a child, he did not think, feel, or speak like his peers. Like the nameless main character in Ralph Ellison's *Invisible Man* (1952), Thelonious is engaged in a struggle for self-definition. By virtue of his "brown skin, curly hair, wide nose, and slave ancestors," he is African American; by virtue of the fact that he comes from three generations of medical professionals and graduated summa cum laude

from Harvard, he lives a middle-class existence whose traits often do not match contemporary stereotypes regarding African Americans.

The concept of "erasure" is central to Percival Everett's novel, since each of its characters offers evidence of some form of personal deletion. Ironically enough, for example, the main character achieves his greatest success, both critical and popular, when he assumes the identity of a fictitious alter ego. Much of the poignancy of the novel is derived from the main character's belated attempts to reconnect himself to his parents, his siblings, and his racial identity, only to be left in the end with an overwhelming sense of displacement.

In addition to depicting the main character's simultaneous journeys of personal discovery and deconstruction, the novel enacts its author's abiding preoccupation with the prevailing definitions of the nature of mainstream African American literature. Ellison's career mirrors much of Everett's own résumé as a writer. Everett's many novels, all of which reflect his ongoing exploration of content and form, posit the question of whether the common reader, regardless of race, will ever be receptive to a writer whose work resists popular expectations and aspires to the status of art.

According to general estimates, *Erasure* is the most reviewed and most acclaimed of Everett's fictional works since the publication of his groundbreaking first novel, *Suder*, in 1983. Critics have praised *Erasure* as a skillful commentary on the dubious merit of some fixtures of contemporary African American pop culture, including pulp fiction purporting to be inspired by the realities of ghetto life in the country's urban centers and the wildly successful and arguably disproportionately influential television book club of Oprah Winfrey. Many reviewers have also seen the novel as the author's plea for the publishing world and its readers to acknowledge the existence and legitimacy of a broad range of African American experience and artistic intention—a range matching the breadth of experience found in the work of European American writers. In particular, Everett chooses to parody a work of literary naturalism to emphasize the limitations of defining a broad literary tradition in terms of a single genre.

American Desert

American Desert, Percival Everett's fifteenth novel, opens with Theodore "Ted" Street on his way to drown himself. Ironically, Ted dies before he can kill himself. A UPS truck dodging a poodle with painted nails collides with Ted's car; Ted is decapitated. The plot progresses chronologically with startling, unexpected events. This irony produces a dark comedy. Symbolically, on the third day after his death, Ted rises up from his casket at his funeral. Remarks from a preacher who does not know him and unflattering comments from his department chair precede Ted's revival.

Reactions to Ted's restoration vary. The chair and dean, never Ted's allies, suffer heart attacks and die. The congregation riots. Ted's family does not celebrate; they experience embarrassment and fear. Ted's wife selects her next husband. Society is more concerned with defining death than with Ted. A religious cult shows no compassion, calls Ted a demon, and captures him for execution. Ironically, Ted remains decent in the decadence. He escapes the commune and returns to rescue the children.

Everett's figurative language and stylistic devices enhance the plot. For instance, Ted notes the approaching deadline for meeting requirements for permanent faculty status; Everett uses the metaphor of the "ticking of the giant tenure clock." At Ted's funeral, Everett humorously describes how Rachel Ruddy, Ted's replacement, pepper-sprays herself out of the church.

Everett's characterization includes realistic diction and omniscience. Ted's explicit messages state (1) that silence is as important as words, (2) that death is not frightening, and (3) that even flawed people can contribute to society. The denouement is abrupt and closed. Ted removes the stitches from his neck, places his head on his lap, closes his eyes, and stays dead.

Wounded

One of a number of novels that reflect Percival Everett's interest in the culture of the American West, *Wounded* focuses on one man's rediscovery of himself as a result of his reengagement in the lives of others. Cut off from the larger world in part because of geographical distance (his ranch is thirty miles from the nearest town), in part because of race (he is one of very few African Americans in the rural West), and in part because of the psychological and emotional walls that he has built around himself since the death of his wife Susie six years earlier, John Hunt must redirect the course of his life when he is forced to respond to events in the local community.

It is clear that John is more comfortable with animals than with people. The first half of the novel is peppered with bits of wisdom that he has acquired from his years of training horses, such as the dictum that "the horse isn't supposed to make decisions." It comes down to control; John believes that he understands and can therefore control horses, but people are another matter. The landscape is also an object of fascination and a source of comfort for John, who responds deeply to the "dramatic land, dry, remote, wild." John himself admits that he has "no affection necessarily for the history of the people" of the West. "It [is] the land for me," John affirms. It may, however, be the sheer inhospitality of the landscape that necessitates some sort of communal bonding; to survive in this space, people need to band together in common cause.

Just as horses find him to be a calming force, people are drawn to John's quiet authority. A man of few words but strong of character, independent of mind, and compassionate to those victimized by others, John Hunt fits the mold of the archetypal Western hero. As signaled by the novel's title, a single man, "wounded" by the course his personal life has taken—particularly the loss of his wife—finds the strength to shelter and defend others "wounded" by prejudice and bigotry. In taking a stand, John rediscovers himself; he admits near the end of the novel, "I can't recognize my own tracks until I stop moving."

The Water Cure

Another example of Everett's ongoing experimentation in the genre of the novel, *The Water Cure* recounts the harrowing story of the aftermath of the kidnapping and murder of a young girl told through the perspective of her father. Like his other novels, the story contains multiple layers, one of which can be read as an allegory of the American condition in the age of the war on terrorism.

The narrator, Ishmael Kidder, earns his living writing romance novels under the pseudonym Estelle Gilliam, but he has submerged his work and identity into finding and punishing his daughter's killer. The man has been freed on a technicality, allowing Kidder to find and kidnap him. He subjects the man to torture, interrupting the narration of revenge with philosophical discourses featuring Socrates, René Descartes, and Pope Gregory as he interrogates both the kidnapper and the nature of evil. The novel also contains passages of Joycean language experimentation in which the narrator transforms ordinary speech through a process

of multilingual puns and interchanging of syllables. The blending of words reaches the edges of intelligibility, as does the blending of identities between criminal and victim. The pages of the novel also contain progressive line drawings that gradually build up to readable images, once more raising the theme of the written word versus the drawn image seen in *Glyph*. This question, of course, as the narrator of *The Water Cure* makes explicit, originates in Plato's discussion of the arts in the *Republic*.

Analysis: Short Fiction

Damned If I Do

Everett once said he does not want to talk about race; he just wants to make art. And, he might have added, make us laugh at ourselves in the process. In the delightful collection *Damned If I Do*, even stories about racial prejudice are treated with a light satirical touch. In "The Appropriation of Cultures," a young black man buys a pickup truck with a confederate flag on the back and, by driving it around, gradually undermines a symbol of racial injustice more successfully than conventional protests. In another story that centers on a pickup truck, a romance novelist who is just trying to earn a living, enjoy his privacy, and protect the environment, finds a way to make Hollywood pay through the nose and, in the process, staves off real estate and commercial encroachment. Everett is a writer who makes readers laugh and does not preach, a writer whose only agenda is exploring the vulnerability and absurdity of the human condition.

Other Literary Forms

In addition to writing long fiction, Percival Everett has published short stories, poetry, and works he has characterized as "multimedia," such as *Re: f (gesture)* (2006). In 1992, he published a children's book, *The One That Got Away*. His most notable collections of short stories are *Big Picture* (1996) and *Damned If I Do* (2004). Everett also served as the fiction editor for the journal *Callaloo* (1994), and his work was featured in a special issue of that journal in 2005. His collection of poetry *Abstraktion und Einfühlung* was published in 2008.

Everett, a prolific and eclectic writer, challenges the conventions of genre in works such as *A History of the African-American People (Proposed) by Strom Thurmond*, a collaborative work that plays with the conventions of the epistolary novel and the slave narrative. His novel *Walk Me to the Distance* was adapted as a film for television under the title *Follow Your Heart* (1990). In his work, Everett draws on a background in ordinary language philosophy from his academic studies as well as his passions for horse training, woodworking, and fly fishing. He has said that he would rather paint than write, and he has exhibited his abstract paintings.

Bibliography

Bell, Bernard W. *The Contemporary African American Novel: Its Folk Roots and Modern Literary Branches.* Amherst: U of Massachusetts P, 2004. In a section labeled "The New Black Aesthetic," Bell acknowledges the merit of *Erasure* as a semiautobiographical experiment, but he is essentially critical of what he sees as the author's apparent lack of regard for how his racial identity has informed his aesthetic practice.

Brown, Rosellen. "The Emperor's New Fiction." *Boston Review* 11 (Aug. 1986): 7-8. While praising *Walk Me to the Distance* for its skillful organization and its essential hopefulness, Brown laments the fact that Everett has avoided the issues of African American identity, both personal and societal.

Dickson-Carr, Darryl. *The Columbia Guide to Contemporary African American Fiction.* New York: Columbia UP, 2005. A brief article argues for Everett's inclusion among the ranks of literary modernists such as Ralph Ellison; it provides some information on the critical reception of *Erasure*.

Eaton, Kimberly. "Deconstructing the Narrative: Language, Genre, and Experience in *Erasure*." *Nebula* 3 (Sep. 2006): 220-32. Explores how the novel questions the reliability of language, genre categories, racial identity, and belief in stereotypes.

Everett, Percival. "The Satiric Inferno." Interview by Peter Monaghan. *Chronicle of Higher Education* 51, no. 23 (2005): A18-20. Everett answers questions about his influences, his style, and his intended audience. Provides overview and analysis of Everett's major publications.

Gray, Paul. "Laugh Track." *New York* 122 (22 Aug. 1983): 70. The novel abandons its promising beginning, Craig Suder's many-layered professional and personal predicament, and opts for jokes at the expense of character development.

Hemesath, James. "*Walk Me to the Distance*." *Library Journal* 110 (1 Mar. 1985): 102. After a rather thin but pleasing first half, Hemesath writes, the novel turns serious and ugly. Unfortunately, he claims, the characterization, description of setting, and general tone lacks the weight sufficient to maintain the author's sober purpose.

Hoffman, Alice. "Slumps and Tailspins." *The New York Times Book Review* (2 Oct. 1983): 9, 26. Describes the novel's humor as often overstated. Calls "redeemingly evocative" the flashbacks involving Suder's youth, wherein the author captures the "terrors of childhood."

Masiki, Trent. "Irony and Ecstasy: A Profile of Percival Everett." *Poets and Writers* 32, no. 3 (2004): 33-39. Focuses on Everett's life and work with a special emphasis on the contention that art transcends the boundaries of race and ethnicity.

Maus, Derek C. *Jesting in Earnest: Percival Everett and Menippean Satire.* Columbia: U of South Carolina P, 2019. Contends that "the best way to analyze Everett's varied oeuvre is within the framework of Menippean satire, which focuses its ridicule on faulty modes of thinking, especially the kinds of willful ignorance and bad faith that are used to justify corruption, violence, and bigotry." Examines "fourteen of Everett's novels and several of his shorter works" through this lens.

Mitchell, Keith B, and Robin G. Vander, eds. *Perspectives on Percival Everett.* Jackson: UP of Mississippi, 2013. Contains nine chapters on such topics as knowledge, certainty, identity; "forclusion"; preservationist impulses; the mind-body split; blues, jazz, the journey to the self; Everett's critique of race, religion and science; from stereotype to cosmopolitan to grotesque; corporeal landscapes; and when the text becomes the stage.

"Percival Everett: A Special Section." *Callaloo* 28, no. 2 (Spring 2005): 291-342. Volume of the noted African American literary journal devotes a substantial section to Everett. Includes an interview, personal tributes, images of Everett's paintings, and substantial critical essays on *God's Country, Glyph, Erasure,* and *Watershed.* Fiona Macrae, Everett's editor at Graywolf Press, contributes a brief discussion of *Frenzy,* and a dialogue is presented between Everett and James Kincaid, a professor of English at the University of California and Everett's collaborator on *A History of the African American People.*

Ramsey, W. M. "Knowing Their Place: Three Writers and the Postmodern South." *Southern Literary Journal* 37, no. 2 (Spring 2005): 119-39. First formulates the concept of the "postmodern South" and then places African American authors Yusef Komunyakaa, Percival Everett, and James McBride within that context. Offers substantive analyses of Everett's novels *Glyph* and *Erasure.*

Review of *Suder,* by Percival Everett. *The Atlantic* 252 (Sep. 1983): 124. The narrative does not live up to initial expectations, and the ending is especially unsatisfactory. "Even daffiness provides no escape from a daft world."

Review of *Walk Me to the Distance. Kirkus Reviews* 52 (15 Dec. 1984): 1156-57. Although praising *Suder* as "intriguing but strained," the review finds *Walk Me to the Distance* hard to enjoy and hard to believe. Argues that there is "emotional power" in the "David/Sixbury/Patrick triangle," but that the rest of the narrative is encumbered by clumsy plotting and dialogue marked by "Gary-Cooperish grunts."

Review of *Walk Me to the Distance. Publishers Weekly* 226 (21 Dec. 1984): 81. States that *Walk Me to the Distance* is hampered by a spare prose style that leaves too much to reader interpretation. Argues that the novel nevertheless provides an evocative treatment of one veteran's "repatriation."

Rozié, Fabrice, Esther Allen, and Guy Walter, eds. *As You Were Saying: American Writers Respond to Their French Contemporaries.* Champaign, IL: Dalkey Archive Press, 2007. Includes an exchange between Everett and French writer Grégoire Bouillier; provides insight into Everett's literary investments, tastes, and poetics.

Russett, Margaret. "Race Under Erasure." *Callaloo* 28, no. 2 (2005): 358-68. One of the most extensive readings of the novel, drawing many parallels between the main character and Everett himself.

Sanchez-Arce, Anna Maria. "'Authenticism' or the Authority of Authenticity." *Mosaic: A Journal for the Interdisciplinary Study of Literature* 40 (Sep. 2007): 139-55. Provides a close reading of Erasure as part of a general discussion of the notion that a work of literature needs to be tied to its origins in order to be properly evaluated.

See, Carolyn. "*Suder.*" *Los Angeles Times Book Review* 31 July 1983: 1, 8. The novel is a comic masterpiece that tells how an individual can achieve transcendence over problems.

Smith, Wendy. "*Walk Me to the Distance.*" *The New York Times Book Review* 24 Mar. 1985: 24. Argues that the novel can be read as a cautionary tale concerning the misplaced desire to escape the problems of the modern world, including the increasingly problematic relationships between men and women, by seeking some imagined frontier. Asserts that the book's theme and characterization, however, are undercut by a "terseness that verges on blankness."

Weixlmann, Joe, ed. *Conversations with Percival Everett.* Jackson: UP of Mississippi, 2013. An important collection of interviews.

— Amee Carmines; Thomas S. Mack; Charles E. May; Anita Price Davis; Robert C. Evans

Jessie Redmon Fauset

Novelist and Journalist

Born: Snow Hill, New Jersey; April 27, 1882

Died: Philadelphia, Pennsylvania; April 30, 1961

LONG FICTION: *There Is Confusion*, 1924; *Plum Bun: A Novel Without a Moral*, 1928; *The Chinaberry Tree: A Novel of American Life*, 1931; *Comedy, American Style*, 1933.

Achievements

Jessie Fauset was one of the most prolific novelists of the Harlem Renaissance of the 1920s, when her works were highly praised for introducing the reading public to a class of African Americans unknown to whites. Perhaps more important than her own works was her publishing and nurturing of other Harlem Renaissance writers as literary editor of *The Crisis*, the journal of the National Association for the Advancement of Colored People (NAACP), from 1919 to 1926. In that capacity, she published works by Langston Hughes, Claude McKay, Nella Larsen, Jean Toomer, and Countee Cullen. In 1920, Fauset also became the managing editor of the short-lived *The Brownies' Book*, writer W.E.B. Du Bois's magazine for children. Her first novel, *There Is Confusion*, was nominated for the Harmon Award in Literature in 1928.

Biography

Jessie Redmon Fauset, the youngest of seven children born to Redmon Fauset, an African Methodist Episcopal minister, and Annie Seamon Fauset, was born in New Jersey on April 27, 1882. She attended the public schools in Philadelphia and graduated as an honor student from the Philadelphia School for Girls. When she sought admission to Bryn Mawr College, rather than admit her, they supported her application to Cornell University. Fauset graduated Phi Beta Kappa from Cornell in 1904. Whether she was the first black woman to attend Cornell or to be elected to Phi Beta Kappa, both of which are often speculated, Fauset has been called "one of the best-educated Americans of her generation."

Denied employment in Philadelphia's integrated schools, Fauset began teaching high school in New York in 1905. After a year there and a year in Baltimore, she moved to the M Street High School (later named Dunbar High School) in Washington, D.C., where she taught for fourteen years. In 1921, a few months after receiving her master's degree from the University of Pennsylvania, Fauset joined the staff of *The Crisis* as literary editor. In 1924 she published her first novel. Fauset left *The Crisis* and returned to teaching in 1926. In 1929, she married a businessman, Herbert Harris, and between 1929 and 1933, she completed three other novels. When her husband died in 1958, Fauset returned to Philadelphia, where she died in 1961.

Photo courtesy of Bernard Botturi

Analysis: Long Fiction

Although she had been writing for *The Crisis* since her undergraduate days, it was not literary aspiration that spurred Fauset to write novels, but rather the 1922 publication of T. S. Stribling's novel about a middle-class mulatto, *Birthright*. Realizing that there was "an audience waiting to hear the truth about" African Americans, Fauset felt that those who were better qualified than whites to present the truth should do so. In presenting such truth, Fauset wrote about characters she knew best: educated African Americans from respectable family backgrounds, whose values and goals were, as she stated, "not so vastly different from other Americans." Fauset used traditional literary forms in her writing, such as the sentimental novel, Greek tragedy, and fairy tales, and was criticized for offering nothing innovative during a time when African American writers were experimenting with cultural forms and themes. In addition, because Fauset's novels focused on women and women's issues, they were dismissed in the 1930s by both white and black male critics. With the burgeoning interest in African American women's literature in the 1970s, female critics began to discover the complexity of Fauset's novels and to note her treatment of gender, class, and race issues. As a result, Fauset's works have become the focus of increased critical attention.

There Is Confusion

Fauset's first novel, *There Is Confusion*—a tale of two families—is structured by three separate but connected plotlines, the first of which focuses on the Marshalls, a well-to-do family. Joanna, the youngest of the four children, encouraged by her father's thwarted dreams of greatness, wants to become a dancer. The second plotline focuses on Peter Bye, the fourth-generation descendant of a family whose lives are intertwined with their wealthy white former owners. While Peter's grandfather, Isaiah, refuses to accept his relative's offer to serve as their coachman and goes on to found a school for black youths in Philadelphia, Peter's dreams of becoming a surgeon are thwarted because he longs to be recognized by the white Byes and is not. Meriwether, Peter's father, deciding instead that "the world owes [him] a living," does nothing. Influenced by his father's attitude, Peter becomes entangled in the legacy of racial hatred and aspires to nothing. It is only when he becomes attracted to Joanna and is influenced by her goals of greatness that he decides, in order to win her love, to become a doctor.

The third plotline, the story of Maggie Ellersley, the daughter of a washerwoman, involves a conventional marriage. Aspiring to the middle class, Maggie begins working for Joanna's father, where she meets and takes an interest in his son, Philip. The interest appears to be mutual; however, Joanna intervenes and tells Maggie that she should marry someone in her own class. A hurt Maggie does so, then becomes a successful businesswoman when the marriage fails. After a second failed marriage, Maggie goes to France to volunteer during the war and encounters the dying Philip. They marry, and she takes care of him until his death.

Within each plotline Fauset heavy-handedly reveals the obstacles to the achievement of each character's dreams: Joanna's dream of becoming a professional dancer is thwarted by race, Peter's dream (or lack thereof) is influenced by family legacy, Maggie's dream is hindered by class. Yet Fauset also reveals how each character achieves despite the obstacles. Unable to dance in a white theater troupe, Joanna starts her own dance class but is asked to dance the role of the colored American in "The Dance of the Nations" when the white woman chosen for the part lacks the technique. Joanna attains instant success and is eventually asked to perform three roles.

Peter, because of his love for Joanna, becomes a surgeon; however, she has no interest in assuming the conventional roles of wife and mother. Therefore, caught in the web of circumstances characteristic of sentimental novels, and through a series of contrived coincidences, Peter ends up in Europe during the war and meets one of his white relatives. Young Meriwether dies in Peter's arms, but not before extracting the promise that Peter would visit the senior Meriwether. By moving beyond hate, Peter not only receives the long-awaited recognition from the white Byes but also wins Joanna as his wife.

As evidenced by the many hardships that Maggie undergoes, Fauset suggests that Maggie's aspiration—to transcend one's class through marriage—is the most problematic. Maggie achieves her desired middle-class status not through her marriages but rather through her business acumen. Moreover, by developing a political and racial consciousness and selflessness and traveling to Europe to aid black soldiers, she is reunited with her first love. *There Is Confusion* ends, as do all sentimental novels, on a happy note. While there are many ideas introduced in the novel, critic Carolyn Sylvander states that the theme that dominates is that "surviving the hardships engendered by discrimination places the black person and the race in a position of superiority."

Plum Bun

Fauset's second novel, *Plum Bun*, is considered by most critics her best. As with *There Is Confusion*, a middle-class African American family is at the novel's center, but unlike *There Is Confusion*, its plot is centered on one protagonist, Angela. In addition, the novel is structured in five parts, using a nursery rhyme as its epigraph and unifying element:

> To market, to market
> To buy a plum bun;
> Home again, home again, Market is
> done.

In the first section, titled "Home," Fauset's readers are introduced to the Murray family: Junius and Mattie and their two daughters, Angela and Virginia. This section also provides the background information important to the rest of the novel. Angela and Virginia are exposed early on to their mother's fairy-tale view of marriage. Just as important, they are exposed to her views on color. Although Junius and Virginia are both brown-skinned, Mattie and Angela are light enough to pass— which they often do "for fun." Junius is not opposed to this as long as no principle is being compromised. The result is, however, that Angela grows up seeing her mother on occasion publicly ignore her dark husband and daughter. When the parents die within two weeks of each other, Angela decides to move to New York in order to further her personal and professional goals. In "Market," Angela becomes the art student Angele Mory and is indoctrinated in the worldly ways of courtship. In section 3, entitled "Plum Bun," Angele meets Roger Fielding, an affluent white man, whom she dates and eventually hopes to marry. Roger does not propose marriage but rather cohabitation. Angele does not agree, and he eventually ends the relationship, but not before Angele has publicly denied Virginia, who has also moved to New York.

In "Home Again," the novel's fourth section, Angele, in search of companionship, admits her love for Anthony Cross, a fellow art student who is also passing. Having resolved never to marry a white woman, Anthony rejects Angele and becomes engaged unknowingly to her sister.

In the final section, "Market Is Done," Angele decides to focus on her art. She wins a scholarship to study in Paris but forfeits it by revealing that she, too, is black when fellow student Rachel Powell is denied money for her passage because of her race. Angele decides to support her own study in Paris. Before she leaves the United States, she returns "home" to Philadelphia and is reunited with a former admirer, Matthew Henson. Knowing that Virginia is really in love with Matthew, and learning that Matthew loves Virginia, Angele does not interfere. Instead she moves to Paris, seemingly destined to be alone; however, Anthony appears that Christmas Eve, sent with Matthew and Virginia's love. Like *There Is Confusion*, *Plum Bun* has a happy ending.

By including the nursery rhyme and fairy-tale motifs within the marriage plot, Fauset explores the choices and compromises women make regarding marriage. The novel "without a moral" indeed has one: Adhering to the traditional conceptions of marriage is problematic when race, class, and gender are factors.

The Chinaberry Tree

Fauset's theme of the effects of race, gender, and class as focused within two-parent, multiple-sibling families is abandoned in her third novel. *The Chinaberry Tree* relates the story of two cousins, Laurentine Strange and Melissa Paul, who are both products of illicit relationships.

Laurentine is the product of an illicit romantic relationship between a master, Colonel Halloway, and his former slave, Sarah (Sal). Accepting the community's opinion that she has "bad blood," Laurentine isolates herself from the community, and rejection from a suitor reinforces her feelings of inadequacy and propels her to further isolation. Melissa, the product of an adulterous relationship between Judy Strange and the married Sylvester Forten, is sent to Red Brook to live with her relatives. She meets and falls in love with Malory Forten, who, unknown to her, is her half brother. The novel explores both women's responses to being innocent victims of fate.

The Chinaberry Tree is not merely Fauset's attempt to reveal that "negroes are not so vastly different" nor that their lives are elements of a play falling together, as stated in its foreword. It is a subtle illustration of women making choices and accepting the consequences: Both Sal and Judy Strange choose forbidden loves. In spite of their "bad blood," as the daughters are seemingly tainted by their mothers' choices, Laurentine and Melissa are able to find true love at the novel's end. What appears to be another example of Fauset's blind acceptance of the values of nineteenth century sentimental fiction is a subtle commentary on women refusing to adhere to the constrictions placed on their lives.

Comedy, American Style

Fauset structured her final novel around the elements of drama, with its chapters entitled "The Plot," "The Characters," "Teresa's Act," "Oliver's Act," "Phebe's Act," and "Curtain." In this, Fauset's darkest work, she returns to the format of the two-parent family. The novel chronicles the life of Olivia Blanchard Cary, a light-skinned African American, who, shaped by two incidents in her childhood, chooses a life of passing. She marries a black doctor, not for love but rather for status, and they have three children. Nonetheless, Olivia's obsession with color consciousness destroys the family. When the oldest child, Teresa, falls in love with the dark-skinned Henry Bates, Olivia intervenes and forces her to marry a French man.

The youngest child, Oliver, suffers the most because of his bronze skin color. Rejected by his mother from birth and often made to play the role of servant or denied in public, he commits suicide. Only Christopher survives intact through his marriage to Phebe Grant. When the novel ends, Olivia has finally achieved her objective: Living alone in France—her husband has divorced her, and her children have abandoned her—she passes as white. In this, her only novel that does not have a happy ending, Fauset's useof satire is quite evident. One critic, pointing to Fauset's subversion of the Cinderella motif, notes that neither mother nor daughter is happily married, and both are poor. Another critic illustrates the ironic use of the Snow White motif: Olivia pronounces the bitter truth in her pregnancy with Oliver that he would be "the handsomest and most attractive of us all," and by doing so she unwittingly proclaims that black is beautiful.

Other Literary Forms

In addition to the four novels, Jessie Redmon Fauset wrote short stories, poems, nonfictional pieces, and works for children. She also translated the work of some Haitian writers.

Bibliography

Ahlin, Lena. *The "New Negro" in the Old World: Culture and Performance in James Weldon Johnson, Jessie Fauset, and Nella Larsen.* Lund, Sweden: Almqvist & Wiksell, 2006. Argues that Johnson, Fauset, and Larsen questioned the standard assumption that Europe was a place of relative freedom and acceptance for black Americans.

Hale, Anthony. "Nanny/Mamma: Comparing Lady Gregory and Jessie Fauset." *Cultural Studies* 15, no. 1 (January, 2001): 161173. An essay centered on the importance of servants in the work of Lady Augusta Gregory and Jessie Redmon Fauset, particularly with respect to class, race, gender, and socioeconomic status.

Harker, Jaime. *America the Middlebrow: Women's Novels, Progressivism, and Middlebrow Authorship Between the Wars.* Amherst: University of Massachusetts Press, 2007. Fauset is one of four authors examined in terms of their efforts to use their fiction to promote secular and progressive Americanism.

Levison, Susan. "Performance and the 'Strange Place' of Jessie Redmon Fauset's *There Is Confusion.*" *Modern Fiction Studies* 46, no. 4 (Winter, 2000): 825-849. A review of Fauset's book.

McDowell, Deborah. "Jessie Fauset." In *Modern American Women Writers*, edited by Lea Baechler and A. Walton Litz. New York: Charles Scribner's Sons, 1991. A general discussion of Fauset's role in the Harlem Renaissance as editor and writer, the article provides an analysis of Fauset's four novels to illustrate their "thematic and ironic complexity."

Miller, Nina. "Femininity, Publicity, and the Class Division of Cultural Labor: Jessie Redmon Fauset's *There Is Confusion.*" *African American Review* 30, no. 2 (Summer, 1996): 205-221. A review of *There Is Confusion* focused on the importance of the Harlem Renaissance and African American culture in general.

Ransom, Portia Boulware. *Black Love and the Harlem Renaissance: The Novels of Nella Larsen, Jessie Redmon Fauset, and Zora Neale Hurston.* Lewiston, NY: Edwin Mellen Press, 2005. Deals with such topics as black men, black women, love, and the "politics of intimacy." Also discusses the influence of these writers on later African American women authors.

Sato, Hiroko. "Under the Harlem Shadow: A Study of Jessie Fauset and Nella Larsen." In *The Harlem Renaissance Remembered,* edited by Arna Bontemps. New York: Dodd, Mead, 1972. While asserting that Fauset "is not a first-rate writer," Sato argues that race is the central concern of the novels' middle-class characters.

Sylvander, Carolyn. *Jessie Redmon Fauset: Black American Writer.* Troy, N.Y.: Whitston, 1981. In this definitive critical biography on Fauset, Sylvander argues that reading Fauset's novels as compared to her life is too simplistic.

Wall, Cheryl. *Women of the Harlem Renaissance.* Bloomington: Indiana University Press, 1995. Wall provides an excellent discussion of all of Fauset's works yet believes Fauset achieved distinction as a journalist and essayist.

— *Paula C. Barnes; Robert C. Evans*

Charles Fuller

Playwright

Born: Philadelphia, Pennsylvania; March 5, 1939

DRAMA: *Sun Flowers, The Rise*, pr. 1968 (one acts); *The Village: A Party*, pr. 1968, pb. 1969 (as *The Perfect Party*); *In My Many Names and Days*, pr. 1972; *The Candidate*, pr. 1974; *First Love*, pr. 1974; *In the Deepest Part of Sleep*, pr. 1974; *The Lay Out Letter*, pr. 1975; *The Brownsville Raid*, pr. 1976; *Sparrow in Flight*, pr. 1978; *Zooman and the Sign*, pr. 1980, pb. 1982; *A Soldier's Play*, pr., pb. 1981; *Sally*, pr. 1988; *Prince*, pr. 1988; *Eliot's Coming*, pr. 1988 (pr. as part of the musical revue *Urban Blight*); *We*, pr. 1989 (combined performance of *Sally* and *Prince*, parts 1 and 2 of five-part play series); *Jonquil*, pr. 1990 (part 3 of *We* play series); *Burner's Frolic*, pr. 1990 (part 4 of *We* play series).

SCREENPLAYS: *A Soldier's Story*, 1984 (adaptation of his play); *Zooman*, 1995 (adaptation of his play).

TELEPLAYS: *Roots, Resistance, and Renaissance*, 1967 (series); *Mitchell*, 1968; *Black America*, 1970-1971 (series); *The Sky Is Gray*, 1980 (from the story by Ernest J. Gaines); *A Gathering of Old Men*, 1987 (adaptation of the novel by Ernest J. Gaines); *Love Songs*, 1999.

Achievements

Charles Fuller is one of a growing number of African American playwrights who have entered the mainstream of American drama. Previously, plays dealing with the black experience, such as Louis Peterson's *Take a Giant Step* (pr. 1954), Lorraine Hansberry's *A Raisin in the Sun* (pr., pb. 1959), and Ossie Davis's *Purlie Victorious* (pr.

1961), were rueful reproaches of white intolerance. Probably because of the period during which they were written (the late 1950s and early 1960s), they did not seek to stir up violent passions but rather to nudge the audience's sensibilities; as a result, they could enjoy a modest run in a commercial theater on Broadway. By the end of the 1960s, however, the Off-Broadway theater, which was always more daring (and less expensive), encouraged plays such as *Dutchman* (pr., pb. 1964) by Amiri Baraka (LeRoi Jones), *Ceremonies in Dark Old Men* (pr. 1965) by Lonne Elder III, and *No Place to Be Somebody* (pr. 1967) by Charles Gordone, the first black playwright to win a Pulitzer Prize, in 1970; these works paved the way for a more aggressive theater reflecting more militant times. As a result, when Fuller appeared on the scene, while he was able to dramatize the plight of African Americans for audiences that were more receptive than they had been in the past, he differed from his fellow playwrights in that he examined the effect of violence *among* black people as resulting from their environment.

Several of Fuller's plays deal with black-on-black murder and are constructed as mysteries; the hunt is on to discover not only the killer's identity but also the cause of the crime. His plays are less traditional in structure, freely moving back and forth in time. His characters often break the illusion of the fourth wall by actively engaging the audience in soliloquies, so that although his subject matter is realistic, his technique is expressionistic. In addition to his own screen adaptation of his drama *A Soldier's Play* (the film version is entitled *A Soldier's Story* and was a great success), he has contributed an adaptation of an Ernest J. Gaines story to public television and an original script to network television. He has also taught at Temple and Toronto universities. Fuller has been the recipient of two Obie Awards, of Rockefeller and National Endowment for the Arts grants in 1976, of a Guggenheim Fellowship in 1977, and in 1982 of a New York Drama Critics Circle Award, an Outer Critics Circle Award, and a Pulitzer Prize—the second awarded to an African American playwright.

Biography

Charles Henry Fuller, Jr., was born in Philadelphia, Pennsylvania, on March 5, 1939. In the course of time, his parents housed twenty foster children, eventually adopting two of them. The family lived in a Philadelphia housing project until Fuller's father, a printer, went into business for himself and became one of the first African Americans admitted to the local printer's union. Soon, the family moved to a racially mixed neighborhood in North Philadelphia, where the Fullers, devout Roman Catholics, sent their children to integrated parochial schools.

As a young boy, Fuller became interested in books by helping his father correct galley proofs; when he was thirteen and had gone to the theater for the first time in his life to see Molly Picon performing in Yiddish (a language he did not even understand), he was so exhilarated that he was convinced he wanted to do nothing but write plays. In high school, he formed a lifelong friendship with Larry Neal, to whom he later dedicated *A Soldier's Play* and after whom he modeled its leading character, Captain Richard Davenport. Because Neal also was devoted to literature, eventually becoming

a published poet and critic, the two young men buoyed up each other's ambitions. After graduation from high school in 1956, Fuller, an English major, attended Villanova University, where he was discouraged from writing because of his race. He left in 1959 to enlist in the army in Japan and South Korea, an experience he prefers not to discuss although it must have served as material for his plays. Returning to civilian life in 1962, he registered at La Salle College, studying at night while supporting himself by working as a bank loan collector in a loan company, as a student counselor at Temple University, and later as a housing inspector for the city. During this time, he kept alive his love for drama by helping to found and run the Afro-American Art Theater in Philadelphia, creating a kind of street theater for ghetto inhabitants. After his first play was produced at Princeton's McCarter Theater in 1968, Fuller left La Salle College without graduating and devoted himself full-time to his literary career. His plans included work on a musical and a cycle of plays concerning the African American experience from 1866 to 1900. Drawing from that experience, he created a series of five plays set during the American Civil War and post-bellum America, produced by the Negro Ensemble Company between 1988 and 1990.

Analysis: Drama

While the plays of Charles Fuller, like those of other African American dramatists, explore the tensions in a society in which the African American minority is constantly exploited and repressed by the white majority, Fuller has set his sights on changing the way Western civilization perceives black people. At the same time, he attempts to avoid stereotyping whites, insisting that groups are formed of individuals, and all are different, some good, some bad. As a consequence, his characters have greater depth and complexity, and he avoids the cliched situations that afflict so many problem plays. He is also deeply interested in telling a story, which is the point at which he usually begins his plays. First, what happened; then, to whom; and finally, why? Even after these questions appear to be answered, the results often raise greater issues that lead to even more perplexing questions. Ambiguity, not resolution, is at the heart of Fuller's work.

Fuller's major concern is not only the violence in today's universe and the way it erodes character but also the violence that black people employ against one another. Although they occupy a world originally shaped by whites who enslaved and abused them, African Americans continue to prey on one another while accepting the role of victim at the hands of their oppressors. The cycle is always the same: sullen passivity that erupts into armed rebellion, followed by chaos, before subjugation and a relapse into bitter acceptance. All of his plays possess this cycle, regardless of the difference in subject matter; artistically, they are a poignant echo of real life, of the race riots that have burned American cities since the 1960s. Yet, though Fuller's canvas is large, his use of the personalized grief of his characters gives the plays a human scale; he is never didactic.

Early Plays

In his first full-length play, *The Village: A Party*, he builds the story around a community composed of five interracial couples. When the black leader falls in love with a black woman, against all the rules of their society, disaster occurs. What is original here is the way Fuller turns accepted convention upside down: In real life, obstacles to marriage confront people of different races. If the play, however, is taken as a metaphor for the barriers encountered by slaves who were forbidden to marry, it becomes clear that Fuller is condemning any law that

arbitrarily decides what is right or wrong without considering its effect on human beings. Another early work, *In My Many Names and Days*, consists of six one-act plays about a black family, a structure he would adopt again when planning his five-play cycle of full-length dramas. *The Candidate* represents his study of a black man's campaign to become mayor of his city and the struggles this entails, revealing Fuller's growing attraction to political themes.

The Brownsville Raid

Fuller, who was becoming increasingly engrossed by the Civil War (he dates the African American relation to the United States from the Emancipation Proclamation), blended politics with history in his greatest success to date, *The Brownsville Raid*. While working in New York with the Negro Ensemble Company, which had previously staged his first play for the group (*In the Deepest Part of Sleep*), Fuller showed the direction that his future plays would take. Using a historical event as its basis, *The Brownsville Raid* dramatizes the story of a company of black soldiers who, in 1906, were wrongfully accused of causing a riot in Texas and shooting a man. In the play, Fuller also explores the relationship between President Theodore Roosevelt and Booker T. Washington, who asks his black editors to play down the "incident" to preserve the peace. The soldiers are dishonorably discharged, and only sixty years later are they vindicated when the truth is discovered. For all of them, however, it is too late.

Zooman and the Sign

Although Fuller returned to a smaller-scale play with *Zooman and the Sign*, he again used the device of a murder investigation, which had already appeared in *The Brownsville Raid*, to propel the story. In addition, he began experimenting with the title character's soliloquies, which alternated with the general action, giving the play an abrupt, stop-start rhythm. The situation in *Zooman and the Sign* is one all too recognizable today: A twelve-year-old girl is accidentally killed in a fight between two street gangs, and the play charts the efforts of her anguished parents to discover the killer. Equally harrowing is the underlying theme: The father, in despair that none of his neighbors will come forward to identify the killer (because they are afraid that as witnesses they will have to deal with the police, though they themselves are innocent), puts up a sign outside his house proclaiming that his daughter's killers are free because of the community's indifference. The neighbors, in turn, are so incensed by the accusation that they threaten his life and attempt to tear down the sign. Their rage, in short, is turned against one of their own people; they have lost their sense of responsibility to one another because it has been destroyed by the very institution that should be protecting them: the law. Here, Fuller has touched on a universal theme, for in just such a way were Nazi concentration camp monitors, though prisoners themselves, wont to ally themselves against their fellow captives because of their own brutalization. Meanwhile, the killer, Zooman, has proclaimed himself to the audience and in his soliloquies explains his way of life, noting that if a black man kills a black man and is not caught immediately, the authorities forget about it. In an ironic twist, the dead girl's uncle, unaware of the murderer's identity, accidentally shoots him, just as the niece was accidentally killed. When the parents look at the dead face of the "perpetrator," it is thatof a teenage boy who, in his mind, has made virility synonymous with violence.

A Soldier's Play

In his finest and most successful work, *A Soldier's Play*, which Fuller says was inspired by Herman Melville's *Billy Budd, Foretopman* (1924), he combines and perfects the themes and technique of his two previous dramas. Calling on audience imagination, he sets his story in a space almost Elizabethan in its use: minimal scenery, few props, and areas that could be transformed from outdoors to indoors or from an office to a soldier's bunk. In addition, as one character is narrating an event in the present moment, by crossing from one side of the stage to the other, he moves into time past.

The play is a mixture of fact and fiction. It depicts an actual unit of black soldiers in the 1940s, stationed in a small southern town while awaiting transfer to Europe. One of the ironies of the situation is the fact that while they are fighting for freedom abroad, they are still segregated at home. The play opens with true Elizabethan violence: A black sergeant is murdered by someone unseen, and he cries out in his death agony, "They still hate you," the sense of which is obscure until the pieces fall into place. The murder worries the white officer in charge of the group because of the suspicion that it was committed by the Ku Klux Klan, resentful that black soldiers had been quartered in the Klan's vicinity. A black officer, Captain Richard Davenport, who is also a lawyer, is sent to investigate; his presence disconcerts the white officers, one of whom confesses that he cannot accustom himself to the sight of an African American in charge. The black soldiers, who are pathetically proud of Davenport's status, are nevertheless unresponsive to his questions because, like the uncooperative neighbors of *Zooman and the Sign*, they are fearful that anything they reveal will cause trouble for them with the white authorities.

What finally emerges is the portrait of the murdered: He is the sadistic Sergeant Waters who, ashamed of being black, drove his men unmercifully, particularly one private, C. J. Memphis. Waters was infuriated by the good-natured, slow-moving, guitar-strumming C. J., who, he believed, prevented ambitious African Americans from moving ahead because he seemed to represent the traditional "nigguh" as seen by whites. Waters harassed C. J., first accusing him of a shooting in town, of which he was innocent, and then provoking him into a fight so that he could be arrested for attacking his superior. Unable to endure being imprisoned like a caged bird, C. J. killed himself; in revenge for what Waters has done, Private Peterson, the most intelligent and, therefore, the most rebellious man in the unit, shot Waters and fled, accompanied by his friend, Private Wilkie, who had witnessed the murder.

When the two are caught, Davenport asks why Wilkie stood by and did nothing while one African American murdered another; all Wilkie can stammer is that he was afraid. Before his death, Waters had gone on a drunken binge to erase the memory of what had happened to C. J.; encountering two white officers, Waters had found in alcohol the courage to speak disrespectfully to them. They, in turn, had beaten him brutally and left him on the road at the moment when Peterson found him, began an argument with him, and finally shot him. In Peterson's eyes, Waters is the real villain, not because he drove C. J. to suicide but because he was so full of hatred for his own blackness. The scene dissolves to the beginning, and suddenly, it becomes clear what Waters meant as he was dying: There is no use in struggling because no matter what black people do, white people will always hate them. At that moment, Waters becomes not a villain but the product of a society that has used him, first to destroy his fellow African Americans and then to turn his rage on himself. At the end, the unit is transferred to Europe, where, Davenport tells the audience, it was wiped out by a German advance. Grudgingly, the white captain admits that he will have to get used to the idea of African Americans in positions of authority.

Some black critics believe that Fuller softened the conclusion to make the play palatable to white audiences: The truth triumphs, the innocents are exonerated, the white captain apologizes, and the black captain has proved himself worthy of his assignment. This play, however, has no happier ending than a Shakespearean tragedy. There are resolutions, but they leave a bitter taste because there are no real winners, only an overwhelming sense of wasted lives.

We

Once more, Fuller moved back to American history. After watching the classic film *One Third of a Nation* (1939), with its infamous depiction of black-white relationships, Fuller decided to counter with his own perspective and planned his five-part opus, *We.*

Directed by Douglas Turner Ward of the Negro Ensemble Company in 1989, *Sally* and *Prince*, the first two plays in Fuller's projected cycle, provide a panoramic view of the American Civil War and its aftermath from an African American perspective. The mood of both plays is that of trust betrayed. *Sally*, set in South Carolina in the middle of the war, has a title character who is a recently freed slave and widow with a teenage son; she wishes for her son's safety, some land, and a man of her own. In one of several episodes dealing with freed slaves at loose ends or serving as Union soldiers, the black soldiers, resentful at being paid less than their white counterparts, bring about a strike and a betrayal. A black sergeant named Prince, who gains Sally's attention but has no wish to settle down, has the same kinds of ambitions and dreams common to white men. Forced to be an intermediary between the strikers and the sympathetic but firm-minded white general in charge, he is persuaded by the latter—who sees the strike as a rebellion against his authority—to identify the ringleaders, who are then shot. Prince faces a moral dilemma; he must choose whether to betray his fellow black soldiers or the army system of which he approves and in which he flourishes.

Recalling some of the same characters and more focused than the first play, *Prince* deals with the protagonist, a Union prison guard in Virginia, who fatally shoots a ruthlessly taunting Southern captive and runs off. Other characters include former slaves on a farm, who have long waited to be paid for picking cotton for the North. One worker named Burner (the title character of *Burner's Frolic*, the fourth play in the cycle) objects to the delay and is imprisoned by the well-meaning but benighted Northerner running the plantation. Burner's lover is a tough black businesswoman who makes a living selling sweetcakes and wants to have her own store. When Prince, ready to pursue his dream of heading west, refuses her request to free Burner, she stabs him, but he survives and continues on his way.

The third play in the cycle, *Jonquil*, reveals Sally with other freed women slaves being abused and raped by Klu Klux Klan members. Sally's rapist, she discovers from the blind Jonquil who recognizes him from his voice, isa judge known for his benevolence toward slaves and malignance toward those freed. Sally persuades her reluctant husband to form a black militia to fight against thuggish whites, but the results have sad consequences.

The plays received mixed but not largely positive reviews, owing to problems of focus and structure. In Fuller's plays, the focus is on the injury that blacks do to blacks, which always results ultimately from the racist infrastructure in which they find themselves. Fuller does not focus on problems between blacks and whites but rather the experiences of blacks among themselves. "I wanted," he said, "to put blacks and whites onstage as people. I didn't want to do the usual black and white confrontation piece."

Bibliography

Anadolu-Okur, Nilgun. *Contemporary African American Theater: Afrocentricity in the Works of Larry Neal, Amiri Baraka, and Charles Fuller.* New York: Garland, 1997. From the series *Studies in African American History and Culture.* Includes bibliographical references and an index.

Asante, Molefi Kete. *The Dramatic Genius of Charles Fuller: An African American Playwright.* Universal Wright Publications LLC, 2015. An accessible introduction to Fuller's work and career.

Ballard, Audreen. "Voices of the '90s." *The New Crisis* 106, no. 1 (January/February, 1999):68-73. Profiles a number of prominent African Americans, including Fuller, on the most important events and people of the last century.

Banham, Martin, ed. *The Cambridge Guide to World Theatre.* New York: Cambridge University Press, 1988. Errol Hill, a black writer and educator, contributes an article on African American theater, its history and development, which are important factors in the career of Fuller. Hill also discusses the playwright's two best-known plays in terms of their favorable reception by white critics and the more reserved attitude of black critics.

Boardman, Gerald. *The Oxford Companion to American Theatre.* New York: Oxford University Press, 1984. Contains a long and useful discussion of black playwrights in American theater, giving invaluable insights into the struggle of African American artists, particularly playwrights, to find a place for themselves. How Fuller emerged from such a background is amply documented.

Draper, James P., ed. *Black Literature Criticism.* Vol. 4. Detroit: Gale, 1992. Contains an informative article on Fuller with a biographical/critical introduction including an interview, chronology, and five excerpted critical reports in chronological order by Harold Clurman, Amiri Baraka, Richard Gilman, William Demastes, and Richard Hornby. Baraka clearly states his reserved attitude toward Fuller's depiction of black characters, as white critics present more positive reactions.

Fuller, Charles. "Charles Fuller." Interview by N. Graham Nesmith. *American Theatre* 16, no. 8 (October, 1999): 99-102. An interview with the playwright that focuses on *Love Songs* and on the author's relationship to the stage. Also features Fuller's advice for playwrights.

_____. "Pushing Beyond the Pulitzer." Interview by Frank

White. *Ebony* 38 (March, 1983): 116. In this interview, Fuller appraises what the Pulitzer Prize has meant to him and discusses the kind of plays he wishes to write—broader in scope, freer in style. He offers some illuminating details about his association with the Negro Ensemble Company and his method of work with its director and playwright, Douglas Turner Ward.

_____. "When Southern Blacks Went North." Interview by Helen Dudar. *The New York Times*, December 18, 1988, p. C5. This interview was conducted with Fuller after the two plays in his cycle, *We*, opened at the Negro Ensemble Company's theater. Fuller explains his plan to dramatize the lives of men and women as they moved North to escape slavery in the South. Fuller's goal has been to give literary permanence to black history that has been handed down largely through oral tradition.

Harriot, Esther. "Charles Fuller: The Quest for Justice." In *American Voices: Five Contemporary Playwrights in Essays and Interviews.* Jefferson, N.C.: McFarland, 1988. Harriot's critical essay places Fuller as one of five Pulitzer Prize-winning playwrights of the same generation who have provided an image of the United States as a violent and unstable society. The other writers are Sam Shepard, Lanford Wilson, David Mamet, and Marsha Norman. Fuller is identified as a writer consistently focusing attention on social issues; his major plays' leading characters are cogently discussed. Harriot's interview reveals Fuller's motivations, aspirations, working methods, and his attitude on racism.

Moritz, Charles, ed. *Current Biography, 1989.* New York: H. W. Wilson, 1989. The article on Fuller deals with his early career in the theater that he ran in Philadelphia. It also emphasizes his conviction that black-white relationships must be seen in all their complexity if they are ever to be understood.

Richardson, Riche. "Charles Fuller's Southern Specter and the Geography of Black Masculinity." *American Literature* 77, no. 1 (March, 2005): 7-32. A thought-provoking analysis of the ways in which *A Soldier's Play* informs and effects modern concepts of what it means to be black. The author argues that southern African American culture seen and judged through northern eyes have exacerbated racial tensions.

Savran, David. *In Their Own Words: Contemporary American Playwrights.* New York: Theater Communications Group, 1988. Includes one of the best and most comprehensive articles on Fuller. It offers a brief critique of his major plays and then records an interview held between Fuller and Savran in the former's apartment on November 28, 1986. In this free-ranging discussion, Fuller touches on everything from his taste in literature (Franz Kafka, Jean-Paul Sartre) to his experiments in dramatic technique and his experience in adapting *A Soldier's Play* for the screen. Photographs.

—*Mildred C. Kuner; Christian H. Moe;*
Robert C. Evans

Ernest J. Gaines

Novelist and Short-story Writer

Born: Oscar, Louisiana; January 15, 1933

Died: Oscar, Louisiana; November 5, 2019

LONG FICTION: *Catherine Carmier*, 1964; *Of Love and Dust*, 1967; *The Autobiography of Miss Jane Pittman*, 1971; *In My Father's House*, 1978; *A Gathering of Old Men*, 1983; *A Lesson Before Dying*, 1993; *The Tragedy of Brady Sims*, 2017.

SHORT FICTION: *Bloodline*, 1968; *A Long Day in November*, 1971; *Mozart and Leadbelly: Stories and Essays*, 2005.

MISCELLANEOUS: *Porch Talk with Ernest Gaines*, 1990.

Achievements

Ernest J. Gaines won the Joseph Henry Jackson Award of the San Francisco Foundation in 1959 for the short story "Comeback." He received a Rockefeller Foundation grant (1970), a John Simon Guggenheim Memorial Foundation Fellowship (1971), and a John D. and Catherine T. MacArthur Foundation Fellowship (1993). The Commonwealth Club of California honored him with the fiction gold medal in 1972, for *The Autobiography of Miss Jane Pittman*, and in 1984, for *A Gathering of Old Men*. Gaines also won the American Academy of Arts and Letters literary award in 1987 and the National Book Critics Circle Award in 1993, for *A Lesson Before Dying*, which was nominated for a Pulitzer Prize. A few of Gaines's novels, including *The Autobiography of Miss Jane Pittman*, *A Gathering of Old Men*, and *A Lesson Before Dying*, were turned into made-for-television movies, and "The Sky Is Gray," a short

story, was dramatized for the Public Broadcasting Service short-story series. He was awarded the National Humanities medal in 2000 and was nominated for the Nobel Prize in Literature in 2004. He received honorary degrees from such institutions as Loyola University (1995); Tulane University (1995); the University of Miami (1999); Centenary College (2000); Elmira College (2000); Lewis and Clark College (2001); Xavier University (2005); the University of North Carolina-Ashville (2007); the University of Louisiana-Lafayette (2008); Emory University (2008); and various others. He was the subject of a documentary film in 2009 and received the Aspen Prize for Literature in 2010. He was awarded the National Medal and the Sidney Lanier Prize for Southern Literature in 2012. Various other awards followed in the final years of his life.

For more than fifty years, Gaines was a serious and committed writer of fiction. He always worked slowly, frustratingly slowly to his admirers, but that was because of his great devotion to and respect for the craft of fiction. His novels are all set in rural Louisiana, north of Baton Rouge: Gaines, like William Faulkner, has created a single world in which his works are centered. Even though Gaines wrote during a time of great racial turmoil and unrest, he resisted becoming involved in political movements, feeling that he could best serve the cause of art and humanity by devoting himself to perfecting his craft. This does not mean that he

Photo courtesy of Slowking

remained detached from political realities. Taken together, his novels cover the period of 1865 to the near-present, reflecting the social movements that have affected black Americans during that time. Gaines has said again and again, however, that he is primarily interested in people; certainly it is in his depiction of people that his greatest strength lies. His focus remained on the universals of life: love, pride, pity, hatred. He aspired thus not to have an immediate political impact with his writing but to move people emotionally.

Biography

From birth until age fifteen, Ernest J. Gaines lived in rural Louisiana with his parents. As a boy, he often worked in the plantation fields and spent much of his spare time with his aunt, Miss Augusteen Jefferson. He moved to Vallejo, California, in 1948 to live with his mother and stepfather, and he attended high school and junior college there before serving in the army. After his military service, he earned a B.A. degree at San Francisco State College. On the basis of some stories written while he was a student there, he was awarded the Wallace Stegner Creative Writing Fellowship in 1958 for graduate study at Stanford University.

In 1966 Gaines received a grant from the National Endowment for the Arts, and from then on he garnered many awards and honors, especially in the wake of the 1974 television version of *The Autobiography of Miss Jane Pittman.* He was a Guggenheim Fellow in 1971 and won an award from the Black Academy of Arts and Letters in 1972. In 1987 Gaines received a literary award from the American Academy and Institute of Arts and Letters, and in 1993·he was awarded a John D. and Catherine T. MacArthur Foundation Fellowship. Also in that year, *A Lesson Before Dying* won the National Book Critics Circle Award.

From 1958 until late in his life, Gaines lived, impermanently, by his own testimony, in or near San Francisco, feeling that living elsewhere enabled him to gain a perspective on his southern material that would be unavailable were he to live in the South full-time. By making yearly trips back to Louisiana, where he held a visiting professorship in creative writing at the University of Southwestern Louisiana in Lafayette, he retained contact with his native region. He moved back to Louisiana permanently and lived during his final years in a home he built on land worked by his ancestors, who were slaves.

Analysis: Long Fiction

Before it became fashionable, Ernest J. Gaines was one southern black writer who wrote about his native area. Although he lived much of his life in California, he has never been able to write adequately about that region. He tried to write two novels about the West but has failed to finish either of them. Thus, while he physically left the South, he never left emotionally. His ties remained with the South, and his works remained rooted there. When he first began reading seriously, Gaines gravitated toward those writers who wrote about the soil and the people who lived close to it, among them William Faulkner, John Steinbeck, Willa Cather, and Ivan Turgenev. He was disappointed to discover that few black writers had dealt with the black rural southern experience. (Richard Wright had begun his career by doing so, but his subject matter eventually moved away from the South.) Thus, Gaines began his career with the conscious desire to fill a void. He felt that no one had written fiction about his people.

This fact helps explain why his novels always concentrate on rural settings and on the "folk" who inhabit them. One of the great strengths of his work is voice; the sound of the voice telling the story is central to its meaning. Among his works, *Of Love and Dust*, *The Autobiography of Miss Jane Pittman*, and all the stories in *Bloodline* are told in the first person by rural black characters. The voices of the storytellers, especially Miss Jane's, express the perspective not only of the individual speakers but also in some sense of the entire black community, and it is the community on which Gaines most often focuses his attention.

Louisiana society, especially from a racial perspective, is complicated. Not only blacks and whites live there, but also Creoles and Cajuns. Thus there are competing communities, and some of Gaines's more interesting characters find themselves caught between groups, forced to weigh competing demands in order to devise a course of action.

Several themes recur in the Gaines canon, and together they create the total effect of his work. Generally, he deals with the relationship between past and present and the possibility of change, both individual and social. Using a broad historical canvas in his works, especially in *The Autobiography of Miss Jane Pittman*, Gaines treats the changes in race relations over time, but he is most interested in people, in whether and how they change as individuals. The issue of determinism and free will is therefore a central question in his work. Gaines has been very interested in and influenced by Greek tragedy, and in his fiction, a strain of environmental determinism is evident. In his works prior to and including *The Autobiography of Miss Jane Pittman*, a growing freedom on the part of his black characters can be seen, but the tension between fate and free will always underlies his works.

Some of Gaines's most admirable characters—for example, Marcus in *Of Love and Dust*, and Ned, Joe, and Jimmy in *The Autobiography of Miss Jane Pittman*—have the courage, pride, and dignity to fight for change. At the same time, however, Gaines reveres the old, who, while often resistant to change, embody the strength of the black people. In his work, one frequently finds tension between generations, a conflict between old and young which is reconciled only in the character of Miss Jane Pittman, who even in extreme old age retains the courage to fight for change.

Other recurring tensions and dichotomies are evident in Gaines's novels. Conflict often exists between men and women. Because of slavery, which denied them their manhood, black men feel forced to take extreme actions to attain or assert it, a theme most evident in *Of Love and Dust*, *The Autobiography of Miss Jane Pittman*, *A Gathering of Old Men* and the stories in *Bloodline*. Women, on the other hand, are often presented in Gaines's fiction as preservers and conservers. Each group embodies a strength, but Gaines suggests that wholeness comes about only when the peculiar strengths of the two sexes are united, again most clearly exemplified in Miss Jane and her relationship with the men in her life.

Among the male characters, a tension exists between fathers and sons. Treated explicitly in Gaines's fourth novel, *In My Father's House*, this theme is implicit throughout the canon. Though young men look to the older generation for models, there are few reliable examples for them to follow, and they find it difficult to take responsibility for their lives and for the lives of their loved ones.

Gaines's characters at their best seek freedom and dignity: Some succeed, and some fail in their attempts to overcome both outer and inner obstacles. Viewed in sequence, Gaines's first three novels move from the almost total bleakness and determinism of *Catherine Carmier* to the triumph of *The Autobiography of Miss Jane Pittman. In My Father's House*, however, reflects a falling away of hope in both individual and social terms, perhaps corresponding to the diminution of expectations experienced in America during the late 1970s and early 1980s.

Catherine Carmier

Gaines's first novel, *Catherine Carmier*, based on a work he wrote while an adolescent in Vallejo, has many of the characteristic weaknesses of a first novel and is more interesting for what it anticipates in Gaines's later career than for its intrinsic merits. Though it caused barely a ripple of interest when it was first published, the novel introduces many of the themes which Gaines treats more effectively in his mature fiction. The book is set in the country, near Bayonne, Louisiana, an area depicted as virtually a wasteland. Ownership of much of this region has devolved to the Cajuns, who appear throughout Gaines's novels as Snopes-like vermin, interested in owning the land only to exploit it. Like Faulkner, Gaines sees this kind of person as particularly modern, and the growing power of the Cajuns indicates a weakening of values and a loss of determination to live in right relationship to the land.

Onto the scene comes Jackson Bradley, a young black man born and reared in the area but (like Gaines himself) educated in California. Bradley is a hollow, rootless man, a man who does not know where he belongs. He has found the North and the West empty, with people living hurried, pointless lives, but he sees the South as equally empty. Feeling no link to a meaningful past and no hope for a productive future, Bradley is a deracinated modern man. He has returned to Louisiana to bid final farewell to his Aunt Charlotte, a representative of the older generation, and to her way of life.

While there and while trying to find a meaningful path for himself, Bradley meets and falls in love with Catherine Carmier. She, too, is living a blocked life, and he feels that if they can leave the area, they will be able to make a fulfilling life together. Catherine is the daughter of Raoul Carmier, in many ways the most interesting character in the novel. A Creole, he is caught between the races. Because of his black blood, he is not treated as the equal of whites, but because of his white blood, he considers blacks to be beneath him. He has a near incestuous relationship with Catherine, since after her birth his wife was unfaithful to him and he considers none of their subsequent children his. Feeling close only to Catherine, he forbids her to associate with any men, but especially with black men. A man of great pride and love of the land, Raoul is virtually the only man in the region to resist the encroachment of the Cajuns. His attitude isolates him all the more, which in turn makes him fanatically determined to hold onto Catherine.

Despite her love for and loyalty to her father, Catherine senses the dead end her life has become and returns Bradley's love. Though she wants to leave with him, she is paralyzed by her love of her father and by her knowledge of what her leaving would do to him. This conflict climaxes with a brutal fight between Raoul and

Bradley over Catherine, a fight that Bradley wins. Catherine, however, returns home to nurse her father. The novel ends ambiguously, with at least a hint that Catherine will return to Bradley, although the thrust of the book militates against that eventuality. Gaines implies that history and caste are a prison, a tomb. No change is possible for the characters because they cannot break out of the cages their lives have become. Love is the final victim. Catherine will continue living her narrow, unhealthy life, and Jackson Bradley will continue wandering the earth, searching for something to fill his inner void.

Of Love and Dust

Gaines's second novel, *Of Love and Dust,* was received much more enthusiastically than was *Catherine Carmier;* with it, he began to win the largely positive, respectful reviews which continued throughout his career. Like *Catherine Carmier, Of Love and Dust* is a story of frustrated love. The setting is the same: rural Louisiana, where the Cajuns are gradually assuming ownership and control of the land. *Of Love and Dust* is a substantial improvement over *Catherine Carmier,* however, in part because it is told in the first person by Jim Kelly, an observer of the central story. In this novel, one can see Gaines working toward the folk voice which became such an integral part of the achievement of *The Autobiography of Miss Jane Pittman.*

The plot of the novel concerns Marcus Payne, a young black man sentenced to prison for murder and then bonded out by a white plantation owner who wants him to work in his fields. Recognizing Marcus's rebelliousness and pride, the owner and his Cajun overseer, Sidney Bonbon, brutally attempt to break his spirit. This only makes Marcus more determined, and in revenge, he decides to seduce Louise, Bonbon's neglected wife. What begins, however, as simply a selfish and egocentric act of revenge on Marcus's part grows into a genuine though grotesque love. When he and Louise decide to run away together, Bonbon discovers them and kills Marcus. Even though he dies, Marcus, by resisting brutalizing circumstances, retains his pride and attempts to prove his manhood and dignity. His attempts begin in a self-centered way, but as his love for Louise grows, he grows in stature in the reader's eyes until he becomes a figure of heroic dimensions.

Through his use of a first-person narrator, Gaines creates a double perspective in the novel, including on the one hand the exploits of Marcus and on the other the black community's reactions to them. The narrator, Jim Kelly, is the straw boss at the plantation, a member of the black community but also accepted and trusted by the whites because of his dependability and his unwillingness to cause any problems. His initial reaction to Marcus—resentment and dislike of him as a troublemaker—represents the reaction of the community at large. The older members of the community never move beyond that attitude because they are committed to the old ways, to submission and accommodation. To his credit, however, Jim's attitude undergoes a transformation. As he observes Marcus, his resentment changes to sympathy and respect, for he comes to see Marcus as an example of black manhood which others would do well to emulate.

Marcus's death gives evidence of the strain of fate and determinism in this novel as well, yet because he dies with his pride and dignity intact, *Of Love and Dust* is more hopeful than *Catherine Carmier.* Gaines indicates that resistance is possible and, through the character of Jim Kelly, that change can occur. Kelly leaves the plantation at the end of the novel, no longer passively accepting what fate brings him but believing that he can act and shape his own life. Though Marcus is an apolitical character, like Jackson

Bradley, it is suggested that others will later build on his actions to force social change on the South. *Of Love and Dust* is a major step forward beyond *Catherine Carmier* both artistically and thematically. Through his use of the folk voice, Gaines vivifies his story, and the novel suggests the real possibility of free action by his characters.

The Autobiography of Miss Jane Pittman

Without a doubt, *The Autobiography of Miss Jane Pittman* is Gaines's major contribution to American literature. Except for an introduction written by "the editor," it is told entirely in the first person by Miss Jane and covers approximately one hundred years, from the Civil War to the Civil Rights movement of the 1960s. Basing the novel on stories he heard while a child around his aunt, Augusteen Jefferson, and using the format of oral history made popular in recent decades, Gaines created a "folk autobiography" which tells the story of people who are not in the history books. While the work is the story of Miss Jane, she is merely an observer for a substantial portion of its length, and the story becomes that of black Americans from slavery to the present. Gaines's mastery of voice is especially important here, for Miss Jane's voice is the voice of her people.

From the very beginning of the novel, when Miss Jane is determined, even in the face of physical beatings, to keep the name a Union soldier gave her and refuses to be called Ticey, her slave name, to the end of the novel, when she leads her people to Bayonne in a demonstration against segregated facilities, she is courageous and in the best sense of the word "enduring," like Faulkner's Dilsey. In her character and story, many of the dichotomies that run through Gaines's work are unified. The differing roles of men and women are important elements in the book. Women preserve and sustain—a role symbolized by Miss Jane's longevity.

Men, on the other hand, feel the need to assert their manhood in an active way. Three black men are especially important in Miss Jane's life, beginning with Ned, whom she rears from childhood after his mother is killed and who becomes in effect a "son" to her. Like Marcus Payne, Ned is a rebel, but his rebellion is concentrated in the political arena. Returning to Louisiana after the turn of the century, he attempts to lead his people to freedom. Though he is murdered by whites, his legacy and memory are carried on by Miss Jane and the people in the community. Later, in the 1960's, Jimmy Aaron, another young man who tries to encourage his people to effective political action, appears. Again the members of the older generation hang back, fearful of change and danger, but after Jimmy is killed, Jane unites old and young, past and present by her determination to go to Bayonne and carry on Jimmy's work. Thus Marcus's apolitical rebellion in *Of Love and Dust* has been transformed into political action. The third man in Jane's life is Joe Pittman, her husband. A horse-breaker, he is committed to asserting and proving his manhood through his work. Although he too dies, killed by a wild horse he was determined to break, Jane in her understanding and love of him, as well as in her affection for all her men, bridges the gap between man and woman. In her character, the opposites of old and young, past and present, and man and woman are reconciled.

Miss Jane's strength is finally the strength of the past, but it is directed toward the future. When Jimmy returns, he tells the people that he is nothing without their strength, referring not only to their physical numbers but also to the strength of their character as it has been forged by all the hardships they have undergone through history. Even though the people seem weak and fearful, the example of Miss Jane shows that they need not be. They can shake off the chains of bondage and determinism, assert their free spirit through direct action, and effect change. The change has only begun by the conclusion of *The Autobiography of Miss Jane Pittman,* but the pride and dignity of Miss Jane and all those she represents suggest that ultimately they will prevail.

In My Father's House

Gaines's fourth novel, *In My Father's House,* was the first he had written in the third person since *Catherine Carmier;* the effect of its point of view is to distance the reader from the action and characters, creating an ironic perspective. Set during a dreary winter in 1970, in the period of disillusionment following the assassination of Martin Luther King, Jr., the novel suggests that the progress which was implicit in the ending of *The Autobiography of Miss Jane Pittman* was temporary at best, if not downright illusory. The atmosphere of the novel is one of frustration and stagnation.

Both the setting and the protagonist of *In My Father's House* are uncharacteristic for Gaines. Instead of using the rural settings so familiar from his other works, he sets his story in a small town. Rather than focusing on the common people, Gaines chooses as his protagonist Philip Martin, one of the leaders of the black community, a public figure, a minister who is considering running for Congress. A success by practically any measure and pridefully considering himself a *man,* Martin is brought low in the course of the novel. His illegitimate son, Robert X, a ghostlike man, appears and wordlessly accuses him. Robert is evidence that, by abandoning him, his siblings, and their mother many years previously, Martin in effect destroyed their lives. Having been a drinker, a gambler, and irresponsible, he tries to explain to his son that his earlier weakness was a legacy of slavery. Even though he seems to have surmounted that crippling legacy, his past rises up to haunt him and forces him to face his weakness. Martin wants to effect a reconciliation with his son and thus with his past, but Robert's suicide precludes that. *In My Father's House* makes explicit a concern which was only implicit in Gaines's earlier novels, the relationship between fathers and sons. No communication is possible here, and the failure is illustrative of a more general barrier between the generations. While in the earlier novels the young people led in the struggle for change and the older characters held back, here the situation is reversed. Martin and members of his generation are the leaders, while the young are for the most part sunk in cynicism, apathy, and hopelessness, or devoted to anarchic violence. If the hope of a people is in the young, or in a reconciliation of old and young, hope does not exist in this novel.

A Gathering of Old Men

Hope does exist, however, in Gaines's *A Gathering of Old Men,* for which Gaines returns to his more characteristic rural setting. Here he returns as well to the optimism with which *The Autobiography of Miss Jane Pittman* ended. This time, as at the end of that novel and in *In My Father's House,* it is up to the old among the black community to lead the struggle for change, this time primarily because there are no young men left to lead. All of them have escaped to towns and cities that promise more of a future than does rural Louisiana.

In this small corner of Louisiana, however, as elsewhere in Gaines's fiction, Cajuns are encroaching on the land, replacing men with machines and even threatening to plow up the old graveyard where generations of blacks have been buried. When Beau Boutan, son of the powerful Cajun Fix Boutan, is shot to death in the quarters of Marshall plantation, where Marshall blacks have worked the land since the days of slavery, the old black men who have lived there all of their lives are faced with one last

322   *Ernest J. Gaines*

chance to stand up and be men. They stand up for the sake of Matthu, the only one of them who ever stood up before and thus the most logical suspect in the murder. They also stand up because of all the times in their past when they should have stood up but did not. They prove one last time that free action is possible when eighteen or more of them, all in their seventies and eighties, arm themselves with rifles of the same gauge used in the shooting and face down the white sheriff, Mapes, each in his turn claiming to be the killer.

As shut off as the quarters are from the rest of the world, it is easy to forget that the events of the novel take place as recently as the late 1970's. Beau Boutan's brother Gil, however, represents the change that has been taking place in the world outside Marshall. He has achieved gridiron fame at Louisiana State University by working side by side with Cal, a young black man. Youth confronts age when Gil returns home and tries to persuade his father not to ride in revenge against Beau's murderer, as everyone expects him to do. Gil represents the possibility of change from the white perspective. He convinces his father to let the law find and punish Beau's murderer, but he pays a heavy price when his father disowns him. He cannot stop other young Cajuns, led by Luke Will, who are not willing to change but would rather cling to the vigilantism of the old South.

In spite of their dignity and pride, the old men at Marshall risk looking rather silly because after all these years they stand ready for a battle that seems destined never to take place once Fix Boutan decides not to ride on Marshall. Sheriff Mapes taunts them with the knowledge that they have waited too late to take a stand. Ironically, they are ultimately able to maintain their dignity and reveal their growth in freedom by standing up to the one person who has been most valiant in her efforts to help them: Candy Marshall, niece of the landowner. In her effort

to protect Matthu, who was largely responsible for rearing her after her parents died, Candy has gone so far as to try to take credit for the murder herself. What she fails to realize is that the days are long past when black men need the protection of a white woman. She is stunned to realize that she too has been living in the past and has been guilty of treating grown black men like children.

The novel does eventually end with a gunfight, because Luke Will and his men refuse to let the murder of a white man by a black one go unavenged. It is fitting that the two men who fall in the battle are Luke Will, the one who was most resistant to change, and Charlie Biggs, the real murderer, who, at fifty, finally proves his manhood by refusing to be beaten by Beau Boutan and then by returning to take the blame for the murder that he has committed. Charlie's body is treated like a sacred relic as each member of the black community, from the oldest to the youngest, touches it, hoping that some of the courage that Charlie found late in life will rub off. Apparently it already has.

With *A Gathering of Old Men*, Gaines returns to first-person narration, but this time the history is told one chapter at a time by various characters involved in or witnessing the action. His original plan was to have the narrator be the white newspaperman Lou Dimes, Candy's boyfriend. He found, however, that there was still much that a black man in Louisiana would not confide to a white man, even a sympathetic one, so he let the people tell their own story, with Dimes narrating an occasional chapter.

A Lesson Before Dying

A Lesson Before Dying, set in Gaines's fictional Bayonne during six months of 1948, reveals the horrors of Jim Crowism in the story of twenty-one-year-old Jefferson, a scarcely literate manchild who works the cane fields of Pichot

Plantation. Jefferson hooks up with two criminals who are killed during the robbery of a liquor store, along with the store's white proprietor. Jefferson is left to stand trial before a jury of twelve white men who overlook his naivete despite his lawyer's argument that he is a dumb animal, a "thing" that acts on command, no more deserving of the electric chair than a hog. When this description causes Jefferson to become practically catatonic, his grandmother enlists the local schoolteacher, Grant Wiggins, to help Jefferson gain his manhood before he is put to death. Thus, like *A Gathering of Old Men*, this novel questions the traditional devaluing of black males in the south.

Reluctantly, Wiggins agrees to help Jefferson by encouraging him to speak and to write, visiting him often and giving him a journal in which to record his thoughts. Finally, right before his execution, Jefferson has a breakthrough when he tells Wiggins to thank his students for the pecans they sent him in jail. Wiggins himself becomes the central character as he learns the real lesson of the novel, that all people are connected and responsible for each other. Wiggins comes to terms with his own role in the system that victimizes Jefferson, and the entire community learns from how Jefferson faces his execution. The novel pays a tribute to those who persevere in the face of injustice, and it also puts forward hope for better racial relationships, especially in the character of Paul, the young white jailer who is sympathetic to Jefferson and to Grant Wiggins's attempts to bring forth his humanity.

If *In My Father's House* represents a falling away of hope for human progress and perhaps also a falling away in artistry, one finds once again in *A Gathering of Old Men* and *A Lesson Before Dying* evidence of the same genuine strengths that Gaines exhibited in *The Autobiography of Miss Jane Pittman*: a mastery of the folk voice, a concern for common people, a reverence for the everyday, a love of the land, and a powerful evocation of the strength, pride, and dignity people can develop by working on and living close to the soil.

Analysis: Short Fiction

Strongly influenced by the folkways of rural Louisiana, Ernest J. Gaines's narratives all reflect a cultural heritage enriched by a strong oral tradition. Although his fiction's main focus is on the African American community, the author's work also reflects the cultural diversity of his native parish, Pointe Coupee, by Creoles, Cajuns, and Anglo-American entrepreneurs, overseers, and law officials. Among Gaines's acknowledged literary mentors are the nineteenth century Russian masters, for their treatment of peasantry; Ernest Hemingway, for his understatement and "grace under pressure" theme; and William Faulkner, for his mastery of locale and the oral narrative.

Bloodline

Gaines, although popular, was a very serious and methodical writer. He worked very hard to fashion a distinct voice richly imbued with its unique traditions. He also spun compelling stories, which were collected in the single volume *Bloodline*, first published in 1968. *Bloodline* contains five long stories, all of which deal with a place and a people Gaines expresses so fully and so vividly that they are recognized as his own exclusive fictional property: the southern black communities living on a stretch of low-lying cotton and sugarcane country between the Atchafalaya and Mississippi Rivers, west and northwest of Baton Rouge. Setting is a central force in Gaines's work, and his fiction often focuses on this distinctive Louisiana region.

All the stories in *Bloodline* take place in and around the fictional town of Bayonne, a small country town not too far from the actual city of

Baton Rouge. The lives of Gaines's men and women are shaped by fields, dirt roads, plantation quarters, and the natural elements of dust, heat, and rain. Whatever the differences among his characters—he has a rich diversity of race and culture to work with—the Cajun sharecroppers, the black tenants, and the white plantation owners all consider the soil and the crops part of their daily weather. Bayonne and the surrounding countryside provide local and cultural unity for the stories in *Bloodline.*

Equally important to the unity of *Bloodline* is the way the stories are presented. All of them are written in the form of oral narratives told by the characters in their own words. The first four stories are told by individual African Americans who participate in or are deeply affected by the stories they tell. The tellers range in age from the six-year-old boy of "A Long Day in November" to a seventy-year-old man in the title story. The final story, "Just Like a Tree," is told by a group of relatives and friends, each in turn, as they attend the leave-taking ceremonies surrounding Aunt Fe, an old black woman who has been invited North to escape white reprisals against the Civil Rights movement. In all these stories the sound of individual voices rings out clearly and convincingly. Gaines has a keen, sure ear for his native speech patterns and recognizes the power of language in a predominantly oral culture to assert, affirm, and keep hold of personal and collective values. His stories deliberately call attention to the special virtues of the spoken word as a rich storehouse capable of keeping alive an otherwise impoverished community.

There is, however, a deeper unifying force to the stories than a common setting, race, and dependence on the spoken word. It consists of the movement of the stories through individual lives toward a sort of communal consciousness. There is a hint of this movement in the successive voices of the five stories. The first two are accounts of two young boys, the third of a young man in jail, the fourth of an old man of seventy, and the fifth of a household of friends, relatives, and one stranger. *Bloodline* begins with the private experience of a little boy and ends with a public event that affects the entire community. The impression of development is strengthened by the recurrence in each story of one of Gaines's major themes, the impact of personal and communal codes of honor colliding with various forms of hostility, especially, in the last four stories, the discrimination, injustice, and violence the African American faced in the segregated South. This is not to imply that polemics or ideologies ever prevail over character in Gaines's stories. What interests him first and foremost is black experience, and some of his best writing centers on the lives and relationships of southern blacks within their own community, with sometimes little direct reference at all to the world of the whites around them. Inasmuch as discrimination and the crimes of segregation were an inescapable fact of southern black experience, the world Gaines describes is always—overtly or not—conditioned by the tensions of racial claims. In *Bloodline,* the questions raised by such claims become progressively more insistent, and the stories themselves roughly follow the chronology of the changing mood among blacks in modern times. Specific dates are not mentioned, but the stories obviously stretch back to the 1940s rural South of "A Long Day in November" up to the 1960s Civil Rights movement in Louisiana alluded to in the last story, "Just Like a Tree."

"A Long Day in November"

In the first story, "A Long Day in November," there are no direct references to racial struggles. It is a long tale told in the voice of a six-year-old boy, Sonny, whose world is suddenly shattered by the separation of his parents. His mother, Amy, leaves her husband, Eddie, because she feels he has become overenthusiastic about his car to the point of neglecting his family. She takes Sonny to her mother's house, and the remainder of the story charts Eddie's unsuccessful attempts to bring his wife home. Finally, on the advice of the local Voodoo woman, Madame Toussaint, Eddie burns his car publicly, and Sonny and Amy return home. For the entire story, Sonny does not act; he observes and suffers. He sees the world in terms of basic feelings— warmth, cold, hope, fear—and desires simply that his disrupted world be restored. The story ends where it began, with Sonny in bed, snug and safe under the blankets, only this time the night is not disturbed by his mother's calls or crying. Instead, Sonny is rocked to sleep by the sound of the springs in his parents' bed.

Gaines is a master at recreating the words and sensations of children, and one of his main concerns in "A Long Day in November" is to contrast Sonny's simple, innocent needs of love and security with the complex world of adult conflicts. Neither his parents nor his grandmother seems to offer him what he needs most. His mother has become hard and bitter, and his father, more gentle, shows a weak streak and tends to use Sonny to win back his wife. The grandmother's irritability may be comic for the reader, but for Sonny she is the most hateful person in his life, rough spoken, harsh, and complaining. She is the one person Sonny would most like to be free of: "Lord knows I get tired of Gran'mon fussing all the time." The main character in the story, however, is Sonny's mother. She may be harsh and bitter, but she has forged for herself a code of personal behavior that finally brings her family into a new relationship. She forces the change at a great cost, especially in regards to her son.

One important feature of "A Long Day in November" is the presence of a well-defined community—the schoolteacher, the preacher, the schoolchildren, the Voodoo woman, Eddie's

friends, and Amy's relatives—where conflict and separation may occur, but whose shared assumptions are not questioned. Increasingly, as the stories progress, not only individual codes but also communal values are brought under pressure.

"The Sky Is Gray"

The second story in *Bloodline*, "The Sky Is Gray," is also narrated by a small boy. One of the most successful stories in the volume, it consists of thirteen episodes spanning the day. James, eight years old, goes with his mother to a dentist in Bayonne. Like Sonny in "A Long Day in November," James suffers more than he acts, but already, even at eight years old, he is beginning to adopt the code of stoic pride his mother is constantly encouraging. His world is even bleaker than Sonny's. His father has been called into the Army, and his mother is left with three children and great poverty. Throughout the story, her hard words and harsh judgments must be measured against the fact that she has been placed in a situation in which mere survival is not always certain. She feels compelled to teach her oldest son how to take care of his family and to survive with dignity as a man.

While waiting in the dentist's office, James watches a young, educated African American argue with an older man who looks to James like a preacher. The young black has no faith in religion but reacts in such an extreme, self-confident way that he challenges their religious beliefs. Still, when he is hit by the "preacher," a man who maintains that no questions at all should be asked about God or traditional beliefs, it is the young man who wins the admiration of James: "When I grow up I want be just like him. I want clothes like that and I want keep a book with me, too."

The point seems to be that given the extent of black suffering, most reactions tend to assume extreme, absolute forms that destroy man's full nature. The preacher is at once too submissive and too aggressive; the young man asserts his right to disbelieve but is unable to make sense out of his contradictory certitudes; and James's mother so overemphasizes stoic resistance that, in a later episode, she is incapable of compromising her rigid pride even when it means a meal for her son. Fortunately, the white lady who offers the meal knows exactly how to circumvent such pride so that natural help is not construed as demeaning charity. Such generosity has been too rare in the past, however, even among her fellow blacks, and the mother's attitude remains unchanged. At first, the story as a whole seems to reveal a world where gentleness and love and flexibility have no place: "The sleet's coming down heavy, heavy now, and I turn up my coat collar to keep my neck warm. My mama tells me to turn it right back down. 'You not a bum,' she says. 'You a man.'" James nevertheless knows that his mother loves her children and that they love her.

"Three Men"

The third story, "Three Men," may have been placed at the center of the collection as a sort of hub toward which the first two stories approach and around which the whole book swings to return to the traditional rural society of the final stories, still rural and traditional, but now in the new context of the Civil Rights movement. Certainly it is the only story in which the central character undergoes anything resembling a change of heart or self-discovery.

Again, like the other stories, "Three Men" centers on a personal code of honor, this time specifically related to racial domination. A nineteen-year-old youth, Proctor Lewis, turns himself in to the law in Bayonne after stabbing another man in a fight over a girl. The story takes place in jail where his cellmates, an old convict, Munford, and a homosexual, Hattie, argue with each other and talk to Proctor. Munford, full of

hate for a society based on racial stereotypes, hates himself for allowing his life to gratify the expectations of those same stereotypes. Recalling the way his own past has swung back and forth between fights and jail, he poses the dilemma of the story: whether Proctor should choose to get out of jail by accepting the bond he initially hopes the white plantation owner will pay, or whether he should stay in jail, suffer the certain beating of the guards, and eventually go to the state penitentiary. Munford claims that the latter choice is the only way for Proctor to keep his manhood, something both Munford and Hattie have surrendered.

As the story ends, Proctor has almost made up his mind to refuse the bond and to abide by the code Munford has described. Although he is finally not sure if he can stand by his decision, a shift of attitude has been made, and the right questions have been clearly articulated. "Three Men" looks back to the seemingly fatalistic rounds of poverty, frustration, and rigid codes of the first two stories and anticipates the last two stories, in which individual acts of self-affirmation seem to offer something more than mere stoic resistance.

"Bloodline"

The last two stories are best treated together, since they both return to the rural world of the plantation suddenly introduced to the rising violence of black activism. "Bloodline," the title story of the collection, raises the old southern problem of mixed blood, but in a new context, the "post segregation" South. The story is told by a seventy-year-old African American, Felix, who works for the plantation's present owner, Walter Laurent. Copper, the half-white illegitimate son of Laurent's dead brother, has returned to the plantation seeking what he considers his birthright, the land on which his "father" raped his mother. He calls himself the General and refuses to go through the back door of the plantation house to meet his uncle. Finally, after Copper has thwarted all attempts by Laurent to force him through the back door, Laurent relents and goes to meet him. Their meeting symbolizes the old order making way for the new. Laurent does not change his mind about the old rules; he simply stops applying them for a time. Copper represents the transformation that will eventually change the caste system of white over black and rewrite the rules Laurent is constantly talking about: "I didn't write the rules, and I won't try to change them."

The old men, Walter and Felix, are clearly part of the old order, but Gaines is careful to show how they both, especially Felix, manage to retain their individual dignity even though bound to the established tradition. There is a give and take between "master" and "servant" common to men who speak the same language, know the same people, and who have lived near each other all their lives. From this perspective, Copper comes back to his birthplace as an outsider, isolated from the rest of the blacks, whom he considers childlike lackeys. He embodies the same sort of absoluteness and aloofness represented earlier by the young man in the dentist's office in "The Sky Is Gray," but he also embodies the necessary wave of change that will eventually sweep through the plantation, a change whose consequences are already being felt in the final story, "Just Like a Tree."

"Just Like a Tree"

"Just Like a Tree" revolves around Aunt Fe, an old black woman who is being taken North to escape the violence that has begun on the plantation. A young man, Emmanuel, has begun working for change, and in retaliation a tenant house has been bombed and a woman and her two children killed. More than any other story in the collection, "Just Like a Tree" affirms the force of the community. The only outsider, an African American from the North, is clearly alien to the shared assumptions and beliefs of the others. He speaks a different "language"; he sets himself apart by his loud manners, his condescension, and his lack of feeling. The other people gathered in the house, even the white lady who has walked to the house to say good-bye, form a whole, united by shared speech and shared feelings. The ceremony itself of farewell, and the narrative mode of the story—told in turn by several of the visitors—affirm the strong communal bonds of rural black society. Unlike the young man in "The Sky Is Gray" or the General in "Bloodline," Emmanuel belongs to the community even as he acts to change the old ways. He is a type of activist represented best in Gaines's work by Jimmy in *The Autobiography of Miss Jane Pittman.*

Aunt Fe's longtime presence in the community, her having touched, in some loving way, every member of the community, and her impending removal to the North provide clues to the tree symbolism of the story's title: Like a great, old, shade tree she has protected and sheltered other living creatures, and her departure will leave a spiritual hole in the life of the community, like the hole that the removal, roots and all, of a large tree will leave in a meadow. Aunt Clo predicts that Aunt Fe will die when she is "transplanted" to the North. The personal diaspora being forced upon Aunt Fe also represents the mass diasporas suffered by African Americans through the centuries.

The story and the book end with Aunt Fe's death. She has refused to be moved, and once again the strong vital roots of individual pride show their strength. The difference is that Aunt Fe's pride affirms its strength within the community, not in aloof isolation from it. In terms of *Bloodline* as a whole, "Just Like a Tree" offers the conclusion that change must involve sacrifice, but that change must take place. The farewell ceremony and Aunt Fe's death also offer the reminder that the traditional community had values that the new order can deny only at its own peril and loss.

The stories of *Bloodline* illustrate two other major themes in Gaines's writing. First, there is the presence and influence of strong female figures such as Aunt Fe and Amy, who are, in various ways, early prototypes of such heroines as Miss Jane Pittman in Gaines's later fiction. Manhood becomes a significant achievement for several male characters in *Bloodline*—James, Eddie, and Proctor—who anticipate even larger treatment of the male-maturation theme in Gaines's novels from *The Autobiography of Miss Jane Pittman* through *A Lesson Before Dying*, one of his most powerful works.

Bibliography

Auger, Philip. "A Lesson About Manhood: Appropriating 'The Word' in Ernest Gaines's *A Lesson Before Dying*." *Southern Literary Journal* 27 (Spring, 1995): 74-85. Auger explains the novel as a biblical allegory, focusing on Grant Wiggins's subversion of the white Christian mythos as a rhetorical act that helps Jefferson transform himself into a New Testament God-figure as he gains control over language.

Babb, Valerie Melissa. *Ernest Gaines.* Boston: Twayne, 1991. This volume in Twayne's United States Authors series offers a chapter on each of Gaines's books through *A Gathering of Old Men.* Its insightful final chapter places Gaines in the larger context of African American literature, explaining how Gaines balances politics and his vision of the artist.

Beavers, Herman. *Wrestling Angels into Song: The Fictions of Ernest J. Gaines and James Alan McPherson.* Philadelphia: University of Pennsylvania Press, 1995. This thoughtful analysis of the literary kinship of Gaines and McPherson with their precursor Ralph Ellison focuses on all three writers' characters' sense of community, storytelling, and self-recovery. While beginning with a look at their southernness, Beavers examines all three as American writers and discusses all Gaines's work through *A Lesson Before Dying.*

Burke, William. "*Bloodline*: A Man's Black South." *College Language Association Journal* 19 (1976): 545-558. This study centers on the design of the five stories in *Bloodline* and argues that they are a coherent record of changing race relations prompted by the African American male's recovery of his masculinity.

Carmean, Karen. *Ernest J. Gaines: A Critical Companion.* Westport, Conn.: Greenwood Press, 1998. Presents an introductory overview of Gaines's work, with analysis of each of his novels and short-story collections. Includes a thorough bibliography of primary and secondary sources.

Clark, Keith. *Black Manhood in James Baldwin, Ernest J. Gaines, and August Wilson.* Urbana: University of Illinois Press, 2002. Chapter on Gaines's work focuses on the "neo-masculinist literary imagination." The opening chapter of the book outlines the aesthetics of black masculinist protest discourse since 1940, contextualizing the later discussion.

Doyle, Mary Ellen. *Voices from the Quarters: The Fiction of Ernest J. Gaines.* Baton Rouge: Louisiana State University Press, 2001. A celebration of Gaines's characters. Doyle examines the ways in which Louisiana's bayous and cane fields are peopled by Gaines with characters that exemplify their real life counterparts.

Estes, David C., ed. *Critical Reflections on the Fiction of Ernest J. Gaines.* Athens: University of Georgia Press, 1994. Fourteen essays that cover all six novels to 1994 and *Bloodline* as well as film adaptations of Gaines's work, offering detailed explications in addition to broad analyses of pastoralism, humor, race, and gender. An excellent introduction highlights important biographical facts, secondary sources, and literary themes in Gaines's work.

Gaines, Ernest J. *Conversations with Ernest Gaines.* Edited by John Lowe. Jackson: University Press of

Mississippi, 1995. This collection offers twenty-five interviews conducted from 1969 to 1994, all but the last previously published. Arranged chronologically, the interviews explore Gaines's thoughts on key aspects of all his work through *A Lesson Before Dying*, especially African American males' search for identity. Includes a useful topical index.

_____. "Ernest J. Gaines." Interview by Bernard Magnier. *The UNESCO Courier* 48 (April, 1995): 5-7. In this interview, Gaines discusses his childhood and family background, the books that most influenced him, his feelings about Africa, and other topics.

_____. "Talking with Ernest J. Gaines." Interview by Marcia G. Gaudet and Carl Wooton. *Callaloo* 11 (Spring, 1988): 229243. In this interview, Gaines provides useful information about how his background influenced his art. He discusses his training as a writer, including the early lack of African American models and the effects of his small-town upbringing. He also analyzes his use of point of view and his treatment of black men and women.

_____. "A Very Big Order: Reconstructing Identity." *Southern Review* 26 (Spring, 1990): 245-253. In this memoir, Gaines recalls his move from Louisiana to Vallejo, California, where he first had access to a public library but did not find there books about the South that he knew. He traces the movement in his writing back into his southern past as he attempted to write for the African American youth of the South the works that did not exist for him.

Gaines, Ernest J., Marcia G. Gaudet, and Carl Wooton. *Porch Talk with Ernest Gaines: Conversations on the Writer's Craft*. Baton Rouge: Louisiana State University Press, 1990. A transcription of an intimate interview conducted by colleagues of Gaines, this work offers an insightful look at how the author has transmuted his Louisiana heritage, familial experiences, literary influences, and strong folk tradition into fiction with a distinct voice.

Gaudet, Marcia, ed. *Ernest J. Gaines: Conversations*. Jackson: University Press of Mississippi, 2019. Contains fifteen interviews with Gaines, ranging from 1994-2017, dealing with such topics as religion, spirituality, regionalism, multi-art forms in his fiction, and many of his longer and shorter works.

Jones, Suzanne W. "New Narratives of Southern Manhood: Race, Masculinity, and Closure in Ernest Gaines's Fiction." *Critical Survey* 9 (1997): 15-42. Discusses Gaines's deconstruction of stereotypes and presentation of new models of black and white southern manhood. Asserts that Gaines suggests that in order to reconstruct the South, black and white men must reject the traditional Western model of manhood that links masculinity and violence.

Lowe, John, ed. *Conversations with Ernest Gaines*. Jackson: University Press of Mississippi, 1995. Collection of interviews with Gaines, ranging from 1994 to 2017, provides information about his life, his themes, and his works. Includes index and chronology of his life.

Papa, Lee. "'His Feet on Your Neck': The New Religion in the Works of Ernest J. Gaines." *African American Review* 27 (Summer, 1993): 187-193. Claims that Gaines is concerned with characters who must make a personal test of religion, not accept it as imposed by institutional Christianity.

Peterson, V. R. "Ernest Gaines: Writing About the Past." *Essence* 24 (August, 1993): 52. A brief biographical sketch that discusses Gaines's background, his typical themes, and the development of his writing career.

Shelton, Frank W. "Ambiguous Manhood in Ernest J. Gaines' *Bloodline*." *College Language Association Journal* 19 (1975): 200209. Shelton notes that although the African American males in Gaines's stories strive for manhood and dignity, they are only partially successful in their quests.

_____. "*In My Father's House*: Ernest Gaines After Jane Pittman." *Southern Review* 17 (Spring, 1981): 340-345. In his detailed analysis of *In My Father's House*, Shelton explores the relative neglect of the novel by reviewers, attributing their less than enthusiastic response in part to the distance achieved through a third-person narrator. Where Miss Jane Pittman symbolizes human survival, the later novel's Philip Martin symbolizes human failing and provides a vehicle for Gaines to explore two earlier themes: the nature of African American manhood and the relationship between fathers and sons.

Simpson, Anne K. *A Gathering of Gaines: The Man and the Writer*. Lafayette: Center for Louisiana Studies at the University of Southwestern Louisiana, 1991. Simpson's study, well documented with excerpts from Gaines's personal papers, offers a biographical sketch, an examination of his stylistic influences and characteristics, and a critical overview of his fiction. It includes an unannotated but thorough bibliography.

—John W. Fiero; Ben Forkner; Frank W. Shelton; Rebecca G. Smith; Philip A. Tapley; Robert C. Evans

Henry Louis Gates, Jr.

Essayist and Critic

Born: Keyser, West Virginia; September 16, 1950

NONFICTION: *Figures in Black: Words, Signs, and the "Racial" Self*, 1987; *The Signifying Monkey: A Theory of Afro-American Literary Criticism*, 1988; *Loose Canons: Notes on the Culture Wars*, 1992; *The Amistad Chronology of African-American History, 1445-1990*, 1993; *Colored People: A Memoir*, 1994; *Speaking of Race, Speaking of Sex: Hate Speech, Civil Rights, and Civil Liberties*, 1994; *The Future of the Race*, 1996 (with Cornel West); *Thirteen Ways to Look at a Black Man*, 1997; *Wonders of the African World*, 1999; *The African-American Century: How Black Americans Have Shaped Our Country*, 2000 (with West); *The Trials of Phillis Wheatley: America's First Black Poet and Her Encounters with the Founding Fathers*, 2003; *America Behind the Color Line: Dialogues with African Americans*, 2004; *Finding Oprah's Roots: Finding Your Own*, 2007; *In Search of Our Roots: How 19 Extraordinary African Americans Reclaimed Their* Past, 2009; *Faces of America: How 12 Extraordinary People Discovered Their* Pasts, 2010; *The Trials of Phillis Wheatley: America's First Black Poet and Her Encounters with the Founding Fathers*, 2010; *Black in Latin America*, 2011; *Tradition and the Black Atlantic: Critical Theory in the African Diaspora*, 2010; *Life Upon These Shores: Looking at African American History, 1513-2008*, 2011; *A Henry Louis Gates, Jr. Reader*, 2012; *Finding Your Roots: The Official Companion to the PBS Series*, 2014; *And Still I Rise: Black America since MLK* (with Kevin M. Burke), 2015; *Finding Your Roots, Season 2: The Official Companion to the PBS Series*, 2016; *100 Amazing Facts about the Negro*, 2017; *Stony the Road: Reconstruction, White Supremacy, and the Rise of Jim Crow*, 2019; *Dark Sky Rising: Reconstruction and the Dawn of Jim Crow*, 2019.

EDITED TEXTS: *Black Is the Color of the Cosmos: Essays on Afro-American Literature and Culture, 1942-1981*, 1982 (Charles T. Davis's essays); *Our Nig: Or, Sketches from the Life of a Free Black, in a Two-Story White House, North, Showing That Slavery's Shadows Fall Even There*, 1983 (by Harriet E. Wilson); *Black Literature and Literary Theory*, 1984, 1990; *The Slave's Narrative*, 1985 (with Davis); *"Race," Writing, and Difference*, 1986; *Wole Soyinka: A Bibliography of Primary and Secondary Sources*, 1986 (with James Gibbs and Ketutto Katrak); *The Classic Slave Narratives*, 1987; *The Schomburg Library of Nineteenth-Century Black Women Writers*, 1987 (30 volumes); *Reading Black, Reading Feminist: A Critical Anthology*, 1990; *Bearing Witness: Selections from African-American Autobiography in the Twentieth Century*, 1991; *Black Biography, 1790-1950: A Cumulative Index*, 1991 (3 volumes; with Randall K. Burkett and Nancy Hall Burkett); *Alice Walker: Critical Perspectives Past and Present*, 1993; *Gloria Naylor: Critical Perspectives Past and Present*, 1993; *Langston Hughes: Critical Perspectives Past and Present*, 1993; *Toni Morrison: Critical Perspectives Past and Present*, 1993; *Richard Wright: Critical Perspectives Past and Present*, 1993; *Zora Neale Hurston: Critical Perspectives Past and Present*, 1993; *Identities*, 1995 (with Kwame Anthony Appiah); *The Dictionary of Global Culture*, 1996 (with Appiah);

The Norton Anthology of African American Literature, 1996 (with Nellie Y. McKay); *Pioneers of the Black Atlantic: Five Slave Narratives from the Enlightenment, 1772-1815,* 1998 (with William L. Andrews); *Black Imagination and the Middle Passage,* 1999 (with Maria Diedrich and Carl Pedersen); *The Civitas Anthology of African American Slave Narratives,* 1999 (with Andrews); *The Souls of Black Folk,* 1999 (with Terri Hume Oliver); *The Bondwoman's Narrative,* 2002 (by Hannah Crafts); *Unchained Memories: Readings From the Slave Narratives,* 2002; *In Search of Hannah Crafts: Critical Essays on "The Bondwoman's Narrative,"* 2004 (with Hollis Robbins); *African American Lives,* 2004 (with Evelyn Brooks Higginbotham); *Africana: The Encyclopedia of the African and African American Experience,* 2005 (with Appiah); *Annotated Uncle Tom's Cabin,* by Harriet Beecher Stowe (with Hollis Robbins), 2007; *The New Negro: Readings on Race, Representation, and African American Culture, 1892-1938* (with Gene Andrew Jarrett) 2007; *The African American National Biography* (with Evelyn Brooks-Higginbotham), 2008; *Lincoln on Race and Slavery* (with Donald Yacovone), 2009; *Harlem Renaissance Lives from the African American National Biography* (with Evelyn Brooks Higginbotham), 2009; *Encyclopedia of Africa* (with Appiah), 2010; *Call and Response: Key Debates in African American Studies* (with Jennifer Burton), 2011; *Gordon Parks: Collected Works* (with others), 2012; *The Oxford Handbook of African American Citizenship, 1865-Present* (with others), 2012; *Dictionary of African Biography* (with Emmanuel K. Akyeampong), 2012; *African American National Biography. Supplement 2008-2012* (with Evelyn Brooks Higginbotham), 2013; *African American National Biography* (with Evelyn Brooks Higginbotham), 2013; *Basquiat: The Unknown Notebooks* (with Dieter Buchhart, et al.), 2015; *The Collected Essays and Memoirs,* by Albert Murray (with Paul

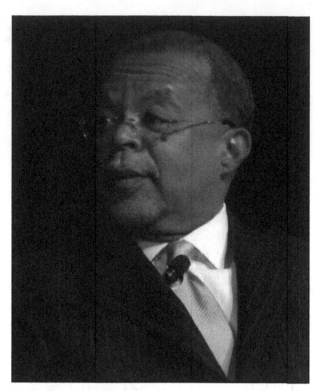

Photo courtesy of Jon Irons

Devlin), 2016; *The Portable Frederick Douglass* (with John Stauffer), 2016; *Dictionary of Caribbean and Afro-Latin American Biography* (with Franklin W. Knight), 2016; *Twelve Years a Slave, by Solomon Northup* (with Kevin M. Burke), 2017; *The Portable Nineteenth-Century African American Women Writers* (with Hollis Robbins), 2017; *Image of the Black in African and Asian Art* (with David Bindman and Suzanne Preston Blier), 2017; *Collected Novels and Poems,* by Albert Murray (with Paul Devlin), 2018; *Annotated African American Folktales* (with Maria Tartar), 2018.

Achievements

Henry Louis Gates's story is much like Horatio Alger's. Gates quickly rose from relatively obscure beginnings and, before he was forty, became a full professor at Harvard University and chair of its African American studies department. By then, he had already achieved the rank of full professor at two prestigious universities, and within two years of his arrival he had tripled Harvard's enrollment in the program he directed. He received one of the so-called genius awards from the MacArthur Foundation in 1981, following Phelps and Mellon fellowships and grants from the Ford Foundation and the National Endowment for the Humanities. By 1995, he had received honorary degrees from nineteen institutions of higher learning, largely in recognition of his developing a branch of critical theory particularly relevant to the study of black writers. The Heartland Prize for nonfiction was awarded him in 1994, and the following year he was named West Virginian of the Year. In 1997, *Time* magazine included him among the twenty-five most influential Americans. He was elected to the American Academy of Arts and Letters in 1999. During the 2003-2004 academic year, he was a visiting scholar at Princeton University's Institute for Advanced Study. In 2005, Gates was elected chair of the Pulitzer Board, which is responsible for awarding Pulitzer Prizes. Over the past thirteen years, Gates has received awards from numerous entities, including the Education Alliance of West Virginia (2006); PBS Channel Thirteen (2006); the Oxford African American Studies Center (2006); the Modern Language Association (2006); the Columbia University School of Journalism (2007); the National Arts Club (2007); the Gordon Parks Foundation (2007); the Woodrow Wilson Foundation (2009); the Corporation for Public Broadcasting (2009); CNN (2009); the NAACP (2010); Harvard University (2011); and Columbia University (2015), among many others.

Biography

West Virginia was racially segregated when Henry Louis Gates, Jr., was born in Keyser on September 16, 1950. Keyser's schools were not integrated until Gates was in secondary school, and integration came to Keyser with less protest than it had elsewhere in the South. In 1968, Gates, named valedictorian of his high school graduating class, gave a militant speech heavily influenced by his study of African history.

Gates's father, Henry Louis Gates, Sr., was a loader in Keyser's paper mill, the major employer in town. He also moonlighted as a janitor for the telephone company. Given his family's financial situation, it had not occurred to Gates to attend college outside West Virginia. In September, 1968, he enrolled in Potomac State College of West Virginia University, where he anticipated studying pre-med.

One of Gates's Potomac State professors, Duke Anthony Whitmore, recognized Gates's promise and urged him to transfer to an Ivy League institution. Gates applied for admission to Yale University and was admitted. In 1970-1971, still interested in medicine, Gates worked as general anesthetist at the Anglican Mission Hospital in Kilimatinde, Tanzania, but he returned to Yale to complete his bachelor's degree summa cum laude in 1973.

Following his graduation from Yale University, Gates continued his studies at Clare College, Cambridge University, and received a master's degree in 1974 and a Ph.D. in 1979. He then became a staff correspondent for *Time* magazine's London bureau. From 1976 until 1979, he was a lecturer at Yale University, after which he became director of Cornell University's undergraduate Black Studies Program.

Gates advanced from assistant to associate professor and, in 1985, was named W. E. B. Du Bois professor of literature at Cornell. In 1988, he assumed the John Spencer Bassett Professorship in English and Literature at Duke University. He left that position in 1990 to become W. E. B. Du Bois Professor of Humanities, professor of English, and director of the African

American studies program at Harvard University, which had struggled to attract students interested in African American history and culture.

Gates immediately enlivened Harvard's African American studies program by bringing in a variety of exciting lecturers, including Jamaica Kincaid, Wole Soyinka, and Spike Lee. Within a short time, Gates's dynamic efforts resulted in a three-fold increase in the number of African American studies majors.

Gates made a major contribution to black studies with the publication in 1988 of *The Signifying Monkey: A Theory of Afro-American Literary Criticism.* This book offered a new theoretical approach to viewing writing by blacks. A landmark work, it was informed by the critical theories of major theorists such as Jacques Derrida, Jacques Lacan, and Claude Levi-Strauss, but reconsidered such theories in the light of the uniqueness of literature produced by blacks both in the United States and abroad.

Besides his academic achievements, Gates is one of the three most prominent black public intellectuals in the United States, sharing that distinction with Cornel West and Kwame Anthony Appiah. Gates has produced two Public Broadcasting Service (PBS) series, *The Image of Black in the Western Imagination* (1982) and *Wonders of the African World with Henry Louis Gates, Jr.* (1999).

Analysis: Nonfiction

Perhaps Gates's greatest contribution is his editing and coediting the works of more than a dozen black writers in the Perspectives Past and Present Series (published by Amistad). He discovered the first black woman novelist, Hannah Crafts, and edited her novel, *The Bondwoman's Narrative* (written in 1850), providing proof of African American intellectual and creative activity before the Civil War. He also produced a book on Phillis Wheatley, the celebrated eighteenth century slave who wrote and published remarkably graceful poetry.

The Signifying Monkey: A Theory of Afro-American Literary Criticism

Gates dealt with some of the questions raised in this book in his first major work, *Figures in Black: Words, Signs, and the "Racial" Self,* published in 1987, one year before *The Signifying Monkey.* Gates's use of the term "signifying," sometimes rendered "signifyin(g)" to suggest the dialect of many blacks, posits the notion that many writers of all races have to deal with the oppressive weight of their literary predecessors and often do so initially by trying to copy them. They then reach a second stage in which they seek to transfigure them, to move beyond them, and to create their own literary worlds.

Gates attempts to determine the boundaries of an African American literary tradition by showing how it intentionally misquotes itself. For Gates, past and future are deconstructed into a river-like strand, a continuous present. Signifying generally refers simply to denoting or representing, but Gates suggests a difference that is present in denoting or representing black literature by rendering the term with a capital *S* and a parenthesized *g:* Signifyin(g). The final *g* in words that end with *-ing* words is often dropped in the black vernacular.

Gates analyzes some dialogue—actually passages of a rap monologue—by H. Rapp Brown, carefully interpreting all its rhymes, rhythms, and repetitions. The Brown lyrics have a remarkable originality that imparts a calculated exhilaration to those who hear them. These are the lyrics of black street talk, and even though one can legitimately compare them to some of Walt Whitman's most excessive writing, they are the unique lyrics of the black culture that produced H. Rapp Brown.

Although Gates is quite aware that many black writers were directly influenced by their white colleagues, in *The Signifying Monkey* he limits his literary-historical definition of signifying to the influence of black texts on other black texts, an important limitation that gives his argument the focus it demands.

Colored People: A Memoir

Having grown up in the segregated South, Gates might well have viewed his past as a period of repression and unhappiness. Such is certainly not the case in *Colored People*, which is an intimate, mellow account of Gates's youth and of his relationship to the community where he lived. Many people write memoirs to sort out their experience and come to a better understanding of themselves, and this appears to be the case in this elegantly written and beautifully recollected glimpse into Gates's past.

Keyser, in Piedmont, West Virginia, was a one-industry town. Its paper mill, which cast a malodorous pall over Keyser most of the time, employed blacks only as loaders of its trucks and machines. Gates's father was employed in this capacity, but he earned so little that he took a second part-time job as a janitor.

Gates's mother was bipolar, and her illness began to surface when Henry (nicknamed Skip) was about twelve. Bewildered by the changes in his mother's personality and disposition, he turned to religion, joining a Baptist church that he describes as restrictively fundamentalistic. For many years, Gates did not know that his mother had been active in the Civil Rights movement before his birth, and that she had led one of the early civil rights protest marches in the United States.

A yearly event in Keyser was a picnic hosted by the paper mill for all of its black employees. Gates always looked forward to and greatly enjoyed this event. The fact that it was segregated did not seem important to him. He writes with great nostalgia and warmth about this picnic, and also about the sense of community that blacks had in this small town. Members of the black community were protective and were truly kind and generous toward one another. Keyser's blacks did not want whites at their picnic because their celebration would have been restrained by white attendees.

Gates was unaware of the color line in Keyser until he was twelve or thirteen. Until then, he, like many young people brought up under segregation, considered the separation of the races normal. Also, he was probably influenced by his father's disdain for blacks. Like many black people, the elder Gates had harsh opinions of blacks who brought dishonor upon their race.

Gates writes frankly about his religious fanaticism during the mid-1960s and about his repressed romance with a white girl. He comments on the transition from "colored" society in the 1950s—note the title of his book—to the "Negro" society of the early 1960s and then to the "black" society of the later 1960s. In the choice of terms to describe themselves, African Americans more or less chronicled a significant change in outlook and attitude.

Changes came with the civil rights advances of the 1960s, and most blacks in Keyser learned about them through television and newspaper reports. As a result of new legislation, blacks could eat in restaurants once open only to whites. They could sit where they wished in movie theaters, and schools were now integrated. But Gates believes that the introduction of these freedoms also ushered in the disappearance of the sheltering institutions that protected blacks within their own communities.

Among the most touching accounts in the book is that of how Gates's mother, Pauline, who looked down upon whites, dreamed of one day owning a house of her own. When the Gates family tried to buy the house of a white family for whom she had worked, she hesitated. Finally she broke down in tears, saying that this house reminded her of the cruelty and humiliation she had received from the owners as their domestic servant.

Loose Canons: Notes on the Culture Wars

Loose Canons is a collection of essays and speeches Henry Louis Gates, Jr., made between 1986 to 1973. Gates concerns himself with examining the implications of nationalistic upheavals and the politics of identity for various aspects of American culture and education. His book is divided into three sections, "Literature," "The Profession," and "Society."

Gates compiled this book with a broad readership in mind. He avoids the professional jargon of his earlier writing, which made it too specialized for many readers. As a result, *Loose Canons* is great fun to read. Gates takes outrageous jabs at many academics involved in critical theory. With tongue in cheek, he accuses Harvard's Helen Vendler of doing the dirty work of the literature and cultural mafia. He cites the spurious contention that Harold Bloom, who is credited with doing a great deal of canon formation, killed off a whole list of venerated writers— from Matthew Arnold to Robert Lowell—consigning them to obscurity.

In reading Gates's book, one must remember that he is trying to justify an expansion, long overdue, of the literary canon to include black literature. Many works by African Americans have been not only ignored but, until recently, had not even been discovered. Gates's herculean efforts to correct this omission are commendable; his struggle to reexamine, redefine, and renew the canon are both understandable and admirable.

The Future of the Race

Gates collaborated with Cornel West on this book, which is often read by young adults. The authors take their lead from W.E.B. Du Bois's brief essay, "The Talented Tenth," published in 1903 in *The Souls of Black Folk*. In it, Du Bois issues a clarion call to gifted young blacks, "the talented tenth," who are well-educated, to dedicate themselves to working for the betterment of their race.

Du Bois's call to educated blacks fell short of its mark, largely because he overestimated the altruistic motives of educated blacks and underestimated the power of an individual's desire to gain an education and elevate his or her socioeconomic status. Gates and West question the wisdom of establishing a black elite, as Du Bois initially suggested in his essay (he shrank somewhat from this position in a 1948 revision).

Gates describes his experiences as a student at Yale, and he writes about two of his talented black classmates there who did not survive and to whom the book is dedicated. Interestingly, he notes that contemporary blacks may find more antiblack racism within their own black communities that in the white community. At least in the white community, one might anticipate such a sentiment and proceed with caution, but many blacks make the mistake of thinking that they can depend upon the support of their black brothers, which is sometimes unrealistic. Gates knew that his own father harbored a deep antiblack prejudice.

The Bondwoman's Narrative

The Bondwoman's Narrative, a novel by Hannah Crafts, was discovered by Gates after he acquired the manuscript through an auction. It is believed to be the earliest novel written by an African American woman. As such, the work is of immense historical significance, quite apart from its literary value. It is Victorian in style, and some scholars argue that the novel is indeed an autobiographical account of Hannah Crafts, a slave who passed for white after escaping from North Carolina to freedom in the North.

Before its publication in 2002, Gates went to great lengths to authenticate the manuscript and to determine that it was written in the mid-1850s. The 2002 edition includes a detailed scholarly introduction by Gates, in which he details his discovery of the novel and the subsequent steps he took to authenticate it, including commissioning a scientific investigation of the manuscript's ink, binding, and paper. The edition concludes with several appendixes that provide evidence to back up Gates's evaluation.

Tradition and the Black Atlantic

Perhaps the most appealing feature of *Tradition and the Black Atlantic* is Gates's unique ability to blend the complicated theories of a broad range of scholars with a deeply personal, often humorous narrative. Gates begins this compelling book by tracing the development of the field of Cultural Studies from the unlikely figure of Edmund Burke to more familiar twentieth century scholars like Raymond Williams, Stuart Hall, Frantz Fanon, and others. Gates argues that Burke's staunch anti-colonialism compares favorably with many of the more celebrated aspects of contemporary multiculturalism.

After a brief comparison of the controversy surrounding Burke's life and politics with the controversies that plagued the Black Arts movement of the fifties and sixties, Gates provides an informative gloss of some of the pioneers in the field of Cultural Studies. He discusses the treatment of Burke by British scholar Raymond Williams. Gates suggests that the field of cultural studies did not die so much as "fade to black." It became a field uniquely positioned to explain the conditions of the African Diaspora.

Following a brief synopsis of Frantz Fanon, a theorist who experienced a revival in the late-twentieth century, Gates concludes with an examination of the culture wars. Gates sees the culture wars as being dominated by a series of false dichotomies antithetical to the multicultural movement but one often created by the effort of both sides to police the ideas of the other. He views the movement away from this unproductive either-or exchange as the greatest challenge for Cultural Studies scholars in the decades to come.

Other Literary Forms

Gates is essentially an essayist, but his editing of lost texts by black writers of the nineteenth and early twentieth centuries has helped to establish a canon of black writing. He is also an anthologist and a much-respected public speaker. The oratorical tone of much of his writing comes directly from his speeches.

Bibliography

Adell, Sandra. "A Function at the Junction." *Diacritics: A Review of Contemporary Criticism* 20 (Winter, 1990): 43-56. Compares Gates's approach to African American literature with that of Houston Baker.

Brooks, Rodney A. "In Gates's Hands, Black American History Is Alive and Growing." *USA Today,* May 25, 2004, p. 5D. Gates discusses his plans for creating the most comprehensive set of African American biographies available, as well as his thoughts on Harvard's recent controversy over faculty-university relations.

Bucknell, Brad. "Henry Louis Gates, Jr., and the Theory of 'Signifyin(g).'" *Ariel: A Review of International English Literature* 21 (January, 1990): 65-84. Presents a thorough analysis and discussion of Gates's ideas. Also discusses Gates's critical position in relation to the positions of other scholars who disagree with his theories.

Eberhart, George M. Review of *Africana: The Encyclopedia of the African and African American Experience,* edited by Kwame Anthony Appiah and Henry Louis Gates, Jr. *College and Research Libraries News*

66, no. 7 (July/August, 2005): 539. A brief review of Gates's latest contribution to African American studies.

Gates, Henry Louis, Jr. "Resurrecting the Texts: A Conversation with Henry Louis Gates, Jr." Interview by Bruce Cole. *Humanities* 23 (March/April, 2002): 6-16. Cole focuses largely on how Gates has found previously unpublished texts by black writers, some of them writing before the Civil War, and has edited them in Amistad's Critical Perspectives series. Gates touches on the need to establish a whole new perspective for evaluating black fiction and poetry, like the one he outlined in *The Signifying Monkey.*

Gates, Henry Louis, Jr. "An Interview with Henry Louis Gates, Jr." Interview by Charles H. Rowell. *Callaloo: A Journal of African American and African Arts and Letters* 14, no. 2 (Spring, 1991): 444-63. Presents interesting and enlightening reflections by Gates on his ideas and his experiences.

Gates, Henry Louis, Jr. "Interview with Henry Louis Gates, Jr." Interview by Jerry W. Ward, Jr. *New Literary History: A Journal of Theory and Interpretation* 22 (Autumn, 1991): 927-35. Presents interesting and enlightening reflections by Gates on his ideas and his experiences.

Gates, Henry Louis, Jr., and Hollis Robbins, eds. *In Search of Hannah Crafts: Critical Essays on The Bondwoman's Narrative.* New York: Basic Books, 2003. Written by authorities on African American history and literature, this collection of scholarly articles analyzes Craft's novel, which was discovered and first published by Gates.

Greene, Meg. *Henry Louis Gates, Jr.: A Biography.* Santa Barbara, California Greenwood, 2012. A roughly 200-page overview of Gates's life, career, and ideas.

Gruesser, John Cullen. *Confluences: Postcolonialism, Afro-American Literature Studies, and the Black Atlantic.* Athens: University of Georgia Press, 2005. This book's third chapter, "Signifyin(g)," examines some of Gates's most influential work. The balance among the four essays in this collection is excellent. There is an especially worthwhile (though challenging) introductory chapter that connects postcolonialism with African American literary studies by exploring the concept of the Black Atlantic.

"Harvard Professor to Step Down as Chairman of Black Studies." *The New York Times*, April 17, 2005, p. 22. Discusses Gates's departure from his position of chairperson of the African and African American Studies department at Harvard University and the recent controversy at that institution.

Kjelle, Marylou Morano. Henry Louis Gates, Jr. Philadelphia: Chelsea House, 2004. A biography intended for younger readers.

Magubane, Zine. "Call Me America: The Construction of Race, Identity, and History in Henry Louis Gates, Jr.'s *Wonders of the African World.*" *Cultural Studies/Critical Methodologies* 3, no. 3 (August, 2003): 247-271. A critique of Gates's documentary that includes analysis of the debates it engendered. Contains a critical examination by scholar Molefti Asante.

Marrouchi, Mustapha. *Signifying with a Vengeance: Theories, Literatures, Storytellers.* Albany: State University of New York Press, 2002. Marrouchi's insights into Gates's work, particularly *The Signifying Monkey,* raise compelling questions. An excellent, original approach.

Naden, Corinne J., and Rose Blue. *Henry Louis Gates, Jr.* Chicago: Raintree, 2006. A brief biography intended for younger readers.

Ogletree, Charles J. *The Presumption of Guilt: The Arrest of Henry Louis Gates, Jr., and Race, Class, and Crime in America.* New York: Palgrave Macmillan, 2012. An account of a famous incident involving Gates that provoked national attention about police prejudice against African Americans.

—*R. Baird Shuman; Paul McCann; M. Casey Diana; Anne B. Magnum; Robert C. Evans*

Roxane Gay

Novelist, Essayist, and Memoirist

Born: Omaha, Nebraska; October 15, 1974

LONG FICTION: *An Untamed State,* 2014

SHORT FICTION: *Ayiti,* 2011; *Difficult Women,* 2017

NONFICTION: *Bad Feminist,* 2014; *Hunger: A Memoir of (My) Body,* 2017

EDITED TEXTS: *Not That Bad: Dispatches from Rape Culture,* 2018; *The Best American Short Stories: 2018,* 2018.

Achievements

Roxane Gay's achievements include a 2015 Pen Center USA Freedom to Write Award and several awards presented in 2018: a Guggenheim Fellowship for Creative Arts in General Nonfiction; an Eisner Award for Best Limited Series, for the comic book *World of Wakanda* (with Ta-Nehisi Coates and Alitha Martinez); a Lambda Literary Award Trustee Award; and a Lambda Literary Award for Bisexual Nonfiction, for *Hunger.*

Biography

Roxane Gay was born on October 15, 1974 in Omaha, Nebraska, the daughter of immigrants from Haiti. In an interview with Hannah Levintova, she recalls being part of "the only black family in my neighborhood for many years. Wherever we lived, we were often the only black family, and certainly the only Haitian family." But she notes that her "parents were really great at providing a loving home where

we could feel safe and secure. There were definitely challenges, but it wasn't as pronounced as you might imagine." She remembers being teased by young friends because her parents spoke with Haitian accents. In another interview, she says that when she was young she "grappled with being black in America and being Haitian in black America and being black American in Haiti and being middle class when that was rarely considered a possibility for someone who looked like me." She was also, she says, "trying to make sense of desire and sexuality and wanting so much for myself that felt forbidden."

Gay recalls being "a very lonely child" who was "very socially awkward" and who "always [had] trouble making friends. And so reading and writing allowed me to have friends and to have an active imaginary life that really sort of kept me sane." She wanted to be a writer even at age four. She reports being gang-raped when she was twelve. Sent to a boarding school in New Hampshire, she began putting on weight, partly to repulse men. Her book *Hunger* deals with this and other aspects of her life as a large woman.

Gay says that when she went to college, she "tried to major in pre-med and architecture and other serious things, but ... really wanted to be a writer." As she worked toward that goal, she took jobs in the student loan business, in telemarketing, and even tending bar, sometimes choosing jobs that would help her overcome her shyness.

After receiving a master's degree from the University of Nebraska at Lincoln and then a Ph.D. at Michigan Technological University, she began teaching English firstat Eastern Illinois University, then at Purdue, and then at Yale. She has contributed to numerous anthologies, periodicals, and newspapers and has been a prominent figure online. She credits her involvement with the online periodical *The Rumpus* for helping her win attention from agents and publishers. Commenting on ugly attacks she sometimes receives online, she says "Nasty emails I delete. I read them, and of course it hurts. I'm human, and I allow myself to feel that hurt. But I also try to keep it in its proper place. This is not someone who deserves my time. They don't deserve my pain. I try to remember that."

Analysis: Long Fiction

Gay's fiction, like much of her nonfiction, often deals with issues of class, gender, race, and violence and particularly with the experiences of people who, for one reason or another (or even for multiple reasons combined) feel alienated from mainstream American culture.

An Untamed State

In *An Untamed State*, the Haitian-American protagonist, Mireille Duval Jameson, is kidnapped as she leaves her parents' gated mansion in Haiti. Although she becomes a focus for her captors' rage, she resists their attempts to justify their actions as class warfare. Gang-raped, beaten, and imprisoned, she is stripped of her privileged identity and left with nothing except a fierce will to survive.

Each of *An Untamed State*'s forty-two chapters is headed by hash marks, as if marked on a wall by a prisoner counting the days of her captivity. Mireille's actual captivity lasts thirteen days, but

Photo by Gabirel Olsen, courtesy of Getty Images

her sense of bondage lasts much longer; when, toward the end of the novel, a therapist tells Mireille that she will get better but will never again be the person she was, Mireille thanks her for this honesty.

Told almost entirely from Mireille's point of view, with only a few chapters focusing on events seen from her husband's perspective, *An Untamed State* is both compelling and uncomfortable to read. Gay's close first-person narration pulls readers into Mireille's consciousness, even as Mireille is forced to endure acts that unmoor her mind from her body. Again and again, Mireille describes herself as "no one": a person with no identity, someone who is already dead. To keep even a small island of sanity, she disassociates herself from the woman she was, the successful American lawyer, the wife of Michael and mother of Christophe, the daughter of a man who refuses to pay a million-dollar ransom to end her torture.

At one point, Mireille begins talking about herself in the third person, as if her former identity has no connection to the person she has become. The first half of the novel is a taut, almost unbearably intense narrative of captivity and escape; the second half depicts, with almost equal intensity, the protagonist's struggle to reconcile the strong, unafraid woman she was before with the still-strong but scarred and wary survivor she has become.

Barefoot, bleeding, and disoriented, the eventually ransomed Mireille is reunited with her family but is too traumatized to allow a medical exam. She and her husband leave Haiti for their home in Miami. But Mireille's terrifying flashbacks of being trapped persist, and she runs from Michael, driving across the country and finally ending up at his parents' farm in Nebraska. There, Lorraine, Michael's mother, gives Mireille both the caring and distance she needs to begin healing, a process that eventually brings her back to Haiti some years later to face her aging father.

In an April 2014 interview with Tomi Obaro for *Chicago* magazine, Gay said the idea for the novel came from hearing her parents talk about kidnappings in Haiti. In creating a character who survives a series of violent sexual assaults, Gay also drew upon her own experience as a rape survivor. Some of Mireille's actions after the kidnapping—she refuses medical attention, leaves her husband and son, and puts herself in a dangerous situation in a bar, where she is nearly raped again—may seem irrational or self-destructive, but they are consistent with Gay's stated determination to create realistic characters who, like most people, sometimes make bad decisions.

The complex, fully developed protagonist here is smart, loving, and determined, yet can at times be stubborn, impulsive, and quick-tempered. Mireille is, by any definition, a strong female character. She is strong enough to survive

the unthinkable, yet she does not come through her ordeal without scars. This same multidimensionality can be found in all the characters in *An Untamed State*, even the kidnappers, whose lives of extreme poverty contribute to but do not excuse their actions; like everyone else, they bear their own scars.

Analysis: Short Fiction

Gay's short stories are often very short indeed. They reflect her interest in the increasingly popular genre of "flash fiction." Other stories, however, are of more conventional length. But however long they are, Gay's short stories often deal with the same subjects found in her nonfiction and novel-length writing, including race, gender, class, violence, and the identity of feminists in general and feminists of color in particular.

Difficult Women

In this collection of short stories, Gay imagines the lives of a diverse group of women, focusing on their romantic relationships and challenging popular notions of certain women as "difficult." The stories glimmer with gorgeous prose and craft, demonstrating both her razor-sharp intellect as a social commentator and her skill and inventiveness as a writer.

Some readers have defined Gay's difficult women simply in terms of their active sexual agency and refusal to subordinate their desires to the men in their lives or to society in general. More interesting readings recognize Gay's complex understanding of the inextricable link between "difficult" and "difficulty," as the women in these stories are not simply wild and hungry but often emerge conflicted, even damaged, from deeply troubled personal histories.

It would be easy to fault Gay for indulging in static sketches rather than consistently creating fully realized characters based on their life histories and circumstances. Some shorter pieces are simply underdeveloped. They suggest rich potential for the characters they introduce, but they seem like the beginnings of stories and are less compelling than the collection's longer, more complex stories.

Other sketches, such as the title piece, invoke stereotypes in an effort to dismantle them. Stereotypes, in fact, are not uncommon in this collection, but Gay often deploys them complexly. Several stories mobilize stereotypes to show the ongoing effects of racism, sexism, and child abuse. In "La Negra Blanca," Gay powerfully challenges readers to witness how racism, classism, and sexism frequently interact and overlap. Stories often show how oppression reduces people to its basest claims. This strategy may account for some stories' occasionally clichéd language and strained dialogue, which some reviewers have singled out for criticism. More controversial is that Gay portrays some women's trauma as leading them to find pleasure in being hurt. Here, the message seems to be that oppression does its work in part by forcing victims to internalize it in order to survive. Some of the best stories—often evoking fantastic worlds—show how characters develop rather than merely react to difficult circumstances.

A key feature of the women in Gay's stories is that all of their difficulties arise from their interpersonal relationships. Her women too often are valued only as wives, mothers, sisters, friends, or lovers. These stories never imagine that a woman's difficulty might be rooted, for example, in her own intellectual or spiritual life. But the volume's unevenness is itself interesting, as Gay allows readers to see examples of some of her finest writing along with pieces that do not work so well. The collection is not a finished masterpiece. It shows its seams, and there is something satisfying about that. In a sense, this approach reflects Gay's philosophy in her

New York Times Best Seller *Bad Feminist* (2014), an essay collection arguing that women need not perfectly practice feminist ideals in order to identify as feminists. *Difficult Women* demonstrates that every story need not be a masterpiece. Overall, the stories reveal Gay as a deeply gifted writer of fiction as well as an astute social commentator.

Other Literary Forms

Until recently, Gay has perhaps been even better known as a writer of nonfiction than as a novelist or author of short stories. Her essays and autobiographical prose often explore the same issues as her fiction—class, gender, race, body image, immigration, sex, sexual violence, and nonbinary forms of sexual identity. One of her most persistent concerns involves feminism as a way of thought and a way of being. Titles of essays in her collection *Bad Feminist* include "How to Be Friends with Another Woman," "The Careless Language of Sexual Violence," and "A Tale of Three Coming Out Stories."

But Gay has found all these issues in some ways easier to discuss than her own identity as a large woman and the ways fat people are often discriminated against in modern culture. In her memoir *Hunger*, Gay describes how, as a young woman, she "ate and ate and ate in the hopes that if I made myself big, my body would be safe. I buried the girl I was because she ran into all kinds of trouble. I tried to erase every memory of her, but she is still there, somewhere. . . I was trapped in my body, one that I barely recognized or understood, but at least I was safe."

Bibliography

Bergman, Megan Mayhew. "Roxane Gay's Powerful New Story Collection, Difficult Women." *The Washington Post* 3 Jan. 2017: n.p., www.washingtonpost.com/entertainment/books/roxane-gays-powerful-new-story-collection-difficult-women/2017/01/03/ad937ee4-d1e7-11e6-945a-76f69a399dd5%5fstory.html. Bergman praises Gay for taking "rewarding risks in form, placing traditional narratives about failed relationships alongside inventive stories that dive into surrealism."

Charles, Ron. Review of *An Untamed State*, by Roxane Gay. *The Washington Post* 27 May 2014: n.p. Charles finds the novel difficult to recommend simply because of the graphic depiction of the violence the protagonist endures and the unrelenting tension of her ordeal; Charles calls the novel "riveting" and brilliantly written, yet so intense and brutal that it was "emotionally exhausting" to read.

Fassler, Joe. "What Zadie Smith Taught Roxane Gay: Identity Is Drag." *The Atlantic* 13 May 2014: n.p., https://www.theatlantic.com/entertainment/archive/2014/05/identity-is-drag-what-zadie-smith-taught-roxane-gay/370794/. In this wide-ranging interview, Gay touches on her childhood but mostly describes her interests as a writer.

Levintova, Hannah. "Roxane Gay Will Make You Proud to Be a Bad Feminist." *Mother Jones* 24 July 2014: n.p., https://www.motherjones.com/media/2014/07/roxane-gay-bad-feminist-interview. In this interview, Gay discusses her early life and her life as a writer.

Newman, Sandra. "Bold Feminist Stories." *The Guardian* 10 Feb. 2017: n.p., www.theguardian.com/books/2017/feb/10/difficult-women-by-roxane-gay-review. Newman admires Gay's talent but sometimes finds it flawed. Most significantly, she warns that Gay, in *Difficult Women*, risks "suggesting that women can find abuse both cathartic and sexually satisfying."

Review of *An Untamed State*, by Roxane Gay. *Kirkus Reviews* 1 Apr. 2014: n.p. This review notes the novel's difficult subject matter and praises Gay's reserved, matter-of-fact handling of violence. "The more bluntly Gay describes Mireille's degradations," the reviewer wrote, "the stronger the impact."

Review of *An Untamed State*, by Roxane Gay. *The New Yorker* 4 Aug. 2014: 69. This review calls the novel a "commanding début" and finds Gay's handling of Mireille's internal struggle to maintain her identity especially well handled.

Seaman, Donna. Review of *An Untamed State*, by Roxane Gay. *Booklist* 1 May 2014: 46. Seaman calls the novel "ferocious, gripping, and unforgettable."

Sieff, Gemma. "No Shrinking Violets: A Short Story Collection from Roxane Gay." *The New York Times* 3 Jan. 2017: n.p., www.nytimes.com/2017/01/03/books/review/roxane-gay-difficult-women.html. Sieff emphasizes "the cryptic, claustrophobic relationships described in these pages and the strange detours that riddle Gay's imaginary landscapes." She concludes that in this book, "you really have no idea what's going to happen next."

White, Ashanti. Review of *An Untamed State*, by Roxane Gay. *Library Journal* 1 Feb. 2014: 62. White praises the book's balance of external drama and internal turmoil.

—Ashleigh Imus; Kathryn Kulpa; Robert C. Evans

Nikki Giovanni

Poet

Born: Knoxville, Tennessee; June 7, 1943

POETRY: *Black Feeling, Black Talk,* 1968; *Black Judgement,* 1968; *Black Feeling, Black Talk, Black Judgement,* 1970; *Re: Creation,* 1970; *Poem of Angela Yvonne Davis,* 1970; *Spin a Soft Black Song: Poems for Children,* 1971, revised 1987 (juvenile); *My House,* 1972; *Ego-Tripping, and Other Poems for Young Readers,* 1973 (juvenile); *The Women and the Men,* 1975; *Cotton Candy on a Rainy Day,* 1978; *Vacation Time,* 1980 (juvenile); *Those Who Ride the Night Winds,* 1983 (juvenile); *Knoxville, Tennessee,* 1994 (juvenile); *Life: Through Black Eyes,* 1995; *The Genie in the Jar,* 1996 (juvenile); *The Selected Poems of Nikki Giovanni,* 1996; *The Sun Is So Quiet,* 1996 (juvenile); *Love Poems,* 1997; *Blues: For All the Changes,* 1999; *Quilting the Black-Eyed Pea: Poems and Not Quite Poems,* 2002; *The Collected Poetry of Nikki Giovanni, 1968-1998,* 2003; *Just for You! The Girls in the Circle,* 2004 (juvenile); *Acolytes,* 2007; *Lincoln and Douglass: An American Friendship,* 2008; *Jimmy Grasshopper versus the Ants,* 2008; *Bicycles: Love Poems,* 2009; *Chasing Utopia: A Hybrid,* 2013; *A Good Cry: What We Learn from Tears and Laughter,* 2017; *I Am Loved,* 2018.

NONFICTION: *Gemini: An Extended Autobiographical Statement on My First Twenty-five Years of Being a Black Poet,* 1971; *A Dialogue: James Baldwin and Nikki Giovanni,* 1973; *A Poetic Equation: Conversations Between Nikki Giovanni and Margaret Walker,* 1974; *Sacred Cows . . . and Other Edibles,* 1988; *Conversations with Nikki Giovanni,* 1992 (Virginia C. Fowler, editor); *Racism 101,* 1994; *The Prosaic Soul of Nikki Giovanni,* 2003 (includes *Gemini, Sacred Cows,* and *Racism 101*).

EDITED TEXTS: *Night Comes Softly: Anthology of Black Female Voices,* 1970; *Appalachian Elders: A Warm Hearth Sampler,* 1991 (with Cathee Dennison); *Grand Mothers: Poems, Reminiscences, and Short Stories About the Keepers of Our Traditions,* 1994; *Shimmy Shimmy Shimmy Like My Sister Kate: Looking at the Harlem Renaissance Through Poems,* 1996; *Grand Fathers: Reminiscences, Poems, Recipes, and Photos of the Keepers of Our Traditions,* 1999; *Hip Hop Speaks to Children: A Celebration of Poetry with a Beat,* 2008.

Achievements

Nikki Giovanni has earned an impressive array of honors throughout her literary career. In the late 1960s she won grants from the Ford Foundation, National Endowment for the Arts, and the Harlem Cultural Council. She was named one of ten "Most Admired Black Women" by the *The New York Amsterdam News* in 1969. In 1971 she won an outstanding achievement award from *Mademoiselle,* an Omega Psi Phi Fraternity Award for outstanding contribution to arts and letters, and a Prince Matchabelli Sun Shower Award; in 1972, a life membership and scroll from the National Council of Negro Women and a National Association of Radio and Television Announcers Award for her recording of *Truth Is on Its Way,* and Woman of the Year Youth Leadership Award from *Ladies' Home Journal;* in 1973, a National Book Award nomination for

Photo courtesy of John Mathew Smith

Gemini and a Best Books for Young Adults citation from the American Library Association for *My House.* In the 1980s, she won a Woman of the Year citation from the Cincinnati Chapter of the Young Women's Christian Association, was elected to the Ohio Women's Hall of Fame, received an Outstanding Woman of Tennessee citation, won the Post-Corbett Award, and was named Woman of the Year from the National Association for the Advancement of Colored People (Lynchburg chapter). In the 1990s, she won the Jeanine Rae Award for the Advancement of Women's Culture and a Langston Hughes Award.

She has received numerous honorary degrees from academic institutions, including Wilberforce University, Fisk University, the University of Maryland (Princess Anne Campus), Ripon University, Smith College, Indiana University, Albright College, Cabrini College, and Allegheny College. Several cities have honored her with keys to the city, including Dallas, New York City, Cincinnati, Miami, New Orleans, and Los Angeles.

Recent awards include a Caldecott Honor Book Award (2006); a Carl Sandburg Literary Award (2007); The National Council of Negro Women Appreciation Award (2007); The Legacy Award from the National Alumni Council United Negro College Fund (2007); the Sankofa Freedom Award (2008); the Carter G. Woodson Book Award (2009); the Moonbeam Children's Book Award (2009); a Maya Angelou Lifetime Achievement Award (2017); and numerous "Image" awards from the NAACP.

Biography

Yolande Cornelia Giovanni was born on June 7, 1943, in Knoxville, Tennessee, but grew up in Wyoming and Lincoln Heights, Ohio, suburbs of Cincinnati, where she currently resides. She described her childhood as "quite happy" in the poem "Nikki-Rosa," and her reminiscences in *Gemini* testify to her devotion to relatives, especially her sister Gary (who nicknamed her "Nikki") and her grandparents, John Brown Watson, one of the first graduates of Fisk University, and his wife Louvenia, whose strength of character she admired and emulated. Giovanni herself entered Fisk at sixteen and was graduated magna cum laude in 1967 with a bachelor of arts degree in history. At Fisk, her independent spirit led to her being expelled after one semester; but when she reentered in 1964, she immediately became involved in politics, reestablishing the university's chapter of the Student Nonviolent Coordinating Committee (SNCC). She also became greatly interested in literature and participated in John Oliver Killens's writers' workshop. She also briefly attended the School of Social Work at the University of Pennsylvania. It was black politics and black art, however, that held her interest. In 1967, a Ford Foundation grant enabled her to complete and publish her first book of poetry, *Black Feeling, Black Talk,* and its success led to a National Foundation of the Arts grant on which she attended Columbia University's School of Fine Arts in 1968. Instead of completing her proposed novel or work toward a graduate degree, she continued to work on a volume of poetry, *Black Judgement,* published through a grant by the Harlem Cultural Council on the Arts.

Her impact on black American literature was immediate and electric. Her celebration of blackness and her militancy placed her in the avant-garde of black letters. Hailed as the "Princess of Black Poetry," she began touring the United States, lecturing to college audiences, spreading her message of black cultural nationalism, "ego-tripping," and love. To raise black cultural awareness and to foster black art, she became an assistant professor of black studies at Queens College, Flushing, New York in 1968 and taught creative writing at Livingston College, Rutgers University, from 1968 to 1970. She organized the Black Arts Festival in Cincinnati in 1967, editing *Love Black,* a magazine of the people—"what the brother thought and felt"; participated in the 1970 National Educational Television program "Soul!"; and took part in the two-week black festival "Soul at the Center" at Lincoln Center in New York in 1972.

The core of Giovanni's life and work is love and service; the focus is the family: her own, the black community, humanity. In 1969, her son Thomas Watson Giovanni was born: Her concern for him—indeed, for all children—was the springboard for her volumes of children's poetry, which include *Spin a Soft Black Song, Ego-Tripping, and Other Poems for Young Readers,*

Vacation Time, and *The Genie in the Jar.* She also worked with the Reading Is Fundamental (RIF) Program in Harlem, the Jackie Robinson Foundation, and the President's Committee on the International Year of the Child (1979). Her poetry reflects a life of meditation and domesticity. She is also an active member of black service organizations and an editorial consultant and columnist for *Encore American and Worldwide News Magazine,* a black news monthly with a Third World focus.

In the 1980s and 1990s she taught at a number of colleges and universities throughout the country, as both a faculty member and a visiting professor, including College of Mount St. Joseph on the Ohio, Mount St. Joseph, Ohio, as professor of creative writing; Ohio State University, Columbus, as visiting professor of English; and Texas Christian University, as visiting professor in humanities. She started her long tenure as professor at Virginia Tech, Blacksburg, Virginia in 1987. She also contributes a great deal of her time to public service and directing a variety of art festivals and writing workshops. She directs the Warm Hearth Writer's Workshop, was appointed to the Ohio Humanities Council in 1987, served from 1990 to 1993 as a member of the board of directors for Virginia Foundation for Humanities and Public Policy, and participated in the Appalachian Community Fund from 1991 to 1993 and the Volunteer Action Center from 1991 to 1994. She was a featured poet at the International Poetry Festival in Utrecht, Holland, in 1991. She gives numerous poetry readings and lectures worldwide and appears on numerous television talk shows. When a mass shooting famously occurred in 2007 on the Virginia Tech campus, Giovanni—who had actually taught the shooter, sensed that he might be dangerous, and threatened to resign rather than continue teaching him – delivered a stirring address at a massive on-campus event to pay tribute to the victims.

Analysis: Poetry

From the beginning of her career, Nikki Giovanni has combined private with public concerns, and her development has been toward the exploration of the inner life of one black female—herself—as a paradigm for black women's aspirations in contemporary America. An individualist who early admired Ayn Rand's concept of rational self-interest, Giovanni has a unique black identity. Her example of self-actualization embodied in her poetry has been not only influential but also inspirational, especially to black youth.

In *The Souls of Black Folk* (1903), W. E. B. Du Bois expressed the dilemma of the black American writer—a double consciousness of being both an American and a black. Nikki Giovanni, however, has never felt this division. In *Gemini* she asserts, "I've always known I was colored. When I was Negro I knew I was colored; now that I'm Black I know which color it is. Any identity crisis I may have had never centered on race." The transition from Negro to black represents for her, as for Amiri Baraka and other adherents of the Black Consciousness movement, a transvaluation: black becomes a "sacrament." It is an outward and visible sign of an inward and spiritual grace, making a poetry reading a "service" and a play a "ritual." Rather than a mask that prevents the inner man from being seen, as in Ralph Ellison's *Invisible Man* (1952), color becomes a sign of worth itself. In her early poems and pronouncements, she proves herself a true Gemini, dividing the world into either/or, into mutually exclusive categories. Everything is literally black or white: "Perhaps the biggest question in the modern world is the definition of a genus—huemanity. And the white man is no hueman." Her concerns, in her first two books of poems, like the audience she both addresses and represents, are exclusively black. Her early ideas about poetry are closely connected with her ideas about race. In her essay "The Weather as a Cultural Determiner" she elaborates on the thesis that black people are naturally poets: Indeed "we are our own poems": "Poetry is the culture of a people. We are poets even when we don't write poems; just look at our life, our rhythms, our tenderness, our signifying, our sermons and our songs." Her poems were originally composed for polemical, not lyrical, ends—for the black community: Poetry is "just a manifestation of our collective historical needs. And we strike a responsive chord because the people will always respond to the natural things."

Political Poems

Throughout her poetry run two main themes, revolution and love—one destructive, the other creative. Even in her earliest verse both strands are evident; only the emphasis shifts from the former to the latter. For example, in an early poem, "Detroit Conference of Unity and Art (For HRB)," the "most valid" of the resolutions passed "as we climbed Malcolm's ladder" was "Rap chose me." The revolution that she calls for in *Black Judgement* is, on one level, literal: In "Reflections on April 4, 1968," the date of the assassination of Martin Luther King, Jr., even her poetic structure collapses in the face of the need for violence:

> What can I, a poor Black woman, do to destroy America?
> This is a question, with appropriate variations, being
> asked in every Black heart. There is one answer—I can kill.
> There is one compromise—I can protect those who kill.
> There is one cop-out—I can encourage others to kill. There are no other ways.

The revolution is also symbolic, striking out at the poisonous racial myths that have devalued blacks in America. In "Word Poem (Perhaps Worth Considering)" she writes: "as things be/ come/ let's destroy/ then we can destroy/ what we be/come/ let's build/ what we become/ when we dream." The destruction here is of values and attitudes, seemingly in accord with the statement in *Gemini:* "Nobody's trying to make the system Black; we're trying to make a system that's human so that Black folks can live in it. This means we're trying to destroy the existing system." Giovanni's poems attack the American political establishment in a sweeping, generalized way; her analysis is simple— exterminate the white beast. Her real contempt is directed toward "Negroes" still in the service of white America: "The True Import of Present Dialogue, Black vs. Negro" is "Can you kill/ Can you kill a white man/ Can you kill the nigger/ in you." Her "Black Judgement" is upon "...niggerish ways." Aware that with children lies the future, she urges in "Poem for Black Boys" new revolutionary games:

> Ask your mother for a Rap Brown gun
> Santa just may comply if you wish hard enough
> Ask for CULLURD instead of Monopoly
> DO NOT SIT IN DO NOT FOLLOW KING GO DIRECTLY TO STREETS
> This is a game you can win.

Poetry of denial, vilification, and decreation (what she calls her "nigger-nigger" phrase) is essentially dead-ended; the main rhetorical problem of the new black poets was how to restore value to the black experience. Giovanni has accomplished such a restoration through the affirmation of her own life and the transforming power of poetry. In her volume *Cotton Candy on a Rainy Day*, "The Beep Beep Poem" has a "song of herself " almost like Walt Whitman's:

> i love the aloneness of the road when I ascend descending curves
> the power within my toes delights me
> and i fling my spirit down the highway i love the way i feel
> when i pass the moon and i holler to the stars i'm coming through

Such elation, however, is unusual. The tone of "Nikki-Rosa," "Mothers," and "Legacies" is more bittersweet. Giovanni gradually realized that writing itself is creative of value: She says in "Boxes," "i write/ because/ i have to." In the 1960s, writing appeared to be a luxury: In "For Saundra," she notes:

> maybe i shouldn't write at all
> but clean my gun
> and check my kerosene supply
> perhaps these are not poetic
> times at all.

My House

In the 1960s, poetry was to be a witness of the times—"it's so important to record" ("Records"), but her poetry proved to be her house: *My House* shows her assimilation and transformation of the world into her castle. In "Poem (For Nina)" from that volume, she begins by asserting that "We are all imprisoned *in the castle of our skins*"; though her imagination will color her world "Black Gold": "my castle shall become/ my rendezvous/ my courtyard will bloom with hyacinths and jack-in-the-pulpits/ my moat will not restrict me but will be filled/ with dolphins." In "A Very Simple Wish" she wants through her poetry to make a patchwork quilt of the world, including all that seems to be left behind by world history: "i've a mind to build/ a new world/ want to play."

In *My House* Giovanni began to exhibit increased sophistication and maturity. Her viewpoint had broadened beyond a rigid black revolutionary consciousness to balance a wide range of social concerns. Her rhymes had also become more pronounced, more lyrical, more gentle. The themes of family love, loneliness, and frustration, which Giovanni had defiantly explored in her earlier works, find much deeper expression in *My House*. Her change from an incendiary radical to a nurturing poet is traced in the poem "Revolutionary Dreams": from dreaming "militant dreams/ of taking over america," she:

> . . . awoke and dug that if i dreamed natural dreams of being a natural woman doing what a woman does when she's natural i would have a revolution

This changed perspective accords with the conclusion of "When I Die": "And if ever i touched a life i hope that life knows/ that i know that touching was and still is and will/ always be the true/ revolution." Love and sex form the subject matter of many of her poems. She will "scream and stamp and shout/ for more beautiful beautiful beautiful/ black men with outasight afros" in "Beautiful Black Men" and propose "counterrevolutionary" sex in "Seduction" and "That Day": "if you've got the dough/ then i've got the heat/ we can use my oven/ til it's warm and sweet."

This bold and playful manner, however, is usually modulated by the complications of any long-term relationship between men and women. While she explains in *Gemini*: "to me sex is an essence. It's a basic of human relationships. And sex is conflict; it could be considered a miniwar between two people," marriage is "'give and take—you give and he takes.'" In "Woman" her acknowledgment of the difficulty of a black man maintaining his self-respect in America has led to her acceptance of his failings: "she decided to become/ a woman/ and though he still refused/ to be a man/ she decided it was all/ right."

Cotton Candy on a Rainy Day

This poem, like many others in *Cotton Candy on a Rainy Day*, bespeaks the tempering of her vision. When Giovanni published *Cotton Candy on a Rainy Day*, critics viewed it as one of her most somber works. They noted the focus on emotional ups and downs, fear and insecurity, and the weight of everyday responsibilities. The title poem tells of "the gray of my mornings/ Or the blues of every night" in a decade known for "loneliness." Life is likened to nebulous cotton candy: "The sweet soft essence/ of possibility/ Never quite maturing." Her attitude tired, her potential stillborn, she is unable to categorize life as easily as before, "To put a three-dimensional picture/ On a one-dimensional surface."

One reason for her growth in vision seems to be her realization of the complexity of a woman's life. The black woman's negative self-image depicted in "Adulthood" was not solved by adopting the role of Revolutionary Black Poet. In "Woman Poem," "Untitled," "Once a Lady Told Me," "Each Sunday," and "The Winter Storm," the women with compromised lives are other women. In "A Poem Off Center," however, she includes herself in this condition: "maybe i shouldn't feel sorry/ for myself/ but the more i understand women/ the more i do." A comparison of "All I Gotta Do" ("is sit and wait") to "Choice," two poems alike in their subject matter and their syncopated beat, shows that a woman's only choice is to cry.

Africa and Black Music

Two other themes in her poetry also ally Giovanni with the new black poets—Africa and black music. The romantic and exotic Africa of the Harlem Renaissance writers appears only in "Ego Tripping," where Africa is personified as a beautiful woman. Her own African experience has produced poems that give a balanced recognition of the African's separate identity. In

"They Clapped," African Americans are treated like any other tourists and African life is seen realistically:

> they stopped running when they learned
> the packages
> on the women's heads were heavy and
> that babies didn't
> cry and disease is uncomfortable and
> that villages are fun
> only because you knew the feel of good
> leather on good pavement.

Her conclusion—"despite the dead/ dream they saw a free future"—opens the way for a new hope in "Africa": "i dream of black men and women walking/ together side by side into a new world/ described by love and bounded by difference."

Black music forms the basis of many of her poems: Aretha Franklin emerges as her personal idol, lines from popular songs are woven into "Revolutionary Music" and "Dreams," and several of her poems are based on traditional black American music. She has written a blues tune, "Master Charge Blues," in which a modern woman lets her credit card cure her troubles, and a song which could be set to music, "The Only Song I'm Singing."

The use of the ballad stanza in "On Hearing 'The Girl with the Flaxen Hair'" is effective in building a narrative about white and black art: The girl with flaxen hair gets a song; the black woman does not because her man is tired after working. Her most successful adaptation of musical form comes in "The Great Pax Whitie" which recalls gospel music (indeed, on her recording she read this poem to the tune of "Peace be still," which is also a refrain in the poem). Here Pax Whitie (a bitter parody of the Pax Romana) is described first in an inversion of the words beginning St. John's gospel: The word "was death to all life." Western history, its wars and brutality, is recounted with two alternating calls and responses: "ain't they got no shame?" and "ain't we got no pride?" Her historical account is heavily ironic:

> So the great white prince
> Was shot like a nigger in texas
> And our Black shining prince was
> murdered
> like that thug in his cathedral
> While our nigger in memphis
> was shot like their prince in dallas.

The irony here and in other political poems, such as "Oppression," will be directed in *Cotton Candy on a Rainy Day* toward herself in "Being and Nothingness" and "The New Yorkers."

Human Relationships

As Giovanni's poems turned toward human relationships, there was a marked increase in her lyricism and especially in her use of imagery, both decorative and structural. Her lover's hands are compared to butterflies in "The Butterfly"; she feels like a falling leaf after a night of passion in "Autumn Poems"; getting rid of a lover is just so much "Housecleaning." "Make Up" sustains the image of cosmetics to talk about the life of pretense that a woman must live. On the whole, her verse descends from William Carlos Williams and Langston Hughes, but her voice is her own. While she is not a stylistic innovator, nor a stunning image-maker, she has an ingratiating style, one that proceeds from the energy of her personality, and an increasingly sure command of phrasing.

In "The Wonder Woman (A New Dream—for Stevie Wonder)," Giovanni reviewed her life up to 1971: "i wanted to be/ a sweet inspiration in my dreams/ of my people but the times/ require that i give/ myself willingly and become/ a wonder woman." If her subsequent history has fallen short of this ideal, it is still her strong clear voice that one remembers after reading her poetry; her poems are ultimately the self-expression of a black woman who has discovered that "Black love is Black wealth" and who has brought many people, both black and white, to poetry.

Children's Poetry

Giovanni devoted much of her writing to children's poetry in the 1980s and early 1990s. She describes her writing for children as an opportunity to "share a bit of the past with children. Black kids deserve to hear their history. My kids books are serious but not dour." Her movement toward this type of poetry reflected her time spent as a mother and time spent enjoying her extended family. More than anything, the poems in her children's collection *Vacation Time* showcased her growing lightness of spirit and inner stability. Similarly, *Those Who Ride the Night Winds* revealed a new and innovative form and brought forth Giovanni's heightened self-knowledge and imagination. In *Those Who Ride the Night Winds*, she echoed the political activism of her early verse as she dedicated various pieces to Phillis Wheatley, Martin Luther King, Jr., and Rosa Parks. A decade passed between the publication of *Those Who Ride the Night Winds* and her 1994 title *Knoxville, Tennessee*, a time during which she devoted energy to public causes and arts development, wrote essays, and contributed to edited texts.

The Middle Years

During the 1980s and the 1990s—Giovanni's "middle years"— her work continued to reflect her changing concerns and perspectives. *The Selected Poems of Nikki Giovanni*, which spans the first three decades of her career, was lauded by critics as a "rich synthesis [that] reveals the evolution of Giovanni's voice and charts the course of the social issues that are her muses, issues of gender and race."

Her collection titled *Love Poems* has an interesting pop-culture twist to it. Ever an unwavering supporter of black youth, Giovanni was devastated by the murder of rap singer Tupac Shakur in 1997 and had the words "Thug Life" tattooed on her left forearm in his honor. She then dedicated *Love Poems* to Shakur. "A lover whose love was often misunderstood," begins the dedication. Giovanni noted in an interview that she was frustrated with those who would confuse the message and the messenger:

> Rap is expressing the violence that's there, and we weren't even looking at that until rap came up and talked about it. It gave voice to the conditions that people are living under.

While there are somber, sociopolitical pieces here—the burning of black churches and the aforementioned role of "gansta rap"—most of the poems find Giovanni upbeat and domestic. Most of the poems are about friendship and sexuality, children and motherhood, loneliness and sharing, "beautiful black men" and "our faith and our energy and loving our mamas and ourselves and the world and all the chances we took in trying to make everything better." Her celebration of creative energy and the family spirit of African American communities dominates this collection.

Blues: For All the Changes

As the twentieth century came to a close, readers found a bit of the younger, more political Giovanni in several of the poems of her collection *Blues: For All the Changes*. While sociopolitical commentary in poetry often fails because it loses touch with humanity, Giovanni continues to keep focus on people: Here she spars with ills that confront Americans, but every struggle has a human face. There is a real estate developer who is destroying the woodland adjacent to

Giovanni's home in preparation for a new housing development ("Road Rage"). There is a young basketball star ("Iverson"), who, when harassed for his youth and style, finds a compassionate but stern sister in Giovanni. And there is President Bill Clinton, who is subject to Giovanni's opinions ("The President's Penis"). Giovanni writes in this collection with an authority informed by experience and shared with heart-stealing candor.

Pop culture and pleasure find a place in the collection as well. She writes about tennis player Pete Sampras and her own tennis playing; pays tribute to Jackie Robinson, soul singer Regina Belle, the late blues singer Alberta Hunter, and Betty Shabazz, the late widow of Malcolm X. She also writes fondly of her memories of going to the ballpark with her father to see the Cincinnati Reds.

Her battle with illness is captured in "Me and Mrs. Robin," which deals with Giovanni's convalescence from cancer surgery and the family of robins she observed with delight and sympathy from her window. Yet this gentle poem also revisits the real estate developer, who, the poem notes, has destroyed trees and "confused the birds and murdered the possum and groundhog." As she identifies with an injured robin, Giovanni's language invokes a gnostic cosmogony: God takes care of individuals; Mother Nature wreaks havoc left and right. "No one ever says 'Mother Nature have mercy.' Mother nature don't give a damn," Giovanni says; "that's why God is so important."

Other Literary Forms

Besides her volumes of verse, Nikki Giovanni has made several poetry recordings. Some, such as *Truth Is on Its Way* (Right On Records, 1971), have gospel music accompaniment. Her recordings, as well as her many public performances, have helped to popularize the black oral poetry movement. Her two books of conversations with older, established black writers, *A Dialogue: James Baldwin and Nikki Giovanni* and *A Poetic Equation: Conversations Between Nikki Giovanni and Margaret Walker*, offer the contrasting attitudes of two generations of black American writers on the aims of black literature in white America. The first book is especially interesting for its spirited discussion about the changing relationships between black men and black women, a topic of many of Giovanni's poems. The second clarifies her literary development and contains an impassioned plea for blacks to seize control of their destinies. She has edited several texts, written syndicated columns—"One Woman's Voice" (*The New York Times*) and "The Root of the Matter" (*Encore American and Worldwide News Magazine*); and contributed essays to many black magazines and journals. *Sacred Cows . . . and Other Edibles* collects a number of her essays. A collection of her work has been established at the Muger Memorial Library at Boston University.

Gemini

Gemini: An Extended Autobiographical Statement on My First Twenty-five Years of Being a Black Poet, which was nominated for a National Book Award in 1973, offers scenes from her Giovanni's life as a child and mother. This book contains not only autobiography but also essays concerning many of the issues that were foremost in the late 1960s. Thus the subtitle, *An Extended Autobiographical Statement on My First Twenty-five Years of Being a Black Poet*, is entirely accurate. *Gemini* is both an autobiography and a statement. Giovanni wrote about events that shaped her as a poet, and then as that poet commented on such topics as black artists and the black liberation movement.

Giovanni's family background does not suggest the revolutionary that she would become.

Her parents, both graduates of Knoxville College, maintained a middle-class lifestyle. Her mother was a supervisor in Cincinnati's welfare department, and her father was a social worker. Like many other middle-class parents, they encouraged piano lessons and college. At the age of seventeen, Giovanni enrolled at Fisk University in Nashville, Tennessee, but she was expelled when, without permission, she visited her grandparents at Thanksgiving. She returned a few years later, graduating with honors. She describes herself as an "Ayn Rand-Barry Goldwater" conservative who became radicalized, partly because of the influence of a roommate, Bertha, who introduced her to the ideas of the Black Power movement but also because of the example of her grandmother, Louvenia, who was "terribly intolerant when it came to white people." Giovanni's early collections of poems, *Black Feeling, Black Talk* (1968) and *Black Judgment* (1968), reveal her as a revolutionary poet who could ask "Nigger can you kill?" She argued for black power and social change, advocating violence to effect that change. In the late 1970s and subsequent years, her work focused more on the humanity of all people. During the time that *Gemini* was written, she was at her most radical.

The 1960s, a time of Vietnam protest, the rise of contemporary feminism, and the Civil Rights movement, was a turbulent period. In 1968 alone, Eugene McCarthy won the primary in New Hampshire, Lyndon Johnson announced that he would not seek reelection, Martin Luther King, Jr., and Robert Kennedy were assassinated, and street violence erupted in Chicago during the Democratic Convention. A few days after King's assassination, Giovanni wrote the poem "Nikki-Rosa," the title suggesting a transformation from the naïve girl Nikki to the more politicized Rosa, the name alluding to Rosa Parks, who in 1955 refused to give up her bus seat, thus precipitating the Montgomery bus boycott. The radical 1960s provided both the backdrop for *Gemini* and the catalyst for writing it.

About half of *Gemini*'s thirteen chapters contain what one commonly associates with autobiography. In the first chapter, "400 Mulvaney Street," Giovanni, a recognized poet, has been invited to give a reading in Knoxville, the city where her maternal grandparents had resided, where her parents met, where she was born, and where she lived for two of her high-school years. The visit provides an occasion for reminiscing about such things as ten-cent double features, street vendors, and Sunday chicken and biscuits. Most important are the reminiscences about her grandmother, Louvenia Terrell Watson, who, as readers learn in subsequent chapters, left her hometown of Albany, Georgia, "late at night under a blanket in a buggy" because her outspokenness made lynching a possibility. Racism could not defeat her, but progress, under the guise of urban renewal, did. When Louvenia was forced to move to a new home which "was pretty but it had no life," she lost her roots. Without her memories, the old woman was left with little. Louvenia had already taught the young Giovanni about the necessity of belonging somewhere, of having a sense of identity, and of accepting her responsibility to other African Americans. When her grandmother's friends attend her poetry reading even though they "shouldn't even have been out that late at night," Giovanni realizes that she belongs, and she also knows that she must instill that sense of community in her son: "I thought Tommy, my son, must know about this. He must know we come from somewhere. That we belong."

The second chapter, "For a Four-Year-Old," presents Giovanni as a four-and five-year-old who is both vulnerable and tough. All summer, she readies herself for school: "I was going to knock kindergarten out. When fall finally came

I was over-prepared. I had even practiced nap time." As a little child would, however, she cries when her mother leaves her at school the first day. The young Giovanni is also a fighter who, often against larger and older opponents, defends her beloved but timid sister Gary. Even at the age of five, Giovanni is politically acute. She writes of her challenge to a fifth-grade boy: "Sure, all the kids knew I could handle myself but teachers never know anything. I had him in a double bind. All the grown-ups ever saw was big brown eyes, three pigtails and high-top white shoes. He would really catch it if they saw him fighting—me especially. My stock in trade was that I looked so innocent. So he backed down." Giovanni, in kindergarten, would challenge Gary's fifth-grade nemeses, including Skippy, Gary's boyfriend. She is tough but also vulnerable: She cries after her mother leaves her in her kindergarten classroom for the first time, and she is confused when Gary is "mortified" that she challenged Skippy. The autobiographical sections illustrate the importance of belonging not only to a place but also to a family, ideas later developed in her poetry.

Other autobiographical segments include anecdotes about her parents, her grandparents, her roommate Bertha, and her son. The emphasis is always on belonging, sometimes to a specific place but often to a family. Her father was reluctant to move to a new house in a black suburb of Cincinnati, a house with a big kitchen, separate bedrooms, and space for a garden, until his family asked, "Who will promise to build a barbecue pit if you don't come?" Giovanni, though she might resist her parents' guidance, demands her place in the family. In the fifth chapter, "Don't Have a Baby Till You Read This," Giovanni describes her pregnancy, which for the first four months she thought was constipation, and the birth, four weeks premature, of her son. The birth was difficult, and

Giovanni's heart stopped during the Caesarean delivery. The love and support of her family are evident, but Giovanni, because of her parents' attention to the new baby, feels displaced: "ALL YOU CARE ABOUT IS TOMMY AND I WON'T STAND FOR THAT. I'M YOUR BABY AND DON'T YOU FORGET IT." Other chapters, primarily in the second half of *Gemini*, constitute an overt political statement. Giovanni views her development into a militant radical as natural, considering her background: "My family on my grandmother's side are fighters. My family on my father's side are survivors. I'm a revolutionist. It's only logical."

As a revolutionist, she rails against the injustice that she observes. She suggests that African Americans have been killed deliberately not only through assassinations but also through drug overdoses, accidents, and illnesses because they, through their ability to unite other black people, threatened the white power establishment: "Anybody the honkie wants to take off he not only can but will." Political figures such as Medgar Evers and Martin Luther King, Jr., are targeted, but so are musicians such as Otis Redding, Jimi Hendrix, Sam Cooke, and John Coltrane, because "Music has been the voice of the Black experience most especially here in America." As a revolutionist, Giovanni advocates change: "We're trying to make a system that's human so that Black folks can live in it. This means we're trying to destroy the existing system." She suggests that racial injustice will cease only when African Americans acquire the power to control their own lives and to tell their own stories, which have been distorted or erased by white narrators. With power comes obligation and responsibility to the black community. Giovanni, although arguing that violence is necessary to counteract the violence directed toward African Americans, is saddened because "the world . . . doesn't have to be that way." She concludes on an optimistic note: "I really like to think a Black, beautiful, loving world is possible. I really do, I think."

In the 1970s, Giovanni was hailed as an important black poet and thereafter maintained a large following. Part of *Gemini*'s importance lies in the fact that it shows the influences, both familial and cultural, that shaped Giovanni into a poet. She presents her decision to be a poet somewhat more modestly: "I can't do anything else that well. If I could have held down a job in Walgreen's I probably would have." It is clear that her grandmother, her sister, and her parents were instrumental in shaping her consciousness. Her decision to be a poet rests in her desire to be a voice for African Americans and to tell their stories; she believes that poets pass on the truth of a people.

In *Gemini*, she explores what threatens the black community: fragmentation as various groups focus on fulfilling their own group's needs rather than on working together; appropriation by whites of black achievements, especially in the field of music; and the determination of whites to maintain their hold on power and to keep African Americans in a state of submission. As Giovanni notes, "Angela [Davis] is wanted and may be destroyed because she is Black. Her capture and destruction serve . . . to show Black people . . . what will happen if they step out of line." Giovanni's antiwhite stance is understandable in the context of the political events of the 1960s. Although she reacts strongly to racism, her venom is directed more toward "honkies," those who perpetuate racism, rather than toward whites in general, who "all clearly are not evil."

Gemini is also a book about love. Both in the autobiographical sections and in the political passages, Giovanni envisions a strong black community, and she suggests ways to achieve that goal. She stresses the importance of a strong, supportive family. Her own family serves as an example. She recalls that her grandmother "was the first to say and make me understand, You're mine, and I'll stick by you no matter what. Or to quote her more accurately, 'Let me know what you're doing and I'll stand between you and the niggers.'" She also relies on her parents and her sister. Family for Giovanni is not limited to the traditional family. She chose to have a child without marrying, a decision she does not regret. She emphasizes the importance of belonging someplace. Her grandmother, forced to move, "died because she didn't know where she was." She also emphasizes the importance of the support of a larger group, the community, that promotes and values black endeavors. In *Gemini* she recounts how, as a young woman, she organized the Black Arts Festival in Cincinnati and also published a small magazine, *Love Black*. Both activities were directed at instilling pride in a black audience.

Even though *Gemini* is prose, Giovanni the poet is evident in the language, especially in the autobiographical sections, where the style is often warm and humorous and at times self-deprecating. For example, on a visit to her parents, she writes of playing cards: "And we were up late playing bid whist because I love bid whist and since most of my friends are ideologists we rarely have time for fun." Even in the more serious political segments, she is still aware of the effect of language, often engaging in wordplay and rhythmic repetitions: "And none of us is free. The guns should be toward the West. Nix(on) him. Spear o Agnew. Won't we ever learn?"

Although *Gemini* received a National Book Award nomination, reviews of it were mixed, primarily because of its combination of autobiography and manifesto. Most critics praised the autobiographical sections as witty and engaging but criticized the militant rhetoric in the other sections as foolish, boring, or abstract. *Gemini* presents Giovanni at an important stage in her life and in her work. Her early poetry collections, such as *Black Feeling, Black Talk* and *Black Judgement,* contain in poetic form some of the militant ideas found in *Gemini,* while her later collections, such as *My House* (1972) and *The Women and the Men* (1975), focus on the more personal moments that are recorded in the autobiographical sections. Thus *Gemini* both explains her militancy and indicates her interest in more universal themes—the need to belong, to have a home, to love, and to be loved—that appear in the later collections.

On a broader scale, Giovanni, in voicing her own concerns, also voiced the concerns of many African Americans in the early 1970s. The 1960s saw the beginning of the Civil Rights movement, a heady time in which the hopes and aspirations of African Americans were raised only to be dashed by resistance that was sometimes subtle but often not. The realization came to many African Americans, as it did to Giovanni, that the only way to achieve equal rights and to have equal opportunity was to fight, responding to violence with violence. In *Gemini,* she gives expression to frustration and issues a call to revolution.

Gemini can also be placed in the context of the black-is-beautiful movement. Giovanni and other black leaders of the 1960s promoted black pride. As she has written elsewhere, "We must . . . rediscover that we are Black and beautiful and proud and intelligent." To that end, *Gemini* contains tributes to various black political leaders such as Angela Davis and to artists such as Lena Horne and Charles Chesnutt. Giovanni's goal is to contribute to building a strong black community.

"A Revolutionary Tale"

In this short story, Kim, an African American woman in her early twenties, is explaining to someone that it is her roommate Bertha's fault that she is late. Kim was politically conservative until she became friends with Bertha, a black activist. Under Bertha's influence, Kim has grown her hair out into an Afro and has stopped getting involved with white men. This ideological decision, however, has cost her money, for she had been receiving some financial support from white men. Now that she has no income, Bertha suggests that she get a job; however, Kim decides to go on welfare instead.

When the caseworker discovers that Kim's parents both work at the welfare office, she angers Kim by huffily announcing that she is not eligible. As Kim chases the caseworker down the hall, her mother comes down the hall crying. Kim tries to convince her mother that it is important to the black revolution that she get welfare, but her mother orders her to either go to graduate school or get a job. Kim is shocked because her mother usually goes along with whatever she wants to do. Her mother, however, says that she has read all of the black revolutionary literature Kim has given her and listened to her many speeches, and now it is time for Kim to listen to her.

Kim calls her father to take her to lunch. When she complains about her mother's orders, he agrees that it is not fair and says her mother never should have said such a thing— Kim should simply get a nice job and not even worry about going back to school. Her father patiently explains that if she wants to improve black people's lives, she must set a good example. He criticizes the black leaders whom she admires because they have never held real jobs requiring them to punch a time clock. Her lunch ruined, Kim goes home to type her résumé.

After making several typing errors, she stretches out on the floor and dozes off. She dreams of a university chasing her down the street; as she runs away, she is swallowed up by a social agency. She wakes up screaming, sure that whatever fate befalls her, she will be destroyed. Then she thinks about all the students whom she could convert if she were back in school and realizes that if she applies to a graduate program in social work, both her parents will be pleased.

When Kim is accepted to a program that is to start in nine months, Bertha is excited but Kim cries. She finally decides she has survived worse things—such as missing out on having sex with an attractive white man while on a civil rights march in Mississippi—so she surely can survive this unpleasantness. She dresses and goes to a bar, where she runs into a black man whom she knows, and goes back to his apartment and spends the night. Kim becomes convinced that if she tells the college placement office that she has been having sex and enjoying it, they will rescind their acceptance. To her surprise, they send her a letter applauding her willingness to try new things and congratulating her on her honesty.

When Bertha does not sympathize with Kim for not being rejected from graduate school, Kim puts drain cleaner in her coffee. When it has no effect other than loosening Bertha's bowels, Kim decides that she is a failure. She sends a second telegram to the school:

> please be advised stop have put drano in roommate's coffee stop she lives stop i am a failure you must reject me stop

They reply with a long letter apologizing for not having completed her placement, explaining that they are a bit behind, and admiring her ingenious way of expressing her needs. Kim is becoming terrified that if she does not come up with a scheme to get out of this, she will end up with a degree, working for an agency, and becoming decent and responsible—the very things that she hates.

Kim next decides that she can escape this fate by telling the school that she has no money, and will need a grant and a stipend. Convinced that she has finally gotten out of returning to school, she goes back to devoting her time to the revolution. First she works on a black arts festival; then she helps start an underground paper, *Love Black*, aimed at black people who seldom read. Her deeper involvement with the Black Power movement refines her ideas on the social system in which the movement is operating, and gives her the impetus to attend graduate school. She decides, however, to walk there, not realizing how long it will take. That, she says, is why she is late.

Nikki Giovanni's story is in the form of a lengthy monologue to an unnamed listener, apparently someone at the college in which Kim has enrolled. Through the monologue, Giovanni portrays the evolution of a young, privileged, previously conservative, middle-class black woman from slogan-spouting radicalism to responsibility. She also uses the story to introduce her audience to some of the leaders of the Black Power movement, and, in the last part of the story, provides a grounding in some of the ideas regarding class, economics, and politics that informed the movement.

Kim's father and mother, seen only briefly at the beginning of the story, are remarkably tolerant of her flirtation with the black revolution. It is not made clear whether they simply have been indulging their high-spirited daughter as she flirts with a radical new philosophy, or if they are really in tune with her but feel unable to express such radical views in the light of their middle-class achievements and lifestyle. When Kim's mother tearfully confronts her in the welfare office, it is clear that she is not merely embarrassed by Kim's applying for welfare, but feels threatened by Kim's bringing her radicalism into her workplace. After recounting how she and Kim's father tolerated Kim's being expelled from school for drinking, getting involved with men they did not like, and even being featured in the newspaper for protesting the Vietnam War by dancing on a table during President Lyndon Johnson's speech at the Democratic Convention, she wails, "But this is my job! Your father and I have worked very hard to give you everything we could."

"A Revolutionary Tale" relies on the self-centered, first-person narration of an educated but unfocused young woman. Although its time frame is the length of a single conversation, the narrator matures greatly over the course of the story. When the story begins, Kim is self-centered and refuses to take responsibility for her actions. First she whines that her troubles are all the fault of her roommate, then she proceeds to implicate the system and her parents as well. After she finally decides to apply for graduate school, she sits back "while others stronger and wiser than I would determine my fate." Once she is accepted into graduate school, she attempts to get them to reject her rather than withdrawing her application, although in an amusingly creative way.

Giovanni's use of language in "A Revolutionary Tale" helps to make the narrator credible. There is a believable balance between standard English, which befits the educated young woman who was "Ayn Rand-Barry Goldwater all the way" before coming under Bertha's influence, and the slang appropriate to a street-smart young black woman in the 1960s.

In line with the narrator's maturation, the tone of the writing changes fairly abruptly in the middle of the story. The story begins in a farcical vein, as Kim and others describe her attention-getting antics in a deadpan fashion. When Kim begins making a real contribution to the black revolution through her work on the magazine *Love Black*, however, she changes from a spoiled girl focused on partying to a concerned citizen of the society that she hopes to help create. The narrative then abandons its comic tone to address more serious issues. It is unlikely that the ideas she is spouting are original to her, but she has moved far beyond the girl who was distressed because she could not contribute to the revolution just by sleeping with financially generous white men and sharing the wealth.

At the end, she informs her listener that one of the reasons she is late is because she decided to walk to school rather than fly or hitch a ride. Wherever Kim has gone in reality, or how she has gotten there, metaphorically, she has traveled a life-altering distance from the spoiled party girl to someone who will be a contributor to the revolution that was previously only a game to her.

Bibliography

Baldwin, James, and Nikki Giovanni. *A Dialogue: James Baldwin and Nikki Giovanni.* Philadelphia: Lippincott, 1973. Based on a conversation aired by the Public Broadcasting Service as *Soul!* in 1971, this friendly, informal conversation sheds light on Giovanni's opinions regarding race and gender identity in America—foundational themes in much of her poetry. Includes a foreword by Ida Lewis and an afterword by Orde Coombs.

Bigsby, C. W. E. *The Second Black Renaissance: Essays in Black Literature.* Westport, Conn.: Greenwood Press, 1980. Bigsby analyzes many recent contributions to African American literature, including the work of Giovanni. Useful to any student of contemporary African American literature. Contains bibliographical references and an index.

Bonner, Carrington. "An Interview with Nikki Giovanni." *Black American Literature Forum* 18 (Spring, 1984): 29-30. Covers topics ranging from contemporary writers, such as Amiri Baraka, to the feminist movement.

Cook, Martha. "Nikki Giovanni: Place and Sense of Place in Her Poetry." In *Southern Women Writers: The New Generation,* edited by Tonette Bond Inge. Tuscaloosa: University of Alabama Press, 1990. Good biographical information. Good analysis and discussion of Giovanni's poetry collections, including a favorable assessment of *Those Who Ride the Night Winds* (1983). Places Giovanni within the Southern literary tradition because of her use of place and history.

Fowler, Virginia C. *Nikki Giovanni.* New York: Twayne, 1992. Focusing on Giovanni's poetry, this book-length study not only offers a comprehensive analysis of Giovanni's poetry (with the exception of her children's poetry) but also provides the reader with some invaluable source materials on the poet's life and work, such as a chronology, a selected bibliography, an index, and an appendix. The appendix is a long, formal interview that Fowler conducted in Giovanni's study on October 12, 1991.

_____. *Nikki Giovanni: A Literary Biography.* Santa Barbara, CA: Praeger, 2013. An accessible biography that deals with such issues as gender, the Black Arts Movement, Giovanni's youth, her academic career, and her development as a writer.

_____, ed. *Conversations with Nikki Giovanni.* Jackson: University Press of Mississippi, 1992. A collection of twenty-one interviews dealing with such topics as race, age, sex, gender, black pride, violence, black leaders, and controversy.

Giddings, Paula. "Nikki Giovanni: Taking a Chance on Feeling." In *Black Women Writers, 1950-1980: A Critical Evaluation,* edited by Mari Evans. Garden City, N.Y.: Anchor Press/Doubleday, 1983. Praises Giovanni's poems written in the 1960s and early 1970s but argues that Giovanni never matured and developed as a poet. Suggests that her technique and craft are inferior in her poems of the early 1980s.

Giovanni, Nikki. "Author Spotlight: Nikki Giovanni." *Ebony* 59, no. 2 (December, 2003): 30-32. An interview with the author that centers on her recent work, particularly her work about her experience with cancer, as well as her views on creative writing and its relationship to hip-hop.

_____. *Conversations with Nikki Giovanni.* Interviews by Virginia C. Fowler. Jackson: University Press of Mississippi, 1992. A collection of interviews with Giovanni containing invaluable biographical information and insights into her writing.

_____. "Nikki Giovanni." http://nikki-giovanni.com/. Accessed September 1, 2005. In addition to a very complete summary of her works, this Web site contains a biography, video clips, photographs, and Giovanni's vitae.

_____. Giovanni, Nikki. "A *MELUS* Interview: Nikki Giovanni." Interview by Arlene Elder. *The Journal of the Society for the Study of the Multi-Ethnic Literature of the United States* 9, no. 3 (Winter, 1982): 61-75. In this first major interview with the mature Giovanni, the poet talks about the impact of a writer and the relationship between the reader and the writer (the writer has the power over the reader but, at the same time, is vulnerable to the reader).

_____. "Nikki Giovanni Gets Real." *Essence* 33, no. 7 (November, 2002): 130-131. Giovanni talks about the late rap artist Tupac Shakur, basketball player Allen Iverson, and how both have been misrepresented in the media. She also gives advice to women on raising boys and young men.

Giovanni, Nikki, and Gloria Naylor. "Conversation: Gloria Naylor and Nikki Giovanni." *Callaloo* 23, no. 4 (Fall, 2000): 13951409. Naylor and Giovanni discuss the importance of black people raising their tolerance of one another and resisting the stereotypes that suggest black men cannot be close to one another.

Gould, Jean. "Nikki Giovanni." In *Modern American Women Poets.* New York: Dodd, Mead, 1984. As treatments of this affable, self-confident poet are wont to be, Gould's discussion of Giovanni is warm and personal. Stresses her biography and particularly her precocious personal achievements; provides little direct examination of the poetry.

Harris, William J. "Sweet Soft Essence of Possibility: The Poetry of Nikki Giovanni." In *Black Women Writers (1950-1980): A Critical Evaluation*, edited by Mari Evans. Garden City, N.Y.: Anchor Press/Doubleday, 1984. Noting the contradictory fact that Giovanni has a large popular audience but has not gained the respect of critics, Harris claims that much of Giovanni's value as a poet derives from her insistence on being herself. She is a serious artist "because she tries to examine her life honestly."

Loyd, Dennis. "Contemporary Writers." In *Literature of Tennessee*, edited by Ray Willbanks. Macon, Ga.: Mercer University Press, 1984. Provides a mixture of biographical information and analytical discussion of Giovanni's poetry. Some discussion of her Tennessee heritage and her use of it in her poetry. General discussion of her poetry up to and including *The Women and the Men*.

Madhubuti, Haki R. *Dynamite Voices*. Detroit: Broadside Press, 1971. Radical African American poet Madhubuti offers a history and criticism of some poets of the 1960's, of which Giovanni was one. Valuable, because he offers a contemporary look at the African American poetry scene. Contains a bibliography.

McDowell, Margaret B. "Groundwork for a More Comprehensive Criticism of Nikki Giovanni." In *Belief vs. Theory in Black American Literary Tradition*. Vol. 2 in *Studies in Black American Literature*, edited by Joe Weixlmann and Chester J. Fontenot.

Greenwood, Fla.: Penkevill, 1986. Contains biographical information, discusses the need for serious criticism of Giovanni's poetry, argues that critics should assess the whole body of her work, and suggests that she is more than the revolutionary poet who wrote militant poems. Her shift to a more personal mode in *My House* should not be viewed as betrayal but instead as development.

Walters, Jennifer. "Nikki Giovanni and Rita Dove: Poets Redefining." *The Journal of Negro History* 85, no. 3 (Summer, 2000): 210-217. The poetry of Nikki Giovanni and Rita Dove is discussed. Both women are examples of self-defined African American women who found a voice through writing.

White, Evelyn C. "The Poet and the Rapper." *Essence* 30, no. 1 (May, 1999): 122-124. Discusses Nikki Giovanni and cultural rapper and actor Queen Latifah, racism, rap music, and politics, topics which have abundantly influenced Giovanni's poetry.

— Sarah Hilbert; Honora Rankine-Galloway; Barbara Wiedemann; Irene Struthers Rush; Robert C. Evans